ACCENTS:
A Manual for Actors

ACCENTS:
A Manual for Actors

Revised and Expanded Edition

by Robert Blumenfeld

LIMELIGHT EDITIONS

NEW YORK

ACCENTS: A Manual for Actors
Revised and Expanded Edition July 2002

Copyright © 1998, 2002 by Robert Blumenfeld

Manufactured in the United States of America

Library of Congress Cataloging-in-Publication Data

Blumenfeld, Robert.
    Accents: a manual for actors / by Robert Blumenfeld.—1st Limelight ed.
        p.   cm.
    Includes bibliographical references.
    ISBN 0-87910-967-X
    1. Acting.   2. English language—Pronunciation by foreign speakers.
    3. English language—Dialects.   I.   Title.
    PN2071.F6B48   1998
    792'.028—dc21   98-19867
        LCCN 2002104721   CIP

Design by Bryan McHugh

To my wonderful parents,
Max David Blumenfeld (1911-1994)
and Ruth Korn Blumenfeld,
with deep gratitude and eternal love.

Table of Contents

Acknowledgements

I would like to thank my many language teachers at Princeton High School and at Rutgers and Columbia Universities. Thanks also to the staff of the Stella Adler Conservatory; to Mr. Albert Schoemann, Ms. Pamela Hare, and Mr. Mark Zeller at the National Shakespeare Conservatory; to my students at both those schools; to my good friend Mr. Anthony Henderson, Assistant Manager of Talking Book Studios; to a very dear, kind man, Mr. William Howle (1918-1997), Manager Emeritus of Talking Book Studios and my high school English teacher; to Mr. John Behan, Manager of Talking Books, for his encouragement; to Mr. Derek Tague, sound engineer at Talking Books, for lending me rare books on accents; to Mr. Patrick Horgan, for his advice; to Mr. George Holmes and Mr. John Horton, for information on things English; to Ms. Terry Donnelly, for advice on Irish accents; and to Mr. David Cerutti and Mr. Richard Bekins for helpful information and advice. I want to express my thanks and gratitude to the following very dear close friends: Mr. Roland M. Davis for his encouragement and support and for his very helpful excellent advice after reading parts of my manuscript; Mr. Albert S. Bennett for encouraging me in this project; Mr. John Stratton, for his very helpful advice; Mr. Michael Roeschlein, for reading parts of my manuscript and offering excellent suggestions and support; Mr. William P. Hammer and his wife Ms. Laura Inman for their legal advice; and Mr. James Hatch for all his help, not only in reading the manuscript in its early stages and commenting very usefully on it, but also in helping me find a publisher. Many thanks to my friends and great actors Troy Sostillio, John McAdams, Greg Steinbrunner and Michael Emerson, a superb Oscar Wilde, from the original cast of the Off-Broadway hit play *Gross Indecency: The Three Trials of Oscar Wilde* by Moisés Kaufman, and to the admirable James Coyle, who later joined the cast, for helping me to clarify my thinking on certain subjects. Great thanks are due also to Professor Ronald Schwartz of New York University for his generosity in contacting publishers on my behalf. I would also like to thank my brothers Richard Blumenfeld and Donald Blumenfeld-Jones, my sister-in-law Corbeau Blumenfeld-Jones and their children, Rebecca and Benjamin, my aunt Mrs. Bertha Friedman and my cousin Ms. Rita Korn and her parents, my uncle and aunt, Seymour and Shirley Korn for their unfailing love and support, and my wonderful maternal grandparents from Galicia in the Austro-Hungarian Empire, Morris (1886-1979) and Harriet Korn (1886-1980). I owe a great debt to all the authors of the books listed in the Bibliography, without whose work this book would have been impossible. I want to thank Ms. Zina Saunders, whose excellent line drawings illustrate the Introduction. To Mr. Bryan McHugh, the designer of this book, I give special thanks for his beautiful work. Special thanks are also due to Mr. Bruce Kitovich, recording engineer for the CDs, to Ms. Nancy Shore, whose copy editing of my manuscript has been invaluable, and to Mr. Mel Zerman, founder and publisher of Limelight Editions, who has been not only very helpful throughout the process of getting this book published, but is also a kind, charming, and erudite man.

List of Phonetic Symbols Used in This Book

Vowels and Semi-Vowels
A: like "a" in *father*
a: like "a" in *that*
aw: like "aw" in *law*
ee: like "ee" in *meet*
e: like "e" in *met*
é: the "e" in French *pré* (meadow)
è: the "e" in French *très* (very); close to the "e" in *met*
ǝ: the schwa; the sound of "e" in *the* before a consonant; close to the French "mute e"
i: like "i" in *bit*; "i:" lengthens it and makes it closer to the "i" in French, Italian, German and so many other European languages
o: like "o" in *not*
oo: like the "oo" in *book*; "u" in *pull*
o͟o: like the "oo" in *pool*
u: like the "u" in *but*
ö: like the "o" in *work* and the German umlauted o (ö)
ü: the French "u" in *dur* (hard; düR); the German umlauted "u" (ü)
y: the semi-vowel spelled "y" in *yes*
w: the semi-vowel spelled "w" in *where* and *we* and "o" in *one*

Diphthongs
ay: the diphthong composed of "e," which is the stressed half of the diphthong, and "ee"; spelled "ay" in *say*
I: the diphthong composed of "A," which is the stressed half of the diphthong, and "ee"; spelled "i" in *fight*
O: the diphthong composed of "u," which is the stressed half of the diphthong, and "o͟o" in American English, of "e" and "o͟o" in British English; spelled "o" in *home*
ow: the diphthong composed of "a," which is the stressed half of the diphthong, and "o͟o"; spelled "ow" in *how* and "ou" in *house*
oy: the diphthong composed of "aw," which is the stressed half of the diphthong, and "ee"; spelled "oy" in *boy*
yo͟o: the diphthong composed of the semi-vowel "y" and the vowel "o͟o," which is the stressed half of the diphthong; spelled *you*. This diphthong is the name of the letter "u" in the English alphabet.

Consonants
The consonants "b," "d," "f," "g," "k," "h," "m," "n," "p," "s," "t," "v," and "z" have the standard phonetic values of General American English. No special symbol is used in this book to differentiate initial, middle, or final

versions of these consonants. The following additional symbols are used:

ch: like "ch" in *church*; a combination of the sounds "tsh"

d: the aspirated tapped consonant sometimes heard in words like *ladder* (La' *de*R)

dg: like "dg" in *edge* or "j" in *just*; a combination of the sounds "dzh"

KH: like "ch" in Scottish *loch*; a guttural consonant in Arabic, Hebrew, Yiddish and German

kh: like "ch" in German *Ich*; also, a softer final version of "KH"; the initial sound substituted for "h" by some Russian and Spanish speakers

L: like the General American "L"

l: like the French liquid "l" in *elle* (she)

L: like the Russian dark "l"

m and n: follow a vowel to indicate that the preceding vowel is nasal, as in French "bo*n*" (good)

ng: like "ng" in *thing*; indicates that the preceding vowel is slightly nasalized

nk: like "nk" in *think*; indicates that the preceding vowel is slightly nasalized

R: the standard retroflex American and British "R"

R: the guttural "R" in German and Yiddish and its softer version in French; one of the guttural sounds in Arabic

r: the tapped or trilled "R" in Italian, Spanish, etc.

sh: like "sh" in *shadow*

t: the very breathy, aspirated tapped "t" sometimes heard between vowels in the U.S. Middle West and British RP accents, as in *water*: wA' *te*R (Middle West); waw' *te* (RP)

TH: voiced, as in *this*

th: voiceless, as in *thing*

ts: like "ts" in *sets*; German pronunciation of the letter "c"

zh: like "s" in *measure*; spelled "j" in French *je* (I)

Other Symbols

? : glottal stop

: : indicates that the preceding vowel is lengthened, as in wo:k (British pronunciation of *work*)

' : indicates that the preceding syllable is stressed, as in "la'-bor" ("lay'-beR," American pronunciation; "lay'-be," British pronunciation)

/ : rising tone

\ : falling tone

Foreword:
What This Book Is and How to Use It

This book is a work of fiction. It is a work of fiction because accents are fictions, in that they are descriptions of models of the way groups of people speak, and in reality everyone speaks in an individual way. Accents cannot be completely captured simply by reading about them and attempting to reproduce the sounds of them from the printed page; you have to hear them. The goal of the actor is to create an individual accent, while adhering to the general phonetic rules you will find in this book. For example, to do a correct upper-class British accent you must pronounce the word *been* to rhyme with *bean* and not with *bin* and you must say *can't* as "kAnt" and not as "kant." But you must also learn to speak with an accent that is specific to the character.

This book is meant to be an introduction to the study of accents for actors and acting students. It is also a practical reference manual for the working actor, with precise, authentic information on how to do more than one hundred accents. As a faculty member of both the Stella Adler Conservatory and the National Shakespeare Conservatory in New York City, and as a private and production coach, I have experienced first-hand the problems and challenges actors and students face in mastering this sometimes difficult subject, and I have devised methods of teaching that provide an easy and workable approach to the study of any accent.

Any actor wishing to do the work of learning accents will find the possibilities for employment considerably widened. As a professional actor, I have been working with accents on stage and screen and in voice-overs and radio commercials for more than 25 years. In addition I have recorded more than two hundred books for Talking Books at the American Foundation for the Blind, many of which have required not only the use of various accents to bring characters to life vocally, but also the use of actual languages. The amount of work requiring accents in recording books and commercials, and in the theater, television, and cinema, both on camera and in dubbing, is enormous.

To use this book, first familiarize yourself with the List of Phonetic Symbols on pages xi-xii. Continue to consult it as you read the text. This list is the simplest and most logical I could devise for English-speaking actors, and requires no knowledge of the International Phonetic Alphabet (IPA), so there is nothing confusing and complicated to learn. The IPA is problematic in its own way in any case. It cannot possibly cover all the variations in sound represented by each of its symbols—although it comes close. It will not tell you, for instance that its symbol for "sh," an elongated "s," stands for a consonant that is pronounced in German with the lips slightly protruded and in General American English with the lips less protruded.

Remember that work on accents consists of memorizing a new pattern of sounds and drilling them so they become easy and habitual. In order to study accents you must learn not only to hear, but also to analyze what you hear. You must then learn to reproduce, or imitate, the sounds which are different from your own way of speaking, and to do that you must drill. This entails recording yourself and listening for accurate reproduction of the sounds. If you learn what to do physically with the vocal apparatus this should facilitate your task. You must teach the muscles of the vocal apparatus to remember and to be flexible. Since you must train your ear to hear, listen to tapes of foreign languages, and do the exercises on them.

No technical knowledge of linguistics is required to use this book, and although I have avoided many technical linguistic terms, I have used such terms where I think it necessary to do so. Every chapter includes an introductory section on cultural and linguistic matters, followed by "How to Do a _____ Accent," which contains detailed linguistic information on phonetics, stress and pitch in the order necessary for the particular accent. (If sections on pitch or stress are not included for a particular accent, it is because they are not necessary.) This section is preceded by "A Quick Reference," which is a summary of the main features of the accent. You should find this a helpful place to begin your work, since it tells you exactly what to concentrate on. Note that the section on phonetics, "The Most Important Sounds," does not always contain detailed descriptions of absolutely every sound in another language, but concentrates on the sounds of English which do not exist in the other language, and are therefore important in creating an accent, or which do not exist in English, but may be carried over into the accent because they are close to English. Do the practice exercises included in each chapter. They will help you get the correct general positioning of the vocal apparatus—sometimes quite different from that of English, sometimes very close to it. Read the Introduction carefully. It is intended to point you in the right direction, and to provide you with useful definitions and concepts.

Because of space limitations a good many accents have been left out. For instance, Turkish and Uzbek have been included as examples of the accents of Turkic languages, but not all Turkic-language accents could be included. The same is true for some Asian accents. Laotian and Cambodian are not to be found in this book, but the accents of Indonesia, Thailand, Burma and Vietnam are here. There are many African accents (there are about 1300 total!) which could not be included, but you will find a number of important South, East and West African accents. Romany and other Gypsy accents are also not included, because today Gypsies speak the languages and have the accents of the countries in which they reside, or from which they may have emigrated, e.g. England or Romania. There is, incidentally, a very interesting English Romany dialect with a unique vocabulary. Some cultural, historical and geographical information is included along with linguistic information for each accent, not only because it is interesting, but because the actor should have the same general knowledge his or her character would have.

We all take our native language and the sounds of our native language for granted. If this book will show you anything, it will show you that there is a great repertoire of sounds beyond those of English. The study of accents can be almost as difficult as learning another language, and, indeed, learning at least some of another language is part of learning a foreign accent. I advise you to study at least one other language. Such a study not only opens your ears and your speech organs, but expands your knowledge of this planet, of this global village in which we all live, as communication becomes increasingly easy and the world increasingly accessible.

It has taken centuries for the world to become this small. And still, wars rage and people kill each other. The theatre in such a world provides, of course, entertainment, distraction, and amusement, but it also provides education. Part of your education as an actor is to explore and master cultures other than your own, to break the bonds of narrow parochial provincialism, and to portray these other cultures for your audience for their greater understanding and enlightenment. The study of the ways in which people express themselves, of the accents with which they speak, is a part of this education, and teaches us something about the common bond of humanity, which transcends the particular accent.

In *The Origin of Language* (John Wiley and Sons, 1994), the brilliant linguist Merritt Ruhlen has elucidated the theory that all languages are derived from one ancestral tongue. If this is true, all the Indo-European, Asian, African, Polynesian, Australian and Amerindian languages, and by extension the people who speak them, must perforce be related, however distantly after tens of thousands of years of human evolution. In other words, we are all quite literally one big human family.

Good luck! Enjoy yourself. That's the main thing. I trust I have been clear and concise in my explanations, and that you will learn and profit from this book.

Practice Exercises and Sentences

The lips, the lower jaw, the vocal cords, the tongue, and the muscles around the mouth must all be trained. Do the following mouth exercises in repetitive sets:

1) Smile and relax.
2) Push the lips forward and back.
3) With the mouth closed and then open, move the muscles around the lips up, down and sideways and around.
4) Hum, feeling the resonance produced by the sound of "m," as you repeat *ma, ma, ma, ma, ma.*
5) While expelling as much air as possible, tap the tip of the tongue repeatedly in various places in the mouth to make the sounds "ta," "la," "da" and a trilled "r" in "ra."
6) Say *ga ga ga ga ga ga* then *key key key key key key.* Feel the placement of the consonants and vowels in the mouth.
7) Say "i i: ee" progressively lowering the tongue for each of the three vowels, and feel their placement.
8) Say *ha ha ha ha ha ha ha* expelling the air forcefully.

Use any or all of the following exercises to practice any accent in the book. Do the same exercise using every accent.

It is absurd to divide people into good and bad. People are either charming or tedious.—Oscar Wilde

Why, sometimes I've believed as many as six impossible things before breakfast.—the White Queen in *Through the Looking-Glass* by Lewis Carroll

"When I use a word," Humpty Dumpty said in a rather scornful tone, "it means just what I choose it to mean—neither more nor less."—from *Through the Looking-Glass* by Lewis Carroll

Another damned, thick, square book! Always scribble, scribble, scribble! Eh, Mr. Gibbon?—The Duke of Gloucester to Edward Gibbon, author of *The Decline and Fall of the Roman Empire*, on the publication of another volume of that monumental work

If I reprehend anything in this world, it is the use of my oracular tongue, and a nice derangement of epitaphs!—Mrs. Malaprop in *The Rivals* by Richard Brinsley Sheridan

He had been eight years upon a project for extracting sun-beams from cucumbers, which were to be put into vials hermetically sealed, and let out to warm the air in raw inclement summers.—from "A Voyage to Laputa" in *Gulliver's Travels* by Jonathan Swift

We are not negotiating. We are negotiating. We are attacking the town. The elections will be free and democratic. We take you now to outside the courthouse. There is no news as yet.—Sentences heard ubiquitously on television news broadcasts

Practice exercises are included in every chapter. You can add these to them. Write them down phonetically, and record them on a cassette, leaving space to repeat them. Listen and repeat them over and over, until they are not only in your mind, but also in your ear and mouth.

ACCENTS:
A Manual for Actors

Introduction
General Principles and Advice; General American English Compared to Standard British English (RP)

The focus of this book is on a particular aspect of the English language: the accents with which it is spoken, native and foreign. Estimates of the number of languages spoken in the world today vary considerably, but there are probably between four and five thousand extant languages. Possibly as many as two thousand more have died out. All these languages are (or were in the case of the dead languages) spoken, of course, with accents native to the languages themselves, and with the accents of foreigners who have learned the languages. It doesn't always seem possible, and in fact it may be nearly impossible, to learn another language perfectly, particularly after the age of about 12, unless you have hours and hours and hours to spend in a language lab listening to language-instruction tapes and repeating drills. Who has the time, except for students whose business it is to do just that? So people learn another language as well as they can, but as they have been used to making sounds differently from the way we make them natively in English, they reproduce the sounds of English as best they can, and they have accents.

Nothing in the world of accents is absolutely hard and fast or written in stone. We say that someone "has a German accent," but what do we mean? There are perhaps as many German accents in English as there are Germans who have learned English. Some people will speak with perfect and undetectable Standard British English, also known as Received Pronunciation (British RP), or General American accents, others with heavy Bavarian or Hanoverian accents, and we also hear everything in between. What this means in terms of acting is that the accent should be as specific to the character as possible.

Apart from but intimately connected with the basic communicative function of language itself are the paralinguistic aspects of language: the ways in which language expresses needs, emotions, feelings and desires; the kind of voice a person has (rough, raspy, creaky, whispery, smooth, tenor, soprano, bass, baritone, contralto, etc.); the particular tempo of an individual's speech. This book is partly concerned with some of those paralinguistic functions where languages and accents differ from English in the way or manner of their expression of emotion for linguistic reasons. For example, in Hungarian, a question, whether emotional or simply interrogative, normally falls in pitch at the end and sounds to speakers of English, accustomed to a rising pitch at the end of most questions, like a declaration. This way of asking a question often carries over into a Hungarian accent in English.

What Is an Accent? How Should the Work Begin?

What we mean by the word *accent* in this book is the way in which a language is pronounced. An accent is a characteristic speech pattern, or, in other words, a distinctive system or mode of pronunciation, and consists of a system of particular vowel and consonant sounds and a characteristic pitch or intonation pattern (music) and a rhythmic pattern (stress and length of syllables), all of which together form the accent. From the general characteristics of a person's accent we can usually tell where that person is from and very often what social class he or she belongs to. As an actor you can use the prototypes or models of accents presented in this book as a basis for developing an individual accent which nevertheless has the characteristics of a recognizable national or regional or class accent. This is a part of the actor's external technical work, but the accent itself must be internalized and become simply the character's unconscious manner of talking.

When we talk about vowel and consonant sounds we are talking about the science of phonetics, which studies the repertoire of human linguistic sounds and how they are produced, and it is usually a good idea to begin the study of an accent by looking at its particular phonetic aspects, especially the most important sounds for developing the accent. There are sounds in English which do not exist in other languages, and many sounds in other languages which do not exist natively in English, but are heard in foreign accents in English. When you are creating a foreign accent find out which sounds of English do not exist in the parent language (there is no initial "w" in German, for example, and most languages do not have "th" sounds), and are consequently hard for someone learning English to pronounce. What are the sounds which replace or substitute for the English sounds? When creating a native English accent, say upper-class British RP or one of the accents of the South in the United States, look at the sounds which differ from standard General American, which is the accent of reference for this book. Studying these sounds and comparing them to General American sounds is a bit like learning a new language.

Every chapter in this book contains a section called "How to Do a _____ Accent," and within that section you will find a list entitled "The Most Important Sounds," along with practice words and sentences. After assuming the correct basic general position of the jaw, lips and tongue (the vocal apparatus), which is explained first, and which differs slightly for every accent, as the muscles of the mouth are used or "held" differently, begin your study of those important sound "shifts," the shift from the sound of General American English to whatever the sound in the accent is. For example, in an upper-class British accent the "a" in many words "shifts" to "A," so *bath* is pronounced "bAth." A list of these words is found in Chapter One in the section entitled "The Most Important Sounds."

Rhythm, which is such an important aspect of any accent, is created partly by the stress patterns of an accent. Stressed syllables are usually longer (and louder, and spoken on a pitch differentiating them from adjacent pitches) than the shorter unstressed syllables, just as a half note is longer than a quarter note. By *stress* I mean which syllables in a word are emphasized or most prominent. In English almost every word has its own particular unvarying primary stress, and there is secondary stress in longer words, but unless you have grown up speaking English, and thus learned English stress patterns automatically, you have to make an effort to learn the stress for every word. Stress in English is called "random": words could be stressed on any syllable, and you don't know where the stress is unless you have, in fact, learned it. There are languages in which the first syllable of every word is always stressed, and other languages in which stress is always on the last syllable. Languages in which a particular syllable is always stressed are said to have "uniform" stress. You always know how to stress words correctly even if you have no idea what they mean. This information is very important in creating a foreign accent, as you will see.

When we talk about the *pitch* in an accent we mean the actual notes or tones which give that accent its characteristic music. *Intonation* means the pattern of pitch changes in connected speech, that is, in a sentence, phrase or general utterance. All languages communicate by using a combination of pitch and stress, and the pitch and stress patterns are different in different languages. The actor must study these patterns along with the phonetic aspects of the particular accent he or she is learning. There are patterns of pitch (intonation patterns) in English and these patterns of high and low tones express and convey emotion and meaning (the paralinguistic functions referred to above). In English we can choose to emphasize any word by saying it on a different pitch, higher or lower, from the surrounding pitches. For more information on the important subject of native pitch patterns in English see the section near the end of this chapter, and the chapters on accents native to English.

Everyone has an accent, since you can't speak a language without one. Individuals speak their native languages with their own particular way of expressing themselves, and although this may include individual phonetic variations, at the same time their accents share the characteristics of the area they are from or of the social class to which they belong. People who moved a great deal when they were children for military or diplomatic reasons very often speak with a standard accent with few if any regional variations. A foreign accent is created by carrying certain largely unconscious linguistic habits, linguistic characteristics which are absolutely natural to the speaker, from another language into English. A particular stress pattern, for instance, may be carried into English, so that a Czech, let us say, will almost always stress the first syllables of at least most English words, while a French person or an Israeli will stress the last syllables, except if they contain schwas. The French film actors Simone Signoret, Charles Boyer and Maurice Chevalier all spoke English with recognizably French accents, and they each spoke it in a recognizably individual manner. I have heard all of these people speaking French, and when they speak English they speak it exactly the way they speak French, with the same recognizable individual characteristics. If you want to do a French accent, begin by learning some French.

Lesson: **When you have learned some of the language as accurately as possible, keep your whole vocal apparatus in the same basic position and speak**

English exactly as you have been speaking the foreign language.

Every language has regional accents and dialects and these influence the way English is spoken. Even though they are all Italian, a Sicilian learning English will have a different accent from a Venetian or a Florentine. Dialects and accents are not the same thing, despite the fact that the two words are often used interchangeably in the theatre. Every version of a language with its vocabulary and grammar is actually a dialect, including the standard versions of languages taught in school. Some people speak a dialect which is a non-standard variety of a language and is characterized by its own grammatical features and vocabulary, as in the case of the Scots dialect used by the poet Robert Burns, who wrote mostly in a literary, somewhat anglicized version of Scots, which is a separate Germanic language, and the most closely related language of any to English. Scots is clearly quite different from English spoken with a Scottish accent, such as the widely spoken variety of English called Scottish Standard English (SSE), which incorporates some Scots locutions and vocabulary, but is very much like RP in its grammar. SSE has its own features of pronunciation that are standard only in Scotland (see Chapter Four). You will therefore not find Scottish pronunciations in the *Oxford English Dictionary* or in *Random House*, although you will find some Scots words that have become part of English vocabulary, such as *loch*, pronounced "LoKH," meaning a Scottish lake or fjord. (For an interesting discussion of what we mean when we use the words *dialect* and *language*, see J. K. Chambers and Peter Trudgill's *Dialectology*, Cambridge University Press, 1980.)

Speaking the Scots language or speaking English with a Scottish accent is completely different from speaking Scottish Gaelic, which is another language entirely, a member of the Celtic branch of Indo-European languages. Scottish accents are derived from both Scots and English spoken with a Gaelic accent. Centuries ago, when speakers of Scottish Gaelic learned English, their Scottish accent was a foreign accent, as Welsh, Irish, and Indian accents once were. But generations of native English speakers have spoken with those accents, and their ways of pronouncing English have become the proper and accepted manner in the areas they live in. These once foreign accents are now considered accents native to the English language.

Uta Hagen says in her seminal book *Respect for Acting* (Macmillan, 1973) that people who learn another language do not *try* to speak with an accent. They try to speak their new language as well as possible. It is their native linguistic habits which interfere with that attempt. Sometimes there is no exact equivalent sound in their native tongue, or sometimes they hear inaccurately, and sometimes they simply cannot coordinate what they hear with their vocal apparatus. Of course, as I mentioned earlier, there are people who learn to speak English or any other language they study with virtually no discernible foreign accent. Playing an aristocratic, high-ranking Nazi officer in the film *Man Hunt* (1941), George Sanders, for instance, (born in Russia of British parents) spoke the perfect Hanoverian German which was his character's native language, and the perfect Standard British English his character would have learned. The first language of Leslie Howard, the romantic leading man who spoke quintessential British RP in such films as

The Scarlet Pimpernel (1934), was the Hungarian of his immigrant parents.

Accents, like languages, evolve over time. There are now only a relatively few upper-class Americans who speak as President Franklin D. Roosevelt did in 1941, and the British accents recorded on Edison's wax cylinders by Florence Nightingale and the poet Alfred, Lord Tennyson, among others, no longer exist. The native New York City accents of the 1920s and 1930s, preserved in films of the period, such as *Dead End* (1937), are largely a thing of the past, though still well remembered, but the American stage diction of the late 19th century as recorded by Edwin Booth in 1890 is something nobody now recalls, and it is different from the recorded British stage diction of the same period.

It is fortunate that we have so many recordings from the past. Any actor playing Oscar Wilde, for instance, is in a position to know approximately how he sounded. We know from various sources that Wilde spoke not with the accent of his native Dublin but with the upper-class English accent he learned at Oxford. There is a recording once thought to be of Wilde's own voice. It was exposed as a hoax in a 1987 magazine article by Jonathan Vickers and Peter Copeland in *BASC News*, published by the British Library. Even Wilde's son, Vyvyan Holland, thought at first that he was listening to a recording of his father's voice, and then realized his mistake. Still, the recording, with its very upper-class Victorian English accent, must sound enough like Wilde for an actor to be able to make use of it.

The accents on the authentic recordings of other Victorians, such as the English playwright W. S. Gilbert and the Anglo-Irish composer Arthur Sullivan, sound slightly like American upper-class accents. In fact, upper-class American and British accents were generally closer to each other at the turn of the century than they are today. Miriam Margolyes, the English actress playing the New York dowager in *The Age of Innocence* (1993), spoke with the upper-class American accent of the 1890s, an accent which one hears on the recordings of opera divas Geraldine Farrar and Emma Eames. For more on the upper-class accents of the Victorian era, and on the probable sound of Elizabethan English, see the last section of Chapter One: Standard Upper-Class British RP.

General Principles

The goal of the actor is to internalize, to assimilate, and to integrate the accent so that it becomes simply the character's natural individual way of speaking. When we speak we are not conscious of all the technical processes of speech, and a character with an accent different from our own individual accent must also be unconscious of such processes. In other words the accent must become a habit.

Questions for the Actor to Ask:

1) What is the character's social and educational background? There are accents native to English associated with social classes.

6

2) If from a foreign linguistic background, how did the character learn English? A professor of physics who learned English at his European or African or Asian university may speak with a more upper-class accent in English than a laborer who learned English on the streets of an English or American city. Did the character learn English at school; or on the streets of New York or London or Sydney or Johannesburg? For example, a Yiddish accent in Mile End Road in London sounds quite different from a Yiddish accent on the Lower East Side in New York.

3) How well and how grammatically does the character speak the English language, as indicated in the script? This will often tell you how heavy the accent should be.

4) How thick or heavy or light is the accent? We sometimes hear such a slight accent that we cannot quite identify it. As an actor you may wish to create such an accent, or you may want to do an accent that is just a bit more identifiable to an audience. People can also be inconsistent within their own accent, and will sometimes pronounce "R" or "TH" correctly, and sometimes not. I have heard a German, for instance, who pronounced initial "R"s absolutely correctly, and indeed had an impeccable British RP accent, but who pronounced almost all "R"s after another consonant with the German uvular "R."

5) At what age did the person learn English? Below the age of 12 a heavy foreign accent is very rare, if indeed any exists. Einstein and Freud, who learned English comparatively late in life, both spoke with very thick German and Viennese accents respectively. The Russian journalist Vladimir Posner, who grew up in New York City at the Soviet consulate, sounds like a New Yorker speaking General American and has not even a trace of a Russian accent.

Study the Phonetics of the Parent Language.

You will learn a new set or system of sounds. For a convenient summary of the phonetics of any language consult the phonetics guide pages in a dictionary of that language. For example, *Cassel's German-English Dictionary* will tell you which English sounds do not exist in German, and which German sounds do not exist in English.

Look also at the pages on pronunciation in any foreign-language textbook. In other languages the letters of the alphabet often have different phonetic values (actual sounds) attached to them from the ones we native speakers of English associate with them. For example, in German the letter "w" has a sound very close to our "v," and in fact the initial sound we associate with "w" in words like *what* and *we* does not exist in German. Sometimes the speaker simply cannot say it, or even perhaps hear it, so it is reproduced as the closest sound to it in German, and we often hear "vat" and "ve" in a German accent, or, more accurately, a sound in between "w" and "v." All that is required is that the upper teeth be pressed lightly against the lower inside lip for a "v" to come out. Many Germans are quite aware of this sound, and they learn it very well, but their accent contains other inaccuracies which still make it recognizably German, such as the shift from final voiced consonants to voiceless. The *end* becomes the "ent," for instance.

Learn a Little of the Language Itself.

See the Bibliography for a list of language audiotapes and books. "Feel" the placement of the language in your mouth and judge the general position of the vocal apparatus as you listen to and repeat what you hear on the tape. Memorize a few words or phrases or sentences to use in launching you into the accent. Say them to yourself whenever you need to in order to position the vocal apparatus correctly before speaking with the accent. Work on accents is in part a study in imitation, listening, repeating, and drilling so that the accent becomes habitual and natural. Train your ear to hear the sounds of other languages accurately. You can do this by listening over and over again to the language instruction tapes and by repeating what you hear. Study the stress and pitch patterns and the music of the parent language. Listen to native speakers who are an authentic source and really have the accent you wish to acquire. You can hear them in films, at restaurants and embassies or consulates, cultural centers and organizations, tourist offices, web sites for languages and accents (some with audio recordings) and on recordings of plays. Ask people if you can record them speaking. When working on the accent, record yourself. Listen to yourself and train your ear to hear what you are saying. Avoid the clichés which arise from imitating inauthentic sources, such as a friend or fellow actor doing an imitation. Listen to people in the streets. You can learn a great deal that way.

When working on the play out loud, use some semblance of the accent even if it is not perfected. The reason for this is so that you don't attach your natural American or British or Canadian speech patterns to the character's emotions. The accent you have selected should become habitual and be secondary when you really begin work on the interpretation of the role. If you do the work suggested in this book and really learn some of the language, you should achieve this result.

Study the Four Elements of Any Accent:

1) The Physical Positioning of the Vocal Apparatus; 2) Phonetic (Sound) Changes, Shifts and Substitutions; 3) Stress Patterns (Rhythm); 4) Pitch Patterns (Music; Intonation).

Of course, all these elements must be combined to make an accent. But they may be studied separately.

The Physical Positioning of the Vocal Apparatus

When we speak of a general position of the vocal apparatus (Fig. 1, facing page) and of general places or points of articulation and resonance, what do we mean? First, the musculature of the vocal apparatus is used in a different way in every language or accent, and a priori in a different way from what the actor learning another accent is accustomed to in his or her own accent or language. There is perhaps a limited number of such basic placements or positions, but

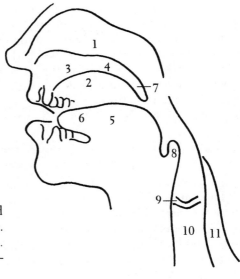

Fig. 1. The Vocal Apparatus
1. Nasal cavity. 2. Mouth. 3. Hard
palate. 4. Soft palate. 5. Tongue.
6. Blade of tongue. 7. Uvula. 8.
Epiglottis. 9. Vocal cords. 10. Tra-
chea. 11. Esophagus.

whatever they are, they change the way things sound and give each accent its
own particular resonance.

Sounds, of course, use the entire vocal cavity for resonance, including the
nasal cavity, but the stream of air is directed against a particular area where a
sound thus has its main point of resonance; in other words a certain part of the
bone forming the front of the face (the masque) and the hard palate in the
mouth vibrates. We speak, for instance, of vowels as *back* or *front vowels*, depending on where the stream of air is directed towards the hard palate. This idea
of a general point of resonance for an accent is not scientific, strictly speaking,
but is rather a "feeling" for the actor to have as to the general placement of the
accent. The muscles around the mouth are employed, sometimes in unaccustomed ways, to change its shape to produce unaccustomed sounds. The tongue
goes to slightly different positions from its usual ones, and it *is* scientific to
speak of a point or place of articulation for consonants, for example.

At the end of my first full day in Paris many years ago I was exhausted from
speaking only French all day long. To speak French with a good accent one is
required to keep the tongue generally slightly raised, thus narrowing the "tunnel" formed in the vocal cavity; to tense the muscles at the corner of the mouth
slightly while protruding the lips a bit; to articulate many of the consonants
with the tongue in a more forward position than when articulating their American counterparts; and to use the French uvular "R." At the end of the day my
mouth was very tired and I longed to relax it into its usual position for speaking
English. Of course this tiredness disappeared as I grew accustomed to speaking
French constantly.

Lesson: **To create a light foreign accent it is sometimes sufficient to have the vocal apparatus positioned for the correct pronunciation of another language.** The accent may then be thickened by adding certain phonetic changes, or by using incorrect stressing or foreign pitch patterns. The general thrust of the position of the vocal apparatus during speech is determined principally by the place of articulation of the consonants and the positioning of the tongue when uttering the consonants. We can define the point or *place of articulation* as the place where the air is blocked or stopped by the action of some part of the vocal apparatus, such as the tongue, lips or teeth. For an example see the section comparing American and British English in this chapter, under "Position of the Vocal Apparatus," where you will find a comparison of the British and American "d."

A Quick Reference: Comparison of the General Position of the Vocal Apparatus During Speech for Some Accents

General American: jaw fairly relaxed; mouth in medium open position; tongue held in middle of mouth; lips relaxed; muscles at corners of mouth relaxed.

Some Southern USA: jaw relaxed; mouth in wide open position; tongue held in middle of mouth; lips relaxed; muscles at corners of mouth relaxed.

Some Middle Western USA: jaw fairly tight; mouth in somewhat closed position; tongue held up; lips slightly tensed; muscles at corners of mouth drawn back slightly and tightened.

British RP: jaw fairly tight; mouth in very closed position; tongue held up and forward; lips relaxed and slightly protruded; muscles at corners of mouth slightly tensed.

London Cockney: jaw loose; mouth in open position; tongue held in medium position and forward; lips relaxed and slightly protruded; muscles at corners of mouth slightly tensed.

Many Irish accents: jaw loose; mouth in open position; tongue held up and forward; lips relaxed; muscles at corners of mouth relaxed.

French: jaw slightly tensed; mouth in somewhat closed position; tongue held slightly raised and forward; lips relaxed and slightly protruded; muscles at corners of mouth slightly tensed.

Spanish: jaw loose; mouth in medium open position; tongue held slightly raised and forward; lips relaxed; muscles at corner of mouth slightly tensed.

North German (Prussian): jaw tight; mouth in somewhat closed position; tongue held slightly raised and forward; lips relaxed and slightly protruded; muscles at corners of mouth slightly tensed.

Russian: jaw loose; mouth in fairly wide open position; tongue held raised and slightly back; lips relaxed and slightly protruded; muscles at corners of mouth relaxed.

Hungarian: jaw relaxed; mouth in slightly closed position; tongue held in medium position and slightly forward; lips relaxed and slightly protruded; muscles at corners of mouth slightly tensed.

Phonetic (Sound) Changes, Shifts, and Substitutions: Some Definitions

Vowel: A single sound made by passing air through the vibrating vocal chords and then through the vocal cavity without the flow of air being stopped. The shape of the vocal cavity changes with each vowel; the tongue is higher or lower; the vocal cavity more open or more closed; and the lips are relaxed or protruded or retracted, rounded or unrounded. The stream of air is directed up and either primarily to the back or middle or front of the palate (the "sounding board" of the mouth), and this is called the *focal point*, or what I mean by the *point of resonance*. Hence we refer, as I have said, to back and front vowels, which can be open or closed, rounded or unrounded. The vowel "A" in *father*, for example, is an open back unrounded vowel. There are also, as in French and Portuguese, nasal vowels, pronounced by lowering the soft palate at the back of the mouth and allowing some air to flow through the nasal cavity just above it, as when articulating the consonants "m" or "n."

Every language has its own vowel system. There is a great confusion on the part of English speakers as to what constitutes a vowel. We Americans are all taught that of the 26 letters of the alphabet used in English, five are vowels: A, E, I, O, and U. The names of the vowels in English are all actually diphthongs, so that one letter stands for two sounds, and as a consequence we mistakenly think of those diphthongs (two sounds) as vowels (one sound). No French or Italian person would think of the letter "A" as the diphthong "ay" in *say*, but rather as the "A" in *father*, and that sound is also the name of the vowel, thus matching one letter to one sound. In many other languages the names of the vowels are pronounced as follows: A (like the "a" in *father*), e (like the "e" in *met*), i: (like the "i" in *bit*, but slightly longer, yet not as long as "ee" in *meet*) (Fig. 2, below), o (like a very short version of the "aw" in *law*, or like the British

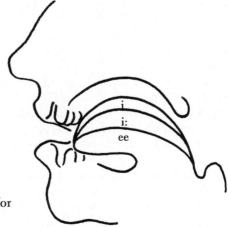

Fig. 2. Position of the tongue for the vowels "i," "i:," and "ee."

"o" in *not*), u (like the "oo" in *boot*). You will find the intermediate vowel "i:" very useful in foreign accents; it often substitutes for both "i" and "ee." Vowels often have at least two versions: open and closed. There are many other vowels, and different "inventories" (an "inventory" is a list of a particular linguistic item) of vowels even in accents native to English, all of which will be discussed as they occur in different accents.

Semi-Vowel: **A vowel during the pronunciation of which the flow of air is beginning to be stopped by the action of tongue or lips and therefore has almost a consonantal quality.** The two semi-vowels in English are "w," during which the lips are beginning to close and are slightly rounded, in *what*; and "y," during which the sides of the tongue move up towards the roof of the mouth touching it very lightly, in *yes*. They can be called semi-consonants or semi-vowels interchangeably. Both "y" and "w" combine with many vowels to form diphthongs: ya, ye, yi, yo, yu, wa, we, wi, wo, wu, etc.

Diphthong: **Two vowels or a vowel and a semi-vowel spoken on one breath, one of which is stressed.** The unstressed half of the diphthong is always very short. An example is "I," from "A" in *father* and "ee" in *meet*; "A" is stressed. In the case of diphthongs formed from a semi-vowel and a vowel, the vowel is always stressed: the letter "U" (semi-vowel "y," vowel "oo") in the English speaker's alphabet. A diphthong occurs when the jaw relaxes slightly immediately after the pronunciation of a vowel and while sound is still issuing from the vocal chords. The tongue "glides" to a different position.

Consonant: **A sound in which the flow of air is impeded or hindered by the action of tongue, lips or teeth.** Every language has its own consonant system, its own inventory of consonants. In English there are two versions of certain consonants: voiced, in which there is sound from the vocal chords, and voiceless (or unvoiced), in which there is not. The pairs are, voiced and voiceless respectively: "b" and "p"; "d" and "t"; "dg" (dzh) and "ch" (tsh); "v" and "f"; "g" and "k"; "z" and "s"; "zh" and "sh"; voiced "TH" and voiceless "th." To differentiate further, there actually are also other versions of these same consonants, including initial aspirated as well as middle and final unaspirated versions, and in some cases a more heavily aspirated version; the final unaspirated version is often referred to nontechnically as the "softest." One letter is used in spelling to indicate what is actually a range of sounds. For example, the slightly aspirated "t" at the beginning of a word is actually a different sound from the "t" in the middle of a word, different yet again from the sound at the end of a word: ţip, maţter, piţ. In the more heavily aspirated tapped version sometimes heard in the middle of a word like *matter* the tongue hardly touches the gum ridge and more air is forced through the vocal cavity. The tapped "*d*" heard as a substutute for "th" in some native and foreign accents in words like *other* (u' *de*, New York; u' *dA*, some German or Spanish accents) and in some native accents in words like *whatever* (wA *de' ve*, New York) is also very important in accent work.

In other languages the sounds are also different from those of General American, even though, once again, the same letter is used to spell them. French "t"s, for example, differ slightly in their points of articulation (in this case, where exactly the tip and blade of the tongue touch the upper gum ridge) from American or British "t"s, which also differ slightly from each other. The other English consonants are: "h," "KH" (as in Scottish *loch*; not really an English consonant, since it only occurs in words of foreign derivation), "ts" (as in *sets*), "l," "m," "n," "ng" and "nk" (which indicate that the vowel preceding it is slightly nasalized as in *thing, song* and *think*) and "r" (trilled and retroflex).

For all accents, native and foreign, always look at the consonants "L/L/l," "R/ R/r" and "TH/th." When creating a foreign accent find out which of these sounds occur in the parent language and are carried over into an accent in English as substitutes for native English sounds. In foreign accents look generally at the consonants first, then at the important vowels and diphthongs. The important sound shifts in foreign accents are often from English consonants to foreign consonants substituted for them, because those particular English consonants do not exist in the foreign language, and are therefore pronounced in English with consonants as close as the speaker can get them to the correct sound of English. In accents native to English look first at vowels and diphthongs, because consonants tend to be very much the same in all accents native to English. There are some differences in the use of "R" and "L" and in "th" and "TH" sounds and in other consonantal phenomena in native accents, and points of articulation differ in some British RP and General American consonants, so consonants have to be looked at as well, but it is largely the shift in vowels and diphthongs which create the variations in native accents.

A Quick Reference: L, Rhotic (R) and TH Sounds

1) L Sounds

1) In all "L" sounds, which are voiced consonants, the blade (the little area just behind the tip) of the tongue is raised and the tongue is slightly grooved; the tip and the blade of the tongue touch an area of the gum ridge near the upper front teeth and slightly block the opening behind the gum ridge into the hard palate; the back of the tongue is low; and air is allowed to pass around the slightly retracted sides of the tongue. In the articulation of the American "L" the contact of the tongue and the gum ridge is light, and "L" resonates in the same place as the vowel "e." But in the formation of one typical Russian "L," for example, the tongue is tensed and its tip pressed against the back of the upper front teeth (Fig. 3, page 14. It resonates where the back vowel "o" does. Another Russian "l," described as dark, is "palatalized," that is the tongue is raised to touch the back of the mouth, and forms the semi-vowel "y" just after the "l" when pronounced before "i" or "e," and resonates where "e" does, so *let* is pronounced "lyet," which means "flight" in Russian, but is also heard in a Russian

accent in English. Very different is the French "l," which resonates where the vowel "o" does. During the pronunciation of "l" the tongue is raised slightly as its tip lightly touches the upper gum ridge where it curves into the upper palate.

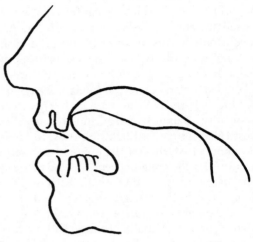

Fig.3. Position of the tongue for a Slavic "L."

2) Rhotic (R) Sounds

1) Rhotic sounds are the voiced consonants spelled with the letter "R." The sound associated with this letter in another language is often carried into English in a foreign accent.

2) Is the language or the accent **rhotic** (from the Greek letter *rho* for "R") or **non-rhotic**? In other words, is the "R" after a vowel and in final position, or before another consonant, (RatheR, woRk), pronounced (**rhotic**) or not pronounced (**non-rhotic**)? In accents native to English if "R" is not pronounced it still often influences the vowel which precedes it, because the tongue is beginning to curl upwards as if to articulate an "R," thus giving an impression of the letter "R," and we speak of "R-influenced" vowels.

3) Is the "R" trilled frontally (symbol: r); pronounced from the back of the throat (a uvular R), as in French or German; or pronounced in the middle of the mouth, with the tip of the tongue curving upward slightly so that the bottom of the tongue is toward the palate (this is called a "retroflex consonant") as in General American English or Mandarin? (Fig. 4, facing page, top.) "R" and "L" are called "continuants," because the sound of these consonants can be continued as long as the speaker has breath.

4) To pronounce a **trilled** "r" (with one or more taps or flaps) heard in many other languages, including Spanish, Italian, Swedish, Finnish, Basque, Portuguese, Polish, Russian and Czech (Fig. 5, facing page, bottom): Begin by saying

14

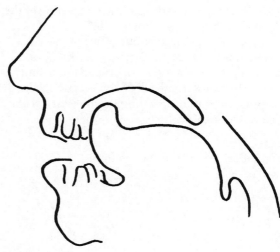

Fig. 4. Position of the tongue for a
retroflex "R."

a tapped "*d*," then the word *very* with a "*d*" instead of an "r." Draw the tip of the
tongue back a very little bit and drop your tongue slightly until you have the
impression of saying "r." Do not curl the bottom of your tongue towards the
roof of the mouth. The tip of the tongue should be just at the opening of the
palate in back of the gum ridge. Alternatively, you may begin a trilled "r" by
saying *hurrah* and shortening the vowel in the first syllable until it is entirely
eliminated, leaving you with a ·

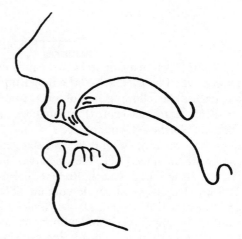

Fig.5. Position of the tongue for a
trilled "r."

tip of the tongue lightly against the opening of the palate, hardly touching it at all. You can then eliminate the "h."

5) To pronounce the guttural or **uvular** voiced "R" (Fig. 6, below) heard in various versions in French, German, Yiddish, Dutch, Danish, Norwegian and Hebrew, first lower the tip of the tongue so it touches the back of the lower front teeth, then raise the back of the tongue so the uvula vibrates against it, as in gargling, or as in articulating its voiceless version, the "KH" heard in Scottish *loch* or German *Ach!*

Fig.6. Position of the tongue for a uvular "R."

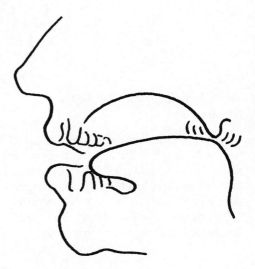

3) TH Sounds

1) "TH/th," which are dental consonant sounds pronounced with the tip of the tongue touching the back of the upper front teeth, do not exist in most other languages. The following pairs of substitutions (voiced and voiceless: THis, thing) are often heard in accents from languages which have no "TH/th": "z" and "s" (French, Northern German, etc.); "d" and "t" (Canadian French, Austrian German, Italian, etc.); "v" and "f" (Russian, etc.). A tapped "*d*" is often heard as a substitute for voiced "TH" between two vowels in German, Dutch and Yiddish accents, as well as in Czech, Russian, Polish and other accents.

2) Some languages which do contain "TH" sounds: Greek; Icelandic (voiced and voiceless); Albanian; Danish (voiced only, with the tip of the tongue in front of the upper teeth, and with more air forced through, and the back of the tongue lower than in English); Spanish (in Castilian only, not in South American Spanish: voiceless "th," spelled "z" or "c" before "i" or "e"; the soft "d" in both Iberian and South American Spanish is often a voiced "TH," or a sound very close to one).

16

Stress Patterns (Rhythm)

In English every word has its particular stress which does not vary. If the stress changes, the meaning changes. *Fre' quent* means "often"; *frequent'* means "to go someplace or to be someplace often." Other examples: *im' port* (noun) and *import'* (verb); *insult'* (verb) and *in' sult* (noun); *pro' gress* (noun) and *progress'* (verb). (Some rare words, such as *besant* [an ancient coin] and *prolix* [unnecessarily wordy] can be stressed on either syllable without changing their meaning; so can some less rare words such as *detail*.) The most important stressed syllable, from the speaker's point of view, is called the *nuclear tone*, because it is the "nucleus" of the sentence, and is usually spoken on a longer, stronger and often higher pitch. The schwaed vowels in British RP in the unstressed syllables, for example, lead the speaker to his or her emphasis as quickly as he or she wishes, without necessarily rushing to make a point, and give the sentence a characteristic British rhythm. In an American rhythm, vowels in unstressed syllables are given a fuller value; they literally take more time to utter.

Other languages, as the list below will show you, have *uniform* stress patterns; that is, every word is stressed on the same syllable. The following information applies to patterns of primary stress, since all these languages have secondary stresses as well.

A Quick Reference: Some Notes on Stress Patterns

For more information see the chapters on the individual accents.

1) Polish uniformly stresses the penultimate syllable of every word.

2) **Some languages which uniformly stress the first syllable**
Hungarian (the following syllables are evenly stressed; in compound words the first syllables of affixes are given a secondary stress, a very slight one)
Czech (accent marks indicate long vowels, not stress, but often sound like stress to English speakers' ears)
Finnish

3) **Some languages which uniformly stress the last syllable**
French (last syllable of a *rhythmic group*, also called a *breath group* or *stress group*, except for syllables ending in the mute "e" as in *table*; there is some secondary stressing on the first syllables of some words for the purpose of expressing strong emotion)
Hebrew (except for certain endings)
Turkish (almost always; see Chapter Twenty-Two for the details)

4) **Some languages with random stress**
English
Russian
Greek

Spanish (usually the penultimate syllable is stressed, except for words ending in a consonant, and then the last syllable is stressed; accent marks indicate unusual stress)

Italian (usually the penultimate syllable is stressed, but by no means always; accent marks are used to indicate unusual stress)

German (often accented on first syllable, except in words beginning with prefixes such as "ge-" as in *geboren*, meaning "born"; the stress is on "-bor-")

Arabic (the syllable with the long vowel is always stressed, but the long vowel can occur in any syllable, although generally not in the last syllable)

5) Some languages with even stress

Japanese (vowels in polysyllabic words are often elided in the middle syllables; that is, turned into a schwa (*e*). This sometimes gives the inaccurate impression of stress to native speakers of English.)

Amharic (Ethiopia) (vowels are often elided)

People who are speakers of foreign languages with random stress patterns will have less difficulty learning to stress English words correctly than people whose languages have uniform stress patterns. Habits of uniform stressing are very difficult to overcome apparently, if one may judge by the frequency of stress patterns carried over into French or Hungarian accents, for example.

Pitch Patterns (Music, Intonation)

All languages communicate emotion by means of pitch patterns, and every language has its own music. In fact, it is a good idea to listen to the music of another culture for clues as to the nature of the spoken language, especially its vocal music. Composers, although they play with melody and rhythms, often set words in correct pitch and stress patterns. Listen to the rhythms in the setting of the aria "Mon coeur s'ouvre à ta voix" (mon kor soov rA tA vwA; my heart opens to [at the sound of] your voice; note that a trilled "r" is used in classical sung French, as opposed to the uvular "R" of spoken French), from Saint-Saëns's *Samson and Delilah*, for example, and you will have a good idea of both the pitch (intonation) pattern and the stress pattern of the spoken language, patterns which are easily carried over into a French accent in English.

In English and in Indo-European languages generally, all stressed and important syllables, that is, whichever syllables the speaker wishes to emphasize, are spoken on a differentiated pitch, often a high pitch, sometimes on a much lower pitch, and with more muscular force than is used in unstressed syllables. Such stressed syllables are therefore louder than unstressed syllables. All unstressed and unimportant syllables are usually spoken on a lower pitch.

Pitch patterns (intonation) are very important in both foreign and native accents. Languages are either *intonational* (non-tonal), as English is, or *tonal*. Tonal languages communicate meaning partly by means of tones or fixed pitches, such as all of the Chinese languages. Cantonese has nine tones. Mandarin, the Standard

Chinese of government, literature and education, has four tones: an even high-level pitch; a high rising (from low to high) pitch; a low falling-then rising pitch; and a falling (from high to low) pitch. Vietnamese has six tones. In a tonal language the same syllable has a different meaning when spoken on a different tone. See the chapters on African and Asian languages. Africa has many tonal languages. Ewe, pronounced "ay' way'," spoken in Togoland and Ghana, has five tones. Ethiopic is also a tonal language. Tonal languages are not to be confused with tonal qualities in non-tonal languages such as Swedish, which also has rising and falling tones that are obligatory but do not always change the meaning of a word. There are about a hundred pairs of words in which tone does change the meaning in Swedish, but this phenomenon still does not make it a tonal language.

Question: What happens to stress patterns in a tonal language? Answer: Lengthened vowels and certain tones give indications of stress for paralinguistic purposes, such as the expressson of emotion.

The music in various accents of Spanish (Mexican, Puerto Rican, Castilian) varies tremendously, and helps determine accents in English. The music of Northern Ireland is as different from a Dublin accent, for example, as the music of Standard British is from General American; a Belfast, or Northern Irish accent is, however, very close in its music to that of Liverpool, which has a large population descended from Irish immigrants. The music of accents from the American South owes something to English provincial accents, and also to Scottish and Irish immigration; immensely important also is the contribution of African languages through the slaves brought here from the West Coast of Africa—Fulani-Adamawa (Nigeria) for example, or Wolof, another important language spoken by many of the early African slaves.

Notes on General American English Compared to Standard British English (RP)

General American, which is standard American English without regionalisms, is the accent of reference in this book. In the List of Phonetic Symbols Used in This Book on pages xi-xii the vowels, semi-vowels, diphthongs and consonants are meant to be pronounced as they are in General American, except when otherwise indicated. An excellent book on American speech is Edith Skinner's *Speak with Distinction* (Applause Theatre Book Publishers, 1990). She discusses the accent called General American, and also describes what she calls Good Speech, also known as Eastern Standard or Theater Standard, by which she means a clearly articulated, non-rhotic accent, very pleasant to the ear. It is close to the old-fashioned upper-class speech of the 1930s, exemplified by President Franklin D. Roosevelt, or Walter Hampden, Gary Merrill and Hugh Marlowe in the film *All About Eve* (1950). Most Americans, however, do not speak Theatre Standard. Their accent is standard rhotic General American, although, strictly speaking, it is nonsense to talk of only one standard speech where so many variations exist.

A good guide to General American pronunciations is the second edition of the *Random House Unabridged Dictionary* of 1993, which includes pronunciations once considered non-standard or even unacceptable, but now considered acceptable. In the 1927 edition of *Webster's New International Dictionary* the pronunciation of *abdomen*, for instance, is given as being stressed on the second syllable only, but Random House now gives first place to what has for decades been the usual pronunciation, with the stress falling on the first syllable, showing how language changes over time. For the pronunciation of Standard British English (RP) refer to the *Oxford English Dictionary*. There are two standard English accents and dialects which people learning the language are taught: Standard British English or RP (Received Pronunciation), which I call British RP in this book for the sake of clarity, and General American, once also called Network English, although there is no longer any reason to call it that, since the standards of pronunciation on television and radio vary so tremendously. Incidentally, it is more difficult to determine what is standard as a spoken language than as a written language. The standard version of a language is a dialect which has become accepted as standard. It is spoken with a standard accent.

The existence of standard versions of languages is as much a political as a linguistic phenomenon. It will not surprise you perhaps to learn that the standard version evolves from the dialect of the governing classes. There is always a great deal of prestige and status attached to that dialect and to the accent with which it is spoken. People wishing to "get ahead" in certain social and political circumstances, certainly in the past, had to, and still sometimes have to learn to speak in the accent of the upper classes, to *sound* sophisticated and educated, as the former Prime Minister Margaret Thatcher did for example. In Great Britain, British RP is spoken generally by the upper economic and educated classes as well as on the stage and in the media, where it was also long known as "BBC English."

How did Standard British become Standard British, and why is it different from standard General American? After the Norman Conquest in 1066 the language of the court and the governing classes in England was French. English was considered an inferior dialect or jargon spoken by commoners, the peasantry and the urban poor. The English spoken in London, the great metropolis and capital city, was just another dialect of medieval English, descended from Anglo-Saxon. Since it was necessary to communicate with the native English-speaking population, a kind of language arose which was a hybrid of the Southern British dialect of English spoken in London, and Norman French. The grammar of this language was Anglo-Saxon, much simplified, shorn of its case endings for nouns and its complicated verb tenses. Much of its new vocabulary, added to that of the native English, was French with an anglicized pronunciation. This language was used at first mainly for administrative purposes. At court the nobility continued to speak French, but because of the gradual integration of the native population with the conquerors, the governing classes finally found it expedient to learn what had become the standard English of their day.

In the early 13th century King John lost possession of his Norman territories to the French, and this event marked the beginning of the decline of the hegemony of the French language in England. Those members of the French-speaking aristocracy who chose to give up their Norman estates and remain in England began to adopt the English tongue as their own and to have their children taught in English and Latin, the common language of higher education everywhere in Europe. The children of the lower economic classes had been taught in village schools in French, but now English began to replace French. This would clearly make it easier for the native English speakers to learn, once the added difficulty of having to be educated in a foreign language was removed.

In 1362 King Edward III opened Parliament with a speech in English, though his native language was French, as was that of every king until Henry IV. The Roll of Parliament which records this speech is in French! In fact the records of parliamentary proceedings would not be generally kept in English until after the middle of the 15th century.

It was not until the reign of Henry V, in the early 15th century, that the governing classes had begun to speak English regularly. This was the language which Chaucer and other writers had been using to create literature since the late 14th century. Chaucer's English is almost the same English used in the great masses of documents surviving from the Royal Chancery of Henry V called Chancery English. With its bilingual legalistic phrases such as *last will and testament*, in which *will* is Anglo-Saxon and *testament* French, it became more or less a standardized written English, and was also used in the courts of law as a spoken language. In fact, an Act passed under Edward III in 1362 had made it the official oral language of the law courts and government departments, superseding French. As a reason for making English the language of the law, the Act states (in French) that most people in the kingdom are unacquainted with the French language and thus have no idea what is being alleged for or against them in court. Written records of legal proceedings must, however, continue to be kept in French and Latin, while oral proceedings at all levels of government are to be conducted in English. The Act was not always obeyed, but its importance lies in the very fact that it was passed.

The spoken language was continuing to gain so much ground in everyday use, as Anglo-Saxon tutors and nurses raised the children of Norman aristocrats, that by the time of the Wars of the Roses it was the native language of many members of the governing classes. Even though the English kings had long possessed territory in Aquitaine in the south of France, and had fought to gain the French crown, despite the loss of Normandy, French seemed rather foreign in the nationalistic political climate of the time.

In British RP today final "R"s in such words as *father, mother, sister, brother,* and in the middle of such words as *first* and *work*, are dropped, but in the days of Henry V and for several centuries thereafter they were pronounced. At the time of the discovery and colonization of America by Europeans final "R"s were still being pronounced. Of course the English colonists crossing the ocean in the 16th and early 17th centuries brought their accents with them.

The dropping of the final "R" appears to have begun in the 17th century among the upper classes in England; nobody knows quite why. Perhaps it was simply easier and lazier not to say final "R"s; perhaps it was considered vulgar to pronounce "R"s too distinctly. Final "R" dropping was already a well-established phenomenon in the 18th century, reinforced by grammarians, lexicographers and teachers. As early as the late 17th century the phenomenon had also spread to the coastal cities of America and the aristocratic plantation owners of the southern colonies who attempted to imitate the speech of their English counterparts, as did the American upper classes generally in the 19th century. Inland the original accents of English were maintained; final "R"s were pronounced, and these accents were later brought west by the pioneers, where they became the standard version of American English, spoken even by many members of the governing classes. Standard or General American is widely spoken today on the East and West Coasts and in the Northwest, Southwest and Middle West states, and increasingly in the southern states as well, despite the existence of many regional variations. That, all too briefly, is the history of the origin of some of the native accents of English.

Position of the Vocal Apparatus

As compared to British English, the position of the lips in General American is generally a bit farther back and the jaw a bit slacker. The language "feels" (as an image) as though it is spoken in the middle of the mouth. British English "feels" much more forward in the mouth, at the point where the tongue stops to form the consonants "t" and "d." That point of articulation is very slightly forward of the American point of articulation for "t" and "d." What this means is that in articulating a British "t" or "d" the tip of the tongue is more forward and the tongue itself raised slightly above the position it assumes in articulating an American "t" or "d." For American English the major point of resonance is slightly behind the British position, where the consonant "R" is formed.

The main point of resonance, speaking figuratively, is determined more by the general placement of the consonants than by the dimensions of the opening for the vowels. In English there are only four consonants whose place of articulation is near the back of the mouth: "g," "ng," "k," and "h." British consonants differ slightly from their American counterparts in having generally a more forward place or point of articulation. The vocal cavity is generally more closed during speech in upper-class British English than it is in American English. On the other hand during Cockney speech the vocal cavity is more open than in either upper-class British or General American speech, which accounts for the different, generally more open quality of the vowels, diphthongs and Cockney triphthongs. However, the point of articulation of the consonants remains the same in Cockney as it does in upper-class British. Therefore, despite the open back vowels and the more open vocal cavity generally, the main point of resonance and the general position of the vocal apparatus is forward. This is not to say that there are no differences between Cockney and upper-class British consonants. (For instance, a medial or final "L" can be replaced by "oo"; "miook" for *milk* is a case in point.)

Phonetics

Aside from the information above, there are some other very important changes in consonants and vowels between the two accents. There are also many differences in the pronunciation of words, many details of which will be found in Chapter One. Americans say *necessary* as "ne se se' Ree" and *egotist* as "ee' ge tist" and *demolition* as "de' me Li' shen," and the British say "e' ge tist" and "dee' me li' shen" and "ne' se sRee" or "ne' se se Ree," for example.

Consonants
R: See the chapter on Standard British English for the changes in the sound of the "R." General American English is **rhotic** as opposed to British RP, which is a **non-rhotic** accent. In other words in General American the "R" is lightly pronounced at the end of a word and before another consonant; in British RP it is not.

L: Another example of a consonant with a forward point of articulation is the consonant "L." There are, of course, a number of versions of this consonant. In an American initial "L," as in the word *like*, the tongue is slightly relaxed and its tip touches the gum ridge lightly. In a British initial "L," in both upper-class and Cockney accents, the tongue is raised slightly more than in an American initial "L"; at the same time the tip and blade of the tongue are pressed slightly more against the upper gum ridge just forward of where it curves up to form the cavity below the palate than in articulating an American "L." The British use a dark "l" (notice that the phonetic symbol for this consonant is different from "L"), with the tongue slightly thickened toward the palate, and the position of the tongue also conditions how the vowels surrounding the "l" sound. This positioning is a key to how the accent should generally "feel" in the mouth, indicating the place in the mouth where the stream of air is generally directed to resonate.

Vowels and Diphthongs
e (schwa): The schwa (the short vowel heard in the word *the* before consonants; "*e*" in my phonetic transcription) so widely used as a substitution for the vowel in unstressed syllables in British RP is much more rarely heard in General American. In the phrase "Secretary of State for the Home Department" all the underlined letters are schwas in British RP (Secretery ef State fe the Home Department). Only the "e" in "-re-" and in *the* are schwas in General American.
A: The broad "A," the sound of the "a" in *father*, so widely used in British English, sounds in American English like the "a" in *that*. See the list in Chapter One on Standard British English.

aw: The "aw" in *law*, *talk*, and *water* never sounds like "A" in *father*. This is a Middle Western and Western regionalism. It is a slightly longer vowel in British than in American.

O: The long diphthong "O" in American English is a combination of "o" and

"<u>oo</u>," o'<u>oo</u>. In British English it is a combination of the schwa "*e*" and "<u>oo</u>": *e*'-<u>oo</u>. Elongate the lips for the British sound.

o: The short vowel "o" in words like *hot, not, got,* etc. sounds almost like the "A" in *father* in General American, like a very short "aw" in *law* in British RP.

u: In General American the vowel "u" in *but* never sounds like the "A" in *father,* as it so often does in British RP.

Stress

Stress on particular words sometimes differs in England and North America and in various native accents. In America we say *an'cillary,* in Great Britain *ancil'lary.* You put your car in a *garage'* in the United States, but in England you park it in a *gar'age,* although even in Britain one hears the American pronunciation nowadays, because of the homogenizing influence of television. For some reason British pronunciations are seldom adopted by Americans.

Pitch (Intonation, Music)

In English stressed and important syllables, whatever syllables the speaker wishes to emphasize, are spoken on an upper pitch, literally with more muscular force, and they are louder. Unstressed and unimportant syllables are spoken on a lower pitch. However, in emphasizing a particular syllable the speaker may use a lower rather than a higher pitch, and this has to do with the paralinguistic functions mentioned at the beginning of this chapter. This pitch pattern (intonation) creates the typical rise and fall of a sentence in English.

The nuclear tone is usually spoken on a slightly higher pitch than the other stressed syllables in the group, especially in British English. Stressed syllables may also be spoken on more than one pitch, with a rising or falling tone. Because of the prevalence of diphthongs in English it is easy to use falling and rising tones; one half of the diphthong is at one end of the rise or fall and the other half is at the other end.

At the end of a simple declarative sentence the pitch is lowered slightly.

At the end of a question the pitch rises, but this pattern may change in certain circumstances. If the word *are* is stressed in *How are you?* it is also often spoken on an upper pitch and *you* on a lower one, for example.

An imperative, or a command, is usually spoken with a falling tone.

Emotional utterances, such as expletives, may add several pitches to the pattern.

There generally are four or five pitches in a typical sentence in American English. There are possibly a few more tones or pitches in a typical British RP sentence. One of the features of other native accents is that they have their own typical intonation patterns. See the chapter on Irish, Scottish and Welsh accents, for example.

Some final words of advice: As an actor you must be understood by your audience. Do not, for instance, do such a thoroughly authentic Cockney or Glasgow accent that most of your audience will find everything you say utterly incomprehensible. Instead do an authentic-sounding version, and always keep your diction clear by articulating consonants strongly. Sometimes all you need to do to sound French or Italian or Swedish or Viennese is to capture the musical pattern or rhythm of the original language, or to use two or three sound substitutions which will give an authentic flavor and a reality to your work. Of course the thickness of the accent is a function of the character you are playing. Walter Matthau in *I.Q.* (1994) accurately captured Albert Einstein's heavy German accent, but spoke much more clearly than the real Einstein, who had to be subtitled in newsreels. It is also possible to do an outrageous distortion as an accent, basing it loosely on linguistic reality, as Peter Sellers did as the hilarious Inspector Clouseau in *The Pink Panther* (1964) and its sequels.

Whether you do a real or comically distorted accent, it must be organic and therefore internal to the character. When Harold Prince was doing the musical *The Petrified Prince* at the New York Shakespeare Festival, he directed Alan Braunstein (excellent in the role of Napoleon, to whom he bore a remarkable resemblance when he was in costume and makeup) to do a French accent. All Mr. Prince wanted the actor to do was to replace the voiced "TH" and the voiceless "th" with "z" and "s." That was all Mr. Braunstein really had to do to have an absolutely clear and convincing French accent. I suggested to him that he also add a bit of the typical rhythmic French phrasing (see Chapter Eight), and he did. His accent was perfect, and just what was required. So, indeed, as the old saying goes, sometimes less is more.

As I have said in the Foreword, people speak as individuals, and so will you, bearing in mind that there are also specific, recognizable characteristics for any accent. It is very important to maintain the general position of the vocal apparatus during speech. In other words, don't lose the general placement of the accent. For instance, in a Russian accent the tongue is generally held high during speech in a position that feels unnatural and uncomfortable to most Americans, but if you let the tongue slip down to a more comfortable position during the pronunciation of vowels and diphthongs, you immediately lose the accent. Russian is full of palatalized consonants, which by definition can only be pronounced with the tongue in an upper position (see Chapter Seventeen). You may lose the accent for only one or two words before you assume the correct position again, but the audience will have found the slip an immediate distraction (they won't even always know why), and they will be less convinced by your performance. After all, you want them simply to accept what you are doing. Instead they think, and probably say afterwards, "That person was in and out of the accent." It helps, too, if you think in the accent even when you are not speaking.

While the general position of the vocal apparatus is consistent, the phonetic shifts from General American consonants are not always consistent, although they usually are. For instance, a character of German background may pronounce initial "R" with its usual retroflex pronunciation, but use a guttural "R" after other consonants. You may, of course, make a choice to do that for your character's accent. Similarly, in various accents there may be a rule that initial ìwî shifts to "v," but the same speaker may sometimes pronounce "w" as "w," sometimes ás "v."

English orthography may be inconsistent and difficult, but, generally speaking, where actual sounds are concerned, as opposed to the letters that we perceive as representing them, there is a consistency within each accent, particularly when it comes to vowels and diphthongs. (The letters don't always represent the sounds we think they represent: See the section above on vowels, for instance. On the other hand, the phonetic symbols in this book, like all such symbols, are meant to represent actual sounds.) Any accent contains its inventory of vowel and diphthong sounds, and a person who substitutes "e" for "a" in such words as *cat* and *back* usually does so all the time, as opposed to what speakers do with the examples just given for the consonants "R" and "w." In Scottish accents, to take another example, the sound "oo" usually does not exist, and "oo" is heard in those words where in General American we use "oo," such as *boot, pool,* and *fool.* You should be consistent with vowel sounds, and consistent even in your choice to be inconsistent with regard to particular consonant sounds. Be absolutely consistent as regards the general position of the vocal apparatus. Remember, too, that what you have to do is make a choice based on your character's circumstances, and the director's requirements ("I want a light, or a heavy accent"), and stick with it.

Watch films or television programs in which the actors speak with an authentic accent, and imitate what you hear. Once you have listened carefully to whatever material you have and accurately reproduced what you have heard, the key to authenticity is habit. Select the accent to suit the character and make it your own by constant repetition and drilling. Begin your work by reading the summary of the most important information about the accent, entitled "A Quick Reference," immediately accessible before "How to Do a _____ Accent." When you feel you have achieved sufficient mastery of the accent, use books, newspaper and magazine articles and read them aloud or silently to yourself using the accent. Work with the texts you have selected by marking them phonetically, then read them aloud slowly. When you feel comfortable with the new sounds, read more quickly, until you feel the accent is absolutely natural. Record and listen to yourself. You can do the same thing with the "Practice Exercises and Sentences" on pages xvi-xvii. It may also help to mark your script phonetically, perhaps on a separate copy from the one you carry in early rehearsals. Make using the accent your habitual way of speaking in rehearsal so that you no longer have to think about it, and it will simply be the way your character naturally speaks. If you are convinced, your audience will be.

Part One

The British Isles and Commonwealth

Introduction

English, which began to assume its modern form in the days of Shakespeare in the later 16th century, is a member of the Germanic family of Indo-European languages. Languages are classified by grammar, not by vocabulary content. Although a great deal of the vocabulary of English comes from Norman French, English grammar is Germanic, as are many of its basic words, such as *it, be, is, this, that, will,* and *was.*

English, carried all over the world by English merchants and colonists and by the agents of the British Empire, is spoken by hundreds of millions of people in the British Isles, North America, the Caribbean, East, West and South Africa, India, Hong Kong, Singapore, Australia, and New Zealand, and serves as a general language of commerce and diplomacy all over the planet. It is one of the official languages of the United Nations.

In the horrendous days of the African slave trade, English was used as a trading language in West Africa, where it gave rise to the first Pidgin varieties of the language in the 16th century, and then to Creoles. The word *Pidgin* is a corruption of the Cantonese pronunciation of the English word *business.* A Pidgin is a language devised for commercial purposes and used between traders who speak one language and an indigenous population which speaks another language. When a Pidgin becomes the first language of the indigenous population of an area, it is called a Creole, a corruption of the 17th-century French word *criar,* meaning "nurse." Most of the nurses, governesses and other servants, slave or free, of the colonists were African, and they brought their own children up to speak Pidgin. Creole languages take on a life and a development of their own. English itself can be said to be a kind of Creole, having evolved from a combination of Anglo-Saxon and Norman French, as outlined in the first section of this book. In areas where the parent language, such as English, is spoken alongside the Creole language there is also a tendency towards a process of decreolization, where the main features of the Creole language are dropped in favor of the original language, which then retains influences from the Creole language, as happened in Jamaica and other Caribbean islands.

There are a vast number of regional accents of English both in the British Isles and North America, and wherever the far-flung British Empire brought English to the colonies as the language of administration and colonization. We shall cover in detail the accents most useful to actors, and content ourselves with a briefer survey of the accents less likely to be encountered in plays and films.

Chapter One
Standard Upper-Class British (RP)

The accent known as RP (Received Pronunciation) is used by Oxford and Cambridge graduates, the aristocracy, and the upper economic classes generally. *Received* refers to the phrase *received in the best society*. RP is the accent learned and used in the English Public Schools all over England, the Public Schools being elite private schools, such as Eton or Harrow, preparatory schools for the great universities of Oxford and Cambridge. They are called *public* because the students are not tutored privately at home, but in public in classes with other students. Incidentally, the students there are not in *grades*, but in *forms*. There is, incidentally, a once well known phrase, which seems to me a middle-class, rather than an aristocratic, expression of smug contempt: He, or she, is *NOCD*, meaning "not our class, dear."

There is a modern variant of RP known as "Sloane Ranger," which takes its name from the trendy area around Sloane Square in London where the well-to-do scions of aristocratic families, called Sloane Rangers, live and play. They go "dinetine" to purchase "Spade" china ("downtown"; "Spode") and they speak through smiling, closed lips. They probably wouldn't be caught dead having afternoon tea at Fortnum and Mason's, and needless to say they would never have *high tea*, which is the term for a working-class evening meal—chops and sausages and so on.

In the 1920s there was an affectation, ably done by Ian Carmichael as Lord Peter Wimsey in the PBS *Mystery* series based on Dorothy Sayers's novels, on the part of some members of the upper class: They dropped the final "g" in "-ing" endings, and went "huntin', shootin', and fishin'." This affectation soon disappeared, as had the Victorian affectation of saying *don't* for *doesn't*: *He don't know*. There is actually a great variety of upper-class accents, including the very precise, well-articulated Oxford University accent. In fact, every school has its own slight variation. There are also those drawling, affected accents in which "R" is pronounced either as "v" (veally tvue) or as "w" (weally twue) or slightly swallowed as a kind of guttural "R." All rather *twee*, don't you think? *Twee* is fairly recent British slang for "cloyingly sweet," derived from baby talk.

The accent of RP is changing somewhat from what it was earlier in the century, and there is a tendency to use glottal stops at the end of some words, an influence from London lower- and middle-class accents (see the end of this chapter). A glottal stop (phonetic symbol: ?), which you may think of as a kind of catch in the throat, is the substitution of a pause during which the glottis is closed for a split second to replace the letter "t" in such words as *it* and *bit*: i?; bi?. In RP it is not used in the middle of such words as *bottle* and *battle*, as it is in London lower-class accents. Some people also insert the semi-vowel "y" in the words *too* and *do*, when those words are not stressed, which never used to be done: ty<u>oo</u>, dy<u>oo</u>. Another change occasionally heard is the shift from "<u>ooe</u>" to "aw" in certain words such as *poor* (pooe, p<u>oo</u>e or paw) and *sure* (shooe, sh<u>oo</u>e or shaw).

The dialectical features of British RP, as well as those of other British accents, include lexical (vocabulary) differences from General American. Where an Englishman would say "That vase is meant to be on the mantlepiece," an American would be more likely to say "That vase is supposed to be over the fireplace" or "on the mantle." But, as they say in England, "You weren't to know that," meaning, to Americans, "You couldn't have known that." In a London restaurant do not ask for a *napkin*, or *nappie*, which is a baby's diaper in England. Ask instead for a *serviette*. In an English kitchen you might find a *fish slice*, which is not a slice of fish, but what Americans call a *spatula*. You wear a *dressing gown* in England, not a *bathrobe*, and you might live in a *block of flats*, which is an apartment house. In England the word *block* used simply by itself also means an apartment house, and not a city street. If someone says they will "come round and knock you up" it does not mean they will make you pregnant, which is what the phrase means in the United States, but simply that they will come over to your place and knock on your door. (By the way, a *rubber* in England is what Americans call an eraser). Perhaps you will play *draughts* (pronounced "dRAfts"), but never *checkers*, which, with a capital "C" rhymes with the name of the Prime Minister's country residence, Chequers. In England there are no *exits*, but there are plenty of *ways out*, not to mention *ways in*, instead of *entrances*. "I'll catch you up" means what Americans mean by "I'll catch up to you." Something that is *jolly good* in England is *great* in America. If something is *bloody awful* in Great Britain, it is *terrible* in the United States. In England garbage is called *dust*, and a garbage pail is called a *dustbin*. The people who collect the garbage are *dustmen*. These sorts of expressions and lexical variations will, of course, be written by an author in a script. Look at Harold Pinter's plays, for instance, for typical British locutions.

The sometimes tenuous relationship between English orthography and pronunciation has led to some unusual discrepancies between what the eye sees on the printed page and what the ear hears. Some examples of British proper names illustrate my point: *Alcester* (awl' ste); *Aveton Gifford* (a' ve ten gi' fed, or, aw' ten dgi' fed); *Badgworthy* (ba' dge Ree); *Beauchamp* (bee' chem); *Biddlesden* (bilz' den; a town in Buckinghamshire); *Blemundsbury* (blemz' bRee; House in London); *Cholmondeston* (chum' sten); *Cholmondely* (chum' lee); *Cirencester* (pronounced as you might expect: sI' Ren ses te, or, sis' i te); *Claughton* (pronounced variously klaw' ten, klaf' ten, or klI' ten; the first two for two different villages in Lancashire, the third for a family name); *Dalziel* (dal' zel, or, dee' el); *Earl Granville Leveson Gower* (gRan' vel l<u>oo</u>' sen gaw'); *Marjoribanks* (mAch' banks); *Worcestershire* (woo' ste she). My favorite, however, is *Featherstonehaugh*, which has *five* pronunciations: fe' the sten haw; fe' sten haw; feee' sten haw; fee' sen hay; and, the least likely, fan' shaw!

There are innumerable examples of Standard British accents in the many British films and television and stage dramas. Among the incomparable actors to listen to are Ian Richardson, Ian McKellen, Diana Rigg, Maggie Smith, John Gielgud, Ralph Richardson, Laurence Olivier, Joan Plowright, Joan Greenwood, Robert Donat, Peter Ustinov, Charles Laughton, Henry Daniell, James Mason, Basil Rathbone, Peggy Ashcroft, Derek Jacobi, John Mills, Trevor Howard (who is wonderful in Noel Coward's *Brief Encounter* [1945], with the brilliant Celia Johnson), Peter Cushing, Christopher Lee, the Redgraves (Michael, Vanessa and Lynn), Claire Bloom, Claude Rains, Alastair Sim (although he was from Edinburgh, in *The Belles of St. Trinian's* [1954] and *A Christmas Carol* [1951]), Margaret Rutherford as Miss Marple in such films as *Murder She Said* (1961) and as Miss Prism in *The Importance of Being Earnest* (1952), with Edith Evans as Lady Bracknell and Michael Redgrave as Jack, and the list goes on and on. You will find the titles of more films in some of the notes to the Practice exercises. And here are some more of my favorite British films, in which you can hear a variety of upper-class and other accents: *The Lavender Hill Mob* (1951), with Alec Guiness and Stanley Holloway; *The Ladykillers* (1955), with Alec Guiness, Cecil Parker (always a pleasure to listen to; hilariously befuddled in Danny Kaye's Hollywood film *The Court Jester* [1956]), Frankie Howerd (as a Cockney fruit vendor), and a wonderfully sweet, genteel Katie Johnson, whose accent you really should listen to for old-fashioned, very clear diction; *The Man in the White Suit* (1951), with Alec Guiness, Cecil Parker, Michael Gough and Joan Greenwood; *I'm All Right Jack* (1959), with Ian Carmichael, Richard Attenborough, Peter Sellers(as a union leader with a marvelous working-class accent), and the inimitable Terry-Thomas, whose accent is hilarious; *Goodbye, Mr. Chips* (1939, a USA-British collaboration), with Robert Donat; *The Servant* (1963) with Dirk Bogarde, Sarah Miles and James Fox (whose accent is always very plummy and upper-class); *The Wrong Box* (1966), based on a novel by Robert Louis Stevenson and his stepson Lloyd Osborne, with Ralph Richardson and John Mills; *Her Majesty Mrs. Brown* (1997), with the brilliant Judi Dench as Queen Victoria, Billy Connolly as the Scottish Mr. Brown, Anthony Sher, who is superb as Disraeli, and a generally wonderful cast, including Geoffrey Palmer; *The Chalk Garden* (1964), with John Mills, Hayley Mills, Deborah Kerr, Edith Evans and Felix Aylmer (excellent also as Polonious in the Olivier *Hamlet* [1948] and as Isaac of York in Hollywood's version of Sir Walter Scott's *Ivanhoe* [1952]); *The Great Gilbert and Sullivan* (1953), with Robert Morley, Maurice Evans, Eileen Herlie, Peter Finch and Martyn Green (whose diction is always superb; listen to him on the series of Gilbert and Sullivan recordings made in the late 1940s and early 1950s, now available on Pearl CD); Mike Leigh's *Topsy-Turvy* (1999), with Jim Broadbent and Alex Corduner and a wonderful British cast; and that, of course, is only the merest sampling.

A Quick Reference

1) When speaking, keep your mouth slightly more closed than in American English.
2) Drop the final "R" and the "R" before another consonant.
3) Learn and use a correct British "L." (See below.) This sound is the key to the placement of the accent.
4) Use schwas in most unstressed syllables.
5) See the list below for words which shift from American "a" in *that* to the British "A" in *father*.
6) Use the British short "o" in *hot, not, got*.
7) Learn and use the British diphthong "O."
8) Check throughout the chapter for words which are pronounced differently in British English from American English, whether for reasons of stress or phonetics. *Been* rhymes with *bean*, for instance.

How to Do an Upper-Class British Accent

1) Position of the Vocal Apparatus

To get the correct position, push your lips forward and say *oo*. Push the lips back slightly and you will have the correct general position in which the mouth should be held for this accent. The lips are held slightly more together and both the lips and the tongue are slightly more forward than in American English. In general the language feels as if it is frontally pronounced, whereas American often feels as if it is in the middle of the mouth. The **point of resonance** is just forward of where it is in General American; that is, the stream of air passing across the vibrating vocal cords is directed towards the front of the mouth, where the palate acts as a sounding board. It is at the point where the tongue touches the opening into the palate to form the sound of "d" (the **point of articulation** of the "d") that the general resonance of British RP lies; in General American that point of resonance is just where the tip of the tongue leaves a space to form the consonant "R." **Practice** by repeating *da da da do do do hello hello hello* several times until you get the feeling you can direct the stream of air forward to that point in the mouth, so the language skips and plays about.

2) **Very important words** which American actors often get wrong:

1) *Been* rhymes with *bean* in a British accent 99 times out of a hundred, and not, as in General American, with *bin*.
2) *For* is often, though not always pronounced with a schwa ("fe") before a consonant or a semi-vowel, as in *for you* and *for me*: "fe yoo"; "fe mee." *For* is pronounced "feR" before a vowel, when the final "R" in *for* is linked to the vowel, as in *for us*: fe Rus. *For* is not usually stressed.
3) *To* is almost always pronounced with a schwa ("te") before the semi-vowel "y" or before a consonant, as in *to you* or *to be*: te yoo; te bee. *To* is pronounced "too" before a vowel, as in *to act*: too akt. *To* in a verb infinitive is almost never stressed. The word *today* is usually pronounced "te day'." Note that the General Ameri-

can pronunciation "too" before a consonant in precise speech sounds pedantic to British ears, since "te" is usual. The pronunciation "too" was used to create the effect of pedantry by Michael Redgrave, brilliant in the superb 1951 British film *The Browning Version* by Terence Rattigan.

Practice
To do, today, to try, to go, to be, to have, to say, to come, to go, for you, for me, for him, for her, for us, for them, for this, for that.

4) *room* (usually Room, with the vowel in *book*, as opposed to General American Room, with the vowel in *boot*); *again, against* (two pronunciations: *e* gen' or *e* gayn', *e* genst' or *e* gaynst'; the first pronunciations are also General American); *anything* (the "y" is usually heard as a schwa: e' ne thing; in a phrase the last two syllables can both be heard as schwas: *Has he given you anything else?* [hez hee gi' ven yoo e' ne theng, or e' ne thing, else]); *everything* (the "y" is often heard as a schwa: e' vre thing); *everybody* (the "y" and "o" can both be heard as schwas: e' vre be dee, especially in a phrase such as *everybody else*, or, alternatively, as e' vre bo' dee); *anybody* (same as with *everybody*); *circumstances* (three pronunciations, the first, if the "R" is pronounced, being also General American: so' kum, or kem, stan' siz, or sez; so' kem sten siz; so' kem stAn siz).

3) The Most Important Sounds

Consonants
L: This consonant feels more forward in the mouth than in General American, and is sometimes more like the French lateral liquid consonant (phonetic symbol: "l"). The tongue is higher than in American. In articulating an "L," the tip of the tongue touches the upper gum ridge behind the front teeth lightly for an American "L," and is pressed against the gum ridge a bit more for the British "L."

R: Standard British English is **non-rhotic**, that is:
1) The "R" in a final position (at the end of a word) is dropped and "R" is dropped as well when the next word or syllable starts with another consonant.
2) The "R" is also dropped following a vowel and preceding a consonant in the middle of words like *first, work, word,* etc.
It may help you to think of "R" before another consonant and in final position as a silent letter, like the "b" in lamb or the "gh" in daughter .
   At the beginning of a word the "R" is the same as it is in American pronunciation; it is a "retroflex" consonant, with the bottom of the tongue curled up toward the roof of the mouth (palate).
   At the beginning of a syllable in the middle of a word between two vowels the "R" is often, but by no means always, given one tap or trill: "r."
   As in many non-rhotic accents there is an "intrusive R." Words like *drawing* become "drawRing" and phrases like *Diana and I* become "Diana Rand I" or even "Diana rand I" (where the "R" or "r" is really linked to the "a" in *and*).

33

There is also a "linking R," where an "R" at the end of a word is linked to a vowel at the beginning of the following word, as in the phrase *my brother and I*.

A few members of the upper classes sometimes drop "R" in the middle of a word, so that *very* is pronounced either "ve" or "vay," as in *very true*: "vay true." Sometimes also there is trouble pronouncing "R" and it is sounded almost like "w," but with the tongue curled up slightly as if to make an "R," but without the tongue's reaching its correct position.

Practice

Write out the following sentences and draw a line through all the "R"s which occur before another consonant, whether at the end of or in the middle of a word.
The firemen at work saw the fire first near the far door.
Barbara was very barbaric, very, very barbaric indeed.

Vowels and Diphthongs
The schwa, *"e"*: This symbol represents the schwa, the sound *"e"* (the vowel in *the* before a consonant) in unstressed syllables. The symbol for this sound in the International Phonetic Alphabet (IPA) is an upside-down, reversed "e." The schwa is often substituted for a longer vowel. This substitution shortens the syllable, eliminating the vowel almost entirely. It is much more widely used in British than in American English today.

Practice

(Note: The apostrophe indicates that the preceding syllable is stressed. Nearly all other vowels are schwas. Remember to drop the final "R.")
The o'ther day' I' was go'ing to say' some'thing amu'sing.
Phonetic pronunciation: THee u' THe day I wez gO' ing te say sum' theng e myoo' zing

Sec'retary of State' for the Home' Départ'ment.
Phonetic pronunciation: sek' Re tRee, or sek' re te ree, or sek' Re te Ree, ev stayt fe THe hOm de pAt' ment

se'parate; prepos'terous; labo'ratory; ga'rage; vi'gilant; believe'; tribu'nal; police'.
Phonetic pronunciations: sep' Ret, or sep' e Ret; pre pos' te Res, or pRe pos' tRes; le bo' re tRee; ga' Redg; vi' dge lent; be leev'; tre byoo' nel; pe lees'

The use of the schwa is perhaps the most important phonetic key to the accent of all, and the one least easily assimilated. The frequent use of the schwa makes the language sound a bit swallowed up on occasion and one has the impression of hearing nothing but consonants, although the articulation can be very strong.

A: Very broad and open-throated. This is the most open vowel in English and only occurs in this accent, where it is widely used in words which in American

34

English are pronounced with the "a" in *that*, except for certain regional variations such as New England, where, however, very few of these words are pronounced in the broad British way.

Partial List

Use these words for practice. Record them and listen to yourself.
advantage, after, words beginning and ending with *after: afternoon, afterwards, hereafter,* etc., *answer, ask, aunt, banana, basket, bastard, bath, blast, branch, brass, broadcast, calf, can't, cask, casket, cast, caste, castle, chance, chancellor, chant, clasp, class,* words beginning with *class: classmate, classroom, classy,* etc., *command, countermand, daft, dance, demand, disaster, downcast, draft, enchant, entrance* (verb), *example, fast, fasten, gala, ghastly, glass, graft, grant,* words ending in *-graph: telegraph,* etc. (But note that the word *graphic* is pronounced "gra' fik"; words ending in "-graphic" are pronounced "gra' fik"; *graphite* is pronounced "gra' fIt"; words ending in "-graphical" such as *geographical* are pronounced "-gra' fi kel"), *grasp, grass, half, lance, last, lather, laugh, lithograph, mask, mast, master, nasty, outcast, paragraph* ("a" in first syllable, "A" in last syllable: pa' Re gRAf), *pass, Passover, past, pastor, pastoral, path, perchance, phonograph, photograph, plant, plaster, prance, raft, rascal, rasp, raspberry* (RAz' bRee), *rather, reprimand, salve, sample, shaft, shan't, slander, slant, staff, stanch, surpass, task, tomato* (Note: The "a" in *potato* is as it is in General American), *trance, transcript, transport* and other words beginning with the prefix "trans-," *vast, waft, wrath*
Note: The "a" in *fancy, gas, mass,* and *glacier* (sounds like "glassier" without the "R"; but note: *glacial* is pronounced "glay' shel") sound like the "a" in *that.*

o: This is the short "o" in *hot, not,* and *got.* In RP it is like the "aw" in *law, bought,* but shorter. In General American *hot, not,* and *got* are pronounced with the "A" in *father.* An **important sound** for a good RP accent.

O: The diphthong in *know* and *own* combines the schwa "*e*" with the "oo" in *boot;* the "*e*" is stressed. Keep the lips forward to pronounce it. (Note: The first part of the diphthong is sometimes incorrectly thought of as being like "e" in *met.*) It is used in the nouns *process* (pRO' ses) and *progress* (pRO' gRes), where American uses the "A" in *father:* pRA' ses'; pRA' gRes'. Note the double stress in the American pronunciation, and the schwa in the British unstressed second syllable.

Practice

I know I don't know how to get over to the road.
I made a great deal of progress in my rehearsal process.

yoo: The long sound in *duke* and *tune* is a diphthong combining the semi-vowel "y" with the "oo" in *boot.* The full diphthong is almost always pronounced in *duke, tune, flute, lure, lute, institution, constitution, delusion, illusion, lunatic,*

Tuesday, newspaper, etc. When the semi-vowel "y" is inserted after a consonant, that consonant is said to be *palatalized.* Literally this means that the tongue has been pushed upwards to touch the upper, or hard, palate, the roof of the mouth. Any consonant (or vowel) can be palatalized. Palatalization is much more widespread in RP (and is ubiquitous, for instance, in Russian) than in General American. To drop the "y" is satirical in the upper classes: *dook,* etc., and an affectation of the 1920s and 1930s. There are some words in which a simple consonant is pronounced without adulteration before "oo"; for example the "d" in *graduate* does not sound like the "dge" in "edge", nor the "x" in *sexual* like "ksh": gra dyoo ayt'; seks' yoo el (although the pronunciation "sek' shel" is also heard, but note that it is not like General American "sek' shoo eL"). A contemporary trend is the dropping of "y" after "l" and "s," so that *lute* (lyoot) becomes "loot," and *super* (syoo' pe) becomes "soo' pe."

More Words in Which the Simple Consonant Is Sounded
Before Fully Pronounced "yoo"

gradual, individual, procedure, sensual, issue (is' yoo), *tissue, schedule* (Notes: "sch" sounds like "sh," not like American "sk." The plurals of *picture* and *lecture* (pik' tyuh, lek' tyuh) become "pik-tshuhz" and "lek-tshuhz.")

Further Phonetic Information

See the very important information in Stress below. Bear in mind particularly the non-rhoticity of the accent and the use of the broad, open-throated "A." The important thing is to select the specific accent to use in playing a specific character, such as the Major in the British television series *Fawlty Towers,* or Lord Emsworth of Blandings Castle in dramatizations of P.G. Wodehouse novels. Remember that people speak in individual, idiosyncratic ways, as well as in ways which are characteristic of a particular region and social class. It is also worth bearing in mind that the same speaker can pronounce the same words differently in different circumstances: *education* (e dyoo kay' shen; more formal); (e dye kay' shen or e dge kay' shen; less formal).

Consonants
There are very few changes from American consonants, except for the fact that some consonants have a more forward point of articulation, namely "d," "t," "k," and "g." In articulating "b" the lips are pressed together for a slightly longer time than in an American "b."

Vowels and Diphthongs
ay: the diphthong in *late, say*; much as in General American. This sound is often but not always shortened in words ending with *day,* so *Monday* becomes Mondee, *holiday* holidee, etc., but *weekday* retains the full long "ay."

a: the vowel in *that, cat*; as in American, but sometimes shortened so it sounds like the "e" in *met.* Occasionally a schwa will be inserted after the vowel, so *that* sounds like "thaet"; this is sometimes exaggerated for satiric effect.

aw: the vowel in *law, awful, bought*: This is a longer sound than in American, with the lips more forward.

e: the vowel in *met*: much as in General American; lips a bit more open.

ee: the vowel in *meet*; much as in General American. Note: In RP the word *been* is usually pronounced to rhyme with *bean*, and not, as in General American, with *bin*.

"es" word endings: These are usually pronounced not with a schwa but with the sound "eez" or with a lengthened "i:."

Practice

bases, catches, snatches, batches, masses, brasses, dances. Note that the last syllable of *women* is also pronounced "i:n."

I: This diphthong, heard in *I, fight, might,* and *right,* combines the broad "A" discussed above with the "ee" in *meet*; the "A" is stressed. The full long diphthong is used in "-ile" endings as in *facile, missile, mobile, projectile, servile,* etc. The "ee" half of the diphthong is dropped in some words when they are unstressed, such as *I'm,* for example, which becomes "Am" or even "em."

i: This vowel in *bit* is the same as in General American.

ow: The diphthong in *how, house* combines the "A" discussed above and the "oo" in *boot*; the "A" is stressed. (The American diphthong combines the "a" in *that* with the "oo" in *boot*). The second half of the diphthong is sometimes dropped; this sounds very pretentious and like the Sloane Rangers.

Practice

How now brown cow.
The outhouse is out back.
Out and about.
u: The short "u" in *but, cup, up, love,* and *above* is a vowel often pronounced like the "A" in General American *father.*

Stress

One of the phenomena that gives a particular "music" to British speech different from the American "music" is that the *nuclear tones,* the most important stressed syllables in the most important words in a sentence, are spoken with their vowels lengthened and usually on a higher pitch.

In English accents many words are differently stressed than they are in General American. Note the differently stressed words in the practice sentence below; the apostrophe indicates that the preceding syllable is stressed. Such words as *secondary, territory, ordinary* and *extraordinary* lose the secondary stress they have in General American on the "-or" or "-ar" syllables, which are pronounced in British English with a schwa, or which even disappear entirely: "sek' endeRee" or "sek' endRee," "te' ReteRee" or "te' RetRee," etc. Note also that the "R" may be trilled when it is between two vowels: "te' reteree" or "te' retRee." Words ending in "-ization" are pronounced with the diphthong "I" instead of the schwa one might expect: *civilization* (si' ve lI zay' shen); *organization* (aw' ge nI zay' shen), and so forth. The ending "-ess" in such words as *princess, countess,* and *stewardess* (but not in *actress*) is often stressed in RP. Among other words differently pronounced in RP from General American are: *believe* (bleev, occasionally); *cigarette* (sig e ret'; stress on the last syllable, as opposed to American stress, which is on the first syllable); *corollary* (ke RA' Le ree, as opposed to American kA' Re la ree); *dictate* (as a verb prononced "dik tayt' "; as a noun it is pronounced "dik' tayt," but Americans use this last pronunciation for both the verb and the noun), *disciplinary* (dis i pli' ne ree); *discriminatory* (dis kri mi nay' teree); *fashionable* (fash' ne bl); *February,* often terribly mispronounced even by newscasters on American television as "feb' y<u>oo</u> ar ee," is pronounced occasionally in Britain as "feb' ree"; *frontier* (frun' teee; stress on first syllable); *government* (guv' ment); *library* (occasionally lI' bRee); *literary* ("li' te Re Ree" or "li' tRe Ree" or "li' tRee," but seldom like American "Li' te Re' Ree"); *literature* (li' tRe che); *mandatory* (man day' te Ree, as opposed to American "man' de taw Ree"); *manufacture* (ma' ne fak' tye; ma' ne fak' tshe, as opposed to American "man' y<u>oo</u> fak' tsheR"); *national* (nash' nel); *ordinary* ("aw' dn Ree" or "aw' den e' ree," with or without a trilled "r," as opposed to General American "awR' din e' Ree"); *perhaps* (pRaps; phaps; pe haps'); *police* (plees); *premature* (pRe' me tyooe', as opposed to American "pRee' me tsh<u>oo</u>R' "); *temporary* (tem' pRee; tem' pRe Ree; tem' pe re ree). For British proper names consult the *BBC Pronouncing Dictionary of British Names* (Oxford University Press, 1990).

Practice (The underlined words are pronounced differently in RP from General American.)
"I don't mean to arouse <u>contro' versy</u> or to appear <u>discrimina' tory,</u> but I would <u>suggest</u> in an <u>ecumenical</u> way that it is <u>necessary</u> to take one's <u>medicine</u> and <u>vitamins</u> on <u>schedule</u> to avoid getting <u>migraines</u>", said the <u>Nicaraguan lieutenant narra' ting</u> a story to his <u>homosexual nephew,</u> the <u>labo' ratory clerk</u> and <u>saxo' phonist,</u> whose car was in the <u>ga' rage.</u>

Phonetic Pronunciations of the Underlined Words:
ken tRA' ve see; dis kRi me nay' te Ree; se dgest', *and not as in American* sug dgest'; ee ky<u>oo</u> me' ni kel; ne' se sree, or ne' se se ree; med' sin; vit' e mins, *not* vIt-; shed' y<u>oo</u>l; mee' grayns; nik e Rag' y<u>oo</u> en; lef or lef ten' ent; neRay' ting; hA me seks' y<u>oo</u> el; nev' y<u>oo</u>; lebA' Retree; klA: k; saks Af' en ist; ga' Redg

Pitch

See the general information in the Introduction on pitch. The following are some useful comparative examples of British and American pitch patterns for practice.

Note: "/" is the symbol for a rising tone; "\" is the symbol for a falling tone. These tones divide a diphthong.

Example:

Oh, I say!

```
        \sa-
    I
/Oh,        y!
```

Oh is spoken on a rising tone, *I* on an upper tone, and *say* on a falling tone. Because of the prevalence of diphthongs in English it is easy to use falling and rising tones; one half of the diphthong is at one end of the rise or fall and the other half is at the other end, as in the example just given.

Another Possible Pattern

```
        \sa-
Oh,
    I       y!
```

At the end of a simple declarative sentence the pitch is usually lowered slightly.

At the end of a question the pitch rises, but this pattern may change in certain circumstances. If the word *are* is stressed in *How are you?* it is often spoken on an upper pitch and *you* on a lower one, for example.

An imperative or a command, is usually spoken with a falling tone at the end: Come \here! A rising tone at the end would seem most unnatural.

Emotional utterances, such as expletives, may add several pitches to the pattern:

```
                dare
        idiot! How
                    you?!
You
```

There are four or five pitches or tones or notes in a typical sentence in American English. There are a few more tones or pitches in a typical British RP sentence. (One of the features of other native accents is the change in these typical pitch patterns. Compare Irish, Scottish and Welsh accents to British RP or General American, for example. The reason the same language is spoken with different accents is simply that languages change. They evolve over time and in different social circumstances as their speakers spread out to different places and sometimes retain older forms of a language which has continued to evolve in its place of origin. Contrariwise, a language may evolve in a new place as it remains conservative at its point of origin.)

Some More Examples of Intonation Patterns in British RP

Would you care for some tea?
(British Pattern)

Would you care for some
                                        /tea? (rising tone) or tea? (flat tone)

(American Pattern)

                                        tea?
Would you care for some

Phonetic Pronunciations Compared:
British RP: wed y<u>oo</u> ke:*e* f*e* sem tee
General American: wood y<u>oo</u> ke:R foR sum tee

Note: In the following examples it is possible to hear the so-called American pattern, which is, I emphasize, only one of several possible patterns in British RP, but you would almost never hear the British pattern in General American.

Were you going there today, if I may ask?
(British Pattern)

                            /da-
            going there to-   \y,   ask?
Were you   if I may

(American Pattern)

                            day, if I may ask?
            going there to-
Were you

Emphasizing the word *there* changes the pattern.
(British Pattern)

                                            ask?
                        day if I
            /there to-   may
Were you going

  or

Were you going   ask?
                    \there   if I may
                        today,

(American Pattern)

                            today, if I may ask?
                    there
Were you going

It was an extremely good plan.
(Three British Patterns)
Note: The first pattern would only occasionally be heard in General American,
and is more typical of British intonation; the next two patterns could be heard
in both British RP and General American.

                                    plan.
                    tremely
            ex-   good
It was an

                                    good
                    tremely
            ex-
It was an   plan.

                    tremely good
It was an ex-   plan.

Unfortunately, it's not quite the right shade of blue.
(British Pattern)

                                    not quite the
        \for-   it's   right shade of
                tun-   y,   \blu-
        Un-   ate/l-   e.

American Pattern:

                                                        blue
                                            shade of
            for-   not quite the right   or
        Un-   tunate-   it's   blue.
                    ly,

41

More Practice

So I said to him "What are you standing there for, man? Fire!" Well, he fired, all right. Hit the choir stalls, as it turned out. "Good gracious," I said, "what did you want to do that for?" "Well, you told me to fire!" he said. Can you imagine? Bloody cheek! How dare he contradict me? I could use a whiskey and soda...

Phonetic pronunciation: sO I sed te him wA' ty<u>oo</u> stand' eng THaye faw man' fA' weL, or wel, hee fAd' awL rIt' hit THe kwA' stawlz ez i tond owt', or It, or owt, or It good gRay' shes man I sed wAt dyoo wAn te d<u>oo</u> THat', or THat, faw weL, or wel, yoo tOLd mee te fA hee sed ken yoo madg' en bLu' dee cheek' how dee hee kon' tRe dikt' mee, or may I kood y<u>oo</u>z e wis' kyen sO' de

Notes: The word *well*, when completely unstressed, can also be heard just as a consonant: "l." You will notice, too, that the first syllable of *imagine* is not pronounced in this transcription; if it is pronounced, it is as the briefest of schwas in this very "swallowed" accent, associated in plays and films with the character of ex-colonial officers serving the empire in the days of imperialism, and much caricatured, as it is here. For good examples of this type of military character see Major Gowen, played perfectly by Ballard Berkeley, in the television series *Fawlty Towers*; and the General played by Sir Alec Guiness in *Kind Hearts and Coronets* (1949), in which Guiness plays eight victims, and Dennis Price, their murderer, has the plummiest of upper-class accents, as does Joan Greenwood. The ironic title comes from the verse "Kind hearts are more than coronets,/And simple faith than Norman blood" in Alfred, Lord Tennyson's *Lady Clara de Vere*. A much more real example of such a character is C. Aubrey Smith, who makes no attempt to put on anything in the way of a special accent, as the bluff, good-hearted Colonel Julyan in Alfred Hitchcock's first American film, Daphne du Maurier's *Rebecca* (1940), with Laurence Olivier as an English aristocrat, Joan Fontaine as the American who marries him, George Sanders (another wonderful plummy accent) as Rebecca's unctuous cousin, and the superbly villainous Judith Anderson, who was born in Australia, but who sounds absolutely English, as Mrs. Danvers.

May it please you, m'lud [or my Lord], if I may offer your Lordship some idea of the circumstances in which my client most unfortunately found himself, I think your Lordship will realize the extreme provocation he was under.

Phonetic pronunciation: may it pleez yoo mlud', or mI lawd', if I may o' fe yaw lawd' ship sAm I deee' ev THe se' kem sten sez, or stAn' siz, or stan' siz, in wich mI klAnt un faw' chne tlee fownd him self' I think yaw lawd' ship wel Reee' LIz THee iks tReem' pRA ve kay' shen hee wez An' de

Notes: The very clear diction of this accent, with strong final consonants, is very similar to those accents I heard from judges and lawyers during a trial I attended in a law court in London. For examples of similar pear-shaped tones, listen to Robert Donat as Sir Robert Morton in Terence Rattigan's *The Winslow Boy* (1948); Francis X. Sullivan as Mr. Jaggers in David Lean's adaptation of Charles Dickens' *Great Expectations* (1946); and the lawyers in the television series based on the John Mortimer stories *Rumpole of the Bailey*, starring Leo McKern as

Rumpole. "M'lud," a shortened form of "my lord," was particularly used when addressing a judge who was also a knight or an aristocrat. This pronunciation was once ubiquitously heard, but the full "my lord" is now more usual. "M'lud" is an authentic Victorian pronunciation. Otherwise, two usual forms of address to a judge were "sir" or "your worship." You will notice that there are three pronunciations for the word *circumstances*; all three can be heard, sometimes used by the same person, in British RP; in the second two pronunciations the word has two stresses, as shown. Also, try to use the British liquid "l," as opposed to the American "L," which you will still find occasionally indicated in some of these exercises, beacause it is sometimes heard, particularly when it is a final sound in a syllable (see, for example, the exercise beginning *As your Lordship may recall*).

Very well, but don't be too long about it. We haven't got all day, you know.
Phonetic pronunciation: ve' ree, or Ree, wel bet don't bee too lAng e bIt', or bowt', it wee ha' vent got awl day yoo nO.
Note: Be sure to do the British "O" diphthong, not the American.

As your Lordship may recall, I had sent to your Lordship's chambers the papers regarding the original brief.
Phonetic pronunciation: ez yaw, or zyaw, lawd' ship, or shep, may re kawL' I hed sent tyaw Lawd' sheps chaym' bez THe pay' pez Ri gA' ding THee e Ridg' neL, or e neL, bReef

Yes, yes, get on with it. We know all about that.
Phonetic pronunciation: yes yes get An weth it, or it wee nO awL e bowt', or bIt', THaet

I most respectfully submit to your Lordships that twenty years is much too long.
Phonetic pronunciation: I mOst re spekt' flee, or fe lee, seb mit' tyaw, or te yaw, lawd' ships THet twen' tee yez, or yeeez, iz mAch, or much, too lAng
Note: The variations in the pronunciation of a number of words in several of these exercises shows that in upper-class speech there is great variety. In other words, there is no monolithic system of pronunciation, and everyone actually speaks idiolectically (in his or her own individual way).

Do you really think so?
Phonetic pronunciation: dyoo reee' lee, or re:' lee, think sO?
Note: Don't forget the British long O diphthong.

This court is adjourned sine die.
Phonetic pronunciation: THis kawt iz e dgo:nd' sI' nee dI' ee
Note: *Sine die* is Latin, meaning "without a day [being named for the court to sit again]." The pronunciation of this phrase is rather oddly anglicized; such anglicizations of Latin date from the Elizabethan era, and there are a number of

other anglicized Latin phrases used in British and American courts of law. For more of them, and for the pronunciation of Latin, see the Introduction to Part Three: Romance Language Accents.

I wish to say that you have performed an invaluable service for the crown.
Phonetic pronunciation: I wish te say THet yoo hev pe fawmd' en in val' yoo e bl se' vis fe THe, or fthe, kRown

That is, I believe, the task with which history has charged us.
Phonetic pronunciation: THat iz I bLeev THe tAsk weth wich his' tRee hez chAgd us, or es

From Reginald Bunthorne's song in Gilbert and Sullivan's *Patience:*
If you're anxious for to shine/ In the high aesthetic line/ As a man of culture rare/ You must get up all the germs/ Of the transcendental terms/ And plant them every-where...
Phonetic pronunciation: if yaw an' kshes, or yaw Ran' kshes, faw te shIn' in THe hI es the' tik LIn' ez e man ev kuL' che Re'e yoo mest get up awL THe dgo:mz' ev THe tRan, or tRAn, sen, or sen, den' teL to:mz' end pLAnt Them, or THem, e' vRee we'e

The idea is this: It should not be impossible to meet both objectives, but the demo-cratic process must take priority.
Phonetic pronunciation: THee I di' Riz THis it, or t, shood not bee im pos' bl, or i bel, te, or t, meet bOth eb dgek' tivz bet THe dem' e kRat', or kRat, ik prO' ses must tayk prI o' Re tee
Note: This is the sort of remark you can hear during proceedings of the House of Commons, whose proceedings are shown on the cable television channel C-Span.

Some Notes on Chaucer's English

Geoffrey [phonetic pronunciation: dge' fRee] Chaucer (1349-1400), best known as the author of *The Canterbury Tales,* written in what was then almost newfangled English, probably spoke French at home with his wife, who was from a knightly French-speaking family in Flanders. He probably also spoke the East Midland dialect of late medieval English and he was enamored enough of the Chancery English he heard and learned, no doubt at the royal court (see the Introduction), to take the unprecedented step of writing the first work of litera-ture in the language. Nobody knows how this language was pronounced, be-cause the knowledge of its pronunciation was lost as Early Modern English took over, but such scholars as F. N. Robinson, who edited the Cambridge edition of Chaucer's works and wrote a superb introduction, and the brilliant linguist Helge Kökeritz have made excellent educated guesses. As you will see from the excerpt below, French still had a very heavy, direct influence on English. Such words as *flour* (the word of Anglo-Saxon origin is *bloom*) and *engendred* (the Anglo-Saxon equivalent is *grown*) are examples of words which have become absolutely English as *flower* and *engendered*. How the consonant "L" was pronounced is unknown; I have indicated it as the French liquid "l," but this is an arbitrary choice.

The opening of the "General Prologue":
Whan that Aprill with his shoures soote/ The droghte of Marche hath perced to the roote,/ And bathed every veyne in swich licour/ Of which vertu engendred is the flour;…"

Literal translation: When [that] April with his showers sweet/ The drought of March has pierced to the root/ And bathed every vein in such liquor/ Of which virtue engendered is the flower;…
Phonetic pronunciation: hwAn THAt A preel' with his sh<u>oo</u>' res sO' te   The dRoo' KHte Of mARch' hAth per' sed tO TH' rO' te And bA' THed e' vree vayn in swich li k<u>oo</u>R'   uf hwich ver t<u>oo</u>', or tü', en gen' dred iz THe fl<u>oo</u>R'
Note: Notice the pronunciation of *which* as "hwich," still heard today in certain **regional American** and **Welsh** accents, among others.

Early Modern English:
The Standard Speech of Shakespeare's Day

In the 15th and 16th centuries there occurred what linguists call the "Great Vowel Shift," which altered English pronunciation and made it very close to our own. Apparently Shakespeare's pronunciation of English, while differing markedly from that of a century before him, did not differ very much from ours. What happened (nobody seems to know exactly how or why) was that vowels became diphthongized in a gradual process. Short vowels were shorter than they are today. Spelling was not standardized, but a pure vowel was possibly represented by a single letter. In regional accents of English some of these Elizabethan sounds still exist. See Walt Wolfram and Natalie Schilling-Estes *Hoi Toide on the Outer Banks* (The University of North Carolina Press, 1997) for a discussion of this subject with regard to the "Ocracoke brogue," which some linguists have conjectured is fairly close to the pronunciation of Early Modern English. The "Hoy Toyders" pronounce the dipththongs "I" and "ow" as described below, and, unlike most other coastal accents in the southern USA, their accent is rhotic (see Chapter Six under "Southern Accent Practice"). The following list shows the difference in Shakespearean pronunciation from that of today:

Standard Elizabethan English was rhotic, and final "R" and "R" before a consonant was pronounced.
"I" in *fight* was "*e'ee*" instead of "*A'ee*."
"ay" in *say* was "*e:'*" instead of "ay" (as it is in Irish accents today).
"O" in *home* was "o:," a lengthened "aw," instead of "o'<u>oo</u>" (as it is in Irish accents today).

"ee" in *meat* was "ay" instead of "ee." But in *meet* it was pronounced as we pronounce it now. Apparently the letter combinations "ea" and "ae" were always pronounced "ay," and the combination "ee" was always pronounced "ee," even though spelling was scarcely standardized.

"ow" in *house* and *how* was "e'<u>oo</u>" instead of "a'<u>oo</u>."

"u" in *but* was "oo" in *book* instead of having its present day sound.

"y<u>oo</u>" was either the palatalized, or liquid, "u" after a consonant, or simply either "<u>oo</u>" or "oo."

The letter "y" in a final position was pronounced "ee," as it continued to be through the 19th century, so *my* and *by* were "bee" and "mee": *by my troth* would have been "bee mee trawth," with the "aw" a very short vowel, as in modern British RP.

Initial consonants which are now silent were pronounced, such as "k" in *knee*. The "g" was pronounced at the end of "ing" words, much as it is on Long Island today.

"To be or not to be" must have sounded like "Toe bay or not toe bay," with all the vowels short. "Brutus hath told you Caesar was ambitious" must have sounded something like this: "br<u>oo</u>' toos, bR<u>oo</u>' toos, bry<u>oo</u>' tes, or possibly bry<u>oo</u>' toos, hAth tawld y<u>oo</u> say' zeR wAz Am bi' see es."

Here is a list of some of the more obscure or difficult, and often mispronounced, names of characters and places in some of Shakespeare's plays, together with their correct (and sometimes, to us, very odd) pronunciations. For proper names in the histories consult the BBC *Pronouncing Dictionary of British Names* (Oxford University Press, 1990). For the pronunciation of the names of Shakespeare's other characters as well as for the period pronunciation of place names consult Helge Kökeritz's Shakespeare's *Names: A Pronouncing Dictionary* (Yale University Press, 1972). The pronunciations shown are American; simply use the system of British RP if you wish to practice them with an upper-class English accent.

All's Well That Ends Well: Marseilles (mAR sayLz'); Lyons (LI' enz); Lafeu (LA fy<u>oo</u>'); Parolles (pe rO' Leez); Countess of Rousillon (R<u>oo</u> siL' yen); Lavache (Le vash'); Helena (he' Le ne)

Antony and Cleopatra: Domitius Enobarbus (de mi' shee es ee nO, or ne, bAR' bes); Proculeius (pRA ky<u>oo</u> Lay' es); Thyreus (thI' Ree es); Menecrates (me nek' Re teez); Diomedes (dI e mee' deez)

As You Like It: Amiens (a' mee enz, or enz); Jaques (jay' kweez, or jay' kes)

The Comedy of Errors: Solinus (se LI' nes); Aegeon (i dgee' en); Antipholus (an ti' fe Les)

Coriolanus: Titus Lartius (tI' tes LAR' shes); Menenius Agrippa (me nee' nee es e gri' pe); Sicinius Velutus (si si' nee es ve l<u>oo</u>' tes); Tullus Aufidias (tu' Les aw fi' dee es)

Cymbeline: Posthumus Leonatus (pAs ty<u>oo</u>' mes Lee e nA' tes); Guiderius (gwi dee' Ree es); Arviragus (AR vi' Re ges, or AR vi RA' ges)

Julius Caesar: Popilius Lena (pe pi' Lee es Lee' ne); Decius Brutus (dee' shee es bRoo' tes); Metellus Cimber (me te' Les sim' beR); Clitus (kLI' tes); Strato (stray' tO); Dardanius (dAR day' nee es); Marullus (me Ru' Les)

King Henry the Eighth: Wolsey (wooL' zee); Cromwell (krum' eL)

King Richard the Third: Sir James Blount (bLunt); Sir James Tyrrell (ti' ReL)

Love's Labor's Lost: Berowne (be roon'); Boyet (boy' it); Holofernes (hAL e feR' neez); Rosaline (RA' ze Lin); Jaquenetta (dgak e ne' te)

Macbeth: Hecate (he' ket)

Measure for Measure: Vincentio (vin sen' shee O); Escalus (es' ke Les); Pompey (pAm' pee); Abhorson (ab hawR' sen); Barnardine (bAR' neR deen)

The Merchant of Venice: Gratiano (grA shee A' nO); Salanio (se LA' nee O); Salerino (saL e Ree' nO)

The Merry Wives of Windsor: Dr. Caius (kI' yes)

A *Midsummer Night's Dream:* Egeus (e dgee' es); Philostrate (fiL' e stRayt); Titania (ti tay' nee e, or ti tA' nee e); Helena (he' Le ne)

Pericles, Prince of Tyre: Antiochus (an tI' e kes); Escanes (es' ke neez); Simonides (si mA' ne deez); Lysimachus (LI si' me kes); Thaisa (thay' i se); Lichorida (LI kaw' Ri de)

The Taming of the Shrew: Petruchio (pi troo' kee O, or pi troo' chee O)

The Tempest: Stephano (ste' fe nO); Milan (mi' Len)

Timon of Athens: Alcibiades (aL si bI' e deez); Flavius (fLay' vee es); Apemantus (a pe man' tes); Caphis (kay' fis); Philotus (fi LO' tes); Phrynia (fRi' nee e); Timandra (ti man' dRe)

Titus Andronicus: Saturninus (sat eR nI' nes); Bassianus (ba see ay' nes); Chiron (kI' Ren)

Troilus and Cressida: Troilus (tRoy' Les); Deiphobus (dee i' fe bes); Margarelon (mAR ga' Re Lon); Antenor (an tee' nawR); Thersites (thoR sI' teez)

Twelfth Night: Feste (fes' tee); Viola (vI O' Le); Aguecheek (ay' gyoo cheek)

Two Gentlemen of Verona: Duke of Milan (mi' Len)

The Winter's Tale: Cleomenes (kLee A' me neez); Archidamus (AR ki day' mes); Perdita (poR' di te)

Practice

Sonnet 29
When in disgrace with Fortune and men's eyes,
hwen in dis gRe:s' with foR' tyoon and menz e'eez

I all alone beweep my outcast state,
e'ee ol e lawn be weep mee e'oot ka:st ste:t

And trouble deaf heaven with my bootless cries,
And tRoo' bel de:f he:' ven with mee boot less kRe'eez

And look upon myself and curse my fate,

And look e pawn' mee self' and kARs, or keRs, mee fe:t

Wishing me like to one more rich in hope,
wish' ingg me le'eek to woon mo: Rich in hawp

Featur'd like him, like him with friends possess'd,
fe:', or fee', tyooRd le'eek him le'eek him wiTH fRendz pe ze:st'

Desiring this man's art, and that man's scope,
de ze'ee Ringg THis manz ARt and THat manz skawp

With what I most enjoy contented least;
wiTH hwAt e'ee mawst en dgoy kon ten' ted le:st

Yet in these thoughts myself almost despising,
yet in THe:z tho:ts mee self' ol mawst' de spe'ee zingg

Haply I think on thee, and then my state,
hap' lee e'ee think on THee and THen mee ste:t

Like to the lark at break of day arising
le'eek to THe lARk at bRe:k oov de: e Re'ee zingg

From sullen earth, sings hymns at heaven's gate;
fRoom soo' len e:Rth singgz hi:mz at he:' venz ge:t

   For thy sweet love remembered such wealth brings,
Fo:R Thee, or THe'ee, sweet loov re mem' bRed sooch we:lth bRinggz

   That then I scorn to change my state with kings.
THat THen e'ee sko:Rn to che:ndg mee ste:t with, or wiTH, kinggz

Notes: This phonetic pronunciation is based on the information in Helge Kökeritz's brilliant, amazing *Shakespeare's Pronunciation* (Yale University Press, 1953.). The phonology of the Elizabethan accent is disputed. Professor Kökeritz, for instance, tells us that such words as *sessions* and *precious* (which occur in Sonnet 30: "When to the sessions of sweet silent thought/...For precious friends hid in death's dateless night"), were pronounced much as they are today: se' shenz; pRe' shes. However, based on other evidence, it is possible that the pronunciations were closer to the French from which these words were adopted into English: ses' syenz; pRe' syes. He also prefers "deeR" to "de:R" for the word *dear*, but the pronunciation of the spelling "ea" is disputed, and "de:R" is certainly possible, considering certain other words where the pronunciation is clearer: *earth, heaven, death*. Incidentally, it is interesting that in **contemporary British RP** the word *dear* is often pronounced "de:e" (see the end of this chapter). The pronunciation of the sounds spelled "ir," "er," and "ur," as in the word *curse* (see the text of the sonnet, below), is also a matter for conjecture. Professor Kökeritz gives no indication as to how "l" was articulated, and I have chosen the more liquid "l" as seeming to me in keeping with the closed diphthongs, indicating a general forward resonance, of this accent. It is interesting to note that the "l" may have been pronounced in words where it is now silent, but still exists orthographically, as in the words *could, would* and *should.* On the other hand there are various indications in some of Shakespeare's rhymes that "l" may have been silent in those words even then. Note that the words *wishing, desiring, despising, arising, sings, brings,* and *kings* are pronounced with an "ngg," as they are to this day by some Long Islanders. Pronounce final "R" lightly.

Victorian Pronunciation and Some Notes on the Accents of the British Royal Family

Victorian pronunciation did not differ substantially from ours, but there are a few differences which one hears on recordings made on wax cylinder in the 1890s and in the 1930s on records by people reminiscing about the Victorian era. Victorian English, British and American, was a non-rhotic accent. The position of the vocal apparatus was slightly different from today's British RP; the tongue was held up more towards the roof of the mouth, as a general position. This phenomenon accounts for the pronunciation of "m'lud" for *my lord,* the usual formula for addressing a judge in an English law court; the word *lord,* in fact, was pronounced like *lard* (LAd). The principal difference, which brought American and English upper-class accents closer together than they are today, was that the schwa was less widely used, so a word like the noun *record* would not have had a schwa in its second syllable, as it does today: "Rek' ed." Instead that syllable was pronounced to rhyme with *board:* "Rek' aw:d" in American, "Rek' awd" (with a shorter vowel) in British. As a verb *record* had a schwa in the first syllable, as it does today. The British "O" diphthong was then like the American diphthong "o'<u>oo</u>" instead of present-day British "e<u>oo</u>." Other than that the accents were very much the same as they are now, with the British pronouncing a broad "A" in such words as *can't* and *bath,* while most Americans said an "a" in those words, except for New Englanders and some members of the upper class. President Franklin D. Roosevelt's upper-class American accent is very close to the American accent of the 1880s.

It is instructive to listen to recordings of such British Victorian actors as Ellen Terry (1848-1928) and Henry Irving (1838-1905), although we are hearing the heightened, very clear stage diction of the period, not everyday speech. Even though the stage speech of British and American actors, as well as the everyday speech of the upper-class British and Americans, was fairly close (and certainly closer than it is today), there are differences that clearly mark one person as British and another as American (see the description of Edwin Booth's and the American politicians' accents in Chapter Six).

Here is Ellen Terry speaking Portia's opening lines in her most famous speech in *The Merchant of Venice*, Act Four, Scene One, recorded in 1911:
"The quality of mercy is not strain'd/It droppeth as the gentle rain from heaven/ Upon the place beneath..."
Phonetic pronunciation: THe kwA' li tee ev mo' see iz not stRaynd'   it dRop' ith az THe dgen' tel Rayn fRem he' vn   e pon THe plays bi neeth'

Pitch Pattern

```
                                                    rain
                         It droppeth        gentle        from
                 strain'd/            as the                      heav'n
          mercy
The quality of        is not


          place
Upon the        be-
                neath.
```

Note: Notice where the stresses fall; she only stresses the syllables indicated in the Phonetic pronunciation. She takes a pause after the word *droppeth* and draws out the diphthong on a rising tone in the word *strain'd*. The rather attractive, appealing tremolo of her high voice, full of restrained emotion, must have been striking to the audience. Ellen Terry's accent is very recognizable British RP as described in this chapter. Quite apart from the obviously artificial, stagey delivery, with the pitch rising from low to high on the first line and falling on the second line (though only the pronunciation of the word *heav'n* sounds actually meant for the stage), it is much the same accent as the one heard in British films thirty years after the recording was made.
And here is how Irving speaks the opening lines of Richard III's speech in Act One, Scene One, recorded on a wax cylinder in 1898:
"Now is the winter of our discontent/Made glorious summer by this son of York..."
Phonetic pronunciation: now' iz THe win' ter uv Ar dis ken tent'   mayd glaw' ree es su' me bI THis sun' ev yaw:k'

Pitch Pattern

```
Now                                        \sum-
                         tent                     mer       son of
     is the winter of    discon-   Made glorious       by this      Yo-\
                 our                                                 rk.
```

Notes: Again, look at the stress pattern; the only stressed syllables are the ones indicated. Beginning on a very high pitch on the word *now* he descends to quite a low pitch on the word *is*. Having delivered the entire first line in staccato rhythm in his rather sharp and penetrating powerful baritone, he slows slightly; and stays low in pitch for the second line, rising on the word *summer*, then drawing out the word *York* at the end on a falling tone. He draws out the vowels slightly on the syllables *Now, sum-,* and *son* as well. This is stage diction and delivery, obviously, and it almost seems to be sung. Despite the artificiality this is a delivery full of charisma and vocal energy. Irving pronounces final "r" (he generally uses "r" elsewhere also, and not "R") quite artificially on the words *winter* and *our,* as shown. He drops the final rhotic sound in the usual British way on the words *summer* and *York.* His accent, like Ellen Terry's, is very much the British RP described earlier in this chapter.

Sir Arthur Sullivan's (1842-1900), accent in the recording he made for Edison in 1888, on the other hand, is slightly different, although still recognizable mid-Victorian British RP. He does not use the British "O" dipththong, but the sound we associate with American accents, and all his "R" sounds are slightly trilled, as in the word *very* (ve' ree). He does, of course, drop his final "R"s and also uses the British liquid "l." The general placement of all three accents is slightly higher than it is in contemporary accents, as mentioned above.

Queen Victoria's own accent probably contained at least a hint of German, since she was raised by a German mother and German governesses. She spoke German before she spoke English, and married the German Prince Albert, whose English was apparently excellent, but heavily accented. They spoke German together almost exclusively. According to Lytton Strachey, in his debunking biography *Queen Victoria,* recordings of her voice on wax cylinder were destroyed by the royal family, who did not want the British public to hear their Queen speaking with a German accent. The voice-over of Queen Victoria in the film *Young Winston* (1972) seems to me an accurate representation of what she must have sounded like: very upper crust with just a slight touch of German. Her son, the Prince of Wales, later Edward VII, also notoriously spoke English with a guttural German "R."

In the present-day royal family, the Prince Consort Philip, whose first language was German, speaks undetectable and perfect British RP. However, he speaks French with a German accent, as I have heard him do in French news interviews.

Recordings of George V and George VI show them speaking also with perfect British RP accents. Some of their more remote ancestors, on the other hand, undoubtedly did not. George I, from Hannover, Germany, spoke hardly any English, and George II spoke what English he did with a heavy German accent. His courtiers, not wishing to be impolite, pronounced the name of the river which flows through London with an initial "t": the *Thames* became the "temz." In New London, Connecticut, the original pronunciation is retained, and the *Thames River* there is pronounced "thaymz." Charles I, who, like his father James I, probably had a Scots accent, stuttered. Alec Guinness played him superbly and with just the right accent, it seems to me, in *Cromwell* (1970). George VI, who reluctantly succeeded his posh, popular, not very bright brother Edward VIII, later the Duke of Windsor, was also a stutterer. His voice can be heard in World War Two documentaries. He was very nervous about speaking in public, but expert tutoring helped him overcome his stammer, noticeable only as a slightly prolonged occasional pause.

The Duchess of Windsor, an American from Baltimore, spoke with a posh imitation British RP accent, but she did not escape sounding as if she were from Baltimore. Both she and the Duke and other upper-class English people can be heard in the documentary film *A King's Story* (1967). In the contemporary royal family, from the Queen Mother on down the line, everyone speaks with perfect RP pronunciation. However the use of the glottal stop, mentioned at the beginning of this chapter, is common in the ladies who married into the family— the late Princess Diana used it, as does Fergie—and is evidence of linguistic change.

Contemporary Speech (Thames Estuary English)

Aside from the glottal stop, and the occasional disappearance of final "L," both of which you will notice in the exercises below, and both of which we usually associate with working-class London speech, there are two important sound shifts which are often, but not always, heard in contemporary upper-class British English:
1) The vowel "<u>oo</u>" (sometimes heard as the diphthong "<u>oo</u>e"), in such words as *poor, moor, boor,* etc. shifts to "aw": paw, maw, baw;
2) The diphthong "eee" in such words as *clear, peer, bleary,* etc. shifts to "e:e."

Practice

I believe the police solved the problem, and did it very handily, too.
Phonetic pronunciation: I bLeev THe pLees sawvd THe pRob' lem en did i? ve' Ree hand' lee t<u>oo</u>
Notes: You will notice the dropping of the middle syllables in the words *believe, police* and *handily.* This is quite common. Look at the section on Stress, above. In contemporary upper-class speech even more syllables are sometimes dropped than are indicated there, so that *civilization* is pronounced "siv LI zay' shen" and *cigarette* "sig Ret'," to take just two examples. The articulation of "L" varies between "l" and "L."

What I really wanted to tell you was that I enjoyed dinner the other evening. It was wonderful. I was so happy eating that delicious food.
Phonetic pronunciation: wA? I ree' lee wan' tid te tel, or te, y<u>oo</u> wez THa? I in dgoyd' di' nA THee u' THA eev', or Reev, ning i? wez wAn' de fel, or f<u>oo</u> I wez s<u>oo</u> ha' pee ee' ting THa? di li' shes füd, or f<u>oo</u>d
Note: This is very close to a standard middle class London accent, and quite similar to the speech of Michael Caine, except for the pronunciation of the word *food* as "füd," which sounds almost Scottish.

So that's not what I actually meant to say, you see. I hope that's clear enough, you poor dear.
Phonetic pronunciation: s<u>oo</u> THas no? wA? I ak' shlee men? te say, or tsay, y<u>oo</u>

see   I hOp THas kli:', or kle:, or kle:*e*, Ree, or Ri, nuf yoo paw dee'*e*, or de:'*e*.
Note: Don't forget the British long "O" diphthong in the word *hope*. Also, there is almost a glottal stop at the end of the word *hope*. Notice, too, the shift from "*eee*" to "*e:e*" in the pronunciation of the words *clear* and *dear*.

Do you plan to do some hang-gliding or some water-skiing when you get there? I mean, when you get there, what do you plan to do? Can't you tell me what you're going to do?
Phonetic pronunciation: dy<u>oo</u> plan te d<u>oo</u> sem hang glI' ding *e* sem waw' te, or waw' te, skee' ing wen, or wen, y<u>oo</u> ge? THe: I meen wen y<u>oo</u> ge? THe: wA de y<u>oo</u> pLan te d<u>oo</u>   kAn? y<u>oo</u> teL, or te, mee wA? yaw geng te d<u>oo</u>

Your judgements have been made hastily, as they so often must be. We all fear that parliamentary yawn.
Phonetic pronunciation: yaw jAdg' mints hev been mayd hay' stLee, or ste Lee, ez THay sO A' fn mAst' bee   wee awL, or aw, fee*e*, or fe:*e*, THa?, or THat, pA' lye men' tRee yawn

Chapter Two
General London and Cockney

"When a man is tired of London, he is tired of life; for there is in London all that life can afford," said the brilliant 18th-century wit, intellectual and lexicographer Dr. Samuel Johnson, in an oft-quoted phrase. If you go to London, you can visit his house, and then partake of such fare as roast beef and Yorkshire pudding at the old Cheshire Inn, and sit there in the place where he sat. What Dr. Johnson said is as true today as it must have been when London was the thriving, bustling port called Londinium, founded by the Romans in the first century B.C.E. Despite the plague of 1665 and the great fire of 1666 and the terrible, destructive German Blitz bombing of World War Two, London survived, and the brave Londoners have rebuilt their incomparable metropolis several times. The London of the unfortunate King Richard II (his portrait, the picture of a slightly bewildered, hopeful youth, terribly serious in demeanor, hangs just inside the entrance to Westminster Abbey); the city of King Richard III (whose story is now a paradigm for fascistic political manipulation because Shakespeare maligned him to please his Queen, Elizabeth I, granddaughter of Henry VII, who deposed Richard); Tudor London; Stuart London; Georgian London (see the films *Tom Jones* [1963] and *The Madness of King George* [1994]); Victorian London—vestiges of all these cities survive amidst the modern skyscrapers in the teeming, fascinating capital of the United Kingdom, the center of commerce and the arts. Just visit the National Portrait Gallery in Trafalgar Square, and you will get a feeling for the rich pageantry of English history.

You can take yourself on a literary or historic walking tour with the help of a guidebook. As you look at the spot in the Tower where Anne Boleyn, the unfortunate second wife of Henry VIII was beheaded, or gaze at Buckingham Palace and wonder what the Queen is like in the few moments of privacy she ever has, and how she feels about the antics of her royal family, keep your ears open and listen to the various London accents—North, South, the West End, the Jewish accent of Whitechapel, working-class accents, and the accent of middle-class London shopkeepers. The authentic Cockney accent is heard in the East End of London among the working class, and it is commonly said that to be a true Cockney you have to have been born within the sound of Bow bells. The church of St. Mary-le-Bow was destroyed in the Blitz, so the bells can no longer be heard, but I suppose you still have to be born in the neighborhood to be considered a real Cockney. There are, as with RP, lexical (vocabulary) differences from General American in the English of London and different grammatical usages as well. These differences in vocabulary and grammar are dialectical features of London English, quite apart from the different accent. A working-class phrase like "Half a mo', Guv' " (usually with the "h" in *half* dropped) is pure British. An American would say "Just a moment, sir." One can translate the British working-class phrase "I don't half think so" into the American "I hardly think so," which would be English upper-class usage as well.

Cockney "rhyming slang" is a fascinating phenomenon, in which the first word of a phrase is used to mean something the phrase rhymes with, as in the following examples: *apples and pears* rhymes with *stairs*; the second part of the phrase is dropped and *apples* means *stairs*. "I went up the apples on my plates." *Plates of meat* rhymes with *feet*. For authentic examples of London accents, listen to Michael Caine, who does a middle-class version in many of his films, such as *The Wrong Box* (1966), and a lower-class London accent in *Alfie* (1966), and to Stanley Holloway as Alec Guiness's partner in crime in *The Lavender Hill Mob* (1951), as the Station Master in Noel Coward's *Brief Encounter* (1945), and as Eliza Doolittle's father Alfred Doolittle in *My Fair Lady* (1964). The television series *East Enders* provides a variety of London accents to listen to. The wonderful Cockney actress Irene Handl in *I'm All Right, Jack* (1959), with Peter Sellers also doing a superb Cockney accent, is also an excellent source, as is the music hall comedian Frankie Howerd, very famous in England, as the fruit vendor in Alec Guiness's *The Ladykillers* (1955), and the television versions of Gilbert and Sullivan's *Trial by Jury* and *H.M.S. Pinafore*. Bob Hoskins, who can do any accent perfectly, is a native Londoner with a broad, delightful accent.

The story is told that when Julie Andrews came to New York to do Lerner and Loewe's Broadway musical *My Fair Lady* (based on George Bernard Shaw's *Pygmalion*; you might want to read it for its phonetic information), her Cockney accent was so perfect as to be nearly incomprehensible. The producers had to hire a dialect coach to teach her how not to do Cockney. Whether apocryphal or nor, the anecdote contains a caveat that cannot be too often repeated: Your audience must understand you. Incidentally, the musical's title is a very ingenious play on words: It is, of course, the last line of the famous nursery rhyme "London Bridge is falling down" (the nursery rhyme tells you perfectly what the musical is about, with its upsetting of a rigid class system based in part on people's accents); and its first two words are an imitation of the Cockney pronunciation of the name *Mayfair*, one of the aristocratic sections of London.

A Quick Reference

1) Keep the jaw slightly dropped and the general "feeling" of the accent forward in the mouth.
2) Drop final "R" and "R" before another consonant.
3) Drop initial "h" and "g" in "-ing" endings for working-class accents. Retain them for middle-class accents.
4) The all-important diphthong shifts: "ay" to "I"; "I" to "oy"; "O" to "ow."
5) The point of articulation of "d" and "t" is the same as for British RP, with the tip of the tongue slightly forward of its position in General American.

6) There is often a glottal stop replacing a "t" in words like *bottle*.

7) Drop final consonants in consonant clusters for a working-class accent ("las'" instead of *last*, etc.)

8) Substitute "v" and "f" for "TH" and "th."

9) *Been* rhymes with *bean*, not with *bin*.

How to Do a London Accent

1) Position of the Vocal Apparatus

Drop your jaw and say "Ah." This gives you the general position of the vocal apparatus for this accent. The jaws are held loosely with the lips a bit forward, and the language sometimes sounds a bit swallowed. Vowels and diphthongs are open; that is, the throat and vocal cavity are more open than in either General American or British RP. A **clearer London accent** would restore dropped consonants, such as the "l" in *milk* and would eliminate glottal stops, pronouncing "t" almost too distinctly. Initial "h" might be pronounced as well, at least at times. Vowels and diphthong substitutions would be very much as in Cockney, but the jaw would be held more tightly, thus shortening and closing the vowels and diphthongs a bit. For practice in the music of the language see the information under "Pitch" below, at the end of this chapter.

2) The Most Important Sounds:

Pay particular attention to the vowel and diphthong substitutions. A **middle-class** London accent should sound clear, with well-articulated consonants, even including a pronounced "h." A **working-class** accent should include some or even all of the consonant shifts, dropping "h" and final consonants in clusters, as well as some initial consonants.

Consonants:

R: These accents, like British RP and other Southern British accents, are non-rhotic, that is, "R" is not pronounced at the end of a word or before another consonant. As in many non-rhotic accents an "intrusive" R is often heard: drawRing; DianaR and I.

h: Initial "h" is absent: 'and; 'at; 'ow for *hand; hat; how*

-ing endings: Final "g" in "ing" endings is absent very often: goin'; runnin'.

There is a tendency to drop the final consonant in a **consonant cluster**, as in *hold fast*, which is sometimes pronounced " a<u>oo</u>L fAs." On the other hand, consonant clusters are sometimes found in more complicated forms, so that *stupid* is variously pronounced "sty<u>oo</u>pid," "shch<u>oo</u>:pid," "shchy<u>oo</u>:pid," or "shchyi<u>oo</u>pid."

?: The **glottal stop** (phonetic symbol: ?) is common. It is a stoppage of vocalization and represents the sound of "t" between vowels and before a pause, and is here indicated by a question mark. **Practice words**: bu?erfly; bo?le; ba?le; wa? if (*butterfly; bottle; battle; what if*).

TH and th: Voiced "TH" is often replaced by "v" (*together* is pronounced "tegevA"). In initial positions voiced "TH" is often replaced by "d" (dis, dat). Initial voiced "TH" is often dropped completely (" 'ass roy?" is heard instead of *that's right*; note the glottal stop for the final "t" in "right"). Voiceless "th" (*think, thin*) is often replaced by "f" ("fin"; "kafee"; "bOf" instead of *thin*; *Cathy*; *both*). Use the preceding words for practice.

Vowels and Diphthongs
A: The vowel "A" in *father* is a pure open vowel, as in British RP. In middle-class London accents it is, however, less open.

Partial List

Use these words for practice. Record them and listen to yourself.
advantage, after, words beginning and ending with *after: afternoon, afterwards, hereafter*, etc., *answer, ask, aunt, banana, basket, bastard, bath, blast, branch, brass, broadcast, calf, can't, cask, casket, cast, caste, castle, chance, chancellor, chant, clasp, class*, words beginning with *class: classmate, classroom, classy*, etc., *command, countermand, daft, dance, demand, disaster, downcast, draft, enchant, entrance* (verb), *example, fast, fasten, gala, ghastly, glass, graft, grant*, words ending in *graph: telegraph*, etc., *grasp, grass, half, lance, last, lather, laugh, lithograph, mask, mast, master, nasty, outcast, paragraph* ("a" in first syllable, "A" in last syllable: pa' Re gRAf), *pass, Passover, past, pastor, pastoral, path, perchance, phonograph, photograph, plant, plaster, prance, raft, rascal, rasp, raspberry* (RAz' bRee), *rather, reprimand, salve, sample, shaft, shan't, slander, slant, staff, stanch, surpass, task, tomato* (Note: the "a" in *potato* is at it is in American), *trance, transport* and other words beginning with the prefix "trans-," *vast, waft, wrath*

ay: The diphthong "ay" in *paper* and *say* shifts to "I." *Paper* becomes "pI' pe." Note: Do not make this sound too open.
Practice words: *paper, say, day, bale, tail, sail, mail, brain, gain, tame, lame, blame*.

ee: This vowel sometimes, but not always, shifts to the diphthong "ay."

I: The diphthong "I" in *I* and *right* shifts to "oy" in *boy*; sometimes "I" shifts to "aw" before a consonant. *I am* becomes "oy am," or even "oy yam." Note: Do not make this sound too open. **Practice words**: *night, blight, fright, fight, five, tiger, fiver, fine, dine, rhyme, bind, find*. Note the glottal stop at the end of the first four words.

O: The long diphthong "O" in *know* shifts to "ow" in *now* and *how*. *I know* becomes "oy now" or "aw now." Note: Do not make this sound too open.

Practice words: *know, how, now, go, bow, low, so, broke, bloke* (the equivalent of American *guy*), *stoke, stroke, slow, blow*.

ow: The diphthong "ow" in *down* and *town; surround* becomes a triphthong: "a'e<u>oo</u>." *Downtown* becomes "dau<u>oo</u>n tau<u>oo</u>n." *How nice* is pronounced "ow noys'," if the word *how* is unstressed.
Practice sentence: *How nice to go downtown!* Phonetic pronunciation: ow, or a, noys te gow da'e<u>oo</u>n ta'e<u>oo</u>n, or dan ta'e<u>oo</u>n
Note: The "t"s in *to* and *town* and the "d" in *down* might be dentalized: dzan tsan.

Further Phonetic Information

L: Final "L" is often replaced by "<u>oo</u>": mi<u>oo</u>k (*milk*); tayb<u>oo</u> (*table*). Otherwise the pronunciation of "L" is either the same as in General American, or else "liquid," as it sometimes is in British RP.

t: The consonant "t" itself is sometimes dentalized and sounded like "ts." The point of articulation is with the tongue forward of its position in General American.

y<u>oo</u>: The diphthong "y<u>oo</u>" in *duke* and *tune* is very long, when it occurs. Often it does not, and *duke* is pronounced "dzh<u>oo</u>k" or "dzhy<u>oo</u>k" or "d<u>oo</u>k," while *tune* becomes "ch<u>oo</u>n" or "chy<u>oo</u>n."

Stress

There are no particular differences in stress patterns from RP. As in RP the most important syllable in the most important word in a sentence, the *nuclear tone*, has its vowel lengthened, and is spoken on a higher pitch. This gives a characteristic English rhythm which is different from the American rhythm, where words are stressed more evenly and where the pitch is also more even. See the sections on "Stress" in the previous chapter and in the Introduction.

Pitch

There are more tones used in London lower- and middle-class accents than in British RP or in General American. Some typical patterns are:

Practice

I think that's stupid.
Phonetic pronunciations: aw fink as shchy<u>oo</u>pi?; oy think das sty<u>oo</u>pid

```
                    stu-
I           that's
    think          pid.
```

I'll have a nice cup of tea with a little bit of milk and sugar.
Phonetic pronunciation: aw wev e noys kA' e tsee wif e Li?' <u>oo</u> bi? e mi<u>oo</u>k en shoo' gA

```
                    cup of                        milk        su-
           nice                      little bit of        and
       a                     tea
     have                          with a
I'll                                                                 gar.
```

How about a glass of milk?
Phonetic pronunciation: ow e ba?, or bow?, e gLAs e mi<u>oo</u>k
NOTE the dropping of "f" in *of.*

```
                              milk?
How a-              glass of
          bout
                    a
```

I know that's what I said; at least I thought so.
Phonetic pronunciation: Oy now ass wa? oy sed a? Leest oy faw? sow

Note the linking of the "t" in *least* to I (oy). It is possible instead to use a glottal stop: "Lees?." The vowel in *thought,* represented here by "aw" as in the word *law,* is quite long. Other choices are possible, for instance "d" for "th" in *that's,* or pronouncing a correct "th" in *thought,* particularly in a clearer London accent.

```
     know                              thought
          that's          said,     least
I                  what          at        I
                      I                          so.
```

Note that the final word, *so,* is spoken with a rising inflection, on a rising tone.

Can I do you now, sir?
Phonetic pronunciation: kin, or ken, oy d<u>oo</u> ye na'e<u>oo</u> su

```
          you          sir?
     do
Can  I
          now
```

Notes: Note that the only stress in the sentence is on the word *now,* which is also the nuclear tone, on a differentiated lower pitch rather than the more usual higher pitch. Notice the stressed Cockney triphthong (the only stressed syllable in the entire utterance), on the word *now*: "a'e<u>oo</u>." During World War Two there was a very popular radio show called *ITMA* (Phonetic pronunciation: it mA), an acronym for "It's That Man Again," starring the comedian Frank Findley. (Originally "That Man" was a bitter, sarcastic and mocking reference to Hitler.) He was always getting into scrapes, and at the most inconvenient moment his office door would open and the charwoman Mrs. Mop would say "Can I do you now, sir?" This became a catch phrase used all over Britain to lighten heavy moments during the darkest days of the war. In the face of some disaster someone would be sure to say "Can I do you now, sir?" and people would burst out laughing. The phrase is, of course, mildly obscene.

So I says to him, I says, what's the big idea? I mean, what's that all about then?
Phonetic pronunciation: sow oy sez t<u>oo</u> im oy sez wos e big oy' deee, or deeeR oy mayn wos a? awL e ba'e<u>oo</u>w? en, or den
Note: If you wish to link the two sentences, you might say: "wos e big oy dee Roy mayn," etc. Also, for purposes of comprehension, you might want to restore some dropped consonants, for instance the "TH" sounds in the phrases *what's the big idea* and *what's that all about then*, which will also give you a more middle-class, shopkeeper's accent.

"Well, I never," I says. "Of course not, of course you never" he says, "Right, I don't think!" He didn't believe me, you see! But I saw her and she was all tarted up, dear! Of course he wouldn't believe it, now would he?
Phonetic pronunciation: weL oy ne' vA, or ni' ve, Roy sez, or ne' vRoy sez   e kaws no? e kaws y<u>oo</u> ne' ve Ree sez Roy? oy down fink ee di?' n bLeev' mee ye see be doy saw Re, or ReR, an shee wez awL tA' tid Ap, deee e kaws ee woo?' n bLeev i? na, or now, woo' dee

Well, it's a lot of rot, that's what I think, and that's what I told him, you can be sure of that! I don't think he knew what he was talking about.
Phonetic pronunciation: we' Lis, or weL' is, e Lo? e Ro? as we? oy fink en as we? oy tow' Lim y<u>oo</u> ?en bee shaw Re da?, or va?   oy down fink ee n<u>oo</u> wo? ee wez taw' kin e bow?', or ba?', or ba'e<u>oo</u>?
Notes: Use this exercise to practice glottal stops. Notice the pronunciation of *can*, which begins with a glottal stop and is almost swallowed, despite the nasality of the final "n." You might pronounce this word more distinctly, if you wish to be more easily understood. You have two possibilities for the pronunciation of *that*, the final word in the exercise.

I believe you. Thousands wouldn't, but I do. I believe you.
Phonetic pronunciation: oy be leev', or be layv, or bleev, y<u>oo</u>   e tha'e<u>oo</u> zenz wood' ent be doy d<u>oo</u> oy be leev' y<u>oo</u>

                                    do.
        lieve   I   lieve
    be-   be-
I   you.   but   I   you.

            Thou-   n't,
                sands would-

I was walking down there the other day and what should I see but the most beauti-
ful girl on the other side of the street, but she was too busy to see me, and when I
looked round again she had disappeared. Easy come, easy go. That's life.
Phonetic pronunciation: oy wez waw:' kin down, or dan, or da'e̲o̲o̲n, ve: vee A' ve
dI an wA? she doy say be de mows byee' dee fooL goL A' nee A' ve soy' de ve
stRay? be? shay wez to̲o̲ bi' zee de say may an wen oy Lookt Raown e gayn shee ad
dis' e peeed   ay' zee kum ay' zee gow, or ga'e̲o̲o̲   as Loyf

Whatever may come your way, take advantage of it. It's later than you think.
Phonetic pronunciation: waw' de ve mI kAm yaw wI tIk id vAn' tidg ev i? is LI'
te, or LI? e, ven yo̲o̲ fink, or, is lI' de Ren yo̲o̲ fink

Chapter Three
English Provincial Accents

There are innumerable accents in the provinces of England, generally classified as Northern and Southern accents. It has been variously estimated that
only 3 to 5 percent of English people actually speak with the British RP accent,
so the accents described in this chapter are those used by most of the population of England. The Southern accents include those in the first two chapters of
this book, namely the non-rhotic RP and London accents; the non-rhotic accents of East Anglia, which is the area just north of London; and the (largely
rhotic) accents of the southwest, including those of Bristol, Somerset,
Worcestershire, Cornwall and Devon. The Northern accents include those of
the Midlands (Birmingham) and, farther to the north and east, of Yorkshire and
the "Geordie" accent of Newcastle-Upon-Tyne, which is the main city of Tyne
and Wear, and the accents, to the west, of Manchester and Liverpool. The BBC
made recordings of some 30 of these accents from villages as close as 10 miles
distant from each other, and some are very hard to distinguish, in my opinion.
You can also hear wonderful examples of English provincial accents and other
native accents of English on the PBS series hosted by Robert MacNeil, *The
Story of English*, available on videotape, and there are several wonderful books
with more information on the subject listed in the Bibliography.

Dialectical features of these accents, that is, differences in grammar and vocabulary from standard varieties of English, are not dealt with here; you will find
them, of course, in any script which might require such accents.

A Quick Reference
Common Phonetic Features of English Provincial Accents

1) These accents are largely non-rhotic (drop "R" before another consonant and
at the ends of words) in urban areas, and rhotic (pronounce all "R"s) in the
countryside.
2) There is a shift as you go north to the Midlands and above from the "u" in
such words as *but* to the "oo" in *look*: *but* is pronounced "boot," *love* "loov," and
so forth. This sound is sometimes heard as a schwa (*e*): "bet"; "lev."
3) In most of these accents, except among the upper economic classes, who
largely speak with an RP accent anyway, the words on the list of "A"-words (*can't,
grass, command,* etc.) found in Chapter One, are pronounced very much like

General American *can't, grass, command*, etc., but slightly more openly.
4) *Been* rhymes with *bean*.
5) Pitch patterns are usually much as in British RP, except in Liverpool.

How to Do English Provincial Accents

East Anglia

Norfolk and Suffolk are the two main areas of East Anglia, and we shall include here a general example of the many accents which exist there. These accents are often said to be very close to American accents, and most of the early settlers in New England were from East Anglia, but the accents do differ considerably, although they are certainly among the ancestors of General American.

How to Do an East Anglian Accent

1) Position of the Vocal Apparatus
The general position of the mouth is pretty relaxed and the jaw is loose, as in General American.

2) The Most Important Sounds
Consonants
The accent is non-rhotic, so drop the final "R" and the "R" before another consonant.

The final consonant or another consonant in **consonant clusters** is often dropped, so *minutes* is pronounced "min' is" and *last* is pronounced "las."

h: Pronounce initial "h" for this accent, unlike London accents.

? for t: A glottal stop is usual in both urban and rural East Anglian speech, replacing the "t" in such words as *bottle*, but also at the end of such words as *what* and *but*. The glottal stop also serves to eliminate the ends of words after it occurs and to replace them with a schwa.
Practice words: *bottle, battle, forty-two, twenty-two*
Phonetic pronunciations: bo' ?L; ba' ?L; faw' ?e t<u>oo</u>; twen' ?e t<u>oo</u>

Vowels and Diphthongs
Vowels and diphthongs not listed here follow the British RP system of pronunciation.

A: Pronounce the "A" in *father, can't, ask*, etc. as it is pronounced in British RP.

a: This vowel should be said with the jaw opened more than it is in General American or British RP.

63

Practice words: *cat, that, hat, bat, mat, sat, matter, batter, gather*

ay: This diphthong should be pronounced with the jaw dropped.
Practice words: *face, gate, late, plate, date, mace, place*

O: This diphthong should be pronounced as it is in General American in such words as *home* and not as it is in British RP.

oo and u: In this accent the "u" in *but, love,* and *above* is pronounced as it is in General American, and the "oo" in *put* is also pronounced as it is in General American, thus preserving the distinction which we have in General American, but not, for instance, in the Midlands accents described next.

Practice

I can't draw the bath until I've finished my bottle of water at twenty-two minutes past five, but they won't be home until then anyway.
Phonetic pronunciation: I kAn? dRaw THe bAth un tiL' Iv fin' isht mI bo' ?L uv waw ?e a twen' ?e too min' is pAs fIv bu? THay: won? bee hOm un tiL THen e' nee way:

Never mind what I might have had. I'm happy as I am.
Phonetic pronunciation: Ne ve moynd wA, or wA?, oy moy? ev ad   oym a' pee ez oy am

I wanted to see what time it was, so I was looking at my watch.
Phonetic pronunciation: oy wAn ?id e see wA? toym i? wez sO oy wez Loo?' in, or Loo kin, a? moy wawch

Whatever you said to me was well said indeed, and I paid strict attention to it.
Phonetic pronunciation: wA?' ev e yoo sed te mee wez weL sed in deed' an oy payd stRikt e ten' chen too i?

You can have anything you want, provided you know how to go after it.
Phonetic pronunciation: yoo kin av a' nee thing yoo wawn? pRe voy' did yoo nO ow de gO Af' te Ri?

Have you got a problem with rabbits in your meadows? We have. There were a lot of them.
Phonetic pronunciation: av yoo go? e pRA' bLim wi Ra' bi?s in yaw me' dez   wee av   deR weR e LA? ev dem

The Midlands (Birmingham)

These are the accents of Britain's industrial heartland. Birmingham (incidentally, the British pronunciation is "bo' ming em," unlike the city in Alabama, which is "boR' ming ham" in General American, and "boy' ming ham" to someone from Alabama) is a thriving metropolitan center, with a population of several millions. In the drama *Breaking the Code*, starring Derek Jacobi as the man who broke the German Enigma code in World War Two, shown on PBS, you have perfect, authentic examples of the Midlands accent. One of the characteristics of some of the rural Midlands accents is the lengthening of vowels and diphthongs in some stressed words, as you will see in the Practice section below. This gives the accents their characteristic rhythms and also influences the pitch, since the lengthened, stressed syllables are spoken on a differentiated pitch.

How to Do a Midlands Accent

1) Follow the information in Chapter One for British RP, with the addition of the vowel shift from "u" to "oo" and (for rural, but not urban accents) the advice about the "A" words. The upper-class and businesspeople usually have accents very close to RP, with the vowel shifts just mentioned.

2) Position of the Vocal Apparatus
Say *book book book* several times and you will have the correct general position. The jaw is looser than it is in RP, but not so loose as in London acccents. The lips are half open, half closed, much as in General American.

3) The Most Important Sounds
Consonants
In the cities the accent is close to British RP, and is largely non-rhotic. Not so in the countryside, where the final "R" is often pronounced. Often "h" in initial position is dropped, as in Cockney accents. Otherwise there are no shifts in consonants, and it is the following section which provides the necessary information for this accent.

Vowels and Diphthongs
A: This vowel shifts to "a," and is therefore much like General American, where British RP uses "A." See the list of words in Chapter One.

I: This diphthong is usually pronounced "oy," with the lips held tight, so it does not have the open quality of the same shift in Cockney accents.

o: This vowel in *work* and *first* shifts to a lengthened "e:." *Work* and *first* are pronounced "we: k" and "fe: st." Notice that the "R" is dropped.

oo and u: The vowel in General American *book* is the sound heard in *but*, instead of "u." In this accent *but* and *put*, as pronounced in General American, rhyme.
Practice words: *but, put, butt, buck, book, luck, look, above, love, dove, rough, tough, bluff, muck*

ow: Instead of the sound in either General American or British RP, the sound made in the Midlands is the diphthong "O." Thus *out* is pronounced "Ot," etc.

yoo: There is a shift in this sound, especially in the countryside, to "ee' oo," so *news* is pronounced "nee' ooz," and *duke* is "dee' ook." This is considered in Britain to be a very rural, peasant accent.

Stress and Pitch

There are no special variations in stressing English words. Pitch patterns are somewhat "flat," that is, less musical than the Southern British accents, but there is sometimes a tendency to rise at the end of a declarative sentence, making it sound like a question, and a bit like Liverpool or Northern Ireland accents, especially in the non-rhotic urban varieties. This pattern must not be overused when doing this accent, however.

Practice

Now look here, but that's not what I told you to do, now is it? You've got to work harder.
Phonetic pronunciations: **Urban**: nO Look ee' ye, or ee' ya, boot THats not wet I tOld yoo te doo nO i:' zit yoov go te we:k a:' de; **Rural**: nO Look ee' eR boot THa:ts no:t wa:t I tOl ee, or ee'oo, te doo nO i zit ee'oov go: te we:Rk a:R' deR
Note that *you* is often pronounced "ee" in the rural Midlands accents, and in Yorkshire as well. The "O" dipthong is close to the American sound.

Things have really changed around here today. It's really completely different. Things were good then. It's good now, too, but not what it was, really. It started to change a long time ago, and you haven't got to be so careful now as in my childhood.
Phonetic pronunciation: thingz av Ree' Lee chay:ndgd e rown deee ti day' its Ree' Lee kAm pLee?' Lee dif' Rin thingz wo good THen its good now too bu? no? wA? i? wAz Ree' Lee i? stA:' tid ti chayndg e LAng toym e go' An yoo av en go? ti bee sO, or se, ke:' fool now az in moy choyLd' ood
Note: Notice the very strong "t" in the second syllable of *started*, the dropped "h" sounds, and the different pronunciation of "R" sounds: R or r, depending on phonetic context.

Whatever I happen to be doing at the time is what I prefer, at least while I am doing it, of course.
Phonetic pronunciation: wA te' ve I ha?', or a?', pn, or pm, te bee doo' ing a? THe tIm iz wA? I pRi fo: a? Lees? wIL Im doo' ing i? u kaw'es

I love Birmingham. It's a wonderful city, when you get to know it.
Phonetic pronunciation: I Luv bom ' ing em is e wun' de feL si' tee wen yoo ge te nO i?

We went down the road in a lovely motorcar.

66

Phonetic pronunciation: wee we:n down THe RO:d in *e* Loov', or Luv, Lee mO:' te kA

Note that for a rural pronunciation you should pronounce the final "R" sounds in *motorcar*. The same thing applies to all final "R" sounds in the other exercises. The vowels are the same for both a general urban and a general rural accent.

The other thing I told him, but he didn't want to listen to me, was that what he was doing was was not going to lead to anything particularly productive.
Phonetic pronunciation: THee oo' THe thing I tOl deem boot ee did' n wawn te, or waw' ne, Lis' en te mee wez THa? wA? ee wez d<u>oo</u>' ing wez not, or no?, gO' ing te Leed t<u>oo</u> a' nee thing pA tik' ye LA Lee pRe dook' teev

Yorkshire, Manchester and the North

The rough country of England's North Riding and the scene of *Wuthering Heights* is gorgeous in the splendor of its hills and moors, even seen from a train passing through. Great gray stone churches and spires and great green farms fill the landscape. York Minster is one of England's great cathedrals. If you go wear your sturdiest parka, for the wind blusters and whistles and blows cold down the Yorkshire hills and dales. For good examples of these accents watch videos of *The Full Monty* (1997) and the television series *All Things Bright and Beautiful*. For **Durham** accents see *Billy Elliot* (2001).

For another northern accent, that of **Lancashire**, which borders Yorkshire on the west, listen to Stanley Holloway's marvelous performances in the CD *Stanley Holloway: "Pick Oop Tha Musket": The Great Monologues* (Pavilion Records, PAST CD 7021). As the back of the album informs us, these monologues are "comic and linguistic gems—and they are *extremely* funny." Although a London Cockney, he does the northern accent perfectly. The accent is similar to that of the greater **Manchester** area, which is just south of Lancashire on the borders of Yorkshire, in the middle northland. See the British version of the television series *Queer As Folk* for **Manchester**; Charlie Hunnam, who plays Nathan, is a Manchester native.

How to Do a Yorkshire Accent

1) Position of the Vocal Apparatus
To attain the correct position, in which the lower lip is thrust a bit forward and the jaw is tightly held, say *you you you* several times, drawing the sound out.

2) The Most Important Sounds
Consonants
The accent is largely non-rhotic, that is, the final "R" and the "R" before another consonant are not pronounced, although there is occasional rhoticity. There is a tendency to shift voiced consonants to voiceless before a voiceless consonant beginning another word or syllable, as in the practice example below: *cloud passing* becomes "kL<u>oo</u>t pa:' sing." The phrase *told to me* would be pronounced "tawLt te mee."

h: "h" is regularly dropped in Yorkshire and most rural Northern accents.

R: There is a uvular "R" in Northumberland and in parts of nearby Yorkshire. This is the only accent native to English in which this sound is regularly heard, although occasionally it is heard in the speech of native Glaswegians. Where in a London accent you might hear a glottal stop, particularly at the end of a word like *but* (London pronunciation "bu?") before another word, in Northumberland and in Yorkshire you will hear a slight uvular linking "R": *but I know* (buR I naw).

TH and th: Before a vowel, especially in older accents, the "TH" in the word *the* often shifts to a "t," so *the other* is pronounced "too' THeR."

Vowels and Diphthongs
Vowels are generally longer than in the Southern English accents, and fewer schwas are heard. The shifts mentioned at the beginning of the chapter apply here, with the following additions:

A and a: These vowels are often reversed, so *what* is pronounced "wat" and *that* is pronounced "THAt."

ay: This diphthong usually shifts to a single lengthened vowel "e:," so *say* is pronounced "se:."

O: This diphthong is usually shifted to the single vowel "aw" in *law*.

ow: In Yorkshire, as in much of the North this diphthong is regularly heard as the sound of "oo." *Cow, cloud, loud, how* and *now* are all pronounced with "oo": k<u>oo</u>; kl<u>oo</u>d; l<u>oo</u>d; h<u>oo</u>; n<u>oo</u>.

Practice

But as I say, do you see that cloud passing overhead? That means rain, that does, before the afternoon is out. No, it's not over yet, this rainy season.
Phonetic pronunciation: be Ra:z oy se:' d<u>ge</u> see THA kL<u>oo</u>t pa:' sin awv Red' THA meenz re: n' THA dooz' bee faw' tA' fta noon' i z<u>oo</u>t' naw snawt <u>oo</u>' vA yet THis re: nee see *zen*
Note the dropping of the final "t" in *that*, the "t" not being replaced by a glottal stop.

I think it was at eight o'clock or so that he came down the street on his own bicycle, must have been.
Phonetic pronunciation: oy think, or tink, twez day de kLAk eR saw THe dee kay:m de<u>oo</u>n dstRayt awn eez awn boy' skeL moost e been

There was not another person to be seen for near two miles round.
Phonetic pronunciation: THeR wez naw *de* noo' THeR poR' sn dbee seen feR nee' eR tee<u>oo</u> moyLz Re<u>oo</u>nd

Well, you can go down there all you want but you'll never see what I saw on that fateful day when I went down and came back having had the fright of my life.
Phonetic pronunciation: weL ye kn gaw d<u>oo</u>n THeR awL ye wawn boo cheL ne' veR see we doy sA awn THat fayt' feL day wen oy wen d<u>oo</u>n an kaym bAk A' ve nAd dfRoy dev moy Loyf

The weather on the moors is nigh unpredictable and you can find yourself in a storm before you know it.
Phonetic pronunciation: dwe' THeR awn dm<u>oo</u>Rz znoy oon' pRe dik' tbL an ye kn foynd yeR seLf' in e stawRm bfawR' ynawt'

(From *Wuthering Heights* by Emily Brontë; the following sentences are excerpts from the dialogue of Joseph, the old Yorkshire servant)
"What are ye for? T'maister's down i' t' fowld. Go round by th' end ot' laith if ye went to spake to him... There's nobbut t'missis; and shoo'll not oppen't an ye mak yer flaysome dins till neeght... Nor-ne me! I'll hae no hend wi't..."
Phonetic pronunciation: Wo tAR ye fawR' tmay' steRz down it fowLd' gaw Rownd' bi tend' ot Layth' if ye wen te spayk' tim THeRz naw' bit tmis' is en shooL' nawt u' pint en ye mAk' yeR fLay' sem dinz' tiL ni:KHt' nawR' ne mee' AL he: naw hend' weet

Translation: What are you meaning to do? The master's down in the fold. Go round by the end of the fence if you want to speak to him... There's nobody but the mistress; and she won't open it if you make your loud noises till night... Nor I! I'll have no hand in it!

Notes: This is a historic Yorkshire dialect, the book having been written in 1845 and published in 1847. Notice the similarity to Scots accents, with the use of the word *hae* for *have* and *neeght* for *night*, for example. The "R" may be a trilled "r," instead of the retroflex consonant. In a Yorkshire accent the word *wuthering* would be pronounced "woo' THe R̦ing, or ring."

Manchester Practice

Manchester is a lovely city.
Phonetic pronunciation: man' che ste iz, or Riz, or riz, e loov' lee si' ?ee

We're not far from Liverpool and not far from Leeds. But we're not too near London.
Phonetic pronunciation: weee no? fA: fRoom li' vA p<u>oo</u>l and no? fA: fRoom leedz boot weee no? t<u>oo</u> neee loon' den

That was a terrible thing he did, that man who went by on his motorcycle. He might have had an accident.
Phonetic pronunciation: THA? wooz e te' ri: bel thing ee did THA? mAn <u>oo</u> went bI dgoost now An eez mO:' ?e sI' keL ee mI? ev ad en ak' si den?
Notes: Notice the lengthened vowels and diphthongs, the dropped initial "h"

and the lightly trilled "r," as well as the liquid "l," and the glottal stops.

He's got a mouth on him. Just terrible.
Phonetic pronunciation: eez go? e mu'üth An eem   dgoos? ta' ri: bel
Note: The dipththong "ow" shifts in this accent, particularly in rural areas, to "u'ü," reminding one of some Scottish accents.

He sang for his supper, but I only put my tongue out.
Phonetic pronunciation: ee sAngg fe' reez soo' pA boo? I awn' lee poo? mI toongg u'üt
Notes: Notice the "g" added to "ng" in *sang* and *tongue*. The vowel "A" in *sang* is really a very broad and open "a."

I was there, yes indeed. I went straight home afterwards, though, I can tell you.
Phonetic pronunciation: I wooz THeee yes in' deed   I went stre:? Om A:f' te woodz THaw I kn tel ye
Notes: The lengthened vowel "e:" substitution for the diphthong "ay" in the word *straight* is absolutely typical, as is the substitution of "oo" for "u," as you will have noticed. Notice, too, the lengthened vowels.

Geordie

This is the accent of Tyneside and Newcastle-upon-Tyne, where Captain Cook learned his trade as a seaman, and of the surrounding area on the northeast coast, not very far from Scotland. The vowels and diphthongs of Geordie resemble those of the Scottish Lowlands, which are both geographically and linguistically close. Pitch patterns can also be similar.

How to Do a Geordie Accent

1) Position of the Vocal Apparatus
First set the correct position: The jaw is fairly loose. The lips are drawn a bit to the side, as when smiling, and the mouth is half open, half closed, as in General American.

2) The Most Important Sounds:
Consonants
This accent is largely non-rhotic: The "R" before another consonant is not pronounced. The vowel before the "R" is considerably lengthened, in words like *cart* and *farm*, which are pronounced "ka:t?" and "fa:m."

h: Initial "h" is pronounced.

r: A trilled "r" is heard, instead of "t," as a link between words: *He got it.* (hee gawr it?)

?: The particularity of the glottal stops heard *after* "p," "t," and "k" is what really characterizes this accent. These consonants sound almost like an aspirated version: *p, t, k*. In this phenomenon the accent resembles Danish, and it is possible that there was a Viking influence which passed over into English.

Vowels and Diphthongs
The shifts at the beginning of the chapter in "A Quick Reference" apply here. Also, as in Yorkshire, the diphthongs "ay" and "O" shift to the single lengthened vowels "e: " and "aw," respectively.

aw: This vowel shifts to "A," much as in the American Midwestern states, so *walk* is pronounced "wAk."

I: In this accent the diphthong "I" usually shifts to the diphthong "ay." *I know* is pronounced "ay naw." "I" is also often heard as "A."

o: The sound of "*o*" in *work* and *first* shifts to a short "aw," so those word are pronounced "wawk" and "fawst."

wa: This is the diphthong heard in this accent in *was* (waz) and *what*, (wat) as opposed to either British RP (wAz; wot) or General American (wuz; wAt). The pronunciation of *work first* (wawk fawst) can easily be confused by a speaker of British RP as meaning *walk fast*. In a Geordie accent this would be pronounced "wAk fa:st."

Practice

I know, I was going to walk the dog, but I can't, because I have to go to work now.
Phonetic pronunciation: ay naw ay waz gawing te wAk THe dAg boot ay kant be kAz ay haf te gaw te wawk now

I went to a show in town about eight years ago.
Phonetic pronunciation: A wen tA shaw in town bow? ayet yayez a gaw
Note: A slight "R" may be heard in the word *years.*

At the time I was having problems up and down my legs, so I went to our local doctor.
Phonetic pronunciation: At THe tIm I wez hAv' in pRawb' Limz oop An down may Ligz saw A win tAR law' ?eL dAk' teR
Note: Notice the glottal stop in the word *local*. It occurs before the vowel, and is often heard in this accent not only replacing "t," but also "k" and "p."

I went walking and climbed onto the steps.
Phonetic pronunciation: A wen? wA' kin An kLImd An? THe stayps

It happened she was baking a cake.

Phonetic pronunciation: it hA' pind shee wez bay:*e'* kin, or ?in, *e* kay:ek

I asked him where he got it, and he told me in that very shop.
Phonetic pronunciation: ay aks' dim waye' ree gA ri? an ee tawL mee in THA? vu' ree shawp, or shaw?

Liverpool

The speech patterns of the Beatles made the Liverpudlian accent world famous. Known as "Scouse," the working-class accent of the city of Liverpool sounds very much like that of the city of Belfast. This is not surprising, because the large immigration from just across the Irish Sea contributed more than anything else to the accent of Liverpool.

How to Do a Liverpudlian Accent

1) Position of the Vocal Apparatus
Say *la la la low low low loo loo* to attain the correct general position. The lips are slightly protruded and the mouth rounded, with a fairly loose jaw. In a characteristic Liverpool speech pattern, the back and blade of the tongue are usually raised towards the roof of the mouth when speaking, a phenomenon known as *velarization*.

2) The Most Important Sounds:
Consonants
The Liverpool accent is non-rhotic, unlike most other Northern British accents. The "R" is usually given one trill: "r." The surrounding countryside accent of Lancashire, however, is rhotic.

h: Initial "h" is usually dropped, but not always.

-ing: "-ing" participle endings drop the nasal "ng" and become "in." However, other words ending in "ing" or with "ing" in medial position, such as *thing* or *singer*, are pronounced with a "g" added: "thingg" and "sing'*ge*"; *singing* is pronounced "sing'gin." The "i" is lengthened.

k: "k" is often heard followed by a slight "KH" sound, in all phonetic positions. The *king* is the "kKHingg."

t: "t" is usually pronounced as "ts" in initial or final position, but not after another consonant. *Street* is pronounced "streets," and *two* is pronounced "ts<u>oo</u>." In certain words, when the ending is followed by a vowel, "t" is pronounced as a light trilled "r": *What a...* is said as "wA *re*" and *get a...* and *but a...* are pronounced "ge *re*" and "boo *re*." It is also pronounced as a tapped "*t*" between vowels so *at home* might be heard as "a *t*Om."

TH: Initial voiced "TH" is sometimes said as "*d*" or, between vowels, as a tapped "*d*."

Vowels and Diphthongs
The vowel shifts mentioned at the beginning of the chapter apply to a Liverpool accent. Vowels in stressed syllables are lengthened. In addition the following important vowel shifts occur:

O: This diphthong is like the General American "O," not like the "O" in British RP.

oo: This vowel shifts to "<u>oo</u>," so that *book* and *cook* and *nook* are pronounced "b<u>oo</u>kKH," "k<u>oo</u>kKH," and "n<u>oo</u>kKH."

Stress and Pitch

There is nothing to worry about when it comes to stress. With pitch patterns we enter an area similar to that of Belfast, where a declarative sentence often rises at the end, instead of falling in pitch. Listen to *A Hard Day's Night* (1964) or any of the other Beatles movies for the very clear musicality of a Liverpudlian accent.

Practice

He was going to be at home all night and his house is on my street, but he went out to the store.
Phonetic pronunciation: ee wooz gO' in tse bee a *t*Om awL nIts an diz ows iz awn mI sreets boo *t*ee wen tsowts tse *d*e stsaw

I was thirty-two years old at the time.
Phonetic pronunciation: oy wez tho:' tsee ts<u>oo</u> ye:z OLd a de tsoym

Possible Pitch Pattern

I
   was   old
      thirty-   at the
          two
             years   time\.

Notes: Notice the falling tone at the end of the sentence. You will notice as well that this pattern is very similar to a **Belfast** intonation (see Chapter Four).

I came into town and I had been there a few minutes when I decided to go into a pub and have myself a pint of beer.
Phonetic pronunciation: oy kay:m in' tse tsown an I Ad been de: Re fy<u>oo</u> min' its wen oy dzi sI' dzidz tse gO in' ts<u>oo</u> e poob an Av moy' seLf' e poyn', or pIn', tse beee

I was just walking down the street, all peaceful like, when it happened.
Phonetic pronunciation: oy wiz dgist waw' kin down de stsReet awL pees' fooL
Loyk wen it Ap' ind

You can tell me that till the cows come home and I won't believe you.
Phonetic pronunciation: y<u>oo</u> kin tseL mee dat tiL de kowz koom Om an oy wOn
be Leev y<u>oo</u>, or ye

Where were you when we needed you?
Phonetic pronunciation: we: we y<u>oo</u> wen we nee' did ye

Bristol, Somerset, and the Southwest

The accent of Bristol is particular to the city, and that of Somerset shares some of its characteristics as far as vowels and diphthongs are concerned. The Bristol accent might be useful in playing a number of the characters in a stage or film version of Robert Louis Stevenson's *Treasure Island*, including Long John Silver, Jim Hawkins, Squire Trelawney, Doctor Livesey, and some of the pirates. The squire and the doctor are usually played with British RP accents, but they are from the Bristol area.

How to Do the Southwestern Accents

1) Position of the Vocal Apparatus
The general position is very close to that of British RP. The position of the jaw is slightly forward and the lips are protruded very slightly.

2) Stress and Pitch
Stress and pitch patterns are important with these accents. Stressed syllables are usually long and spoken on a rising, then falling tone, giving these accents a characteristic rhythm and pitch pattern a bit different from other provincial accents.

3) The Most Important Sounds
Consonants
The accents of Bristol and Somerset are rhotic, with a hard retroflex "R," almost as in Ireland, but with the tongue farther back and up toward the palate.

l: There a particular phenomenon associated with a Bristol accent, and that is the addition of an "l" to words ending in a vowel, just after the vowel: tomorrowl, Eval, bananal. Ida is idle; perhaps she can tangle (tango). Ideas are ideals in Bristol, so the well-known joke goes. This consonant is typically dark and hard.

s: In Somerset "s" shifts to "z." The name of the county is thus "zoo' me zet." This is an old pronunciation, however, and is apparently not heard much any more. It is useful in 18th- and 19th-century plays in which rural characters from the West Country appear.

t and ?: There is some glottal stopping at the endings of words finishing with "t": but (be?).

th: As in a Cockney accent "th" is sometimes replaced by "f" in Bristol.

Vowels and Diphthongs
A and a: Words which in British RP are pronounced with "A" generally are pronounced in Bristol and Somerset with "a" (See the list in Chapter One), but the "a" is an intermediate, more open sound.

I: In Somerset (but not in Bristol) this diphthong usually shifts to a tight "oy," that is, the jaw is tightly held and more closed than, for example, the similar shift in Cockney.

u and oo: Unlike the northern provincial accents, the accents of Bristol and Somerset keep the typical southern British distinction between these two vowels, represented in the words *but* and *book*. However, there is no clear distinction between "u" and the schwa "*e.*"

Practice

I   that's tr-
  know   ue.

Phonetic pronunciations: **Somerset**: oy naw THAts tR<u>oo</u>. **Bristol**: i nO THAts tR<u>oo</u>.

Well, you know, I can tell you what happened, because I expect you want to know.
Phonetic pronunciation (**rural**): weL ye nO I kin teL ye waw? a' pind bkiz I spek, or ik spek, ye waw ne nO

What was that book you were reading there? Is it hard to read?
Phonetic pronunciation (**rural and urban**): waw? wez dad book ye wuR ree' ding de:R iz i? Ard de Reed

The summer was lovely that year and the sun shined bright over meadow and farm and lake and moor.
Phonetic pronunciations
Bristol: fsoom' eR wez Loov' Lee fat yeeR an fsoon shoynd bRoyt O' veR med' O an fARm an Layk an mooR
Somerset: de zoom' ER wez Loov' Lee dat yeeR an de zoon shoynd, or zhoynd, bRoyt O' veR med' eR an fARm an Layk an m<u>oo</u>R

They were hard winters we had to endure and lots of frost and snow and ice.
Phonetic pronunciarions
Bristol: vay weR hARd, or ARd, win' teRz wee had t<u>oo</u> en dy<u>oo</u>eR an LAts e fRAst an snO an oys
Somerset: day weR hARd, or ARd, win' teRz wee had to en' dy<u>oo</u>eR an Lats oo vRAst an znO an oyz

Bristol is a grand city, and we have the Old Vic, which is a really great theater, if you ask me.
Phonetic pronunciation (**Bristol**): bRis' teL iz e gRand si' dee an wee av dee Ol vik wich iz Ree' Lee e gRayt fee' *de*R if y<u>oo</u> ask mee

Cornwall and Devon

Cornish is a Celtic language resembling Welsh, Breton and Manx, still spoken until recently by inhabitants of the Isle of Man. In 900 C.E. the Kingdom of Cornwall was conquered by the Anglo-Saxons, whose language predominated in the region, existing alongside the Cornish of the local population. Its last speaker died in the mid-18th century, sometime after 1776, the last year in which records exist of its still being spoken by native speakers. Despite the fact that this was before the advent of recording, written records of it have been well preserved, and it is a well-known language to scholars of the Celtic tongues. There are various literary works, including 14th century Passion plays, written in Cornish.

The contemporary accents of Cornwall and Devon are very close to that of Bristol.

How to Do Cornish Accents

1) Position of the Vocal Apparatus
Say *me me me him him him* several times to set the correct general position. The jaw is tightly held, with the lips protruding slightly, which accounts for the short diphthongs. The short diphthongs give the accent a typically rather staccato quality. The pitch pattern can be said to be rather flat, and somewhat like General American.

2) The Most Important Sounds
Consonants
Consonants are heavily pronounced. The accents are rhotic, with a heavy retroflex "R." The tongue is even farther back towards the palate than it is in Irish accents.

h: This consonant is sometimes dropped.

L: This consonant is typically very dark, approaching the French "l."

?: There is a often a glottal stop in words ending in "t": *but* is pronounced "be?."

Vowels and Diphthongs
Diphthongs are typically short, and this is the main difference between the accents of Cornwall and Devon, and the accents of Bristol and Somerset.

A and a: Both these vowels typically are pronounced as a less open-throated "A."

ee: In the names of the days of the week, this is the final sound: *Monday* is pronounced "Men' dee," etc.

u: The "u" in *but* shifts to a schwa (*e*). Otherwise, the difference between "u" and "oo" is apparent, as is typical of southern British accents.

Practice

But I know you can't express it more clearly than that, now can you?
Phonetic pronunciation: be? I naw ye kAn? iks pRis' i? mawR kLiR' lee THAn THA? now kAn ye

He was a local farmer, just a person from a Cornish village.
Phonetic pronunciation: hee we ze LO' keL fAR' meR dgus' te poR' sen fRe me kawR' neesh vi' Leedg
Note: Notice the strong "L" sounds, with the back of the tongue raised. Note, too, the strong "R" sounds and the lengthening of the vowel to "ee" in the unstressed syllables of the words *Cornish* and *village*—not untypical, by the way, of Middle Western and some Californian accents in the United States. Notice, too, the strong linking of consonants to the vowels which follow them, as in *was a*, *just a*, *Cornish*, and *village*. The diphthong "O" sounds American.

The world was inside out or upside down.
Phonetic pronunciation: The wawRLd wez in' soy da<u>oo</u>? eR up soy da<u>oo</u>n
Note: I have used the symbol "a<u>oo</u>" instead of the usual "ow" to indicate the lengthened, specific version of this diphthong. It is not quite a triphthong, but almost.

We started going around together, she and I. Well, we had a wonderful time. You know what it is: we just enjoyed our company.
Phonetic pronunciation: wee stawR' deed gO' eeng Ra<u>oo</u>n te ge' THeR shee an I weL wee ha *de* wun' deR fool toyme   ye nO wA teez' wee dgist in dgoyd' AR kump' nee
Notes: The phrase *what it is* could also be pronounced "wAt teez," with two distinct "t" sounds: a soft one at the end of the word *what* and a hard "t" at the end of the word *it* linked to the word *is*. Notice that the speaker sometimes says "I' and sometimes "oy."

They had given us up for good, I think, because they thought we were gone for good.
Phonetic pronunciation: THayd giv' em es up feR goo' dI think' be kez THay thawt wee weR gawn feR good
Notes: Notice the shift from "n" to "m" at the end of the word *given*. The final "t" in *thought* should be very lightly pronounced.

The ships used to go out to sea to fish and they came back full. Those were great days, I tell you.
Phonetic pronunciation: THe ships y<u>oo</u>s de gwow te see te fish an THay kaym bak fooL   THOz weR gRayt dayz I tel y<u>oo</u>

Worcestershire

Worcestershire is on the Welsh border country. This is a rural accent.

How to Do a Worcestershire Accent

1) Position of the Vocal Apparatus
The mouth is fairly relaxed, but the lips tighten on certain sounds, notably "I" and "ee" (described below).

2) The Most Important Sounds
Consonants
R: The accent is heavily rhotic, that is, the final "R" and the "R" before another consonant are pronounced.

Vowels and Diphthongs
A: Words pronounced with "A" (*ask, bath, can't,* etc.) in British RP are pronounced with the sound of "a" in that, as in General American. See the list of such words in Chapter One.

aw: In words like *law* this sound is pronounced "A": *law* is pronounced "LA."

ee: This is shortened to "i," so *sheep* rhymes with *ship.*

I: This is pronounced "u'-ee." It is a short diphthong combining the "u" in *but* and the "ee" in *meet.*

o: Similar to the "aw" described above, the "o" in *cross,* etc., is pronounced "A": *cross* is "crAss."

oo: The "oo" in *book* or *put* is pronounced like the "u" in *but,* so *book* is pronounced "buk" and *put* (poot) as "putt." *Book* rhymes with *buck* and *put* with *putt.*

Practice

The sheep were going across the field, but stopped at a ditch of water that I saw them drink out of.
Phonetic pronunciation: THe ship weR gaw' ing e krAss THe fee' eLd bit stApt et e ditsh ev wA' teR THat eee sA THem dRink owd ev

I've quite often been to the other side of the field. You can go round there if you like. I'm going myself.
Phonetic pronunciation: ueev kwoy dAf' ten been tu THu' THeR sueed vTHe fee' eLd   ye kin gu reoond THeR if ye Lueek   ueem goo' en muee' seLf
Note: The sounds of "I" and "ow" are very close to the presumed Elizabethan sound (see Chapter One).

Worcestershire Sauce is a great invention, delicious with meat and all kinds of things.
Phonetic pronunciation: woos' teR sheR sAs ez e gRay din ven chen di Li' shes wi meet an AL kueendz e thingz

The farmers in these parts are very mindful of the environment.
Phonetic pronunciation: THe fAR' meRZ neez pARts eR ve Ree mueend' feL vee,or ev THee, en vuee' Ren ment

I've often had occasion to remark that the weather hereabouts is uncertain from one day to the next.
Phonetic pronunciation: ueev Af' ten had e kay' zhen tRee mARk' THat THe we' THeR heeR' e beoots' zin soR' ten fRim win day te THe nikst

You can enjoy your vacation in these parts wandering through these hills and dales, hiking around and stopping by a farm to see how they work it and to have some great local food.
Phonetic pronunciation: ye kin in dgoy' yeR ve kay' shn neez pARts wAn' dRing thRoo THiz hiLz n dayLz hueek' in e Reoond n stAp' en buee e fARm te see heoo THay woRk it ntav sim gRayt Law' keL food

Chapter Four
Irish, Scottish and Welsh Accents

Irish, Scottish and Welsh accents are all based originally on Celtic languages. Irish is originally from Gaelic, or Erse; Scottish accents from Scottish Gaelic (and from Scots, a dialect of English); and Welsh from the Welsh language. The linguistic hegemony of English in the British Isles never killed these languages, which are still spoken.

Irish Accents

Gaelic was the original language of Hibernia, as the Romans called Ireland. It was never latinized under Roman rule, as so many other European languages were. Nor did the medieval invasions of Anglo-Saxons and Norsemen destroy the language. Today it is the native tongue of perhaps one million people.

Ireland, like Scotland, was ruled on a clan system, and divided into small kingdoms. There was constant warfare, but the Celtic artists and craftsmen continued to produce brilliant work in spite of it. The island's conversion to Christianity was completed in the fifth century by St. Patrick. The Catholic monks in the Middle Ages kept Irish literary and philosophic culture alive, and they illuminated manuscripts with gorgeous Celtic artistry. In 1170 the first English invasion, under King Henry II, who had been granted the island by Pope Adrian IV, began. For eight centuries of bloody war and conflict the English governed Ireland with an oppressive hand.

The English noble families who moved to Ireland and were granted estates by the crown gradually began to think of themselves as Irish. At the same time as they added their accents to those of Ireland, the native Irish were learning English with a variety of Gaelic accents. The hegemony of the English also led to a reverse immigration, and an Anglo-Irish community developed in England. Such opponents of home rule for Ireland as Lord Carson, who always spoke with an Irish accent (he was already well-known, though not yet a lord, when he crushed his former Trinity College classmate Oscar Wilde in the libel suit Wilde brought against the Marquess of Queensberry), made their homes in England. Even among the anglicized Irish in Ireland, English was the prestigious language. A great many very famous authors writing in English were Irish, among them Jonathan Swift, Oliver Goldsmith, Richard Brinsley Sheridan, William Butler Yeats, George Bernard Shaw (who never lost his heavy Dublin brogue), and Oscar

Wilde. (When Wilde was asked how he felt about home rule for Ireland, he said "Ah, well, my idea is that Ireland should rule England.") Ireland produced one of the literary geniuses of the 20th century in James Joyce.

In the 17th century the attitude of the English ruling classes was particularly hostile. The bitterly anti-Irish Oliver Cromwell, in his attempt to subdue the rebellious island, was responsible for infamous massacres at Drogheda (Anglicized pronunciations: draw' e de or droy' de; the Irish say "draw' khe de," from the Gaelic *Droichead Atha*) and Wexford. Religion was at the bottom of the conflict, and the Puritan Cromwell was not alone in being anti-Catholic. (A man of contradictions, he did have English Catholic friends, although Catholicism was a proscribed religion.) You can read more about the tragic history of this century and the terrible treatment of the Irish in their own land in Antonia Fraser's *Cromwell The Lord Protector* (Alfred A. Knopf, 1973).

The Irish language and culture were disparaged by those who governed Ireland. As late as 1900, for instance, the Anglo-Irish composer Sir Arthur Sullivan wrote an operetta (his last), called *The Emerald Isle*. Some of the comic characters speak with broad accents, and Irish folklore is satirized. The music, sometimes very beautiful, is often mock-Irish. Even though all of this is meant to be very charming and "quaint," it betrays much of the supercilious, patronizing attitude of the Victorians towards things Irish. There are also, however, authentic Irish light operas from the same period, such as Charles Villiers Stanford's beautiful *Shamus O'Brien* (1896).

As a result of famine and terrible economic conditions, there was massive Irish emigration to North America in the 18th and 19th centuries. See *Far and Away* (1992), both for some of the history, and for the authentic accents of such Irish actors as Cyril Cusack.

Once Irish independence from England was achieved in 1921 (in the south, with six of the nine Ulster counties remaining under British rule in the north), the cultural nationalism of the Celtic revival could assert itself without fear. The attempt to revive the Irish language is ongoing in Ireland and many people speak and read it as a second language.

There are many examples of Irish accents available on film, video and records. The gorgeous Irish accents in the Abbey Theatre recordings of Sean O'Casey's plays are not to be missed. For more contemporary accents listen to the many supporting players in the wonderful film *A Man of No Importance* (1994), set in Dublin, starring Albert Finney, whose accent is perfect as a man who admires and emulates Oscar Wilde; the views of the city are superb. Also listen to Milo O'Shea and the other Irish actors in the film of James Joyce's *Ulysses* (1967). Worth hearing as well is Dublin-born Barry Fitzgerald in such Hollywood films as *The Quiet Man* (1952), despite the intentional exaggeration of his accent. You should also see Carol Reed's magnificent film *Odd Man Out* (1947), with James Mason as a hunted Irish rebel leader; *The Crying Game* (1992) with Stephen Rea, for northern accents; and *Michael Collins* (1996) set during the 1916-1921 rebellion, with Liam Neeson in the title role. There are a number of videos which will give you a great impression of Ireland, such as the 1997 PBS documentary *Danny Boy: In Sunshine or in Shadow*. Also excellent is the A&E video *The Irish in America*. For **Limerick** accents see the moving film *Angela's Ashes* (1999), based on Frank McCourt's wonderful, Pulitzer Prize book. Very much worth seeing and listening to is John Huston's last film, *The Dead* (1987), based on James Joyce's short story in *Dubliners*. The atmosphere of the film and the performances by the Irish cast are superb. Be sure to see the PBS videotape *The Irish and How They Got That Way*, with the marvelous, vivacious Ms. Terry Donnelly and Mr. Ciarán Sheehan, who has the most beautiful voice you will ever hear. If you can find them, listen to the now rare recordings of Siobhán McKenna, such as her reading of Molly Bloom's soliloquy in the Caedmon Spoken Arts LP (TC 1063, ca. 1960) of James Joyce's *Ulysses*, which she reads with the American actor E.G. Marshall, and her cassettes of *The Collected Stories of Katherine Anne Porter, Irish Verse and Ballads* and *The Poetry of Yeats*. The following CDs are also useful: *John McCormack in Irish Song* (Pearl, Gemm CD 9338), in which you not only hear the gorgeous voice of the famous tenor singing, but also speaking, on track 20 when he introduces *The Londonderry Air; The Irish Songbook: 21 Treasured Irish Songs by Timeless Voices of Yesteryear* (Moidart Music Group, MID CD 006); "*The Minstrel Boy*": Irish Singers of Great Renown (Pearl, Gemm CD 9989). Browse in the folk music section of record stores, and you will find many authentic examples of accents. From County Cork in the southeast to Sligo and Donegal in the northwest of the Republic you will thus hear a great variety of Irish accents, rural and urban. On the east coast of the Republic of Ireland are its capital city of Dublin, with County Kildare (stress on the second syllable) just southwest of it and County Meath just north of it. On the southeast coast is County Cork. Limerick is just north of County Cork, and County Clare and Galway, both on the west coast, are north of Limerick. Northwest of Galway is County Mayo (pronounced in Ireland with the stress on the second syllable, but usually strssed in America on the first; from Gaelic *Mhuigheo*, pronounced "vwee O'"). The counties of Louth, Monaghan, Cavan and Leitrim, all in the Irish Free State, border Northern Ireland (UK) on the south. Derry and Belfast are in Northern Ireland (UK), which has been divided into districts since 1974, replacing the former system of counties.

With all these accents and many more, there is nevertheless a common set of phonetic characteristics, particularly as regards vowel and diphthong shifts, but you should look at how the accents vary in this regard in specific locales. The Irish "R" and "l" (see below) are common to most of the accents, which vary between rhotic (the majority of accents), and some non-rhotic, particularly in the north (**Meath** [pronounced "meeTH"]; **Belfast** [sometimes;], some other areas of Northern Ireland, etc.). When people from the **Belfast** area speak non-rhotically, the accent may remind you of New York City or Boston accents, as Bernadette Devlin did me when I heard her speaking in television interviews, except for the pitch/intonation pattern which you will see below. In some accents both retroflex "R" and trilled "r" are heard (**County Cork, Galway, Mayo** [the "R" shifts to a trilled "r" between two vowels], **Kerry**). Many accents (**County Cork, Limerick, Dublin** [sometimes], **Wexford** [sometimes], **Mayo**, etc.) shift

"TH" and "th" to "d" and "t"; some to "dTH" and "th" or "tth" (**County Cork, Galway, Dublin working class,** who live in **Inner Dublin**). Note that in **County Mayo** you can hear all three versions of "TH/th": TH, th, d, t, dTH, tth. In **Galway** "s" before consonants is often pronounced "sh," but this is not the case in other accents. You can see some variations in the comparative Phonetic Pronunciations in the Practice section, which include the southern accents of **Kildare** (not far from Dublin; a very clear, easily comprehensible accent, similar to **middle- and upper-class Dublin suburban and urban** accents, which I will call for our purposes **General Dublin** speech); **County Mayo** (because of the large immigration from Mayo to the USA many Americans think of this as the most typical Irish accent, but of course, as you can see, there are many others); **Galway; County Cork; Inner Dublin** (usefeul for Sean O'Casey plays, for instance); and the northern accents of **Belfast** and **Derry.**

As you might expect, British RP pronunciations such as "se dges' chen" (as opposed to General American "sug, or seg, dges' chen) for *suggestion* and "teR' i tRee" (against General American "teR' i tawR' ee") for *territory* are usual, but Irish English is also marked by the use of "a," and not "A," in such words as *ask, answer, after* and *can't* (see the list in Chapter One). The vowel "a" in Irish English is more open than it is in either British RP or General American. Dublin and Belfast, as well as every one of the 32 counties in the green isle—in the Republic of Ireland, formerly known as *Eire* (e:' Re), and in Northern Ireland— have their own accents.

A Quick Reference

1) The first question is where in Ireland your character comes from, **north** or **south**.
2) In the **south** there is a heavily retroflex final "R" and "R" before another consonant. In the **north** the final "R" is often dropped.
3) The consonant "l" is dark, liquid, and slightly retroflex (the bottom of the tongue curls upward), especially in the **south**. This "l" is a key to the general placement of the accent.
4) The vowel "a," slightly open, is used where British RP uses "A."
5) The vowel shifts are: "a" to "A"; "aw" to "A"; "e" to "a." The "o" in such words as *hot, not, got, gone* and *on* is pronounced either as it is in British **RP (Kildare/ General Dublin)**, or else it shifts to "A" (**Belfast, Limerick, County Mayo, County Cork, Galway,** etc.), or to "aw" (**Inner Dublin,** etc.). You see how specific you have to be to do an authentic accent. For example, the usual shift from "aw" to "A" in such words as *law* and *water* (as in the accents of **Belfast, Mayo,** or **Dublin**), does not occur in either **Derry,** which is in the north (actually, it does occur there sometimes); or in the southern city of **Limerick,** where the "aw" in a word like *fortune* is pronounced as it is in General American (fawR' chen), but lengthened slightly: faw:R' chen. All vowels in all accents are lengthened slightly before "R" or "r."
6) The all-important diphthong shifts: "ay" to "e:"; "ee" to "e:," especially in the

south; "O" to "aw"; and "I" to "oy," this last one in the **south**; in the **north** "I" remains "I." In both **north** and **south** there is sometimes a tendency to turn the diphthong "ay" into a triphthong, so a word like *basis* is pronounced "baye' sis."
7) "TH" and "th" are often heard, especially in the west of Ireland, but also often in the **north** and **south**, as dental plosives "d" and "t" (with the tongue against the back of the upper front teeth). A tapped "d" is sometimes heard between vowels in such words as *other* (u' *deR*). Occasionally (not always), a tapped "t" is heard in such words as *forty* (**north**: faw:' *tee*; **south**: fawR' *tee*). The consonants "TH" and "d" are are sometimes pronounced "dTH"; "t" and "th" are either "th" or "tth" in ceertain phonetic positions in some accents (**Cork, Inner Dublin, Galway,** etc.); see the Practice section.
8) *Been* mostly rhymes with *bean*, and, especially in the **north**, with *Ben*; and sometimes with *bin*.

A Quick Reference: Comparative Pronunciations of Selected Words

tomorrow, anything, paper, through, theater; more; floor; been; there; poor; drive; mile; work
Belfast: t*e* mA' R*e*; a' n*e* theng; pe:' peR, or or pe:'*e* peR'; thRi'<u>oo</u>; the:' *deR*; mawR, or maw; fLA, or fLaw; ben, or ban; THe:R, or THeeeR; pawR; dRIv; mIL; wo:Rk
Derry: t*e* mawR' A, or t*e* m<u>oo</u>' RA; *e'* n*e* then; pe' peR; thRee, or thRi:ü; thi:' *deR*; m<u>oo</u>R, or mawR; fLawR; ben; THeR, or THeR; p<u>oo</u>eR; dRoyv, or dRIv; mIeL; wo:Rk
Galway: t*e* mAR' aw; i' n*e* ting; pe:' peR, or pe:' per; tthr<u>oo</u>, or tR<u>oo</u>; tay' ttheR; mAR; flAR; been; de:R; p<u>oo</u>r; dTHroyv; moyl, or mIl; weRk, or werk
Mayo: t*e* mA' R*e*; *e'* nee ting; pe:' peR; tR<u>oo</u>, or thR<u>oo</u>, or tthRoo; tee', or thee' *e*, teR; mAr; flAR; been; de:eR, or dTHe:eR ; p<u>oo</u>eR; dRoyv; moyl; waw:Rk, or waw:rk
County Cork: t*e* maw' re'; a', or o', nee ting; pee' per; tthr<u>oo</u>; tee' *e* ther, or tther; mawr; flawr, or fl<u>oo</u>r; been, or bin; de:er; p<u>oo</u>r; dTHroyv; moyl; we:rk
Kildare/General Dublin: t*e* maw' RO; *e'* nee, or n*e*, thing; pay:' peR; thR<u>oo</u>; thee' *e* teR; mawR; flawR; been; THe:R; p<u>oo</u>R; dRIv; mIl; woRk
Inner Dublin: t*e* mA' R*e*; *e'* nee thing; pay:' peR; thR<u>oo</u>, or tsR<u>oo</u>, or tthRoo; thee' *deR*; m<u>oo</u>R, or m<u>oo</u>eR; fl<u>oo</u>R, or fl<u>oo</u>eR; been; de:R, or deeR; p<u>oo</u>eR or py<u>oo</u>eR; dRoyv, or dTHRoyv; moyl; wawRk, or wawk, or wawrk, or weRk

How to Do Irish Accents

1) Position of the Vocal Apparatus
There are two basic positions. For **northern** accents the position is a bit in be-tween the General American and British RP positions, slightly more closed than in General American. The jaw is relaxed. For **southern** Irish accents the jaw is fairly loose and open generally, more than in General American, but more closed than in London accents. Practice the Irish retroflex "l" to get the general position. An exception to this relaxed position of the jaw is **County Cork,** where the general position of the vocal apparatus is tighter and more closed.

2) The Most Important Sounds
   Vowel and diphthong shifts, similar in both **north** and **south**, and these sounds change radically from British RP or General American. Vowels are lengthened before "R." For further phonetic information see below under the specific accents. For consonants, especially the all important "R" and "L," see below under the different Irish accents.

The Different Irish Accents

Northern Irish (Belfast, Derry)

The accents of **Belfast City** vary from non-rhotic to rhotic. **Derry** has a distinctly rhotic accent. There is a music to northern Irish accents that is quite different from the southern pitch patterns, and it varies from a flatness that almost sounds American to the kind of intonation described below under "Pitch," and further detailed in the Practice section.

The Most Important Sounds
Consonants
Consonants are generally the same as in Standard English, but the "L" is like the liquid "l" of Italian or French. However, in the **Belfast** area and in **Derry** you may to hear an "L" approaching the General American sound. Sometimes "TH" and "th" are heard as "d" and "t." See number 7 under "A Quick Reference."

Vowels and Diphthongs
A: Pronounce words like *ask, bath* and *can't* on the model of General American, rather than British RP. See the list under "A" in Chapter One. The vowel should, however, be lengthened and slightly more open-throated in an Irish accent than in General American.

a: The "a" in words like *bad, that,* and *cat* is heightened, close to the "A" in *father*.
Practice words: *bad, cat, sat, mat, that, hat*

aw and A: The "aw" in words like *law, talk,* and *because* are close to the "A" in *father*.
Practice words: *law, talk, water, ought, bought, sought, long*

ay: This diphthong shifts to a pure lengthened vowel "e:." The first part of the diphthong is the vowel which is retained and lengthened. Sometimes it actually sounds close to "ee," so *say* would rhyme with *see*.
Practice words: *say, day, hay, may, paper, later, greater*

e and a: The "e" in words like *met, bet,* and *bed* is broadened, close to the "a" in (standard) *bad* (working-class: "be: ed").

85

I: The "I" diphthong is close to "oy" in *boy*, but in **Belfast** it is often close to the General American diphthong.

i and e: The short "i" sounds like short "e" in *met, bed. Killed* becomes "kelled"; *think* becomes "thenk," etc. In some areas of the city of **Belfast** there is a shift from "i" to a schwa "e": *sit* shifts to "set" and *sit down* is pronounced "set dAün." The word *inward* is pronounced "en' weRd" or "en' wed."

O: The pure lengthened vowel "aw" is the shift from the diphthong "O" as in the word *home.* The first half of the diphthong is retained.
Practice words: *home, alone, bone, known, grown, blown, stone*

o: The vowel is such words as *work, first* and *girl* is longer than it is in General American, and tends almost towards "aw," but is otherwise the same vowel.

ow: In many accents "ow" is pronounced as in General American (not British RP). In the north (and sometimes in **Inner Dublin** in the south), this dipththong occasionally shifts to a tight, closed version of "O": e'<u>oo</u>. This is not to be confused with the "O" of British RP; rather it is more like the "O" described in the section of Chapter One on Early Modern English. In **Derry** "ow" shifts to "I" or to "e'<u>oo</u>."
Practice words: *mouth, south, how, now, brown, cow, down*

u and oo: The "u" in *but* is like "oo" in *book.* It is also sometimes like a schwa in (working-class): *butcher* shifts to "betshuR."

Pitch

There is a particular sort of musicality in this accent, which often has a rising tone which we associate with questions, at the end of a declarative sentence.

Practice

And that was the sort of thing he wanted to tell me, you see.
Phonetic pronunciation: An THAt wez THe saw te thing hee want' ed te tel mee yoo see
Note that the "t" in *sort of* is very aspirated, almost like a flap with more air in it, instead of a hard "t."

One Possible Pitch Pattern:

```
                                              me,
        that                                          you see.
And          was the sort of thing he wanted to
                                      tell
```

I know I met him in the road a short time ago.
Phonetic pronunciation: oy naw oy mat em in THe Rawd e shawt toym e gaw

In **Derry** "ay" in *say* or *paper* shifts to "e" in *met*, so *paper* rhymes with *pepper*. The "u" in *but* is pronounced as it is in General American. The "a" in *that* and *marry* is pronounced very broadly, like "A" in *father*. However, the accent in this area varies, so you will often hear *law* and *cross* pronounced as they are in General American. The dipththong "ow" in words like *out*, *down*, *house* and *now* shifts to "I" or to "e'oo": It, dIn, hIs, nI; e'oot' de'oon, he'oos, ne'oo. The sound of "oo" shifts to "ee" or to "i:ü," so *through* is pronounced "thRee" or "thRi:ü." The "aw" in *law* and *cross* is also pronounced like the "A" in *father*. The "o" in *work* and *first* is pronounced like the "aw" in *law*: "wawrk," "fawrst." *Want to* is contracted to "wanna." Some "oo" words are palatalized, as in *move*, which is pronounced "myoov" and *school*, "skyool."

Border Accents

Near the border between the Northern counties and the Republic of Ireland the accents remain largely non-rhotic. This is the case, for instance in the accent of **Meath** (not directly on the border, but very close), in which, however, you do hear an occasional final "R" or even "r" pronounced, as well as R-influenced vowels; the initial rhotic sound is usually a trilled "r." The advice below will give you the Irish midlands accents, particularly with the vowel and diphthong shifts. As usual, there are some exceptions, and in **Meath** the shift from "I" to "oy" does not occur: "I" remains "I."

The Most Important Sounds
Consonants
R: In initial position a trilled "r" is often heard.

TH and th: The "TH" in such words as *this* is pronounced like a dental "d," and the "th" in words like *think* is pronounced "t": tink.

Final "g" in "-ing" endings is often dropped: *nothing* is pronounced "nut' en."

Vowels and Diphthongs
Vowels are as above for Northern accents. Diphthongs are lengthened: *before* is pronounced "be fO' e"; *hear* and *here* are pronounced "hee' e"; *more* becomes "mO' A."

Southern Irish (Dublin; County Cork, etc.)

These are rhotic accents, except among those portions of the population who imitate British speech. There are class differences in Irish accents; see below under specific information for **Dublin** accents, for example. Following the phonetic indications below will give you a **Kildare** or **General Dublin** (suburban; **middle** and **upper class**) accent, some of the clearest Irish speech.

The Most Important Sounds
Consonants
Consonants are generally the same as in standard varieties of English. Take note of the following important changes, however:
L and l: Often "L" is liquid ("l"), as in French or Italian. The "l" is also slightly retroflex; the bottom of the tongue curls upward as the "l" is articulated.

R: The very retroflex final "R" is pronounced with the tongue curled farther back than in General American, so that the sides of the bottom of the tongue really touch the inner sides of the upper gum ridge.

TH and th: These sounds are often substituted for by "d" for the voiced "TH" and "t" for the voiceless "th," but by no means always. In **Dublin** "th" before "R" is often heard as "t" or even "ts," as in the word *through* (tsR<u>oo</u>), in working-class speech. The educational background and social class of the speaker must be considered here.

Vowels and Diphthongs
The shifts in vowels and diphthongs are similar to **Northern Irish** substitutions. **Practice words** for many of these sounds will be found under that section.

ay: The long "ay" diphthong often shifts to a lengthened pure vowel "e:."

ee: Long "ee" in words like *tea* becomes like "ay" in *say*; *tea* becomes "tay."
Practice words: *tea, meat, Jesus, leave, here* (rhymes with *hair*), *beer, teach, reach, believe*

I: This diphthong often loses the schwa which follows it in words like *mile* and *trial*. Sometimes it shifts to "oy." *Mile* (General American pronunciation: mI' eL) and *trial* (General American pronunciation: tRI' eL) are pronounced either "moyl" and "tRoyl," or "mIl" and "tRIl." The first two pronunciations can be heard in **County Cork** (except that in Cork *trial* would be pronounced "tthroyl"; notice the "tth" and the trilled "r"), and in **Inner Dublin** (working class), and the last two in **General Dublin** (middle and upper class and in suburbia) and in **Limerick**.

o: The vowel in such words as *work, first* and *girl* varies from the same pronunciation as in General American (**Kildare/General Dublin**) to "aw" (**Inner Dublin, Mayo**) to a long "e:" (**County Cork**) to a short "e" (**Galway**). In all cases the vowel before the "R" or "r" is lengthened slightly.

oy: The shift of the "oy" in words like *boy* to the "I" diphthong is much more marked in the **south**.

u: The "u" in *but* becomes like "oo" in *book*: *occur, nurse, work, first* (sometimes leaning towards "awR" in **Dublin**).

yoo: Words like *tune, duke*, etc., add the semi-vowel "y" before the vowel "oo," but in working-class speech (where a word like *true* is triphthongized, becoming "tReeyoo"), the consonants change instead of the semi-vowel "y" being inserted between the consonant and the vowel "oo," so *tune* is pronounced "choon" and *duke* is pronounced "jook."

County Cork: Initial "TH" and "th" are pronounced "d" (voiced) and "t" (voiceless), but voiceless "th" is sometimes substituted in the middle of a word for "t": *theatre* is pronounced "tayther." Often a "t" is heard before the "th," so an alternative pronunciation, in **Cork City**, would be "tay' tther" or "tee' ther." The "TH" sometimes shifts to "dTH," especially before "r" (as it does also in **Galway**). The "r" is pronounced with one trill in all positions. There is also an up and down lilt, which you must hear in order to reproduce it accurately. The diphthong "ay" shifts to "ee," so words like *wait* and *paper* are pronounced "weet" and pee' per." The sound of "a" in words like *chance* is very flat, almost like the sound heard in the American Middle West or in some New York City accents in the word *avenue*. The accent discussed here is a general one for the county and for **Cork City**, but it is not what you would hear in Cork high society, where people speak with what is called a "Montebello" accent, named for the hill where they live.

In **Dublin**, "I" ranges from "oy" to "ooee"; but see above under "I." *Mile* sometimes has a schwa inserted before the "L" and is pronounced "moyel," and sometimes "mIeL," rhyming with *trial*. The vowel "o" as in the word *work* does not exist in **working-class** speech; "oo" is the usual substitute: "wooRk." It is usual to say initial "h." Also particular to Dublin is a schwa inserted before "R" in words like *beer, square, floor, pair, horse* (beeeR, skweeeR, flooeR, payeR, hooeRs). Voiceless "th" is sometimes heard as a "ts," especially before "R." Also common, in working-class speech, is the insertion of a schwa between consonants. *Dublin* is pronounced "du' be lin," for example. For an **upper-class** Dublin accent do a dark Irish retroflex "l," with the bottom of the tongue curled very slightly up towards the roof of the mouth. The upper-class accent is very lightly rhotic; the final "R" is softly pronounced. The vowels are more as in General American than British RP. There is no schwa after "I" in words like *mile* and *trial*, which are pronounced "mIl" and "tRIl." Even in upper-class Dublin speech "TH" and "th" are often pronounced as dental plosives "d" and "t," although not always. See number 7 under "A Quick Reference" for more information on "TH" and "t" sounds.

On the **southwest coast** there is a particular phenomenon to consider: the semi-vowel "y" is sometimes inserted after an initial consonant, especially after "k" and "g." *Car* is pronounced "kyAR," and *garden* becomes "gyAR' din." *Doctor* is pronounced "dyak' teR."

Pitch

The southern Irish accents are famous for their lilt, a kind of up-and-down melody. In fact, the intonation patterns are very close to those of British RP, and adding the phonetic shifts of the Irish accent to those patterns will give you the effect of the lilt. Listen to the Irish raconteurs in the video of *The Irish in America,* and you will hear what I mean. You can use the sentences in Chapter One for practice, as in the following example from that chapter:

```
                              not quite the
        \for-                 it's              right shade of
            tun-        y,                            \blu-
Un-             ate/l-                                       e.
```

General southern Irish phonetic pronunciation: un fawR'che net lee its not kwoyt THe, or de, Royt, or Royt, she:d ev bLoo

A particular phenomenon in the Irish intonation of yes-or-no questions is the falling tone at the end:

```
Would you care to go \o-
                         ut?
```

Phonetic pronunciation: woo' dge, or dyoo, ke:R, or kayeR, te, or te, gaw owt, or owt

Practice

Like I said to yous, that's really very true, and sure you'll be after knowin' the truth of it, somewhere along the road anyway.
Phonetic Pronunciations:
Belfast: LIk I sad te yez, or yiz, THats Ree' Lee va' Ree tRi'oo an shawR, or shooR, yiL, or yi'ooL, or yooL, bee af' teR nawn, or naw' in, THe tRi'ooth ev et soom' we:eR e LAng' THe Rawd a' nee we:'
Derry: loyk oy sed tee yeez THAts Ree' lee ve' Ree tRee, or tRi:ü, an sheeR yeel bee af' teR nawn THe tReeth ev et, or uv ut sem' we:eR e Lawng THe Rawd e' nee we
Galway: loyk I sid te yez dats Ray' lee ve' Ree tRoo an shoor yel bee af' ttheR nawn de troot ev it soom wi:' er e lAng de Rawd, or rawd, i' nee we:
Mayo: loyk oy sed ti yiz dats Ree' lee ve' ree tRoo An shooer yil bee af' theR nawn di tRoot ev it soom' hwee' er e' lAng de, or dTHe, Rawd e' nee we:
County Cork: loyk oy sed te yez dats ree' lee, or ray' e lee, ve' ree tthRoo an shawr yel bee, or bay, af' ther nawn de tthroot ev it soom wee' er e lAng de rawd o' nee wee

90

Kildare/General Dublin: lIk I sed te yez THats Ree' lee ve' Ree tRoo and shooeR yel bee af' teR nO' in THe tRooth ev it, or it, sum' hwe:eR e lAng THe ROd e' nee way

Inner Dublin: loyk, or lIK, oy sed, or sad, te yez dats, or ats, Ree' lee ve' Ree tsRoo an shawR yel bee af' ter nawn de tsRoot ev it soom', or sum', wee:eR e lAng de Rawd a' nee wee

Irish Folk Ballad
(Irish folk songs, when sung by such Irish singers as John McCormack, Margaret Burke Sheridan and James Joyce's favorite baritone J.C. Doyle, are a great source for Irish accents and culture, quite apart from the beauty and inspiration of the songs themselves.)
Oh, did you not hear of Kate Kearney?/ She lives on the banks of Killarney;/ From the glance of her eye,/Shun danger and fly,/ For fatal's the glance of Kate Kearney!

Phonetic pronunciations
Northern: aw: did ye nAt heeR e kay: t ka:' nee; shee livs awn THe bAnks ev ki la' nee; fRem THe glAnts ev heR I, shoon day: n' dgeR an flI faw fay:' tlz THe glAnts ev kay: t ka:' nee

Southern: aw: did ye nAt heeeR ev kay:t kAR' nee; shee livs awn THe bAnks ev ki lAR' nee; fRem THe glAnts ev hawR oy shoon da:n' dgeR An floy, fawR fay: tlz THe glAnts ev kay:t kAR' nee

Note: The voiced "TH" sounds could certainly be pronounced as "d." The "t" in *Kate* could be heard as a tapped, aspirated "*t.*"

Fortune smiled upon him in Ireland.
Phonetic pronunciations:
Belfast: faw', or fA', or fawR', chen smIld u pAn' im in AR', or IeR', or A', lend
Derry: fawR' chen smoy' eld e pawn' um un oyR' Lund
Galway: fAR' chen shmoyld e pAn him in oyr' lend
Mayo: fAR' chen smoyld e pAn him in oyR' lend
County Cork: fawr' chen smoy' eld A pAn' im in oy' er, or oyr', lend
Kildare/General Dublin: fawR' chen, or tyen, smoy' eld, or smIld, e pawn' him in IR' lend
Inner Dublin: fooR' chen smoyld, or smIld, e pawn' im in IR', or AR' lend

Pitch pattern (Belfast)

```
                        upon
For-                          him in
    tune                           Ireland.
            smiled
```

What's the matter? Cat got your tongue?
Phonetic pronunciations:

Belfast: wAts THe or MA' teR   kat gAt yeR tung
Derry: wAts THe mA' teR   kat gAt yeeR tung
Galway: wAts de ma' ttheR   kat gAt yer, or gAT cher toong
Mayo: wAts de ma' teR, or theR   kat gAt yeR, or gA' cheR, toong
County Cork: wAts de ma' ther, or tther, kat gAt yer, or cher, toong
Kildare/General Dublin: wAts THe ma' teR   kat, or kat, got, or got, yeR tung
Inner Dublin: wats de ma' teR kat gawt yeR, or cheR, toong

Sure, and that'll be the end of it.
Phonetic pronunciations:
Belfast: shooR an THa' tL bee THee and *ev* ut
Derry: sheeR An THA' tl bee THee end uv et
Galway: sh<u>oo</u>r en da' *tl* bee dee ind *ev* it, or i*t, et*
Mayo: sh<u>oo</u>eR an da' tl bee dee end *ev* it
County Cork: shawr n dA' dL bee dee end *ev* it
Kildare/General Dublin: shooR, or sh<u>oo</u>eR and THa' tl bee THee end *ev* it
Inner Dublin: sh<u>oo</u>eR An da, or dA, or THa, orTHA, tl bee dee, or THee, end *ev* et

It's not what you're thinking at all, I can assure you. We only went to the theater, then he walked me home through the lane. And I met him there anyway. He didn't pick me up first. That's all. It wasn't a date, the way you're thinking. I'm done with telling you. You're an idiot to be so jealous. Come to my arms. It's you I love, you know, my darling.
Phonetic pronunciations:
Belfast: ets nawt wet yeR thank' en e *d*AL I kin e shy<u>oo</u>R, or sheeR, y<u>oo</u>, or yi:<u>oo</u> wee awn' Lee wan te THe theee' teR THan hee wAkt mee hO:m thR<u>oo</u> THe Le:n   nI mat im THayeR a' nee we: hee did', or ded', ent pik mee up, or oop, fo:Rst   THats AL   it wAz' ent e de:t THe we: y<u>oo</u>R, or yeeR, thenk' en   Am dun, or doon, with taL' in ye   yAr, or yawR an i' *dee* it ti bee saw dgaL' es   kum, or koom, te mI Amz   its y<u>oo</u> I Loov ye naw, or nO, mI dAR', or dA, Ling
Derry: ets nAt wAt yeeR think' in a *t*awL I kan a sheeR' yee   wee awn' Lee wen te THe theee' *de*R THen hee wawkt mee hawm thRee THe Len   an I me *di*m THe:eR e' nee we   hee did' en pek me up fo:Rst   THats awL   it wAz' nt e det THe we yeeR think' en Im dun wi tel' in yee   yeeR an i' *dee* ut te bee saw dga' Lus   kum te mI awRmz   its yee I Luv yi naw mI dAR' Lin
Galway: its nAt wAt cher tink' in e *t*Al I ken e shooR ye   wee awn' lee wint te de tay' ttheR   din hee wAkt mee hawm tthr<u>oo</u> de len   en I mit him de:R i' nee we: hee did' ent pik me oop feRsht   dats Al   it wAz' ent e det, or det, de we: y<u>oo</u>r tink' in   Im doon wit tel' en ye   yeR an i:' *dget* te bay saw dgel' *es*   koom te mI Armz   itsh y<u>oo</u> oy loov ye naw mI dAR' len
Mayo: its nAt wAt yeR, or wA' cheR tink' in at Al oy kin e sh<u>oo</u>eR y<u>oo</u>   wee awn' lee wen te de tthee' e teR den hee wAkt mee hawm tthR<u>oo</u> de le:n   an oy met him deeer e' nee we: hee did' en pik mee oop faw:Rst   dats Al   it wooz' ent e de:t de we: yAR tink' in   oym doon wit tel' in ye   yAR an i:' dgit ti bee saw dgel' is   koom te moy A' remz   its y<u>oo</u> oy loov yi naw moy daR' ling

92

County Cork: its nawt wet yer tink' in e tAl oy kin e shawr ye wee awn' lee wen te de, or de, teee' ttheR den ee wAkt mee hawm tr_oo_ de Leen en oy met im deeer o', or a:', nee we: hee did' en pik me oop fe:rst dats Al twez en e de:t de we: yawr tink' in oym doon wit tel' in ye yawr an ee' dget ti bee saw dgel' es koom te moy Armz its y_oo_ oy loov ye naw moy dar' lin

Kildare/General Dublin: its not wet yeR, or yawR, think' ing a _tawl_ I kan e sh_oo_R y_oo_ wee On' lee went te THe theee' teR THen hee wAkt mee hawm thR_oo_ THe Le:n And I me_t_ him THay:R e' nee way Hee did' ent pik mee up foRst THats awl, or Al it wAz' ent e de:t THe we: y_oo_R think' ing Im dun with tel' ing y_oo_ yawR an i' _dee_ et te bee sO dge' _les_ kum te mI ARmz its y_oo_ I luv y_oo_ nO mI dAR' ling

Inner Dublin: its nAt wAt, or cheR, yeR think' in e dAl oy kin e sh_oo_eR y_oo_ wee awn' lee wen te de theee' teR den hee wAkt me haw:m tsR_oo_ de Le:n an oy met him dayeR, or dTHayeR, e' nee way hee did' en pik mee oop fawRst dats Al et wooz' ent e de:t de we: y_oo_eR tink', or tsink', in oym doon, or dun, wit tel', or tsel', in ye yeR en i:' dgit, dyet, te bee saw dgel' _es_ koom ti moy A' Remz its y_oo_ oy loov ye naw moy daR' len

I'm just taking a break from my work. I'm reading the papers.
Phonetic pronunciations:
Belfast: am dgoost te:' kin e bRe:k, or bRe:'ek, fRoom mI woRk, or wawRk Am Reed' en THe pe:' peRz, or pe:'e peRz
Derry: Am dgist te' kin e bRek fRoom mee wawRk Am Reed' en THe pe' peRz
Galway: Im dgoost te:' ken e bRe:k fRoom mI werk oym Ray' dn de pe:' peRsh, or peRz
Mayo: oym dgoost te:' kin e bRe:k fRoom moy wARk oym ree' dn de pe:' peRz
County Cork: Am dgoost tee' ken e breek froom mee, or moy, wawrk oym reed' en de pee' perz
Kildare/General Dublin: Im dgust tay:' king e bRay:k fRAm, or fRem, mI wo:Rk Im Reed' ing THe pay:' peRz
Inner Dublin: Am dgust te:' kin e bRe:k fRem moy wawRk, or woRk oym Reed' in de pay:' peRz

Wait till I tell you what I read in the papers, says I. I never heard the like in my life.
Phonetic pronunciations:
Belfast: way tiL I teL, or taL, ye wA dI Ra' din THe pe:' peRz, or pe:'e peRz, sez I I na' veR ho:Rd THe LIk en mI LIf
Derry: wet til oy teL yee wAt oy Red, or Rad, in THe pep' eRz sez oy I na' veR ho:Rd THe LIk in mI LIf
Galway: we: _tl_ I til ye wA_t_ I Rid in de pe:' peRz, or perz, sez I oy ni' ver herd de loyk in moy, or mee, lIf, or loyf
Mayo: we:' tloy tel ye wA' _toy_ Re dn de pe:' peRz sez oy oy ni' veR hawRd de loyk in moy, or mee, loyf
County Cork: wee' tl, or dl, oy tel ye we' toy red in de pee' perz se' zoy oy ni' ver he:rd de loyk in moy, or mee, loyf

93

Kildare/General Dublin: way *tel* I tel y<u>oo</u> wA *t*I Red in THe pay' peRz *sez* I I ne' veR hoRd THe lIk in mI lIf

Dublin working class: we: tl oy tel *ye we d*oy Red in *d*e pe:' peRz *sez* oy oy ne' veR hawRd, or hawrd, or haw:d, de loyk in moy, or mee, loyf

Possible Pitch Pattern (Cork)

```
                                    says
                                      I.
Wait                         papers,
     till      you what I read in the            ne-
      I                                        ver
        tell                            I      heard the like in my    fe.
                                                                    li-/
```

Notes: This is one example of the sometimes lyrical intonation one hears in **Cork City**. Listen to the cassette *Accents for Actors:Ireland, Wales, Scotland and England* for an authentic example of **Cork** and other accents.

I want some butter to my bread. It's just too dry without it.
Phonetic pronunciations:
Belfast: I wAnt sum bu' *te*R te mI bRad its dgest t<u>oo</u> dRI wu thOw', or the'<u>oo</u>, det

Derry: I wawnt *se*m bu' *de*R de moy bRad ets dgus tee dRI wu thow *d*ut

Galway: I wAnt soom boo' *te*R, or *te*r, or the*R te mI, or moy, bRed itsh dgisht t<u>oo</u> dTHroy *we d*ow' *te*t

Mayo: oy wAnt soom boo' *te*R ti moy bRed its dgoost t<u>oo</u> dTHroy wi thow' *ti*t

County Cork: oy wawnt soom but', or bu', the*R ti moy bRed its dgoost ti<u>oo</u> dTHRoy wu thow' *di*t

Kildare/General Dublin: I wAnt sum bu' *te*R te moy, or mI, bRed its dgust t<u>oo</u> dRI with ow' *ti*t, or it

Inner Dublin: oy wAnt soom boo' *t*theR te moy bRed its dgoost te<u>oo</u> dTHRoy wu thow' *te*t

Possibly I'll keep it there in the future for easy reference. It's only a mile down the road.
Phonetic pronunciations:
Belfast: pA' su bLee AL keep, or kayp, et THay:R en THe fyee' cheR feR ee, or ay, zee Raf' Rents its awn' Lee *e* moy' eL dOn THe Rawd

Derry: pA' su bLee AL keep ut TheR feR ee' zee Ref' Runts ets awn' Lee *e* mIL dan THe Rawd

Galway: pA' *se* blee oyl kayp *et*, or et, de:r, or de:R, in *de* fy<u>oo</u>' cheR fer ay' zee Ri' frents, or frentsh itsh awn' lee *e* moyl, or mIl, down *de* Rawd, or rawd

Mayo: pAs' *e* blee oyl kayp it dayer in *de* fy<u>oo</u>' cheR fer ay' zee Ref' Rents its awn' lee *e* moyl down *de* rawd

County Cork: paw' si blee oyl keep it de:r in de fyoo cher fer ee' zee ref' rents its awn' lee *e* moyl down de rawd

Kildare/General Dublin: po' si blee Il keep it THe:R in THe fyoo' cheR feR ee' zee Re' fe Rents, or Re' fRents its awn' lee *e* mIl down THe ROd

Inner Dublin: paw' si blee oyl kayp it day:eR, or THay:eR, in de, or THe, fyoo' cheR feR ay' zee Ref' Rents its awn' lee *e* mIl down de Rawd

Note: Notice that in the **Belfast** and **Derry** accents the "L" is much like the General American consonant, whereas in the other three accents the "l" is the dark, liquid sound.

He went down south there and the words stuck in his mouth.
Phonetic pronunciations:
Belfast: hee want dOn sOth THay' eR An THe wo:Rdz stook, or stuk, in i:z mOth

Derry: hee went dan sath THeR an THe wo:Rdz stuk en ez math

Galway: hee wint down sowt de:r an de werdz, or weRdz, or weRdsh, shtook in hiz mowt

Mayo: hee went down sowt de:R an de waw:Rdz stook in hiz mowt

County Cork: hee went down sowt de:R and de we:rdz stook in iz mowt

Kildare/General Dublin: hee went down sowth THe:R and THe woRdz stuk in hiz mowth

Inner Dublin: hee went down sowt dee' eR and de wawrds stook in hiz mowt

Tomorrow I can do anything I want.
Phonetic pronunciations:
Belfast: *te* mA' Re I ken di'oo e' ne theng I wAnt

Derry: *te* maw', or moo', RA I kin dee a' ne then I wawnt

Galway: *te* mA' Re I ken doo i' nee ting I, or oy, wAnt

Mayo: *te* mA' Re oy kin doo e' nee ting, or thing, oy wAnt

County Cork: *te* maw' re oy kin doo e', or o', ne ting oy wawnt

Kildare/General Dublin: *te* maw' RO I, or oy, kan doo e' nee thing I, or oy, wawnt

Inner Dublin: *te* mA' Re oy kin doo e' nee thing oy wawnt

There are more things in heaven and earth than are dreamt of in your philosophy.
At all.
Phonetic pronunciations:
Belfast: 1) THeR eR mAR, or maw:R, thengz in hav' en An o:Rth THan eR dRamp toov in yawR fe LA', or Law', se fee a dAL' ; 2) THeR *e* maw thengz in hev' en an o:th, or e:th, THen *e* dRamp' toov in yaw fil A' se fee a daw:L'

Derry: THeR eR mooR thengz en he' vn en o:Rth THan eR dRemp, or dRamp, tuv en yeeR fi LA' *se fee* a tawL'

Galway: de:R AR mAR tingz in hi' vn an eRt, or eRtth, dan AR drimp' toov in yooR fi' lA se fee *at* Al

Mayo: der eR mAR tingz in hev' en an awrt, or awRth, dan eR dRemp' toov in

95

yAR fi lA' *se* fee   a tAl'
County Cork: d*er* *er* mawr tingz in hevn an e:rt den *er* dremt' thoov in yer fi law'
se fee   a tAl'
Kildare/General Dublin: THe:R AR mawR thingz in he' ven and oRth THan
AR dRem' tuv in yaw:R fi lA' *se* fee   a *t*Al, or *t*awl, or tawl
Inner Dublin: de:R *e*R m<u>oo</u>eR thingz, or tingz, in hev' en *en* awRth, or awRt,
THan, or dTHen, or den, *e*R dRemp', or dTHRemp', toov in y<u>oo</u>eR fi LA' *se* fee
e tAl'

Oh, says I, and isn't that the truth then?
Phonetic pronunciations:
Belfast: aw sez I And ez' ent THAt THe tRi'<u>oo</u>th THan
Derry: okh sez I An e' zen THat THe tReeth THan
Galway: aw siz I an iz' ent dat de tR<u>oo</u>t din
Mayo: o sez oy An iz' nt dat de tR<u>oo</u>t den
County Cork: aw *sez* oy' an iz' en dat de tr<u>oo</u>t, or tthr<u>oo</u>t, den
Kildare/General Dublin: O sez I, and iz' ent THat THe tR<u>oo</u>th THen
Inner Dublin: aw sez oy an iz' en dAt de tR<u>oo</u>t den

Scottish Accents

Scottish Gaelic (pronounced "gay' Lik" in English; spelled "Gàidhlig" and
pronounced "gA' lik" in Gaelic), which is still spoken in some remote areas of
the Highlands, for example on the Isle of Skye, as well as a 15th century North
British dialect confusingly called Inglis and later renamed Scottis, then Scots,
form the bases of the Sottish accents in English. British RP, with minor grammatical and some lexical variations, is spoken widely all over Scotland. English
spoken with a Scottish accent, and again with some grammatical variations from
British RP and General American, is called **Scottish Standard English** (SSE).
The rules given under A Quick Reference are for SSE (and some of its important variations), and more rules are indicated throughout this chapter. Following the rules for SSE will give you a good, general Scottish accent.

Scots is a separate Germanic language with five principal dialects of its own:
Lallans (the name is based on the Scots pronunciation of *Lowlands*), a somewhat artificial dialect based actually on Central Scots, and used widely in literature; North; South; Central; and Islands. It has its own lexical features (such
words as *gloaming* [twilight] and *greet* [weep]); its own grammatical features:
"the woman that her dog got run over" (quoted in Wells); its own morphological features: "dinnae" for *does not*, "whaur ye gaun?" for "where are you going?", etc. If someone says to you "Ye muckle sumph!" you should feel insulted
at being called "You big jerk!" On the other hand "Mony a mickle maks a
muckle." In other words "Many a small thing makes a big thing," or, as the
English say "Take care of the pence, and the pounds will take care of
themselves."

There is an interesting French lexical influence on Scots, dating perhaps from the era of the French-educated Mary, Queen of Scots, and from the Auld (Old) Alliance of the French court and the Stuarts. This influence is seen in such Scots words and phrases as *ashet* (plate; pronunced "ash' et"; from French *assiette*, pronounced "ass ee yet' "); *on the kee vee* (on the alert; pronounced as it looks; from French *qui vive?* pronounced "kee veev'," meaning "who goes there?", literally "who lives?"); and *dinna fash yersel* (don't get annoyed or angry, or do not anger yourself; pronunced "di' na fash yer seL' "; from French *ne vous fâchez pas*, a reflexive verb meaning literally "do not anger yourself" or "do not get angry").

Robert Louis Stevenson uses occasional lexical and grammatical elements of Scots in *Kidnapped* to create authenticity and the atmosphere of the Highlands. His illustrious predecessor, the immensely popular Sir Walter Scott, did the same sort of thing in such novels as *Rob Roy* and the Waverley series. Some of his characters talk in a highly anglicized Scots dialect, seemingly very real and accurate and all rather new to the English reading public of the 1810s and 1820s.

Robert Burns of Ayrshire wrote his poetry sometimes in English; sometimes in a literary dialect of English incorporating Scots features; sometimes in a literary Scots dialect. "I gaed a waefu' gait yestreen" (phonetic pronunciation: A gayd e way' foo gayt yes treen') seems so like English with a Scottish accent, that we think we ought to understand it immediately, but we don't, because it is really written in pure Scots, although there are a few lines farther on in this poem which are pure English ("...Her heaving bosom, lily-white...").It translates literally "I goed a woeful go yesterday evening," or, more meaningfully, "I walked around in a sorrowful manner yesterday evening." "Gaed a gait" means "went a go" and is a poetical repitition, much like "did the deed."

Such words as *wee* (little) and *dirk* (dagger) have become a part of standard English vocabulary, as have *lad* or *laddie* (boy) and *lass* or *lassie* (girl). There are also some well-known Scots words like *bairn* (child), *ken* (know) and *bra* (good; of Scandinavian origin), which retain their dialectical associations. Everyone knows the words of the song "we'll drink a cup o' kindness yet for auld lang syne," which means "...for old long since," or, less literally, "...for the sake of what happened a long time ago." Spelling reflects Scottish pronunciation in such words as *guid* (good), *auld* (old), *anither* (another), *tae* (to), *dae* (do), *gae* (go), *nocht* (nought), *a'* (all), and *wi'* (with). On the other hand words like *hae* (have) and *frae* (from) are pure Scots. There are mony ither differences, but this is all enof tae begin wi'. Sae on wi' yur guid work!

After the 1745 rebellion of the Highland clans led by Bonnie Prince Charlie, the Stuart claimant to the thrones of England and Scotland, ended disastrously at the battle of Culloden, the Hanoverian monarchs, in an attempt to avoid any such revolts in the future, tried to stamp out Highland culture. The brutal slaughter of the Highlanders, the burning of their farms and villages, and the enforced emigration of many more meant not the death of the culture, but its stubborn underground resistance. The playing of the bagpipes and the wearing of the kilt were forbidden, and the Gaelic language was suppressed. It survived, as did the bagpipes and the kilt, to be revived by the Romantics in the 19th century.

The Scottish film industry has prospered in recent years, and wonderful authentic examples of Scottish accents can be heard in such films as *Local Hero* (1983), among many films by Glasgow director Bill Forsyth. I also particularly recommend his wry and charming *Gregory's Girl* (1979). *Trainspotting* (1996), Danny Boyle's powerful, upsetting film starring Ewan McGregor and Robert Carlyle, is based on Irvine Welsh's novel set in the underground drug scene in Edinburgh, and is excellent for listening to authentic accents as well. Listen to Dougray Scott in *MI2* (1999) for the clear accent and elegant diction of Fife in eastern Scotland. Avoid the imitations in the various versions of Robert Louis Stevenson's *Kidnapped*, such as Walt Disney's film, but do listen to James Robertson Justice in Disney's *Rob Roy* (1954). Gordon Jackson in *The Prime of Miss Jean Brodie* (1969) (in which Maggie Smith in the title role also does an excellent Edinburgh accent, as does Celia Johnson as Miss McKay) and as the butler Hudson in the British television series *Upstairs/Downstairs* has a wonderful light Scots accent. The accents in such films as *Rob Roy* (1995) and *Braveheart* (1995) vary tremendously, and you should only listen to the actors who really are Scottish in those films, although Mel Gibson, whose work with accents is uniformly excellent, sounds perfectly authentic as Braveheart.

Sean Connery, perhaps Scotland's most famous contemporary actor, occasionally uses his real Scottish accent, although in the James Bond films he sounded deliberately more English. In one of his latest films, *The Rock* (1996), he used his own accent. In older films, listen to Finlay Currie as Magwitch in David Lean's *Great Expectations* (1946) and as Queen Victoria's gruff Scottish retainer John Brown in *The Mudlark* (1950), with Alec Guinness as Disraeli. Alec Guinness stars in *Tunes of Glory* (1960), about a Scottish regiment, and you can hear Duncan Macrae, among other Scottish actors.

The following CDs are also useful: *"I Love a Lassie": the voice and songs of SIR HARRY LAUDER* (Pavilion Records, PAST CD 9719), grand performances by a grand old music hall performer; *Ewen MacColl: The Real MacColl* (Topic Records, TSCD 463), for wonderful Highland folk songs; *The Scottish Songbook: 20 Treasured Scottish Songs By Timeless Voices Of Yesteryear* (Moidart Music Group, MIDCD 001); and the series *Robert Burns: The Complete Songs* in 12 albums (Linn Records, various CD numbers). Many more examples of authentic accents can be found in the folk music section of record stores.

The Scottish accents can be divided roughly into three large groups:
1) the Northern accents of the Western and Middle Highlands and Islands (Skye, the Hebrides);
2) the Southern Border and Lothian accents of the Lowlands, including those of Edinburgh, perhaps the clearest Scottish speech, and Glasgow, which sounds slightly slurred and "swallowed," urban accents both quite different from each other);
3) Central, Ayrshire, or Scottish Midlands, which is Robert Burns country.

For the application of some of this complicated phonetic information to **Highlands, Lowlands** (largely rural), **Ayrshire** (Midlands), **Glasgow** (there is A Quick Reference for this accent in the Practice section), **Edinburgh, Orkney** and

Shetland Island accents, see the Practice section, below.

A Quick Reference

1) In all Scottish accents pronounce final trilled "r" and "r" before another consonant, sometimes lightly, sometimes heavily.
2) See the important information below about the consonant "L."
3) Lengthen the vowel "o" to "aw" in *hot, not, got,* etc., and lengthen vowels generally before "r" and before nasal consonants "m" and "n."
4) Words which in British RP are pronounced with the broad open-throated "A" in *father* are often pronounced in Scottish accents with a slightly open "a" as in the word *cat*.
5) In Glasgow and in the Highlands there is often a glottal stop replacing "t" in words like *bottle*.
6) In words spelled with "wh," such as *where, what* and *when,* pronounce an initial "h": hwe:er; hwot; hwen.
7) Keep initial "p," "t" and "d" quite soft, with only a little aspiration.
8) There is no distinction between the long "oo" sound in such words as *cool, pool* and *boot* and the short "oo" in *cook, pull* and *book*; all such words are pronounced with "oo," so *fool* rhymes with *full,* etc.
9) *Been* rhymes with *bean*.

How to Do Scottish Accents

As with Irish accents you must know specifically where your character comes from. There are several Scottish accents, as discussed above.

1) Position of the Vocal Apparatus
The general position of the vocal apparatus for all Scottish accents is with the lips forward and the tongue up and towards the front of the mouth.

2) The Most Important Sounds
Consonants
All Scottish accents are rhotic, that is, a final "R" or an "R" before another consonant is pronounced.

h and wh: Scots pronounce their initial "h." Words beginning with the spelling "wh" are often pronounced with "hw," so a word like *where* would be pronounced "hwere." There is an interesting substitution of "f" for "wh" in words like *where, what, when* in the **Far Northwest,** and even for the "h" in *how*. Example: "fusti kat?" ("How is't ye ca' it?", meaning "What is it called?"; Phonetic pronunciation: foo' sti kawt)

KH: The sound of the voiceless consonant "KH," called a *velar fricative,* is the same as in German *Ach!,* and is made by vibrating the back of the tongue against the uvula, almost as with a French uvular "R," but without using the voice. It occurs in expletives, in words such as *technical* and *patriarch,* and in place names

99

like *Loch* (Lake) *Lomond*.

L, *L* and l: This consonant is extremely important in Scottish accents, and there are several points to bear in mind, and in mouth:
1) There are three versions of this consonant in Scottish accents. In the **Highlands** and sometimes in **Glasgow** "L" is pronounced with the tip of the tongue more forwardly placed behind the upper front teeth and the blade of the tongue thickened, just as in a Slavic "L." Then there is an "L" like the General American L, heard in the **Lowlands** and **Midlands**.
Practice these two sounds with the word *Lowlands* (Phonetic pronunciations: Law' Lenz; Law' Lenz). The word *Lowlands*, incidentally, gave rise to a sort of modern poetic Scots dialect, called "Lallans."
  Also in the **Lowlands**, and sometimes farther north in the **Midlands**, a more liquid "l," as in French, is heard. The blade of the tongue is not thickened, and the tip of the tongue is not pressed and held against the upper gum ridge. This sound is not heard in initial position, but only after another consonant. Practice with the words *please* and *middle* (Phonetic pronunciations: pleez; mi' dl).
2) In some urban working-class accents, in **Glasgow** and in **Edinburgh**, and in **Highlands** accents as well, "L" in final position or before another consonant is sometimes dropped or replaced with the vowel "<u>oo</u>", so *salt* is pronounced "sawt" and *full* is pronounced "foo." *Careful* is pronounced "kay:r' foo." Scots orthography reflects this. *Salt* is spelled "saut" and *full* is spelled "fou."

r: "r" is given one trill or tap, sometimes more than one, in all accents. In **Edinburgh** it is more lightly pronounced in the final position within words like *work, first, word*, where the preceding vowel is also lengthened. In **Glasgow** there is sometimes heard a uvular, guttural "R," similar to the French sound; this is perhaps best avoided by the actor, except in a heavy working-class accent. Note that in an **Inverness** accent the "R" is not trilled, but retroflex, like an Irish or American "R." Final "R" is still pronounced, giving the accent an almost Irish sound. In **Scottish Standard English** the "R" is either given one light trill, or is a very lightly pronounced retroflex "R." Also, a phenomenon of **Glasgow** speech is the shift from voiced "TH" to "r" in initial position: *My brother and my father and my mother went to the market*. Phonetic pronunciation: me bru' rer an me fo' rer an me mu' rer wen te re mAr' ke?

?: A **glottal stop** is heard frequently at the ends of words like *bit*, but only sometimes in the middle of words like *better*. It is a more frequent sound in the **Highlands** and in **Glasgow** than in the Lowlands, but it is heard ubiquitously. However, it is not used in **Scottish Standard English**.

th: The consonant "th" in a final position, as in the word *with*, is often dropped.

zh, sh and j, ch: An interesting feature of **Highland** speech is the use of voiceless for voiced consonants (very Gaelic), so that *pleasure* becomes "plea*sh* (instead of *zh*) ure" and *enjoying* becomes "en*ch*oying."

Other consonants remain the same as in British RP.

Vowels and Diphthongs

Vowels are always lengthened slightly before "r." The schwa is much less in evidence than it is south of the border in England, and full, if short, vowels appear in every syllable in more careful Scottish speech, but not always in working-class speech. As far as many Scots in the **Midlands** and **Highlands** of Scotland are concerned, words like *fern, fur* and *fir* do not rhyme as they do in General American and British RP (but note that the word *girl* is usually pronounced "gurL," "gerL" or "gu' reL"). *Fern, fur* and *fir* have three distinct vowels, as they do in their spelling: fern, or, sometimes fe:ern; fur; fi:r. In **Scottish Standard English** and in **Edinburgh**, however, these words do rhyme, and the vowel heard is either "u" or "e." In **Glasgow** words spelled with "u," "i" and "o" all take the vowel "u," but words spelled with "e" or "ea" are pronounced with "e:": *fur* and *fir* are pronounced "fur"; *fern* is pronounced "fe:rn" and *heard* is pronounced "he:rd." In **Edinburgh** and in the **Lowlands** generally *coat, cot* and *caught* all rhyme, and are pronounced with a lengthened "o" close to the "aw" in *law*.

A: In *bath, father, grass, can't, after* this sound is close to American *that*. Scots spelling indicates this pronunciation. For example, *father* is spelled "faither."

a: The "a" in *that, cat,* etc. is pronounced like General American *father*. **Practice words:** *that, cat, bat, hat, hatch, batch, bachelor, platter, clatter*

e: The pure vowel "e" is open in words like *dress; perfect* (diphthongized and pronounced "payr' fekt' " as both noun and verb); *square* (where it is lengthened before the "r": "skwe:r").

ee: The "ee" is long in words like *please* and before "r" in words like *beard*.

i: The "i" is short in words like *bid, lid, lit,* etc.

I: In **Edinburgh** the diphthong "I" is often flattened to a long "ay" diphthong, as in the word *say,* so *price* is pronounced "prays" or "pRays," with a retroflex "R," as in General American. The pronoun, however, often drops the second part of the diphthong, so "I" is pronounced "A," which is also generally true in **Central** dialects, where *price* is "prAs." In the **Highlands** "I" is often pronounced like "ee" in *wee: Highlands* becomes "Hee' Lenz," spelled in Scots: Hielands.

O: In **Edinburgh,** instead of being diphthongized, the lengthened pure vowel "o" is heard in words like *go* and *home* in **educated** speech. In the **Highlands** this diphthong shifts to "ay" in *say:* (Scots spelling) *Gae hame* (Go home). The lips are not rounded and protruded as they are in the British or American versions of this sound. Scots spelling indicates this in another way, as well. For example, *stone* is spelled *stane*, and *home* is spelled *hame*.

o: In *not, got, hot* this vowel is lengthened, so it is a bit like "aw" in *law*. In general "o" is lengthened before "R."

oo: There is no long "<u>oo</u>" vowel in words where one might expect it; only its short version is heard, so that the vowel in *book* rhymes with the vowel in *food*; *pool* rhymes with *pull*; *brooding* with *pudding*; *woman* with *human*; *wool* with *tool*, etc. In the **Highlands** the French "u" (phonetic symbol "ü") is also heard in words like *to, do, book* and *true*, in which word it is also sometimes lengthened and preceded by a very short "ee," i.e., *true* ("treeü"). Scots orthography tries sometimes to indicate that this is the sound, so *moon* is spelled *muin*, and pronounced "mün."

ow: The diphthong "ow" in *how, mouth,* and *house* is pronounced in **Edinburgh** like the "<u>oo</u>" in *pool*. More accurately, the "<u>oo</u>" is usually diphthongized by being preceded with a slight stressed schwa: *e'oo*. (Bear in mind that "*e'<u>oo</u>*" only replaces "ow," and that, as described above, there is no distinction in Scottish accents between "<u>oo</u>," which does not exist in such words as *pool* and *fool*, and "oo" in such words as *pull* and *full*, whereas in General American and British RP the distinction exists.) In **Ayrshire (Midlands)** and **Glasgow** accents the "ow" shifts to "<u>oo</u>" without a schwa before it, so *down*, for instance, is pronounced "d<u>oo</u>n." In **Scottish Standard English** "ow" is usually pronounced as it is in British RP (see Chapter One); alternatively, it can be pronounced "*e'<u>oo</u>*." In the **Highlands** it is often heard with the same sound as the French "ü" as the second half of the diphthong: haüs. But some regions pronounce it as in Edinburgh.

u: The "u" in *but*, also spelled with an "o" in words like *love, above*, etc., is pronounced like the "o" in *work* or like a German umlauted "o" (böt, möther, etc.) in **Edinburgh**, like a short "i" in the **Highlands** (bit, mither, etc.).

Stress

In words like *organize*, and other words ending in "ize," and some ending in "ate," such as *adjudicate*, the last syllables are stressed. This is a phenomenon of Scots stress patterns carried over into Scottish accents of English. Some more words stressed on syllables different from those in British RP or General American: *discord'; po'lice; advertise'; consequence'; illustra'ted; otherwise'.*

Pitch
The Music of Scottish Speech

There are two patterns which are very Scottish: 1) a rising and falling curve in a declarative phrase, where the falling last note is still a fairly high one; 2) A series of falling tones in a phrase on an accented syllable, even in questions.

102

You should not have done that nor should I.
Phonetic pronunciations
Edinburgh: ye shood nawt hAv dun THAt, or, THA? naw:r shood ay
Highlands: ye shüd, or, shid nay, or, naw, hA doon THA? noor shid ee

Pitch Pattern One:
You

       should   nor
              not   done   should
                 have   that   I.

Did I see you hanging out the washing a short time ago?
Phonetic pronunciations
Edinburgh: did ay see y<u>oo</u> hAng ing aüt, or, oot THe waw shing e shaw:rt taym a gaw
Highlands: did A see ü hAn gin oot, or, üt THe waw shin e shawert, or, shoort, or, shooert te: m e gay, or, a gaw

Pitch Pattern Two:
Did I

      see
             you
                  hanging   wash-
                         out the   ing   a
                                            short time
                                                 ago

From Robert Louis Stevenson's *Kidnapped*
Note: Stevenson himself spoke English, according to friends and biographers, with a very pleasant Edinburgh accent.
Chapter One
(Mr. Campbell and David Balfour speak with **Lowlands** accents)
"Are ye sorry to leave Essendean?" said he, after a while.
"Why, sir," said I, "if I knew where I was going, or what was likely to become of me, I would tell you candidly. Essendean is a very guid place indeed, and I have been very happy there; but then I have never been anywhere else..."

Phonetic pronunciation: "Ar yi saw' ree ti leev e' sn deen?" sed hee Af' te re hwIl; "hwI, ser," sed I, "if I ny<u>oo</u> hwayer I wez gaw' ing, awr hwawt wez lIk' lee te be kim ev mee, ay wed tel y<u>oo</u> kAn did lee. e' sn deen iz e good play:s in deed', And I hAv been ve' ree hA' pee THayer; bit THen I hAv ne' ver been e' nee hwayer els..."

Chapter Twenty-Three
(Cluny Macpherson and Alan Breck Stewart speak with **Highland** accents)

"Well, Mr. Stewart, come awa', sir!" said he, "and bring in your friend that as yet I dinna ken [do not know] the name of."

"And how is yourself, Cluny?" said Alan. "I hope you do brawly [well], sir. And I am proud to see ye, and to present to ye my friend, the Laird [Lord] of Shaws, Mr. David Balfour."

Phonetic pronunciation: "weL mis' ter styü' ert, kim e wA' se:r!" sed hee, "An bring in yer, or, yoo:r, fre:nd THA? Az ye? A di' ne ken THe ne:m ev." "An hoo ez yer-, or, yoo:r- self, kloo' nee?" sed A' len. " A hawp ye dü braw' lee, ser. And I Am prood, or, prAüd, te see ye, An ti pri zent' te ye mA fre:nd, THe Layerd u shawz, mi' ster day:' vid bAL' fer."
Note the lengthened vowels before "n" and "r," as in the word *Laird*.

Scottish Folk Song, **Highlands** Accent
Note: For superb, authentic Scottish accents listen to recordings of Scottish folk songs, and to the CD series *Robert Burns The Complete Songs* (LINN Records), gradually being released in 12 volumes.
(From "The Auld [old] House" by Lady Nairne)
"Oh! the auld house, the auld house,/What tho' the rooms were wee [small]!/ Oh! kind hearts were dwelling there,/And bairnies [children] fu' [full] o' glee."
Phonetic pronunciation: aw! THee awld hoos, or, hAüs/ hwaw? THaw THe roomz wayr wee!/ aw! kInd hayrts wayr dwe' Ling THayer, An bayr' neez foo u gLee

No, I'm, er, not happy about it and that but… It's not a useful thing, old fellow, but we'll go away, just the two of us, take a room, and take the waters there by the sea. Do you want to? It will make you feel better.
Phonetic pronunciation (**Glasgow**) : naw Am er nay ha' pee e boo? e? na? bi? is naw e yis' foo thing awL fe' Le bi? wiL gay e wA' dgis re, or e, twA' vis tak e rim an tak re wA?' erz ray' er bre see dgi wA' ne i? L mak yi feeoo be? er
Notes: In addition to the vowel and diphthong shifts listed elsewhere, some keys to a **Glasgow** (pronounced "gLes' ke" by Glaswegians) accent are:

A Quick Reference: Glasgow

1) Substitute "r" for voiced "TH."
2) Shift from General American "yoo" to "yi."
3) Drop final "L" and use raised back "L."
4) Use the ubiquitous glottal stop.
5) It is also worth bearing in mind that the accent tends to sound "swallowed" and that one often hears a guttural uvular "R," usually associated with French or German.
6) The dipththong "ow" shifts to "oo."
7) The diphthong "ay" shifts to "A."
8) Words spelled with "or" and "ur" and "ir" (*work, fur, fir, girl, bird*) are all pronounced with "u"; words spelled with "er" and "ear" are pronounced with "e:" (*fern, earth, certain*).

104

The accent is particularly difficult to understand for non-Glaswegians, partly because of the dialectical features of Glaswegian speech, such as the use of tag words and syllables such as *er* or the word *see* in introducing a subject: *See me and my friend, see, we er went there.* Phonetic pronunciation: see mee nme fren see wi er wen? ray' er. Two more examples: *All those people down there and that, I don't know.* Phonetic pronunciation: aw ray pi poo d<u>oo</u>n ay' er, or ray' er, a na? A dnaw. *I'm,er, not sure and that, but I think I'll go there tomorrow.* Phonetic pronunciation: A mer na shi:r a na? ber A then? AL gay ray' er re maw' re, or rer. The stereotyped accent of the middle-class Glasgow area called **Kelvinside** is considered a pretentious attempt to ape upper-class English speech, and is thus a subject for parody. It shares some characteristics of the **Sloane Ranger** accent described briefly in Chapter One, but with a Scottish twist: the diphthong "I" is pronounced "ay" and the vowel "a" is pronounced "e." An example: *I don't know why you should think that. Actually I'm quite apprised of the situation, having been told of it five times.* Phonetic pronunciation: ay dawnt naw hway y<u>oo</u> shood think THet ek' ty<u>oo</u> e Lay aym kwayt e prayzd' ev THe si ty<u>oo</u> ay' shen hev' ing been tawLd ev it fayv tayms. See the further note on **Morningside**, below, in the sentence beginning *I went down into the glen.*

I swim without worrying about it.
Phonetic pronunciations:
Scottish Standard English: I swi:m wi:' thowt, or the'<u>oo</u>t, wu' ree ing e bowt', or be'<u>oo</u>t, it
Glasgow: A s<u>oo</u>m e th<u>oo</u>? weR' ee en e b<u>oo</u>? e?
Highlands: A s<u>oo</u>m e thoo? wer' ee in e b<u>oo</u>', or beü, dit, or di?
Lowlands; Edinburgh: A swi:m we the'<u>oo</u>t wer' ee in a bowt, or b<u>oo</u>t, or be'<u>oo</u>, tit
Notes: Notice the guttural "R" in the Glasgow accent. The "w" dropped in the words *swim* and *without* is typical of the **Highlands** and **Glasgow** accents, and is sometimes heard in the **Lowlands** as well. In Scots initial "w" is regularly dropped, and this carries over into accent in English.

Birds on a fir tree or in the ferns certainly don't wear fur coats. It's your turn now.
Phonetic pronunciation
Scottish Standard English/Edinburgh/Lowlands: burdz, or berdz, awn e fur, or fer, tree awr i:n THe furnz. or fernz, sur', or ser', ten lee dawnt we:r fur, or fer, kawts i:ts yoor tu:rn, or tern, now, or ne'<u>oo</u>
Ayrshire/Highlands/Glasgow: bu:rdz awn e fi:er (Glasgow: fur) tree awr i:n THe fe:renz se:r' ten, or ?n, lee daw:n't, or dawn?, way:er fur kawts i:ts yoor tu:rn, n<u>oo</u>
Notes: Remember that in the **Highlands** and **Midlands** the distinction observed orthographically in such words as *fir, fern* and *fur* is also often observed in pronunciation. In **Scottish Standard English** and in **Edinburgh**, however, all these words do rhyme. Keep the initial "t" in *turn* soft for **SSE**, harder in other accents. In **Ayrshire** and in the **Highlands** notice that the vowels are long and many are diphthongized. The diphthong on the word *now* is very open in all accents.

I caught him on the cot wearing my coat, and I pulled him off and threw him in the pool.
Phonetic pronunciation (**Edinburgh/Lowlands**): I kawt, or kot, him awn the kawt, or kot, we:r' ing mI kawt, or kot, and I poold him of and thrü, or three, hi:m i:n THe pool

There's nae a sair hairt but what it can be mended.
Phonetic pronunciation (**Highlands**): THe:rz nay a sayr hayr?, or hayrt, bu? hwA? i? kAn, or kan, bee men' did, or men' it

Don't look so worried, my friend.
Phonetic pronunciation (**Highlands**): dawn? Lük, or Lik, saw wu' reed mA, or mI, frend, or freend

Possible Pitch Pattern

```
                      my friend\.
            ried,
Don't
     look      wor-
          so
```

Will we not do that? We ought to do that.
Phonetic pronunciation (**Highlands**): wuL wee naw dü THA? Wee awkht, or awkh, ti dü THA?
Note: The "t" is such words as *ought* and Scots words such as *bricht* (bright) and *nicht* (night) is sometimes dropped.

In summer the flowers bloom, and it's a pleasure to be on the hills.
Phonetic pronunciations:
Scottish Standard English: in sum' er THe flow' erz bloom and i:ts e ple' zhoor, or zher, too bee awn THe hi:lz
Highlands: in sim' er THe fLoorz bLüm An i? se pLay' sher ti bee awn THe hiLs, or hi:'eLz, or heLz
Lowlands: in sum', or sem', er THe fLow' erz, or flArz, bLoom And its e ple:' zhoor ti bee awn THe hi:Lz, or hi:lz
Note: Notice the pronciation of *bloom* with "oo," not "oo"; the liquid "l"; and the long "i:" in the **Scottish Standard English** pronunciation. In the **Highlands** pronunciation notice the shift from the voiced "zh" in the word *pleasure* to "sh." This shift, carried over from Gaelic, is also typical of the **Orkneys** and the **Shetland Islands,** where there is also the interesting phenomenon of adding "kh" before "w": The word *wheel* is pronounced "khweeL"; *which* is pronounced "khwi:ch"; and *white* "khwIt," etc. (In old Scots this was the usual pronunciation. It is possible that the letter "q" was meant to indicate this sound in old Scots spellings. According to the *Oxford English Dictionary* the letter "q" was

usual in Middle English orthography in such words as *qwat* [what] and *quele* [wheel], but "wh" was used also, and in Old English "hw" was a usual spelling. Scottish and northern English scribes preferred such spellings as "quh," "qvh" and "qwh," indicating that the sound for "q" was probably "kh.") Also pronounced are consonants long silent in other accents of English (but present in old Scots), such as the "gh" in *daughter*, the "k" in *knee* and *knife* and the "g" in *gnaw*. In the islands "TH" and "th" are pronounced "d" and "t." The grammar and vocabulary of this dialect are absolutely fascinating.

I had some herring and it come back on me.
Phonetic pronunciation:
Highlands: A hAd sim, or süm, ha' ring An i? kim, or küm, bAk en mee
Lowlands: I ha:d sim, or soom, her' ing an it kim, or koom, bAk awn mee

He wrote it down and sent the letter.
Phonetic pronunciations:
Scottish Standard English: hee rawt it down, or de'<u>oo</u>n, and sent THe le:' ter
Highlands: hee, or hi, rayt, or raw?, et d<u>oo</u>n, or dün, An saynt THe Lay' ter, or Lay?' er
Ayrshire/Glasgow: hee raw? i? d<u>oo</u>n An se:n? THe Le:?' er
Lowlands/ Edinburgh: hee rawt e daün an se:nt THe Le:' ter, or Le:' ter

I went down into the glen and met my girl there, and we talked of a better world and I don't know what else, but that we hope everything will be fine more times than not.
Phonetic pronunciations:
Scottish Standard English: I went down, or de'<u>oo</u>n, in' te THe gle:n and me:t mI gurl, or gerl, THe:er and we taw:kt uv e be:' ter wurld, or werld, and I dawnt naw hwawt els but THat we hawp ev' ree thing wil bee fIn mawer tImz THan nawt
Ayrshire: A went d<u>oo</u>n in' te THe gLen An met mA gu' reL THay' er An wee tAkt ov e be' ter wur' eLd An A dunt naw hwaw? els bit THAt wee hawp ev' re thing wuL bee fayn m<u>oo</u>' er taymz THe nawt
Edinburgh: A went d<u>oo</u>n, or down, or de'<u>oo</u>n, in' te THe gLen an met mA gurl THe:r an wee tawkt ov e be' ter wArLd an A dawn? naw hwawt eLs bet THat wee hawp ev' ree thing wiL bee fIn m<u>oo</u>' er, or mawr, tImz THan nawt
Notes: In the general refined **Scottish Standard English** and **Edinburgh** accents remember that the initial "t" in such words as *talked* and *times* is very soft, and tends to sound almost voiced, like a soft "d." Actually, as with all urban areas, there are several Edinburgh accents: upper- and working-class; the accents of the middle class neighborhood of **Morningside**. See the notes about **Glasgow** accents, above. The satirized and stigmatized accent called **Morningside and Kelvinside** is usually considered one accent, even though associated with two different cities. It's very much the sort of speech Maggie Smith used in playing the pretentious Jean Brodie in the film *The Prime of Miss Jean Brodie.*

From the Jacobite song *Will Ye No Come Back Again?* (wuL yi naw koom bAk e gen')

*Bonnie Charlies's noo awa (now away)// Safely o'er the bounding main// Many a heart will break in twa (in two)// Should he no come back again*ÖBetter lued ye canna be *(Better loved you cannot be)*

Phonetic pronunciation **(Highlands)**: baw' nee chayr' Leez n<u>oo</u> e wA' sayf' Lee ow:er THe baün' ding me:n mo' nee e hay:r?, or hay:rt, wuL brak in twA shid, or shüd, hee naw koom bAk e gen be' ter, or be? er, l<u>oo</u>d yi, or ye, ka' ne, or ne:, bee

Scots Sentences; Central **(Ayrshire)** pronunciation, unless otherwise indicated:
I asked at him and he did it in a crack and it was by.
Phonetic pronunciation: A Askt A? im, or Aks dA dim An hee de de?, or di di?, in e krAk An i? wez bI, or bay
Translation: I asked [it] of him and he did it in a flash and it was over/past.

Hae a thocht mair parritch.
Phonetic pronunciations:
Ayrshire: hay e thokht, or thokh, may:r pA', or paw', ritch
Edinburgh: hAv e thaw?, or thawt, mayr paw' ridg
Translation: Have a thought [a little bit] more porridge/oatmeal.
Note: The "t" in *tocht* may be dropped.

Och, bide a wee and hover a blink. Ye'll tak a wee dram.
Phonetic pronunciation: awkh bId, or bayd, e wee an hu', or ho', or hi', ver e bLink yi:L tak e wee dra:m
Translation: Ah, stay a bit and rest a moment. You'll take a little drink [of whiskey].

She was at me again and she threw a gruntle. Och, she's no in. A maun dree ma weird and dree out ma born days.
Phonetic pronunciation: shee wez a? mee e gen an shee thrü e grin' tL okh sheez naw in A mawn dree ma wee:rd, or weeerd, an dree aü?, or <u>oo</u>?, or <u>oo</u>t, mA bawrn, or baw' ren, deez, or day:z
Translation: she was nagging/scolding me again and she made a face. Ah, she's not in [she's nuts/out to lunch]. I must endure my fate and live out my lifetime.

Welsh Accents

Welsh is still spoken as a first language by perhaps six hundred thousand people. Until the mid-18th century it was the native language of the vast majority of the population, despite centuries of English in a few Welsh areas, such as Pembroke. Only in the large industrialized areas did English have a really strong hold, until recently. But even in Shakespeare's day Welsh people were learning English and participating in English life, as witness his characters Owen Glendower in *The First Part of King Henry IV* and Fluellen in *The Life of King Henry V*.

Until the 1930s Welsh was the first language of most people living in Wales, who learned English as a second language, but succeeding generations have spoken English as their first language. For beautiful Welsh accents listen to the original recording of Dylan Thomas's *Under Milk Wood*, with Thomas himself as the First Voice. Anthony Hopkins has a touch of his native Welsh accent overlaid with British RP. Emlyn Williams's *The Corn Is Green* (1945) contains good, authentic Welsh accents. An *A&E Biography* of Richard Burton contains early footage of him speaking in a Welsh accent.

One of the colorful Welsh traditions is to give people nicknames based on their profession or on some salient personal characteristic. There was a woman in one town called "Margaret Slow-Rising," so named because her face was pasty white and a bit puffy, like slow-rising bread flour. (If she had been a man the sobriquet might have had other connotations.) In *Under Milk Wood* there is Dai Bread the Baker and then there is Dai Milk the Milkman, you see. The phrase *you see* is often added at the end of a sentence, much as Americans say *you know*.

A Quick Reference

1) To do most Welsh accents, drop the final "R" and the "R" before another consonant, but see below for Welsh Border accents.
2) There is very little use of the schwa, and all vowels in stressed and unstressed syllables receive their full value.
3) Generally speaking, all syllables are pronounced.
4) Vowels in stressed syllables are longer than they are in British RP or General American.
5) See below for information about Welsh pitch patterns, which give a characteristic music to the accent, an intonation pattern somewhat like that in the accents of India.
7) *Been* rhymes with *bean*.

How to Do a Welsh Accent

While Welsh accents do vary from North to South and from East to West, the information under "The Most Important Sounds" really applies to all of them. They tend to be more rhotic near the eastern border with England, but the vowels and diphthongs retain their purity. The rhythms are also very similar all over the Welsh map.

1) Position of the Vocal Apparatus
The general position is with the lips generally slightly closed and a bit forward. The lips are slightly, almost imperceptibly pursed.

2) Pitch

The pitch or musical pattern of Welsh accents is very important. A Welsh accent is often said to be "sing-song," because of the constant up-and-down rise and fall of the pitches, making it less even-toned that British RP or General American. One possible pattern is shown below. This characteristic should not be exaggerated, but it is true that there is a delicious musicality to a Welsh accent.

Practice

The sentence goes down, you see, then up again and so forth, you see.
Phonetic pronunciation: THe sen' tens gOz down y<u>oo</u> see THen up a gen' and sO fawth y<u>oo</u> see
Note that in a **North Welsh** accent the final "z" sound of *goes* would be "s," and the "R" in *forth* would be pronounced.
One Possible Pitch Pattern:

The sentence				again	forth	
goes		you see,	up			
	down,	then,		and so		you see.

3) The Most Important Sounds

In these accents they are the **vowels and diphthongs**, and it is also very important to know that most Welsh accents are non-rhotic, except in the areas of the **Welsh Border** with England, where words like *farm* and *storm* have a schwa inserted between the trilled "r" and the "m": fA rem; staw rem. The "r" in a word like *very* is often given one trill, and is often trilled at the beginning of a word as well. The consonants are very clearly articulated, and a Welsh accent is known for its clear, strong liquid "l."

schwa: There is almost no use of the schwa in unstressed syllables (but see below under "u" and "y"). Instead every vowel and diphthong is clearly pronounced, except in past participle verb endings like "-ed" (as in the words *unstressed* and *lengthened*) and usually follows the phonetic value of the letter representing it. A name like *Margaret*, for instance, is pronounced with all its syllables: mA' gA ret. Diphthongs are long. Vowels in the middle of a word are lengthened slightly. In one-syllable words vowels are lengthened, and they are lengthened also before the dropped "R" in stressed syllables.

A: In a **Cardiff** accent this vowel is often heard as the "a" in *that*.

O: The "O" diphthong is sometimes heard as if it were the "<u>oo</u>" in *boot*; *home* rhymes with (the all but obsolete) *whom*.

u: In **South Wales** the vowel "u" in *but* is often heard as a schwa in all words. *Butter* is pronounced "be' tA." In **urban** areas the same vowel, "u," is heard in

110

both syllables.

y: This semi-vowel is often inserted between two vowels. *Fire* is pronounced "fl' yA." In such words as *news* and *duke* the "y" is always pronounced after the initial consonant: ny<u>oo</u>z; dy<u>oo</u>k. On the other hand, in words containing "l," such as *regular* and *particular* a schwa is sometimes heard before the "l": re' ge lA; pA tik' e lA. The word *articulated* could be heard either as "A tik' e lay ted" or as "A tik' y<u>oo</u> lay ted."

Further Phonetic Information

Consonants
h: This consonant is often dropped in **urban** Welsh accents, unless the speaker wishes to emphasize a particular word.

dg: This sound does not exist in Welsh, so its voiceless counterpart, "ch," is often substituted for it, especially in the mountainous **north**, so *just* is pronounced "chust." Even Shakespeare in *Henry* V has his Welsh character use this sound. Fluellen says, of the Irish Captain MacMorris in Act Three, Scene Two, "By Cheshu, he is an ass, as in the world: I will verify as much in his peard."

z: This sound does not exist in Welsh. As a result, particularly in the **north of** Wales, an "s" is substituted, especially in final position, so *is* is pronounced "is," instead of "iz."

Stress

The only unusual feature of Welsh stressing is that secondary stresses are often eliminated, and the primary stress is slightly more forceful. A word like *eliminated* will have a very strong stress on "-lim-" and almost no secondary stress on "-at-," where we would expect it in General American or British RP. The pitch of "-at-" is also consequently lower. In **South Welsh** accents in particular the vowel in a stressed syllable is often lengthened, which gives the accent a typical musical rhythm, usually accompanied by a pitch pattern which is also typical.

Practice

Well, you see, it was not so much what he did as what he became. There was that awful thing that happened in the marketplace. Do you know about that? You don't, now, do you?
Phonetic pronunciation: wel y<u>oo</u> see it wAz not sO much hwAt hee did az hwAt hee bee kaym' THe: wAz THat aw' fooL thing THat ha' pend in THe mA' ket pLays' d<u>oo</u> y<u>oo</u> nO A' bowt THat y<u>oo</u> dOnt now d<u>oo</u> y<u>oo</u>

Possible Pitch Pattern

```
        you              not
Well,      see,  was          much         did                    came.
           it          so          what he      as what he be-

                                                              place.
                      ful thing that happened in the      ket-
There was that                                        mar-
              aw-

              about that?
Do you                      don't,            you?
     know              You
                             now
                           do
```

Note: This is a **South Welsh** pronunciation. For **North Welsh** devoice some consonants, so that *the*, for instance, would be pronounced "the" instead of "THe."

It was a close thing. In fact, I never saw such a close thing in my life. He made a beautiful shot to win the game for which we were eternally grateful.
Phonetic pronunciation (**South Welsh**): it wAz e kL<u>oo</u>s thing in fAkt I ne:' vA saw such e kL<u>oo</u>s thing in mI Lif hee me:d a by<u>oo</u>:' ti fooL shawt t<u>oo</u> win THe gay:m faw which wee we: ee te:' ne Lee gRe:t' fooL
Note: Notice the lengthened vowels in these sentences and the ones below.

They were a very loving couple. He had dark curly hair and she had fair hair and they were wickedly in love.
Phonetic pronunciation (**South Welsh**): THay we:' RA, or rA, ve' ree lu:' ving ku:' peL hee had dA:k ko:' Lee he: And shee hAd fe: he: And THay we: wi:' ked Lee in Luv

The investiture of the Prince of Wales at Caernarvon Castle is an ancient ceremony, and a most impressive pageant, gorgeous in colorful uniforms and the castle all draped in flags and banners.
Phonetic pronunciation (**South Welsh**): THee in ves' ti tye uv THe pRints uv wayLz at kIR, or kAR, nAR' von kA' seL iz an ayn' chent se' Re me nee and e mOst im pRes' iv pa dgent gaw' dgus in ku' Le feL y<u>oo</u>' nee fawmz and THe kA' seL awL dRaypt in fLagz and ba' nuz
Note: The "R" sounds in the word *Caernarvon* can be dropped. Alternatively, a very lightly trilled "r" may be heard instead of the retroflex "R" in such words as *Caernarvon, prince* and *draped.* For a **North Welsh** accent, devoice the final consonants in the words *is, uniforms, flags* and *banners.*

112

Well, you see, it was a wonderful thing and we could not have enough of it, you understand, but everything in this life is finite, you see, and as all good things must come to an end, so did this.

Phonetic pronunciation (**South Welsh**): weL y<u>oo</u> see it wAz e wun' de feL thing and wee kood not hav ee nuf' uv it y<u>oo</u> un' de stand but ev' e Ree thing in THis Lif iz fI' nIt' y<u>oo</u> see and az awL good thingz must kum t<u>oo</u> an end sO did THis

Note: For **North Welsh** devoice final consonants, so *was* will be pronounced "wAs" and *as* "as," instead of "az."

We were very enthusiastic as young boys and we loved when they told us stories. We had our dinner that we sat down to, and after we had eaten the whole thing we commanded them to tell us stories and they did.

Phonetic pronunciation (**North Welsh**): wee wu ve' Ree en th<u>oo</u>' see as tik as yung boys and wee luvd hwen thay tawLd us staw' Rees   wee had ow' e din' e that wee sat down t<u>oo</u> and Af' te wee had ee' ten the hawL thing wee ku' man did them t<u>oo</u> teL us staw' Rees and thay did.

Note: Notice that the final "z" sounds in the word and syllable endings shift to "s" in the words *enthusiastic, boys, stories*. Also, in the word *commanded* the "A" of British RP shifts to the same pronunciation as in General American.

The Welsh mining towns, the hills and the countryside of Wales, are so very beautiful, that just to see them makes you stand in awe.

Phonetic pronunciation (**North Welsh**): THe weLsh mI' ning towns THe hiLs and THe kun tRee' sId uf wayLs A sO fe' Ree by<u>oo</u>' ti fooL THat dgust t<u>oo</u> see THem mayks y<u>oo</u> stand in aw

Note: All the voiced "TH" sounds can shift to the voiceless "th" sounds for a more rural accent.

Chapter Five

Accents of the British Commonwealth: India, Sri Lanka, Australia, New Zealand and the Caribbean

India

India has been free of British rule since 1947 and an independant state since 1950, but for nearly two centuries it was the crown jewel of the British Empire. The Portuguese and French also occupied parts of the subcontinent, which includes the country of Pakistan, with its Moslem majority. Ornate, symbolically decorated Buddhist temples dating back to 250 B.C.E. survive, architecturally rich, graceful and gorgeous, and the culture of the Jains, of Hinduism and of the Sikhs continues to flourish. The luxurious palaces of the rajahs, who lived in splendor and were surrounded by squalor, still exist in all their ironic grandeur, alongside the 18th- and 19th-century government buildings, grandiose monuments to colonial rule, which were meant to impress and subdue the population.

In the 18th century the British were fascinated by the discovery of ancient Sanskrit, the Indian language of the *Baghavad Gita* and other classics of Hindu literature. Sir William Jones, a British lawyer and amateur linguist living in India, published a paper in 1786, in which he discussed the relationship of Sanskrit to Greek, Latin, Gothic, Celtic languages and Old Persian. Modern scientific Indo-European linguistics was born. Sanskrit was thought to be the oldest of the Indo-European languages until 1915, when inscriptions in Hittite (a more ancient, Anatolian language) were identified as Indo-European by the Czech linguist Bedřich Hrozný.

It is conjectured that all these languages and their descendants derive from a lost tongue called Proto-Indo-European. To discover what that language might have been like has proved very difficult, if not impossible. Linguists have said that if one knows Latin and one knows the Romance languages, it is easy to figure out how they evolved from Latin, but that if one did not know Latin, one could never arrive at it from studying the modern Romance languages. Where the Indo-European tongues originated, whether in India, Mesopotamia, or somewhere else, is not known. Be that as it may, many of the languages of India are related to the other Indo-European languages of Europe through the branch known as Indo-Persian.

There are 845 languages spoken in India, Pakistan and Bangladesh. The foreign accents of India result from the various languages of the subcontinent, some of which are descended from Sanskrit, among them Hindi and Urdu (closely related to each other), Gujurati and Bengali, but there are many Indians whose first language is English, and who speak with an Indian accent that their parents have learned. Indian accents are often called "Bombay Welsh." This is because they share the quality with a Welsh accent of pronouncing all vowels as they are written, except the final silent "e" in verb endings with "ed." The schwa is almost absent in both Welsh and Indian speech. The word *pronounced* is pronounced without a schwa: "pRO nownst'." However, in an Indian accent the stress may shift to the first syllable: "pRO' nownst."

You can hear good examples of Indian and Pakistani accents (very similar to Indian) in *My Beautiful Laundrette* (1985); *Gandhi* (1982); *A Passage to India* (1984); and the PBS *Masterpiece Theatre* drama *The Jewel in the Crown*, available on video.

A Quick Reference

1) Look at the information under "Consonants" about retroflex (bottom of tongue curving towards roof of mouth) consonants "d" and "t," which are such a hallmark of these accents.
2) Use the vowel system of British RP.
3) There is a lilt, an up-and-down intonation pattern, which is frequent in Indian accents.
4) Drop final "f" and "v."
5) Substitute initial "v," very lightly pronounced, for initial "w" at the beginning of words or syllables, and initial "w" for initial "v."
6) *Been* rhymes with *bean*.

How to Do an Indian Accent

1) Position of the Vocal Apparatus
For the general position: Curve your tongue up towards the roof of the mouth and say *ra ra ra ta ta ta da da da*. You are now pronouncing "retroflex" consonants. The position of the tongue is generally farther up near the opening where the upper gum ridge curves up to the palate while speaking. The reason for this is the number of retroflex consonants in the original languages. The mouth is wider open than in either General American or British RP.

2) Pitch
Pitch and musical patterns are extremely important, especially in a **heavy** Indian accent. There is an up-and-down lilt to an Indian accent, which is why it is sometimes referred to as "Bombay Welsh." This is the music of the original Hindi carried over into English.

3) The Most Important Sounds
Consonants
Pay special attention to the consonants, especially the retroflex "d," "t," and "r."

115

Indian accents are rhotic, often with a trilled "r" in initial position and a light American "R" in other positions, the tip of the tongue being farther back and up than in the American "R." This "R" is called a "retroflex R," because the bottom of the tip of the tongue is turned towards the roof of the mouth when pronouncing it. Sometimes an American "R" is inserted in a word where no "R" exists: *melodic* is pronounced "mil AR' dik." *Farther* and *father* (with an "R" inserted in *father* before the "TH") can rhyme in an Indian accent.

f and v and w: There is no final "f" or "v." A word like *twenty-five* is pronounced "tventy-fi'." There is often a confusion between "v" and "w," and a reversal of these two consonants, so the Indian pronunciation of *development*, "dee' velepment," shifts to "dee' welepment; *very* and *violence* to "wery" and "wiolence." *We* and *work* shift to "ve" and "vork". The "v" is very lightly pronounced.

t and d: In Hindi these consonants, which have non-retroflex versions, both also have retroflex versions. They are pronounced with the bottom of the tongue touching the roof of the mouth, in this case just behind the upper gum ridge into the opening of the palate. It is the retroflex "t" and "d" which one hears in Indian accents in English. In a sentence like "What are you doing?" the "w" shifts to "v" and "t," "d," and "r" are all retroflex consonants.

TH and th: When these consonants are not correctly pronounced, the substitutions for them are a retroflex "d" for the voiced "TH" and a retroflex "t" for the voiceless "th."

Further Phonetic Information

Vowels and Diphthongs
The vowel and diphthong system of British RP is followed, as a natural result of centuries of British rule in India. See Chapter One for this system, and use it for an Indian accent. Because there is no initial "s" in Hindi, one often hears an "i" inserted before a word beginning with "s": "istation."

Stress

There are stresses particular to Indian accents. de' velopment (dee' welepment), incumbent', un' rest, mor' tars', vi' olin (vwI' lin), etc. Often words, no matter what their stress in General American or British RP, are stressed on the penultimate (next to the last) syllable: presi' dent; de' cline; re' sult; penulti' mate; excell' ent; logi' cal, etc.

Practice

Notes: The following exercises are based on the accents of northern speakers whose first language is **Hindi**. For the accents of the speakers of **Bengali** and the southern **Dravidian** languages, make the retroflex consonants even more retroflex, i.e. curl the tongue farther back when articulating "t," "d," "r" and so forth,

116

and maintain the tongue curled back as a general position for it when speaking. For **Bengali** and **Dravidian** accents the retroflex slightly trilled "r" is very soft, the trill being articulated farther back toward the roof of the mouth, with lots of space between it and the curled tongue, than it is for a **Hindi** accent.

I don't know what you mean. It could be anything.
Phonetic pronunciation: I dO nO vA ty<u>oo</u> meen. it kood bee e' nee ting
Note that "d" and "t" are retroflex consonants in this accent.
One Possible Pitch Pattern:

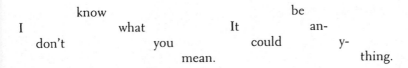

Don't be silly. He is old, but very eminent in his area of endeavor.
Phonetic pronunciation: dOn bee sil' lee   hee i:s wold bAd we' ree yem' i nen in hi:s yay' ree yA o en' de wer
Note: The intrusion of "w" before initial "a"," "o" and "u" and of "y" before initial "e" and "i" is typical of speakers whose parent language is one of the **southern Indian Dravidian** languages. It is not to be used for other Indian accents.

He was elected to the government five times and was Prime Minister, most unusual.
Phonetic pronunciation: hee vas i' lek te t<u>oo</u> di gawR' mend pfI tIms an vas prI min is' ter mOs un' y<u>oo</u> dg<u>oo</u> al
Note: The shift from voiceless "zh" to voiced "dg" is typical of **Bengali** speakers.

I would like not to go, but we can find another place.
Phonetic pronunciation: I vood lIk nARt t<u>oo</u> gO bARt vee kan fInd a nu' de, or deR, plays

The only thing I must say is that it is difficult to handle these things.
Phonetic pronunciation: dee On' lee ting I mAst say i:z dat i:t i:z dif' ee kult t<u>oo</u> han' del deez tingz
Note: The phrases should be clipped, with short vowels.

Possible pitch pattern

```
                                              handle
                                          to
                I can              icult
         only thing    say    diff-
The                        is                           these
                  that it is                                  things.
```

In what sense do you mean difficult?
Phonetic pronunciation: in wARt, or vARt, sens d<u>oo</u> y<u>oo</u> meen dif' ee kult

So we can go to the station and there we can buy a muffin and we can eat on the train.
Phonetic pronunciation: sO vee kan gO t<u>oo</u> dee stay' shun an de:r vee kan bI ay mu' fin an vee kan eet on dee train.
Note: Again, all the phrases should be clipped, with short vowels. Remember that the "t" sounds should all be retroflex and very soft.

Possible pitch pattern

```
        to the                         muf-
    /go      sta-         there we can     a                        eat on the
So we can         tion and          buy         fin and we can         train
```

I don't feel like doing that now.
Phonetic pronunciation: I dOn feel lIk d<u>oo</u>' ing dat now.
Note: Be aware of the liquid "l" sounds, not quite like the French, but much softer than the usual American "L."

After a while we can get off. There is an Indian restaurant not far away and we can get something there. It is a very popular place.
Phonetic pronunciation: ARf' ter ay vIl vee kan get awRf de:r i:z an in' dee an rest' aw rAnt not far ay vay' an vee kan get sum' ting t<u>oo</u> eet de:r it is e we', or ve', ree pop' ler plays
Notes: The retroflex "p" sounds in *popular* and *place* should be very soft, and almost voiced to "b." The retroflex "R" sounds intruded into the words *after* and *off* (and into other words in these exercises) should be very softly pronounced, generally speaking, although sometimes these sounds are rather strong. They are unintentional, and result from the raising of the tongue to articulate a consonant following a vowel, while air is still being forced through the vocal cords. Bear in mind that in a lighter accent the retroflex "R" in these words does not occur.

It takes half an hour. That is not a vast amount of time.
Phonetic pronunciation: i: tayks hAf, or hARf, an owr dat is nARt e wAst, or wARst, or vARst, e mawRnt' ev, or ef, tIm
Note: The "t" sounds in *takes* and *time* are very soft retroflex consonants, and are almost voiced to a "d." The "d" in *that* is also a retroflex consonant.

Sri Lanka (Ceylon)

For centuries Sri Lanka (Ceylon) was under the cultural sway of India. Since 1948 it has been a member of the British Commonwealth, and quite independent. A Sri Lankan accent is, in fact, not very different from an Indian accent, except for the absence of retroflex consonants. It follows the British model in being non-rhotic and in using the British broad, open "A" where General American uses "a." See the list in Chapter One. The "r" in initial position is given a light trill. The two principal languages of Sri Lanka are the official language, Sinhalese, which is Indo-European and derived from Sanskrit, and Tamil, one of the Dravidian languages of the south of India, but spoken by a large majority in Sri Lanka. The political troubles in Sri Lanka, which means "resplendant island," stem in part from the problems between these two ethnic groups.

A Quick Reference

1) Drop the final "R" and the "R" before another consonant. Give the "R" one light trill or tap at the beginning of a word.
2) Use the vowel system of British RP, but make the broad "A" in such words as *can't* a less open vowel, and do a General American diphthong "O," but with the lips slightly rounded. Also, lengthen diphthongs slightly.
3) The point of articulation of "d" and "t" is as forward as possible, with the tip of the tongue landing in a much more forward position than in either British or American English, but not retroflex as in Indian accents. This point of articulation is the key to the accent.
4) Do the liquid "l" which is specific to this accent. See below.
5) Substitute a light initial "v" for an initial "w."
6) *Been* rhymes with *bean*.

How to Do a Sri Lankan Accent

1) Position of the Vocal Apparatus
To assume the correct position, push the lips slightly forward, keeping the jaw relaxed.

2) The Most Important Sounds
Consonants
R: The non-rhotic accent of British RP is followed. The "R" is often, though not always, trilled (r) in initial position, especially at the beginning of a syllable in the middle of a word. The consonants "t," "p" and "g" in word endings are pronounced with a hard sound. All the consonants have a hard quality.

l: The "l" in this accent has its point of articulation slightly forward of the American "L" or the British liquid "l." The tip of the tongue is close to the upper front teeth.

Vowels and Diphthongs
Again, the vowel system of British RP is the one to use. Instead of the schwa in unstressed syllables, however, a short "e" is often heard. *Secretary* is pronounced "sek re te' ree." On the other hand diphthongs are often lengthened, but only slightly.

A: The British pronunciations are followed for the list in Chapter One, but the vowel is less open-throated than the British, and is really intermediate between "A" and "a." This means specifically that the tongue is in a position between its positions for "A" and "a."

O: The sound of this diphthong for this accent is "e' oo," not the British RP "e' oo."

Practice words: *home, go, know, blow, so, show, known, sewn, throne*

w: Substitute a lightly pronounced "v" for initial "w," by which I mean that the upper front teeth should articulate a "v" by lightly touching the inside lower lip and glancing off it quickly.

Pitch

There is a slight up-and-down musicality to a Sri Lankan accent, coming in part from a lengthened quality to vowels before "R."

Practice

The cuisine of Sri Lanka, or Ceylon as it used to be called, is quite superb and can be very spicy.
Phonetic pronunciation: THe kwi zeen' uv sree lAn kA aw si lAn' az it yoos too bee kawld iz kwIt syoo po:b' and kan bee ve' ree spI' see
Note that the diphthongs should be long, and note as well the absence of a schwa in the word *to.*

Of course, darling, if you want to go home we can leave. I don't really care if we stay or not.
Phonetic pronunciation: uv kaws dA' ling if yoo wAnt too gO hOm wee kan leev I dont ree' lee ke: if wee stay aw not
Note: Don't forget to do the particular "O" diphthong, described above. Notice the absence of a linking "R" between the words *care* and *if.*

Hot peppers are delicious, but not to every taste, especially if you are not used to them.
Phonetic pronunciation: hawt pe' puz A di li' shus but nawt too ev' Ree, or ree, tayst es pesh' A Lee i:f yoo A not yoost too THem

You have to acquire the skills necessary to get you through life.
Phonetic pronunciation: yoo hav too a kwIe THe skilz ne se se' Ree te get yoo thRoo lIf
Note the liquid "l" and the characteristically dropped final "R" sounds.

The great natural beauty of the island of Ceylon, which we call Sri Lanka now that we are independant, is a remarkable combination of lowland and highland,

120

and the coast is surrounded by high cliffs and great lagoons.
Phonetic pronunciation: THe gRayt na' choo rel by<u>oo</u>' tee Av THee I' lend *ev* si
lAn' which we kawl sRee lAn' ke now THat wee A in dee pen' dent iz *e* Ree mAk'
e bel kom bee nay shen uv lO' Lend and hI' Lend and THe kOst i:z *se* Rown' did
by hI klifs and *le* goonz'

*There is a heavy monsoon season which drenches the island with water from May
to October, and which is wonderful for the production of spices and tea.*
Phonetic pronunciation: THe: iz *e* he' vee mon s<u>oo</u>n' see' zen which dRen' chez
THee I' lend wi:th waw' tu frum may t<u>oo</u> ok tO' be and which i:z wAn' *de* fool
faw THe pRO duk' shen Av spI' sez and, or an, tee
Notes: be sure to use very clear diction, with well-articulated consonants. Again,
you will notice the lack of a linking "R" between the words *there* and *is*. Also,
notice that both "R" and "r" are used.

Australia

Once Captain Cook claimed the east coast of Australia for the English crown
in 1770, British colonization was inevitable, and by 1829 the continent
first sighted by Portuguese and Spanish explorers was completely under British
domination.

The Australian accent of English, which sounds to American ears very close to
the Cockney of London, in fact derives from the 18th century London accent.
The first English settlers were convicts from the London prisons, sent to Botany
Bay, south of present-day Sydney, in 1788. There are, of course, many differences
between the two accents. For example, there is no glottal stop on the "t" in such
words as *bottle* or *but*, as there often is in Cockney.

There was in the 18th century a large aboriginal population, descendants of
the natives who had lived on the continent for some tens of thousands of years,
and they spoke some 250 languages, many wholly unrelated to each other, although phonetically they appear to have in common many nasalized vowels, and
retroflex and palatalized consonants. Each clan apparently had its own language
and dialects. In the 19th century, as the British occupied the entire continent,
many of the aborigines died or were killed, and, of course, their languages died
with them, not before enriching the vocabulary of Australian English with such
words as *boomerang* and *kangaroo*. From perhaps as many as a million aborigines,
the population dwindled to some 70 thousand. An attempt is being made to
keep those languages that did survive alive by teaching them in bilingual schools.
The Aborigines today mostly speak with the same Australian accents as the majority population.

The Australian accent throughout the continent is pretty much the same,
with some local Outback (back country) and urban variations, which most non-
Australian actors will not need to concern themselves with. It is characteristically "flat" and even the open vowels sound more closed.

Australian dialectical features include a colorful vocabulary and a rhyming slang similar to that of Cockney. *Captain* means "look," because *look* rhymes with—what else?—"Captain Cook." The word *onka* means "finger," because "finger" rhymes with *onkaparinga*, which is a kind of Aboriginal wool rug. In non-rhyming slang, *Woolies* is "Woolworth's" store; a *shrewdie* is "a shrewd person"; a *barbie* is a "barbecue grill"; *footy* is "football"; and *brekkie* is "breakfast," and let's hope it doesn't *look like a dog's breakfast*, which is *Aussie* (Australian) for "a horrible mess." The famous national song "Waltzing Matilda" contains wonderful Australian words, such as *swagman* (hobo), *jumbuck* (sheep), *billabong* (waterhole), *tuckerbag* (knapsack, or a bag for holding *tucker*, British and Australian school slang for "food"), and *billy* (a tin container used for boiling something). The troopers ride up and ask the poor *jolly swagman*: "Where's that jolly jumbuck you've got in your tuckerbag? You'll come a-waltzing, Matilda, with me..."

There is a thriving Australian film industry, so there are many examples of Australian accents to listen to, aside from that of Paul Hogan of *Crocodile Dundee* (1986) fame. Earlier films include *Gallipoli* (1981) and *Breaker Morant* (1979). Films with authentic accents include *Outback* (1987), *Strictly Ballroom* (1994) and *Priscilla, Queen of the Desert* (1994). Also wonderful are the films of Peter Weir, including *Picnic at Hanging Rock* (1975).

A Quick Reference

1) Keep the lips fairly closed and drawn very slightly to the sides during speech. The general resonance of the accent (where the stream of air is directed) should "feel" fairly far back in the mouth.
2) Drop the final "R" and the "R" before another consonant.
3) See the information below under "A" for the Australian use of this vowel, which differs from both British and American in that it is sometimes used as the British use it, and sometimes as Americans use it.
4) Lengthen "e" before (dropped) "R." Shorten "e" to "i" elsewhere. See below for an explanation and practice sentence.
5) Do the following diphthong shifts: "ay" to "I"; "I" to "oy"; "O" to "ow"; "ow" to a lengthened "a." These important shifts distinguish the accent.
6) "L" is often dropped in the middle of a word, such as *Australian*, pronounced "stRIn."
7) Pronounce "t" as an aspirated "d" in the middle of a word like *butter*.
8) Initial "h" is sometimes dropped.
9) *Been* rhymes with *bean*.

How to Do an Australian Accent

1) Position of the Vocal Apparatus
The lips are kept fairly closed, but move flexibly to make the different sounds, without ever opening too widely and sometimes being thrust farther forward for words with the sound "<u>oo</u>" than in American or British English. The corners of the mouth are slightly drawn back as in a smile. The general **point of resonance**

is the back of the mouth. Standard Australian English, as opposed to American or British standard accents, feels generally far back in the vocal cavity.

2) The Most Important Sounds
The Australian accent is non-rhotic, that is "R" is not pronounced at the end of a word or before a consonant.

Vowels and Diphthongs
schwa (e): The schwa is used in unstressed syllables almost more than it is in British English (see Chapter One). Thus, for example, *enable* is heard as "en ay' bel," rhyming with *unable*. The last syllables of *Alice, salad, valid,* and *torches* (which thus rhymes with tortures, the "R" being silent, of course), are all schwas.

A and a: The broad, open-throated "A" of British RP (see the list in Chapter One) is also heard, slightly less open, in Standard Australian. However, there are some exceptions, notably in words where the "A" is followed by "n" plus another consonant. In these words the sound "a" as in General American *that*, slightly more open, is used: *advantage, chance, dance, demand, example, plant,* etc. The sound "a" is also used before "R" and in non-rhotic words as well. For example, the word *car* is pronounced "ka:" (notice the lengthening of the vowel), and *hard* is pronounced "ha:d." In unstressed syllables "a" is often replaced by "i."

ay: This diphthong often shifts to "I," very close to the Cockney sound.

Practice

Made your bed yet? Make it up quick and pick up the paper.
Phonetic pronunciation: mI dge bi dgit mIk it kwik en pik Ap THe pI' pe

e: This vowel is lengthened before "R": *shared* is pronounced "she:d" and is distinguished from the word *shed* only by the length of the vowel. Also important to note is that "e" often is shortened to "i" in words like *pen* and *ten*.

Practice

They shared ten pens in the shed.
Phonetic pronunciation: THI she:d tin pinz in THe shid

I: This dipththong often, though not always, shifts to a very short "oy." Unstressed it is sometimes heard as a schwa (e).

O: This diphthong often shifts to "ow" or (more rarely) to "ay." It also shifts quite often, especially in urban areas, to "o'ü." *Home* is pronounced variously "howm," "haym," or "hoüm."

ow: This diphthong shifts often to a lengthened "a:" or even sometimes to a lengthened "e:," so *sound* rhymes with *sand* or *send*.

The sound of the bells was heard in the house.
Phonetic pronunciation: THe sa:nd ev THe biLz wez ho:d en THe ha:s

Further Phonetic Information

Consonants

g: Final "g" is often dropped in working-class and rural speech in "-ing" endings, and a schwa is heard before the "n": *coming* is pronounced "ku men," the schwa itself being a very short vowel.

h: Initial "h" is sometimes dropped, but by no means always.

L: The sound of this consonant in an Australian accent is fairly close to the Slavic dark "*L*," but without the tongue flattened. It is distinctive and must be heard. Also, it is not always used. Sometimes "L" disappears altogether, to be replaced by the semi-vowel "y": *Australia* is pronounced "os tRI' ye" or even "stRI ye." *Australian* is "stRIn."

t: Sometimes "t" is pronounced as a very soft "*d*" in the middle of a word: *butter* is pronounced "bA' *de*," *mutter* "mA' *de*," and so on.

Stress

The frequent lengthening of vowels and diphthongs gives Australian its characteristic broad rhythm.

Pitch

There is nothing particularly distinguishing about Australian pitch patterns, which resemble British RP more than other pitches. However, there is an occasional tendency in declarative sentences to start on a low pitch and end on a higher pitch, almost as if asking a question, with most of the pitches being high, as in the following example:

Practice

right, I think,   far as I know.
That's   as
Phonetic pronunciation: THits Roy*t* e think ez fa Rez oy now

He just stood and stared at him.
Phonetic pronunciation: ee dgist stood n ste:d ed em.
Note that *stared* rhymes with *instead*.

Where are you from? I'm from Sydney, Australia, down under.
Phonetic pronunciation: we: Re y<u>oo</u> fRAm Am fRem si' nee stRI' ye da:n An' de

The town council met downtown in the town council building. It had a remarkably flat roof and not enough windows.

Phonetic Pronunciation: THe ta:n ka:n' seL met da:n ta:n in THe ta:n ka:n' seL biL' ding it hed e ri ma:k' e bLee fLet ri'<u>oo</u>f en no' di nAf win' dez

Note: There are different "L" sounds heard even in the same person's accent, as you will notice above.

It was great. He did this three hundred sixty-degree rollover. It just shows that the darkest day dawns bright.

Phonetic pronunciation: i? wez gRIt, or gRIt. hee, or ee, di:d THi:s thRee hAn' dRi:d si:ks' tee di gRee' RoüL ow' ve it dgist, or dgis, showz THet THe da:k' es, or is, dI dawnz bRoyt

Note: Remember that final consonants, such as the "t" in *bright*, should be very soft.

There were brilliant students of singing who went abroad and were great successes, such as Melba and Sutherland, but I tend to want to stay at home, because I don't need to go away. No, I don't need it.

Phonetic pronunciation: THe: we bRiL' yent styee' dents ev sing' ing hee wint e bRawd' end we gRIt sek si' sez sAch ez MiL' be en sA' THe Lend be dI, or doy, tind te wawnt te stI et hIm, or hoüm, be kez oy, or I, daynt nayd te gay, or gO, e wI nay, or noü, oy daynt, or down, nay det

Note: Notice the unusual diphthong "oü" in the word *home* and in the word *rollover* in the previous exercise. This sound, which replaces a long "O" diphthong, is quite typical of Australian accents.

New Zealand

New Zealand and Australian English sound very much alike to outside ears, but not to Australians or New Zealanders, and, indeed, there are a couple of distinct differences. The speech of New Zealanders also tends to be very clear and not slurred or run together, as in some Australian Outback accents.

In the early history of New Zealand, first settled by the British in the 18th century and annexed to the crown in 1839, the Maori accent would have been a foreign one, of course, derived from the Polynesian language of the first inhabitants of the islands. Maori is still spoken and taught in New Zealand, but Maoris today mostly speak like all other New Zealanders.

For good examples of the New Zealand accent, see two films made by Australian director Jane Campion: *The Piano* (1993); and Janet Frame's autobiographical *An Angel at My Table* (1990).

A Quick Reference

1) This accent is non-rhotic. Drop the final "R" and the "R" before another consonant.

2) Pronounce "A" on the Australian model. See above.

3) Substitue a "schwa (e)" for "i."

4) Substitute "aw" or "ow" for "O," but only in a heavy accent; otherwise use the British diphthong.

5) In "ee" before "R" do a pure vowel instead of a diphthong.

6) Articulate all consonants clearly. Pronounce the initial "h" and use the British dark liquid "l."

7) Substitute an aspirated "*d*" for "t" in the middle of words like *butter* in a heavy New Zealand accent. A tapped "*t*" is often heard at the end of words like *get* and *it.*

8) *Been* rhymes with *bean.*

How to Do a New Zealand Accent

1) Position of the Vocal Apparatus

The position is more relaxed than the Australian. The jaw is a bit looser. The lips are drawn to the side, but a bit less than in Australian.

2) The Most Important Sounds
Consonants

New Zealand accents are non-rhotic, that is "R" is dropped before another consonant and at the end of a word. Consonants are very clearly articulated. New Zealanders pronounce the initial "h," and pronounce "l" darkly. An aspirated "*d*" is often heard in the middle of such words as *butter* and *matter*. In Maori names beginning with "ng," in which both consonants are pronounced in Maori, the anglicized pronounciation is "n," so the name of the mystery writer Ngaio Marsh is pronounced "nI' O mAsh."

Vowels and Diphthongs

A New Zealand accent often sounds very close to the Australian accent because the vowels are often quite similar.

A: This vowel is pronounced on the Australian model.

ay: This diphthong sometimes, but not always, shifts to an Australian-sounding "I."

ee: Before "R" this vowel is often not diphthongized, at least in a heavy accent, so that a word like *clearly* would be pronounced "klee' lee," instead of "kleee' lee."

i: This vowel is shifted to a schwa (e) or sometimes to the "u" in *but. This* rhymes with *thus*, and *six* with *sucks*, while in New Zealand you have "dunner," not *dinner. Bill* and *bull, fill* and *full* also all rhyme, all pronounced with "u."

126

I: This diphthong often shifts to a vowel, either "aw" or "A."

aw and O: There is sometimes no distinction made between the diphthong in *home* and the vowel in *not*, although the "O" sometimes shifts to "ow" as in a Cockney accent. Thus *goal* and *Gaul* rhyme. *He scored six goals* is pronounced "hay skawd suks gawlz." This makes for a very heavy accent, and you would often hear the British "O" used in New Zealand. You also hear an Australian "O," a combination of the vowels "o" and the French "ü": "o'ü."

w (semi-vowel): The initial "hw" for words spelled with "wh" is usual in New Zealand.

Practice

I'll be home at six o'clock for dinner. Right. As far as I know, that's it.
Phonetic pronunciation: awL, or AL, bee haym, or hoüm, et seks e kLok fe de' ne Royt, or, RIt, or Royt ez fa Re zI now, THets i:t, or, ut, or i:t, or ut

Where did you get it? Did your Dad give it to you?
Phonetic pronunciation: we: ded yi<u>oo</u> git et dud yaw ded giv et e yi<u>oo</u>

Get over here when I call you.
Phonetic pronunciation: gi deow ve hee win oy, or I, kawL yi<u>oo</u>

From here to the next town is not too far. You can see the church steeple if you go out on the road. I've visited that town.
Phonetic pronunciation: fRem hee de THe nikst teown iz not t<u>oo</u>, or t<u>oo</u>, faw y<u>oo</u> kin see THe cho:ch stee' peL ef ye gO eowt awn THe Rowd Iv, or oyv, ve' ze ted THat teown

I had a delicious piece of fruit from the orchard, and I couldn't resist. I stood there on the spot and ate it.
Phonetic pronunciation: I hed e di Li' shes pees ev fri<u>oo</u>t fRem THee aw' chud end oy koo' dnt ri zist' I stood THe:' Ron THe spawt en It ut, or et

The best thing to do in those circumstances is to grin and bear it.
Phonetic pronunciation: THe bist thing te di<u>oo</u> An' de THoz so:' kum sten' suz iz te gRin un bayR ut

The Caribbean

The accents of British former possessions, such as Barbados and Jamaica, are very similar, but those of the other islands have many variations. There are nevertheless some common phonetic characteristics which will enable you to do an authentic accent. As a general rule, for instance, the accents of **Barbados** and

Jamaica, as well as that of **Guyana,** are rhotic, while those of the **Bahamas,** **Trinidad** and many of the other islands are non-rhotic. It is worth noting that the language of the islands has undergone a process of decreolization. Pidgin English was used between the English merchants and planters and the African slave population. For further information see the Introduction to Part One on page 28. In the islands English continued to exist alongside the Creole which developed there, and gradually took over as the first language of the population, hence the decreolization of the island language. Creole left its mark on the accents of the Caribbean.

A Quick Reference

1) The music (pitch patterns) and stress patterns of Caribbean accents are very important. See below.
2) Drop the final "R" and the "R" before another consonant (Bahamas, Trinidad, small islands). Pronounce final "R" for the accents of Barbados and Jamaica.
3) Substitute "A" for "a," but make the "A" more closed, that is, lift the tongue slightly above its position for a broad, open-throated "A."
4) Do the following vowel and diphthong shifts: the "schwa" (e) to "i"; "ay" to lengthened "e:"; "aw" to a slightly closed "A"; British RP "o" to General American "A"; "O" to a lengthened "aw:."
5) Insert "y" after "A" when "A" follows "g" or "k."
6) Drop the initial "h" and the final "t" in a consonant cluster at the end of a word.
7) *Been* usually rhymes with *bean*, but may sometimes rhyme with *bin*.

How to Do the Accents of the Caribbean Islands

1) Position of the Vocal Apparatus
The general position of the vocal apparatus is much as in General American. The jaw is half open, half closed.

2) Pitch
One of the most important features of Caribbean accents is the pitch pattern, the specific music of these accents. Sentences often begin on a high pitch and go step by step to a lower final pitch. There are more notes used in this accent than in almost any other accent in English. It goes up and down, man (pronounced "mAn"). Up and down. Otherwise the usual pattern of ending a declarative sentence on a falling tone and a question on a rising tone is followed.

Practice

Oh, man, I think he's walking in the garden.
Phonetic pronunciation: aw: mAn I tink heez wA' king in di gyA' din.

One Possible Pitch Pattern:
Oh,
   man,
      I
        think
          he's
            walking
               in the
                  gar-
                    den.

3) Stress

Stress patterns are very important in these accents. Where American and British stress is on the first syllable of such words as *celebrate* and *realize*, Caribbean stress is on the last syllable. In fact, the general tendency in stressing is to stress the last syllable, except for "-ed" past participle endings, giving this variety of English its characteristic rhythm. A word like *accentuated*, stressed on the second syllable in both British RP and General American, is stressed in the Caribbean accents on the fourth syllable, as in certain Irish accents. There is an even quality to the stress patterns of this accent, due to the tendency not to differentiate stressed and unstressed syllables very much. On the other hand, the lengthening of some vowels gives the accent a less even rhythm occasionally.

4) The Most Important Sounds

The first thing to listen for are the shifts in the vowels and diphthongs. Also, the accents are strongly non-rhotic, that is, "R" is dropped at the end of a word and before another consonant.

Vowels and Diphthongs

schwa: Instead of a schwa (e) being used in unstressed syllables, "i" is used, as in a New York accent. Vowels in unstressed syllables remain strong.

a: This vowel characteristically shifts to "A." *That's right, man* is pronounced "dAts RIt mAn."

aw: This vowel often shifts to "A." *Law* is pronounced "LA" and *corn* is pronounced "kAn" or "kyAn."

ay: This dipththong shifts to a single lengthened vowel "e:."

o: This vowel sometimes shifts to "A." Thus *not* is pronounced "nAt."

O: This diphthong shifts to a single lengthened vowel "aw:."

y: This semi-vowel is often inserted after a "k" or a "g" and before an "A." So *car*

129

is pronounced "kyA" and *garden* is "gyA din."

Consonants
h: In Jamaica initial "h" is usually dropped, as in London.

L and l: Very often a dark, liquid "l" is heard in these accents, as opposed to the usual General American "L." You can substiiute this "l" for the "L' in any of the exercises in the "Practice" section below.

t: Final "t" is dropped at the ends of consonant clusters in word endings. *Don't* is pronounced "daw:n," *left* is pronounced "Lef," etc.

TH and th: These sounds usually shift to "d" for "TH" and "t" for "th."

Practice

It's my sister, you know. She's on vacation. She goes places and calls me. She takes the car. My uncle goes, too, but he doesn't call me, man.
Phonetic pronunciation: its mI sis' tA y<u>oo</u> naw: sheez awn vay ke:' shn shee gaw:z ple:' siz An kawLz mee shee te:ks di kyA mI An' kL gaw:z t<u>oo</u> bAt ee dAz' in kaw:L mee mAn
Note the lengthened vowel "e:" in the second syllable of *vacation*, and the absence of the schwa in the last syllable of *vacation*.

Pitch Pattern

```
                                          pla-   and
          sister,        She's            goes   ces      calls me.
It's my                    on       She
          you know.            vacation.


She                     uncle          he          call
    takes the           goes, too, but  doesn't   me,
          car. My                                      man.
```

Note: For the following exercises see "A Quick Reference" for when to pronounce or drop final "R," depending on which island or country the character is from.

So my family is against it, but I want to buy that building. With good tenants it will pay for itself, man. It's a good investment, I tell you, man. It's right there, in my grasp.
Phonetic pronunciation: saw mI fAm' Lee i:z A genst' i:t bAt I wAn t<u>oo</u> bI THAt bi:eL' di:ng wi:t g<u>oo</u>d te' nAnts i:t wi:L pe: faw Ri:t seLf' mAn i:ts A g<u>oo</u>d i:n vest' ment I teL y<u>oo</u> mAn its RIt THayeR, or THeeeR, in mI gRasp

They can each have a garden of their own and enjoy the fruits of their labor.
Phonetic pronunciation: de: kAn eech hAv e gyA', or gyAR, den awv de: Rawn'

130

An en' dgoy dee fR<u>oo</u>ts Av de:, or dayeR le:' bAz, or bARz

Oh, you know, the beaches down here are gorgeous and there is always lots of sun-shine and the food is delicious, nice and spicy sometimes, too, like I told you. But you can wash it all down with a nice glass of milk.
Phonetic pronunciation: aw y<u>oo</u> naw dee bee' chez down hee: A gaw' dgus An de: Ri:z awL we:z lawts uv sun shIn' An dee food i:z dee Li:' shus nIs An spI' see sAm tImz' t<u>oo</u> lIk I tawl y<u>oo</u> bu ch<u>oo</u> kAn, or kan, or kn, wAsh i dAl down wi: de nIs glAs e milk, or meeelk

Did you ever take a vacation on a Caribbean island?
Phonetic pronunciation: di:d y<u>oo</u> e' vA te:k ay ve: ke:' shun awn ay kA' Ri: bee' an I' LAnd

There is no end to the wonders of life in this paradise of ours.
Phonetic pronunciation: de: Ri:z naw end t<u>oo</u> dee wAn' dAz Av Lif i:n dees pA' RA dIs' Av ow' Az, or Az

Part Two

North American Accents

Introduction

Although English is the most widely spoken language in the United States, it is by no means the only one. Spanish and Chinese are extensively spoken as well, and Italian, Russian, Japanese and Korean are also quite common, especially in large urban areas. In New York City, home of the United Nations, you can hear almost every language in the world. The Native American languages, also known as American Indian languages, are numerous and fascinating, but because of the tragic history of the decimation of the "Indian" nations there is very little in the way of specifically Native American accents of English today. Native Americans speak mostly with the accents of the regions they come from.

It is a wonderful phenomenon that even though many Native American languages are now gone, many are still spoken, in fact, by tens of thousands of people. There are two Native languages spoken in Alaska, Greenland and Canada: Eskimo and Aleut. American Indian languages number more than a thousand, of which more than one hundred are spoken in North America. One of the principal families of Native American languages is the Algonquin, mainly spoken in the northern Midwest. It includes Chippewa and Blackfoot. The Delaware language spoken in the Midwest is also Algonquin. They took their language with them when they were driven West from what is now New Jersey, New York, Pennsylvania and Delaware. The most widely spoken language of the Algonquin family today is Cree, which alone has 85 thousand speakers in northern Montana and in Manitoba, Canada. The famous word *How!* is actually Cree for "Greetings!" The Iroquois family of languages includes the Cherokee of North Carolina and the Mohawk and Seneca in New York. Dakota or Sioux, as it is also called, numbers some 15 thousand native speakers. The languages of the Siouan family include Crow and Osage. Navajo and Apache are related languages of the Athapascan family. Hopi, Ute and Comanche are all Uto-Aztecan languages. Both Navajo, with more than one 150 thousand speakers, and Hopi with five thousand speakers, are still heard in the Southwestern states.

In Central America and Mexico there are more than three hundred Native languages, including Nahuatl, the language of the Aztecs, and Mayan. There are probably about a thousand languages in South America, including the Quechua of the Incas in Peru, Jivaro, Tupi, Arawak, and the numerous languages of the Amazon.

Among the great linguistic legacies of Native Americans are the names of places: *Delaware, Manhattan, Wichita, Mississippi, Manitoba, Saskatchewan,*

134

Oneida, Penobscot, Merrimac, Connecticut, Kennebec, Passaic—the list goes on and on. *Wigwam, pecan, hickory, hominy, chipmunk* and *moose* are all Native American words.

In colonial days and in the era when the West was so bloodily invaded by settlers of non-native origin there were Native American pidgin languages, first developed in Massachusetts (an Indian name) and Virginia, and Native American accents as well, of course. For a fascinating and authentic example of Native American language and accents see the film *Dances With Wolves* (1990), in which the Lakotan Sioux language is spoken. In this admirable film Mary McDonnell, playing a European-American who has lived with the Lakota so long that she has forgotten English, speaks with a highly convincing accent as she relearns English with Kevin Costner, playing a soldier who has gone west. In *Windwalker* (1980) you can hear the Cheyenne and Crow languages, and in *The Scarlet Letter* (1995) Algonquin is spoken. In all these films the Native American languages are subtitled.

Today the hoary clichés from old Hollywood westerns of the Pidgin English spoken by Native Americans are a thing of the past. Yet such sentences as "Me no can do," "Me makem heap big fire," "Me go on warpath," "Me sittem down," and "Long time no see" are certainly actual Pidgin phrases. A script containing such language will certainly not require the actor to worry about doing an accent, which will be implied in the language of the script itself and merely requires to be spoken out loud for the audience to think it is hearing an accent. On the other hand, the next chapter, which is about regional accents in America, should certainly prove useful to anyone who has to do a role in a play by Tennessee Williams or to portray a New England sea captain in one of Eugene O'Neill's dramas.

Chapter Six

Regional Accents in the U.S.A., Hawaii, Samoa

Roughly speaking, continental American regional accents are divided into two broad belts: Northern and Southern.

Southern accents are characteristically non-rhotic, with certain pockets of rhotic accents, using Southern vowels and diphthongs, in Texas, Oklahoma and Tennessee and in some mountain areas. In the Ozarks *a right far piece down the road* is "a rat fur piece..." In the Southwestern states of Arizona and New Mexico, General American is widely spoken, and these states are therefore not classified as having Southern accents.

Northern accents are characteristically rhotic, with a very pronounced American "R" in the Midwest, for instance in Detroit and Minneapolis and northern Wisconsin, which also has a heavy Scandinavian influence. There are pockets of non-rhotic accents on the East Coast from New York City through Boston and up through New England. For an explanation of the history of this linguistic phenomenon see the Introduction.

Of course American regional accents have changed over time, as the attempts by Mark Twain, for example, to write them phonetically show. Thomas Jefferson's younger brother Randolph, whose spelling is erratic, to say the least, writes in letters to his brother in a way which may well indicate pronunciation. He spells *again* as "a gayn" and *at all* as "a tall," indicating a hard "t," and he spells *really* as "raly," indicating that it may have been pronounced "ray' lee."

When Samuel Johnson published his *Dictionary of the English Language* in England in 1755, he wrote that he had published a book "by which the pronunciation of the English language may be fixed." Although this was a vain hope, which took no account of the many English or American accents or of the fact that languages evolve, Dr. Johnson helped set standards for pronunciation of the language for his own social class and in his own day. He had a great influence on the attitude of the American lexicographer Noah Webster, who believed in standardized pronunciation. Many vain attempts to fix pronunciations and accents in a constantly changing linguistic world have been made by rhetoricians and lexicographers from the eighteenth century, and even earlier, to our own. Elizabethan linguists deplored the dropping of the letter "l" from such words as *calf* and *half,* but they were obviously powerless to change it. How many native speakers of English even realize today that the "l" was once pronounced? And in America two centuries later Thomas Sheridan published a book in Philadelphia in 1783 with the amusing and typically unwieldy eighteenth-century title *A rhe-*

136

torical grammar of the English language, calculated solely for the purposes of teaching propriety of pronunciation, and justness of delivery, in that tongue, by the organs of speech.

On the other hand, Benjamin Franklin, devising his own system of phonetics, attempted not to prescribe, but to record the pronunciation of his era, although he did call for spelling reform. In 1768 Franklin published *A Scheme for a New Alphabet & reformed mode of Spelling, with Remarks & Examples concerning the same...* (The title continues for some time.) You will immediately notice the inconsistent capitalization. Apparently a reformed system of punctuation was also needed, and, indeed, punctuation was later standardized, due to the system of public education, among other things. It is in part thanks to Franklin, with his lists of words and their pronunciations, that we know how Americans talked in the mid-eighteenth century, and they talked very much like the English people they were before the Revolution. But Alexander J. Ellis (see below) thinks that even then his pronunciations must have been old-fashioned, because Franklin was already sixty-two when he published his book.

According to Franklin's description, such words as *certain* and *rain* rhymed, as the last syllable of *certain* was pronounced with a full diphthong, not with a schwa, and that was also apparently the pronunciation in England. And, apparently, both words were pronounced with the long vowel "ee": Reen; soR' teen. So were words spelled with "ay," so *pay* and *paper* were pronounced "pee" and "pee' peR" (as they are in Cork, Ireland to this day). On the other hand, here we see the problem of trying to interpret Franklin's (and others') attempt to spell words phonetically: Does the "ee" with which Franklin spells *rain* mean the contemporary sound (for which I use the symbol "ee" in this book), or is he following the Continental or Italian system, where "e" stands for a sound similar to "ay"? If the latter, the pronunciations would be "Rayn" and "soR' tayn." In fact, this is almost more probable, when you consider that Franklin says the word *compared* is pronounced "kem peeRd." He may mean "-payRd," or he may not. The sound of "e" was apparently quite long, and such words as *men, lend, name* and *lane* all had the same vowel, namely "e:." It is certainly possible, however, that they all were pronounced with the diphthong "ay," retained in *name* and *lane* today, whereas the shorter vowel became the norm in *men* and *lend*. The sound of "I" was apparently much as it had been in Shakespeare's day: "e'ee" (see the section on Early Modern English in Chapter One).

The foregoing is all obviously conjectural, but the accents of eighteenth-century Americans could not have been that dissimilar to our own, judging by recordings of the voices of people whose grandparents were born in the late eighteenth century. Of course, accents obviously continued to evolve and diversify, and to absorb elements from the accents of the huge numbers of immigrants who helped build this country, along with the great working force of African-Americans, first forcibly brought here as slaves. And all of their accents heavily influencedAmerican speech.

The pronunciations of the early to mid-nineteenth century have been preserved in such rare books as John Walker's *A Critical Pronouncing Dictionary,*

137

which went through many American editions from 1818 through the 1830s, but of course we cannot hear the accents, so we have the same interpretive problem as we do with Franklin's descriptions. (Walker, incidentally, published his first dictionary in London in 1775, entitled *A Dictionary of the English language, answering at once the purposes of rhyming, spelling and pronouncing. On a plan not hitherto attempted.*) And Alexander J. Ellis wrote an exhaustive pioneering study of the history of English pronunciation in 1869 entitled *On Early English Pronunciation* (see Bibliography). His system of phonetics is not easy to follow, and the phonetic values he attributes to letters are sometimes problematic, i.e. one has to guess at what he means. Still, it is fairly easy to make educated guesses as to how eighteenth-century accents sounded, and we don't have to guess at all as to the sound of mid to late nineteenth-century accents. We can hear them!

The stage diction of Edwin Booth (1833-1893), recorded on an Edison wax cylinder in 1890 in excerpts from Shakespeare's *Hamlet* and *Othello,* is surely most instructive. You can compare the description that follows with those of British actors Sir Henry Irving and Ellen Terry in Chapter One.

Here is how he pronounces the first lines of Othello's speech to the Venetian Senators in Act One, Scene Three:

"*Most potent, grave and and reverend signiors/My very noble and approved good masters...*"

Phonetic pronunciation: mOst pO' tent grayv' and re' ve rend see nyawz'/mee ve' ree nO' beL and e proovd' good' ma' stez

Pitch Pattern

```
                              gnors/
Most potent, grave and reverend          ble      proved    mas-
                         si-   My very no-  and ap-    good
                                                            ters
```

Notes: Booth's voice is quite low in pitch and very sonorous, and he delivers the speech in a very "grave and reverend," rather melancholy tone, for which he was famous. Even through the scratchy static surface noise his power as an actor is apparent, and he is rather surprisingly natural, especially for his day and age. Other actors of the period are far more artificial; some are quite hammy, in fact (Lewis Waller and Arthur Bourchier, for example). The very first word, *Most,* is spoken on quite a low note. There are actually slight pitch changes in the line *Most potent, grave and reverend,* but the basic impression is of a monotone. Notice the stressed syllables, which give you his rhythm, which is purely Shakespearean iambic pentameter, without that fact being at all emphasized by the actor. As for phonetics, you will notice that he says "mee" for *my;* that he uses the American "a" in the word *masters;* that he uses a slight trill on the "r," that final "R" is silent (non-rhotic); that the "O" diphthong is the American, not the British, version; and that he does not use a schwa in the final syllables of the words *potent* and *reverend.* His diction is obviously meant for the stage. But

138

working-class New Yorkers back then often said *my* as "mee"; and the clearly American "O" diphthong, and the "a" in such words as *masters* must have been distinguishing marks of General American speech, then as now. The trilled initial "r" was surely widely heard back then, giving the accent its old-fashioned sound for us today. Final "R" was either dropped or lightly pronounced, and this was done inconsistently by the same person.

You can hear the voices of Presidents Woodrow Wilson (born 1856), Theodore Roosevelt (born 1858), William Howard Taft (born 1857) and presidential candidate William Jennings Bryan (born 1860) on a CD from Marston Records (see Bibliography). Their accents are fascinating to listen to.

It is instructive to hear the upper class **New York** accent of Teddy Roosevelt, which is already quite different in some ways from that of his cousin, upper-class New Yorker Franklin D. Roosevelt (born 1882), whose voice you can hear in numerous documentary films. Some examples: Whereas Franklin Roosevelt would pronounce the words *first* as "fost," *thirty* as "tho' dee," or "tho' tee" and *third* as "tho:d," Theodore Roosevelt, whose speech is notable for his very clear diction and strong final consonants, said "foyst," "thoy' tee" and "thoyd," a pronunciation similar to one we now associate with working-class speech of the 1930s and 1940s, as in the famous Brooklyn phrase "thirty-third [street] and third [avenue]," pronounced "toy' dee toyd an toyd." T.R. says "woyd" for *word*, and Franklin says "wo:d." However, both pronounce *certain* as "so' ten" and *purpose* as "po' pes!" Incidentally, although both Theodore Roosevelt's and the old Brooklyn pronunciations are almost gone in New York (but see the section on New York City accents, below), in **Alabama** people still say "foyst," "thoy' dee thoyd" and "woyd" for *first, thirty-third* and *word*. And they pronounce *purpose* as "poy' pes."

Woodrow Wilson (who says "thoRd" for *third*), governor of the state of New Jersey before he was president of the United States, was born in **Virginia**. He has just a very slight, occasional touch of the southern in his refined, patrician speech, in words like *never* (ne' ve) *other* (o' thu), *want* (wawnt) and *party* (which he pronounces variously as "pawR' tee." or "pawR' tee"). Taft and Bryan say "pAR' dee"; Roosevelt says "paw' tee," with a real R-influenced vowel in the first syllable.

Wilson, Taft, and Bryan, despite individual differences, all have remarkably similar accents, although they were from three different states; William Howard Taft was from **New Jersey**, William Jennings Bryan from **Nebraska**. Roosevelt sounds a bit different from the other three, because he generally drops final "R." But they all spoke with what must have been the standard patrician accents of their day, with excellent, very clear diction and distinctly articulated consonants, so *trusts* is pronounced "tRusts," with all its consonants; so is *governmental* (guv eRn men' teL). (Roosevelt, however, says "guv' ment" for *government*, sounding rather British.) Nor are their accents very different from contemporary accents. Bryan, Wilson and Taft generally pronounce distinct final "R." All four politicians lengthen word endings and syllables containing the vowel "i" in such words as *American* (e meR' ee ken); *finish* (fin' eesh); *democratic* (dem' e kra' teek);

imperialistic (im piR' ee a Lis' teek); *issue* (eesh' <u>oo</u>); *punish* (pun' eesh); *breaches* (bReech' eez); *motive* (mO' teev); *management* (man' eedg ment); *tariff* (ta' Reef); *characterize* (ka' Reek te RIz); *character* (kaR' eek teR); *added* (a' deed); *wages* (way' dgeez); *political* (pe Li' tee keL); *needed* (nee' deed); *prevented* (pRe ven' teed). As late as 1953, in his inaugural address, President Eisenhower (who does not have a heavy regional accent, although he was bon in Denison, Texas in 1890), says "bRi' teesh" for *British* and "pRi' ve leedg" for *privilege,* showing that these pronunciations had by no means died out. Indeed, they are still heard in areas of the **Middle West,** although on fewer words than in 1900. Taft pronounces the word and syllable *for* as "fAR," with the "R" very lightly pronounced: *performance* (peR fAR' mints); *reform* (Ree fARm'); *platform* (plat' fARm); *formulate* (fARm' y<u>oo</u> Layt); *forms* (fARmz); *forces* (fAR' seez). In fact, he usually say "A" in such words as *war* and *long,* while Bryan, Roosevelt and Wilson say "aw" in those words and in the list of words with *for,* just as we do today in a General American accent. (You can hear Taft's pronunciations, with the final "R" dropped, in some areas of **New England** today.) For all four the "a" in such words as *ask* and *class* is an open vowel, not as broad a sound as the British "A," but in between "A" and "a." And any one of the four could have said *But how is he going to do it?* the way Woodrow Wilson said it: "but how i zee goyng te d<u>oo</u> i:t."

For good examples of this accent listen to grande dame Margaret Dumont (1889-1965) in such Marx Brothers classics as *Coconuts* (1929) *A Night at the Opera* (1935); and to Edward Everett Horton (1886-1970), the worried, nervous, endlessly fussy, frazzled character in such Fred Astaire and Ginger Rogers films as *The Gay Divorcee* (1934) and *Top Hat* (1935). Both actors were born in Brooklyn, N.Y. This accent is substantially the one you want in period films and plays made from Edith Wharton or Henry James novels. Again, for good, clear diction and somewhat old-fashioned American speech and stage diction, useful for these plays and films, consult Edith Skinner's *Speak with Distinction* (see Bibliography).

A Quick Reference: Upper-Class Early 1900s Accents

1) Position of the Vocal Apparatus: The mouth is slightly more closed than in contemporary General American, and the general point of resonance is slightly more forward, closer to the British RP of the day, but this is still not a British accent.
2) The accent is non-rhotic, with R-influenced vowels, in northeastern areas, from New York to New England, on the west coast (where it is sometimes rhotic), and on the east coast of southern states: Drop post-vocalic "R" before another consonant. Everywhere else the accent is rhotic, but the "R" is almost always very lightly articulated.
3) Shift "aw" to A in some cases, especially before "R"; see paragraph above.
4) Shift "i" to "ee" or to "i:" in some cases, when this sound occurs at the end of or in the middle of a word; see paragraph above.
5) Lengthen "o" in such words as *work* and *first.*

6) The vowel "a" in such words as *ask, answer, can't, bath, that, cat* and *task* should be more open than it is in contemporary American English.

7) Consonants should be crisp and clearly articulated, and strong even at the ends of words.

Practice

The policies of the government must ensure that the liberties of the people be preserved.
Phonetic pronunciation: THe po' Li seez ev THe guv' ment, or guv' eRn ment, must en' shooeR, or shooeR, or shooe, THat THe Li' beR teez, or teez, uv, or ev, THe pee' peL be pRee, or pRi, zo:Rvd', or zo:vd'

The conditions under which acoustic records were made in the studios were unenviable and really quite difficult.
Phonetic pronunciation: THe ken di shenz un' de wich, or hwich, e koo' stik Re kawdz', or kawRdz, we, or weR, mayd we, or weR, un en' vee e beL and Ree' e Lee dif' i:, or ee, kuLt, or keLt

The imperialistic policies of the United States with regard to such areas as the Phillipine Islands is viewed by some as benign and protective, by others as reprehensible.
Phonetic pronunciation: THee im pi:R' ee e Lis' teek po' Li seez uv THe yoo nI' ti:d stayts wiTH Ri gAd, or gARd, te, or too, such e:' Ree ez az THe fiL' e pen I' Lendz iz vyood bI sum az bi nIn' and pRe tek' teev bI uTH' ez, or eRz, az Rep' Ree hen' see beL

I sensed a certain pain in my abdomen, and it turned out to be a bit of indigestion.
Phonetic pronunciation: I senst e so:', or so:R', ten payn in mI ab dO' men and it to:nd, or to:Rnd, owt too bee e bit ev in dI, or de, dges' chen

I felt I was just a cog in the wheel of the great machinery of life.
Phonetic pronunciation: I feLt I wez dgust e kog in THe weeL, or hweeL, ev THe gRayt me sheen' e Ree ev LIf

My husband was an art dealer, and we had a duplex apartment on West Fifty-Seventh Street, near Carnegie Hall.
Phonetic pronunciation: mI huz' bend wez an At deeL' e and, or Rand, wee had e dyoo' pLeks e pAt' ment on west fif' tee sev' enth stReet neee kA neg' ee hawL
Note: New Yorkers today generally stress the first syllable of the name *Carnegie* when referring to the concert hall and the famous delicatessen, but the name of the man for whom they are named is still stressed on the second syllable.

For a wonderful selection of regional American accents listen to the daily proceedings of the House of Representatives and the Senate, available on cable television's C-Span channel. The politicians get elected partly because they sound like just plain old folks from home, the people next door. Incidentally, C-Span also regularly shows the British Parliament, both Commons, made up of speakers of all kinds of regional British accents, and Lords, speakers of superb RP; the Irish Dael; and the Australian and Canadian Parliaments.

A Quick Reference
Regionalisms Compared

Comparative pronunciations of the words *pork chop* in various regions of the United States:

General American: pawRk chAp (Note: The "R" is very lightly pronounced.)
East Coast Southern: pawk chop
Alabama and other Deep Gulf rural areas: pOk chAp
Texas and other Plains Southern States: paw:Rk, or paw:eRk, chAp (Note the lengthened vowel and heavy "R.")
Middle West: pawRk chAp (**Michigan**: poRk chap; **Wisconsin**: pARk chAp) (Note: The "R" is very heavily pronounced.)
Boston: pAk, or pok, chop
New York City: paw:k chAp (Note the lengthened vowel.)

Comparative pronunciations of *I know*:
General American (and **Boston, New York City, Northwest**): I nO
Southern: A nO (southern **North Carolina**: a ne<u>oo</u>; southern **New Jersey, Philadelphia, Baltimore**: I ne<u>oo</u>)
Upper Middle West (**Dakotas, Wisconsin, Michigan**): I n<u>oo</u>

Comparative pronunciations of the words *park your car*:
General American: pARk yawR kAR (Note that the "R" is very lightly pronounced.)
East Coast and Deep Gulf Southern: paw:k yaw: kaw: (**Alabama**: paw:k yO kaw:) (Note the lengthened vowels.)
Texas and Plains Southern: pAeRk, or pawRk, yaweR kaweR
Middle West: paRk yeR, or yawR, kAR (**Michigan**: pa:Rk yeR ka:R)
Boston: pAk, or pak, ye, or yaw, kA, or ka:
New York City: pawk, or pARk, yaw kaw, or kAR (Note that the "R," when pronounced, is very light.)

Comparative pronunciations of the words *the law's delay*:
General American: THe Lawz de Lay'
Southern: THe Law:z di lay: ' (lips open; **Alabama**: LOz)
Middle West: THe LAz de Lay' (almost "Lee"; lips closed)
Boston: THe Loz, or LAz, de lay'
New York City: THe Law:z di Lay'

Comparative pronunciations of the sentence *It was a medal made out of metal.*
General American: it wuz e me' deL mayd owt uv me' teL

General Southern: it woz *e* mi' deL may' *da' de* mi' *deL*
General Middle West: it wuz a me' deL may*d* ow' *de* me' teL
Boston: it wez e me' deL may*d* ow' *de* me' deL
New York City: i? wuz *e* me' *deL,* or deL, may' *dow de* me' deL

Comparative pronunciations of the sentences *My upstairs neighbor makes so much noise. It sounds like a herd of elephants up there sometimes. I never heard anybody walk with such a heavy tread.*
General American: mI up' ste:Rz nay' beR mayks sO much noyz it sowndz LIk *e* hoRd uv e' Le fents up THe:R sum' tImz' I ne' veR hoRd e' nee bA *dee* wawk with such *e* he' vee tRed
General Rhotic Southern (Texas, mountainous areas, etc.): mA *o*p stay' *e*Rz nay' beR mayks sO moch nO' eez It sowndz LAk *e* hoRd *e*v iL' *e* fents *o*p THay' *e*R *so*m tAmz A ni' veR hoRd i' nee bA' *dee* wOk with such *e* hi' vee tRay' ed
General Non-Rhotic Southern (Gulf States, East Coast, etc.): mA up' stay*e*z nay be mayks sO much noyz it sowndz LAk *e* ho:d *e*v iL' *e* fents up THay*e* sum' tAmz A ni' *ve* ho:d i' nee bA *dee* wawk with such *e* hi' vee tRe:ed
General Middle West: mI up ste:Rz nay' beR mayks sO much noyz it sowndz LIk *e* hoRd uv eL' *e* fents up THe:R sum' tImz I ne' veR hoRd e' nee bA' dee wAk with such *e* he' vee tRed
Boston: mI up' ste:z nay be mayks sO much noyz it sowndz LIk *e* ho:d *e*v eL' *e* fents up THay*e* sum' tImz I ne' *ve* ho:d e' nee be *dee* wawk with such *e* he' vee tRed
New York City: mI up' ste:z nay' *be* mayks sO much noyz it sowndz LIk *e* ho:Rd, or hoyd, *e*v el' i fints up THe: sum' toymz I ne' *ve* hoyd, or hoR*d,* e' nee bA *dee* dee waw:k with, or wit, such *e* he' vee tRed

Notes: The symbol "e:" in the word *upstairs* in the **Boston** and **New York City** pronunciations actually represents two slightly different sounds: The **New York City** sound is flatter and longer, the **Boston** sound shorter. Also, in **New York City** any final "R" sounds, as in the words *herd* and *heard,* are very light indeed, as are other final consonants. In the words *herd* and *heard,* for instance, if an "R" is heard it is very light; notice the old-fashioned pronunciation, which it is still possible to hear, "hoyd" (for both words). The "R" sounds in the **General Middle West** are a lot harder than they are in the **General American** pronunciation, i.e. the tip of the tongue is rolled up farther back in the **General Middle West** pronunciation. There are a great many **Southern** accents, so the generalized pronunciations above, while servicable, may need to be more specific. For instance, some people from **Alabama,** one of the **Gulf States,** would pronounce the words *heard* and *herd* as "hoyd." Someone from southwestern **North Carolina,** one of the **East Coast** states, might pronounce the word *like* as "Lak," instead of "LAk."

It is interesting to compare the pronunciation of the word *orange:* The **General American** pronunciation is "o' Rindg"; in the **South** the pronunciation varies from "aw' Ri:ndg" to "ARndg" to (occasionally) "awndg"; the **Middle West** pronunciations vary from "awRndg" in **Detroit** to "aw' Reendg" in **Indiana** and western **Pennsylvania;** in Boston they say "o' Rendg" with a soft "R"; and in **New York City** people say "A' Rindg." The word *coffee* is also variously pronounced: in **New York** it is "kaw:' fee" and in the **Middle West** it is "kA' fee"; in parts of the **South** it is "kO' fee." But to most of the country it is "ko' fee."

Southern Accents

There are several methods of classifying Southern accents. The simplest, I think, is to divide them into four main areas:
1) East Coast Southern (Maryland, Virginia, coastal North Carolina, coastal Georgia).
2) Mid-Southern (Appalachian Mountains; border states like Kentucky, Tennessee). For a broad Tennessee accent listen to Dolly Parton in *9 to 5* (1980).
3) Deep Gulf Southern (the rest of Georgia and North Carolina, South Carolina, Mississippi, Alabama, Louisiana). These are the accents most useful in plays by Tennessee Williams. A refined Charlotte, North Carolina accent can be heard in the speeches of Billy Graham.
4) West or Plains Southern (Missouri, Texas, Oklahoma, Arkansas). President Clinton, of course, has an Arkansas accent, while Texas is well represented by, among others, Tommy Lee Jones, and Oklahoma by James Garner.

All of these Southern accents have characteristic phonetic features in common. For practice pick a play by Tennessee Williams and use the dialogue, marking the text with the sounds indicated below.

There are many films in which you can hear authentic Southern accents, as well as accents learned by northern actors. Actors from the southern states who use their natural accents when their roles demand it include Sissy Spacek (Texas); Rip Torn (Texas); Geraldine Page from Missouri (see her in the 1961 film of Tennessee Williams's *Summer and Smoke*); Morgan Freeman, from Memphis, Tennessee (see *Driving Miss Daisy* [1989] and *The Shawshank Redemption* [1994]); Miriam Hopkins from Georgia (see her as the aunt in the 1949 film *The Heiress*); Billy Bob Thornton and others with authentic rhotic Arkansas accents in *Sling Blade* (1997), a very upsetting, moving film which Mr. Thornton also wrote and directed; and Elvis Presley, born in Mississippi. There are also actors from the south, such as Ava Gardner and Louise Fletcher, who use no Southern accent, but simply speak General American.

A Quick Reference

Summary of Important Phonetic Differences in the Southern Accents
1) **Non-rhotic:** East Coast Southern; Deep Gulf Southern (Alabama, Mississippi, Louisiana)
2) **Rhotic:** West, or Plains, Southern (Texas, Oklahoma); Mid-Southern (Tennessee, Kentucky, Ozarks, Appalachia)
3) **Consonant Cluster Reduction:** Rural Southern speech generally, Ebonics,

144

Alabama, Georgia, Mississippi. See below.

4) Generally vowels and diphthongs are lengthened beyond what is usual in General American.

5) "I" to "A": ubiquitous; often slightly diphthongized before voiceless consonants (k, p, s, t); pronounced "a" in southern **North Carolina**; often slightly dipthongized in **Plains Southern**; sometimes pronounced "e" (schwa) when unstressed

6) "i" to "e": ubiquitous

7) "e" to "i": ubiquitous

8) For further specifics for the different states see below.

How to Do Southern Accents

1) Position of the Vocal Apparatus
The important general position for Southern accents is with the mouth fairly open and loose jawed, which accounts for the quality of the "lax" vowels.

2) Stress
There is occasional non-standard stressing in Southern accents: *in' surance, ho' tel*. The word *dispute* is often stressed on the first syllable when it is a noun and on the second syllable when it is a verb.

3) Pitch
The pitch patterns or intonation of Southern speech gives these accents characteristic and varied music. The lengthening of diphthongs mentioned below changes the rhythm of a sentence from that of General American by introducing falling and rising tones on the lengthened diphthongs. This is the famous **Southern drawl**. There is also a characteristic rising tone at the end of a declarative sentence, as if it were a question.

4) The Most Important Sounds
For a **light** general Southern accent all you really have to do is to drop the second half of the diphthong "I" so that it is pronounced "A": A know. The other phonetic trait that all Southern accents share is the reversal of "i" and "e." You also have to determine whether the accent is rhotic or non-rhotic. With these three phonetic characteristics you have a Southern accent without half trying.

Vowels and Diphthongs
Vowels are often diphthongized: *glance* becomes "gLaents"; *glass* becomes "gLaes." The semi-vowel "y" is sometimes inserted before the schwa, resulting in a triphthong: gLayents, gLayes. Diphthongs are often lengthened or drawn out, giving a kind of music to Southern accents, often called a Southern drawl, the word *drawl* being pronounced with a very long diphthong; in **Alabama** you would hear the word *drawl* pronounced "dRO<u>oo</u>L." In the South, the word *south* is pronounced "sa:' <u>oo</u>th."

A: "A" in *father* is often sounded like "aw" in *law*.

e and i: There is a reversal of "i" and "e" in general Southern speech generally. Examples: *pen* is pronounced *pin* and *pin*, *pen*. *Memphis* is "Mimphis." A schwa is sometimes inserted between the vowel and the final consonant, in **Tennessee** and **Texas** for example, where *pen* shifts to "peeen," and *condemn* to "kondeeem." **Practice**: *pen, pin, ten, tin, Ben, bin. Ben got ten tin pens out of the ten tin bins.*

I: "I": The diphthong in *fight* usually drops the "ee" and is sounded "A," although as times change and television influences speech, this phenomenon seems to be slowly changing, certainly in upper-class Southern speech. Before voiceless consonants ("k," "p," "t") "I" often retains a slight, very slight diphthongization. In southern **North Carolina** it is often pronounced "a." When unstressed it can be pronounced as "*e*" (schwa).
Practice words: *my, by, tie, die, try, high, dive, jive, live, height, type, like, quite*

Consonants
An important phenomenon in many parts of the South is "consonant cluster reduction" in such combinations as "st," "ld" and "nd," in final position (at the ends of words). Examples: *host* becomes "hos"; *hold* becomes "hol"; *end* is pronounced "en." *My host told me there wasn't going to be a band* sounds like "mA hOs tOl mee THay wadn gawna bee *e* ban (or sometimes: bayen)" (**Georgia**, etc.). In mountain accents, especially when speech is slurred, some medial consonants are dropped, so *everybody* is pronounced "eR bA' di:" or, more distinctly, "ev Re bA' dee." (**Baltimore, Ozarks**, parts of **Texas**). Note the tapped "*d*," often heard.

g: The final "g" in "ing" endings is often dropped in lower-class Southern accents. "I was just going along" is pronounced "A z dgst gOin lawng." Notice, too, the dropping of initial "w" and the vowel "a" in *was*, the absence of a vowel in *just*, and the dropping of "a" in *along*. In the phrase *going to*, the final "g" is sometimes dropped, as is the "t" in *to*, and the final syllable of *going* is sometimes nasalized: "Am awn (or "gawn") gO now."

s: "s" in spelling, pronounced as the voiced consonant "z" in General American, in *isn't* and *wasn't*, is often heard as a soft "d": idnt, wudnt. The final "t" is either very soft or else dropped altogether: idn, wudn. Alternatively the "d" is dropped and the final "t" pronounced: int, wunt. Sometimes the final "t" is dropped: in, wun. These phenomena can all be heard from the same speaker at various times.

Further Phonetic Information

Consonants
h: In old-fashioned rural Southern accents an "h" is sometimes inserted in words beginning with "i," as in *it*, which becomes "hit." "Hit's true."

L: "L" has several phenomena associated with it: "L" is sometimes dropped in

146

medial position: *help* is "hep" (**Mississippi**); *wolf* is "woof." "L" is sometimes sounded like "y": *million* thus shifts to "miyun" ("a miyun dolez"). Sometimes a schwa and a diphthong are inserted before "L," replacing a vowel: *help* is "hayeLp" in **Texas**.

t: The "t" in Southern mountain speech (as in the **Ozarks** and other parts of **Arkansas**) is often heard as a glottal stop (phonetic symbol: ?) in the middle of words: *settler* is pronounced se?la; *battle*, ba?l (as in the **Bronx**). In rural **Georgia** and **Alabama** the spelling combination "t" and "y" where one word ends in "t" and the next one begins with "y," as in *put you* (General American pronunciation: poot y<u>oo</u>) varies from the distinct standard pronunciation to the lower-class "poo' choo" and "poo' ch<u>oo</u>." The word *temperature* is pronounced "tem' pe che" in **Missouri** and in **Mississippi**, and elsewhere in the South. In **Deep Gulf** accents the spelling comination "t" and "h" in *right here* is pronounced "rachye." *I'm going to put you right here* sounds like "Am awn pooche rachye." Notice the dropping of initial and final "g" in *going*, very rural, very lower-class. TH and th: Voiceless "th" in lower-class Southern speech is often heard as "f": *both* is "bOf." Voiced "TH" becomes "v": *breathe* is "breev."

Vowels and Diphthongs
aw: The vowel "aw" in *law*, *thought*, and *bought* is often diphthongized as "O" ("o'<u>oo</u>"). For example, in **Alabama** and the other **Deep Gulf** accents *because* is pronounced "bi kOz'." *Thought* and *bought* are pronounced "thOt" and "bOt." **Practice words**: *because, thought, bought, pork* (Note: Drop the "R"), *drawl, law, ought, brawl*

e: "e" before "zh," as in *pleasure, measure* and *leisure*, is diphthongized and pronounced almost like "ay" in *say* in rhotic Southern accents, as in **Missouri** and parts of **Texas**, but like the "e" in *met* elsewhere.

O: 1) "O" in *home* is much the same as in the North, but in coastal **Maryland** and the southern part of **North Carolina** it is often heard as "o'<u>oo</u>" (with the "o" in *work* as the first half of the diphthong) instead of "o'<u>oo</u>" (with the "o" in *not* as the first half of the diphthong). *Home* becomes "ho'<u>oo</u>m"; *know* shifts to "no'<u>oo</u>." (Note: This is also characteristic of a number of Northern accents, such as **Philadelphia**, **Baltimore**, and **southern coastal New Jersey** [the Pine Barrens], which are, however, rhotic accents, unlike many Southern accents). "O" is also pronounced "e'<u>oo</u>" and "u'<u>oo</u>" in southern **Virginia** and northern **North Carolina**, so *château* is pronounced "sha te<u>oo</u>' " or "sha tu<u>oo</u>'." The General American pronunciation is simply "sha tO'."
2) In words ending with the spelling "-ow" or the pronunciation "O" a schwa is often substituted for the General American "O." (See also below under **New Orleans**.)
Practice words: *fellow, yellow, tomorrow* (te mA' Re), *bellow, jello, mellow*, (but not *hello*, which is still "he LO' ")

o: The sound in "er," "ir," and "or" in the spelling of *fern, fir,* and *work,* while sharing the non-rhoticity of the accent, is sometimes pronounced "eee": feeen, weeek, although *fur* is pronounced "fe" or, alternatively, "fu." In **Alabama** and **South Carolina** these sounds are pronounced with an "oy," a very short sound: "foyn," "foy" ("foy coat"), "woyk." Note: This sound, lengthened, is also heard in the old **Brooklyn** accent, now largely gone, but still heard occasionally, or should I say "hoy:d"?). In various areas of the South, including coastal **Virginia** and as far west as **Alabama**, "oy" is pronounced "aw," thus losing its quality as a diphthong: *boil* is pronounced "bawl" and *spoil* is pronounced "spawl." In **Alabama** "o" also replaces "u," so *of, but, other* and *love* are pronounced "ov," "bot" (or "bo?," with a glottal stop), "o' THe," and "Lov."

ow: In **Deep Gulf** and **Mountain** accents this diphthong often shifts to a flat, lengthened "e:oo," so *grounds* is pronounced "gre:'oondz." The "e:" is close to being a diphthong, "ay."
yoo: "yoo" (spelled "u" and "you") in unstressed final syllables is almost always schwaed: *continue* is pronounced "continye"; *volume* is "volyem." On the other hand "yoo" is often pronounced with a lengthened vowel "i:" replacing the semi-vowel "y" after a consonant: "nyooz" (news) shifts to "ni:ooz," "dyook" (duke) to "di:ook," the "i" being stressed in both cases. It is also pronounced with the mouth closed and the lips protruded.

Southern Accent Practice
(for both lengthened diphthongs and rising final tones)
I thought I was going to go downtown. I never did make it. I tried, but I never did make it downtown.
Note that the underlined diphthongs are lengthened. The underlined and italicized diphthongs are both lengthened and spoken on a high pitch.

(For sound shifts/substitutions)
Nice white rice is my favorite kind of food.
Phonetic pronunciations
General Southern: nAs wAt RAs iz mA fay' vRit kAn e food (Note that the "A" before a voiceless consonant, "s" in this case, may be slightly diphthongized.)
North Carolina (Charlotte): nas wat Ras iz ma fay' vRit kan e fiood
Outer Banks: noys woyt Roys iz moy fay' vRit koynd uv food
Note that in the southern part of **North Carolina**, near Charlotte, the "A" is flattened so it sounds like the "a" in *that*: "a know," instead of "A know"; the town of *Pineville* is pronounced as if it were spelled "Panveal" (where "ville" is diphthongized). In the **Outer Banks** of North Carolina *I* becomes "oy", and the inhabitants are known as "Hoy Toyders." This may be very close to the English of Shakespeare's day. The dipththong "ow" is pronounced "e'oo" and final "R" is heard. Final "d" becomes "t," so *island* is pronounced "oylint."

He got into a dispute. It was awful.

Phonetic pronunciation: hee gA *d*in tu dis' py<u>oo</u>t it *wez* aw:' fL
Note the heavily aspirated "*d*" and the shortening of *into a* to "tu." To pronounce the "y<u>oo</u>" in the Southern way, just close your mouth and protrude the
lips slightly. In **Alabama** the word *awful* would often be pronounced "O' feL."

I'm going to tell you something, fellow. Don't mess with me.
Phonetic pronunciations
General East Coast, Kentucky, Tennessee: Am gaw' ne, or awn, tiL, or (more
rarely) teL y<u>oo</u> sum' thin fe' Le dO mis weth mee
Alabama: Am On tiL y<u>oo</u> som' thn, or som'm, fe' Le dO*n* mis weth mee

I slept on the train.
Phonetic pronunciations
Educated General East Coast Southern: A slipt awn THe* tRay:n
Kentucky, Tennessee, but also Alabama and rural generally: A slip, or slep, aw
ne tRay:n
North Carolina: a slipt awn THe tRay:n
Note that there is sometimes a rising note on the word *train*, making the de-
clarative sentence sound like a question.

Well, you know, I have a few questions about that actually.
Phonetic pronunciation (**Baltimore**): weL ye neO A hav e fy<u>oo</u> kwes' chins e
bowt THat ak' shLee

Every time I go there I have a great time.
Phonetic pronunciation (**Baltimore**): e' Ree tIm I gO THe:R I hav e gRayt tIm,
or (sometimes) toym

It was ghostly, like it was a haunted house or something.
Phonetic pronunciation (**Baltimore**): i wez gOst' Lee LIk i wez e haw' nid hows
eR som' thin
Note: In **southern New Jersey** around the Pine Barrens the "ow" diphthong in
the word *house* is close to the Cockney version, but without being lengthened.

*Everything was fine on Saturday, then we had snow to a total of about sixteen
inches, but they had no snow in Florida.*
Phonetic pronunciation (**Baltimore**): e' Ree thing wez fIn awn saR' day THen
wee had snO t<u>oo</u> e tO' deL, or tOL, uv e bowt siks' teen inch' iz but nO snO in
fLawR' e de
Note: With some consonants added back—the "v" in *everything*; the "t" in *Saturday*—this is a **Philadelphia** pronunciation. As it is, this is a heavy **Baltimore**
accent. See the note above for the pronunciation of "ow" in *about*.

*He was into one thing, you know, and then he goes totally in the other direction
and everything is different.*

Phonetic pronunciation (**Baltimore; Philadelphia**): hee wez in' te wun thing ye nO an THen hee gOz tO' Lee, or tO' de Lee, in THee u', or o', THeR de Rek' shen an e' Ree thing iz di' fRin?

Note: In the exercises above don't forget to do the **Baltimore** "O" diphthong, also heard in **southern New Jersey** and **Philadelphia**.

Earlier you stated that that would be the end of it. That was going to be the end of it.
Phonetic pronunciation (**Kentucky**): eR' Lee eR yoo stay' died, or deed, THe, or THet, THat wood bee THee ind' ev it, or ind ov' it THa dez, or wez, gaw' ne, or gawn', bee THe ind ov it
Note: The final "t" sounds in *that* and *it* should be so light as to be almost glottal stops.

While we're talking about that, isn't it true that you called him on the phone?
Phonetic pronunciation (**Kentucky**): wAL wiR tA', or taw', kin e bowt' THat in, or idn, i tRoo THat yoo kAL', or kawL', deem awn THe fOn

I feel that it was done in cold blood and I feel that we have to try to make an issue of it.
Phonetic pronunciation (**Kentucky**): A fiL THat it wez don in kOL blod an A fiL THat wee hav, or haf, te tRA te mayk an ish' e uv it
Note: Notice the liquid "l" in the word *blood*, as opposed to the usual General American "L." This pronunciation, without the liquid "l," could also be heard in **Tennessee**.

I want to find out. How many more times are they going to count?
Phonetic pronunciations
Tennessee: A wawn' te fAn aoo?   how mi' nee mawR tAmz eR THay gO' in te kaoont?
Kentucky (rural): A waw' ne, or wawn, fAn eoo?   haoo mi' ni: mawR tAmz eR THay gawn, or gaw' ne kaoon?
Note: Notice the glottal stops. The **Kentucky** upper-class urban accents of such cities as Louisville (pronounced "Loo' e viL" or sometimes "Loo' veeL" in Kentucky) are closer to **Tennessee** accents, with fewer consonants dropped and shorter vowels. Working-class accents are like the rural accent, as shown.

I want to thank you. Please let me do so.
Phonetic pronunciations:
Tennessee: A wawn te thank yoo, or ye   pLeez lit mee doo sO
Kentucky rural: A waw' ne, or wawn, or wawn, thank yioo PLeez le' mee deoo sO
Kentucky urban: A wawn te thank yoo   pLeez let mee doo sO.
They just orchestrated the whole thing and rolled over.
Phonetic pronunciation (**Mississippi**): THI dgist aw kis tRay' did THe heOL theng n ReOLd eO' ve

150

Were the military ballots even mentioned?
Phonetic pronunciation:
Georgia: we THe mi' Li te Ree ba' Lits ee' ven min' chend
Alabama: we THe mi' Li te:' Ree ba Lets ee' vin min' chind
Notes: For **Alabama** the "R" in *military* should be very hard and the "e" sound in the syllable before it should be lengthened, unlike the short "e" in the **Georgia** pronunciation. **Georgia,** of course, like the other states, has a number of accents, from that of President Jimmy Carter of Plains, to Atlanta, Macon, coastal and interior rural accents.

We want to try to avoid certain kinds of situations before they arise with regard to anybody else.
Phonetic pronunciation (**Texas**): wee waw ne tRA *de e* voyd', or vawid', soR' tn kAn' dze si ch*oo* ay' shenz be f*aw*R THay e RAz' with R*e* gawRd' te i nee bA dee eLs, or eeLs, or iLs, or ieLs
Note: This sentence may be used to practice certain other Southern accents as well. For **Alabama** pronounce the word *certain* as "soy' tn" and drop the final "R' in *before* and *regard.* For **Tennessee** and **Kentucky** the "A" for "I" substitution can be lightened, so that "I" is a slightly lengthened diphthong. Also, say "wee wawn te tRI, or tRA, te e voyd." Say "kAndz ov." Pronounce final "R" lightly in *before* and *regard.*

Texas Practice
Far out on the range the cowboys ride on their horses.
Phonetic pronunciation: fo:R a*oo*d awn THe Rayndg THe ka'*oo* baw'eez RA:*d* awn THay:R ho:R' siz
Note the lengthening of the diphthongs.

I got a good look at you, and you're going to go to town.
Phonetic pronunciation: A gA' *de* good loo' ki ch*oo* en y*oo* awn gO de ta*oo*n
Note the heavily tapped "*d*"s.

There's nothing I can't tell you.
Phonetic pronunciation: THeRz no' thin A, or, Ai, kay:n teL, or tiL, ye, or y*oo*
Note that in Texas the "e/i" reversal does not always occur. Note also the lengthening of "kay:n," although the final "t" is not pronounced.

I don't care what they say, I think he's a dope.
Phonetic pronunciation: A *d*On kayeR wut, or wot THay say. A thenk heez e dOp.

It's an idea whose time has come. There has to be a winner and a loser.
Phonetic pronunciation: its an A' deee, or A deee', or I deee, h*oo*z tAm, or tIm, haz kom   THeR has, or haz, te bee e wi' neR an e l*oo*' zeR.

Well, golly gee, what do you know about that?
Phonetic pronunciation: wayeL gA' Li: dgee wo *de* ye no<u>oo</u> baowt da, or da?, or THaeet

Let me turn just briefly to this issue, because I take it this Board didn't do that and that assumes, of course, that you don't know whether you have a dimpled chad or not.
Phonetic pronunciation: Le' mee toRn dgist bReef' Lee te THis i' she bi kOz A tayk eeet THis bOeRd di? n d<u>oo</u> THat n THa *de* s<u>oo</u>mz' e kawRs THet y<u>oo</u> dO nO wi' THeR y<u>oo</u> hav *e* dem' pLd chad eR nAt, or nA?
Note: The word *issue* could also be pronounced "i' sh<u>oo</u>." The pronunciation "i' she" is a typical **Gulf States** and **Tennessee** pronunciation. Words such as *course, board,* and *briefly* can be heavily diphthongized for a more rural accent.

African-American Accents

Descended from and influencing in turn Southern non-rhotic accents is a variety of English known as Ebonics, or Black Street Speech. It has its own dialectical variations from General American, and its own varieties as well. (See below under Gullah for an example of such a variety.) This African-American speech, though descended from rural Southern accents, is also an urban phenomenon, widely heard in the inner-city ghettos of northern as well as southern cities. The subject of Black English is, needless to say, surrounded by much controversy involving class prejudice, as well as racism. See John Baugh's *Black Street Speech* (University of Texas Press, 1973) and J. L. Dillard's *Black English: Its History and Usage in the United States* (Vintage Books, 1973) for superb studies and analyses of this subject. There are highly expressive idioms and vocabulary and variations in grammar in Ebonics. "I be talkin' about it"; "He done told me"; and "It don't make no difference" are just a few examples of such grammatical variations. It would be a mistake to suppose that the first speech of most African-Americans is Ebonics, or to characterize Ebonics as sub-standard, more a sociologically prejudicial than a linguistic characterization; they are, rather, valid non-standard dialectical variations, just as valid as those one hears in English Provincial or Scottish dialects. Of course, most African-Americans either speak General American, or speak with the accents of the regions they come from, whether New York City, Detroit, Boston, Alabama or California, and many whose first speech is Ebonics also speak General American. Some of the characters in the films of Spike Lee provide excellent examples of Ebonics. See *Mo' Better Blues* (1990) and *Malcom X* (1992), among others. Also very much worth seeing is *Hollywood Shuffle* (1987), a wry, accurate comedy about the stereotyping of African-Americans in Hollywood, co-written, directed by and starring the endearing, handsome Robert Townsend.

The Most Important Sounds
R: Black Street Speech is characteristically non-rhotic.

Consonant clusters are often reduced ("wha's up" for *what's up*; "prob'ly" or

152

even "pro'ly" for *probably*; "regu'ly" for *regularly*; "don' " for *don't*; "las' " for *last*; "excep' " for *except*, etc.); and the final "g" in "-ing" present-participle endings is often dropped.

dg: The combination "d" and "y" is often pronounced "dg," as in *did you*, heard as either "di dg<u>oo</u>" or "dg<u>oo</u>."

t: The combination "t" and "y" is often pronounced "ch," as in *don't you*, heard as "dOn ch<u>oo</u>."

TH and th: The "TH" in such words as *this* and *that* is often heard as a "d," but the voiceless "th" in *thing* is usually pronounced as "th." Sometimes, especially in an older form of Ebonics, voiceless "th" is pronounced "f" and voiced "TH" is virtually eliminated in the context of a phrase, or replaced by a very soft "b": *both of them* might be heard as "bOf u' bm." This pronunciation, generally obsolete in contemporary Ebonics, is generally heard in contemporary rural **Alabama** and **Mississippi** accents, whether in the speech of African-Americans or European-Americans.

Two other characteristic Southern linguistic phenomena are also heard in this accent:
I: the dropping of the second half of the "I" diphthong, so that "I" is pronounced "A."

i and e: The reversal of "i" and "e," so that *thing* is pronounced "theng" and *pen* is pronounced "pin."

i for y in word endings: Often, although by no means always, a word ending orthographically in "y" will be pronounced with an "i": *very* is pronounced "ve' Ri"; *very true* is pronounced "ve' Ri tR<u>oo</u>," when the "i" is not dropped altogether; *ordinary* is pronounced "aw den e' Ri." Note that this an older phenomenon in Ebonics, and is fast disappearing, although it is still heard among Southerners who are European-American, especially in **Alabama**, north **Florida**, and **New Orleans**.

wh: Words spelled with "wh" are sometimes pronounced, as in other Southern accents, like "hw," so *what* and *when* may be heard as "hwet" and "hwin" or "hwien."

Pitch

There are more notes used in intonation patterns in Ebonics than in General American, and higher pitches can be quite common, especially in situations where people are joking around with each other with pleasant bantering. Again see the section on Gullah for an example, and under "3) Pitch" near the beginning of the section "How to Do Southern Accents."

African-American Practice

Note: Use the exercises under "Southern Practice" as well.

What are you all [often spelled "y'all," a general Southern expression meaning "all of you," or "you," plural or singular] *thinking about?* [This might actually be phrased as "What y'all be thinkin' 'bout?"]
Phonetic pronunciation: we, or hwe, chaw:L [bee] the*n'* kin ba<u>oo</u>?
Note the glottal stop at the end of *about*.

What do you all [y'all] *want to do?* [or, *be wantin' to do*]
Phonetic pronunciation: we, or hwe, chaw:L waw' ne, or wawn, d<u>oo</u> [bee wawn' ne d<u>oo</u>]

Let's go. I finally got the change.
Phonetic pronunciation: Les gO A fAn' Lee gAt de chayndg

(Sentences overheard on the New York subway and the New Jersey Transit trains)
What's up, bro? [brother] *What do you think?*
Phonetic pronunciation: wo sup bRO wo, or we, ch<u>oo</u> thank
Note: The phrase *What's up?* s also frequently pronounced "su?" with a glottal stop, or "sup."

You jivin' me? I ain't going to do that.
Phonetic pronunciation: y<u>oo</u> dgA' vin mee A ayn gawn d<u>oo</u> da

Yo, man, he's over there, if you're looking for him. And don't you be talking. Don't say nothing. She's not your gal.
Phonetic pronunciation: yO man heez O' ve de:', or de:', fyoo Look' en, or in, fawm an don' ch<u>oo</u> bee tawk' in don say nu' ?n sheez nA chO gaL

Meet me by the number two train.
Phonetic pronunciation: mee? mee bA de num' be t<u>oo</u> tRayn

They might want me to catch a ride, see, so I don't know but I think that's where we met to go to the store that time.
Phonetic pronunciation: day mA? wawn mee de kach e RA:d see sO A dOn nO be dA thank das we: wee me? te gO de de staw da tAm
Note: A single *de*, standing for *to the* in the phrase *to go to the store*, is also possible.

He was, like, doing his thing for a while, you know what I mean?
Phonetic pronunciation: hee ez Lak d<u>oo</u>' en iz theng faw wAL y<u>oo</u>, or ye, nO wA, or we dA, meen, or meen

I'm going to tell you something. I want a glass of milk.

Phonetic pronunciation: Am aw*n* te *ye*, or y<u>oo</u>, sum?' *em*, or su*n*' ?n A waw' ne gLas *e* mi<u>oo</u>k

Note: Notice the dropped "L" sounds, typical of some speakers. Remember the dropped "L" in the **Cockney** accent in Chapter Two. This is typical as well of some **Gulf Coast Southern** accents, as well as of the **Gullah** accent. And, occasionally, it is heard in the **Bronx**.

They was like, yo, they really got on him.
Phonetic pronunciation: day wez Lak yO day Ri Lee gA dawn im, or eem

I'm on AOL, but it takes so long, man, you know what I'm saying? It's always so busy. It dials, then it redials. I can take a shower, get out, and it's still dialing, you know what I'm saying?
Phonetic pronunciation: Am awn ay O eL be *di* tayk sO Lawng man y<u>oo</u> nO wAm say*n* is O' weez sO bi' zee i dALz de ni? Ree' dAlz A kin tayk *e* show' *e* gi dow? an is stiL dA' Lin ye nO wo *d*Am say' in

Note: Notice the two possible pronunciations of the phrase *You know what I'm saying?*. Of course, there are other ways of pronouncing this as well, using more or fewer syllables.

Gullah

This African-American accent from around Charleston, South Carolina is said to take its name from a pronunciation by slaves of their native Angola. There is a great deal of anglicized Bantu vocabulary in the Gullah dialect. For more information see *The African Heritage of American English* by Joseph E. Holloway and Winifred K. Vass (Indiana University Press, 1997). Of course the first Black accents in this country were those of the African slaves, and these African acccents influenced English in the Southern colonies, just as those of other groups did. Gullah is a variety of Southern accent. Its particular characteristics include the dropping of prefixes and of final consonant clusters, (see above). *I suppose so* is pronounced "A spOz sO." *I expect so* is pronounced "A spek sO." A slight aspiration very close to an "h" is added before vowels: *It's true* is pronounced "his tR<u>oo</u>" or even "hish tR<u>oo</u>," with the final "t" in the consonant cluster in *it's* dropped, and the retroflex "R" so light, that is with the tongue not curled very far back, as to become almost a "w." *The oysters was [were] good* is pronounced "de hoy' sez wez goo." Spoken rapidly, this sentence might be quite difficult to understand. Comprehension of this accent by those unfamiliar with it is made even more difficult by the occasional pronunciation of "s" as "sh" particularly after the vowel "i": The word *restaurant*, for example, is pronounced "Rish' tRawn" and *history* is pronounced "hish' tRee" or "hish' Ree" with the "t" dropped. The rhythm, which is quite staccato and rapid, and the music of Gullah are quite particular, and must be heard to be accurately reproduced. In part the intonation pattern consists of a series of high notes rising even higher in a declarative sentence, which then sounds like a question. *I don't know what you're going to do about it* sounds like "A n nO hwu' choo gawn d<u>oo</u> bow' di?." (The "?" represents a glottal stop.)

The pitch might look as follows:

```
                                        di?.
            hwuchoo gawn doo
        nO                        bow
An
```

You could expect really good food at that restaurant.
Phonetic pronunciation: ye koo spek Ri' Lee goo f<u>oo</u> ha, or a, da Rish' tRaw*n*

I suppose you love the oysters because they were so good.
Phonetic pronunciation: hA, or A, spOz y<u>oo</u> Luv de hoy' sez kawz day wez sO goo

You can't hardly get there from here.
Phonetic pronunciation: ye kay*n* haw' Li: gi de: fRem hee:*e*

What did you want to go and do that for?
Phonetic pronunciation: hwu ch<u>oo</u> waw*n* gO nd<u>oo</u> da, or a, fu, or f*e*

It's really true, I tell you, and I can prove it.
Phonetic pronunciation: his, or hish, Ri' Lee tR<u>oo</u> hA, or A, te ye nA k*n* pR<u>oo</u> vi

New Orleans

This French, Spanish and Creole city, with its famous restaurants, its Mardi Gras and its French Quarter (in which the French names of streets are anglicized) has specific accents, different from the rest of Louisiana. The information given here is generalized. Listen to Paul Prudhomme on his television cooking show, or to Justin Wilson's cooking show for a rural Cajun Louisiana accent.

How to Do a New Orleans Accent

Like other Southern accents, this accent is non-rhotic, but otherwise the accent sounds very Northern, almost like Brooklyn accents. A New Orleans accent has also been compared to a Hoboken, New Jersey accent, perhaps because of the substitution of "d" and "t" for "TH" and "th," and the non-rhoticity they share.

In the famous Ninth Ward (phonetic pronunciation: nInt wawd) the accent is supposed to be particularly heavy, and very like that of Brooklyn, New York. The New Orleans pronunciations of streets and places with French names, despite the city's French background, bear little relationship sometimes to the original language, beginning with the name of the city itself. New Orleans (pronounced "ny<u>oo</u> oR' Lenz" or "ny<u>oo</u> oR' Lee enz" in General American) is "awR lé aw*n*" in French, but to most people who live in Louisiana it is either "ny<u>oo</u> aw Leenz' " or "naw' Lenz" or "nyaw' Lenz." Some more examples: *Bourbon* (French: b<u>oo</u>R bon'; New Orleans: beR' ben); *Richelieu* (French: Ri: she lyo'; New Orleans: Reesh' L<u>oo</u>); *Antoine* (French: awn twAn'; New Orleans: an' twAn); *Chartres* (French: shAR' tRe; New Orleans: chAR' teRz); *Pontchartrain* (French: pawn shAR tRe:*n*'; New Orleans: pAn' she tRayn'). The name *Burgundy* is stressed on the second syllable.

The Most Important Sounds
Consonants
ch: In a real **Cajun** accent the final "ch" is often heard as "dg." The word *church* is pronounced "chudg," for example.

TH and th: Voiced "TH" in *this, them, these* and *those* is often pronounced like "d." Voiceless "th" is often "t."
Practice words: *through, think, these, them, those*

Vowels and Diphthongs
A: This vowel sometimes shifts to "aw," so *party* is pronounced "paw" dee' and *part* "pawt," or "paw?," with a glottal stop, which is very occasionally heard in this accent.

-ed: Words ending in "ed," such as *married* shift the ending to "id": "ma' Rid."

I: In lower-class New Orleans accents the "I" diphthong shifts to a vowel and becomes "A," as in the other Southern accents, with the second half of the diphthong ("ee") dropped, although this is not always the case and one sometimes hears the General American diphthong, certainly among the upper class.

-ow: Words ending in "ow," such as *fellow* or *yellow* shift the diphthong in the last syllable to the schwa: "feL' e"; "yeL e."

o: The sound of this vowel in *work* and *first* sometimes shifts to "oy," or, more accurately, to a diphthong "u'ee."
Practice words: *heard, first, work, learn, bird, word*
oy: This sound, whether in *boy* or *boil* shifts to "aw": "baw"; "bawl."

New Orleans Practice

She was married in a yellow gown and I enjoyed the crawfish boil we had for a wedding feast.
Phonetic pronunciation: shee wuz ma' Rid in e ye' le gown en A in jawd' de kRaw' fish' bawl wee had faw Re we' ding feest

We went to a party in the Ninth Ward and everybody had a really good time.
Phonetic pronunciation: wee wen t<u>oo</u> e paw' dee in de nInt wawd an ev' Ree bo' dee had e Reel, or RiL, good tIm, or tAm

They were all dressed up and you should have seen them parading through the streets on Mardi Gras.
Phonetic pronunciation: day weR awL dResst up an y<u>oo</u> shood *ev* seen dem *pe* Ray' ding tR<u>oo</u> *de* stReets awn maw' dee gRaw

It was a private affair and what went on was nobody's business.
Phonetic pronunciation: i? wuz *e* pRA' *ve de* fay' *e* and wAt wen awn wuz nO bo' deez biz' nis, or bi' nis, or bid' nis

They was real good years when he was working down there by Lake Pontchartrain.
Phonetic pronunciation: day wuz RiL good yee:z wen hee wuz woy' kin down de: bA láyk pAn' she tRayn'

You should try Gallatoire's some time. It's just great. And so is the Commander's Palace and Antoine's, and a lot of other terrific restaurants down here.
Phonetic pronunciation: y<u>oo</u> shood tRI ga' *Le* twAz sum tIm its dgus gRayt an sO iz *de ke* man' dez pa' *Le*s an an' twAnz an *e* LA' dev u' THe *te* Ri' fik Res' *te* Rawnz down heee

Northern Accents

Northern accents fall generally into the categories of:
1) the **rhotic** accents of the Middle and Far West (including the interior areas of the Middle Atlantic States); for typical clear Midwest accents, listen to Clark Gable, who was from Ohio; Spencer Tracey, from Milwaukee, Wisconsin; Gary Cooper from Montana; and James Stewart, born in the town of Indiana in western Pennsylvania.
2) **Non-rhotic** East Coast accents (including New England and the coastal areas of the Middle Atlantic states). The Kennedys have real old-fashioned Boston accents, very individual.

The Middle West: Indiana, Chicago, Illinois, Ohio, Montana, Michigan, Nebraska, Wisconsin, The Dakotas, Minnesota and the Pacific Northwest

A Quick Reference

1) Pronounce a hard "R" at the ends of words and before another consonant. In the **Pacific Northwest** (Washington, Oregon, Idaho) make the "R" softer.
2) Consonants are "hard" and well articulated. These are generally very clear accents.
3) The sound of "a" in *cat* is very flat, and sometimes diphthongized to a very flat "ae."
4) Shift "aw" to "A" for the entire area under discussion.

5) For further specifics see below.

How To Do Middle West Accents

1) Position of the Vocal Apparatus
The general position of the vocal apparatus in the Middle Western accents feels very tight and the lips are drawn out to the sides a bit, as in a tight smile.

2) The Most Important Sounds
Consonants
R: These are strongly rhotic accents generally, with a very rolled "R," and the tip of the tongue rolled back and up, more than it is in General American. This is true of upstate New York, western Pennsylvania, Idaho, Indiana, Illinois, Ohio, Montana, Wisconsin, Minnesota, Michigan, Nebraska and the Dakotas. For a good example of this phenomenon listen to the accents in the movie *Fargo* (1996). For a typical, clear Nebraska accent listen to Johnny Carson on videotapes of the *Tonight* show.

Final "d," "k," "p," "t," and "z" can be rather hard, using the middle or initial version of the consonant instead of its usual General American softer version. This is true in **Detroit**.

Vowels and Diphthongs
a: "a": in *that, gather,* and *black* is very flat, and often diphthongized: thaet, blaek. This is the case from upstate New York all the way west to Minneapolis and beyond. In the Middle West *marry, merry* and *Mary* all rhyme and are pronounced like *Mary*.

aw: "aw": in *law* is sounded like the "A" in *father*, except before "R," where it remains as a shortened "aw." In **Wisconsin**, however, it is pronounced like "A" even before "R." *Law* is "LA"; *water*, pronounced "wawteR" in General American, is pronounced "wAteR," and sometimes "wAteR," with a very soft, aspirated (breathy) "t"; *all* is "AL." A slightly flatter version of this sound, still not General American, is heard in **California**. In **Indiana** and elsewhere farther west an "R" is sometimes inserted after "aw," so *wash* (General American pronunciation: wAsh) is pronounced "wawRsh."

ay: This diphthong sometimes shifts to "ee," especially when it is unstressed (**Dakotas, Minnesota, Wisconsin**).

er: In **Chicago**, in addition to the phonetic characteristics described above, there is a tendency to use a schwa in words like *there* and *sure*, pronounced "sheR" in **Detroit**, and also in **Minneapolis**. This pronunciation is perhaps due in part to the influence of Scandinavian accents, and is heard in upstate **Wisconsin** and in **Minnesota** on the Canadian border, and the vowel is shorter than it is in Detroit. A typical Wisconsin and Minnesota phrase, often parodied, and heard in

159

the movie *Fargo* (1996), is *Oh, sure, you betcha* (O: she:R y<u>oo</u> beche). Listen to Joe Mantegna in *Glengarry Glen Ross* (1992) and to Bill Murray in *What About Bob?* (1991) and *Groundhog Day* (1993) for real **Chicago** accents. Listen to the speech of Illinois-born William Holden in *Stalag 17* (1953), *Sunset Boulevard* (1950) and *The Counterfeit Traitor* (1962), or any of his more than 60 films. The comedian Jack Benny, born in Waukeegan, also had a touch of Illinois in his accent. See him in videos of his TV series *The Jack Benny Hour*, and in such films as *To Be or Not To Be* (1942) and *The Horn Blows at Midnight* (1945).

e to ay: Another important shift (true in **Missouri** and parts of **California** as well) is from "e" to "ay," so such words as *measure, leisure,* and *pleasure* are pronounced "may' zheR"; "Lay' zheR"; "pLay' zheR."

O to <u>oo</u>: This shift is typical of northern **Wisconsin** and **Minnesota**. *I know* is pronounced "I n<u>oo</u>."

oo and <u>oo</u>: In **Indiana** and **Missouri** (Southern, properly speaking, but sharing some Midwest characteristics) *roof, root* and *room* are pronounced with the "oo" in *book*, not with the "<u>oo</u>" in *boot*.

oy to I: This shift is typical of northern **Wisconsin**. The infamous Senator McCarthy's phrase "Point of order, Mr. Chairman" is pronounced "pInt ev AR' deR mis' teR che: R' men." Did he say "pint of ardor"? *Department* and *deport-ment* rhyme, as do *depart* and *deport* in this accent.

Wisconsin Practice

Do they know how far we gotta go? Sure they do.
Phonetic Pronunciation: de THay n<u>oo</u> how fAR wee gA de g<u>oo</u> sheR THee d<u>oo</u>

The dairy farms in Wisconsin make the most delicious cheese you could ever hope to eat.
Phonetic pronunciation: THe de:' Ree fARmz in wis kAn' sen mayk THu m<u>oo</u>st du Li' shes cheez y<u>oo</u> kood e:' veR h<u>oo</u>p tu eet

"Oh, brother," I said, "that's really something else!" "Oh, really? What else is it?" he said. He was always a real wiseguy.
Phonetic pronunciation: <u>oo</u> bRu' THeR I sed THaets Ri' Lee sum' thing, or sum?' m, eLs <u>oo</u> Ri' Lee hee sed wA' deLs iz it hee wez AL' weez e ReeL wIz' gI
Notes: Notice the shift from the diphthong "O" in *Oh* to the vowel "<u>oo</u>." The trick here is to think "O" while saying "<u>oo</u>." The pronunciation of *What else is it?* could be heard in **Chicago** as well, but with the "i" in *is* lengthened.

You can't be serious. That's just unheard of.
Phonetic pronunciation: y<u>oo</u> kaent bee si:' Ree es THaets dgust un hoR' duv

Well, you know, that's how we view things out here in the heartland.
Phonetic pronunciation: weL ye nO THaets hO wee vy<u>oo</u> thingz Ot heeeR in THe hARt Laend

He went over there to the next farm, and he never came back.
Phonetic pronunciation: hee went O' veR de:R te de nekst fARM aen hee ne' veR keem baek

Chicago Practice

I'm sure there's nothing at all that can't be made that much simpler with hard work.
Phonetic Pronunciation: Am sheR THeRz nuthing aet AL THaet kaent bee may:d THaet much simpLeR with hARd woRk

I'd really like to get in here.
Phonetic pronunciation:Id Ri' Lee LIk te ge din heeeR

Where in the law does it come from.
Phonetic pronunciation: we:R in THe LA dez it kum fRum

What's the matter?
Phonetic pronunciation: wAts THe me:', or mae', deR

Be serious for a moment. That's just an impossible situation.
Phonetic pronunciation: bee si' Ree es feR e mO' ment   THaets dgust aen im pA' si beL si ch<u>oo</u> ay' shen

I heard of a guy that went down there and lost his shirt.
Phonetic pronunciations: 1) I hoR' duv e gI THaet went down THeR aen Lost hiz shoRt; 2) I hoR' dev e gI det went down eR, or deR aen Lost iz shoRt

A Typical Middle Western Accent: Michigan

The accent has a hard "R" with the tongue rolled up slightly. The sound shifts from General American listed below are very marked.

The Most Important Sounds
a: The "a" in *that* is frequently diphthongized and very flat: "THaet."

aw to A: The shift from "aw" to "A" is very strong: kAl (*call*), wA' teR (*water*), etc.

o to a: All the "o" sounds shift to "a" in *that*. The prefix *non* is pronounced "nan," *comments* becomes "ka' ments" and *acknowledgements* sounds like "ak na' Ledg ments." *Congress* becomes "kang Res."

Michigan Practice

I know that's true and I send my acknowledgements to Congress.
Phonetic Pronunciation: I nO THaets tR<u>oo</u> aend I send my ak na' Ledg ments te kan' gRes

I don't see that at all.
Phonetic pronunciation: I d<u>oo</u>nt see THae' dae dAL

The court has agreed to take up that matter.
Phonetic pronunciation: THe kawRt, or kawRt, haez e gReed' te tayk up THaet ma' teR, or mae' deR

That's just not true. Detroit is a wonderful city and a great place to live.
Phonetic pronunciation: THaets dgust nat tR<u>oo</u> dee' tRoyt iz A wun' deR fooL si' dee aen A gRayt pLays te Liv
Note: People from **Detroit** often stress the first syllable of the city's name; the rest of America stresses the last syllable.

He's the most impossible person. If you have orange juice he wants pear juice, and vice versa. It's such a bother!
Phonetic pronunciation: heez THe mOst im pass' e beL poR' sen if y<u>oo</u> haeve awRndg dg<u>oo</u>s hee wAnts pe:eR dg<u>oo</u>s aend vIs voR' sA its such e ba' THeR

Oh, my God, were you at the Old Cider Mill at the same time? I didn't see you there!
Phonetic pronunciation: O mI gad weR y<u>oo</u> aet THee <u>oo</u>Ld say' deR miL aet THe seem tIm I did' ent see y<u>oo</u> THe:eR

More Middle Western Practice

Note: The following practice sentences range geographically, from Pittsburgh in western Pennsylvania to Seattle in the far west, but they are all varieties of Middle Western accents.

I'm not going to get into that. I have had no contact with them all evening.
Phonetic pronunciations:
Pittsburgh: Am nA? gaw' ne ge din' te da I haev haed nO kAn takt wi dem awL eev' ning
Note: Notice the glottal stops and the pronunciation of *all* as "awl" instead of the usual Middle Western "Al."

I'd like to comment about that. I'd like to say a word about our political process. That's what I want to say.
Seattle: Id lIk te kA' ment e bowt THat Id lIk te say e woRd e bowt AR pLi' di kL pRA' ses THat's wA dI waw' ne say

Note: In **Minnesota** the word *political* might be pronounced "pe Li' dee keL."

I thought they ought to pay cash on the barrelhead just for good measure.
Phonetic pronunciation **(Indiana)**: I thAt THay A' *de* pay kaysh awn THe be:'
ReL hed, or hayd, dgust feR good may' zheR
Note: In **Michigan,** where the flat "a" in *barrelhead* would be very flat indeed,
the words *cash* (kay' esh) and *measure* (me:e' zheR) would also have a very flat
"a" amd "e," respectively.

Did you finish washing up?
Phonetic pronunciation **(Indiana)**: did y<u>oo</u> fin' eesh wawRsh' ing up
Note: This much is the same as a **Nova Scotia** accent, with the intrusive "R" in
washing.

*We all knew him. He liked to sleep late, and I went to wake him up, but he was
always so dramatic that he made a scene and told me to let him sleep. Sleep it off,
I would have said, but I thought he might throw something at me, so I just shut up
and let him be.*
Phonetic pronunciation **(Indiana/parts of Illinois/western Pennsylvania/Ohio)**:
wee AL n<u>oo</u> eem   hee LIk tu sLeep Layt an I wen tu wayk eem up but hee wez
AL weez sO dRe ma' deek THa*et* hee may' *de* seen aen tOLd mee tu le' deem
sLeep sLeep i' dAf I wood ev sed be dI' thAt hee mIt thRO sum' thing aet mee
sO I dgust shu' dup aen le' deem bee

Can you turn that off, or at least turn it down. It's awfully loud.
Phonetic pronunciation: kin, or kaen, y<u>oo</u> toRn THae dAf eR et, or aet, Leest
toRn it down   Its Af' Lee Lowd.
Notes: In **Minnesota** the final consonants such as "d" in *loud,* "n" in *can,* and
"t" in *least* would be very hard; also, the diphthong "ow" in *loud* and *down* is
really pronounced "A'<u>oo</u>" and is very short. In **Michigan** and **Indiana** they would
be softer. In **Michigan** the "a" in *that* is particularly flat, and the "R" is particularly hard. In **Indiana** and **Illinois** all the consonants are softer.

California

A working class **San Francisco** accent sounds something like a **Chicago** accent, with an added nasal "twang." The famous, hilariously funny Gracie Allen
of the Burns and Allen comedy duo was from San Francisco, but her accent is
General American, although non-rhotic. The accents of Gertrude Stein, with
her mellifluous voice, and Alice B. Toklas, with her raspy, somewhat nasal voice,
are preserved on recordings which show them speaking with an upper-class
American accent from the turn of the century; both were from Oakland, California. San Francisco and **northern California** accents are General American.
Listen, however, to the accent of the late former President Richard M. Nixon

from Whittier, with his pedantic, overly precise, almost Middle Western diction, with its rounded "R" and too plosive plosives, and his diptongization of "e" in such words as *measure* and *pleasure*: mayzheR, pLayzheR. While it is dangerous to speculate about psychology, I would guess that his pseudo-intellectual accent was an overcompensation for feelings of inferiority. In **Los Angeles** the non-Standard **"Valley Girl"** accent, with its palatalized consonants and diphthongized vowels (*school* is pronounced "sky<u>oo</u>eL"), is a particular regional and middle-class variation. The pitch in the "Valley Girl" accent is also very specific, with a rising tone on final diphthongs, as in the following example: *I was going to school.* (I wez gOing te sky<u>oo</u>eL), where the last syllable of the sentence is spoken on a rising tone, as if it were a question and not a statement. This accent is frequently used to portray mindless airheads and bimbos; whether this is an accurate perception or not I leave to the reader to decide. Not everyone who speaks with this accent is an idiot.

Valley Girl Practice

It's like, you know, I was at school and my friend said, like, do you, like, want to, and so we went to the movies and it was, like, really awesome.
Phonetic pronunciation: its LIk ye nO I wez at sky<u>oo</u>' eL/ an my fRend sed LIk de y<u>oo</u> wAn t<u>oo</u> an sO wee wen te THe m<u>oo</u>' veez/ an it wez LIk Ri' Lee A' sem/
Note: Notice the three rising tones, on the words *school*, *movies*, and *awesome*.

Like, you know, you do your college thing, like, whatever, you know.
Phonetic pronunciation: LIk ye nO' y<u>oo</u> d<u>oo</u> yeR kA' Lidg thing LIk wA de' veR ye nO'

What am I supposed to tell your Mom, huh, I mean, like, what?
Phonetic pronunciation: wA de mI spO' se teL yeR mAm hu I meen LIk wAt

Hey, dude, how are you? Can you really do that?
Phonetic pronunciation: hay düd how AR yee<u>oo</u> kin y<u>oo</u> Ri' Lee dü Tha?
Notes: The use of the vowel "ü" hardly implies any French accent. In this version of the vowel the lips are protruded while the jaw is opened wide, just the opposite of the French or German vowel. In the pitch pattern below you will notice the rising and falling tones; the vowels in the stressed syllables spoken on those rising and falling tones are very long and drawn out.

Possible Pitch Pattern

```
               are                        that?
Hey,                            ly
     du-\   how     yo-\     /real-
                            you      /do
     de,               u? Can
```

Upstate New York

This accent, a form of Middle Western accent, also has a hard "R" and a tendency to diphthongize the vowel in *that* as in Michigan. The final "g" in "ing" verb endings is frequently dropped. "Ayeh," meaning "yes," is frequently heard, as it is in a **Down Home Maine** accent. A particular pronunciation in the upstate area of New York is "be tay' de" for *potato*, the "d" in the final syllable being very soft. The "aw" in *law* shifts typically to "A."

Upstate New York Practice

I was petting my dog and eating potato chips, ayeh.
Phonetic pronunciation: I wez pe?' en mI dAg aen ee?' en be tay' de chips ay' e

Well, we refinished that house and we had a great time doing it and we had a lot of work to do on it, that's for sure. We didn't want to have to worry about it.
Phonetic pronunciation: weL wee Ree fin' isht THaet hows aend wee haed e gRayt tIm doo' ing it aend wee haed e LA' de woRk te doo awn it THaets feR shooR wee di' ?n waw' ne haef te wu' Ree e bow' dit

Buffalo and Rochester get so snowed in sometimes in the winter because of all the storms and the wind off the Great Lakes. Fifty feet sometimes. Quite a blizzard.
Phonetic pronunciation: bu' fLO aen RA' ches teR git sO snOd' in sum tImz' in THe win' teR bee kez' ev AL THe stawRmz aen THe wind Af THe gRayt Layks fif' dee feet sum tImz'. kwI' de bLi' zeRd

New York City

You can hear every accent in the world in New York City, both because the United Nations is there, and because of immigration from all over the world. There are several native New York City accents in each borough, Bronx, Brooklyn and Queens, all non-rhotic. New York City accents have been influenced by immigrant communities, notably Irish, Italian, Jewish and Hispanic, (so that there are New York City Irish, Italian, Jewish and Hispanic accents), as well as by Black Street Speech. "Uh-uh" for *No* and "Uh-huh" for *Yes* are originally African-American expressions. The original non-rhotic New York accents are undergoing alteration, but are certainly useful for plays set decades ago, as those of Clifford Odets are, for example. Most educated New Yorkers have rhotic accents, with the "R" very lightly pronounced. The working-class accents tend to be more broadly non-rhotic, though this is a vast generality. Queens and Long Island accents, especially lower-class accents, have a reputation for being rather nasal, although this is not always the case.

In films and on stage New York City accents done by people who are not natives of New York City often sound inauthentic. There are two particular pronunciations that are a giveaway, and that I often hear: New Yorkers usually say "An" for the word *on*, almost never "awn"; a flat Middle Western "a" is never

165

heard in such words as *that* and *have*, despite the fact it can be heard (although without the schwa often added to it in the Middle West), in some words, such as *can't, stand* and *avenue*. When I worked as a Dialect Coach for the Broadway production of the musical *Saturday Night Fever*, I had to teach the New York City accent to those members of the cast who came from the Middle West. They all were terrific at getting the authentic sounds, and at pronouncing *married* as "ma' Reed" and not "ma:', or me:', Reed," but they did have to work at it; it was not at all their natural way of speaking English.

See Newark-born Joe Pesci as the slumlord in *The Super* (1991), and as the lawyer in the riotously funny *My Cousin Vinny* (1992), along with the wonderful Marisa Tomei, for great New York City area accents. Among other actors with a variety of native New York City accents are Billy Crystal, Danny Aiello, Armand Assante, Luther Adler, Lee J. Cobb, Long Island-born Rodney Dangerfield, Bronx-born James Caan, Robert De Niro, Al Pacino, Richard Dreyfuss, Hector Elizondo, Burt Lancaster; James Cagney; Jackie Gleason, whose celebrated TV series *The Honeymooners* is set in Brooklyn; Sammy Davis, Jr. (*Ocean's 11* [1960], etc.); Woody Allen; Whoopi Goldberg; Dom De Luise; George Burns; Rosie O'Donnell (from Long Island); Harvey Fierstein (see *Torch Song Trilogy* [1988]); Barbra Streisand (see *Funny Girl* [1968]); Judd Hirsch; Paul Sorvino; Jerry Stiller and Anne Meara; Carl Reiner; Rob Reiner; Groucho Marx; and Mel Brooks, who is married to Bronx native Anne Bancroft. She can use her New York City accent when her roles demand it, as in *Garbo Talks* (1984) and *84 Charing Cross Road* (1987). See George Burns and New Yorker Walter Matthau in Neil Simon's *The Sunshine Boys* (1975), set in New York City, like so many of his comedies. See also Chapter Nine on Spanish accents; Chapter Ten on Italian accents; and Chapter Fourteen on Yiddish accents, especially the section on p. 253, "London and New York Yiddish Accents Compared."

The Most Important Sounds
Consonants
As is usual with non-rhotic accents, there is an "intrusive R" in such phrases as *the idea is* and *law and order*, which are pronounced "THee I deeR' iz"; "LawR an aw' *de*." Note the tapped "*d*."

g: In a stereotypical **Long Island** accent (known also for its flat vowels: "A" shifts to "aw"; "a" is very flat), final "g" is added to the "ng" in such words as *long* and *sing:* Lawngg; singg. This may be due to the influence of Yiddish, where such sounds are a part of the language; on the other hand, this was apparently the usual Elizabethan pronunciation. Language tends to simplify itself: Somewhere around the seventeenth century the extra "g" simply disappeared from most provincial and standard British accents, although it remained in some provincial accents, such as Liverpool's.

-ing endings: The final "g" is typically dropped, especially in lower-class accents.

166

L: A real New York City and Brooklyn phenomenon is the occasional dropping of an "L," as in *almost* and *always*, pronounced "OmOst" and "Owayz," or even "Oweez." Similarly *all right* and *already* are pronounced "e RIt'," "e RIt,' " or even "e RI?' " and "e Re' dee." NOTE the tapped "d" and tapped "t."

? and "t"; t and d: In the **Bronx** a glottal stop (phonetic symbol: ?) is often heard replacing "t" in medial and final position: *bottle* becomes "bA?l." *What* is pronounced "wa?." In New York City **Hispanic** accents the "t" is sometimes simply dropped before another consonant (no glottal stop replaces it), so *What does it mean?* is pronounced "wa dus i meen." Note the final "s" in *does*, also a frequent phenomenon in Hispanic accents, in which the final voiced "z" sound shifts to voiceless "s." This information can be useful in the Puerto Rican roles in the musical *West Side Story*. The consonants "t" and "d" in final position are often heavily aspirated, especially in **Brooklyn**, and there is an occasional tendency (associated most often with **Brooklyn**, **Queens** and **Long Island**, and with New York City Jewish accents) to dentalize "t" and "d" to "ts" and "dz." Also, "tR" in some lower class accents shifts to "chR," so *try* is pronounced "chRI." Similarly, "dR" shifts to "dgR," so *dry* is pronounced "dgRI." A tapped "d" is often heard as a substitute for "t," as in the following examples.

Try to do it.
Phonetic pronunciations:
Queens: tsRI or tsRoy, chRI or chRoy, tse or *de*, d<u>oo</u> or dz<u>oo</u>, it
Note: You also hear *it* pronounced "its" [**Queens**]or "i?" [**Bronx**].
Brooklyn: tRoy *de* d<u>oo</u> it
Note that the final "t" is strongly aspirated, or, alternatively, dentalized.

Forget about it.
Phonetic pronunciation (originally New York Italian, now ubiquitous): fe ge' *de* bow', or ba', dit, or di?, or *dit*
Note that in the pronunciation "dit" the "t" is very lightly pronounced.

TH and th: These consonants typically shift to "d" and "t," respectively. Sometimes certain initial and/or final consonants are dropped. The words *going to* are "gaw' ne", or (lower class) "e' ne," with the initial and final "g" and the "t" in *to* dropped. *I'm going to go now* becomes "Am e' ne gO now." Initial "TH" is often dropped. An example: *Is that so?* is heard as "i zat sO," with the "z" in *is* linked to the "a" in *that*. *That's right* is pronounced "ats RIt."

Vowels and Diphthongs
schwa: Instead of a schwa in unstressed syllables, an "i" is often heard. Examples: *island* is "I' Lind"; *forward* is "faw' wid."

A: The "A" in *father* is often sounded like "aw" in *law*: *park* is "pawk."

a: For a typical lower-class very "flat" pronunciation of this vowel the lips are closed and narrowed to either side, as in the famous phrase *I can't stand it,* pronounced "I ka:n? sta:n' di*t.*"

aw: The "aw" in *law* is lengthened. *New York* is "N<u>oo</u> Yaw:k."

I: This vowel sometimes shifts to "oy." The words *like* and *night* are pronounced "loyk" and "noy?." On the other hand *I'm* is also pronounced "Am." *I'm here* is heard variously as "Am hee*e*" or "oym hee*e*" (New York Jewish); "Am heeR" (general New York City and New York Irish); or "Am hee" (New York Italian), etc.

o: The "o" in *bottle, got, not, on* and *sorry* is like "A" in *father.* Note: In the **South** and in the **Middle West** *on* is "awn"; *Chicago* sounds like "Chicawgo" in **Chicago.** In Chicago *on the table* is "awn the table." New Yorkers always say a rather nasal "An the table."

o: No longer much heard is the tendency associated with **Brooklyn,** discussed above under Southern accents, to pronounce "ir" and "or" in *first* and *work* as "foy:st" and "woy:k."

<u>oo</u>: The consonants followed by "<u>oo</u>," as in the words *news* and *duke* are almost never palatalized in lower-class New York speech: "ny<u>oo</u>z," "dy<u>oo</u>k." Instead these words are pronounced "n<u>oo</u>z" and "d<u>oo</u>k." *Few* is pronounced "fy<u>oo</u>," naturally, and in more educated speech the consonants before "<u>oo</u>" are often palatalized. The sound "y<u>oo</u>" is often called a "liquid u."

General New York City Practice

(Heard in the street)
Like they say "No, he ain't gonna do it." Please!
Phonetic pronunciation: LIk day say nO hee ayn? ge' ne d<u>oo</u> i? pLeez
Notes: The pronunciation could be heard in any ethnic group in New York City. The word *gonna* (going to) could also be pronounced "gaw' ne". Instead of a glottal stop on the "t" in *it* one could hear either a simple or a dentalized "t." In a New York City **Italian** accent, the diphthongs could be lengthened in *do* and *Please!* To make the same sentence into a **Jewish** New York City accent, you could dentalize the "d"s and "t"s; pronounce them with the tip of the tongue touching the back of the upper front teeth (except for the Bronx, where you should do a glottal stop). In a New York City **Irish** accent you might hear the "TH" correctly pronounced, and there might be no glottal stop on the "t" in *it*

The island of Manhattan is almost twelve miles long and absolutely filled with gorgeous buildings and parks and museums.
Phonetic pronunciation: THee I' lind uv man ha?n iz O mOst tweLv moy' eLz law: ngg and ab su l<u>oo</u>? lee fiLd with gaw:' dgis biL' dinggz and pawks and my<u>oo</u> zee' emz

168

1) The "d" at the end of the word *and* is often dropped.

2) The word *museum* is often pronounced "my<u>oo</u> zeem' " in lower-class and **Brooklyn** speech.

3) The glottal stop in *Manhattan* and *absolutely* is typical of the **Bronx**; otherwise say a regular unaspirated "t" in these words.

Didn't you hear what I said? I didn't ask you that. What do you want to do? Nothing? All right. Got to go. You're finished? I'm finished. Baddabing, baddaboom.
Phonetic pronunciation: din' che, or choo, hi:, or hi:R, wA' *d*I sed I din a:sk y<u>oo</u> da?, or da wa' *de* ye, or y<u>oo</u>, wa' ne d<u>oo</u>, or wa' che wa' ne d<u>oo</u> nuth' in, or nu?n. aw, or u, RIt' gA' *de* gO' yaw fin' isht Am fin' isht bA *d*A bi:ng' bA *d*A boom', or b<u>oo</u>m'
Notes:

1) If the final "R" in *hear* is pronounced, it should only be lightly pronounced. A **New York City Jewish** pronunciation of the word *here* might be "heee" and **New York City Irish** could be "heee" or "heeR," with a very light retroflex "R." A **New York City Hispanic** pronunciation could be "hi:R."

2) Notice the ubiquitous tapped "*d*" sounds. The "d" in *do* could also be dentalized: "dz<u>oo</u>." This is not necessarily true in a **New York City Hispanic** accent, where the "d" can be articulated fairly far back, and the lips protruded to form the vowel "<u>oo</u>" with the mouth very closed, forming a narrow opening. The **New York City Italian** version can be somewhat more open.

3) The expression (composed of nonsense syllables) *baddabing, baddaboom* is **Italian-American** and means "quick" or "just like that" or "before you knew it" or "that's it," and it has various other meanings depending on context (as do other expressions, such as the **Yiddish/Russian** *Nu*, meaning literally "Well," with or without a question mark; pronounced "n<u>oo</u>"; see Chapter Fourteen). In the case of the exercise sentence above it means "I'm out of here" (**New York City Italian** pronunciation: Am ow', or a', *de* hi). Notice the long "a:" in *ask*, characteristic of some **New York City Italian** speakers. Watch the HBO television series *The Sopranos* for some authentic examples.

He did it baddabing, baddaboom. And there we were, baddabing baddaboom, it was over.
Phonetic pronunciation: hee di' *d*it, or i?, bA *d*A bing' bA *d*A boom an de: wee wu bA *d*A bing bA *d*A b<u>oo</u>m' i? wuz O: vu

Tell him to put the turkey in the fridge, because there's a whole empty fridge there.
Phonetic pronunciation: teL im *t*e poot THe toR' kee in THe fridg bee kawz THe:z e hOL emp' tee fridg THe:
Notes: The vowel in the first syllable of the word *turkey* is very slightly pronounced, and could be absent altogether. The vowel is said to be "R-influenced," which means that the tongue wants to rise when forming the back consonant "k" (in this case), after the open vowel following the front consonant "t." The

same phenomenon is also heard in such words as *work* and *bird* in other non-rhotic accents, such as Boston and British RP: The tongue, in wanting to rise while air is still being forced through the vocal chords, forms a slight "R" sound.

He needs a new doctor and a new dentist.
Phonetic pronunciation: hee nee' dze n<u>oo</u> dAk' te Ra na n<u>oo</u> den' tist

There's another agenda here that you're aware of.
Phonetic pronunciation: THe:z e nu' THe Re dgen' de THat yaw Re we:' Ruv
Note: In the word *There's* an R-influenced vowel, i.e. a slight "R," may be heard.

There were some guys out there the other day. They were taking a survey on East Fifty-Eighth Street off Park Avenue.
Phonetic pronunciation: THe: we sum gIz owt THe: THee u' THe day THay we tsay' kin e soy' vay An eest fif' tee ayt stReet aw:f paw:k a:' vi ny<u>oo</u>
Notes: The dentalized "t" in the word *taking*, along with the dropped final "g," is perhaps associated with an **Irish** New York accent; with a "g" added to the "ng" and the initial "t" dentalized, it could be a **Jewish** New Yorker speaking, as could also be the case with the word *guys*, if pronounced, with a very short diphthong, as "gaweez" instead of "gIz." The pronunciation of the word *survey* varies, and a strong "soy" sound is seldom heard anymore. The sound could be transcribed as a short "seee." Also, the vowel in the syllable "sur-" is almost always R-influenced. The vowel in the first syllable of the word *avenue* could be very flat, almost an "e:." The pronunciation "a' vi n<u>oo</u>" is also heard, with either a flat "a" or a more open "a" in the first syllable.

(Overheard on the subway):
So Pearl introduces her to Helen's husband and you know what she says? "You're her husband? You have my condolences."
Phonetic pronunciation: sO poRL, or poyL, in tRi d<u>oo</u>', or dzoo' siz hu ti he' Linz huz' bind an ye nO wAt shee sez   yaw hu huz' bind y<u>oo</u> hav mI ken dO' Lin siz
Note: Another example of an R-influenced vowel: The "R" in *Pearl*, should be very light, if it is pronounced at all.

She talks a good game, but she can't do it. That's her problem!
Phonetic pronunciation: shee taw:ks e good gaym bet shee kant dz<u>oo</u>, or d<u>oo</u> i? THats hu pRAb' Lim

So she calls him at seven a.m. in the morning and he says "I can't talk to you now; I have to go to work." So she gets mad at him.
Phonetic pronunciation: sO shee kaw:Lz him at se' vin ay em in THe maw' ning, or ningg, an hee sez I kan, or kan?, or kant, taw:k te y<u>oo</u> now I haf te gO de woRk So shee gets ma:' da dim

That's her problem!
Phonetic pronunciation: THats hu pRAb' Lim

Yeah, well, she's not so easy to get along with either.
Phonetic pronunciation: ye: weL sheez nAt sO ee' zee *de* ge *de* law:ng, or law:ngg,
with ee' THe

That's her problem!
Phonetic pronunciation: THats hu pRAb' Lim

Boston and Massachusetts

There are several Boston and Massachusetts accents. Listen, for example, to
Bette Davis, who was from Lowell, Massachusetts. For a typical upper-class New
England accent listen to Katherine Hepburn, from Hartford, Connecticut. The
individual, distinctive accents of the Kennedy family, which can be heard in
many recordings and documentary films, as well as when Senator Ted Kennedy
speaks on television, is very broad, and is similar to the Boston accents described
below. Among other things, the Kennedys tend to lengthen stressed vowels and
diphthongs slightly. Boston accents are generally non-rhotic, but not always. In
any case a very lightly pronounced "R" is heard. The consonants "b," "d," "p," and
"t" are well articulated and tend to be the harder versions in final position as well
as in initial position.

The Most Important Sounds
Vowels and Diphthongs
schwa: Sometimes, in less educated Boston speech, a schwa is inserted after "e"
and before an "R" in such words as *caring* and *daring*: kee*R*ing, dee*R*ing. In unstressed syllables, in educated Boston speech, the schwa is used somewhat as it
is in British RP, so *business*, for example, is pronounced "biz' nes."

A: Bostonians usually say *bath*, *can't*, and *aunt* with the "A" in *father*. They say
going to as "gonna" or "gunna" (where the "u" is the sound in *but*). In Boston
Boston is "BAsten," whereas to a New Yorker the city is "Bawsten," or even
"Bawstin." In the Back Bay area the "A" in *park* is pronounced like the "a" in
that: pak. Elsewhere it is like General American "A."

a: Where in General American the vowel "A" occurs before "R," as in the word
car, in a Boston accent one either hears the "A" still, or, especially in Back Bay
accents, a shift to "a," so *car* is pronounced "ka:."

aw: "aw": shifts to the "A" in *father*, much as in the Middle West. In the Back Bay
area and even in Cambridge the "aw" often has a schwa inserted between itself
and a final "R," (not pronounced), so that *floor* is "fLOe" and *door* is "dOe." In

a more upper-class accent "aw" shifts to "o," as in British RP *hot*, *not*, and *got*. Note: This phenomenon also occurs occasionally in the non-rhotic Southern accents.

Practice words: *north, law, pork, hot, not, got*

o: "o" in *hot, not, got* is sounded as in Standard British.

oo: As in New York this vowel does not often have the semi-vowel "y" inserted between a consonant and itself in lower-class Boston speech, so *news* and *duke* are pronounced "nooz" and "dook." In upper-class Boston Brahmin speech "oo" is always palatalized: "nyooz" (news); "dyook" (duke).

Boston Practice

Park your car in Harvard Yard.
Phonetic pronunciations:
Back Bay: pak ye ka in haved yad
Upper-class Boston Brahmin: pAk ye kA in hAved yAd
Note that the vowels in the Brahmin accent are R-influenced.
Note, too, that, as in all non-rhotic accents, there is a "linking R." So *car in* could be pronounced "ca Rin" in the above sentence.

The law is very formal and strict in that regard.
Phonetic pronunciations:
Back Bay: The LA Rez ve' Ree fA' meL an strikt in THat Ree gad'
Upper-class Boston Brahmin: THe Lo Riz, or Lo iz, ve' Ree fo' meL an strikt in THat Re gAd'

The weather has cleared up nicely, so we can go out doors again, and the ice on the Charles River is starting to melt.
Phonetic pronunciations:
Upper-class Boston Brahmin: THe we' THe haz kLeee dup nIs' Lee sO wee kan gO owt' dOez e gen' and THee Is An THe chA:Lz Ri' ve Riz stA' ding te meLt
Back Bay: THe we' THe haz kLee: dup nIs' Lee sO wee kin, gO owt' dawz e gen' and THee Is awn THe chaLz, or chALz, Ri' ve iz, or Riz, sta', or stA', ding te meLt

Well, you can go up there if you want to, but I wouldn't recommend it.
Phonetic pronunciations:
Upper-class Boston Brahmin: weL yoo kan gO up THaye' Rif yoo wAn too bu dI wood' en rek' e mend it
Back Bay: weL ye kn gO up THe:' Rif ye wawn', or wAn', too, or waw', or wA', ne, be dI wood' en rek' e mend it

Boston is the cradle of liberty, and it's where the American Revolution began.
Phonetic pronunciations:
Upper-class Boston Brahmin: bos' ten iz THe kRay' deL ev Lib' e tee and its

way*e* THee *e* mer' *e* ken Rev *e* L<u>oo</u> shen bi, or bee, gan'
Back Bay: bAs' ten iz THe kRay' deL uv Lib' *e dee* an its we: THee *e* mer' *e* ken Rev *e* L<u>oo</u> shen bee gan'

There are certain things to be done at certain times, as a last resort, provided that is necessary, as far as what you are describing.
Phonetic pronunciation (**General Boston**): THe' RA so' ?n thingz te bee dun at so' ?n tImz az *e* la:st ri zaw*t*, or zaw?, pRe vI:' did THa diz ne' *se se* Ree ez fa: Rez, or Rez, wAt yaw, or y<u>oo</u> A, di skrI:' bing
Note: Notice the glottal stops in the word *certain*, the flapped "t" or glottal stop (speaker's choice) in *resort*, and the lengthened "a" sounds in the words *last* and *far*. You also have a choice of pronunciations for *you are*.

Down Home Maine

This is largely a coastal accent, but heard inland as well. The accent is strongly non-rhotic. It is perfect for some of the plays of Eugene O'Neill—*Desire Under the Elms*, for example—or the seafaring plays. It is perhaps best to ignore the phonetics as he writes them, though they do inform you that he wants the character to have an accent.

The Most Important Sounds
Consonants
ing: Final "g" in "ing" verb endings is dropped.

t: The combination "t" and "y" as in such phrases as "look at you" is pronounced "ch": lookeche.

Vowels and Diphthongs
This accent shares some of the same vowel shifts as the Boston accent, namely the "a" to "A" shift in such words as *can't* and *bath*; and the dropping of "y" before "<u>oo</u>" in such words as *news* and *duke*. Vowels are quite short in general. "Ayeh," meaning *yes*, is frequently heard.

A: The "A" in *what* is pronounced either as "u" or "e": wut, wet.

aw: The "aw" sound before "R" in words such as *door, important, for, folklore,* and *or* is pronounced like the "A" in *father*: dA, impAtnt, fA, fOkLA, A (meaning *or*). Sometimes, alternatively, a schwa is inserted, as it is in Boston, in such words as *floor* and *door*.

Down Home Maine Practice

Ayeh, there was a boat down there in the harbor last time I looked out the door.
Phonetic pronunciation: ay' *e* THe wez *e* bOt down THay' *e* Rin THe hA' be LAs tIm I look dowt THe dOe

That was quite a storm at sea and there were a lot of ships lost that day in the high winds and gales out there.
Phonetic pronunciation: THat wez kwI' *de* stAm owt THay' eR at see an THe: we' Re LA *de* ships LAst THat day in THe hI windz an gay' eLz owt THay' *e*

Perhaps it might be of some interest to you to remember the old days, when we went strawberry picking in summer and blueberry picking in fall, and everything wasn't available year round from some hothouse somewhere.
Phonetic pronunciation: praps it mIt bee *ev* sum in' trest te y<u>oo</u> te ree mem' be THee Ol dayz wen wee went stRaw' bRee pik' in in sum' *e* an bL<u>oo</u>' bRee pik' in fawL an ev' Ree thing wAz' ent *e* vayL' *e* beL yeee Rown fRem sum hot' hows sum' waye

If it wasn't for all that lightning and thunder them boats would have got in to harbor sooner.
Phonetic pronunciation: if twent fRawL THat lIt' nin an thun' *de* THem bOts woo' *dev* got in te hA' be s<u>oo</u>n' *e*

Well, there was nothing for it but we must go on till we got there.
Phonetic pronunciation: weL THe: wez nuth' in fA' Rit bet wee must gO awn tiL wee got THaye

As sure as I live and breathe these coasts and rocks and ocean waves that shine under the moon and stars are the most beautiful country on the face of the earth.
Phonetic pronunciation: a shooR az I Liv and bReeTH THeez kOsts en Roks en O' shen wayvs THet shIn un' *de* THe m<u>oo</u>n en stAz A THe mOst byoo *de* fooL kun' tRee awn THe fays ev THee oRth, or o:th
Note: The "R" in the word *earth* should be very lightly pronounced, if at all.

Some Notes on Philadelphia, Baltimore and Pennsylvania Dutch Accents

For Philadelphia and Baltimore see the information under "O" in Southern Accents. In Baltimore the "aw" is often sounded like "<u>oo</u>," as in the word *moor*, and diphthongized, and unstressed syllables are schwaed, so the name of the city sounds like "BAltem<u>oo</u>R." The "t" sometimes shifts to a tapped "d" or to an aspirated "t." Consonants in the middle of a word are sometimes dropped, so *everybody* is pronounced "eR bA' dee." For **Baltimore** practice see the exercises under **Southern Accent Practice**; for **Philadelphia** practice see the exercises under **More Middle Western Practice**.

A Pennsylvania Dutch accent is really a kind of German accent; the language of Pennsylvania Dutch is a variety of Plattdeutsch, or Low German. The accent is non-rhotic, with the "R" often shifting to "r," with one trill.

A Quick Reference for Pennsylvania Dutch

1) Do regular General American vowels and diphthongs.
2) Substitute "d" and "t" for "TH" and "th."
3) Substitute initial "v" for initial "w."
4) Shift voiced consonants "b," "d," "g," "v" and "z" at the end of a word to voiceless "p," "t," "k," "f" and "s."

Pennsylvania Dutch Practice

We were making cheese and doing the chores on the farm when the storm broke over the cornfields.
Phonetic pronunciation: vee ve may' kin, or king, chees an d<u>oo</u>' in, or ing, de chaws An de fAm ven de stawm brOk O' ve de kawn' feelts

The rolling hills and woods around York and Lancaster, Pennsylvania are very wonderful at all times of the year.
Phonetic pronunciation: de rOL' ink hiLs ent voots e rownt' yawk ent Lan' ke ste pen' siL vay' nye A ve' ree vun' de fooL a dawL tIms uf de yeee

There are a lot of things that remain to be done.
Phonetic pronunciation: de:r Ar e LA' def tinks dat ree mayn' t<u>oo</u> bee dun

You have got many things to consider if you want to accept his proposition or not. Because he's going to be coming around, and he wants an answer. You're going to have to decide.
Phonetic pronunciation: ye, or y<u>oo</u>, hef got me'nee tinks te, or t<u>oo</u>, kun si' de if ye, or y<u>oo</u>, vawn t<u>oo</u> ak sept' his prAp', or brAp, e si shen aw not   bi kaws' hees gaw' ne bee ku' min e rownt' en hee vawnts en en', or a:n', se y<u>oo</u> Ar, or yaw, gaw' ne hef te di sIt'

I didn't know what to do about it, so I end up doing nothing and just waiting for something to happen.
Phonetic pronunciation: I di' den nO vAt te, or t<u>oo</u>, d<u>oo</u> e bow' dit sO I ent up d<u>oo</u> ink nu' dink en dgust, or chust, vay' dink fe, or faw, sum' tink te, or t<u>oo</u>, hep' en, or em

We should all be happy with our own house and garden and being at peace with the neighbors and the world.
Phonetic pronunciation: vee shoo' dawl bee hep' ee vi' dA rOn' hows en gA' den en bee' in et pees vit, or vi, de nay' bes ent di vawrlt, or velt

Hawaii and Samoa
The Native Accents of the South Pacific Islanders

The population of the Hawaiian Islands consists of native Hawaiians, Americans of European and African ancestry, Puerto Ricans, Spaniards, Philippinos, Chinese and Japanese, all of whom have contributed their linguistic influence to the Hawaiian accent, as did the Hawaiian and Hawaiian Creole languages. After World War Two there was a great immigration of workers from Samoa to the plantations of Hawaii.

Hawaiian and Samoan are related Polynesian languages. They belong to a subgroup of the Malayo-Polynesian family, which contains hundreds of languages. The Hawaiian language has given us the place names on the islands of this Pacific state: Honolulu, Maui, and so forth. General American is the accent usually heard there, as it is in Alaska. There are nevertheless a few phonetic characteristics particularly associated with a native Hawaiian accent. The same phonetic characteristics also apply to Samoa, with the exceptions noted below. These accents would be fine in *South Pacific* by Rodgers and Hammerstein.

Notes on the Phonetics of the Hawaiian and Samoan Languages

Hawaiian has only six consonants: "h," "k," "l," "m," "n" and "p." It has five vowels: A, e, i, o, <u>oo</u> (spelled "u"); and one semi-vowel: w. Syllables begin with either a consonant or a vowel, but all syllables end in a vowel. All of this has heavily influenced the accent of native Hawaiian speakers in English, and has contributed to the accent of people whose first language is English. There is no "R" and no "s." *Merry Christmas* in Hawaiian is *Mele Kelikimaka*, with every syllable evenly pronounced and no schwa substituting for any vowel. *Aloha* and *ukelele* are Hawaiian words.

The phonetics of Samoan are a bit different. There are more consonants: "f," "g," "s," "t" and "v," in addition to the Hawaiian consonants. There are no semi-vowels, the usual five vowels, as above, and no "r," "d," "b," or "z."

How to Do a Hawaiian Accent

The Most Important Sounds
Consonants
Note: Consonants in final position are generally voiceless, where they are voiced in General American.
h: sometimes dropped: *He dropped his hat.* (hee dRAp deez hat)

R: The native Hawaiian accent in English varies between being rhotic and non-rhotic, and when there is a non-rhotic pronunciation the vowels are heavily r-influenced. The Samoan accent is non-rhotic. This is not surprising, since there is no "R" in either Hawaiian or Samoan. However, when the Hawaiian accent is rhotic, it is a heavy, almost Middle West "R" which is heard.

s and z: Final "s" in the spelling of *was* and in plurals, usually pronounced "z" in General American, is voiceless: *was* (wuz) is pronounced "wus."

TH and th: "TH" and "th" are replaced often by "d" and "t."

There is some consonant cluster reduction in final position. The "t" in *last* would be dropped, as would the "d" in *end*. In initial position, on the other hand, some consonant clusters become more complicated. The word *strain* is pronounced "shtRayn," and *train* becomes "chRayn." (The information about initial consonant additives does not apply to a Samoan accent.)

?: Sometimes a final "t" or "k" or "d" is replaced by a glottal stop: bi? (bit); drin? (drink); clou? (cloud). The name of the state has at least six pronunciations in the Hawaiian Islands themselves: hAwI?' ee; hAvI?' ee; hAwoy'; hAvoy'; hAwI'; and hAvI. Glottal stops exist in the Hawaiian language, but this phenomenon in English is perhaps more a reflection of a Chinese influence. In words like *bottle* and *battle*, on the other hand, the "t" is heard not as a glottal stop but as a soft aspirated "t," and sometimes almost like an "s."

Vowels and Diphthongs
a: The "e" in *met* and *dress* and the "a" in *that* are both pronounced, as in the Middle West, "ae": maet, dRaes, THaet.

aw: As in the West and Middle West the "a" in *water* and *call* shifts to "A": wA deR; kAL. Note the tapped "d" in *water*.

oo: This vowel is almost never palatalized after a consonant. "nyooz" (news) and "dyook" (duke) are pronounced "nooz" and "dook." Of course *few* is pronounced "fyoo."

u: There is no difference between the "u" in *but* and the "A" in *father*. Both are pronounced like "A" in *father*.

Stress
There is a tendency, due to Japanese and Philippino influence perhaps, as well as to the influence of Hawaiian Creole, to stress words more evenly than in General American. All the syllables sound fairly even, in other words.

Pitch
In native Hawaiian accents there is sometimes a high-pitched rapid delivery ending on an even higher note on the most important syllable of a question. See below under Hawaiian Practice for an example in the question "Gonna come home late tonight?" The syllable "-night," which is the most strongly stressed of the entire sentence, is pronounced on the highest pitch of the sentence, after a staccato, almost unstressed delivery of the previous words.

Hawaiian Practice
(For actual sounds; Note the Middle Western quality of the hard "R.")
The warriors are here in their boats in the water around the bend in the river.

177

Phonetic pronunciation: THe wA' RyeRz eR heeeR in THeR bo:ts in THe wA' deR e Rownd' THe biend in THe Ri' veR

Gonna come home tonight?
Phonetic pronunciation: gaw' ne kum hOm t<u>oo</u> nI?

Possible Pitch Pattern

night?
Gonna come home late to-

I stopped in to have a little bit to drink with him, but we didn't stay long.
Phonetic pronunciation: I stApt in te haev e li' del bi? te dRink wi' THeem but wee di' dent stay Lang

The spectacular volcanoes of Hawaii are the most incredible sights in the world.
Phonetic pronunciation: THe spek tak' ye LeR vawL kay' nOz uv he wA' yee, or ee, AR THe mOst in kRe' di: beL sIts in THe woRL

You can see the most gorgeous tropical flowers and tropical birds all over the is-lands.
Phonetic pronunciation: y<u>oo</u> kan see The mOs gawR' dgus tRA' pee keL fLowRs an tRA' pee keL boRds AL O' veR THee I' Lendz, or Lents

Once you come here you will never want to leave. The weather is perfect all year round.
Phonetic pronunciation: wunts y<u>oo</u> kum heeeR y<u>oo</u> wiL ne' veR wawn t<u>oo</u> Leev. THe we' THeR is poR' fik AL yeeeR Rown

Chapter Seven
Canada: French and English Canadian Accents

Canadian English, which is very much the same all over Canada, and has been called "Central/Prairie Canadian English," resembles General American very strongly, but differs from it in a few important phonetic points. It is a very clear and well-articulated accent of English. There is a well-known clichéd ending to Canadian declarative sentences, which turns them into questions. It consists of adding the monosyllable "eh?" to the sentence. In General American this would be pronounced with the lips parted downwards, but in a Canadian accent the lips are drawn slightly to the side, as in a smile. The few regional differences which exist in Canada do not change the basic idea of the accent: Speech in the middle prairie provinces tends to be slow in rhythm, and in Nova Scotia an "R" is often intruded in such words as *after* and *wash*, pronounced ARf' teR and wARsh, or wawRsh. In Newfoundland the vowel "A" regularly shifts to "aw," and "TH" and "th" shift to "d" and "t"; and there is a feeling of Somerset in England, with the occsasional shift of "s" to "z": *summer* is pronounced "zu' meR." But you can still follow the rules laid out below.

Canadian French, on the other hand, differs considerably from the French spoken in France, both phonetically and lexically. There are a number of Canadian French accents in French:
1) the accent of Quebec City
2) the accent of Montreal
3) the rural accents of Quebec Province.

For all they have in common, they also have very distinct differences. A Montreal accent, for example, is much more clearly articulated than the accents of the city of Quebec or the countryside.

Canadian French is a descendant of 17th century Norman French, since many of the immigrants came from Normandy to settle in Quebec. In the 1750s, during the colonial wars between Britain and France, Quebec City fell to England after a bloody battle on the Heights of Abraham, just outside the city. Both the Marquis de Montcalm, the French commander, and General James Wolfe, the British commander, were killed. Although the British asserted their hegemony, the French clung proudly and fiercely to their culture and to their language. This era and the aftermath of the war are the sources of the political problems resulting from anti-French discrimination throughout Canadian history. Despite the fact that both French and English are the official languages of Canada, French has less prestige in largely English-speaking Canada, and discrimination on linguistic grounds has persisted to the present day even in parts of Quebec Province, such as the city of Montreal.

For an example of good clear Canadian English diction listen to anchorman Peter Jennings on ABC Nightly News. Listen, too, to Alex Trebek, the host of the television quiz show "Jeopardy." The marvelous television series *The Kids in the Hall* features a group of young Canadian actors (Dave Foley, Bruce McCulloch, Kevin McDonald, Mark McKinney, Scott Thompson) in hilarious satirical sketches. Donald Sutherland, wonderful in such films as *Ordinary People* (1980) and *Eye of the Needle* (1981), and many others, has superb Canadian English diction. His son, Kiefer Sutherland, who also has very fine speech, spent much of his youth in Toronto. You can hear him in *Flatliners* (1990) and *A Few Good Men* (1992), among many other films. The charming Michael J. Fox, the star of the television series "Spin City" and of the *Back to the Future* film series is from Edmonton. Brendan Fraser, the handsome, brilliant, versatile actor whose diction is impeccable, and who stars in such films as *The Passion of Darkly Noon* (1995), *With Honors* (1991), *Gods and Monsters* (1998)—listen to Sir Ian McKellen's wonderful British RP speech—and *School Ties* (1992), as well as such romps as *George of the Jungle* (1997) and *Dudley Do Right* (1999), was born in Indianapolis, traveled much as a child (his father was a Canadian tourism official), and grew up partly in Canada, where he studied theater. And Fay Wray may have come from Canada, but her screams in *King Kong* (1933) are pure Hollywood. The eminent actor Hume Cronyn, who made his stage debut in 1930, and whose career on stage and screen has thus spanned seventy-one years so far, in *Lifeboat* (1944) and *Cocoon* (1985), to name only two of his films, is eminently worth listening to for some of the best and clearest diction you will ever hear. Among other prominent actors of Canadian origin, all of whom speak beautifully, are: Colleen Dewhurst (*Annie Hall*, 1977); the elegant, noble Walter Pidgeon always wonderful and greatly dignified in his dozens of films, including *How Green Was My Valley*, 1941, and *Funny Girl*, 1968, in which he played Ziegfeld; Raymond Massey (many films, including *Abe Lincoln in Illinois*, 1940; he was memorable as Lincoln); Leslie Nielsen (hilarious comedies, including *The Naked Gun*, 1988); the inimitable Walter Huston (dozens of films, including *The Treasure of the Sierra Madre*, 1948); William Shatner (best know as Captain Kirk in the "Star Trek" television series); Raymond Burr (Perry Mason to many); and Lorne Greene (star of the televison series "Bonanza"). To this list you can add the versatile and brilliant Christopher Plummer (who can sound British or American at will), Margot Kidder, Pamela Anderson, Joseph Wiseman, Dan Ackroyd, John Candy, the riotously funny Jim Carrey, Rick Moranis, Martin Short, Mike Myers, Neve Campbell, the stunning Yvonne de Carlo (her career in films has spanned fifty years; see her in *For Whom the Bell Tolls*, 1943, and *The Captain's Paradise*, 1953, with Alec Guiness), Catherine O'Hara, Jennifer Tilly, Meg Tilly and Mary Pickford, "America's Sweetheart," known mostly for her silent films. (I do not include people who were born in Canada but grew up in the United States.) To people who do not know that these actors are from Canada, they simply sound like Americans with exceptionally fine, clear speech, but, if you listen carefully, you will hear individual versions of the Canadian accent, in some cases stronger than in others, of course. Generally absent from the accents of most of the people listed above is the famous Canadian pronunciation of the diphthong "ow" in such words as *out, about,* and *house.* Among French Canadian actors Lothair Bluteau (*Jesus of Montreal,* 1989, in French) has only a slight accent in English, and Geneviève Bujold, in such films as *Anne of the Thousand Days* (1969) has almost no French accent to speak of, except for the softness of her consonants.

A Quick Reference (English Canadian)

1) Canadian accents are heavily rhotic.
2) The vowel "ow" is pronounced "u'<u>oo</u>" when it ends a word or before a voiceless consonant; "ow" before a voiced consonant.
3) The diphthong "I" is often pronounced "*e*'ee."
4) *Been* usually rhymes with *bean,* but may also sometimes rhyme with *bin.*

How to Do an English Canadian Accent

Information on pitch and stress is unnecessary for Americans, as there are no differences. British actors using this book should look at the phonetic indications in Chapter Six on Regional American accents and at the comparison between General American and British RP in the Introduction.

1) Position of the Vocal Apparatus
The position of the vocal apparatus is much the same as for the accents of the American Midwestern states, particularly northern Wisconsin and Minnesota, where the jaw is somewhat tight and the lips a bit more closed and drawn a bit to the side than in General American. This position is not to be exaggerated; it is very slightly different from General American.

2) The Most Important Sounds
The consonants are very strong and well articulated. Canadian English, like the American of the Midwest states, is strongly rhotic. More important are the vowels and diphthongs. Vowels tend to be short, and there are some specific phenomena to bear in mind. In general Canadians use the same vowel system as that of General American.

aw: Close to the sound heard in Midwestern American accents, this vowel shifts to "o," as in British RP *not. Law* and *saw* are pronounced "Lo" and "so." *Thought* and *taught* are pronounced "tho*t*" (Note the aspirated final "t") and "tot." In making this sound the throat is more closed than in most American accents.

e: In an unstressed syllable before an "R," "e" often shifts to a schwa (*e*). For example, the word *there,* when not stressed, becomes "THeR." On the other hand *bury* is usually pronounced "be' Ree," but *strawberry* is usually pronounced "stRo' bRee."

i: Words with final syllables containing the vowel "i" and other words with this vowel in unstressed syllables are often pronounced with the vowel lengthened to either "ee" or "i:." Some examples: *finish* (fin' eesh); *punish* (pun' eesh); management (man' i:dg ment).

I: This is one of the characteristic Canadian sounds, the diphthong being pronounced "*e*'ee" instead of the General American "A'ee."

ow: This is the other typical Canadian sound. Before a voiceless consonant or when it is the end of a word, instead of saying "a'<u>oo</u>," as in General American, the Canadian says "u'<u>oo</u>." *About* and *house* are pronounced "*e* bu<u>oo</u>t" and "hu<u>oo</u>s." *How now, brown cow* sounds like "hu<u>oo</u> nu<u>oo</u> bru<u>oo</u>n ku<u>oo</u>." However, before a voiced consonant it is pronounced "ow," as in words like *cloud* and *clown*.

Further Phonetic Information

A and a: These vowels are pronounced as in General American, and do not change to "A" as they do in British RP.

w: Words spelled with "wh" are pronounced with "hw": *white* is "hweeet." This is true in Toronto and in Ontario generally, but not true in the Western Provinces, where "wh" is pronounced in the same way as it is in General American.

y<u>oo</u>: The "y" is usually not pronounced in words like *news* and *duke*. Canadians say "n<u>oo</u>z" and "d<u>oo</u>k."

L: The Canadian "L" is pronounced with the blade of the tongue more closely pressed to the roof of the mouth than the General American "L," which drops the blade of the tongue slightly. This is called a "dark L."

t: The "t" is sometimes strongly aspirated at the end of a word, and even sometimes in the middle of a word, so *matter* is sometimes pronounced "ma' *te*R." "What's the matter?" is pronounced either "hwots THe ma' *te*R" or "hwots THe ma' *te*R."

Practice

We were out and about on the Canadian plains, just riding our horses.
Phonetic pronunciation: wee we RO?' ne bOt An THe ke nay' dee en, ke nay' dgen, playnz dgust RI' ding AR hawR' siz

Do come in and join us for a cup of tea. Or do you prefer coffee?
Phonetic pronunciation: doo' kmin an dgoyn' es fRe kup' ev tee' awR dy<u>oo</u> pRi feR' ko' fee

Now that's not right, you know.
Phonetic pronunciation: now THats not, or nawt, Rit ye nO

We had a wonderful meal there, and it was so delicious we could hardly finish all of it.
Phonetic pronunciation: wee had e wun' deR feL meeL THe:R and it wez sO di Li' shes wee kood hARd' Lee fin' eesh, or i:sh, or ish, oL, or AL, ev it

We finished about two thirds of it, which was sort of a pity.
Phonetic pronunciation: wee fin' eesht e bOt t<u>oo</u> thoRdz ev it, or it, wich wez sawR tev, or dev, e pi' tee, or tee

Finish what you're doing and come outside. We don't have all day, you know. We're about to leave for a long time. Anyway, it's too hot out there.
Phonetic pronunciation: fin' eesh wu' cheR d<u>oo</u>' eeng an kum Ot' sId   wee don't hav AL day ye nO   wi:R e bOt' te Leev fRe Long tIm   e' nee way its too haw' dOt THe:R

That about completes our survey of Canadian English, eh?
Phonetic pronunciation: THat e bu<u>oo</u>t' kum pLeets AR seR' vay ev ke nay' dee en ing' Lish ay

Two Specific Canadian Pronunciations:
khaki (kAR' kee); *bilingual* (bI, or be'ee, lin' gy<u>oo</u> el)

A Quick Reference (French Canadian)

1) For a heavy accent stress the last syllables of phrases.
2) Substitute "d" and "t" for "TH" and "th."

How to Do a French Canadian Accent

See Chapter Eight on French accents, with particular reference to the advice on the position of the vocal apparatus and stress. Many French Canadians speak English with only a very slight accent, if any.

1) Position of the Vocal Apparatus
In Canadian French the position of the vocal apparatus is slightly different from the position described in Chapter Eight. The jaw is a bit looser and lower than in French French, which makes a Canadian French accent different immediately. It also makes it fairly easy for French Canadians to get the correct positioning in the pronunciation of English.
2) The Most Important Sounds
Consonants
Some of these differ markedly from the French of France. Canadian French veers between being rhotic and non-rhotic.

d and t: In Quebec, but not in Montreal, these consonants are pronounced "dz" and "ts."

r: Instead of the French uvular "R" the "r" is often trilled. One does also hear the uvular "R" in Quebec, however, less often in Montreal. This can sometimes carry over into English, so *thrilled* is pronounced "tri:ld."

TH and th: These sounds do not exist in French. French Canadians usually substitute "d" and "t" for the voiced and voiceless consonants, respectively.

Vowels and Diphthongs
The vowel system of Canadian French does not differ markedly from that of the French of France. See Chapter Eight. However, the following differences are notable:

A: In Canadian French "A" often becomes "aw," so for example *parc* (park) becomes "paw" in Quebec, where endings of words are often dropped, and "pawr" in Montreal. In Standard French the word is pronounced "pARk." I was once walking past a small park with the father and children of the family with whom I was staying one summer in Quebec City, studying French at Laval, and I asked its name. He said, "Oh, c'est le Parc des Braves." Not until I passed a joint statue of Montcalm and Wolfe with the name of the park on its base did I realize that it was called "The Park of the Heroes." He pronounced the French name "le paw dze bRaw." The "e" in "dze" (of the) was so slight as to be almost not there. In Standard French it would be pronounced "le pARk de bRAv."

Nasal vowels: In Quebec City and in the countryside, one usually hears "ye" (the semi-vowel "y" being very slight) inserted after a nasal vowel, diphthongizing the syllable. Thus *quinze* (fifteen) is pronounced by many Quebec City residents as "kayenz." In Montreal it is a shortened "kenz," whereas in Standard French it is "kanz." In Quebec people say "kayenz dzo law' " for *quinze dollars* (fifteen dollars) and in Montreal they say "kenz do lawr'."

Stress

See Chapter Eight. The same rules apply to all dialects and accents of French. Because French Canadians are surrounded by English it is perhaps easier for them to learn correct stressing in English.

Pitch

There is a particular French Canadian pitch pattern which sometimes carries over into an accent in English. It consists of a rising then falling tone at the end of a declarative sentence, which is said on a lengthened and sometimes diphthongized vowel. This is very different from the patterns discussed in Chapter Eight.

Practice

Je peux le dire.
Translation: I can say it/so.
Phonetic pronunciation: zhe po le dzi: e; Standard French would be "di:R"; Canadian French would sometimes be "dzi: eR."

> \di-
>   ire.
>   peux
> Je   le

Note the falling tone on *dire*, diphthongized in a Canadian French accent.

I'm going to tell you, that's right, me, I'm going to make it plain to you what I think.
Phonetic pronunciation: (Note that the stress group endings are indicated by the symbol "//.") Am gaw' ne tel you// das rIt me// Am gaw' ne me: k i:t ple:n t<u>oo</u> y<u>oo</u>// wA dI ti: nk//.

By gar, if that's the way they want it that's the way it's going to be.
Phonetic pronunciation: bI gAR, or gAr, i:f dats de way day wawn i:t dats di way i:ts gaw' ne bee
Note: The expression *by gar* [by God] is an old clichéd version of a Canadian French accent. It's what French trappers say in such forgotten novels as Robert W. Chambers' *The Little Red Foot* (George F. Doran Company, 1921), a story that takes place upstate New York during the American Revolution.

The elections are going to be held whether they want them to be or not. Our voices will be heard!
Phonetic pronunciation: dee i lek' shens AR gaw' ne be held', or eld', we' deR day wawn em t<u>oo</u> awR not' Ar, or AR, voy' si:s wi:l be o:Rd, or ho:Rd, or ho:Rd, or o:Rd

The English may have captured the land of Canada, but they never captured our hearts.
Phonetic pronunciation: dee ing gleesh' may av kap shoRd' dee land ov ka na dA' bu day nev' eR' kap shoRd A rARts'
Note the three different pronunciations "R," "r" and "R" in the same person's speech; people are inconsistent sometimes in their own accents, and this is a good lesson for the actor who wants to sound absolutely real.

Montreal and Quebec have some of the best restaurants in the world.
Phonetic pronunciation: mawn ré Al' an ké bek' av som ov dee bes res taw rawn i:n dee wo:rl'

It's too much, I tell you, just too much, don't you think?
Phonetic pronunciation: i:s ts<u>oo</u> moch A tel y<u>oo</u> dgos ts<u>oo</u> moch dzOn y<u>oo</u> ti:nk
Note: Remember that in Québecois French "t" and "d" are often dentalized, and pronounced "ts" and "dz." This can carry over into an accent in English, but it is rare.

186

Part Three

Romance Language Accents

Introduction:
The Pronunciation of Latin

The principal Romance languages, each of which has many dialects and accents are French, Spanish, Portuguese, Italian, and Romanian. Less widely spoken are Catalan, Occitan, Provençal (the language of the medieval troubadours in France), Gascon, Sardinian (with two dialects, and the closest of the Romance languages to Latin), Romansch (one of the four official languages of Switzerland), and Ladino, also known as Judezhmo or Judeo-Spanish (the medieval Jewish language consisting of Spanish with numerous Hebrew vocabulary elements) which the Jews of Spain brought with them to other Mediterranean lands after the expulsion of 1492.

All the Romance languages have their origin in Latin, the language of the Roman Empire. Each of the Romance languages replaced Latin, which had superseded the local tribal languages of the conquered peoples. These ancient, forgotten tribal tongues contributed elements of vocabulary to the evolving local dialects of Latin and thence to the Romance languages. Thus French contains Germanic elements from the lost languages of the Frankish tribes; Spanish and Portuguese have vocabulary from the tribes of the Iberian Penninsula and from the Arabs who lived there for eight hundred years; and Romanian retains a large Slavic vocabulary. The pronunciation of the Romance languages was unquestionably heavily influenced by the phonetic elements of those forgotten tribal languages. Hence we get *oeil* in French, *occhio* in Italian, *ojo* in Spanish, *olho* in Portuguese, and *ochi* in Romanian, all meaning "eye," and all from Latin *oculus*.

Latin was actually a number of Italic dialects, of which that of the city-state of Rome came to dominate the linguistic, as it did the political, scene. Related languages, now extant only in the form of inscriptions, were Oscan and Umbrian, and one can just imagine some ancient Roman comedy, now lost in the mists of antiquity, in which some comic character speaks with an Oscan accent, and says, as in one surviving Oscan inscription, "kvaisster" for *quaestor* (a Roman court judge, later a high Roman official; presumably pronounced "kwI' stawr").

Latin completely killed off the one non-Indo-European language of the northern part of the Italian peninsula, Etruscan, largely by integrating and Romanizing the Etruscan population. The Etruscan language survives only in the form of inscriptions that nobody has been able to decipher completely to this day. Apparently Etruscan was spoken in ancient Rome for centuries alongside Latin. Once the Etruscan king Tarquinius Superbus (Tarquin the Proud) was deposed and the Republic replaced the Etruscan monarchy, the Latin speakers simply took over the entire government, and the pressure on the Etruscans to assimilate was very strong.

As it evolved, Latin developed several forms. These included the classical literary and administrative Latin of Ancient Rome, the spoken language of Ancient Rome, which, judging by the comedies of Terence and Plautus, must have been somewhat different from the written language, and the dialects of the provinces of the Roman Empire. Medieval Church Latin was, of course, a later development, used not only in the Roman Catholic Mass, but also in universities and schools as the language of education and communication throughout Europe and North Africa.

Since Latin was the everyday language of government and commerce, its hegemony was assured. By the time the Roman Empire broke apart, Latin was so entrenched that it simply continued to survive in the cathedral and the university, and its provincial dialects and accents continued to evolve into the Romance languages which replaced it in ordinary speech and daily affairs.

One of the most important elements of concern for the actor attempting to master Romance language accents is the phenomenon of "rhythmic phrasing," which refers to the habit of stressing one or more syllables in an entire phrase, rather than in an individual word, so that the stress in an individual word can shift depending on its position in the phrase. For a detailed explanation of how this affects the specific accent under discussion, see the chapters on the individual languages, beginning with Chapter Eight on French Accents. French is the extreme example of a language in which rhythmic phrasing is the system of stressing, but all the Romance languages have this tendency to a greater or lesser degree.

Another important thing to bear in mind is that many Europeans learn the standard British accent of English, so that their English is often non-rhotic and follows the British vowel system. Using the accent of RP will make you sound more foreign immediately to an American audience's ears.

In most of the Romance languages the trilled "r" is used. Learning this sound gives you a very useful tool for a great many non-Romance accents as well. (See 4 under "A Quick Reference" for "Rhotic (R) Sounds" on page 13 for the method of learning to trill an "r," if you cannot already do so.)

Learning the exact sound of the European continental version of the vowel "i" will also provide you with a useful tool. This sound can be described as intermediate between the "i" in *bit* and the "ee" in *meet*; quite literally, as the tongue is slightly lower in position than for "i" and slightly higher than for "ee." (See Fig. 2 on page 11.) If you accurately learn these two sounds, "r" and "i," which exist only very rarely in accents native to English, you can begin to create almost any European accent.

Two Systems of Latin Pronunciation

No one knows exactly how the ancient Romans pronounced their language. However, it is conjectured by various scholars, such as L. R. Palmer, S. F. Bonner, A. Ernout and R. G. Kent, that the system described below is as accurate as it can be for the pronunciation of the standard literary language, given inevitable dialectical and accentual variations in the spoken language. There are Elizabethan anglicized pronunciations of ancient Roman names, some of which you can see in Chapter One in the section on the pronunciation of names in Shakespeare's plays, and of legal phrases still used in the courts (see below). When Latin phrases occur in plays, pronounce them depending on the context in which they appear: anglicized in a British courtroom drama; in the medieval way if you are playing an ecclesiastic, etc. If you are playing a cleric who has to recite various portions of services in Latin, I suggest you pronounce the medieval church Latin with the accent of the country's language, which is typically the way it was spoken in the days when Latin was still the language of the Mass. For example, I have heard Latin pronounced with a distinctly French accent at High Mass in Québec City, with a uvular French "R"; with an Italian accent at a church service in Florence; and with an American accent in New York City and in Providence, RI. In the film of Frank McCourt's *Angela's Ashes* (1999) you can hear brief portions of funeral and other services in Latin with an Irish acent.

There are two principal systems of pronunciation of the Latin language: the (conjectural) ancient Roman, Classical pronunciation, that of Julius Caesar, Horace, Catullus and Virgil; and Medieval Church Latin. The Elizabethan anglicized system has given way in Great Britain to the Classical pronunciation, so British students are no longer taught to say "vee' nI vI' dI vI' sI" for Julius Caesar's famous phrase *veni vidi vici* (I came, I saw, I conquered), but "we' nee wee' dee wee' kee," just as we are taught to do in the United States. In Medieval Latin this phrase is pronounced "ve' nee vee' dee vee' chee." Here are the sounds of the two systems, compared:

Vowels and Diphthongs
The vowels in both systems are much the same, but that of the diphthongs differs in the two systems. Pronunciation of pure vowels, all of which have long and short versions, follows approximately the system of Italian:

a: Both systems: A; ae: Classical: always I as in *Caesar* (kI' sAr), from which is derived German *Kaiser* (kI' ze) and Russian *Czar* (zAR) or *Tsar* (tsAR); Medieval: ay; au: Classical: ow; Medieval: ow or (sometimes) aw. Some ancient Romans apparently pronounced "au" as "aw," so the name of the emperor *Claudius* was heard as either "klow' dee oos" or "klaw' dee oos."
e: e; ei: Both systems: ay; eu: Classical: y<u>oo</u>; Medieval: ay'<u>oo</u>
i: Both systems: i: or ee, when a long vowel
o: o; oe: Classical: oy; Medieval: ay
u: Both systems: <u>oo</u> in long syllables; oo in short syllables, as in the ending *-us* in *Julius* (y<u>oo</u>' lee oos); ui: Both systems: <u>oo</u>'ee, but after q: wee

190

y: Classical: like modern French or German ü; Medieval: ee

Consonants

The consonants d, f, h, k, l, m, n, p (the combination ph is pronounced p in the Classical system, f in the Medieval), should be pronounced in both systems much as they are in English. The letter j did not originally exist, although it is used in later Latin writing, and is always pronounced "y." Nor did the letter w exist, and the sound of this semiconsonant was spelled with the letter "u" or "v." During the period of the Roman Republic the previously unknown letters z and k were introduced, to be used in spelling transliterated Greek words. There were no th sounds, and the combination th should be pronounced "t."

b: Classical: b as in English, but the combinations bs and bt were pronounced ps and pt; Medieval: b as in English

c: Classical: always k; Medieval: ch before i, e, ae and oe; k before a, o, u; cc: Classical: always like two k sounds; Medieval: ch before e or i, k elsewhere; ch: Both systems: k

g: Classical: always a hard g; Medieval: dg before i, e and hard g before a, o, u; gg: Classical: always like two hard g sounds in a row; Medieval: dg before e and I, elsewhere like two hard g sounds; gn: Classical: as in English; Medieval: ny

q: Both systems: always in orthographic combination with u; pronounced kw

r: Classical: probably given one trill; Medieval: given one trill. However, in Church ceremonies this sound was pronounced (as I have heard it done) as the rhotic sound is in the country where Mass used to be celebrated in Latin, i.e. R in France or Québec City, r in Italy, R in the United States.

s: Classical: always like English s; Medieval: s, except between two vowels or following a voiced consonant, where it is pronounced z

t: Classical: hard t; Medieval: ts before i, e and hard t before a, o, u

v: Classical: w; Medieval: v

x: Classical: ks; Medieval: ks, except in words starting with ex and followed by h, s or a vowel: gz

z: Both systems: dz

Stress

In two-syllable words, stress the first syllable. In words of three or more syllables stress the penultimate (next to last) syllable with the long vowel, or the antepenultimate (third from the end) if the vowel in the penultimate syllable is short. It is impossible to clarify this rule further without the reader's learning the language, but notice where the stressed syllable falls in the words and passages below.

Some Latin words

caelum (heaven; also spelled *coelum*) Classical: kI' Loom or koy' Loom; Medieval: chay' Loom; *civitas* (city) Classical: ki' wi tAs; Medieval: chi' vi tAs; *gravitas* (weight, heaviness, importance) Classical: grA' wi tAs; Medieval: grA' vi tAs;

humanus (human, humane, cultivated) Both systems: h<u>oo</u> mA' noos; *inclino* (to bend, to turn back) Both systems: in klee' no; *invictus* (unconquered) Classical: in wi:k' toos; Medieval: in vi:k' toos; *miser* (poor, miserable, unhappy) Classical: mi:' se:r; Medieval: mi:' ze:r; *mors* (death) Classical: mawRs; Medieval: mawRz

The opening sentence of Julius Caesar's *de Bello Gallico* (*Of the Gallic War*; phonetic pronunciation: de: beL' o: gA' Li: ko:)
Gallia est omnis divisa in partes tres, quarum unam incolunt Belgae, aliam Aquitani, tertiam qui ipsorum linguae Celtae, nostra Galli appellantur.
Phonetic pronunciation: gA' Lee A est om' ni:s di wee' sA in pAR' te:s tRe:s kwA' room <u>oo</u>' nAm in ko:' loont beL' gI A' lee Am A kwi tA' nee te:R' tee Am kwee ip so:' Room Lin' gwI keL' tI nos' tRA gA' Lee A peL An' tooR
Translation: All of Gaul is divided into three parts, of which the first is inhabited by the Belgae, the second by the Aquitani, the third by those who in their own language are called Celts, in ours Gauls.
Literal translation: Gaul is of-all divided in parts three, of which first inhabit Belgians, second Aquitanians, third who in-own/self language Celts, ours Gauls are-called.

Some religious words and phrases, pronounced in the Medieval Church manner:
Ad majorem Dei gloriam (to the greater glory of God; this is the motto of the Jesuits) Ad mA yaw' rem day' ee glaw' ree Am; *Agnus Dei* (Lamb of God) A' nyoos day' ee (Classical: Ag' noos); *Deo gratias* (God be thanked, or thanks to God) day' O grA' tsee As; *Domine, non sum dignus* (Lord, I am not worthy); do' mi nay non soom dee' nyoos (Classical: dig' noos); *ecce homo* (behold man) e' chay ho:' mo: (Classical: ek' ke:); *in hoc signo vinces* (in this sign [meaning the sign of the cross] you conquer) in hok si:' nyo vi:n' chays (Classical: si:g' no: wi:n' ke:s); *in nomine patris et filii et spiritu sanctu* (in the name of the father and of the son and of the holy spirit/ghost) in no' mee nay pA' trees et fee' Lee ee et spee' ree t<u>oo</u> sAnk' t<u>oo</u>; *in saecula saeculorum* (for ever and ever; literally: in ages of ages) in say' k<u>oo</u> LA say' k<u>oo</u> Law' room (often Anglicized: in sek' ye Le sek sek ye Law' Rem); *Introibo ad altare dei* (I approach the altar of God [the opening phrase of the Mass]); in trO ee' bO Ad AL tA' ray day' ee; *mea culpa, mea maxima culpa* (my guilt/sin, my greatest guilt,or mine is the greatest sin) may' A kool pA may' A mAx' I mA kool' pA

Some anglicized phrases
Legal: *amicus curiae* (friend of the court; an independent expert witness) A mee' kes ky<u>oo</u>' ree ee, or I; writ of *certiorari* (certification, a writ asking an inferior court to make its proceedings available for review by a superior court) soR' shee *e* RA' Ree; *de facto* (in fact) dee, or day, fak tO; *de jure* (in law, by right) dee, or day, dgoo' Ree; *de novo* (again) dee, or day, nO' vO); *habeas corpus* (have the body [brought to the court]) hay' bee es kawR' pes; *in absentia* (in the absence of) in ab sen' che; *in loco parentis* (in place of the parent) in lO' kO pe Ren' tis; *prima facie* (at first sight; on the face of it; self-evident; this phrase is applied to

evidence); *sine die* (without a day [being named for further proceedings]) sI'
nee dI' ee

Common: *ad hoc* (literally, to the this; for a particular purpose, as in an ad hoc
committee) ad hAk; *ad infinitum* (to infinity, infinitely) ad in fi' nI tem; *bona fide*
(literally: in good faith; real; honest; "on the level") bO' ne fId; *curriculum vitae*
(resume of one's life, career) ke Ri' kye lem vI' tee; *dramatis personae* (the persons
or characters or list of characters in a drama) dRa' ma tis poR sO'nee; *ex cathedra*
(from the chair; a pronouncement from the seat of authority; used of the Pope's
pronouncements, for instance; on the highest authority; this expression is also
used ironically) eks ke thee' dRe; *ex officio* (from the office, literally; a pronouncement made by virtue of the fact that someone holds a certain office, therefore not
to be disputed; officially) eks e fi' shee O; *ex post facto* (literally, from after the
fact, or deed; retroactively, as in legislative acts) eks post fak' tO; *in extremis* (near
the end; near death; in dire straits; literally: in the extreme) in eks tRee', or stRe',
mis; *in medias res* (in the midst of things) in mee' dee es Rays', but often pronounced in the Latin way: in may' dee As Rays; *in memoriam* (in memory of) in
mem' aw' Ree em; *ne plus ultra* (the highest point, the greatest height, the acme,
the best; literally: not more over and above) nee, or nay, pLus uL' tRe; *pater familias*
(father of the family) pay', or pa', or pA', teR fe mil' ee es; *sine qua non* (something
absolutely necessary, literally: without which not) sI' nee kway' non', but often
pronounced in the Latin way: see' nay kwA' non'; *tempus fugit* (time flies) tem'
pes fyoo' dgit; *ultima Thule* (the farthest limit; figuratively, the highest thing possible of attainment or achievement; the place farthest north to the ancient Romans; literally:farthest Thule) uL ti' me thoo Lee

Chapter Eight
French Accents

Marcel Proust (1871-1922) was one of the seminal authors of 20th-century literature. His innovative novel, *In Search of Lost Time,* intricately structured and written in elegant, sinuous prose, is a mesmerizing book of profound insight, subtle analysis, astonishing scope, humanity, intellect, and brilliant comedy; it is full of characters so real (because they have in them what we all have: a life of the unconscious mind), that we think they must actually have existed. While the Paris he loved slumbered or enjoyed its glittering nightlife, Proust wrote stretched out in bed all night almost every night during his last few years, so that he could finish his book before death overtook him in the cold, cloistered room in which he tried in vain to shield himself from debilitating attacks of asthma with medications and cups of strong coffee and milk. You can see his room today, with his original furniture and artifacts, recreated in the Musée Carnavalet. That quintessential Parisian author, Honoré de Balzac (1799-1850), whose house is now a museum, also existed sometimes entirely on coffee, grinding the beans for every cup at his desk, and writing feverishly all night to create *The Human Comedy,* splendid, brilliant novels about life in Paris and in the French provinces. For those of us who have no such obsessive habits, it is perhaps enough to know that the coffee in Paris is delicious, and that it is one of the great pleasures in life to sip it outdoors at the Café de Flore on a sunny day while reading Proust or Balzac, and to dream.

French, the native language of 70 to 80 million people, is spoken not only in France but also in Canada, Haiti, French Guyana, Martinique, Belgium, Luxembourg, Switzerland, parts of the United States, namely Maine and Louisiana, North Africa and several other African countries. Until around 1930 French was spoken as a native language in various towns in Illinois and up and down the Mississippi River valley in what had, after all, been French colonial territory.

Supposedly the best Standard French is spoken in and around the city of Tours, and the numerous accents in France itself include those of Paris, with its rich argot, Marseilles, Provence, Toulouse and Alsace. Francien, the dialect of the northern region called the Ile-de-France, where Paris is located, evolved into modern Standard French. As the prestigious language of the king and the court, its ascendance over the other dialects of French, such as Occitan in the south, Norman French in the west, and Burgundian French in the east, was assured. Linguistic standards are maintained by the prestigious Académie Française (French Academy), founded in the 17th century. A great many writers in France aspire to be received *sous la coupole* (under the cupola in the rotonda of the Académie), and to be a member of the esteemed organization which exists to ensure the purity of the French language. Of course, the Academy began essentially as a political organization. The idea was to control the language, and in so doing, to govern the people. It was the dialect of the governing classes which was being promoted as the "best" French.

In the south a dialect evolved from Latin called Occitan or *langue d'oc* (the language or tongue of *oc*), which gave its name to the province of Languedoc. In the north the dialect which evolved into Standard French was called the *langue d'oïl* (the language or tongue of *oïl*). The words *oc* and *oïl* are the two ways of saying *yes* in those dialects. In Latin *hoc ille* (this that) was the phrase for *yes*. In the south *hoc*, with the "h" dropped, was retained to mean "yes." In the north the "h" and the "c" were dropped, the *ille* pronounced as that combination of letters is pronounced in modern French, "eeye," and the words combined eventually became modern French *oui* (yes). The other French word for "yes," *si*, used after a negative question ("N'y es-tu pas allé?" "Si! J'y suis allé!" {Phonetic pronunciation: nee e tü pA za lé? see! zhee süi za lé!} "Didn't you go there?" "Yes! I went there!") comes from Latin *sicut*, meaning "thus" or "yes," the syllable "-cut" being dropped. The words *s*" (yes) in Italian and *s*" (yes) in Spanish are also derived from *sicut*.

Standard French is a rhotic language, and all final "R"s are pronounced. The "R" in French is uvular, in the throat in Standard French, but is given one frontal trill in certain areas in the south of France and in **Montreal**. In **Brussels**, because of the Flemish influence, the "R" is very guttural, very close to "KH" (the sound in Scottish *loch* or German *Ach*).

In Standard French articulation is very clear and very frontal. One has the impression of speaking in the front of the mouth almost entirely, despite the guttural French "R" and back vowels. In the **Parisian** accent the tendency is to swallow sounds, to elide them and to make them slightly guttural. The Parisian "R" is softer and more swallowed than the "R" in Standard French. In Paris "Je ne sais pas" (I don't know; zhe ne sé pA) becomes "J'sais pas" (shé paw). "Je suis allé au restaurant avec mes copains" (I went to the restaurant with my pals; zhe süi za lé o: Re sto RAn' a vek me: ko pen') becomes " J'suis allé au restaurant 'ec mes copains" (shsüi za lé o: Re sto RAn' ek me: ko pen'.) Strictly speaking the "ü" in this sentence is really a semi-vowel, considerably shorter than the phonetic symbol used in this transcription would indicate.

In **Southern** French accents there is a tendency to denasalize nasal vowels, or, in **Provence**, to pronounce them as if they had a "g" after them, as in English *thing*, so *balcon* (balcony; balkon) becomes "balcong." Mute "e" (similar to English schwa; e) is often pronounced, giving the accent an Italian flavor. See any of Marcel Pagnol's films for these accents. An example: "Mais ça tombe très bien." (from Pagnol's *Fanny* [1932]: literally "But that falls very well," i.e., "That's very opportune."). In Standard French: "mé sA tawmb tRè byen'." In a Marseilles accent: "me: sA tom be tRè byeng'."

In **Lyon** and the surrounding countryside the accent is quite clipped, with short clear vowels and clear consonants. Listen to the character Monsieur Brun in *Fanny* for an authentic Lyonnaise accent, and to the other characters for the salty, colorful accent of **Marseille**, where the film takes place.

The **Swiss** French accent is equally clear, and there is a tendency to drawl the vowels slightly.

In **Alsace** the accent has a distinctly German flavor to it, with initial voiceless consonants shifting to voiced, and vice versa, so that *palais* (palace; pA le:') sounds like *balai* (broom; bA le:') and *Je* (I; zhe) sounds like "*she*." An Alsatian accent in English sounds very much like a French accent, with its typical rhythmic phrasing, with German consonants.

The **Haitian** accent is non-rhotic. For example *bonjour* (Hello; bon zhooR') is pronounced "Bonjou' " (bon zhoo'). With typical regional Caribbean vowel shifts, it sounds very much like other accents of the Caribbean and like French accents of **Africans**. See the section in Chapter Five on the Caribbean for these vowels. Each of these accents will give a slightly different French accent in English. Note: **Use all the words and phrases above for practice.**

Some roles which require a French accent are the French Princess and her Lady-in-Waiting, who speak French as well as English with a French accent, in William Shakespeare's *Henry V*; Dr. Caius in *The Merry Wives of Windsor*; Comtesse de la Brière in J.M. Barrie's *What Every Woman Knows* (and Maggie has to speak French); the French Maid in Noel Coward's *Private Lives*, and Emile de Becque in Rodgers & Hammerstein's *South Pacific*.

Aside from the many translations of plays by Molière, Feydeau and Rostand done in English without French accents, there are many plays set in French-speaking environments. These plays may or may not use French accents. Some examples: Langston Hughes's *Emperor of Haiti*, about Toussaint l'Ouverture (in Philip Hayes Dean's *Paul Robeson*, Paul Robeson briefly plays Toussaint l'Ouverture with a Haitian French accent); Arthur Miller's *Incident at Vichy*; Robert E. Sherwood's play, and the musical based on it, *Tovarich*, in the Parisian scenes; and S.N. Behrman's *Jakobowski and the Colonel*, about refugees in Nazi-occupied France. Various French characters have appeared in movies and TV series, among them Hercule Poirot (Agatha Christie's Belgian detective); the characters in the musical based on Marcel Pagnol's *Fanny*; Lafayette in the TV mini-series about George Washington; and the French villagers in the British sitcom series *Allo Allo*, set in Nazi-occupied France, full of deliberately fake French accents. The hilarious fake French accent that Peter Sellers concocted for Inspector Clouseau in the Pink Panther film series is not to be missed, beginning with *The Pink Panther* (1964).

For good examples of French accents listen to Charles Boyer in *Gaslight* (1944), *Arch of Triumph* (1948), and many other films; Simone Signoret in *The Sea Gull* (1968) and *Ship of Fools* (1965); Louis Jourdain in *The Count of Monte Cristo* (1976); and Gérard Depardieu in *Green Card* (1990).

A Quick Reference

1) Stress the last syllable of a group of words, except when it contains a schwa.

196

Stress multi-syllable words evenly, or incorrectly in a heavy French accent.

2) In a heavy accent do a French uvular "R." See below for how to do it.

3) Do a French "l," which is articulated with the tongue raised; the tip of the tongue is just behind where it is in articulating an American "L."

4) Drop the initial "h."

5) Consonants are generally "softer" initially, "harder" in final position.

6) Substitute "z" and "s" or "d" and "t" for "TH" and "th."

How to Do a French Accent

1) Position of the Vocal Apparatus

Push your lips forward and say <u>oo</u> <u>oo</u> <u>oo</u> *out out out not not not*. This will give you the general placement of the accent in the mouth, the correct position of the vocal apparatus. French is spoken with the lips slightly more forward of the position in which we speak General American. The major point of resonance is where the French consonant "d" is formed, with the tip of the tongue just slightly behind the upper front teeth, a tiny bit forward of where the "d" is formed in General American. Again, remember that because there are so many pure vowels in French the vocal apparatus does not relax so much within syllables, which would diphthongize the vowels, and the lips and tongue are more active. When French is spoken, the muscles at the corners of the mouth are held somewhat taut, tenser than they are in speaking General American. To a French person this slight tension is unnoticeable, because it is habitual. It is not at all uncomfortable. Holding these muscles as if you were about to speak French will give you a slight French accent. The forward articulation of classical French can be heard, for example, in *Ridicule* (1996), set in 1783 France, but often contemporary French articulation, as exemplified in the film *Les Voleurs* (1996), is less clear, and the main point of resonance has shifted back a bit toward the middle of the mouth. This clearly influences the accent in English.

2) Stress

The most important feature of a French accent in English is the stress pattern carried over from the French language. This pattern is very hard to eliminate. The French system of stress is quite different from that in English. In English every word is individually stressed. French is spoken in "rhythmic phrases," also called "stress groups" or "breath groups." The last syllable of the group is stressed, except for syllables containing a schwa ("e"), or mute "e." For example in the phrase *la table* (the table; lA tA' ble), the syllable "ta-" is stressed because the last syllable, "-ble," contains a schwa.

A rhythmic phrase, which may consist of one word, usually consists of a group of words which form a logical grammatical entity, such as a noun with its adjectives or a verb with a pronoun subject and an adverb. Stress in a French word changes depending on the position of the word in a rhythmic phrase. For example in the phrase *la maison* (the house; la me: zon') the last syllable "-son" is stressed. If we add an adjective to the phrase and make it *la maison blanche* (the white house; la me: zon blansh') the stress shifts to "blan-," the first syllable of the word for "white."

197

The last syllable, "-che," contains a schwa. French communicates ideas by means of these rhythmic phrases rather than by means of individual words, and the rhythmic phrasing gives the language its characteristic rhythm.

The tendency of French people speaking English is to stress the ends of phrases even in English. Because any French person learning English knows that this is not correct there is usually an attempt to compensate for the stressing by making both syllables fairly even, as if there were a slight confusion as to which syllable should be stressed: "Ev'en' while be'ing' con'cerned' / for my safe'ty', / I res'cued' / the drown'ing' sai'lor'/." To **practice** take a sentence and divide it into rhythmic phrases, with a slash after each phrase. Put a mark over the last syllable of each phrase and read the sentence aloud heavily stressing the last syllables of the phrases. Sometimes there is another overcompensation, which consists of stressing syllables which do not normally receive a stress: "I re' gard/ him/ as ad mir' a ble." *Admirable* would be pronounced "ad mI' Ra bel," with a French "l."

3) The Most Important Sounds
h: "h" in French, which is used in spelling, but not pronounced, tends to be dropped in English and occasionally pronounced in words where we no longer pronounce it, as in *hour*, or inserted intrusively: 'e 'urt 'is harm [arm].

l: The French "l" is pronounced with the tongue up, the tip of the tongue slightly in back of the upper front teeth. The "l" should resonate in the front of the mouth, where the vowel "o" (as in *work*) resonates. **Practice** by saying "o" several times, then say "l."

TH and th: Substitutions for "TH" (voiced and voiceless pairs: "z" and "s"; "d" and "t" are the usual substitutions in a French accent) may or may not be consistently paired; you could hear, for example: "Zat's de ting" (That's the thing). The pair "d" and "t" is more typical of **French Canadian** accents than of European French accents.

R: The French uvular "R," pronounced gutturally (in the throat), is produced by keeping the lips and lower jaw stationary and in the position of whatever vowel will accompany the "R." The tip of the tongue is also motionless and placed behind the lower front teeth. As the larynx gently vibrates the back of the tongue should rise towards the soft palate, but not touch it. The uvula should give a series of taps, so the "R" rolls or gargles slightly. See Fig. 6 on page 15. In the softer Parisian version the uvula does not vibrate. In **French Canada** and the **Midi** (Southern France, referred to in French as the *midi*, pronounced "mi: di:'," meaning "midday," when the sun is hot) the "r" (with a light tap) is usual.

i: : The French vowel "i:" is not exactly like the English vowel "i" in *bit*, but is intermediate between that vowel and the "ee" in *meet*; it is a vowel which does not exist in English and is often heard in a French accent. See Fig. 2 on page 11.

o: A pure open "o" is often a substitution for the diphthong "O" in "hOme." The second part of the "O" diphthong is dropped. Alternatively, both parts of the diphthong could be evenly stressed (and the "h" dropped): aw'<u>oo</u>m'.

Different French Accents

1) For a **very slight** accent simply maintain the position of the vocal apparatus and do not add other sounds.

2) For a **light** accent, in addition to the position of the vocal apparatus, use the French stress pattern. Stressing phrases instead of individual words will give you a French accent even if you do nothing else. You can hear an extremely light, almost nonexistent accent, except at moments, in the PBS *Mystery* dramatization of P. D. James's novel *Original Sin*, in the character of the elder M. Etienne, played by Raymond Gerome. He says "dizappointment" and "Al THe way dA'<u>oo</u>n'" (stressing both halves of the diphthong evenly), and all of a sudden this slight French accent appears in his otherwise perfect British RP.

3) To make the accent **slightly heavier** do all the above and do a correct American "R" with the lips forward. Keep one or more of the sounds from French which do not exist in English. You might choose to nasalize vowels before "n" or "m" in the middle of a word. You might choose to keep a substitution for "TH" sounds. You might choose to keep the French "l."

5) For an even **heavier** accent add pitch patterns (see below) to the stress patterns and you will have a fairly musical French accent.

6) For a **very heavy** accent use the information from the sections on "Stress," "Pitch," "The Most Important Sounds" and "Further Phonetic Information." Use all the sound shifts. You will be pronouncing English as if it were French. Use the French "R" and "l" and the "z" and "s" pair as a "TH" substitution. Drop all "H"s. Nasalize vowels before single "n" in the middle of a word ("condition"). There was a French announcer on cable television who used to say the word *channel* as if it were the name of the French fashion designer Chanel, with the stress on the last syllable: "sha-nel'." He pronounced *cable* to rhyme with French *table* and *TV* as it is pronounced in French, "té-vé." *French* became "fRAnsh." He was, he said, the "A n<u>oo</u>n sayR' fawR ze fRAnsh kA ble té vé sha nel'." Every word he said sounded as if it were actually a French word. He was virtually incomprehensible.

Further Phonetic Information

Consonants
Consonants are generally "softer" in French than in English. The versions of "p," "t," "d," and "v" used in the initial position would be in English the middle or final version of the sound (*ha<u>pp</u>y, be<u>tt</u>er, a<u>dd</u>, e<u>v</u>ery*).

Vowels and Diphthongs

Because most vowels in French are not diphthongized as they are in English, it is harder for a French speaker of English to diphthongize them. Diphthongs tend to sound as if both vowels are evenly stressed. For example, "I" in *fight* sometimes sounds like "A'ee' ": "fA'eet'." Often pure vowels are heard as substitutions for diphthongs.

é and è: The French vowel "é" is similar to the first part of the English diphthong "ay." The opening of the lips is narrow, and the lips are widened as when smiling. This vowel is often heard in a French accent in English as a substitution for the diphthong "ay." The French vowel "è" is similar to the English vowel "e" in *met*, but with the lips open wider. This vowel is often heard as a substitution for the "e" in *met*.

ü: The French "u" ("ü" in my phonetic transcription), is a pure vowel pronounced with the lips forward as if to say "<u>oo</u>" as in *boot*, but with the "ee" in *meet* actually pronounced.

nasal vowels: There are "nasal vowels" in French, indicated by a vowel before "n" or "m" followed by another consonant, as in *impossible*, where "im-" is a nasal vowel close to "en" (the "e" in *met* nasalized).

Pitch and Intonation Patterns

Like English questions, French questions usually end on a higher pitch. There is a musicality to a French declarative sentence, which begins on a lower note, curves to a higher note without making a direct and steep ascent to a higher tone, goes back down slightly and then rises again, falling to a low note to end a simple declarative sentence. The combination of stress and pitch give a French accent its characteristic music.

Example: (The "//" indicates the end of a rhythmic phrase, on the last syllable of which the primary stress falls.) La comtesse de Sérizy, // soeur du marquis de Ronquerolles, // donnait au commencement de la semaine suivante // un grand bal // auquel devait venir // madame de Langeais.—From *La Duchesse de Langeais* by Honoré de Balzac.
Literal translation: The Countess of Sérizy, sister of the Marquis of Ronquerolles, gave at the beginning of the week following a grand ball to-which was-supposed to come Madame de Langeais.

Phonetic pronunciation: lA kon tes de sé Ri: zi: // so:R dü mAR ki: de Ron ke Rol // do ne: o ku mAns mAn de lA se men süee vAnt // un gRAn bAl // o kel de ve: ve ni:R // mA dAm de lAn zhe:.
Note: You will see that in the preceding phonetic pronunciation there is only one diphthong in that entire sentence (the "ui" in *suivante*). All the other syllables contain only pure vowels. The absence of diphthongs means that there is

200

no relaxation within syllables and the mouth moves to change position after every syllable, much more rapidly than in English where the mouth relaxes within almost every syllable to create diphthongs. This phenomenon is carried over into English, and vowels are often not diphthongized in a French accent.

The following is a schematic representation of a possible pitch pattern:

```
                                              rolles,//
La        tesse            zy,//              quis de
    com-       de   ri-        soeur   mar-       Ronque-
           Sé-               du
```

Note that the pitch of *du* should actually be only slightly lower than that of "mar."

```
        nait                  ment                               bal//
don-    au      mence-        de la      maine      vante// un grand
            com-                     se-        sui-
```

The pitch of *un* should actually be slightly below that of *grand*.

```
                  nir//               Lan-
    quel   devait  ve-         dame de
au-                     ma-              geais.//"
```

Note that the pitch of "de" in *devait* should be slightly below that of "vait" and that of "Lan" slightly below that of "nir."

You see how different this is from General American intonation and pitch patterns. It is exactly this sort of music that is carried over into English in a French accent.

Practice

Use the sentences from Balzac and Proust for practice. Say the literal translation of the French sentences aloud, dividing the sentence into the same rhythmic phrases as the original French sentence and using the same pitch patterns for each phrase as in the French sentence. This should produce a characteristic French rhythm and music. Remember that if a person has learned British English, the final "R" will be dropped; if American it will be pronounced. For a **Haitian** accent the final "R" should generally be dropped, even for an accent in the United States.

The opening sentence of Marcel Proust's (mAR sel' pR<u>oo</u>st') *A la recherche du temps perdu* (*In Search of Lost Time*; A lA Re she:Rsh' dü tAn peR dü'; note that in French only the first word of a book title is capitalized, except when there are proper names.)

Longtemps, je me suis couché de bonne heure.

Literal translation: Long time, I myself am bedded [have gone to bed] of good hour.
Translation: For a long time I went, or used to go, to bed early.
Phonetic pronunciation: law*n* tA*n*' zhe me süi: k<u>oo</u> shé' *de* bu no:*R*'

Possible pitch pattern

<pre>
                                    é   bonne
         temps,   couch- de
Long-   je me suis   heure.
</pre>

From *Du côté de chez Swann* [Phonetic pronunciation: dü ko té' *de* she: swAn'] (*Swann's Way; almost literally In the Direction of Swann's House*), the first volume of *In Search of Lost Time*:
Et bientôt, machinalement, accablé par la morne journée et la perspective d'un triste lendemain, je portai à mes lèvres une cuillerée de thé où j'avais laissé s'amollir un morceau de madeleine.
Phonetic pronunciation: e bye*n* to:' mA shi:n al maw*n*' a ka blé pA*R* lA mawR*n* zh<u>oo</u>*R* né' e lA pe*R* spek ti:v du*n* tRi:s' *te* law*n* *de* me*n*' zhe paw*R* té A mé lèv' *Re* ün küi*e* *R*é *de* té <u>oo</u> zhA vé le sé sA mo li:*R*' u*n* maw*R* so: de mA dle*n*'

Literal translation: And soon, mechanically, weighed-down by the melancholy day and the prospect of a sad tomorrow, I carried to my lips a spoonful of tea where [in which] I had let soften a bit of madeleine.

Phonetic pronunciation of literal translation (**light accent**): and s<u>oo</u>n' me ka' ni ka' lee' wayd down' bI TH*e* me' lan' ko' lee day' and TH*e* pRos' pekt' *ov* a sad t<u>oo</u> maw' RO' I ka' Ri:d' t<u>oo</u> mI li:ps' ay spoon' fool' *ov* tee' we:*R* I had let saw' fen' ay bi:t *ov* mA dle*n*'

Notes: Pay special attention to the stress pattern, indicated by the apostrophes. Notice, too, the use of the French "l" and the lengthened "i." Proust himself, by the way, apparently pronounced the name of his character *Swann* as "süAn," according to Lucien Daudet in *Autour de soixante lettres de Marcel Proust* (*Round Sixty Letters of Marcel Proust*; Phonetic pronunciation: o: t<u>oo</u>*R* de swA sawnt le' t*Re* de mA*R* sel pR<u>oo</u>st'; Gallimard, 1928). Proust's friend, Gautier-Vignal (go tyé vi: nyAl') says "svAn." However, most people say "swAn."

Lapérouse, the historic restaurant, was unfortunately not known for its cuisine. But things have changed. There is a new chef and the food is delicious, superb, and the dÈcor is as sumptuous as it was when Victor Hugo and Mark Twain dined here.
Phonetic pronunciation: (**Very heavy accent**) lA pé *R*<u>oo</u>z *de*, or ze, i:s to Ri:k Res to Rawn' wez in, or on, faw ch<u>oo</u> net lee not nawn' faw Ri:ts kwi: zi:n' bot si:ngz Av she:ndg', or che:ndg', or che:ndgd ze: Ri:z e ny<u>oo</u> shef en ze food i:z di li: shes', or shos, sü pe:*R*, or s<u>oo</u> peRb', en *ze* dé kawR' i:z a:z *som* ch<u>oo</u> es az i:t woz wan vi:k taw Rü go:' en mARk twe:n dA ndi:*R*', or dAn deee*R*'.

Well, you know, it's a great film.
Phonetic pronunciation: wel y<u>oo</u> no:', or naw', i:ts, or i:s, *e* gRe:t, or gRe:t, fi:lm'
Note: If you gutturalize the "R" to "R" you will have a heavier accent. If you use a retroflex American "R" and an American "L" you will have a lighter accent. For the lightest accent simply do the French stress pattern, stressing as indicated by the apostrophes.

Be sure when you serve not to put your arm in front of the customer's face.
Phonetic pronunciation: bi: shoo wan y<u>oo</u> seRv' naw t<u>oo</u> pot y<u>oo</u> hAm' i:n fRont ov zee kos ti: me:Rz fe:s'

Possible Pitch Pattern

```
                                                cus-    mer's
                                  arm                   to-
                 serve                                          face.
      sure    you      not to put your     in front of the
Be       when
```

It takes two hours to make this dish properly.
Phonetic pronunciation: i:t te:ks t<u>oo</u> how' eRz' t<u>oo</u> me:k zees deesh pRaw' peR li:'
Note: This is, of course, a very heavy accent, but these sentences were actually said as the phonetic pronunciations indicate, with the overcompensatory "h" where it shouldn't exist.

Possible Pitch Pattern

```
                            dish
              ho-        make this    prop-
        two          to                   er-
It takes          urs                        ly.
```

Don't argue with the customers.
Phonetic pronunciations: (**Heavy**) dawn, or dawnt, hAR gy<u>oo</u>' wi: zee ko sto meR'; (**Medium**) don AR' gy<u>oo</u>' wi:s *de* ko' sto' meRz'; (**Light**) don't AR' gy<u>oo</u>' wi: *de* ku' staw mez'

Possible Pitch Pattern

```
         argue          cus-
Don't         with the    to-
                             mers.
```

I was walking down the Boulevard St.-Michel in the Latin Quarter of Paris one

sunny spring day and I had not a care in the world.
Phonetic pronunciation: A woz waw ki:ng, or wO ki:n, dAn', or dAn', ze b<u>oo</u> lvAR se:*n* mi: shel' in *ze* la ti:n kwaw toR' *ov* pA' Rees won *so* nee spRi:ng de:' an I ad no tay kay Ri:n *ze* wuRl'
Notes: Notice the two different pronunciations of the pronoun "I," depending on the phonetic context of the diphthong: at the very beginning, or in the middle of a phrase. Notice, too, the linked consonants in the phrase *not a care in the world.* To lighten the accent, do a retroflex "R" and correct "TH" sounds throughout the exercise.

Paris is one of the most beauiful cities anywhere, from the point of view of art and architecture, and, of course, the food in Paris is simply spectacularly delicious, from the hot chocolate at Angélina's on the rue de Rivoli to the haute cuisine creations of the quintessential temple of gastronomy, Taillevent.
Phonetic pronunciation: pA Rees i:z wun *ov* ze mOs by<u>oo</u> di: f<u>oo</u>l si *dees* e nee wayeR' fRom *ze* poy*n* to vy<u>oo</u> *ov* AR tan AR ki: tek tyeR' an *ov* kawRs *ze* foo di:n pA Ree i:z spek tAk y<u>oo</u> lAR lee di: li: shos' fRom *ze* ot sho ko lAt' at aw*n* zhé li: nAz' aw*n ze* rü de Ri: vo li:' t<u>oo</u> *ze* ot kwi: zi:*n'* *ov ze* kwi*n* te se*n* shel tem pel *ov* gA stRo no mi:' tAy' vaw*n'*
Note: Once again, this is a very heavy accent. Aside form the usual restoration of "R" and "TH" sounds, you can also lighten it up by not doing nasal vowels in such English words as *point, quintessential, and temple.*

204

Chapter Nine

Spanish Accents: Spain, Central and South America

When the Romans completed their subjugation of the Iberian Peninsula in 133 B.C.E., having taken more than 70 years to do so after their victory over its previous conquerors, the Carthaginians, in the second Punic War, they found in the mountainous north the non-Indo-European Basques, and throughout the land a great many Celtic tribes whose origins were presumably north of the Pyrenees, and who had conquered and either replaced or amalgamated with the earlier Iberians, whose language was largely lost in the process. Possibly Iberian was of North African origin. It may be that Basque is one with ancient Iberian, or it may be a related language, and, if so, it is the only one of the ancient languages to have survived the earlier invasions of the Indo-Europeans as well as the later Roman conquest, perhaps due to the isolation afforded by the Pyrenees. At any rate, Latin soon took over and became the dominant language of the peninsula, evolving into Spanish. Certain Basque words in Spanish attest to the influence of this ancient people even after the Roman hegemony was established. For example, the province of Navarra takes its name from Basque *naba*, which means "a high mountain plain," and *Vega* (as in the name of the famous playwright Lope de Vega) derives from Basque *ibaiko* and means "wooded area near a river."

There is a Spanish-Jewish language called variously Ladino, Judezhmo or Judeo-Spanish. Essentially it is medieval Castilian Spanish, carried by the Jews who spoke it all over the Mediterranean after the expulsion from Spain in 1492, and still spoken in Greece, Turkey, and parts of North Africa by their descendants. A good deal of its vocabulary is derived, as might be expected, from Hebrew and it is written, like Yiddish, in a modified Hebrew alphabet. The Jews were expelled from Spain after a long "golden age" of cohabitation and even assimilation and integration with the other peoples of the Iberian Peninsula. They fell victim, as did the Moors, to the Christian "Reconquista," the reconquest of Spain for Catholicism after centuries of domination by the Moslem Moors who had invaded from North Africa and conquered the Visigoths (who had themselves invaded earlier from the North when the Roman Empire, including the province of Hispania, was destroyed). The monarchs of the Christian kingdoms of Aragon and Castile were determined to unify Spain for the sake of what they fervently believed to be the "one true religion." In doing so they spread their language throughout Iberia.

With the explorations of the 16th and 17th centuries Spanish was carried to the New World by the imperialistic Conquistadors. Over the centuries and through the independence movements and revolutions in South America, Spanish retained its dominance as a language, although the many Amerindian languages continue to exist alongside it. As one might expect, however, South American and Castilian Spanish differ substantially, both in vocabulary content and in accents.

Spanish is not the only language spoken in Spain. Aside from Basque, there are a number of Romance languaguages still widely used, most notably the Galician dialects (*galego* in Galician), and Catalan, with seven million speakers, spoken in Catalonia (Catalunya in Catalan), whose capital is Barcelona, and in the independent country of Andorra, high in the Pyrenees between Spain and France. The orthography and pronunciation of Catalan are quite different from Spanish, despite great linguistic similarities. For example, the letter "j" is pronounced "zh" in Catalan and "kh" in Spanish, and the double "ll," which is "y" in Spanish, is "l" in Catalan. However, a Catalan accent is not very different from a Spanish accent, so you can follow the general advice given below.

Today Spanish is spoken by approximately 325 million people. It is the official language not only of Spain itself, but also of most South and Central American countries, of Mexico and many Caribbean islands, including Cuba. In the United States it is spoken widely in the northeast, for instance by the large Puerto Rican population of New York City, and in Arizona, New Mexico, California and Texas, as all four states were once Spanish possessions, as was Florida, where Spanish is once again heard widely because of the Cuban immigration. If you live in New York or another large center of the Spanish language, listen to the people around you. In films you can hear the late Raul Julia, who had a very slight Puerto Rican accent, in, for example, *Kiss of the Spider Woman* (1985), or listen to Antonio Banderas for a Spanish Spanish accent in several recent films. There are many Spanish (and British) accents in the PBS Masterpiece Theatre dramatization of Joseph Conrad's *Nostromo*; some of the South American accents are so thick they are nearly incomprehensible. You will want to avoid that, of course. Listen to Desi Arnaz for a Cuban accent in the *I Love Lucy* television series.

A Quick Reference

1) Keep the lips slightly parted when articulating bilabial consonants, such as "b" and "v." Consonants in general are "softer" than in General American.
2) Substitute a soft "kh" for initial pronounced "h."
3) Drop the final "t" in consonant clusters containing it (last, most, etc.).
4) Use a trilled "r," which can be heavily rolled sometimes, but if you use a retroflex "R," as in some Mexican accents, make it very "hard."
5) Substitute "s" for "z" sounds.
6) Substitute "d" and "t" for "TH" and "th" and a tapped "d" for "TH" and for "t" between vowels.
7) Substitute a lengthened "i: " for both "i" and "ee."

206

How to Do Spanish Accents

First of all, decide which Spanish accent you wish to create. See the important information under pitch for Mexican, Castilian, and so forth.

1) Position of the Vocal Apparatus

It is very important to relax the vocal apparatus. The lips are fairly loose and barely touch to make consonants. The jaw is relaxed and half closed. Say *wa wa wa* six times, and you will have the idea.

2) The Most Important Sounds

Consonants

Pay special attention to "h," "n," "r," "s" (sometimes retroflex), and "y." All the consonants are softer than they are in English. The lips do not close fully to form "b" or "d," for example. There is a tendency in some accents, notably those of Puerto Rico and Cuba and in other areas where "s" is dropped before a consonant, to reduce consonant clusters, especially those containing a "t" or a "d."

b/v; d/t: The consonants "b" and "v" are very close to each other as, are "d" and "t." This is because the language is spoken with the lips generally kept substantially apart, a position of the vocal apparatus which conditions all the sounds.

ch: In Cuba the sound tends to be relaxed into "sh." In a Cuban accent in English you might sometimes hear people say "shursh" for *church*.

h: There is no pronounced "h," although the letter is used in spelling. For an initial "h" Spanish-speaking people substitute their "j" (*jota*), pronounced like a soft "kh."

ll: Double "ll" in Spanish is like English "y" in Spain, and often like "ly" in South American Spanish. In Argentina it is often heard as "zh": *million* is heard as "mi: zhon'."

n: This sound is often heard as "ng" at the end of a word in Spanish, particularly in Cuba and Puerto Rico. Sometimes it is simply a nasalized vowel. The word *ten* in a Cuban or Puerto Rican accent in English is heard variously as "teng" or "ten" (nasalized).

r: The "r" in Spanish is trilled, usually receiving one tap, or, if doubled, two taps. The "r" is more breathy in Castilian (as it is also in Argentine Spanish). In fact the "r" has a lot of breath in it and can be rolled.

s and z: There is no "z" sound in Spanish, although the letter is used in spelling. In South America it is pronounced "s," and in Spain, in Castilian Spanish, it is pronounced "th." Otherwise "s" is always substituted for a "z" in English, particularly at the end of a word, where the sound is often spelled with an "s":

please, says, does. In South American Spanish there are accents in which all final "s" sounds as well as "s" sounds before another consonant are dropped, as are many final consonants. The letter "c" is also pronounced "th" (as in the American voiceless "th" in *think*) in Castilian Spanish before "i" and "e," and "s" in South American Spanish. The sound of "s" does not exist in Spanish in an initial position when the "s" is followed by another consonant; instead it is preceded by "e": España (e spA' nyA; Spain); español (e spA nyo:l'). Notice that the unstressed syllables retain the full value of the vowel and are not reduced to a schwa. The tendency to pronounce words beginning with "s" in English, as if they begin with "e" gives a characteristic, if somewhat clichéd, touch to a Spanish or various South American accents in English. Occasionally the "s" is pronounced as a retroflex consonant; the bottom of the tongue is turned towards the roof of the mouth.

sh and zh: These sounds likewise tend to be confused with each other, and it is the voiceless "sh" which usually substitutes for the voiced "zh," so that *measure,* for example, is pronounced "may' sher."

t: Final "t" does not exist in Spanish, and is often not sounded in English.

TH and th: Because of the Castilian pronunciation of "c" and "z" as "th," these sounds can be learned by Spanish speakers, usually the voiceless "th" being heard in all positions, so that *this* (THis) is heard as "thi:s." Otherwise substitute "d" for "TH" and "t" for "th."

Vowels and Diphthongs
The vowel system in Spanish consists basically of : a (A), e, i, o, u (oo). The vowels have open and closed versions. Diphthongs often shift to pure vowels in an accent in English.

a: This is an intermediate vowel (between "A" and "e"; the tongue is literally in between its positions for those two vowels) which does not exist in Spanish. Often "e" is substituted for it, so *hat* is pronounced "khet" and *cat* sounds like "ket."

i: This vowel also does not exist in Spanish. Instead there is the vowel intermediate between the vowels "i" and "ee": a lengthened "i:." This is the vowel heard in Spanish accents in English. Sometimes one hears a fully pronounced "ee" (where it should be heard, as in *team* and *teen*), and, more importantly, as a substitution for "i," as in such words as *tin* and *think* (both pronounced with an initial "t").

O: This diphthong shifts to a short "aw," so *home* is pronounced "khawm."

y: This semi-vowel has various pronunciations in Spanish, which carry over into

208

English. In Castilian "y" is almost like its English counterpart, only slightly more closed. In Argentina it sounds like "zh," and in Puerto Rico and Cuba almost like the "j" in *just* or *edge*. *Yo no se* (I don't know) is "yo no se:" in Castilian, "zho no se:" in Argentina, and "dgo no se:" in Puerto Rico. The way this sound is pronounced in Spanish is often the way it is pronounced in English.

Stress

Almost every word in the Spanish language is stressed on the penultimate (next to last) syllable, unless the word ends in a consonant, and in that case the last syllable is stressed. Accent marks in Spanish indicate a stressed syllable. In other words, the stress for the purposes of an actor wanting to do a Spanish accent in English, is random enough so that there is usually no problem for Spanish-speaking people in learning to stress English words correctly. We have to look to phonetics and pitch patterns for the characteristics which create a Spanish acccent in English.

Pitch

Argentine, Mexican, Cuban and Puerto Rican Spanish accents all have different intonation patterns, different kinds of music. These patterns are often carried over into an accent in English. Mexican Spanish, for example, sometimes has a sort of sing-song quality absent in other varieties.

Practice

The opening sentence of Chapter One of *Don Quijote de la Mancha* (don kee kho' te de lA mAn' chA) by Miguel de Cervantes (mi: gel' de ser vAn' tes, or, in Castilian pronunciation, ther vAn' tes):

Remember that all the consonants are softer than their English counterparts, so that "v" is almost like "b," "d" like "TH," and so on.

En un lugar de la Mancha, de cuyo nombre no quiero accordarme, no ha mucho tiempo que vivía un hidalgo de los de lanza en astillero, adarga antigua, rocín flaco y galgo corredor.

Literal translation: In a place/village of la Mancha [an area south of Castille and just west of Valencia] of which the name not wish/care/desire-I to-recall/remember-me, not ago/has-been much time that lived a gentleman of those of lance in rack, shield antique/ancient, nag skinny/lank/scrawny and greyhound for-run/chase/hunt.

Translation: In a village of la Mancha, the name of which I do not desire to remember, not long since there lived a gentleman, one of those with a lance in the rack, an ancient shield, a scrawny nag, and a greyhound for the hunt.

Phonetic pronunciation: en oon loo gAr' de lA mAn' chA de koo' yo nom' bre no kye' ro A kor dAr' me no A moo' cho tyem' po ke vi: vi:' A oon i: dAl' go de los de

lAn' za, or lAn' thA, en As ti: ye' ro A dAr' gA An ti:' gwA ro si:n', or ro thi:n', flA'
ko ee gAl' go kor re dor'

Spanish Phrases

Como està Usted, señor? Muy bien, gracias, y Usted? Muy bien, gracias.
Translation: How are you, sir? Very well, thank you, and you? Very well, thank you.
Phonetic pronunciation: ko' mo es tA' <u>oo</u> sted' se nyawr' mooi:' byen' grA' syAs
ee <u>oo</u> sted' mooi:' byen' grA' syas
Note that the "n" at the end of *bien* is somewhat nasalized, and look at the
section on consonants. Final consonants especially are very soft. The word *gracias*
(thanks) can have three syllables, "grA' si: As" in an educated accent. In **South
American**, **Puerto Rican**, and **Cuban** pronunciations the "s" before "t" in *està*
(are) and *Usted* (you) is silent, as is the final "d" in *Usted*: "ko' mo e tA' <u>oo</u> te:."

English Sentences

I don't know.
Phonetic pronunciation: I daw nO

Pitch Pattern

```
                kno-
I
    don't        w.
```

(Note the falling tone on the word *know*.) The same pattern is heard in a **Mexican**
accent in Spanish itself. *Yo no se* (pronounced as written, with short vowels in *Yo*
and *no* and a lengthened "e" in *se*) means "I don't know," and follows the same
pitch pattern in a Mexican accent, which tends to be carried over into English.

It's true that I told him.
Phonetic pronunciation: i:s tr<u>oo</u> da*d* I to:l KHi:m
Note the hard "KH," which is often heard for an initial "h," although a softer
"kh" is also usual.

Pitch Pattern

```
                told
    true
It's        that I        him.
```

I was going down Main Street.
Phonetic pronunciation: I wus go:' wi:*n* down mayng e stree
Note that this is a very **heavy** accent.

I eat a good piece of meat.
Phonetic pronunciation: I i:*t* A g<u>oo</u> pi:s A mi:t

210

You know what I mean.
Phonetic pronunciations
Spanish: y<u>oo</u> naw hwA *d*I, or khwA *t*I, mi:*n*
Argentine: y<u>oo</u> naw KHwa *d*I mi: n
Cuban, Puerto Rican: zh<u>oo</u> naw hwA*d* I mi:ng
Mexican, Puerto Rican, Cuban: dg<u>oo</u> naw KHwA*d* I mi:ng
Note: Of course the last two represent a very **heavy** Puerto Rican or Mexican accent, depending on the particular **pitch** or intonation or musical pattern joined to it, and are something of a cliché, used to great comic effect by the brilliant Mexican comedienne Charro.

Pitch Pattern (Mexican)

```
                    mea-\
You         what            n.
     know        I
```

Pitch Pattern (Spanish)

```
                    mean.
     know
You          what I
```

It's not very much, only forty-five pesos for that matter.
Phonetic pronunciation (**South American**): i:s no be' ree mAsh aw*n*' li: fawr *t*i: fI pe' sos fawr dA mA' *de*

Pitch pattern

```
                            forty-
            much,              fiye           that
     not very        only           pesos           matter.
It's                                     for
```

A New York Taxi Driver from **Spain** (A real accent heard by me)
I drive him in my taxi to 345 Houston Street. It's very far over. He gets out, and he's off.
Phonetic pronunciation: I drI kheem een mI tA' see ty<u>oo</u> three fawr' *dee* fI KHow' sten stree. ees be' ree fA rO' vA. khee ges ow en KHee sawf

Note the two different pronunciations of "v" in *very* and *over*, and the dropping of the final "v" in *five*. Also notice the linking of final consonants such as "s" in *he's* to the following word *off*. Note, too, the variations between "KH" and "kh" for the initial "h."

211

Possible Pitch Pattern

```
                tax-        Hous-                    o-                  off.
          my         345       ton         ve- far         out      he's
    drive    in      i              Street.      ry   ver.    gets   and
I        him         to               It's           He
```

It's not the best thing in the world, but it's something at least. What else can I tell you? It was a present from me to you. That's all. You don't like it, I'm sorry.
Phonetic pronunciation (**Puerto Rican**): i:s no dee bes ti:ng i:n dee wawRL bu di:s son ti:ng a Lees wA deLs kan, or kang, I teL y<u>oo</u>, or dg<u>oo</u> i wus a pres' en fRo mee t<u>oo</u>, or ts<u>oo</u>, y<u>oo</u>, or dg<u>oo</u> das, or das, awL Dg<u>oo</u>, or y<u>oo</u>, dOn LIk' ee dAm so' Ree
Notes: This accent could also serve for **Mexican** or **Cuban** characters.

You didn't tell me that, you know, cause I would never have agreed if I knew that.
Phonetic pronunciation (**Puerto Rican**): y<u>oo</u>, or dg<u>oo</u>, di' din, or di?' in, tel mee da? y<u>oo</u> nO kaws I woo nef' e haf a gReed if I n<u>oo</u> da?, or da
Notes: Notice the liquid "l." For a **New York Hispanic** accent change the final "f" sounds in *never* and *have* to "v" sounds, and pronounce the final "d" in *would*.

For this cake the fruit is marinating in liquor and it is absorbing the rum.
Phonetic pronunciation (**South American/Peruvian**): fawr dees kayk dee fr<u>oo</u> i:s mA' ree nay deeng i:n dee li:' kor an i: dees a sawr' vi:ng dee rom

It's really freezing in here, because the landlord didn't turn on the heat.
Phonetic pronunciations:
Puerto Rican/New York City/Cuban: is Ree' lee free' sin in kheeR bi kaws de lan lawR di' din toRn An de khee
Notes: For **New York City** pronounce the initial "h" sounds in *here* and *heat* as "h," not "kh." Also, the word *didn't* has various possible pronunciations: di' din; din; di?' in. For a heavier **Puerto Rican/Cuban** accent pronounce all the "R" sounds as "r," with one trill.
South American/Peruvian: i:s ri' lee fri:' si:n i:n kheer bi: kaws dee len' lawr di:' den torn awn di: khee
Mexican: i:s ree' lee free' seen een kheer bee kaws' dee lan' lawr dee' din, or deen, torn An dee khee
Note: For a lighter accent pronounce "r" as retroflex "R."
Spanish: i:s ri' lee fri:'sing i:n kheer bi: kaws' di lan' lawr di:' den torn awn di: khee

Chapter Ten

Italian Accents

The linguistic situation of the Italian Peninsula is unusual, in that the many dialects of Italian continue to exist alongside the standard language, which is usually learned in school. This is partly because Italy was not unified politically until 1861, and then not completely. Rome was annexed in 1870, and the Veneto some time after that. There are also isolated pockets of speakers of German, Albanian and neo-Grecian dialects.

The dialects of the Italian language condition the accent in English as well as in Standard Italian itself; Neapolitan and Roman are as different from each other as both are from the dialects of the Veneto, which includes the Venetian of the city of Venice. Different again is the **Florentine-Tuscan** dialect, which is what we learn in school as Standard Italian. The speech of the Florentines became the de facto standard because it happened to be the language of some of the greatest early Italian literature, of which there is an example in the quotation from Dante below. It also provided the standard, accessible language of musical terminology, and of opera libretti, performed all over Italy. Opera was the popular music of its day, and everybody knew the operas of Rossini, Donizetti and Bellini, as well as Verdi's political, patriotic works. Everybody studied Dante and Leopardi in school. The language of Florence was thus eminently suitable as a standard which everybody could learn while continuing to speak their own dialect. It is the language of film, television and radio. In Italian films characters sometimes speak Standard Italian with various regional accents.

Italian dialects may be divided roughly into 14 categories: seven northern groups of dialects, including those of Venice and the Veneto; three central groups, including those of Florence and Tuscany; and four southern groups, including Roman, Neapolitan, and Calabrian. Sicilian, often classified as an Italian dialect, is so different as to be almost another Romance language, which some people think it is. Indeed, the dialects of Italy are as different from each other as its cities are: Imperial Rome, still filled with the ruins of the ancient city, the architecture of every century in almost every street; the narrow medieval streets and the Duomo of Florence, which evoke the time of Dante, and the palaces which make one dream of the pageantry and splendor of the Medici; proud shimmering sea-girt Venice, so fugitive and so breathtaking. See Visconti's film of Thomas Mann's *Death in Venice* (1971), and read Proust, Ruskin, John Julius Norwich, and Mary McCarthy on Venice, as well as Harold Brodkey's Proustian novel *Profane Friendship* (Farrar, Straus and Giroux, 1994).

213

As an example of dialectical, accentual differences, in **Neapolitan** there are voiced consonants where Standard Italian has them voiceless: *cattivo* (bad; kA ti:' vo) becomes "gaddifo," and word endings are often dropped: "gaddif" (gA di:f'). *Che si dice?* (literally "What is said?", "What do they say?" or by extension "What do you say?," or "How are you?") pronounced "ke' si: di:' che:" in Standard Italian, is "ge:' se deech' " in Neapolitan. *Gumba* (goom bA'), the literal meaning of which is "compatriot" or "someone from the same village or district," means by extension "pal," "friend," or "buddy"; it often has the latter meaning for Italian-Americans. It is a shortened dialectical form of the Standard Italian word *compaesano* (kom pA e zA' no; there is a secondary stress on "pA"). Similarly, the word *paesano* (countryman, someone from the same village or district, peasant; pA e zA' no) is often shortened to *paesan'* (pI zAn'): He's my paesan'. This often means "He's my friend" or "We speak the same (figurative) language," instead of simply "He's my compatriot."

A Neapolitan accent, as opposed to the Neapolitan dialect, is often used in Italian films to give them a general Southern flavor, a notable example being the 1943 film *Rossini*, remarkable for being an anti-Fascist film made right under the nose of Mussolini's censors. Of course there are a great many differences between the Neapolitan and Florentine vocabularies, and it is these differences that make the dialect so difficult to understand by someone who has not learned it, and who speaks Standard Italian. For the actor's purposes, however, we must concentrate on the phonetic characteristics, which are superimposed onto English. A great many southern Italians, from the Naples area, from Sicily, and from Italy's Adriatic coast, emigrated to America and it is their accents that most people probably think of as "Italian," as inaccurate as that idea may be. The broad insertion of "A" or "e" in between words and sometimes in between syllables of the same word, while this phenomenon certainly exists, is not a true representation of an Italian accent. The information in the section "The Most Important Sounds" will tell you when to use this sound.

In the very northern part of Italy the **Tyrolean** accent sounds somewhat German, because a rolled uvular "R" is used. Along with features superimposed from Standard Italian, this "R" is usually heard in a Tyrolean accent in English.

Venetian, with its soft "zh" and "sh" sounds, appears somewhat French. The word *merceria* (marketplace) is pronounced "marzharee' " in Venice, for example. This softer sound is carried into accents in English.

In **Rome** there is a tendency to diphthongize certain pure vowels, so "o" sounds like the British "e_oo_": Roma, the name of the city Rome becomes "re_oo_' mA." *I setti colli di Roma* (the seven hills of Rome), which is pronounced "i: se:' ti: ko' li: di: ro' mA" in Standard Italian becomes "ee set'tee ge_ool_'lee dee re_oo_'mA" in a Roman accent. It is easy for the Romans to pronounce English diphthongs correctly because of the diphthongizations in their parent language.

There is a host of Italian mafiosi, gangsters and mobsters in Hollywood films—characters that have created an unfortunate, prejudicial, defamatory and terribly inaccurate picture of Italian-Americans; absent from such films are the brilliant intellectuals, musicians, artists, doctors, professionals, scientists, chefs, teachers and working people who form the mass of the Italian-American community. In 1931 Edward G. Robinson starred as Rico Bandello in *Little Caesar*, and such films as *The St. Valentine's Day Massacre* (1967), John Huston's *Prizzi's Honor* (1985), excellent and amusing though it is, and the very funny comedy *Married to the Mob* (1988), with Mercedes Ruehl as a jealous mafia wife, have continued to add to the stereotype. So has the *Godfather* series (*The Godfather*, 1972; *Part II*, 1974; *Part III*, 1990) by Italian-American director Francis Ford Coppola; the first of the series is perhaps the best. Many of the accents required in such films are Italian for the older immigrant generation, and General American, New York or Chicago for the second generation Italian-Americans. For a hilarious, satirical send-up of mafia movies see *The Freshman* (1990), in which Marlon Brando parodies himself as the Godfather. There are also portrayals of Italian-Americans on the right side of the law—judges, lawyers and prosecutors—in such popular TV series as *Law and Order*. Among films which counteract the mafia image is *Moonstruck* (1987), starring Cher and New Yorker Danny Aiello, and the charming *Used People* (1992), with Marcello Mastroianni and Shirley MacLaine. The film is set in New York City, and is good not only for Mastroianni's Italian accent, but for New York accents as well.

Sophia Loren in her many films and Anna Magnani in *The Rose Tattoo* (1955) are worth listening to, as is Eduardo Cianelli in his Hollywood films, such as his first, *Reunion in Vienna* (1933) and his last American film, *The Secret of Santa Vittoria* (1969). In 1936 he played the gangster Trask in the film of *Winterset*.

To hear beautiful Italian, see any of Federico Fellini's films, as well as Vittorio De Sica's moving account of Italian Jews during World War Two, *The Garden of the Finzi-Continis* (1971). Ettore Scola's *A Special Day* (1977), starring Sophia Loren and Marcello Mastroianni, is set in Italy in 1938, and is also very much worth seeing.

A Quick Reference

1) Insert a very brief schwa between consonants where the combination does not exist in Italian. See below for details.
2) Drop initial "h."
3) Use a trilled "r" with one tap.
4) Substitute "d" and "t" for "TH" and "th."
5) In stressed syllables lengthen vowels preceding "l," "m," "n," and "r."
6) Substitute the pure vowels "aw" or "o" for the diphthong "O."
7) Substitute the "A" in *father* or the "e" in *met* for the sound of "a" in *cat*.

How to Do a Standard Italian Accent

1) Position of the Vocal Apparatus
The lips are slightly more forward of their position in General American. The tip of the tongue is often at the opening of the palate and the language feels as if it spoken in the middle to front of the mouth. Except for the sound of the consonants "k" and "g," there are no guttural sounds in Standard Italian or in the dialects, aside from the uvular "R" in a **Tyrolean** accent.

215

2) The Most Important Sounds

The **most well-known phenomenon** in a Standard Italian accent occurs because in Italian the vast majority of syllables end in a vowel. (There are short monosyllabic words which end in consonants. These words are simple grammatical words, such as *non* [not], *il* [the masculine definite article "the"], and *con* [with]). This is the insertion of a schwa in between consonants. There are a limited number of "consonant clusters" in Italian, that is groups of consonants found together, and they are mostly in an initial position. It is uncomfortable for many Italians, from whatever dialect background, to pronounce such clusters in English. The insertion of a brief vowel, usually a schwa, is therefore very common in Northern Italian accents in English when one word ends in a consonant and the next word begins with a consonant. There are certain combinations of consonants which exist in Italian, and which would therefore be comfortable for an Italian to pronounce in English, such as "st" (pasta) in the middle of a word, and "sm" (*smarrita*, which means "astray") in initial position, so the word *smile* would present no problem. The following initial consonant clusters also exist in Italian: "s" plus "b," "d," "f," "g," "k," "l," "m," "n," "p," "r," "v," "ch," "dg"; and "b," "c" ("k"), "d," "f," "g," "p," "t" plus the trilled "r"; and "b," "f," "g," "k," "p" plus "l." In English "sb," "sd," "sv," "sf" and "sg" do not exist in initial positions, as they do in Italian. We do have "st" and "sp" as in the words *sport* and *state* and these consonant clusters would present no difficulty to a native Italian speaker learning English. The same thing is true of the consonants which go with "l," namely, they exist in both English and Italian, and therefore present no difficulty to the Italian student of English. There is no insertion of a schwa between the consonants in these clusters. All the consonants in Italian are softer than their English counterparts.

Here are some examples of phrases you can use for **practice** showing the insertion of the schwa in an Italian accent in places where uncomfortable consonant clusters occur, uncomfortable, that is, because these clusters do not exist in Italian: *in the front of the mouth* (ine de front ove de mowt); *sometimes more, sometimes less* (sometImze more, sometImze less); *it's true* (itse troo). Note: The "t" at the end of *front* should be linked to the "o" of *of*. In the **Northern Italian** accent *That's good* is pronounced "datse goode." In more educated speech it might be pronounced "dats (very slight pause) goode," or the final schwa might be dropped altogether.

In some cases in a **Southern Italian** accent you would hear "A": "ine dA front ofA dA mowt"; "sometImzA maw, sometImzA les"; "itsA troo." *That's good* is pronounced "atse goo." Entire word endings are sometimes dropped. My father had a friend from southern Italy who used to go into the woods to gather what he called "ho' ke mush" (oak mushroom, an edible tree fungus).

The Important Consonants

h: Initial "h" is always silent in Italian, and therefore, often, in an accent in English. In Italian spelling, if it follows "c," "g," or "sc" before "i" or "e," it makes those consonants hard: *ghianda* (acorn), pronounced gyAn' dA; *che* (which,

216

that), pronounced ke: ; *schiena* (back), pronounced skye:' nA. Note: *scena* (stage) is pronounced she:' nA.

l: Produced by the tip of the tongue lightly touching the upper palate further forward than for the English "L." You should feel "l" resonate where the vowel "i" resonates. **Practice** by saying the vowel several times, then say "l."

n: Slightly nasalized before the hard sound of "c" or "g": *dunque* (then), *tengo* (I hold). This can carry over into an accent in English.

r: Given one trill. To trill an "R": Keep the lower jaw and lips stationary. Raise the tip of the tongue toward the front part of the hard palate as you vibrate the vocal chords, at the same time giving the tip of the tongue two or three taps as the air is released through the mouth. The tip of the tongue should be very free and only touch the opening into the hard palate very lightly. You should feel the air going through, almost like an "h" sound. The sound of "r" is close to "d."

The consonants "l," "m," "n" and "r" are prolonged when they follow a stressed vowel and precede another consonant: *alto* (high), *campo* (field; city square, in Venice), *tanto* (so much), *arte* (art).

TH and th: These sounds do not exist in Italian. Substitute "d" for voiced (THe); "t" for voiceless (think).

Information on Other Consonants
The consonants "b," "d," "f," "m," "n," "p," "t" and "v" are pronounced sub-stantially as in English, but "softer." Their pronunciation is conditioned by the general position of the vocal apparatus.
Note: Doubled consonants lengthen a preceding vowel.

c (in Italian spelling): Like English "k" except when followed by "i" or "e," when it is like "tsh" in English *church*.

g: Hard, as in English *go*, except when followed by "i" or "e," when it is "dg" like the "g" in English *ginger*.

gl (in Italian spelling): 1) sometimes as in English: negli' gere (neglect) 2) when followed by "i" pronounced as in "lli" in English *William*; *figlio* (son); *gli* (plural definite article "the"). The exact sound of "gl" in Italian does not exist in English.

gn (in Italian spelling): Like "nj" in English *onion*. Magni' fico (magnificent).

s: Two sounds in Italian: voiced (almost a "z"): *cosa* (thing); *quasi* (almost); *sdegno* (scorn); and voiceless "s": *stare* (to stay), *senza* (without); "ss" is always voiceless: *classe* (class).

sc: Hard, like "sk," but when followed by "i" or "e" like "sh" in English *shine*.

z: Similarly, two sounds: voiceless like "ts": *mezzo* (middle); and voiced (like English "dz"): *danzare* (to dance)

Vowels and Diphthongs
The Italian system of pure vowels is as follows: A, e, i, o, <u>oo</u> (spelled "u" in Italian). Each has two sounds: open and closed. This means quite literally that the mouth is either slightly more open or more closed when pronouncing the vowel. Use the Italian words for **practice**. Be careful when practicing not to diphthongize the vowels; do not relax the jaw or glide the tongue when pronouncing them. Record yourself, and listen carefully for any hint of diphthongs. Listen to Italian opera singers, and you will hear that they sing the same vowel for the duration of a coloratura passage.

A: Never made into a schwa, even when unstressed. Pa' pa, Mam' ma, dram' ma (drama), chiama' re (to call).

a: The sound of this vowel does not really exist in Italian. Substitute the "A" in *father* or the "e" in *met*.
Practice words: *can't, cat, that, bat, mat, sat*

e: Closed: *pepe* (pepper); *seta* (silk). Open: *lento* (slow); *senta* (listen), *vento* (wind).

i: Open: *io* (I), *vidi* (I saw). Unstressed and followed by a vowel: (diphthongized) *ieri* (yesterday); *viene* (comes). Not pronounced when unstressed and following "c," "g" or "sc": *Giovanni, scialle* (shawl).

o: Closed: *dopo* (after); *molto* (much). Open: *cantò* (sang); *odi* (hear); *ciò* (that). Note: Accent marks in Italian indicate only stress, not pronunciation.

O: This diphthong does not exist in Italian, except in a **Roman** accent (see the introductory section of this chapter). Substitute the pure vowels "aw" or "o."

<u>oo</u> (spelled "u" in Italian): Open: *luna* (moon); *più* (more); u' nico (only). Unstressed and followed by a vowel: (diphthongized; pronounced like "w" in *wall*): *buono* (good); *questo* (this); *uguale* (equal).

Every letter in an Italian word is pronounced according to the Italian system. Diphthongs are spelled out in two letters: "ei" (ay), "ai" (I), "au" (ow), "oi" (oy), "uo" (wo'), "iu" (y<u>oo</u>'), "ie" (ye').

Stress

Stress in Italian is mostly on the penultimate syllable, but by no means always. Accent marks indicate an unusual stress (*città*, which means "city").

218

Double consonants are divided in Italian syllabification. So a word like *matter* would have the first vowel lengthened in an Italian accent in English.

In Italian all unstressed vowels are short. All stressed vowels are long. This is carried over into an accent in English. What this means is that there is a kind of music similar to "rhythmic phrasing," a rhythm created by the lengthening of stressed vowels, and diphthongs, the stressed half of which is longer than in an accent native to English.

Pitch

The pitch in Italian is high on stressed syllables, low on unstressed syllables. In a declarative sentence the pitch starts low, then rises, then falls again to end a sentence. In a question the pitch rises at the end. In a command the pitch starts high, then gradually falls to the end. There are more musical notes in the typical rise and fall of an Italian sentence than in an English one.

Practice

Note the pure vowels. Remember that most of the syllables end in a vowel. Even without knowing what the words mean you should be able to pronounce these verses. Use the translation for practice in English.

From Dante's *La Divina Commedia: Inferno*
(Opening of Canto III of Dante's *The Divine Comedy: Hell*: The inscription on the Gates of Hell)

"Per me si va nella città dolente;
per me si va nell' eterno dolore;
per me si va tra la perduta gente.

Giustizia mosse il mio alto Fattore;
fecemi la divina Potestate,
la somma Sapienza e il primo Amore.

Dinanzi a me non fur cose create,
se non eterne, ed io eterno duro;
lasciate ogni speranza, voi ch'entrate."

Literal translation
"Through me one goes into the sorrowful/pain-filled/suffering city;through me one goes into eternal sorrow/suffering;through me one goes among the lost people.

Justice moved/motivated my High Maker; Divine Power made me, Supreme Wisdom, and Primal Love.

Before me were no things created, if not eternal, and I last eternally: Abandon/Leave all hope, you who enter."

Phonetic pronunciation
per me si: vA ne:' lA chi: tA' do le:n' te
per me si: vA nel e te:r' no do lo' re
per me si vA trA lA per d<u>oo</u>' tA dgen' te

dg<u>oo</u> sti:' tsi A mo:s' se il mi:'o Al' to fA:t to' re
fe:' che mi: lA di vi:' nA po tes tA' te
lA so:m' mA sA pi en' tsA e il pri:' mo A mo:' re

di: nAn' tsi A me non f<u>oo</u>r ko' ze kre: A' te
se non e te:r' ne ed i:'o e te:r' no d<u>oo</u>' ro
lA shA:' te o' nyi: spe rA:n' tsA vo'i: ken trA:' te

Note the entire absence of the schwa in unstressed syllables and the lengthened pure vowels in stressed syllables, as well as the slight lengthening of the stressed half of diphthongs.

Here is the first line of the above in a possible pitch pattern:

```
            va                  tà do-
    me               nella  cit-     len-
Per   si                                te.
```

You can see how many more notes and how much more music there is than in an English sentence. The next sentence might begin on a higher note than the preceding one began on, and rise to even higher notes before falling to end the sentence, all for dramatic effect. The syllable "do-" in the first line of the pitch pattern, just above, might be on a higher note than is there indicated, at the speaker's discretion, and the final syllable "-te" may go even lower.

Phonetic pronunciations of first verse of Dante translation
Northern/Florentine: tr<u>oo</u> mi: wAn gawz i:n' t<u>oo</u> di: saw' raw foo' le si:' ti: / tr<u>oo</u> mi: wAn gawz i:n' t<u>oo</u> e te:r' nel saw' raw / tr<u>oo</u> mi: wAn gawz e mAng' or mA ng'e, di: law' ste pi:' pel
Southern/Neapolitan/Sicilian: tr<u>oo</u> mi: wA ne gawz i:' ne t<u>oo</u> di: saw' raw foo' le si:' ti: / tr<u>oo</u> mi: wAn gawz I:' ne t<u>oo</u> i: te:r' ne le saw' raw / tr<u>oo</u> mi: wAn, or wAn, gawz e mAng'e di: law' ste pi:' pel
Note the lengthened vowels and very weak schwas between certain syllables in both pronunciations. For a **light Northern** accent you can pronounce the "TH/ th" sounds correctly. In the **Southern** accent note the possibility of a nasalized vowel in the word *one*. As an exercise, write out the other verses phonetically.

You've got to exercise or it's no good. You get home, you sit in a chair, especially in the wintertime. And we had a rough winter so far.
Phonetic pronunciation (**Southern/Sicilian**): y<u>oo</u> gA' de ek' se sIz awR, or awr, i:'

tse naw g<u>oo</u>d, or g<u>oo</u>   y<u>oo</u> ga dom yoo si:' di:n e che: es pe' she lee i:n e wi:n' te
tIm   an wee ad e Ru', or ru', fe wi:n te sO fA

Possible Pitch Pattern

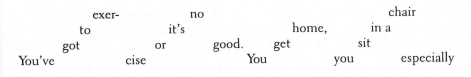

It's a great thing, you know, to ba able to travel, and Italy is especially varied in the beauty of its rolling hills and cities.
Phonetic pronunciations:
Northern/Florentine: i:ts e gray' te ti:ng y<u>oo</u> naw too bee ay' bel t<u>oo</u> trA' vel an i:' tA lee i:z e spe' shA lee va' reed i:' ne de by<u>oo</u>' tee awv i:' tse ro' ling i:ls a' ne si:' ti:s
Southern/Neapolitan/Sicilian: i:' tse gRay' de ti:ng t<u>oo</u> bee ay' be le too tRa' vel an i:' tA lee i:z is pa' shA lee va' ree i:' ne de byoo' dee aw vi:' tse Raw' li:ng i:lz a' ne si:' deez

From a conversation the author had in a trattoria (trA to ri:' yA) in Venice:
Waitress: *Che vuole per il primo piatto?*
Me: *Che c'è?*
Waitress: *Spaghetti colla sepia.*
Me: *C'è altra cosa?*
Waitress: *E tutto.*
Me: *Dunque prendo questo per il primo piatto, grazie.*
Waitress: *E per il secondo piatto abbiamo un pesce grigliato.*
Me: *Meraviglioso!*
Waitress: *Vuole vino o aqua?*
Me: *Aqua, per piacere.*
(After the meal)
Me: *Era tutto veramente delizioso.*
Waitress: *Grazie.*
Me: *C'è una dolce?*
Waitress: *No.*

Translation: What do you want for the first course?/ What is there?/ Spaghetti in squid (cuttlefish) ink sauce./ Is there something else?/ That's all./ Then I'll take that for my first course, thanks./ And for the second course we have a grilled fish./ Marvelous!/ You want wine or water?/Water, please./ Everything was really delicious./ Thanks./ Is there dessert?/ No.

Phonetic pronunciation: ké vwaw' le per i:l pri:' mo pyA' to/ ké che:/ spA ge:' ti: kol' lA se' pyA/ che: Al' tra ko' zA/ e t<u>oo</u>' to/ doon' kwe pren' do kwes' to per i:l pri:' mo pyA' to grA' zye/ e per i:l se go:n' do pyA' to A byA' mo oon pe' she gri' llyA' to/ me rA vi: glio' zo/ vwaw' le vi:' no o A' kwA/ A' kwA per pyA che:' re/ e:' rA too' to ve: rA men' te: de: li: tsi: o' zo/ grA' zye/ che: oo' nA do:l' che/ no:

Notes: The sound represented by the Italian orthographic combination "gl" does not exist in English; you can hear it accurately on the CD or on Italian language learning audio material. Note, too, that the Italian "o" is longer than the English "o" and is close to the "aw" in *law*.

Translation done in Italian accents:
Northern/Florentine: wA d<u>oo</u> y<u>oo</u> wawn faw di: fo', or fer', ste kaws wAt i:' ze de: spA ge:' tee i:n skwi: di:nk sOs' i:' ze de: som' ti:ng els' dats aw:l' den Il tay *ke* da' *te* faw mI fo' ste kaws tanks an faw dee sek' en de kaws wee av' *e* gri:l' de fi:sh mA' ve loos y<u>oo</u> wawn' *te* wIn aw waw' *de* waw' *de* pleez e' ve ree ti:ng wAz ree' *e* lee di: li:' shoos tanks i:' ze de: dee zot no:

Southern/Neapolitan/Sicilian: wA *de* y<u>oo</u> wAn, or wA' ne, fu di: fu', or foy', ste kaws wA di:' ze de: spA ge:' ti: wi: de skwi: di:nk' saws i:' ze de' re so' me ti:ng els ats, or dats, awl den I' le tay' ke da' te faw mI fo' ste kaws tanks a' ne faw dee sek' *e* ne kOs wee a' ve gri:' lde fi:sh mA' ve loos y<u>oo</u> wA' ne wI' naw waw' *de* waw' *de* pleez e' ve ree ti:ng waw' ze dee' lee shoos tanks ee' ze day dee zoy', or zo', te no:

Chapter Eleven
Portuguese Accents: Portugal and Brazil

Portuguese is spoken by about 10 million people in Portugal, and more than 160 million people in Brazil. In 1945, a treaty, the "Acordo Luso-Brasileiro," made the orthography of Portuguese uniform in both Portugal and Brazil. The ancient Romans called Portugal the province of "Lusitania." It actually comprised a large area of present-day Spain, as far as Avila, the western part of León, and Galicia. Portuguese is also spoken in Madeira and in the Azores. There are Portuguese speakers as well in former African and Pacific Portuguese colonies, and there are speakers of Galician, now considered a dialect of Portuguese, in Spain.

The Portuguese language preserves much in contemporary speech from its medieval past, when it developed as a dialect of Galician. Portuguese and Galician were, in fact, one language originally. In the 11th century various wars of conquest resulted in the eventual political, and consequent linguistic, division of Portugal under the son of Henry of Burgundy, Alfonso, who conquered Lisbon in 1147, deposed Alfonso VII, and made himself king. The standard version of the language thus evolved in the political center of power in and around Lisbon.The Douro River is the dividing line between the Southern and Central dialects of Portuguese, on the one hand, and the more archaic, conservative Northern dialects (Entre-Douro-e-Minho and Tras-os-Montes) on the other.

The Portuguese, like the Spaniards, explored the world far and wide, and developed trade with India in the 15th century. Such Portuguese names as Prince Henry the Navigator, Bartolomeu Diaz, Albuquerque, Vasco da Gama and Almeida became widely celebrated. In the New World the Portuguese conquered Brazil, from which they expelled Dutch colonies in 1654, as compensation for the loss of Indian trade to the Dutch 50 or so years before.

There are many differences in vocabulary between Portugal and Brazil, just as there are differences in the vocabulary of English between the United States and Great Britain. One of the principle differences between Brazilian and Portuguese Portuguese pronunciation is the elimination of final "sh" and "zh" sounds, which exist in greater profusion in Portugal itself. Also, Brazilian Portuguese is spoken more slowly, and words are not linked or elided into each other as much as they are in Portugal. The final "e," often silent in Portugal, is usually sounded in Brazil.

The celebrated Brazilian actress and comedienne Carmen Miranda (who died in 1955), is the perfect person to listen to for a Brazilian Portuguese accent. From her first American film, *Down Argentine Way* (1940), to her last, *Scared Stiff* (1953), she is delightful in her fruit-filled hats and broadly ruffled blouses and skirts. Listen to her sing in Portuguese and speak in English. You will notice that she has the same accent in both languages. This is a key to any accent: the way the original language is spoken is often the way English will be spoken.

A Quick Reference

1) Nasalize vowels before "m" and "n."
2) In a heavy accent pronounce the final "s" as "sh."
3) Lengthen the vowel in stressed syllables.
4) Use a trilled "r." Pronounce initial "r" with an "h" before it: "hr." Aspirate "r" in all positions.
5) Substitute "d" and "t" for "TH" and "th."
6) Substitute the "e" in *met* for the "a" as in *cat*, and the "a" in *cat* for the "e" in *met*.
7) Diphthongize "e" to "*ee*."

How to Do a Portuguese Accent

1) Position of the Vocal Apparatus
When you begin to work with the accent, assume the correct general position of the vocal apparatus, which is with the lips open about the same amount as in General American and the jaw relaxed. Keep a light, frontal articulation.

2) The Most Important Sounds
Pay attention especially to the nasal vowels before "n" and "m," and the lengthening of stressed syllables. As in Spanish the stress is on the penultimate syllable, except if the word ends in a consonant or in more than one vowel, and then the stress falls on the last syllable. Accent marks are used to indicate unusual stress. Portuguese is a softly spoken language. The rate of speech is slower for Brazilian Portuguese, with evenly spaced and lengthened syllables, which means that in Brazilian Portuguese a multisyllable word can have secondary stresses. In Portuguese in general the stress is heavily marked and the stressed syllable is longer, its vowel lengthened. This gives not only a characteristic rhythm to Portuguese itself, but can carry over into an accent in English, even when words are correctly stressed.

For the accents of **Madeira** or the **Azores**, ignore the advice on lengthened diphthongs, and pronounce them with the usual length they should have in General American or British RP. In the Portuguese spoken in those Atlantic islands the vowels and diphthongs are generally shorter than they are in Portugal, and the typical Portuguese "lh" (pronounced "ly") is shifted to a simple "l." A *million dollars* is thus pronounced "*e mee:' e lyen* daw:' lAsh" by someone from Portugal or Brazil, and "*e mi:' len daw' les*" by someone from Madeira. Note that the final "s" is often correctly pronounced in English.

Consonants
Consonants in Portuguese are softer than in General American. Initial "t" and

"p" are less pronounced, and closer to their French versions, or to their middle versions in English *dapper* and *little*. In Northern Portuguese "b" and "v" are very similar to their pronunciations in Spanish, with the lips slightly parted as they are pronounced. In the South the lips touch together more strongly.

ch: In the **Lisbon** accent "ch" is softened to "sh," and a Lisbon accent in English might reflect this shift: *church* would be pronounced "sho: sh."

l: The Portuguese "l" is dark, pronounced, especially in final position, with the blade of the tongue pulled back.

r and R: In Portuguese the "r" is lightly trilled. In an accent in English the attempt to pronounce the General American "R" in initial position sometimes results in a heavily aspirated trilled "hr": *right* is pronounced "hrIt." In **Lisbon** especially one hears an occasional uvular "R" much like the one in French, and this "R" can be used for a Lisbon accent in English.

s and zh: Initial "s" is sometimes heard as "sh" in an accent in English. *Self* is pronounced "sheeLf." At the end of a word in Portuguese Portuguese it is usually heard as "sh." At the end of a word "z," similarly is "zh" in Portugal, "z" or "s" in Brazil.

TH and th: There are no "th" or "TH" sounds. The usual substitutions are "d" and "t": *this thing* (di:s ti:ng). Note the lengthened "i:" and the nasal "n" in *thing. Thousand* is pronounced "tow' znd."

Vowels and Diphthongs
There are nasal vowels in Portuguese, similar to those in French, and they can be quite apparent in a Portuguese accent in English. A phrase like *I don't know* sounds very nasal on both the "n"s in *don't* and *know*. Listen to Carmen Miranda. Notice also that the stressed part of any diphthong is lengthened.

Practice

So, that's what you think, isn't it?
Phonetic pronunciation: Saw:' <u>oo</u> das hwA ty<u>oo</u> tee:nk ee:' sen teet

a: This vowel does not exist in Portuguese. "e" is substituted for it: *handle* (hendl). Notice that the "n" is very nasal.

e: This vowel can be diphthongized to "ee," especially before an "l," which tends to sound almost like a Slavic "L" with the tongue down from the roof of the mouth. Listen to Carmen Miranda, for example: *well* sounds like "weeL." *Then* sounds like "deen," and the "n" is rather nasal.

You must see the color, a beautiful red.
Phonetic pronunciation: y<u>oo</u> mAst see di kaw' lAR, ay byoo' tee f<u>oo</u>L hrad
Notice the inconsistent "R" and "r," and the Portuguese "L" in final position.

Pitch

There is a musical rise and fall to Portuguese, which reminds one somewhat of French. In Portuguese, however, the pitch is markedly higher, and the lower pitch is closer to it than is the lower pitch in French. The higher pitch is on the lengthened vowels described above. It is also heard in syllables containing nasal vowels.

Practice

And I have a very important message for you, which I have to deliver by hand.
Phonetic pronunciation (**Brazilian**): eent I hev ay va' Ree im pawR' tint mas' idg fawR y<u>oo</u> wi:ch I hev t<u>oo</u> di Li:' veR bI he:'end

I don't think it's right really.
Phonetic pronunciation (**Brazilian**): I daw*n* thi:*n*k i:ts RIt Reee' Lee
Note: Be aware of the Portuguese "L."

The people want to know the full extent of the problem.
Phonetic pronunciation: THe pee' poo wawn t<u>oo</u> nO THe f<u>oo</u> ik stayent' ev de pRA' bLim

Let me tell you something especially interesting.
Phonetic pronunciation: Lat mi: taL yoo sAm' thi:ng es' pash A Lee ie:n teR as' ti:ng

I wanted to come and see you but I didn't have the time.
Phonetic pronunciation: I waw*n* ned tee<u>oo</u> kAm a*n* see yee<u>oo</u> bA *d*I di:' den av de tIm
Note: The "m" and "n" sounds should be very nasal.

Possible Pitch Pattern

```
                                                    ti-\
                        see                 the
    wanted to come and            didn't have        me.
 I                       you but I
```

There are a lot of social and economic problems, as there are everywhere, but we are going to solve them.
Phonetic pronunciation: de:R AR ay law' *d*uf sO' shee eL ayen ee kO naw' mi:k

pRaw' b*L*ims as de:R AR a' vRee way*e*R bA wee AR gaw*n*g t<u>oo</u> sawLf day*e*m

Nâo, senhor, eu nâo entendo inglês.
Translation: No, sir, I don't understand English.
Phonetic pronunciation: na<u>oo</u>*n* se nyawr' ay' <u>oo</u> na<u>oo</u>*n* e*n* tye*n*' d<u>oo</u> e*n* glaysh'
Note the nasal vowels.

Pitch Practice

```
                           ten-      in-
Nâo             nâo             do
    se-             en-             glês.
        nhor
            eu
```

Chapter Twelve

Romanian Accents

Little is known of the languages of the lower Danube basin before the arrival of the conquering Roman legions in the second century C.E. The Emperor Trajan imposed the Latin language on the area known today as Romania. The modern language, also called Daco-Romanian, descends from the Latin spoken in the province of Dacia near the Black Sea. The local languages, which must have influenced at least the accent with which Latin was spoken, were replaced by it. By the time of the dissolution of the Roman Empire the local dialect of Latin was firmly entrenched, though surrounded mostly by Slavonic languages.

There is a heavy Slavonic influence in the vocabulary of Romanian (principally from Old Church Slavonic and Bulgarian), but not in the grammar, which remains a Romance grammar. As with English there is often a double vocabulary; Romanian includes words from both Slavonic and Latin. There are, for instance, two words for *border*: the Latinate *frontiera* (frawn tyay' re) and the Slavonic *granita* (grA' ni: tse). In the 19th century linguistic nationalists attempted to purge the Slavonic elements from the Romanian vocabulary, which amount to about 20 percent, but without success. There are also minor borrowings from the Greek, Turkish and Hungarian vocabularies.

The official national standard language is the dialect of Bucharest, the center of political power. Aside from other branches of Balkan Romance, there are two principal dialects of modern Romanian: 1) Moldavian, spoken in the north and in Moldavia and the Ukraine; and 2) Muntenian (Wallachian) in the south. Wallachian is the basis of the literary language and of the modern Standard Romanian of Bucharest. The Arumanian dialect of Romanian is spoken in parts of Yugoslavia, Greece and Macedonia and there is a dialect of Romanian spoken in Transylvania. All in all there are probably more than 21 million speakers in all these regions.

A Quick Reference

1) Use a trilled "r" and pronounce it in all positions.
2) Use a dark, liquid "l."
3) Substitute "z" and "s" for "TH" and "th."
4) Substitute "v" for initial "w."
5) Substitute a soft initial "kh" for "initial "h."
6) Substitute "u," "o," or "e" for "A." See below under "A."

7) Substitute "*o*" or "*e*" or "*u*" for the "schwa (*e*)."

8) Look at the section on "Pitch" and do the exercises at the end of the chapter.

How to Do a Romanian Accent

1) Position of the Vocal Apparatus

In Romanian the general position of the vocal apparatus is with the jaw fairly tight and the mouth half open, half closed. There are only two frontally rounded vowels (literally with the lips pushed forward and rounded) in Romanian, "u" (the "oo" in *book*) and "o" (the "aw" in *law*, quite short), so the lips do not get pushed very far forward most of the time. The main points of articulation, on the other hand, are felt to be quite forward in the mouth and very frontal, only "k" and "g" being back (velar) consonants.

2) Pitch

Pitch is very important in this accent. Simple statements end in a falling tone, as in so many languages. The falling tone, however, is not so marked as in English, and is closer in pitch to the syllables which precede and follow it, a trait which is carried over into English and gives the characteristic music of a Romanian accent. Questions which ask for a yes or no end, as in English, on a rising tone. However, in a Romanian accent in English, the speaker sometimes give such questions a falling tone, perhaps out of confusion as to the correct intonational pattern. Questions end on a falling tone, if they begin with an interrogative pronoun. In English this may also be true. See the "Practice" section at the end of the chapter.

3) The Most Important Sounds

Consonants

l: Use a dark liquid "l" for this accent, close to a French or a British "l."

r: A trilled "r" is very important in this accent, and is ubiquitous.

TH and th: The consonants "TH" and "th" do not exist in Romanian. The usual substitutions are "z" and "s."

v: There is no initial "w" in Romanian, and "v" is the usual substitution for it in an accent in English. *What, when* and *where* are pronounced "vut," "ven" and "ve:r." *Right away* becomes "rIt' e vay'."

h: This consonant does not exist in Romanian in its English version, but it is very close to it, lighter than the Spanish *jota* or the Scottish "ch" in *loch* (KH), and it is usually so pronounced in English, very lightly, however. *How are you?* is pronounced "khow er yoo." The reply could be "ve' ri: fIn senk yoo" (very fine, thank you).

Vowels and Diphthongs

There are seven vowels in Romanian: A, e, i, o, and u (oo), plus a schwa (e) and a palatalized "i:," in which the tongue is pressed towards the palate. The sound is close to a "y." There are also 17 diphthongs and two triphthongs: 1) spelled "eai," pronounced "yay"; and 2) spelled "eau," pronounced "yow." A number of these diphthongs do not exist in English, and need not concern us here.

schwa: Substitute the "o" in *work* or an "e" or "u" for the schwa, and make either sound very short. Use the "Practice" section at the end of the chapter.

A: In Romanian the short sound of this vowel, which has long and short versions, is close to English "u" in *but*, or to the "o" in *work*. This is important in a Romanian accent in English, particularly in the attempt to pronounce it in unstressed syllables. Sometimes in an accent in English the sound of "e" in *met* substitutes for "A." The word *rather* would be pronounced like *rudder*, but with "z" instead of "d." See the "Practice" section at the end of the chapter.

a: There is no "a" in Romanian, and "e" is the usual substitution for it. *That* is pronounced "zet." *What's that?* is pronounced either "vAts zet" or "vuts zet."

i: There is no "i" in *bit* in Romanian. Instead the usual substitution is the lengthened intermediate vowel "i:," as in so many languages.

O: This diphthong exists in Romanian, in which it is spelled "ou." In most languages the "O" diphthong is absent, but a Romanian will have no trouble pronouncing it in a phrase like *go home* (gO Om, or gO khOm).

Stress

In Romanian the stress is random. Stressed syllables are only slightly stressed, giving a somewhat even-toned quality to Romanian speech, which can carry over into English. As a result, and with the usual Romance language tendency to speak in stress groups or rhythmic phrases, in order to emphasize a word the speaker has to place it in a prominent grammatical position, which is done in Romanian exactly for purposes of emphasis.

Practice

Romanian Words and Pitch:
Se poate? Bineînteles. (Is it possible? Of course.; se pwA' te   bi: ne in tse les')

Se poa-   Bineînte-
        te?   les.

In the following example the difference between an English and a Romanian intonation pattern is one note.

230

What is it?
Phonetic pronunciations: "vut i:z i:t" or, occasionally with the "A" correctly pro-
nounced, "vAt i:z i:t"
(English)

```
        is
What       it?
```

(Romanian)

```
What is
          it?
```

I would like to discuss this issue.
Phonetic pronunciation: I vood lIk t<u>oo</u> di:s kus' zi:s i:' sh<u>oo</u>

Possible Pitch Pattern

```
                          is-
        like to discuss
    would              this
I                            sue.
```

Note: This is a typical pitch pattern for a declarative sentence in Romanian, and
caries over into an accent in English.

Practice words for "a" and the schwa: *father, rather, important, particular, usual*
Phonetic pronunciations: fu' zor, or fu' zer; ru' zor, or ru' zer; i:m pawr' tunt, or
i:m pawr' tent; por ti:k' yu lur, or pur ti:k' yu lor; yoo' zh<u>oo</u> ul, or yoo' zh<u>oo</u> el

English Sentences
When there was something to write about we wrote a lot of letters.
Phonetic pronunciation: ven ze: vAs sAm' si:nk to rIt e bowt' vee rOt a lot' Af
le' tAs

That property belonged to us in Bucharest.
Phonetic pronunciation: zet pro' pe tee bi: lawnkt t<u>oo</u> As i:n boo' kA rest'

It could not have been what you thought it was.
Phonetic pronunciation: i:t koot nawt khev been vAt y<u>oo</u> sawt i:t vaws

*I thought it was rather important or I would not have interrupted you in the middle
of something.*
Phonetic pronunciation: I tawt i:t vaws ru' zor i:m pawr' tunt awr I voot nawt ur
khef i:n ter up' tet y<u>oo</u> i:n zu mi:' del uf sum' sink

231

Bucharest was once thought of as the Paris of Eastern Europe, but a lot of it was unfortunately destroyed, and it is only now beginning to recover.

Phonetic pronunciation: boo' kA rest' vAs vAnts sawt uv ez ze pA' ri:s uv i:st' ern y<u>oo</u>' rup but ay lot uv i:t vAs un fawr' ty<u>oo</u> nayt lee de stroyt' ent i:t i:z awn' lee now bi gi:n' i:nk t<u>oo</u> ri ku' vur

Part Four

Germanic Language Accents

Introduction

The Germanic branch of the Indo-European languages derives from ancient Gothic, which has survived in the form of inscriptions and literature. Among the Germanic languages are German and its many dialects, among them Swabian (Schwabisch), High German and Bavarian-Austrian; Yiddish, closely related to Middle High German; Dutch and its derivative Afrikaans; Flemish, which is very closely related to Dutch; the Scandinavian languages Danish, Norwegian, Swedish, Icelandic and Faroese; and, of course, English. Frisian, with two main branches: West Frisian and North/East Frisian, spoken on islands off the coast of Holland, is the most closely related of the Germanic languages to English. Frisian grammar is quite different from English, but there is a famous rhyme: "Bread, butter and green cheese/Is good English and good Friese." The spelling is different in the two languages, but the pronunciations are similar: *brea; büter; grien tsiis*, which some people still make on the farm by hand in a *tsjerne*. In Friesland people *sliepe* and English speakers *sleep*, and a Frysk (pronounced fri:sk; the Frisian name for the language) dictionary is a *wurdboek*. And *saturdei* evening is Saturday evening wherever the *muun* shines at night, is it not, *boi*?

Germanic phonetics studies show that many sounds of Anglo-Saxon and Old English, once pronounced, have disappeared. The sound of "KH," as in Scottish *loch* or German *Ach!*, once pronounced in words like *daughter* and *night*, pronunciations preserved in a broad Scots dialect, have been gone from English since before the days of Queen Elizabeth I, and even earlier. Modern English is also much simplified gramatically, having lost declensions and cases for nouns. The second person informal singular, *thou* (nominative) and *thee* (accusative) are also gone, except in the speech of religious Quakers, but in German, Dutch, and the Scandinavian languages this second person informal is preserved, as are the more formal modes of saying *you*, such as the use in German of *Sie*, which, without a capital "s" is the third person singular *she*. In contemporary standard forms of English we have only the word *you* for all forms of second person address. On the other hand English spelling, still influenced by earlier pronunciations, is no longer as phonetic as it once was, and is, in fact, rather complicated to learn. Other Germanic languages, except for Danish, are generally simpler. Learning the phonetics of a parent language will help you enormously in learning its accents in English.

Chapter Thirteen
German Accents: Prussian, Bavarian, Viennese

"...German sounds a thoroughly respectable language, and, indeed I believe is so," says Lady Bracknell, who is arranging a musical evening, during which she cannot possibly allow French songs, because "People always seem to think that they are improper," in Act One of Oscar Wilde's *The Importance of Being Earnest* (1895). In Act Two, Cecily Cardew objects to studying German: "But I don't like German. It isn't at all a becoming language. I know perfectly well that I look quite plain after my German lesson." To which her governess, Miss Prism, replies: "Child, you know how anxious your guardian is that you should improve yourself in every way. He laid particular stress on your German, as he was leaving for town yesterday. Indeed, he always lays stress on your German when he is leaving for town." This is the dual view of the German language which has prevailed for a very long time in the English-speaking world: German is respectable and well organized, and at the same time it is an ugly, harsh and guttural language. Mark Twain also found it to be a very comic language. His essay "The Horrors of the German Language," which he delivered as a speech to the Vienna Press Club on November 21, 1897 is, frankly, hilarious, especially if you speak German and are familiar with the intricacies of its grammar. During World War One German was a subject for mocking humor, and it has never quite recovered from the prejudice against it. Even the English royal family felt compelled to change its name in 1917 from Wettin, the family name of Victoria's husband, the Prince Consort Albert of Saxe-Coburg and Gotha, to Windsor.

The horrors of the German occupation of Europe in World War Two and of the Holocaust made German a despised, hated, and feared language all over Europe. The Nazi criminals ruled Germany for only 12 years, but during that time they not only brought untold suffering on their victims, but in the process destroyed for decades the respect in which German culture, at least before the two world wars, was held by the world. Temporarily forgotten was the humanitarian strain in German philosophy and tradition exemplified in the works of Schiller and Goethe, and in the attitude of King Ludwig of Bavaria, who, mad though he may have been, nevertheless built three superbly beautiful 19th-century castles and who opposed war, hated anti-Semitism and racism and believed in the brotherhood of man. German had been a lingua franca in Eastern Europe before World War One, and to some extent it still is. The attempt in the Austro-Hungarian

Empire (an artificial state founded by the Compromise of 1867 uniting Austria and Hungary under one crown; it lasted 51 years, until the end of World War One), to homogenize all the peoples within its borders and make them into good German-speaking Austrians, and yet to tolerate all the national cultures, was doomed to failure from the start, given the climate of rampant anti-Semitism and nationalistic prejudices, but it was, at least in theory, the opposite of the Nazi disease.

Frederick the Great of Prussia, the autocrat who welcomed the anti-autocratic Voltaire to his court in Potsdam, named his palace *Sans Souci*, which means "without a care" in French. He preferred to speak and write in French, which he considered highly civilized, rather than in German, a language he considered uncouth. Within a language culture certain accents may be considered uncouth as well. In Germany a Saxon accent is considered comic, partly but not entirely for political reasons, since its reputation preceded the era when the ruler of East Germany was Ulbricht, who was from Saxony and had a heavy Saxon accent, like many of the border guards. Still, one can hardly stigmatize a language, but such linguistic prejudices die hard, if at all. To my ears German can be very pleasantly sonorous and elegant, particularly when High German is beautifully pronounced. Listen, for instance, to the beautifully articulated German in the expressive, moving songs of Franz Schubert, whose genius for melody astonishes, as recorded by such outstanding artists as Dietrich Fischer-Dieskau, Hermann Prey, Matthias Görne, Brigitte Fassbaender, Lotte Lehmann, Elizabeth Schumann and the Danish tenor Aksel Schiøtz, whose German is impeccable. It has sounds which have long disappeared from English, but which were pronounced in Anglo-Saxon, such as "kn," in which both consonants are pronounced, or "KH," the same sound heard in Scottish *loch*, and spelled "ch" in German. The word for *daughter* in German is *Tochter*, pronounced "toKH' te," and in older forms of English the "gh" in *daughter* was also so pronounced. Also interesting to note: Nouns are capitalized in German, as they were in 18th-century English.

The German language is highly inflected, with three genders (masculine, feminine, neuter) and four cases (nominative, genitive, dative, accusative) for nouns, and complicated verb tenses, and a grammatical structure in which certain participles go at the end of a clause, and word order can be inverted if the first word of a sentence is not its subject. The usual word order of a sentence in German is subject/ verb/ object. Here is a German sentence which illustrates some of the complications of German grammar, and which you can use for practice:

Doch bin Ich in der Stadt eine lange Zeit gewesen.
Literal translation: However have I in the City a long time been. (However, I have been in the city a long time. I translate *bin* as "have" here even though it literally means "am.")
Phonetic pronunciation: doKH bi:n i:kh i:n dee shtAt I' ne lAng' e tsIt ge ve:' zen.

German, spoken by more than 100 million people worldwide, is the official language of Germany and Austria and one of the four languages of Switzerland. It began to be standardized in the 14th century despite the numerous dialects spoken in the independant principalities and dukedoms, and became the language of literature and civil administration, replacing Latin. The present Standard High German (Hoch Deutsch) is said to be spoken in its purest form in the dialect of Hannover. Some of the principal dialects in Germany (all of which make a difference in speaking English) are: Berlin; Swabian (Schwabisch), spoken around Stuttgart; Bavarian, spoken in the south; and Saxon (Sachisch), spoken in the East.

In **Austria** we find the dialect of Vienna (Wienerisch), and a general rural accent similar to that of **Bavaria**. For stage purposes you generally need to study the **Prussian** (or North German, Hanoverian) and **Austrian** (or South German) dialects. A **Swiss** German accent strongly resembles a Bavarian or Austrian accent, and Schwyzertütsch (Swiss German) is widely spoken in a number of dialects.

The Commandant played by Sig Rumann in *Stalag Seventeen* (1953) and innumerable Nazi officers in films and plays required heavy German accents. There is the Flea Circus professor in the play *The Great Magoo* and the occasional portrayal of famous individuals such as Einstein or Freud. Actors with **Austrian** accents include Walter Slezak in *Lifeboat* (1944); Maximilian Schell; Lotte Lenya in *From Russia With Love* (1963); Anton Walbrook in *The Red Shoes* (1948); Oskar Werner in *Ship of Fools* (1965); Oskar Homolka in *War and Peace* (1951); Paul Henreid in *Casablanca* (1942); and, of course, Arnold Schwarzenegger in his many action-adventure films. For **North German** accents listen to Sig Rumann, who was from Hamburg, as the Opera House Manager in *A Night at the Opera* (1935), and with Jack Benny in *To Be or Not To Be* (1941); Felix Bressart, a wonderful character actor in such films as *To Be or Not To Be* (1941) and *The Shop Around the Corner* (1940); Conrad Veidt in *Casablanca* (1942); Marlene Dietrich in her many films; Armin Mueller-Stahl from East Prussia in *Shine* (1996) and *Avalon* (1994); Lilli Palmer in *The Counterfeit Traitor* (1962); Curt Jurgens in *Battle of Britain* (1969) and *The Spy Who Loved Me* (1977); and Gert Frobe in *Goldfinger* (1964) and *Is Paris Burning* (1966).

A Quick Reference

1) In all German accents drop the final "R" and the "R" before another consonant. For North German accents use a uvular "R"; for South German/Austrian accents use a trilled "r" with one tap.
2) Final voiced consonants ("b," "d," "dg," "g," "v," "z") shift to voiceless ("p," "t," "ch," "k," "f," "s").
3) Initial "w" shifts to "v."
4) Initial "s" sometimes shifts to "z."
5) For "TH/th" substitute "z/s" for North German; "d/t" for South German.
6) Substitute the lengthened pure vowel "o:" for the diphthong "O"; the length-

ened pure vowel "e:" for the diphthong "ay."

7) In South German/Austrian accents, diphthongize vowels, especially before "r." In the German spoken in Vienna, for example, "A" shifts to "aw" and before "R" to a diphthongized "awe" and this carries over into English: Substitute "aw" for "A" in words like *father* (occasionally) and diphthongize "aw" before "R" in words like *of course*.

8) Substitute "e" for "a" in a heavy or medium accent.

9) Use the vowel system for British RP, not General American, and you will sound more foreign to American ears right away.

10) To create a **light** German accent, follow the advice about shifting final voiced consonants to voiceless consonants. This may be the only thing you have to do, perhaps adding a little of the information under "Pitch."

How to Do German Accents

1) Position of the Vocal Apparatus
Push your lips forward and say *avail avail avail*. This will give you the correct general position of the vocal apparatus. The lips are in a slightly more forward position than in General American, much the same position, in fact, as in British RP. The lower jaw is a bit more forward, too. The tip of the tongue is also quite forward. German is often said to be a guttural language, because of certain sounds, (the "ch" in *ach*; the uvular "R"), but in fact it is a very clearly pronounced, frontally articulated language. The consonant "sh," spelled "sch" or as "s" before "p" or "t" is pronounced with the lips protruded, for example, unlike its General American counterpart.

2) The Most Important Sounds
Consonants
Both Standard High German and Austrian German are non-rhotic. The letter "R" in a final position or before another consonant is not pronounced. In **North German** accents "R" is generally lightly guttural (in the throat), and sometimes heavily guttural. In **Vienna** and **Bavaria** "r" is given a frontal trill (usually one flap).

Very important: What would be final voiced consonants in English become voiceless in German, and in a German accent in English. This shift in the sound of final consonants is usually the last thing to disappear. Thus "b" becomes "p"; d" becomes "t"; "g" becomes "k"; "z" becomes "s." In German the letters "b," "d," "g," and "s" are symbols for voiceless consonants when they appear at the ends of words. This phonetic phenomenon is very frequently carried over into a German accent in English, so the word *end* is pronounced "ent." The word in German is *Ende* (all nouns are capitalized in German), and the "d" is voiced, not being in a final position. However, when the German word is shortened to *End*, it is pronounced "ent." As if in compensation, in a somewhat exaggerated comic German accent, some final voiceless consonants shift to voiced: *it's true* becomes "idz tRoo," and *that's right* is pronounced "dedz RId." *Edge* rhymes with *etch*.

Practice words: *rig* (rik, or Rik); *give* (gi:f); *have* (hef); *cab* (kep); *hat* (het); *is* (i:s, as opposed to "iz"); *was* (vAs); *haze* (hays); *end* (ent); *king* (kink, or king, since final "ng" exists in German); *England* (ing' lAnt, or eng' lAnt, as it is in German); *bend* (bent); *bide* (bIt); *abide* (u bIt'); *bins* (bi:nts); *beans* (bi:nts); *rescind* (ri: si:nt', or Ri: sint', or ri: zint'); *blood* (blut); *pad* (pet)

Very important: In German orthography the letters of the alphabet are used differently than in English orthography. Initial semi-vowels and consonants have different sounds associated with the letters of the alphabet than they do in English. In heavy accents the following sound shifts or substitutions carry over into English.

l: This liquid consonant in Standard High German is similar to the French "l" and is the "l" often heard in German accents in English. You should feel it resonate where the vowel "i" resonates. **Practice** by saying "i" several times, then say "l."

s: Initial "s" is close to our "z" sound.

TH and th: The consonants "TH" and "th" do not exist, except in German spelling: In North German accents it is very common to substitute "z" for voiced: *This* is pronounced "zis"; and "s" for voiceless, so *thing* is pronounced "sing." In South German substitute "d" and "t": "dis ting." Between vowels "TH" is sometimes heard as an aspirated tapped "d," so *father* is pronounced "faw' *de*" or "fA' *de*."

v: "Initial "v" is close to our "f" sound in German itself, and this often carries over into an accent in English, so *very* is pronounced to rhyme with *ferry*, and remember to use either a uvular "R" or a trilled "r." Occasionally, as a kind of overcompensation, you might hear an initial "w," learned by the student of English, but inaccurately as far as where it is actually heard, substituted for a "v": "wery."

w: The semi-vowel "w" does not have the sound we associate with it in English in an initial position, although it is used in German spelling in an initial position. It is closer in sound to our "v." When the combination "qu" is used in English spelling it is pronounced "kw." This sound, too, does not exist in German, and the pronunciations "kv" or "kf" are substituted for it. *Queen* is pronounced "kveen" and *quite* is pronounced "kfIt."

Vowels and Diphthongs
a: This vowel often shifts to "e," so *back* is pronounced "bek." Sometimes "e" shifts to "A."
Practice words: *cap* (kep); *hat* (het); *back* (bek); *that* (zet, or det); *rat* (Ret, or ret); *cat* (ket); *balance* (be' lents, or bA' lints); *ballet* (be' lay, or bA le:'); *ballad* (be' let, or bA' let); *salad* (se' lit, or sA' let, or seldom, zA' let)

Further Phonetic Information

Consonants

Other sounds are as in English, but there is a German "KH" ("ch" in German spelling). There are soft and hard versions: the hard is like Scottish *loch* (loKH); the soft close to English initial "h" in such German words as *Ich* (the first person pronoun "I"; i:kh) and *fertig* (finished; fe:' ti:kh), dialectically pronounced sometimes, in **Berlin** for example, as a "k." My phonetic symbol for this sound is "kh." To pronounce it correctly in German say the English word *hue*, than add the sound "i" before it, then drop the "ue."

Vowels and Diphthongs

The vowel system is A, e, i, o u (<u>oo</u>) with some additions: Ö Ü Ä. There are also diphthongs: phonetic symbol "I" (spelled "ei" in German); phonetic symbol "oy" (spelled "eu" in German); phonetic symbol "ow" (spelled "au" in German); and phonetic symbol "<u>yoo</u>" (spelled "ju" in German). The diphthongs "O" and "ay" do not exist in German and lengthened vowels "o:" and "e:" tend to be substituted for them, or else the two halves of the diphthong are evenly stressed. In **Vienna** the tendency is to diphthongize and lengthen vowels in German, giving the accent its special lilt, and reminding New Yorkers, at least, of a Brooklyn accent. This is carried over into an Austrian accent in English: *of course* is pronounced "uf kaw: es" or, alternatively "uf k<u>oo</u>: es." *Sure* is pronounced "sh<u>oo</u>: e" or, alternatively, "sh<u>oo</u>: A." All vowels have long and short versions. Ö is similar to the sound in *work* (minus the "R"): "vok" in a fairly heavy accent, "wok" in a lighter accent. Ü is the French "u," (international phonetic symbol: y; my phonetic symbol: ü). Ä is similar to the "ay" in *say*.

Stress

Stress in German has rather complicated rules, but one can say it is random for the purposes of learning stress patterns in English. In German, the stress is often on the first syllable, but words beginning with prefixes, such as "ge," are often stressed on the second syllable.

Pitch

Pitch patterns vary with the dialect, but in **Standard High German** the pattern is similar to English (stressed syllables are on a higher pitch than unstressed). There is one pattern which sounds rather pedantic to English ears. It consists of a rising tone on a stressed word in a declarative sentence, as in the following example: "That is quite <u>right</u>, I think." The underlined word is spoken on the highest tone of the sentence. There is a musical intonation pattern which is quite different from English, however, in **Vienna**, and it is quite different from the German heard in **Berlin**, and has a very sing-song lilt to it, which you can hear in the dialogue of Strauss's *Die Fledermaus*, on the 1960 London recording conducted by Von Karajan, for example.

From "Die Lorelei" ("The Lorelei," a mythical siren-like creature who dwells in the Rhine; Phonetic pronunciation: dee law' Re lI) by Heinrich Heine.

Ich weiss nicht was soll es bedeuten, dass Ich so traurig bin;
ikh vIs nikht vAs zol es be doy' ten dAs ikh zo tRow' rikh bi:n
Literal translation: I know not what should it mean, that I so sad am;

Ein Märchen aus uralten Zeiten, dass kommt mir nicht aus dem Sinn;
In maye' khen ows ooe' Al' ten tsI' ten dAs kumt mie nikht ows daym zi:n
Literal translation: A tale from ancient times, that comes from-me not out-of the mind;

Die Luft ist kühl und es dunkelt, und ruhig fliesst der Rhein;
dee looft ist kül oont es doon' kelt oont Roo' ikh fleest de: RIn
Literal translation: The air is cool and it darkens (grows dark), and quiet(ly) flows the Rhine;

Die Gipfel des Berges funkelt im Abend Sonnenschein.
dee gip' fel des baye' ges foon' kelt im A' bent zon' en shIn
Literal translation: The tops of-the mountains sparkle in-the evening sunshine.

Translation:
I know not what it betokens, that I am so very sad;
Some ancient mythic story refuses to leave my head;
The river air is cooling, and peacefully flows the Rhine,
And the mountaintops are sparkling in the late evening sunshine.

Practice Sentences

It would have been quite something if what I had said had really happened.
Phonetic pronunciations:
Very heavy accent: i:t voot hef been kvIt zum' sink if vAt I het zet het Reee lee hep' emt
Medium heavy accent: it voot haf been kfIt sum' sink if vAt I het set het reee' lee hep' ent
Lighter accent: it woot hef been kwIt sum' sink if wAt I hat set hat reee' lee hap' ent
Lightest accent: it woot haf bin kwIt sum' think if wAt I hat set hat Ree' lee hap' ent

Notes: 1) You can see from the last phonetic pronunciation that the last thing to disappear from a German accent is the final voiceless consonants, where General American and British RP have voiced consonants. 2) For an Austrian/Bavarian accent trill the "R" and for North German accents use the uvular "R." 3) In words like "really" draw out the diphthongs for Austrian accents; shorten them for North German accents.

My father told me to take up a sure profession.
Phonetic pronunciations:
Prussian/North German: mI fA' ze tawlt mee t<u>oo</u> tayk Ap e sh<u>oo</u> pRO fe' shen
Austrian/Bavarian/Swiss: mI faw' *de* tawlt mee t<u>oo</u> tayk Ap e sh<u>oo</u>'*e* prO fe' shn

Whatever you want to do, do it well and be happy.
Phonetic pronunciations:
Prussian/North German: vAt ef' *e* y<u>oo</u> vawn t<u>oo</u> d<u>oo</u> d<u>oo</u> i:t vel ent bi: he' pi:, or pee
Austrian/Bavarian/Swiss: vaw de' fA y<u>oo</u> vaw ne d<u>oo</u> d<u>oo</u> i:t vel en bee he' pee
Note the tapped "*d*" in *whatever*. For a **lighter accent,** you could pronounce the "v" in the syllable "-ever" in *whatever,* as well as the initial "w"s in *whatever, want,* and *well,* correctly.

From Johann Strauss's *Die Fledermaus* (1874)
Ganz recht! Ich sehe, Sie fassen die Sache von der humoristischen Seite auf.
Literal translation: Completely right! I see you take the thing from the humorous side on.
Translation: Quite right! I see you look at this thing from a humorous angle/point of view.
Phonetic pronunciations
Prussian: gAnts Rekht i:kh ze' *e* zee fA' sen dee zA' KH*e* fon de: h<u>oo</u> mo Ri' sti shen zI' te owf
Austrian/Viennese: gawntz rekht i:kh ze' e zee faw' sen dee zaw' KHe fawn de:*e* h<u>oo</u> maw ri:' sti shen zay' te Of

Pitch Pattern (**Viennese**)
Note the rising and falling tones.

```
        recht!
Ganz                  Sie fas-
     Ich      he      sen    che                    ischen \Sei-
          se-/              die    von der hu-   ist-          te auf.
                            Sa-               mor
```

Pitch Pattern (**Prussian**)

```
        recht!      sehe, Sie fassen
Ganz        Ich                 die Sache
                                        von              ristischen
                                           der humo-          Seite
                                                                  auf.
```

242

It is with great gratitude that I accept this award.
Phonetic pronunciations:
North German (Heavy accent): i:t i:s vi:s gRayt gRe' ti: ty<u>oo</u>t zet, or set, I ek
sept' zi:s e vawt', or A vawt'
Austrian/Bavarian: i:t i:s vi:s, or vi:t, grayt gre' ti: ty<u>oo</u>t det I ek sept' di:s e
vawet'

That was the only way he could get things accomplished, believe me.
Phonetic pronunciations:
North German (Heavy accent): zet vAs zee On' lee vay hee koot get sinks e
kawm' pli:sht bi leef' mee
Austrian/Bavarian: det vAs dee On' lee vay hee koot get tinks e kawm' pli:sht bi
leef' mee

*You must have on a jacket and tie to dine in this restaurant, gentlemen. These are
not my rules. I am terribly sorry.*
Phonetic pronunciations:
North German: y<u>oo</u> mAst hef awn e dge' ket en tI t<u>oo</u> dIn i:n zi:s Res' to: Rant
chen' tl men   zees A no:t mI R<u>oo</u>ls I em te' Rip lee saw', or zaw', Ree
Austrian/Bavarian: y<u>oo</u> mAst hef awn e che ket en tI t<u>oo</u> dIn i:n di:s re staw
rawnt chen' tl men. di:s A no:t mI r<u>oo</u>els I em ta', or te', rip lee saw' ree

*When it comes to the environment, things are quite serious and the weather pat-
terns, for instance, really need to be studied assiduously.*
Phonetic pronunciations:
North German: ven i:t kAms t<u>oo</u> zee en fl' Ren ment sinks A kfIt see', or zee',
Ree es ent ze ve' se pe' tens faw i:n' stents, or stents, Ree' lee ni:t t<u>oo</u> bee stA'
deet, or deet, a si:t', or zi:t', y<u>oo</u> es lee
Austrian/Bavarian: ven i:t kAms t<u>oo</u> di: en fl' ren ment ti:nks aw kfIt see' ree es
ent di: ve *de* pe' tens faw ri:n stents ree' e lee ni:t t<u>oo</u> bee stA' di:t e si:t y<u>oo</u> es lee
Notes: The accents in the sentences above are very heavy. You can lighten them
up by pronouncing "TH" and "th" sounds correctly and by doing a retroflex
"R." Also, initial "w" and "s" can be correctly pronounced. Keep the final shift
of voiced to voiceless or unvoiced consonants and do the vowels as indicated.
Think British RP and not General American and you will sound foreign, and
lighten the accent at the same time.

*There's an upsurge of interest in that kind of thing, and at the same time, I assure
you, it presents no particular danger.*
Phonetic pronunciations:
North German: zay' es en Ap' so:ch Af in' tRest i:n zet kIn awf sink ent et ze
saym tIm I e sh<u>oo</u>'e y<u>oo</u> i:t pRi zents' no pA' ti:k y<u>oo</u> lA dayn' dge
Austrian/Bavarian: dayes en Ap' so:ch Af i:n' te rest in det kInt awf ti:nk ent et
de saym tIm I e sh<u>oo</u>'e y<u>oo</u> i:t pri zents' nO pA ti:k y<u>oo</u> lA dayn' dge

Possible Pitch Pattern

```
                        interest
         up-       of            in that kind of thing              time
              surge
There's                                               at the same
     an                                          and


                                    dan-
                      particular
                  no
         sure
     as-      you   presents
I            it                              ger
```

That's right that things happened, and they were mistaken, but they disappeared and we went back into the theatre right afterwards.

Phonetic pronunciations:

North German: zets RIt zet si:nks hep' ent ent zay vo mi:s tay' kn bAT zay di:s e pi:et ent vee vent bek i:n' t<u>oo</u> ze tee' e te RIt Af' te vets

Austrian/Bavarian: dets rIt, or RIt, det sinks hep' emt ent day vo mis tay' kn bAt day di:s A peeet' ent vee vent bek i:n' t<u>oo</u> de see' A te rIt ef' te voots

Notes: Notice the inconsistency of the rhotic sounds and of the "TH" and "th" substitutions. People are often inconsistent within their own accent, and will sometimes pronounce an accurate "R," and in the next word an "r." The nasalised "n" in the last syllable of *mistaken* is almost an "ng."

Chapter Fourteen
Yiddish and Its Dialects

Yiddish was the first language of most Eastern European Jews before World War Two, and is today the first language of many Hassidim (the ultra-Orthodox sect of Judaism), whether they live in Brooklyn or Jerusalem. In its grammatical and lexical essence Yiddish is the Rhineland dialect of medieval High German. The language is written in a modified Hebrew alphabet, and approximately 15 percent of its vocabulary is derived from Hebrew, the language of religion and religious education for the Jews of medieval Europe, just as it is for contemporary Jews. The pronunciation of these adopted words is "Yiddishized," by vowel shifts and by stressing syllables that are different from the ones stressed in Hebrew. For example, Hebrew *mishpaha* (mish pA khA'; family) becomes Yiddish *mishpukhe* (mish poo' KHe). There are also vocabulary elements derived from Slavic and Romance languages.

The Yiddish language was carried to Eastern Europe by Jews fleeing the Rhineland after bloody pogroms (a Slavic word meaning "officially instigated massacres") during the time of the Black Death in the 14th century. Indeed the process had begun even earlier, during the first crusades in the 11th and 12th centuries, when Jews trying to escape destruction in the western parts of Europe fled to what is now Austria, the Czech Republic, and Slovakia.

The Jews had arrived in the Rhineland from farther south, bringing with them early medieval French and Spanish Jewish languages, and adopting the local Germanic dialects, which they modified by the addition of Hebrew and Romance vocabulary elements.

By the 14th century Jews had been living in the Rhineland for some six centuries. With their different and misunderstood religion, they were looked on by the superstitious much as witches were looked on in Salem in 17th-century America, as if they were in league with Satan, and they were accused of starting the plague by poisoning wells. The Polish kingdom and Eastern Europe in general welcomed the devastated Jews for their presumed commercial abilities, and they lived well and peacefully there until the poisonous virus of anti-Semitism eventually asserted itself, with all its pernicious effects. By the 18th century the vast majority of the legally segregated and isolated masses of Jews, barred from the professions and from owning land, having continued to teach their children the *mame-losh'n* (mA' me lo' shn; mother tongue), lived in horribly impoverished conditions in Russia and Poland and the eastern provinces of the Austro-

Hungarian Empire. Their language was despised and disparaged as a "jargon," much as the African languages of the slaves brought to the United States were called "dialects" by the slave owners, who referred to English as a "language," thus giving it, as they thought, greater weight and dignity. Yiddish was thus both a means of preserving a culture and a badge of oppression. Periodically those who spoke it were slaughtered.

With the murder of so many millions of Yiddish speakers by the Nazi extermination machine it appeared as if the language was doomed. Yiddish has nevertheless proved to have great resilience. Although the number of native speakers is clearly declining, probably several million people still speak Yiddish as a first language, (a mere fraction of the almost 11 million who spoke it before the Second World War), and there are still active Yiddish theatres in various countries. With its colorful expression, vibrant humor and earthiness, it became in the 19th and 20th centuries the vehicle for a brilliant literature expressing among other things the joys and sorrows of the Jewish condition in Eastern Europe.

Yiddish is richly expressive, idiomatic and ironic. For example, one could say *Ein kleinikeit!* (In' kLI' nikIt; meaning literally "a little thing," but the real meaning of the expression is "big deal!" or "who cares?" or, alternatively, an ironic "really?" or "so what?"; the expression means the opposite of the literal meaning of the word) in response to a complaint such as "I can't get my shoelace untied" or "I won't get that paper written on time." Obviously there are many other contexts in which this expression, which makes light of both important and unimportant events, could be used. "The conductor dropped his baton during the concert!" *Ein kleinikeit.* It is very difficult to translate Yiddish idioms, which have so many possible interpretations. The rich and varied vocabulary of "body language," such as shrugs and gestures which may accompany such expressions, is beyond the scope of this book to describe.

Sholem Aleichem, in talking about the Dreyfus Affair in his short story "Dreyfus in Kasrilevke" (kAzRil' efke; the fictitious Eastern European Jewish town he created), begins his tale of the reactions of the local citizens to the accusations of treason in 1894 against the French Army General Staff officer Captain Alfred Dreyfus, who was accused simply because he was a Jew, tried, found guilty, stripped of his rank, condemned to penal servitude on Devil's Island and eventually exonerated, in a wonderfully ironic way. "I don't know if the Dreyfus Affair came to a head anywhere as much as it did in Kasrilevke." And he adds "In Paris, zugt man, hot dos oykh gekokht vee in a kessel." (Phonetic pronunciation: in pA Rees' zoogt mAn hut dos oyKH gi koKHt' vee in A ke' sel; literal translation: In Paris, say they, has it also cooked as in a kettle; real, if figurative translation: In Paris, they say, the pot was also boiling.) The irony, of course, is that nobody has ever heard of the small town of Kasrilevke or its self-important inhabitants. Paris is where it all really happened! The "also" is typical Yiddish humor, as is the deflation of the self-important and the egotistical.

The reports of Dreyfus's second trial, held after he was brought back from Devil's Island in 1899, are read to the local populace by Zaydl (zay' dl), the one man in town who has a subscription to a newspaper, and Zaydl tells them Dreyfus

246

was again found guilty. They are outraged, not at the generals and politicians, but at Zaydl. They refuse to believe he is telling them the truth just because it was in the newspaper. *Blat-shmat!* (blAt shmAt; paper-shmaper!; *shmat* also means "rag," and the rhyming word which begins with "sh" is also a typical Yiddish way of putting something down), they yell at him. The story ends with a further ironic twist, because, as Sholem Aleichem says, "A simn—ver iz gevayn gerecht?" (a si' mn veR iz gi vayn' gi ReKHt'; an omen/a sign—who was right?) about the innocence of the accused Dreyfus. Not the bigwigs and the high mucky-mucks, but the man in the street, who knew all along. Incidentally, you can use the sentences in Yiddish for practice, and to help launch you into the accent.

As a living language of immigrants, Yiddish has always added to its vocabulary from the surrounding majority language. In Paris you might hear someone say *Oy, er iz getombet!* (ooee eR iz gi tom' bit; Oh, he has fallen!). In classic Yiddish the sentence would be the Germanic *Oy, er iz gefallen!* (gi fA' lin). The word *getombet* is derived from French *tomber* (tawm bé'; to fall), and is pure Parisian Yiddish. In Moscow an elderly gentleman said to me, in purely Moscow Yiddish: *Ich hob a zun in Chicago. Er schreibt pismus.* (eeeKH hub u zoon in shi kA' ge eR shRIpt pis' mes; I have a son in Chicago. He writes letters). The word *pismus* is from the Russian word *pismo* (pees maw'; letter), with a Yiddish plural "s" added to it. The Yiddish word for a letter that one writes is really the pure Germanic *brief* (bReef) or *brievel* (bRee' vel; a short letter). The *shammes* (shA' mes; sexton) of the synagogue, giving our group a little tour, pointed to the balcony and said *Un dort oyben zitsen die zhenshchinas.* (oon dawRt oy' bn zi' tsn dee zhen' shchi nes; And there above sit the women). Now, *women* in Yiddish is *veiber* (vI' beR) or *froyen* (fRoy' in), Germanic words once again. The Russian word for woman is *zhenshchina* (zhen' shchi: ne). Again our Moscow speaker had Yiddishized the word by adding an "s" to make it plural.

Certain words which are associated with Yiddish are also Slavic. *Oy* (ooee, stress on the oo half of the diphthong; "oh," said in many contexts, including those of commiseration or complaint) is as Russian as it is Yiddish, even when it has the Germanic words *vey* (vay; woe) or *gevalt* (gi vAlt'; help, but the more literal meaning is force, or even police force originally) added to it in the expressions *oy, vey!*, which is ironic as well as literal, and the equally ironic or literal *oy, gevalt!*. Common to both Slavic and Germanic vocabulary is *nu* or *nu?* (noo; well; so?; so what?, etc.), but *nuzhe?* (noo' zhe; well?) has a typical Russian ending, "-zhe," meaning "then," and reinforcing the *nu*. *Nu, nuzhe,* and *oy* are expressions which can all be found in the plays of Anton Chekhov, as well as in the stories of Sholem Aleichem.

The expression *nu* is susceptible of a variety of meanings and interpretations, expressed by means of different pitches, a long or short vowel, and sometimes accompanied by gestures. Some of them are "I'm waiting; come on already! What's taking you so long?" (rising pitch from low to high, lengthened vowel; or high pitch falling to slightly lower, shortened vowel); "So? What are you waiting for?" (rising pitch, from low to medium high or very high, lengthened vowel); "That's the way it is. I'm resigned to it. What can you do?" (high or low single pitch, lengthened or shortened vowel, with a shrug of the shoulders and opening of the hands, palms out, and, perhaps, a sigh); "So why doesn't the show start already?" (medium pitch, lengthened vowel); "So what did you expect?" (slight rising or slight falling pitch, long vowel); "All right, so, forget it, you know?" (very high pitch, short vowel, a turning away of the head); "I told you so. Didn't I tell you? Now maybe you'll believe me." (medium pitch, very slight rising tone, lengthened or shortened vowel); "So what? Who cares? Big deal!" (any pitch, short or long vowel; perhaps with a shrug and a turning of the head, as the eyes close slightly; it's the intention that counts). Intention and context are everything. Any of the suggested pitches could express another meaning, conveyed by the speaker's intended communication in uttering just that one syllable *nu*. But, in fact, that one syllable can be repeated (*nu, nu*), and can mean any of the above, doubled, or... anything you want it to mean. You can also see how rhythm (stress; long or short vowels; even though we are dealing with a word of one syllable) and music (pitch) work together to create the accent. I am reminded of another expression associated with Jewish irony and humor: *What else is new?*, meaning, of course, that nothing is, that what has just been said is old news, or expected. "He isn't even looking for a job! He just sits around all day doing nothing!" "Nu, so what else is new?"

A great many Yiddish words are to be found in contemporary English, especially in cities with large Jewish populations, such as New York: *chutzpah* (KHoots' pe; nerve; gall); *shmuck* (shmuk; jerk, but literally penis or jewel); *bagel*; *kibbitz* (ki' bits; to tease, to comment while looking over someone's shoulder); *shlep* (shlep; to carry around); *shmooze* (shm<u>oo</u>z; to converse); *meshugge* (mi shoo' ge; crazy). In London you can even buy a jar of *haimishe* (hay' mi she; home-style) pickles, and *nosh* (nAsh in New York, or, in London, nosh; snack) on a bagel or on *gefilte* (ge fil' te; stuffed) fish.

There are two dialects of Yiddish which everyone whose grandparents came from Eastern Europe knows of, *Galitzianer* (Galician), the dialect heard generally in the eastern provinces of the Austro-Hungarian Empire, such as Galicia, in other words in most of what is now eastern Poland and the western parts of the Ukraine, as well as in Romania; and *Litvak* (Lithuanian), which is the dialect in northern and western Russia and in Lithuania, with Slavic vocabulary added to it, as we have seen. There is another dialect of Yiddish which was spoken everywhere else, in the rest of Poland, Russia, the Ukraine, and in what is now the Czech Republic (although before World War One the Jews of Prague, being Austro-Hungarian citizens, largely spoke German as a first language, and not Yiddish) and Slovakia.

The lands in which Yiddish was spoken have changed borders so many times, even in this century, that the geography of these dialects only makes sense if a pre-World War One map of Eastern Europe is consulted. In political terms it is certainly nonsense to speak of a "Standard Yiddish," since the Jews who spoke it were never in a position of power from which to impose their language even on the Jewish part of the population. However, from the literary point of view it does make sense to speak of a standard written language. The standard literary language is spoken with an accent that is a generally accepted system of pronunciation widely used by Yiddish speakers who are neither Galitzianer nor Litvak. It is therefore considered a standard accent by speakers of Yiddish, even though some of the great Yiddish writers, such as Sholem Aleichem, who created the famous Tevye the Dairyman of later *Fiddler on the Roof* fame, were Galitzianers and wrote the dialogue of their characters in a distinctly Galician accent. It is nevertheless the standard accent that is generally used in the Yiddish cinema and theatre, which flourished not only in Eastern Europe, but also on Second Avenue on the Lower East Side of New York at the beginning of the 20th century, with such luminous stars as Maurice Schwartz (who played Tevye the Dairyman brilliantly in a 1939 Yiddish film), Boris Tomashevsky, Bertha Kalish and Jacob Adler.

The differences in pronunciation between Galitzianer Yiddish and Standard Yiddish are quite marked, as is the pronunciation of liturgical Hebrew by the Ashkenazim (Eastern Europeans) from that of the Sephardim (Spanish Jews), the Sephardic accent being close to that of the present-day Israelis. In Galicia, my grandparents, all four of whom came from the same small area near Kolomea in what is now the western Ukraine, but which then belonged to Austria-Hungary, would say *A git'n tug, vus hert zukh?* (u gi' tn toog voos heRt zeKH; a good day, what is heard? or, less literally, hello, what do you hear?, or hi, what's new?); but in the theatre they would have heard these same words pronounced "a gut'n tog, vos hert zikh?" (u goo' tn tog vos heRt zuKH) bringing the pronunciation much closer to German. There is no soft "kh" in Yiddish, only the hard "KH."

For good examples of Yiddish accents listen to Maurice Schwartz in *Salome* (1953), as Ezra, and *Slaves of Babylon* (1953), as Nebucchadnezzar. His film *Tevya* (1939), in which he starred in Yiddish in the title role, is brilliant. Gertrude Berg, Molly Picon and Menashe Skulnik also have Yiddish accents in their rare film appearances. See, for instance, *The Goldbergs* (1950), with Gertrude Berg, David Opatashu and Eli Mintz, about an immigrant Jewish family in New York. *Hester Street* (1975), while excellent and moving, gives a real feeling of turn-of-the-century immigrant New York, but is less authentic, because the actors' first language was not Yiddish.

A Quick Reference

1) Study the section on the all-important pitch (intonation) patterns of Yiddish, which give the accent its characteristic music.
2) In initial position use either a uvular "R" or a trilled "r" with one tap. Before another consonant or in final position these sounds may be pronounced, but for New York or London you may want to drop them.
3) Pronounce final "g" in "-ing" word endings and in general.
4) For "TH/th" substitute "d/t" or, sometimes, a tapped "d" between vowels: "fA' deR" for *father*.
5) For initial "w" substitute "v."
6) For "a" as in *cat* substitute "e" as in *met*.

How to Do a Yiddish Accent

1) Position of the Vocal Apparatus

The muscles of the mouth are held a bit more loosely than in General American. The resonance of Yiddish is behind that of General American, near the back of the throat, and that part of the mouth is open, with the back of the tongue down. Thicken the tongue as for a Slavic "L" (see Chapter Seventeen on Russian accents), and you will have the main point of resonance. The lips are very slightly thrust forward and slightly more open than for General American.

2) Pitch

The music or pitch patterns of a Yiddish accent have tremendous variety, and are very distinctive and characteristic. They have often been described as "sing-song," because they hit many more upper and lower notes than does Standard English. The music of the Yiddish language itself, with its expressive intonation patterns, is one of its most important features, and this is especially so in a Yiddish accent in English.

Practice

Listen to the introduction and opening bars of the Colonel's song "When I First Put This Uniform On" in Gilbert and Sullivan's *Patience*, and you will have a good idea of one intonation pattern, representing an explanation. Recite the following practice phrases, rather than singing Sullivan's tune:

```
        first put this uniform on,     said as I looked in the glass
When I                          I
```

Menachem Begin, Prime Minister of Israel, was from Poland originally, and his speech offers an excellent example of a Polish Yiddish accent. He spoke this sentence in a television interview:

Let us sit together around the table and talk peace.
Phonetic pronunciation: Let As si: t too ge' der e rAn' di tay' beL en tawk pi:s
Note that the final "r," which is given one trill here, instead of being pronounced gutturally, should be very lightly pronounced.

Here is one possible intonation pattern, not his, by the way, which was markedly "flat."

```
                                            talk
                            table
            gether    round            and
Let us   to         a-       the                    peace.
      sit
```

So? What else is new? What can you do?
Phonetic pronunciation: sO vAt eLs iz n<u>oo</u> vAt ken yoo d<u>oo</u>

```
     o?              is new?      can you do?
         What                What
So-
         else
```

I told him, "come here." But did he listen? No!
Phonetic pronunciation: I tawlt im kum heeeR baw did hee lis' in nO

```
  told
       him                              No!
I           come      But        ten?
            here.     did he
                            lis-
```

Note: In a question, a rising tone at the end is usual. In an imperative sentence, a simple lower pitch at the end is usual. However, a falling tone at the end of a question and/or a rising tone at the end of an imperative are sometimes heard, as in the following example, the implication of which is that the person being addressed is an idiot. Note the falling tone on the word *in*.

```
          waiting             \in!
    are you         for?      him
What                 Bring
```

3) The Most Important Sounds
Consonants

Yiddish is a rhotic language, and accents in English tend to be rhotic, although in London and New York you might also hear non-rhotic Yiddish accents because the surrounding accents of English are generally non-rhotic. Other consonants are substantially the same as they are in English, the place of articulation of "d," "t," "b," "p" and "sh" being slightly forward of the General American position; that is, the tip of the tongue is closer to the upper front teeth. The lips are slightly forward. Final voiced consonants are often voiceless: "d" shifts to "t" (*end* is pronounced "ent"); "b" sometimes shifts to "p" (*cab* is pronounced "kep" or "kap" or "keb" or "kab"); "ing" shifts to "ingk" (*thinking* is pronounced "tinkingk"). However "z" does not usually shift to "s," so a *rose* is still a ROz. In final consonant clusters voiced consonants shift to voiceless: *hold* becomes "holt."

"g" in final "ing": In English "ing" is pronounced with a "g" following it, but in Yiddish "ing" is followed by a distinctly sounded "g." The verb *to sing* is *singen* in Yiddish, pronounced "zingen." In English this phonetic characteristic is carried over, so that, for example, *Long Island* is pronounced "lAn gI' lint" or "lawn gI' lint," instead of "lawng I' lend." In Yiddish the word for *long* is *lang* (lAng).

qu: the combination (kw) does not exist in Yiddish. Substitutions are "kv" or "kf": *quite* is pronounced "kvIt" or "kfIt" or even "kevIt." *Quiet* becomes "kfI' yit" or "kvI' yit."

R and r: "R" is the guttural, uvular R, versions of which are also heard in French and German. However there is also a frontal, trilled "r" in Russian Yiddish, and this is sometimes heard in a Russian Yiddish accent in English.

TH and th: Voiced "TH" and voiceless "th" do not exist in Yiddish. The usual substitutes for them are "d" and "t." It would be very rare to hear any other substitutions. These two consonants can also be correctly pronounced in a lighter Yiddish accent.

Vowels and Diphthongs

For the vowels use whichever vowel and diphthong system exists in the surrounding accent native to the English language, paying special attention to those vowels which do not exist in Yiddish and are therefore substituted for with different vowels. For example, there are no umlauted vowels as there are in German (See Chapter Thirteen on German accents), such as ü and ö (phonetic symbol o). The German *schön* (beautiful, pretty, nice) becomes Yiddish *shayn*. Ü does not exist in Yiddish or English, but it does in French, for example, so in a Yiddish accent in French the speaker would pronounce *la rue* (the street; lA Rü) as "lA Ree." The German diphthong "au" (phonetic symbol: ow) as in the word *Frau* (woman; fRow) does not exist either, and "oy" (as in English *boy*) is usually substituted for it. One of the words for woman in Yiddish is *froy*.
Note: This information on vowel shifts applies no matter what native English accent (and vowel system) the immigrant is surrounded by, i.e., New York, London, Sydney, Capetown, etc.

a: "a" does not exist in Yiddish. Close to it is the vowel "e" which, slightly lengthened, often substitutes for "a." For example *cat* is pronounced "ke:t," and *that* becomes "de:t." *That's right* is pronounced "de: ts RIt."

i: "i" does exist in Yiddish. However, the intermediate front vowel "i:" also exists, and this vowel is sometimes substituted for "i" in English words. The term *intermediate* refers quite literally to the position of the tongue, which is in between its position for the vowel "i" and the vowel "ee." The lengthened intermediate front vowel "i:" does not exist in English.

w: There is no inital semi-vowel "w" in Yiddish. A strong "v" is the usual substitution for it: *one* is pronounced "vun," *what* becomes "vAt," and so on. In a lighter Yiddish accent the "w" is correctly pronounced, sometimes with the lips slightly forward. Sometimes, as an overcompensation, words which begin with "v" are pronounced with an initial "w," so *very* may be heard as "we' Ri:" or "we' Ree," and *while what will* may be heard as "vIL vAt viL."

4) Stress
Stress in Yiddish is random. Many words are stressed on the second syllable. Prefixes like the Germanic "ge-" (indicating that a word is the past participle of a verb) are never stressed. Stress in English is generally easy for Yiddish speakers, but occasionally words will be incorrectly stressed. "Car' penter" might become "carpen' ter," for example, as in a famous "dialect" vaudeville sketch from the 1920s.

London and New York Yiddish Accents Compared

The first question to ask is: where did the Jewish immigrant learn English? If it was in the East End of London, as with some of the characters in Arnold Wesker's plays, see Chapter Two on London and Cockney accents, and use the vowel and diphthong shifts you will find there along with the different consonants in this chapter. If the person is more educated use the information in Chapter One on upper-class British accents.

For New York the vowels and diphthong shifts will be found in Chapter Six on Regional American accents.

In the East End of London, in Whitechapel, the old Jewish quarter where Eastern European immigrants settled, there is still an open-air market. You can have a salt beef sandwich at Bloom's delicatessen. (In New York you would go to the Carnegie Deli for a corned beef sandwich; New Yorkers say "kawn beef"). There is a variety of first- and second-generation Jewish accents to be heard, and Yiddish words are used. I once saw an old lady, who was not Jewish, trying to sell cruets and other little stoppered bottles in which to mix salad dressing. "Who wants the cruets, ladies and gentlemen?" she said softly. Next to her a Jewish peddler was rather loudly selling watches. "Get your watches here, real Swiss watches here!" She muttered something about Jews half under her breath. "Oh, shut up! You're so loud!" she said. "Shut up yourself, lady!" he returned. She said "You're *meshugge*, you are, and that's a Jewish word!" "Don't you call me *meshugge*, I'll have the law on you!" Here is a phonetic transcription of the conversation:

"oo wawnts THe kroo' its, lI' deez n dgen' ?l men"
"ge che waw' chiz ee' A, Reel swis waw' chiz ee' A"
"ow shA tAp yaw sow lowd"
"shAt Ap ye self' lI' dee"
"yaw mi shoo' ge yoo aw Ren THets u dgyoo' eesh wod"
"down choo kawl mee mi shoo' ge Rawl av THe law Rawn yioo"

Notice the "intrusive R" in the last two sentences. A first-generation immigrant to London would probably have pronounced "TH" as "d" and would have said "svis vaw' chiz" for *Swiss watches*, and his "R" would have been the guttural Yiddish "R": "awl av de law Rawn yi<u>oo</u>." In New York he would have said "svis vA' chiz" and "Al hev di law RAn y<u>oo</u>," in the unlikely event that he were to use such a British expression. More probably he would have said "I'll call the police!" (Al kawl di pA lees'). Notice that in Cockney Yiddish the initial "h" is dropped, as it is in other Cockney accents. In second-generation accents, i.e., in the accents of the children of Eastern European Jewish immigrants (to both New York and London) there is sometimes heard an overly articulated "d" and "t," particularly at the end of a word, but sometimes at the beginning of a word. These conso-nants are "dentalized," that is the tongue is pushed lightly against the back of the upper front teeth. "Don't tell me" becomes "dzOn tsel mee," in New York for example, or "dzown tsel mee" in London. The word *street* becomes "streets," almost as if it were plural, or, alternatively, is pronounced with a very strong "t." *Bend* is pronounced "benz" or, alternatively, with an overly articulated "d." Be careful of exaggerating these two sounds.

More Practice

A classic Jewish joke:
Man: *I need a suit.*
Phonetic pronunciation: I need' A s<u>oo</u>t'

Tailor: *You need a suit? So we'll take a measurement. I can make it for you in six days.*
Phonetic pronunciation: y<u>oo</u> ni:d A s<u>oo</u>t'   sO viL tayk a me' zhe mint   I ken mayk' it fe y<u>oo</u> in siks dayz'

Man: *Good by me! That's terrific! I'll be back!*
Phonetic pronunciation: Good bI mee'   dAts ti Ri' fik   AL bee bek'

   (Six weeks later)

Man: *Nu, so what happened? Where's the suit? I keep coming to ask. Every week for six weeks. You said six days, it's already six weeks! God made the world in six days!*
Phonetic pronunciation: N<u>oo</u> sO vAt hep' mpt   vez di s<u>oo</u>t'   I ki:p ku' mink t<u>oo</u> esk a' vRee veek' fe siks veeks'   y<u>oo</u> sad siks dayz' its u Ra' dee siks veeks'   gAd mayd di voyLd', or voyld, or voyLt, in siks days

Tailor: *Yeah… Look at it!*
Phonetic pronunciation: ye:'   Look' ed it
Note: The consonant "R" can be pronounced R, r or R. For a lighter accent pronounce initial "w" correctly in such words as *weeks* and *world*.

More sentences
So whatever you are going to do, you have to do it well and thoroughly.
Phonetic pronunciation: sO vA' de' ve y<u>oo</u> gaw' ne d<u>oo</u> y<u>oo</u> hef te d<u>oo</u> it vel en taw' Ro lee

Possible Pitch Pattern

```
                            do-\                      well      thor-
                  you are going to                              and
            ever                        o
        what-                               have to do it                  ough-
  So                                        you                                ly.
```

What do you want from my life? Because you forgot it's my fault?
Phonetic pronunciation: vA' de y<u>oo</u> vAnt frem mI lIf

Possible Pitch Pattern

```
                    want
                                                            got
  What do you
                    from my                      for-            fault?
                life? Be-        you
                        cause                it's
                                                    my
```

All right. I'll be quiet. I'll even sip my tea with my mouth closed.
Phonetic pronunciation: aw Rit Al bee kvI' it Al ee' vin sip de tee vit mI mowt klozd

Possible Pitch Pattern

```
                    quiet.                    tea
        right.                        sip my
                            even                        mouth closed.
  All       I'll be       I'll                 with my
```

Chapter Fifteen
Dutch Accents

Dutch, which has given us such words as *cookie, cruller, waffle*, and *Brooklyn*, is spoken in Holland by approximately 15 million people, and Flemish, which is more like Dutch with an accent than like another language, is one of the official languages of Belgium and is spoken by almost six million people. Dutch is also the official language of the Netherland Antilles and of Surinam in South America. It was also widely spoken in the Dutch colonies, such as Indonesia, where it was, of course, the language of the administration.

Afrikaans, spoken in South Africa, is an offshoot of Dutch and very close to it. The language of the Boers (Dutch for *farmer*), it was brought to South Africa in the 17th century by the colonists and merchants of the Netherlands, and flourishes there to this day, along with English (in the late 18th century the English took over the Dutch colony) and the African languages, Xhosa and Zulu. Dutch itself was originally considered a variety of Plattdeutsch (literally, "flat German"; in other words, Low German).

The Netherlands began political life as a province of the Holy Roman Empire, but became a country in the 10th century. They were occupied first by the Burgundian Dukes in the early 15th century, then by Maximilian of Austria in 1490, and in the 16th century by Spain, under the oppressive, ultrareligious, austere Phillip II. (Verdi's opera *Don Carlo*, based on a play by Schiller, is set largely at Philip's court in Spain; its plot revolves around the Flemish political situation.) During the Flemish Renaissance political awareness and a desire for national independence led eventually to the formation of the present state of Holland in the 16th and 17th centuries. The culture of the Reformation period saw a flowering of Flemish and Dutch culture, with the writings of the humanist philosopher Erasmus, among other brilliant scholars, as well as the rise of the 17th-century Dutch school of painting. Among its greatest and most superb exemplars was Rembrandt, whose chiaroscuro umber portraits and landscapes evoke a dark, brooding, profound, mysterious and loving sense of self; Vermeer, whose painting the *View of Delft* so fascinated Marcel Proust; and van Ruysdael, whose majestic landscapes call forth the stormy and glorious skies of this flat and fertile country.

For good examples of Dutch accents listen to Rutger Hauer, whose English is perfect, but who can put on a Dutch accent, in *Soldier of Orange* (1977) and *Blade Runner* (1982). Joeran Krabbé has a heavier accent in *The Fugitive* (1993).

A Quick Reference

1) The key to this accent is the Dutch retroflex "s," pronounced with the bottom of the tongue curved up towards the roof of the mouth.
2) Substitute "d/t" or "d/s" or a tapped "d" for "TH/th."
3) In a heavy accent substitute initial "v" for "w."
4) Use the Dutch guttural uvular "R" in initial position, but drop this sound before another consonant or when it ends a word.

How to Do a Dutch Accent

1) Position of the Vocal Apparatus
Open your mouth slightly and curl the tip of your tongue up and back while saying "s." The feeling of the language is that it is spoken in the back of the throat and towards the middle of the mouth, with some frontal articulation. The mouth is slightly open, and the lips remain back, not pushed forward as in some other accents, and rather close to the position of General American.

2) The Most Important Sounds
Consonants
R and R: This consonant is very guttural, a uvular sound in the back of the throat and close to "KH." There is also an "R" in a middle position which is close to an American "R," but softer. You can use it in a **light** Dutch accent. To make this "R" do not curve the tongue tip up towards the roof of the mouth as you would normally do, but keep the tongue flat as you raise it.

s: In Dutch this consonant is pronounced with the tip of the tongue up and back towards the opening into the palate. This is an important sound in a Dutch accent in English.
Practice words: *castle, so, said, say, soon, sound, aforesaid, inside, outside, words, sounds, similar, sensible*

TH and th: These sounds do not exist in Dutch. The usual substitutions are "d" for the voiced TH and the Dutch retroflex "s" or "t" for the voiceless th: *this thing* is pronounced "dis sing." Also heard between vowels is a tapped "d." See the "Practice" section below.

Vowels and Diphthongs
Use the vowel system of British RP given in Chapter One, not General American.

u: The vowel "u" in but does not exist in Dutch, and "o" as in the word work is often substituted for it. Sometimes it is pronounced "A."

Further Phonetic Information

Consonants
Dutch has two guttural consonants, "R" and "KH," which last is spelled with

the letter "g." The name of the famous painter *Van Gogh* is pronounced "fAn KHoKH" in Dutch.

L: In Dutch the sound of "L" is dark and rather Slavic, similar to Russian, with the tongue thickened almost into the upper palate. It is a useful sound, but not always heard except in **heavier** Dutch accents.

v: This consonant is often substituted for initial "w" is such words as *where, what, when,* etc. However, an initial "w" does exist in Dutch, so only use a "v" in a **heavier** Dutch accent.

Vowels and Diphthongs
There are some interesting diphthongs in Dutch which do not exist in English, except for their use in certain Scottish accents. For example, the "ui" in *huis* (house) is pronounced "Aü." *Huis* is pronounced "hAüs," as it sometimes is in a Lowland Scots accent. Otherwise the vowel system is the usual system: A, e, i, o, and u (<u>oo</u>), with the addition of the French "u" (ü). The vowel system of British RP tends to be the one taught to students in Holland, as opposed to the system of General American.

Stress

The stress in Dutch is random, although there are complicated rules. Prefixes, for instance, are never stressed, but otherwise first syllable stressing is common. For purposes of learning an accent in English stress can be virtually ignored. There is sometimes an abrupt, staccato rhythm to unstressed words with short vowels and an even, legato rhythm when syllables containing long vowels are stressed. This phenomenon is more noticeable than it is in English. See the example in the "Pitch" section, below, where this principle applies to the exercise sentence.

Pitch

Pitch patterns in Dutch are very close to English, with a higher tone on stressed syllables, a drop at the end of a declarative sentence, and a rising tone at the end of a question demanding an answer other than *yes* or *no*.

The first thing I have to do is to make sure my bicycle is securely locked.
Phonetic pronunciation: se fos si:ng I hef te d<u>oo</u> i:s te mayk sh<u>oo</u>e mI bI' si: kel i:s si ky<u>oo</u>e' lee lokt
Note: Notice the pronunciation of *the* as "se" instead of the more usual "de."

Possible Pitch Pattern

```
                                    bi-            curely
                    do          sure my   cycle
     first thing I              to make            is se-
The              have to    is                             \locked.
```

Notes: Notice the falling tone at the end of the sentence. The words *do, sure,* and the syllables "bi-" and "-curely" should be pronounced with lengthened vowels. All the other words and syllables are more staccato.

Practice

Dutch Words and Phrases

Note: These words and phrases should give you the feeling of the language in the mouth and the correct positioning of the vocal apparatus for a Dutch accent in English.

de school (the school): de sKHo: L;

schrijven (to write): sKHRay' ven;

uit (out): oüt ("oü" is a diphthong, combining the vowel in *work* and the French "ü," particular to Dutch, but heard also sometimes in Highland Scottish accents);

vegen (to wipe): ve:' KHen;

uitvegen (to wipe out): oüt' fe:' KHen;

Ik beloof je, dat hij niet denkt te komen. (I promise you that he does-not intend, literally "think," to come.): ik be Lo:f' ye dat he: ni:t denkt te ko' men

Het ei wordt gekookt. (The egg is being boiled): et ay vawRt KHe ko:kt

English Sentences

The castle bell struck three o'clock.

Phonetic pronunciations:

Medium accent: de kAsL beL stRAk sRee e kLok

Heavy accent: de kAsL beL stRAk sRee e kLok

The retroflex "s" and the tapped "d" for "TH" between vowels would be the hallmarks, to me, of a pretty heavy Dutch accent.

Phonetic pronunciations:

Light to Medium accent: de Re' tRo fleks s en de tapt dee faw tee aych bee tveen' vow' eLs voot bee de hawL mAks t<u>oo</u> mee Af u pRi' dee he' vee dAch ak' sent

Heavy accent: de Re' tRe fleks s en di tept dee faw tee ayh bi tveen' vowLs voot bee de hawL mAks t<u>oo</u> mee Af u pRi' dee he' vee dAch ek' sent

Well, whatever you can say about that, it could be true.

Light to Medium accent: weL wA de' ve y<u>oo</u> kan say e bow' det it kood bee tR<u>oo</u>

Heavy accent: veL vaw de' ve ye ken say e bow det it kood bee tR<u>oo</u>

Notes: Notice the palatalized "L" in *well*. Remember to use a retroflex "s" in *say*. Notice the tapped intervocalic "d" substituted for "TH." Do a uvular "R" in the heavy accent.

Amsterdam is a wonderful and very free city of canals, which we call "gracht," and boats and bridges and bicycles. The Rijksmuseeum is one of the greatest in the

259

world, with its collection of Rembrandts and Vermeers, and the Van Gogh museum is not far away from it, just across the way.

Phonetic pronunciation: Am' ste dAm' i:s e von' de fool ent ve' ree free si:' dee Af ka nals' vi:ch vee kawl KHRAkht ent bOts ent bri:' dges ent bI' si kels   de RIks' m<u>oo</u> say' oom i:s vAn Af de gRay' dest i:n de, or se, vo:lt vi:s i:ts kaw lek' shen Af Rem' bRAnts ent fe: me:es' ent de fAn KHoKH' m<u>oo</u> see' em i:s nawt fA' Re vay fRAm i:t dgAst a kRaws de, or se, vay

Note: In words with pronounced "R" sounds, any of the three (retroflex, guttural or frontally trilled) may be used, depending on how heavy or light you want the accent. The guttural "R" should be very light. It could also be a retroflex guttural sound, very light, again. Don't forget to do a retroflex "s" in such words as *Amsterdam, is, bicycles, greatest, just* and *across* as well as in the exercise following.

So that's the way it is. You have to proceed slowly in order to get things done the way they should be done, you understand.

Phonetic pronunciation: sO sats se vay i:t i:s y<u>oo</u>, or ye, hef t<u>oo</u>, or te, pRO seet' slO:' lee i:n aw' de t<u>oo</u>, or te, get sings, or sinks, dAn, or don, se vay say shoot bee dAn y<u>oo</u> An' e, or de, stent

It's four forty-three now. You have not much time if you want to be there by five.

Phonetic pronunciation: i:ts faw faw' dee sRee now ye, or y<u>oo</u>, hef not mAch tIm i:f ye, or y<u>oo</u>, vawn te, or t<u>oo</u>, bee se: bI fIf

Chapter Sixteen

Three Scandinavian Languages: Danish, Norwegian and Swedish

The three Scandinavian languages, Danish, Norwegian and Swedish, as well as Icelandic, are all descended from Old Norse, the language of the Vikings. They are distinct, but closely related, mutually intelligible languages, belonging to the Germanic family. They are thus related to English, German, Dutch and Yiddish.

It is important to note that the music of all three languages, with the lengthened vowels and glottal stopping in Danish, and the tones in Norwegian and Swedish, must be heard pronounced by native speakers in order to be correctly imitated. An **Icelandic** accent, incidentally, is often very light and sounds either British or American, depending, of course, on which major accent the speaker has learned; when the accent is heavier it resembles a light Norwegian accent without the special pitch/intonation patterns described below. See the list of language tapes in the Bibliography. It is certainly a good idea to learn some of the language and to use the sentences you learn as a means of launching you into the accent, with the correct positioning of the vocal apparatus which you learn along with the actual sounds you will be imitating.

Danish

Danish is spoken by five million people in Denmark, itself, as well as in Greenland, where it is the official language, and the Danish territory of the Faroe Islands, where Faroese, a language closely related to Danish, is also spoken. Even though the population of native speakers of Danish is relatively small, there are a number of dialects of Danish, and a number of accents ranging from the rural speech of the Isle of Fyn, and its principal city Odense, birthplace of Denmark's most famous writer, Hans Christian Andersen, to the urban accent of Copenhagen.

For two good examples of Danish accents listen to the comedy of Victor Borge, whose sophisticated charm, dry wit, and brilliance have made his lovely, soft Danish accent world famous; and to the singing of the superb tenor Aksel Schiøtz (Phonetic pronunciation: Ak' sel shots), whose recordings are now available on CD. He sings, for example, a magnificent "Comfort ye, my people" from Handel's *Messiah* in almost flawless English. Only one or two very slight lapses in specific sounds show us what difficulties there are for even such a magnificent linguist as Aksel Schiøtz to contend with in learning English. Language teaching in Denmark is really excellent, and many Danes learn to speak English with only the slightest of accents. In Copenhagen I once met a Dane who, in talking about the Swedish tenor Jussi Bjoerling, whom he had heard live, said in an almost flawless upper-class British accent "His singing was an absolute miracle"; but he pronounced it as follows: hiz sing' ing wez en ab' se ly<u>oo</u>t mI' re kel. Until he said *miracle* anyone would have thought he was English.Others have heavier accents, among them some of the people interviewed in documentaries on Denmark in World War Two. The heroic resistance of Denmark to the Nazis is legendary. Aksel Schiøtz himself, in fact, was one of the leaders of the Danish Resistance, and was highly decorated after the war.

Learning to pronounce Danish well is enormously difficult for native speakers of English. A glance under the sections detailing the actual phonetics will show you why.

A Quick Reference

1) Pronounce all the consonants as lightly as possible, keeping the lips parted.
2) Pronounce a light uvular "R," if the correct retroflex "R" has not been learned, at the end of a word and before another consonant.
3) Substitute "ks" for "gz" in words like *exact*, and "sh" or "ch" for "dg."
4) Use a dentalized "t," pronounced like a light "ts." In the middle of a word you can, alternatively, use a heavily aspirated "d."
5) Pronounce "L" with the tip of the tongue lightly touching the point of articulation.
6) Substitute a very soft "v" for initial "w."
7) Substitute "s" for "z" in all positions.
8) Pronounce "TH" and "th" correctly.
9) Substitute "A" for "u" in words like *but*.

How to Do a Danish Accent

1) Position of the Vocal Apparatus
The key to this accent is the nature of Danish **consonants**, conditioned by the basic position of the vocal apparatus. Danish is spoken with the lips fairly wide apart and the inside of the mouth more open than in speaking General American or British RP (cf. Spanish). Despite some frontal articulation the language's focal point of resonance is from the back to the middle of the mouth. Keep your mouth much more open than it is in General American and **lengthen the vowels in stressed syllables**. This is the key to the Danish accent. It is also important that in Denmark it is often British, not American, English that is taught. Use the British RP vowel system and make the English non-rhotic, if that is appropriate for the character.

2) The Most Important Sounds
Consonants
There are several important points to bear in mind regarding consonants in

262

Danish:
1) They are generally much softer than their English counterparts, as a result of being spoken with the lips slightly more parted than in English. This is very important for developing a Danish accent in English, where the Danish versions of the consonants tend to be used. In the Danish phrase *mere te?* (more tea?; pronounced in Standard Danish "me:' *Re* te:?'," with a glottal stop after the lengthened vowel in "te," and a very light "R") the words can sound, as I have heard them when taking tea in Copenhagen with Danish friends, almost as if they were the English words *more tea*; the Danish word *mere* is pronounced "moR," with a very soft, slight "R" at the end, the "*e*" dropped, and the "t" very lightly pronounced and aspirated.
2) There is often a **glottal stop** in stressed syllables or in one-syllable words; it does not replace a consonant, but falls as a brief stress, a brief closing of the vocal chords, in between the vowel and the consonant, or sometimes after the consonant or vowel at the end of a word, as in the example above. See the information under "Vowels and Diphthongs," where this is further discussed.
3) Danish is a rhotic language: Final "R" and "R" before a consonant are pronounced.
4) There are a great many silent consonants, used in spelling but not pronounced, just as in the English words *lamb* and *daughter*, where the "b" and "gh" are silent, respectively.
5) The distinction of the voiced consonants "b," "d" and "g" versus the voiceless consonants "p," "t," and "k" is blurred or does not exist, except that "p," "t," and "k" tend to be heavily aspirated. The combinations which are voiced in English ("x" in *exact* pronounced "gz" in English; "j" in *just* or *edge* in English) are voiceless ("x" in *exact* is pronounced "ks": "eksakt"; "j" in *just* or *edge* is pronounced "sh" or "tsh": "shAst"; "esh" or "etsh") in a heavy Danish accent.

ch: The sound of "ch" in *church* is often voiceless, but not accurately, so that it is sounded as "sh" or even "ts" or "tsh" (the "sh" after the "t" being very slight).

L: The Danish "L" is articulated with the mouth more open than in General American. It is always lightly pronounced in all phonetic positions. This is one of the few sounds which Aksel Schiøtz pronounces in the Danish way in the word *people*, the first time he sings the phrase "Comfort ye, my people" from Handel's *Messiah*; the second time he gets it right, and all his other "L's are equally correct, in such words as *Jerusalem* and *wilderness*.

qu: Since there is no initial "w" in Danish the sound "kw" does not exist, but is often learned quite well. Otherwise, substitute a very light "v": kv.

R: The Danish "R" is a very guttural uvular "R," deeper in the throat than either the French or German "R." A more or less correct English "R" can easily be learned, however, but at the end of a word or before a consonant a slight Danish uvular "R" is sometimes heard.

t: The Danish "t" in initial position is sometimes slightly dentalized and sounds like "ts." In the middle of a word like *butter* it is often heard as a heavily aspirated tapped "d."

TH and th: The voiced "TH" exists in Danish, where it is often spelled as a single or double "d." "TH" never occurs at the beginning of a word in Danish, and occurs only after a vowel. In the Danish sound the tip of the tongue is behind the lower front teeth, instead of behind the upper front teeth as in English, and the blade of the tongue is raised towards the roof of the mouth. It is deeper in the throat than its English counterpart, but requires no substitute in a Danish accent in English. There is no "th" sound in Danish, but it does not usually present a problem to Danish speakers learning English, although occasionally you might hear an "s" substituted for it. In general, however, simply use the usual "TH" and "th" sounds.

v: This consonant, articulated with the mouth fairly open, is often pronounced very much like an English semi-vowel "w," (a sound which, strictly speaking, does not really exist in Danish), as in the Danish word *oversæt*, which means "translate," and is pronounced "oweR se?t'." The glottal stop (?) does not replace the "t," which is very lightly pronounced, like the "t" at the end of the English word *set*. The "R" is also very lightly pronounced, and here resembles a Parisian uvular "R."

z: This sound does not exist in Danish. Substitute an "s" for it.

zh: This sound also does not exist. Substitute "sh" for it. The word *measure* is pronounced "me:' shA" in a Danish accent. Note the lengthened vowel in the first syllable, and the non-rhotic ending.

Vowels and Diphthongs
There are eleven vowels in Danish: A, a, e, é, i, o (long and short), o (ö), ü, <u>oo</u> spelled "u," and the schwa (*e*). All of these vowels have long and short versions. **Very important:** The vowels are fairly close to each other, and in Danish the lips often remain open and unrounded for all vowels, just as they remain slightly parted even for plosive consonants. When lengthened they may all precede a glottal stop. In English a glottal stop replaces the consonant "t" in certain accents (London; the Bronx; some Scottish accents), but in Danish it may be heard as a sort of extra very brief sound after any long vowel and before any consonant in a stressed syllable only. The city of Copenhagen is spelled København in Danish, pronounced "ko?(p)n how?(p)n'," with the last syllable stressed. The "(p)" is merely suggested and is hardly heard at all.

u: This sound, heard in the English word *but* does not exist in Danish. The usual substitution for it is the "A" in *father*.

w: There is no initial "w" in Danish. Substitute the soft Danish "v." This is one of the few sounds the tenor Aksel Schiøtz pronounces incorrectly, and then he only does it incorrectly one time; otherwise he does it correctly and perfectly. It is important to note, in other words, that even in a person's own accent there may be inconsistencies; a particular sound may be pronounced perfectly one time, and incorrectly the next.

Stress

Stress in Danish is random, as in English, and is therefore not a problem for Danish speakers learning English. To be more specific, stress tends to fall on the first syllable, except for the first syllable of such words as past participles of verbs, where it is on the second. There are many words as well where the stress falls on a syllable other than the first, as in the many loan words from French, which are stressed on the last syllable.

Pitch

The music of Danish is intimately related to the lengthening of vowels. Long vowels in stressed syllables are spoken on an upper pitch, and there tends to be a somewhat sing-song quality to a Danish accent in English, mirroring the pitch patterns of Danish itself.

You can have a wonderful time in Copenhagen and you just have to put your cares and troubles away.
Phonetic pronunciation: y<u>oo</u> kan haf *e* vun' *e* fool tsIm i:n kO' p?en hay' *gen* en ye zhus hef *te* poo? yaw ke:s en tRo bels *e* vay'

Possible Pitch Pattern

```
                   won-
                        derful                                    have to put your
           have a                  time                       just
        can                             in              and you
    You                             Copen-    gen
                                          ha-


    cares and
            troubles a-
                    way.
```

Practice

rød grød med fløde (red pudding with cream): Ro:TH gRo?TH me(TH) flo:THe Danes say that nobody who is not a native speaker can pronounce the name of this delicious Danish dessert of summer red berry pudding and heavy cream correctly. Note the glottal stop in *grød*, and the lengthened vowels in *rød* and *fløde*, as well as the (optional, but usual) dropping of the "TH" in *med* because of the phonetic context (before a consonant cluster).

From H. C. Andersen's "The Princess and the Pea"
("Prinsessen på Aerten")

   Der var engang en prins. Han ville have sig en prinsesse, men det skulle vaere en rigtig *prinsesse. Så rejste han hele verden rundt for at finde sådan en, men alle vegne var der noget i vejen.*
Translation: There was once [Once upon a time there was] a prince. He wanted to have a princess, but she should be a *real* princess. So he rode round the whole world to find one, but there was always something wrong every time. [literally, something in the way]
Phonetic pronunciation: pRi:n se' sn paw e:' etn; de: vAR en gang' en pRins. hAn vi:' le how si: en pRi:n se' se, men de: sgoo' le ve:' Re en ri:? ti: pRi:n se' se. saw Ray' ste hAn he:' le vee' ?tn Roon? faw A? fi:' ne saw' dAn en, men A' le vay? ne vA de no: Ret i: ve: yen.

Phonetic pronunciation of Translation: de: waws wuns e pRi:ns. hee wa' ned tsoo haf e pRi:n ses' bu? shee shoo bee ay Ree'eL pRi:n ses' sO hee ROd Rown THe hOL wo:L tse fIn wun bu THe: wes awL' ways sum' thing Rawng ef' Ree tsIm

English Sentences
Sixteen people disappeared from a merchant ship and we don't know what became of them.
Phonetic pronunciation (**Heavy** accent): seksh' teen pee' bl dees e peeeR' fRom e moR' syant sheep en vee dOn nO vAt bee kaym' ov dem

These persons asked me if they could come with me and I said sure they could.
Phonetic pronunciation: dees pos' ents Ask mee if day koot kum vi:t mee en I set shooe day koot

You can't think of everything you would like to think or of all the words you would like to put down.
Phonetic pronunciation: yoo kan thing uf e' fRee thing yoo woo lIk tsoo thing awR uf awl de wo:s yoo woo lIk tsoo poo dzown
Note: All the consonants should be very lightly pronounced.

After nine o'clock I can call him, I suppose.
Phonetic pronunciation: Af' te nIn O klog I kan kawl him I si, or syi, pOs'
Note: The final "g" in *clock* is very, very softly articulated, with little pressure between the tongue and the back of the palate. In fact, all the consonants are soft.

For our purposes it is very important to study a little of the Danish language.

Phonetic pronunciation: faw ow:' *e* po:' bo sis it is ve' Ree, or *Ree*, im paw?: tn?
ts<u>oo</u> stA:' dee *e* li?:' l A TH*e* day:' nish lan' gw*e*sh
Note that the consonants "p," "t," "v," "d," and the final "dg" in *language* are all
very lightly articulated. Note also the symbol ":" which indicates that the preceding vowel is lengthened.

Norwegian

From the end of the 14th century until 1814 Norway and Denmark were one
united kingdom, and the written language was a literary Danish. In Norway
various dialects of Norwegian were spoken, differing in the southeast, with its
capital city Oslo, where the prestigious Standard Norwegian originated, and the
northern parts of the country, with their rural dialects. After the political separation of the two kingdoms Norwegian began to come into prominence as a written and spoken language, and there were various spelling and linguistic reforms
in 1907, 1917, 1938, 1951 (when a commission was set up to reform the language) and in 1959.

There are two forms of Norwegian: Bokmål and Nynorsk. The first is the prestigious dialect of the south used in the media and in major literature; the second is that of the west and north. (The letter "å" is pronounced "o"). Henrik
Ibsen wrote his plays in Bokmål. The two dialects were brought into increasing
conformity with each other during the linguistic reforms.

There are approximately four million native Norwegian speakers in Norway.
At the end of the 19th century and even earlier there was a large Norwegian
emigration to the United States, especially to northern Minnesota and to Wisconsin, and an influence on the accents of those areas. "Oh, yeah, you betcha"
is the cliché fake Norwegian phrase, spoken on an upward pitch, of that region.

For a good example of a light Norwegian accent without clichés listen to the
actress Liv Ullmann. The delightful Hollywood film and television series *I Remember Mama* (1948), about an immigrant Norwegian family in San Francisco,
starred Irene Dunne in the movie and Peggy Wood in the TV series, both doing
excellent light accents as Mama. (In that film, incidentally, Oscar Homolka played
Uncle Kris, the irascible curmudgeonly family patriarch with a heart of gold,
using his own native Viennese accent; it was the usual practice in Hollywood to
cast anyone with any accent in any part requiring one, no matter what the accent was supposed to be.)

A Quick Reference

1) Pay special attention to the information under "Pitch" below. Use a falling or
a falling-rising tone to give the Norwegian music to a sentence.
2) Substitute initial "y" for initial "dg" in words like *just*. For final "dg" substitute "tsh."
3) Subsitute initial "v" for initial "w."
4) Substitute "s" for "z."
5) Substitute "d" and "t" for "TH" and "th."

267

6) Substitute "oo" or a "schwa (e) for "u."
7) Generally substitute long vowels for pure diphthongs, so "O" shifts to "aw," for example.

How to Do a Norwegian Accent

1) Position of the Vocal Apparatus
The lips are fairly close together and slightly forward, and the language has a strong frontal articulation.

2) Pitch
The pitch patterns or music of the Norwegian language, and of a Norwegian accent, is very important. As in Swedish, there are two tones in Norwegian, but the tones are different from the Swedish tones. In Norwegian the tone rises from low to high, whereas in Swedish it falls from high to low.
1) Tone One is a simple falling tone, represented by the symbol "\."
2) Tone Two is a falling then rising tone on both syllables of a word, represented by the symbol "∨."
Tone One is often used in monosyllabic words, but also in words borrowed from other languages. Tone Two is used in words of more than one syllable. As in Swedish there are pairs of words whose meaning depends on the difference in the tones. This musical quality of intonation carries over into accents in English.

Yes, well, you know, you can't be certain about that.
Phonetic pronunciation: yes vel yü nO yü ke:nd bee so ten a bow dat

Possible Pitch Pattern

```
                                    cer-\
                          be                  \bout
           kno-\      can't/        tain a-
Yes,   you      w you
     well                                        tha-\
                                                    -at.
```

3) The Most Important Sounds
Consonants
Together with pitch they are the key to the accent. Norwegian itself is not diffi-cult to learn to pronounce, unlike Danish, and the accent is not particularly difficult to do. Most of the consonants are very close to the ones in English, and present no problem in developing a Norwegian accent. They are perhaps a bit softer than the English consonants, and voiceless in final position, even where they are voiced in accents native to English, so "b" becomes "p," "d" becomes "t," "g" becomes "k," and "z" becomes "s."

268

dg: This initial consonant does not exist in Norwegian, and the cliché is the substitution of "y" for it, as in the Norwegian name *Jan*, pronounced "yAn." It is, however, quite a real substitution. *Just a minute* is pronounced "yoost *e* mi:n' et."

qu: This combination, pronounced "kw" in English, does not exist in Norwegian. Substitute "kf."

R, r and R: All three versions exist in Norwegian. A uvular "R" is heard in the south around Bergen and Oslo, a very lightly trilled "r" in the northeast, and a very lightly pronounced "R" in general at the end of a word or before another consonant, as in British RP, but even lighter. Often Norwegian speakers will learn a correct "R," or use one of its other versions, depending on which region of Norway they are from.

TH and th: These sounds do not exist in Norwegian. The usual substitutions are "d" and "t" for voiced, as in *this*, and voiceless, as in *think*, respectively.

z: This sound does not exist in Norwegian. Substitute "s" for it, especially in final position. *Is it true?* is pronounced "is it tR<u>oo</u>."

Vowels and Diphthongs
There are long and short vowels in Norwegian following the usual A, e, i, o, u (<u>oo</u>) system, plus a long "o" (as in the English words *work* and *first*) spelled either "ö" or "ø," and "ü," spelled "y." Vowels are not diphthongized, even when long, and a pure vowel substitution for a diphthong is characteristic of a Norwegian accent.

u: The sound does not exist in Norwegian. Instead it is variously pronounced "oo" (*just* becomes "yoost"); "e" (*but* becomes "bet"); or "A" (*love* becomes "lAf").

w: This sound does not exist initially. Substitute a lightly pronounced "v."

Stress

Stress, as in other Germanic languages, is random, tending often to be on the first syllable. There is generally no problem in learning to stress English words correctly. Lengthened vowels and diphthongs tend to give the accent a characteristic rhythm. Note the tones also in the "Practice" sentence below.

Practice

Some Norwegian Phrases
Han er en god venn av meg.
Translation: He is a good friend of mine.
Phonetic pronunciation: hAn e:R en god ve:n Af me:

Jeg kommer til hotellet.
Translation: I will come to the hotel.
Phonetic pronunciation: yI ku'meR til haw tel' et

Hvor lang vei er det?
Translation: How far away is it?
Phonetic pronunciation: vawR lAng vay eR de:

English Sentences
I just came there to see what he was doing.
Phonetic pronunciation: I yoo:st kay:m\ de:r tü /see: vat hi: vAs /dü:' \ing

Bergen, Norway is home to an annual festival of arts, and it is not far from the home of the great composer Edvard Grieg, on a superb fjord, and it is worth taking a trip to see.
Phonetic pronunciation: ber' yen naw', or nawR' vay i:s hOm ty<u>oo</u> an an' y<u>oo</u>el fes' ti: vel awf dee Arts end i:t i:s not fAr from di hawm ov ed' vARt gReek awn ay sy<u>oo</u> poRp fyawrt end i:t i:s voRt tayk' ing ay tRi:p ty<u>oo</u> see

The month of July is very hot and there is a lot of work to be done outdoors all day long.
Phonetic pronunciation: de mawns ov y<u>oo</u> lI' i:s ve' ree hawt an de:R i:s e Law' dof woRk t<u>oo</u> bee don ow dawrs' awL day Lawng

We were waiting a whole year for that package, but it just never arrived, and we have no idea what happened to it.
Phonetic pronunciation: vee ve vay' ti:nk ay hawL yeeer faw dat pek' ech be' di:t yoost ne' ver ay rIft an vee haf nO I' deee vAt hep' ent t<u>oo</u> i:t

But I am telling you what went on in those days was simply unbelievable.
boo dI am teL' in y<u>oo</u> vAt went awn i:n dOs days vAs si:m' pLee oon bi Leev' e beL

You just listen to what I'm telling you and you can't go wrong.
y<u>oo</u> yoost li:s' ten, or en, t<u>oo</u> vA' dIm teL' in y<u>oo</u> en y<u>oo</u> kent gO rawnk, or rawng

Swedish

Swedish is spoken not only by more than eight million people in the Swedish homeland itself, but by pockets of native speakers in northern Wisconsin and Minnesota in the United States, as well as by several hundred thousand people in Finland, which was once part of the Swedish kingdom, just as Norway and Denmark were once united politically. Thus the most widely spoken Scandinavian language is Swedish.

There are rural and provincial accents of Swedish, and, as you might expect, there is the urbanized Stockholm accent. Swedish was much influenced by French following the election of the French Napoleonic Marshal Bernadotte and his young wife Désirée to the throne of Sweden in the early 19th century. The story is fictionalized in the Hollywood costume drama *Desiree* (1954), with Marlon Brando as Napoleon, Jean Simmons as Désirée, and Michael Rennie as Bernadotte.

The wonderful, very slight accents of the superb movie stars Greta Garbo and Ingrid Bergman are excellent examples to listen to. They are characterized by a slight over-articulation of final consonants, and a Swedish lengthened "ö" in such words as *work* and *first*. Also excellent to listen to for his very light accent is Max von Sydow, who has made so many films in both Swedish and English. The late Viveca Lindfors, who appeared in *Stargate* (1994), also had a light Swedish accent, worth listening to. For the sound of Swedish itself, watch the films of Ingmar Bergman.

A Quick Reference

1) Study the very important "Pitch" section below. The intonation patterns of Swedish are often superimposed on English. Practice exercises for the music of a Swedish accent are included under "Pitch."
2) Generally lengthen vowels and diphthongs, using the Swedish tones on them.
3) Substitute "o<u>oo</u>" or "ü" for "<u>oo</u>."
4) Substitute the sound of "*o*" in "work" or a "schwa (*e*)' for "u."
5) Substitute initial "v" for initial "w."
6) In a heavy accent substitute "y" for initial "dg" as in the word *just*, and "tsh" for final "dg."
7) Use a lightly trilled "r" with one tap and pronounce it in all positions.

How to Do a Swedish Accent

1) Position of the Vocal Apparatus
The lips are half open, half closed and slightly forward. The articulation is between that of Danish, with its open quality, and Norwegian, which is more closed.

2) Pitch
Pitch in Swedish is an enormously important part of the accent, both in the language itself and in an accent in English. There are characteristic obligatory tonal patterns. There are two tones in Swedish, Tone One and Tone Two:
1) Tone One is a single falling tone on the last syllable of a word, or on a monosyllabic word. The vowel in the preceding syllable is lengthened slightly.
2) Tone Two is a double or compound falling tone (which does not rise as in Norwegian) the first part of which falls slightly, the second of which rises a slight bit above the final fall of the first tone and then falls again.

Although Swedish is not a tonal language, it does contain about five hundred contrasting pairs of words which depend on tone for their meaning. For example, *fallet* (fʌ' let\; meaning "the grammatical case"), spoken on a single fall-

271

ing tone (Tone One in Swedish), changes its meaning when spoken on a double falling then rising tone (Tone Two in Swedish): *fallet* (fA\\' let\\) means "fallen."

The first half of the tone is held for a long instant, then falls abruptly, giving a very characteristic music in Swedish, a music which is often heard in Swedish accents in English.

Practice

No, it's not true that he told him he was coming to your house for dinner.
Phonetic pronunciation: no:oo\\ is no\\ troooo\\ dat hee tawld\\ hi:m hee vos köm'\\ ing tyü dee'\\ ner(R)

Note the way the tones fall in the sentence, the lengthening of vowels, and note also that the phrase *not true* is meant to be said with a Swedish Tone Two:

```
___
no
        \
    troooo
```

Pitch can also vary over the course of a sentence. Practice the following sentence in Swedish, and its translation into English using the same pitch pattern, or intonation:

Jag var hem och såg glasena på bordet.
Translation: I was home and saw the (drinking) glasses on the table.
Phonetic pronunciation: ya vAr hem okh saw glAs'\\ en A paw boor' det\\\\
Note: Swedish Tone Two.

```
                        ena        bord-
            hem                    på
Jag var          och såg  glas-              et.
```
Questions have a falling tone at the end, instead of rising as in English.

Practice

Is that really true?
Phonetic pronunciation: i: s dat ree' Lee trooo

```
              tru-\
    really         e?
Is that
```
Note the Swedish Tone One on the word *true*.

Follow this advice under "Pitch" particularly in superimposing the pitch patterns onto English. In combination with information on phonetics this will give you a very **heavy** Swedish accent. To avoid the cliché of a Swedish accent, and to develop a **light** Swedish accent, listen to Garbo and Bergman, who have learned English intonation very well. Their accent comes from their pronunciation of certain vowels and consonants.

3) The Most Important Sounds
These are the lengthened vowels and diphthongs in stressed syllables, which, together with the pitch patterns make the accent.

Vowels and Diphthongs
Vowels in Swedish are long and short versions of the A, e, i, o, u (oo) system, plus a schwa (e), "o," and "ü." The lengthened vowels are intimately related to the tonal quality of Swedish, and this carries over into an accent in English.

oo: This sound has no exact equivalent in Swedish, and "ooo" or "yü" are substituted for it in a heavy Swedish accent: *too much* is pronounced "tyü mech." *True* is pronounced "trooo."

u: There is no exact equivalent in Swedish for the vowel in *but*, so the sound of a schwa (e) or "o" or "A" when the vowel is in a stressed syllable are the usual substitutions.

w: As this has no equivalent, an initial "v" is substituted for it.

Consonants
The same advice applies here as to Norwegian, since the consonants are generally a bit softer than their English counterparts. They are pronounced with the tip of the tongue against the back of the upper front teeth ("d," "n," "l," "t"), but presenting no particular problems, with the following important exceptions:

dg: This sound does not exist in Swedish in initial position. The usual, clichéd but accurate, substitution for it is "y."

m: At the end of a word "m" is voiceless in Swedish, and this is also true therefore of its pronunciation in a Swedish accent in English. Words like *mechanism*, *sarcasm* and *phantom* have a voiceless "m" at the end.

qu: The combination "kw" does not exist in Swedish, but the combination "kv" does exist, and is the usual substitution in English. The Swedish spelling for this combination is "kv."

r: The Swedish "r" is lightly trilled, or tapped, and the tendency even in a light Swedish accent is to have the sides of the tongue a bit too far towards the roof of the mouth and the tip of the tongue a bit too far back, so that the English "R" is incorrectly pronounced, although close in sound to what it should be. Listen to Ingrid Bergman or Max von Sydow.

s: The "s" in Swedish is close to an English "sh," because it is slightly retroflex; it is pronounced with the bottom of the tongue towards the roof of the mouth.

sw: The usual substitution for this sound, which does not exist in Swedish, is "sv."

Stress

Stress in Swedish is random. Vowels are lengthened and often given one of the tones discussed above in stressed syllables, giving a Swedish accent in English its characteristic music.

Practice

You have studied in Sweden? Yes, I studied in Stockholm and found it very beautiful, especially the "Gamla Stan," the Old City.
Phonetic pronunciation: y<u>oo</u> ha stu' deed in swee:' den yes I stu' deed in stok' holm an /found it ve' Ree \by<u>oo</u>' dee fool es pe shA lee THee gAm' lA stAn THee awld /si:' \tee

Notes: The tone of the first sentence rises at the end, as is usual for a question. Notice the tones in the second sentence. For a **very light** Swedish accent all you have to do is drop certain final consonants, such as the "v" in *have* or the final "t" in such words as *at* and *what*, and lengthen some vowels, as the "ee" in "swee" is lengthened in the above example. Note that all the other sounds are perfectly pronounced as in General American.

Stockholm is a city built on a series of islands, and you can take a boat from one to the other, and visit the Gamla Stan, that is the Old City. You will think you are back in the Middle Ages. Or you can go to Södermalm for the restaurants.
Phonetic pronunciation: stok\' /hawlm i:s e si:'\ tee bi:lt/ awn e see' rees ov I'\ lands an yü kan tayk e bawt from von tü dee o'/ der an vi:' si:t de gAm' lA stAn' det i:s dee awld si:'\ tee   yü vi:l ti:nk yü Ar bak i:n de mi:' del ay'\ dges, or dyes awr yü kan go tü so:'/ der mA:lm' fawr di res'/ to rAnz
Note: Pay attention to the falling and rising tones.

If you have never tried a Swedish smörgåsbord, with its tempting array of dishes, you are in for a real treat.
Phonetic pronunciation: i:f yü haf ne' ver trIt e swee' di:sh smor' gos b<u>oo</u>er' vi:t i:ts temp' ti:ng a' ray ov di:' shes yü Ar i:n fawr ay ri:l treet\

Do you care for music? In Sweden we have the most wonderful singers and musicians, like the tenor Jussi Bjoerling, whose voice was meltingly, hauntingly beautiful, or the majestic Birgit Nilsson, magnificent and quite incredible.
Phonetic pronunciation: de yü kay:r fawr myü'\ si:k   i:n swee' den vee haf di mawst vun' der fool si:ng' es an myü' si: shens lIk di te' ner yoo' si: byor' li:ng

274

ho<u>oo</u>s voys vAs me:lt' i:ng lee haw:n' ti:ng lee byü:' ti: fool awr di mA ye:s'\ ti:k
bi:r' gi:t ni:l'\ son mAg' ni: fi: sent an kfIt i:n kred'/ i: bol
Note: Pay attention to the lengthened vowels in such words as *meltingly, haunt-ingly* and *beautiful.* They are a key to the rhythm of the accent.

Drottingholm is also worth a visit, with its opera season and its real, eighteenth-century court theater, where you can see a thunderstorm recreated as they saw it back then.
Phonetic pronunciation: drot' ning holm' i:s awl' saw vort ay vi:' si:t vi:t i:ts aw'
pe: rA see' sen an i:ts reel ay' teent se:n' tye ree kaw:rt tee' *e* ter ve:r yü kan see *e*
ton' der stawrm ree kree ay' ted es day saw i:t bak de:n

Part Five

Slavic Language Accents

Introduction

The Slavic, sometimes called Slavonic, languages include the liturgical language of the Eastern Orthodox churches, Old Church Slavonic, Old Bulgarian (which evolved into Old Church Slavonic), Russian, Ukrainian, Bulgarian and Serbo-Croatian, all written in the Cyrillic alphabet. Polish, Czech and Slovak are all written in the Roman alphabet, and the prevailing religion of those areas was (and is) Roman Catholicism.

Slavic phonetics include two phenomena useful to know in doing Slavic language accents in English. First, there are the agglutinative consonants, combinations of consonants called "consonant clusters," often found at the beginnings of words. While they vary from language to language, they condition the position of the vocal apparatus generally, as the tongue continues to seek a forward, upward position, in order to pronounce the consonants. Secondly, especially in Russian, there is a tendency to "palatalize" consonants, especially the nasal consonants "m" and "n," before "e" and "i." This means that, literally, the tongue touches the roof of the mouth after or during the pronunciation of the consonant, resulting in the insertion of the semi-vowel "y" between the consonant and the following "i" or "e," or other vowel.

There is also a typical Slavic "L," heard in Russian, Serbo-Croatian, and other languages, articulated by pressing the tongue directly against the back of the upper front teeth while raising the blade of the tongue towards the palate (see Fig. 3, page 13). This is in addition to the dark liquid "l," similar to the "l" in French, also heard in Russian and in Polish. In Polish there is also an "l" written with a diagonal line through it; the sound of this consonant is close to the sound of the General American semi-vowel "w." These typical sounds condition the "feeling" of the accents in the mouth and determine their main focal points of resonance.

Chapter Seventeen
Russian and Ukrainian Accents

Russian is perhaps the most important of the Slavic languages, in that it is spoken by some 215 million people in Russia, of whom some 61 million people speak it as their second language.

The first written records in Old Russian, presumably the language from which the East Slavic languages Russian, Ukrainian and Belorussian all evolved, date from around 1000 C.E. They are written in the alphabet invented by the Orthodox Greek Christian missionaries Cyril and Methodius, which is based largely on the Greek alphabet. They devised it in order to write in Old Church Slavonic, which existed alongside Old Russian, and which is the liturgical language of the Slavonic Orthodox churches.

The differentiation of Russian, Ukrainian and Belorussian into separate languages parallels the course of history and the political separation of the countries, which suffered under Lithuanian or Polish domination. All these areas were later reunited, not happily, under the Romanov czars and in the Soviet Union.

Russian was standardized in the 18th century under the westernizing Peter the Great. It is still written in the Cyrillic alphabet, and in order to know the accurate pronunciation of Russian words it is necessary to read this alphabet. The transliteration of Russian words into the Roman alphabet is often problematic. For instance, the Cyrillic letter "ё" is usually transliterated as "e," when in fact it stands for the sound of the diphthong "yaw," sometimes spelled "yo." Among other things this Russian letter tells the reader that the syllable containing it is always stressed. For people who do not know what the letter is in the original Cyrillic, pronunciation of Russian words can be inaccurate. For example, most English speakers would pronounce the name of the battleship in Sergei Eisenstein's 1925 film *The Battleship Potemkin* (and of the prince for whom the ship is named) pretty much as it appears in the Roman alphabet. In fact, in Cyrillic it contains the letter "ё" and is therefore pronounced "PA tyawm' kin." The Cyrillic letter "e" represents the diphthong "ye" and is therefore not in any case a pure vowel in the Cyrillic system, despite its appearance in transliteration, so that the usual mispronunciation of Prince Potemkin's name is wrong on two counts.

Leningrad, Moscow and the various rural areas all have their own accents. The major plays of Anton Pavlovich Chekhov (1860-1904) take place in the Russian provinces; provincial accents are used for certain characters in Russian productions. Incidentally, Chekhov's house in Moscow is a wonderful museum: the first floor recreates the rooms as they were when he and his family lived in them, while the second floor is devoted to exhibitions about Stanislavsky's original Moscow Art Theatre productions of his plays, and the third floor is a small working theatre. The three Prozoroff sisters dream of going to Moscow, where there is life and laughter, but Vershinin calls it a gloomy city, and, indeed, Moscow has a dual aspect: On the one hand, it is a city of light set on a broad river lined with pleasant green parks, and on the other, it is overwhelmed by the awe-inspiring brooding fortress of the Kremlin, whose high walls surrounding a complex of cathedrals and government palaces, with Lenin's impressive tomb at its base in Red Square, bespeak imperial power.

The other major Russian city is St. Petersburg (Leningrad in Soviet days), built on the Neva River (nyi vA') in the early 18th century by Peter the Great, and renowned for its splendid architecture and broad avenues, such as the Nevsky Prospekt (nyef' ski: pro spyekt'), famous in the books of Gogol, Tolstoy and Dostoevsky. In one of the gloomiest of the city's numerous shaded canals the mad mystic monk Rasputin, who held the Czarina in his thrall, was drowned in 1916, having been first poisoned, and then shot by his aristocratic assassins. Near St. Petersburg, Pyetrodvoryets, Peter's palace (destroyed by the retreating Germans in World War Two, and rebuilt and restored under the Soviets), is a monument to the folly and luxury of the czars, heedless of the vast poverty and misery of their empire. The Russian Revolution of 1917 began in St. Petersburg with the siege of the Winter Palace, now the Hermitage museum.

The Russian court spoke French; the czar's daughters had English and French tutors, and spoke both languages extremely well. The famous Anna Anderson, now proved by DNA testing to have been an imposter, passed herself off as the Czar's youngest daughter Anastasia, who supposedly had survived the execution of her family by the Bolsheviks. To me, she has the distinctly Polish accent of the factory worker she is actually supposed to have been; anyway, there is nothing particularly Russian about her accent, no palatalized consonants, etc. In any case, the real Anastasia might have had a better accent than this woman, heard speaking English in the PBS *Nova* documentary *Anastasia Dead or Alive?* (1995), which contains good examples of Russian accents.

For more examples of Russian accents listen to Michael Chekhov, a great actor, acting teacher and theorist and the playwright Anton Chekhov's nephew, as the psychiatrist in Hitchcock's *Spellbound* (1945) and to the great ballet dancer Mikhail Baryshnikov in *White Nights* (1985). Maria Ouspenskaya in *The Wolf Man* (1941) and many other films is not to be missed, with her heavy Russian accent, as heavy as Rudolf Nureyev's in *Valentino* (1977). Yul Brynner in *The King and I* (1956) does not even try to do a Siamese accent, but sticks, as always, with his medium Russian accent. Akim Tamiroff appears in dozens of Hollywood films; notable is his Oscar-nominated performance in *The General Dies at Dawn* (1936) and *For Whom the Bell Tolls* (1943). Incidentally, he studied with Stanislavsky at the Moscow Art Theatre.

A Note on the Pronunciation of Russian Names

It is very useful to understand some of the rules for stressing Russian names if you are doing the plays of Chekhov and Turgenev, for example. Too many English-speaking actors mispronounce Russian names.

Russians have three names: a first name, a patronymic, and a last name. The second name, the patronymic, is the name of the person's father with a masculine or feminine ending, indicating that the person is his son or daughter. The ending is never stressed; instead the patronymic receives the stress of the root name, for example Stepan' Stepan'ovich (Stephen son of Stephen); Stepan'ovna (daughter of Stephen). The "ov" in patronymics is often not pronounced, but the patronymic derived from *Pyotr* (Peter), with its stress on the "o," stresses the second syllable of the patronymic: Petro'vich (son of Peter); Petro'vna (daughter of Peter). *Ivan Aleksandrovich* (John son of Alexander) can be pronounced either "ee vAn' Alyik sAn' dro vich" or "eevAn' A lyik san' drich." "Ivan Ivanovich" is usually pronounced "ee vAn' ee vA' nich." *Ilya*, which in Russian is stressed on the last syllable, also stresses the patronymic on the last syllable, Ilya' (eel yA'), so the name of the character known as "Waffles" in Chekhov's *Uncle Vanya* is pronounced "ee lyA' ee lyich'."

The diminutive endings, indicating endearment, which abound in Russian novels and plays, are not stressed. For example, "Mashenka," the diminutive of "Masha," (itself a diminutive of *Maria*, pronounced "mA ri:' A," meaning "Mary" in English; I count 44 diminutives of *Maria* in a Russian dictionary of first names and patronymics, *Slovar Ruskikh Lichnikh Imyen*, Moscow "Russian Language" Publishers, 1980), used by Anfisa in Chekhov's *Three Sisters*, is pronounced "mA' shen ke" and not, as I have often heard it, "mA shen' ku." If you are not sure of the pronunciation of Russian names, look them up in a dictionary or in a student edition in Russian of the play you are doing, usually available if the play is a well-known one. You will find the stress indicated, usually in the cast list to begin with, and in the text where diminutives are used.

Correct Stress in the Names of Some of Chekhov's Characters

(The symbol " ' " occurs after the stressed syllable).

From *Uncle Vanya*

Alexan' der Vladi' mirovich Serebriakov' (Phonetic pronunciation: syer ryeb ree yA kof')
Yele' na Andre' yevna
So' fia Alexan' drovna
Ma' rya Vasil' yevna Voinits' kaya (Phonetic pronunciation: voy nyits' kA yA)
Ivan' Petro' vich Voinits' ky (Uncle Va' nya)
Mikhail' (Phonetic pronunciation: mi: KHA i:l'; an anglicized "mi: KHII' " is acceptable) Lvo' vich A' strov
Ilya' Ilyich' Telye' gin
Mari' na

From *Three Sisters*

Andrei' Serge' yevich (or Serge' yich) Pro' zoroff
Natal' ya Ivan' ovna
Ol' ga
Ma' sha
Iri' na
Fyo' dor Ilyich' Kuli' gin
Alexan' der Igna' tyevich Vershi' nin
Nikolai' Lvo' vich Tu' zenbach
Vassi' lyi Vassi' levich Solyo' ny
Ivan' Roman' ovich (or Roman' ich) Chebuti' kin
Alyeksei' Petro' vich Fyedo' tik
Vladi' mir Karl' ovich Ro' de'

From *The Seagull*

Iri' na Nikola' yevna Arka' dina
Constantine' Gavril' ovich Tryeplyoff' (often pronounced in English "tre' plef")
Pyotr Nikola' yevich (or Nikola' yich) So' rin
Ni' na Mikhai' lovna Zaryech' naya
Ilya' Afanas' yevich Shamra' yev
Pauli' na Andre' yevna
Ma' sha
Boris' Aleksye' yevich Trigor' in
Yevgyen' yi Serge' evich (or Serge' yich) Dorn
Semyon' Semyon' ovich Myed vyed' yenko

From *The Cherry Orchard*

Lyubov' Andre' yevna Ranyev' skaya
A' nya
Leonid' Andre' yevich (or Andre' yich) Ga' yef
Yermolai' Alekse' yevich (or Alekse' yich) Lopa' khin
Pyotr Serge' yevich (or Serge' yich) Trofi' mov
Boris' Boris' ovich Semyo' nov-Pish' chik
Charlot' ta Ivan' ovna
Semyon' Pantelye' evich Yepikho' dov
Dunya' sha
Ya' sha

A Quick Reference

1) Palatalize "d," "l," "n," and "t," especially before the vowels "i" and "e." See below for an explanation.
2) Do a Russian "L."
3) Substitute a soft "KH" for initial "h."
4) Substitute the pure vowel "aw" for the diphthong "O."
5) Substitute "v" for initial "w," or pronounce "w" correctly: your choice.

6) For "TH/th" substitute "d/t" or "v/f."
7) Substitute the intermediate vowel "i: " for both "i" and "ee."

How to Do A Russian Accent

1) Position of the Vocal Apparatus
The position of the tongue is extremely important in doing a Russian accent. The lips are slightly forward, and the tongue is often forward and up towards the upper, or hard, palate (the roof of the mouth). The dark Russian "l" (as opposed to the heavy "L,"; see below), is one of the keys to this accent: when articulating the "l" the tip of the tongue should be up and forward, and should not touch the back of the upper front teeth. Considering the information which follows, this general positioning of the tongue makes a great deal of sense.

2) The Most Important Sounds
Consonants
One of the phenomena which give the Russian accent its character and its music and rhythm is that long vowels tend to be really long in stressed syllables, and short vowels really short, almost schwas in fact, in unstressed syllables. Especially important is the phenomenon known as **palatalization**, which is something quite particular to Russian accents. Palatalization amounts to the insertion of the semi-vowel "y" after a consonant, as in Russian *Nyet* (No). This ubiquitous phenomenon in Russian phonetics tends to be carried over into English, making words like *duke* and *newspaper* easy to say in their palatalized versions, and intruding into words like *article*, which becomes "archikel" or "artyikel." The consonants which are regularly palatalized in Russian are "d," "l," "n," and "t." These consonants, in other words, are pronounced with the tongue near the hard upper palate, with a "glide" into the "y" semi-vowel. The consonants "ch," "zh," and "ts" are not palatalized when pronounced with "y"; the tongue is not raised to the roof of the mouth when they are articulated. The consonants "b," "d," "f," "k," "m," "n," "p," "t," "v" and "z" are substantially as they are in English, but they have harder and softer versions than the English ones. The soft versions are pronounced with the lips slightly parted. The soft version is always the one heard when palatalized.

If you look at the practice exercises you will see how many consonants come together in clusters, an important feature of the Russian language. Although some of the consonants are preserved in spelling, they are dropped in pronunciation. Such consonant clusters as occur regularly in English therefore present no problems to the Russian speaker learning English. The clusters common to both languages are "bl," "gl," "kl," "pl," "br," "gr," "kr," "pr," "tr," "shr," "st," and "str." There are consonant clusters in Russian which do not exist in English, such as "zhr" and "shch" as in *Khrushchev*. The only time this combination occurs in English is between two words: *rush chair, flush cheek*.

Final voiced consonants become voiceless ("v" shifts to "f," etc.) For example: "Romanov" (the Czar's family name) is pronounced "re mAn' ef." The second syllable is stressed.

h: There is no "h" in Russian. Substitute a soft version of the final sound in Scottish *loch*, a sound which does exist in Russian. Its phonetic symbol is "kh." In Russian itself the "h" is often replaced by a "g," so the name of Shakespeare's play is "Gamlet."

r: "r" is frontally trilled (one flap) in initial position, and often much like an American "R" in the middle of a word as in the author's name *Turgenev* (TooR gen' yef).

L and l: The "*L*" is said with the tongue thickened slightly and with its tip touching the back of the upper front teeth and the blade forward. You should feel its point of resonance where the vowel "o" as in British RP *not* resonates. The "l" is palatalized when soft, and should resonate where the vowel "e" resonates. Practice these sounds by first saying the vowels, then saying "*L*" and "l."

TH and th: There is no voiced TH in Russian and no voiceless th. Substitute "v" and "f" for voiced and voiceless, or "d" and "t." Not often heard is the substitution of "z" and "s." Say "vis fing" or "dis ting" for *this thing*.

v: Sometimes, although initial "v" exists in Russian, there is an overcompensatory tendency to substitute an initial "w" in a very heavy Russian accent, so *very* is pronounced "we' ree." Often "v" substitutes for initial "w" in words like *what, where*, and *when*.

Vowels and Diphthongs
In Russian, vowels have short and long versions, depending on whether they are stressed or unstressed. The system has: A, e, i: , o, u (oo). Notice that "i" is lengthened. In Russian a short version of "i" is palatalized. The palatalized vowels, called "soft" vowels, are really diphthongs with the semi-vowel "y": ya, ye, yaw (the sound "aw" is spelled "o"), yu (yoo), yi (as in Russian *nichevo*, meaning "nothing," pronounced "nyi:' chye vaw"). This particular Russian sound of "yi," with the tongue raised to the roof of the mouth, does not exist natively in English, but is often heard in a Russian accent.

A: "A" is sounded as in *father*.

e: The letter "e" in the Cyrillic alphabet represents the diphthong, or palatalized vowel, "ye" as in *yes*. This is the sound one sometimes hears in words like *that* in a heavy Russian accent: "dyet" or even "dyets," with the final "t" dentalized; one also hears the "a" in words like *that* and *hat* sounded like the A in *father*: dAt, khAt. On the other hand, one also hears this vowel correctly pronounced, or pronounced in words with an "e," such as *let*, pronounced "lat." *Let's go* can be alternatively "lyets gaw" or "lats gaw." (The word *let*, pronounced "lyet," means "year" in Russian, incidentally, but the more usual word for "year" is *god*.)

i and ee: The Russian unpalatalized "i" is the intermediate vowel "i:" between the longer "ee" in *meet* and the shorter vowel "i" in *bit*. The tongue is in a position literally part of the way between those two vowels.

o: This vowel does not exist in Russian. The usual substitutions are either "o" or "aw."
Practice words: *work, first, burn, turn, learn, churn, earn*

O: The diphthong "O" does not exist in Russian. The letter "o" in the Cyrillic alphabet represents the sound of the pure vowel "aw" in *law*, when stressed; when unstressed it represents the sound of "A" in *father*. In a Russian accent in English it is often the "aw" that is substituted for the "O" diphthong in words like *go* and *home*: "gaw khawm," or "KHawm."

w: This semi-vowel is often pronounced correctly in initial position. However, "v" often substitutes for "w."

Stress

Stress patterns are random in the Russian language; therefore not a problem in learning English.

Pitch

There is a rising intonation pattern in the Russian declarative sentence until the end of the sentence, which ends on a falling tone. In a question there is often a falling tone at the end, where we would use a rising tone in English:

> But
> > why
> > > not?

Different Russian Accents

For a **light** Russsian accent, use the Russsian versions of "r" and "R" and the vowel and diphthong substitutions and follow the advice under "Pitch."

For a **heavier** accent add to this the substitution of "kh" for "h" and substitutions for "TH" and "th" and "v" for "w."

For a really **heavy** accent add to this the full use of palatalization.

Practice

Note: Use the translation to practice the accent in English. Say the Russian, and without changing the position of the vocal apparatus immediately say the English. These sentences have been transliterated from the Cyrillic alphabet.

Ya khochu govorit' po-Russki.
Literal translation: I want speak in-Russian.
Translation: I want to speak Russian.

Phonetic pronunciation: yA khaw ch<u>oo</u>' gA vo reet' po r<u>oo</u>' skee
Possible Pitch Pattern

```
                     po-
               rit
         chu
Ya                           Russki.
    kho-      govo-
```

Shto khochesh ot minya?
Literal translation: What want-you from me?—Yelena to the Professor in Act
Two of Chekhov's *Dyadya Vanya* (dyA' dyA vAn' yA), "Uncle Vanya."
Translation: What do you want from me?
Phonetic pronunciation: shtaw kho' chish ut mi nyA'

Ochevo vui vsyegda khoditye v chyornom?
Literal translation: Why you always go-around in black?—from Chekhov's *Chaika*
(chI' kA), "The Seagull."
Translation: Why do you always go around dressed in black?
Phonetic pronunciation: u chye vaw' vwee fsyeg dA' kho dee' tye v chyawr' nem

*Sit down and let me tell you how things are going with me. I'm looking for a job
and I don't know if I'll find one. It depends.*
Phonetic pronunciation: si: dAn en Lat mee taL y<u>oo</u> KHA fi:ngz AR gaw' i:ng
wi:f mee Am L<u>oo</u>k' i:n feR e dgAb, or dgawb, en I daw naw eef AL fInd wAn ee
di: pandz'

I like psychedelic and techno music.
Phonetic pronunciation: I LIk psi: KHe da' Li:k en taKH' naw my<u>oo</u>' zi:k

The party was lasting all night. I had a wonderful time.
Phonetic pronunciation: vi pAR' tyee vaws les' tyi:ng, or tyi:ngg, awL', or eL, nIt'
I khed e vAn' der, or deR, or dyer, or dyeR, fool, or fooL, tIm

Excuse me, can you move? We want to sit down.
Phonetic pronunciation: ek skyooz' mee ke:en y<u>oo</u> moov' vee vawn t<u>oo</u> si:' dAn'

*I had no control over it and I was thrown overboard, right over the side of the ship
into the water and the ship proceeded to sink. It was really terrible.*
Phonetic pronunciation: I khet naw kun' trawl, or trawL, aw' ve i:t ent I vaws
srOn aw ve bawt' RIt aw' ve ve sIt awf ve shi:p i:n t<u>oo</u> vi waw' te en vi shi:p praw
si:' det t<u>oo</u> si:nk i:t vaws ri:' lee ta' ryi beL

*Well, you know, they call it Little Odessa out here in Brighton Beach, because of
all the Russians who now live here. And it's great to walk on the boardwalk.*

Phonetic pronunciation: veL ye naw vay kawL i:t Li:' teL A dyes' e owt kheer i:n bRI' tn bi:ch' bi kaws awf awL di RA' shints khoo now Li:f kheeeR en i:ts gRayt too vawk awn ve bawRd' vawk'

Did you ever read Chekhov's short story "Lady with Lapdog," but, of course, that's really completely different, and it's take place in different kind of resort town. He was great short story writer, besides plays.
Phonetic pronunciation: di:ed yoo av' e Ri:d chye:' khefs shawRt staw' Ree Le:' dee vi:f Lep' daw:g be def kaw:Rs' dets Ri' Lee kawm pLi:' tLee dyi:' fRant en i:ts te:k pLe:s' i:n dyi:' fRant kIn awf Ri: zawR tAn khi: vaws gRe:t shawRt staw' Ree RI' deR bi: sIts' pLe:s, or plye:s

There were a lot of things that happened in those years that we don't like to talk about, but eventually they must see the light of day.
Phonetic pronunciation: de:r ver ay Lawt awf fi:ngs vet khep' ent i:n vaws yeeeRs vet vee dawnt LIk too tawk e bowt' bAt i van' tyoo e lee vay mAst see vi LIt awf day
Notes: All the "TH" and "th" sounds could be "d" and "t" instead of "v" and "f." This would make the accent a little lighter. Notice that both "R" and "r" are used here, because, once again, people are inconsistent within their own accents.

You can say what you like, but it's not going to happen. Of course not.
Phonetic pronunciation: yoo ken, or kyen, say vawt yoo Lik bA di:ts nawt gaw' ing too, or gaw' ne, khe' pen fkawRs' nawt

Possible Pitch Pattern

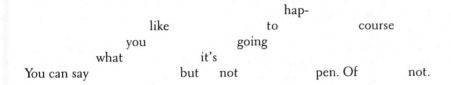

```
                                      hap-
          like                  to              course
      you                   going
   what                 it's
You can say          but   not         pen. Of       not.
```

Ukrainian

Ukrainian, which is also called Ruthenian, especially the variety spoken on the Polish border and in the Carpathians, is closely related to Belorussian and to Russian and is written in the Cyrillic alphabet. More than 40 million people speak it in the Ukraine and in the United States and Canada. The accent in English is very similar to the Russian accent, but Ukrainian does not use palatalized consonants. Nevertheless, the phonetics are so much the same that you can consult the phonetics section for Russian. There is one particular phenomenon that is worth remarking on: the Ukrainian "v," which usually substitutes in an accent in English for the initial semi-vowel "w," shifts in Ukrainian to a sound close to "w" before a vowel. The confusion as to the correct sound in English results in a combination of the two, "vw," so that, for example *why* is pronounced "vwI."

Practice

The announcer on a Ukrainian television station, speaking quite well in English, used Ukrainian intonation patterns just heard in Ukrainian, and which might be schematized as follows:

```
                like
     would           to                     we   are
I                         an-          that
                               nounce


          ing                                      ing
  go-          to                        danc-
                    have          lore
                          folk-


                    sic
              mu-                 the
          folk             for         next
and                                            half   hour.
```

Phonetic pronunciation: I vwood lIk t<u>oo</u> a nownts' det vwee Ar gawng t<u>oo</u> KHev fawk' lawr' den' sing ent fawk my<u>oo</u>' zeek fawr di nakst KHef ow' Ar

Wherever you go in the Ukraine you see fields of wheat and other grains growing, because it is the breadbasket of the region, and the large city of Kharkiv is also very important.
Phonetic pronunciation: vwe: ra' ver y<u>oo</u> gaw i:n di y<u>oo</u> krayn' yoo ken see fi:ldz awf vweet en A' der graynts graw' i:nk bi kos i:t i:s di brad bes' kit awf di ri: dgen en di lardg si:' tee awf KHAr' kef i:s awl' se vwa' ree i:m pawr' tint

Whatever you want, you do it in whatever way you want.
Phonetic pronunciation: vwA' da ve y<u>oo</u> vwawnt y<u>oo</u> d<u>oo</u> i:t i:n vwaw' da ve vway y<u>oo</u> vwawnt

I love to decorate the Easter eggs, and I do it in a very colorful manner.
Phonetic pronunciation: I lAf ti de' ki rayt di i:s' tar aks en I d<u>oo</u> i:t i:n ay va' ree kaw' ler fool me' ner

Pashka, our Easter cake, is a magnificent creation.
Phonetic pronunciation: pAsh' kA ow' er i:s' ter kayk i:s ay mAg ni:f' i sant kree ay' shin

288

Ukrainian food is rich and filling and delicious, with pierogies sprinkled with sautéed onions, and then there is stuffed cabbage and kasha and gravy.

Phonetic pronunciation: y<u>oo</u> krayn' ee en food i:s ri:ch en fi:l' i:ng en di lish' is vi:t pi: raw' gi:s sprin' kilt vit saw' tayt awn' yins en den de:r i:s stawft ke' bich en kA' shA en gray' vee

Chapter Eighteen

Polish Accents

Polish, one of the Slavic group of languages with close linguistic ties to Russian and especially to Czech, which influenced its early development, is spoken by about 35 million people in Poland and the Ukraine and various other countries. Approximately three quarters of a million people speak it in the United States. If you live in New York, go for a walk in the streets of Green Point, Brooklyn, a neighborhood where you will hear Polish and Polish-accented English. Incidentally you can pick up a rye bread and some of the superb Polish cold cuts and sausages from one of the Polish delicatessens there.

Poland had a strong central government as early as the 10th century, and the development and hegemony of Standard Polish began at about that time, imposed on the country as the prestigious language of choice. As Poland is largely Roman Catholic, the usual written language even for administrative purposes was Latin. Church sermons are the first surviving literary documents in Old Polish, however, dating from the late 14th century. At first the seat of the Polish monarchs was in western Poland, but it shifted to Cracow and then, finally, to Warsaw, whose dialect heavily influenced the standard language, both orally and literarily. Today in Poland there are various accents, rural and urban, including those of Warsaw, Cracow, northern Poland and Galicia.

The remarkable job done by Meryl Streep in *Sophie's Choice* (1982) is memorable not only for the fact that she learned some Polish for her dialogue in Polish and learned a Polish accent in English, but also for the fact that in the concentration camp scenes she speaks German with a Polish accent. For authentic Polish accents by native speakers, listen to interviews with Zbigniew Brzesinski, Nixon's national security adviser, who spoke with a very slight accent, and to some of the interviewees in films about the Holocaust, for example *Shoah* (1985) by Claude Lanzmann. For additional examples of Polish see Krzystof Kieslowski's film *White* (its American title), or *Blanc* (1993), set partly in Warsaw. Also worth seeing is the somewhat inaccurate Andrzej Wajda film *Korczak* (1990), set in the Warsaw Ghetto in World War Two. Listen to one of the language tapes listed in the Selected Bibliography and learn some of the language. This is a very important first step, because once you have the "feel" of the language in the mouth you can maintain it in the basic position for speaking Polish and thus launch yourself into the accent.

A Quick Reference

1) Articulate consonants very clearly.
2) Use a light trilled "r" with one tap in all positions, or a General American retroflex "R" in a lighter accent. A Pole living in London might have a non-rhotic accent.
3) Substitute a light "kh" for initial "h."
4) Substitute a lightly pronounced "v" for initial "w."
5) Substitute "d" and "t" for "TH" and "th."
6) Substitute "e" for "o."
7) Substitute "A" for "u."

How to Do a Polish Accent

1) Position of the Vocal Apparatus
Polish is a frontally articulated language. The opening of the mouth is narrowed and the tongue keeps returning to a forward position to form the many consonant clusters of the language. The corners of the mouth are very slightly turned down.

2) Stress
Stress in a Polish accent is very important. Stress in Polish is uniform, always on the penultimate (next to the last) syllable. Cognate words which English speakers associate with a certain pronunciation are thus differently pronounced in Polish, and this may carry over into a Polish accent, although learning correct stress patterns is generally not a problem for Polish speakers. For example, *president* is pronounced "pre zi:' dent" in Polish, stressed on the second syllable. Sometimes there is incorrect stressing in an attempt to compensate for the speaker's inaccurate knowledge of English, which he or she knows is not always stressed on the penultimate. A three-syllable word like *understand*, for example, may be stressed only on the first syllable, instead of receiving a stress on both the first and the last syllables. Because of the length of Polish vowels, discussed below, there is an even quality to the rhythm of a Polish accent in English.

3) The Most Important Sounds
Consonants
Pay attention as well as to the medium length of vowels, and don't forget the even rhythm, despite the strong invariable stress pattern.

It is unnecessary here to go into the entire system of the orthography of Polish consonants, which is very consistent but somewhat complicated. The letters of the alphabet are used differently than in English, and there are some specific Polish letters, such as the "l" with a line through it, pronounced much like an English semi-vowel "w." The combinations "cz," "dz," "rz," and "sz" represent the same sounds as the English "ch," "dz" or (when followed by "i" or with an acute accent over the "z") "dg," "zh," and "sh," respectively, but the Polish sounds are pronounced 1) with harder voicing in the case of "dz" and "rz," that is with

291

more of a slightly buzzing vibration, and the lips a bit forward for all four conso-nants; 2) with more forced air in the case of "cz" and "sz," the latter also being pronounced with a slight hiss, as is the Polish "s." In general Polish consonants are more forcefully pronounced than their English counterparts.

d and t: Both the voiced and voiceless consonants are pronounced in Polish with the tip of the tongue touching the back of the upper front teeth. It is this pro-nunciation which is used in a Polish accent in English.

h: This consonant exists in Polish, but has a quality closer to a light Spanish *jota*, or the harder "ch" in Scottish *loch* (loKH). It is the Polish sound one often hears in a Polish accent. "KH" also exists in Polish, with the spellings "ch" and "h."

r: The Polish "r" is lightly trilled, and is often, but not always, used in a Polish accent in English. The correct "R" is often learned, however.

The following sounds of English do not exist in Polish:

qu: In Polish the spelling "kw" represents the sound "kf," and this is the usual substitution in English.

sw: This combination, which exists in Polish orthography, is pronounced "sv" in Polish, and in a Polish accent in English. The English sound of "sw" in *sweet* does not exist in Polish.

TH and th: Substitute "d" and "t" or, occasionally "s" for the voiced (THis) and voiceless (thing), respectively.

Vowels and Diphthongs
All vowels in Polish are of medium length, including vowels in stressed syllables. Vowels in unstressed syllables have the same length as vowels in stressed syl-lables. No vowel is as open as, let us say, the broad, open-throated "A" of British RP. There are two nasal vowels in Polish ("en" and "an," spelled with a cedilla underneath the vowel), which in an accent in English sometimes gives a nasal-ized pronunciation to an "n" after a vowel and before another consonant, as in the word *indeed*, pronounced "in' di:d." Notice that "ee" does not exist in Pol-ish, and the medium length "i:" is substitued for it. Otherwise the system A, e, i, o, <u>oo</u> (spelled "u") is used.

A and a: Note that the first vowel in the Polish sound system is really closer to "a" and not a very broad "A," and is thus the flatter, medium version of this vowel. Nevertheless, it is a sound closer to "A" than to "a" which is often heard in such words as *carry* (kA' ri:), *cat* (kAt), etc.

o: This vowel, heard in *work* and *first* in English, does not exist in Polish. Substitute "e," so *work* and *first* are pronounced "verk" and "ferst."

oo and o̲o̲: There is a confusion between the two sounds for Polish ears, and the second is usually substituted for the first, so *book*, for example, is pronounced "bo̲o̲k."

u: This vowel does not exist in Polish. Substitute "A," so the words *but* and *love* are pronounced respectively "bAt" and "lAv."

w: This semi-vowel does not exist in initial position in Polish. Substitute a softly pronounced "v." The inconsistencies even in the accent of a given individual are such, however, that the sound of "w" may sometimes be pronounced correctly, at other times incorrectly, as in the phrase *one wish*, which could be either "vAn vi:sh" or "wAn vi:sh," but seldom "vAn wi:sh."

Pitch

Pitch patterns are very similar to English pitch patterns, with a stressed syllable spoken on an upper pitch and an unstressed syllable on a lower. Declarative sentences generally end on a falling pitch, although they may occasionally rise at the end during, let us say, an explanation of some sort, when the speaker wishes to make a point. Questions end with an upward inflection. There is sometimes a kind of lilting inflection in declarative utterances in Polish, and it can carry over into an accent in English. You will find an example in the Practice section. However, you should use this kind of pitch pattern only very occasionally, or you will sound most unreal. It requires a lot of practice to incorporate it into the accent in a natural way.

Practice

Polish Sentences
Kocham morze.
Translation: I love the sea.
Phonetic pronunciation: ko' KHAm maw' zhe

Czy zamykacie okna?
Translation: Are you closing the windows?
Phonetic pronunciation: chi: zA mi: kA' tsye ok' nA

Przepraszam, do zobaczenia.
Translation: Excuse me, I'll see you later.
Phonetic pronunciation: pshe prA' shAm do zo bAch en' yA

English Sentences
We were going one day to see the village castle, when we rembered we had forgotten our guidebook, which gives all the beautiful architectural details.

293

Phonetic pronunciation: vi: ve:r gaw' ing wAn (or "vAn") day t<u>oo</u> see de vi:' lAdg kA' sl ven vi: ri: mem' berd vi: KHed fawr go' ten owr gId' b<u>oo</u>k vi:ch gi:fs awl di: by<u>oo</u> ti:' f<u>oo</u>l Ar KHi: tak t<u>oo</u>' ral di:' tayls

Warsaw, which we call Warszawa in Polish, was destroyed during the Second World War, but it has been rebuilt and there are some lovely sections. Cracow, in Polish Kraków, on the other hand, was largely spared, because it was the Nazi seat of the occupational government.
Phonetic pronunciation: vawr' saw vi:ch vee kawl vAr shA' vA i:n paw li:sh vAs di stroyt dy<u>oo</u>' ri:ng dee se' kent vawlt vaw' bAt i:t hes been ree' bi:lt ent de:r A sAm lAf' lee sek' shens kra' kow i:n paw' li:sh krA' koof awn dee A' der hent' vAs lArdg' lee spe:rt be kOs' i:t vAs di nA' tsee si:t awf dee ok <u>oo</u> pay' shi nel gA' ve ment

I have supposed in the past that I would be transported somewhere away from the place where I was, but it never happened that way.
Phonetic pronunciation: I hef s<u>oo</u> pust' i:n dee pest, or pAst, det I voot bee trens paw' tet sAm' ve:r ay vay' frAm dee plays ve:r I vaws bAt i:t ne' ver hep' ent det vay

The most that you can say is that it was a wonderful time in my life, and that means a lot to me.
Phonetic pronunciation: di mawst det y<u>oo</u> ken say i:z det i:t vAs ay vun' der fool tIm i:n mI lIf en det mi:nts ay lawt t<u>oo</u> mee

What do you suppose he is going to do about the situation?
Phonetic pronunciation: waw *de* y<u>oo</u> s<u>oo</u> pus' khee i:s gawng t*e*, or gaw' n*e*, d<u>oo</u> *e* bow de si: ch<u>oo</u> ay' shun

Whatever he did, he thought he would get away with it.
Phonetic pronunciation: vA te' ver hee di:t he tawt, or tOt, hi: vood gat a vay' vi:t i:t

Possible Pitch Pattern

```
                              would get a-
          he            thought he            way with
What-    er            he                                  
   ev-        did,                                    it.
```

Chapter Nineteen
Czech and Slovak Accents

Czech and Slovak are so closely related that before World War Two the National Theatre in Prague used to perform a play in Czech on one night and in Slovak on the next, and mixed audiences of Czechs and Slovaks would attend any performance and understand the play perfectly. The amazing history of these countries, once part of the vast Austro-Hungarian Empire, is that they were united into one republic, Czechoslovakia, after World War One, separated by the Nazis into two countries, reunited after World War Two, and are now two separate countries again.

For a long time the language of prestige in Czechoslovakia was German, because of the ruling House of Hapsburg. Czech and Slovak in their various varieties were considered peasant languages of provincial people in Bohemia, Moravia and the other provinces of Czechoslovakia. The Jews of the extraordinarily beautiful city of Prague, present-day capital of the Czech Republic, usually spoke German or, if they were from the countryside, Yiddish, and much literature was written in German, the language, for instance, of Franz Kafka. More recent times have seen the music of such composers as Dvořák and Janáček and the literature of such writers as Capek and Vaclav Havel.

The alphabets of Czech and Slovak, which both employ a modified Roman alphabet, are slightly different, but the grammar and vocabulary are extremely similar, and for a long time Slovak was considered a dialect of Czech, rather than a separate languages. Approximately ten million people speak Czech and five million Slovak. For our purposes the accents are so close that we may speak of a Czechoslovakian accent in English.

Standard Czech developed in the 13th century from the dialect of Prague, which was a Central Bohemian dialect. Latin, since before the ninth century and despite the introduction of Old Church Slavonic in Bohemia and Moravia, was the major language of the educated and ruling classes. It was not until the end of the 18th century that Slovak began to be looked upon as a separate language, and that nationalism in both Czechia and Slovakia began to flourish in these then provinces of the Austro-Hungarian Empire.

An example of an extremely light Czech accent is that of the movie actor Herbert Lom, the brilliantly funny Chief Inspector in the Pink Panther series, and one of the crooks in the British film *The Ladykillers* (1955), with Alec Guinness. In fact his accent is so slight that it is hard to place, and sometimes sounds Viennese. *The Ladykillers*, by the way, is excellent listening for a variety of British accents.

A Quick Reference

1) Substitute "A" for "a," but make it slightly more closed, that is, raise the tongue slightly.
2) Substitute "z" and "s" for "TH" and "th" in a heavy accent; "d" and "t" in a lighter accent.
3) Substitute "v" for initial "w."
4) Use a lightly trilled "r."
5) Pronounce initial "s," "z," and "zh" correctly.

Different Czechoslovakian Accents

1) For a **heavy** accent pay special attention to the vowel "A" and to the substitution of initial "v" for initial "w," as well as to the "z" and "s" substitutions for "TH" and "th."
2) In a **light** accent pronounce the "TH" and "th" correctly, and do a General American retroflex "R," which some people I have heard have learned perfectly; some of the correct vowels and diphthongs continue to elude them, however.

How to Do a Czechoslovakian Accent

1) Position of the Vocal Apparatus
The mouth is slightly more open than it is in General American. The lips are slightly protruded, with the tongue tending to assume a forward position.

2) The Most Important Sounds
Vowels and Diphthongs
Vowels with accent marks over them are long, even when unstressed. In an accent in English there is a tendency to lengthen vowels in second, unstressed syllables. Diphthongs tend to be lengthened slightly.

A: This vowel tends to be used both for words pronounced with "A" in British RP and for words pronounced with "a" such as *cat*.

ee and i: The usual substitution for these vowels, neither of which exists in Czech or Slovak, is a lengthened intermediate vowel "i:."

w: This sound does not exist initially in either Czech or Slovak. An open-mouthed "v" is the usual substitute for "w." The word *one* is pronounced "vun." However, in a **lighter** accent, this sound should be correctly pronounced, as it will have been accurately learned.

y: This semi-vowel is usually heard in such words as *newspaper, duke* and *tune*. The combination "tu" (phonetically "ty<u>oo</u>") is often heard as "chy<u>oo</u>."

Consonants
As in all the Slavic languages there are agglutinative consonants, so there is

usually no problem in pronouncing English consonant clusters fully. There is no tendency, as in some accents in English, to devoice voiced final consonants, so *is*, for example, is pronounced "i:z."

h: The "h" is slightly more heavily aspirated than in accents native to English.

qu: The sound of "kw" does not exist in Czech or Slovak. Instead substitute a soft "kv."

r: The "r" is trilled or flapped, and usually the accent in English is rhotic if learned in America, non-rhotic if learned in Britain.

s: Initial "s," unlike many other accents in English, is correctly pronounced.

TH and th: There is no "TH" or "th." Instead a heavily voiced "z" substitutes for "TH" and an "s" for "th." You might hear "d" and "t."

z and zh: Pronounce this sound correctly in such words as *pleasure* and *azure*.

Stress

The stress in Czech and Slovak is uniformly on the first syllable, and this is a trait which tends to carry over into accents in English, sometimes making the accent sound similar to Hungarian. Accent marks indicate the length of vowels only, not a change of stress.

Pitch

The stressed syllable, the first in Czech and Slovak, is spoken on an upper pitch. The syllables with lengthened vowels are also spoken on upper pitches. Together with the stress pattern these phenomena lend a kind of rising/falling music to a Czechoslovakian accent. Also there is a tendency to rise instead of falling at the end of a declarative sentence, if the sentence ends with a one-syllable word.

Practice

Czech Words
velcí vojáci (big soldiers; Phonetic pronunciation: vel' tsee vo' yA tsee); *jeden, dva* (one, two; Phonetic pronunciations: ye' den, dvA); *leden, únor* (January, February; Phonetic pronunciations: le' den, oo' nawr)

In Slovak these words are very similar: there are only minor differences; for example, *January* is "l'aden," pronounced "lA' de nye."

English Sentences
So that is how it was, you see, really.
Phonetic pronunciations:
Heavy accent: saw zAt i: z KHow i: t vAz yoo see ree' A lee

Light accent: saw THet i: z KHow i:t wAz y<u>oo</u> see Ree' a lee

Possible Pitch Pattern:

<pre>
So that   ally.
      is how   was   see, re-
           it   you
</pre>

There were many things that went on in those days of which you know nothing.
Phonetic pronunciations:
Heavy accent: zay:er vayr ma' ni: si:nggz zAt vant awn i:n zawz dayz A vi:ch y<u>oo</u> naw nA' si:ngg
Light accent: THayer wayr ma' ni: thi:ngz THAt want awn i:n THawz dayz Av wi:ch y<u>oo</u> naw nA' thi:ng

We could collect anything we wanted: books, stamps, anything, and we could make up a list of our collections without these things being worried about.
Phonetic pronunciation: vee koot ko' lekt e' nee sink vee vawn' tet b<u>oo</u>ks stemps e' nee sink ant vee koot me:k Ap ay li:st uf ow' er ko' lek shins vi:z owt dees ti:nks bee' ink vaw' reet a bowt

We were gone a long time and we had great experiences.
Phonetic pronunciation: vee ver gawn ay lawnk tIm ant ve het grayt eks' peer ee en ses

Possible Pitch Pattern

<pre>
                   time   perien-
We were gone a long   great ex-
                   and we had   ces.
</pre>

We were taking a walk and I was very surprised at how quickly we returned, so I wanted to take another walk, but nobody else did, so we stayed home.
Phonetic pronunciation (**Heavy Slovak**): vee ver tayk' i:ng ay vawk en I vaws va' ree s<u>oo</u> prIst' et khow kvi:k' lee vee ri' tawrnt saw I vawn' tet t<u>oo</u> tayk a naw' der vawk bAt naw baw' dee als di:t saw vee stayt hawm

The villages and mountains here are very beautiful.
Phonetic pronunciation: di vee' lA dges ent mAn' tens kheer Ar wa' ree byoo' tee fool

Chapter Twenty
Serbo-Croatian and Bulgarian Accents

Like Czech and Slovak, Serbian and Croatian, the languages of the Balkan countries, once united to form Yugoslavia (the first half of the word is from the Slavic word *yugo*, meaning "south"), are so closely related as to be mutually entirely intelligible. They were also both written in a modified Cyrillic alphabet, but Croatian now uses the Roman alphabet, while Serbian retains the Cyrillic. When the territories of Yugoslavia were ruled by the Turks under the Ottoman Empire Serbo-Croatian was also written in the Arabic alphabet, particularly in the region of Bosnia. Approximately 15 million people speak Serbo-Croatian, with its many dialects.

Serbo-Croatian Accents

A Quick Reference

1) Use a lightly trilled "r" with one tap, and a dark liquid Slavic "L."
2) Substitute "a" for "e" and "e" for "a."
3) Substitute "A" for the "schwa (e)" and for "u."
4) Substitute "d" and "t" for "TH" and "th."
5) Substitute "A" for "aw" and "aw" for "o."
6) Substitute "v" for initial "w."
7) Pay special attention to the information under "Pitch," the falling tones of which are characteristic of this accent.

How to Do Yugoslavian Accents

1) Position of the Vocal Apparatus
The mouth is slightly more closed, but otherwise much as in General American. The lips are slightly protruded, and the muscles at the corners of the mouth are heavily used.

2) Pitch
Pitch is a very important element in this accent, and the music of Serbo-Croatian is quite specific. In Serbo-Croatian there is a pitch accent, giving the language, and the consequent accent in English, a musical intonation, which is more pro-

nounced in some regions than in others, and determines for natives the origin of the speaker. The rules for this intonation pattern are complicated, and need not concern us much in any case in doing an accent in English.On most one-syllable words there is either a falling (this is the most frequent pattern) or a rising tone, to be learned word by word. There is likewise either a falling or a rising tone on stressed syllables, again to be learned word by word. These tones are indicated by four accent marks, which, wherever they occur, show vowel length, stress, and pitch all in one. Two accent marks show rising tones for long and short vowels; two show falling tones for long and short vowels. There is also a fifth accent mark for long vowels in unstressed syllables. In questions there is often a rising tone at the beginning followed by a falling tone at the end, similar to Russian possibilities for asking questions.

3) The Most Important Sounds
Vowels and Diphthongs
Although there are long and short vowels, as in English, in Serbo-Croatian the vowels do not change their basic pronunciation, except for their length. In other words there is no differentiation, as there is in English, among "A" and "a" or "e" and the lengthened diphthong "ay." The diphthongs tend to be rather short.

A: This vowel, aside from being pronounced correctly but broadly in words taking it, also substitutes for the schwa in unstressed syllables and for the "u" in *but* and *love*, and also for the "aw" in *law*, so *law* is pronounced "LA." See below under "*o.*"

a: Often there is a reversal of "a" and "e." Another possibility, often heard in a Serbo-Croatian accent, and sometimes in a Norwegian accent, is a diphthongization in which "a" shifts to either "e'e" or "a'e," so *national* is pronounced either "ne' she neL," "ne'e shA naL" or "na'e she neL."

aw: This vowel often shifts to "A," so *talk* is pronounced "tAk."

e: See "a," above.

i: This vowel does not exist in Serbo-Croatian. The often-heard substitution is the intermediate lengthened vowel "i:."

O: This diphthong does not exist in Serbo-Croatian. A short "o" is often substituted for it, so *home* is pronounced "KHom."

o: This vowel does not exist in its English form in Serbo-Croatian, where it is closer to a short English "aw" in *law*, and is the sound usually carried over into a Serbo-Croatian accent. This is very close to the sound of "o" in *not* in British RP.

o: This vowel, heard in *work*, *first* and *murder* is pronounced like the "aw" in *law*:

vawrk, fawrst, mawr' dAr. *Murdered* is pronounced "mawr' dAt" (as I heard on television).

u: This vowel usually shifts to "A." See "A" above.

w: This sound does not exist in initial position. An initial "v" is substituted for it.

Further Phonetic Information

Consonants
The accent tends to be rhotic, unless the speaker, as is the case with some diplomats, has learned the British model of English.

Final voiced consonants shift to voiceless, so "d" becomes "t," "b" becomes "p," etc.

h: There is no "h" in Serbo-Croatian. A sound similar to the Spanish *jota* (KH) is heard instead.

L: A dark "L" is the one to use in a Serbo-Croatian accent, as it is heard in the language itself. It is pronounced with the blade of the tongue thickened and the tip pressed against the upper gum ridge just behind the teeth.

r: The "r" gets one flap, tap or trill.

TH and th: There are no "th" or "TH" sounds in Serbo-Croatian; "t" and "d" are substituted for them: *this thing* (di:s ti:ng).

Stress

The stress in Serbo-Croatian is random, but there is one absolute rule: The stress never falls on the last syllable, even where the vowel is long. In two syllable words, therefore, the first syllable is always stressed.

Practice

Dobar dan. Hvala lepo.
Translation: Good day. Thanks very much.
Phonetic pronunciation: daw'\ bAr dan/ KHvA'/ LA Le'/ paw
Note the rising and falling tones, which in the Cyrillic alphabet would be indicated by accent marks over the letters of stressed syllables; this is not done in the Roman alphabet.

```
               ala      epo.
Do-        an. Hva-    le-
     obar da-
```

301

How are you doing? Fine, I hope.
Phonetic pronunciation: KHow/ Ar y<u>oo</u> doo' ing\ fIn\ I KHOp\
Note the rising and falling tones.

```
            are you do-
     w                       Fi-       ho-
Ho-                   ing?      ne  I      pe.
```

However, we are not ready to accept that yet.
Phonetic pronunciation: KHow a' vAr vee Ar nawt ra' dee to Ak sap' det yat

What has happened in the former Yugoslavia is the worst of tragedies for all concerned.
Phonetic pronunciation: vawt KHes KHep' ent in dee fAr' mer y<u>oo</u> go sLA' vee ye is di /vawrst Av /tredg' e \dees fAr AL\ kAn sernt'

No, it's not possible at this time to determine exactly what went on.
Phonetic pronunciation: naw i:ts nAt pAs' i: bAL a di:is tIm te di' ter mi:n e' zek Lee vot vent An

I don't know how long. Five years, ten years. She was very lovely and I actually thought she was famous, but I did not care about that.
Phonetic pronunciation: I dawn naw KHow Lawnk fIf yi:s tan yi:s shi: vaws we' ree Lawf Lee ant I ek' tchy<u>oo</u> e Lee tawt shee vaws fay' mOs bAt I di:d' en ke: bow dat

Well, it's going to be all right, you know. It just has to be.
Phonetic pronunciation: veL i:ts gong ti bee AL rIt ye no i:t dgost KHes te bee

Possible Pitch Pattern

```
                             kno-\
              ri-\    you              has
        going to be all     ght,      w.   just
Well, it's                         It         to be.
```

Note: Pay particular attention to the falling tones on the words *right* and *know*

Some of the most beautiful forests and coastal cities in the world are to be found here.
Phonetic pronunciation: sAm Af di most byoo' ti: fooL fA' rists ent kos' tAL si:' tees i:n di voreLt Ar te bee fAnt KHeeer.

Bulgarian Accents

Bulgarian is a Slavic language closely related to Serbo-Croatian, using an only slightly modified Cyrillic alphabet, spoken in Bulgaria on the shores of the Black Sea. There have been a number of famous Bulgarian opera singers, among them Zinka Milanov and Boris Christoff. For example of the Bulgarian "L" listen to Boris Christoff in his recording of Verdi's *Simon Boccanegra*; his Italian is heavily accented, but his singing is superb, as was his acting.

In the seventh century the Turkic people calling themselves Bulgars invaded and conquered the territory now known as Bulgaria. They found there a native Slavic population, with which they assimilated over the centuries, although their name remained. Linguistically they adopted the local Slavic dialects, which evolved into the Bulgarian language, today spoken by about eight million people.

Linguistically Bulgarian is the simplest of the Slavic languages, having, uniquely, no declensions for nouns, in other words, no cases to learn. Bulgarian, again unique among Slavic languages, also has a definite article.

A Quick Reference

1) Use a lightly trilled "r" and a liquid Slavic "L."
2) Substitute "v" for initial "w."
3) Substitute "d" and "t" for "TH" and "th."
4) Substitute "e" for "o."
5) At the end of a word or syllable shift voiced consonants to voiceless. See below.
6) Before another consonant shift voiceless consonants to voiced. See below.

How to Do a Bulgarian Accent

1) Position of the Vocal Apparatus
The lips are half open, half closed, much as in General American. Bulgarian is a very frontally articulated language, with the main focal point of resonance in the front of the mouth, except that this point is always relaxed for the typical dark Slavic "L."
2) The Most Important Sounds
Consonants
Note: Pay special attention also to the length of vowels, which are fairly short, although diphthongs tend to be lengthened.

There are a great many consonant clusters in Bulgarian, which means that there are few problems in pronouncing English consonant clusters. At the ends of words voiced consonants shift to voiceless, and this carrries over into an accent in English: final "b" shifts to "p"; "d" shifts to "t"; "g" to "k"; "v" to "f"; "z" to "s." Voiceless consonants occurring before other consonants shift to voiced, so that, for example, the "p" in *lipstick* is pronounced "b" in a Bulgarian accent: "li:b' sti:k'." The accent tends to be non-rhotic.

L: The Bulgarian "*L*" is quite dark and liquid, and is pronounced with the blade of the tongue thickened.

qu: This combination of sounds does not exist in Bulgarian. The usual substitution is "kv" or "kf." *Queen* is pronounced "kveen."

r: The Bulgarian "r" is trilled once, and this is the sound usually heard in a Bulgarian accent. The tip of the tongue is directly behind the upper front teeth in the Bulgarian "r."

TH and th: Substitute "d" and "t" for the voiced and voiceless respectively, or pronounce them correctly.

Further Phonetic Information

Vowels and Diphthongs

All vowels in Bulgarian are short, and diphthongs, almost as compensation, tend to be lengthened. This carries over into English, where vowels are perceived as short and diphthongs as long, giving a characteristic Bulgarian rhythm to an accent in English. The schwa in unstressed syllables, as in British RP, is often heard.

ee and i: The intermediate vowel "i:" is usual in a Bulgarian accent, since neither "ee" nor "i" exist in Bulgarian.

o: This sound does not exist in Bulgarian, and is quite short in a Bulgarian accent in English. It is pronounced either "o" or "e": *work* and *first* are pronounced "vok" or "vek" and "fost" or "fest." If the accent is rhotic a trilled "r" is heard after the vowel: "ferst" and "verk."

u: The exact sound of this English vowel does not exist in Bulgarian. There are a number of possible substitutions for it: "a," "aw" and "A." See the "Practice" section below for examples.

w: This semi-vowel does not exist in Bulgarian. A "v" is the usual substitution. The number *one* is pronounced "vun."

Stress

The stress in Bulgarian, like that in English, is random, and it is therefore not usually a problem for Bulgarians to learn to stress English correctly. There is frequent stressing of final syllables.

Pitch

The pitch in Bulgarian is generally more monotone than in English. As in English the typical declarative sentence drops in pitch at the end, while the typical question rises in pitch. For a change there is no special pitch pattern to pay attention to, although there can occasionally be an up and down, sing-song quality to the accent.

Practice

Bulgarian Words and Phrases (Transliterated from the Cyrillic alphabet)
Az byakh (I was). Phonetic pronunciation: Az byAKH
Az ne byakh (I was not). Phonetic pronunciation: Az ne byAKH
Vie ne byakhte (You were not). Phonetic pronunciation: vee' e ne byAKH' te
portselanova chasha (china cup). Phonetic pronunciation: pawr tse LA' no vA chA' shA
riza ot pamuk (shirt of cotton). Phonetic pronunciation: ree' zA ut pA' mook

English Sentences
And what lovely things are you going to do today, my dear friend?
Phonetic pronunciation: ent vAt LAf' Li: ti:nks Ar y<u>oo</u> gawnk t<u>oo</u> d<u>oo</u> t<u>oo</u> day mI di:' Ar frent

A lot of people wouldn't believe such a thing is possible.
Phonetic pronunciation: ay Lat awf pi:' pL vood' en bi: Li:v sawch ay ti:nk i:s pAs' i: beL

Possible Pitch Pattern

```
        peo-               lieve        thing is possi-
   lot of        wouldn't be-    such a
A          le                                    ble.
```

I can tell you it's true. I know first of all from experience.
Phonetic pronunciation: I ken taL y<u>oo</u> i:ts tr<u>oo</u>   I naw fest awf awL frawm ek spee' ree ents

No, but it doesn't matter.
Phonetic pronunciation: naw, bA di: dAz' en me' ter

Of course, if you would have tried such a thing you would never have gotten away with it.
Phonetic pronunciation: awv kaws i:f y<u>oo</u> voot hef trId sawch ay ti:ng y<u>oo</u> voot na' ver hef gaw' ten ay vay' vi:t i:t

The mountains and the Black Sea resorts attract great crowds in summer.
Phonetic pronunciation: di mAn' tents and dee bLek see ri' zawrts e trekt' grayt krAts i:n saw' mer

305

Part Six

Miscellaneous European Accents

Introduction

There are a number of languages in Europe which are not in the Indo-European family. Among them are Basque, Finnish, Turkish and Hungarian. The latter three may be related to each other; the first is a "language isolate," with absolutely no other living or known dead languages related to it. Albanian and Greek are also language isolates, but Greek has had an enormous influence on all the other Indo-European languages of Europe, particularly with regard to vocabulary. Greek culture, too, of course, has shaped western thought and customs for two milennia now. The Baltic languages, Lithuanian and Latvian, form a branch by themselves; other languages in that group, such as Wendish and Old Prussian, died out long ago. Estonian, geographically next to Lithuanian and Latvian, is related to neither of them, but is related to Finnish.

One of your best sources for any of the accents in the following chapters, as for accents in general, is news broadcasts. If you have to do an Albanian accent, for instance, be alert for news stories from that country. Documentary films are another excellent source for these accents.

Chapter Twenty-One
Greek

Greek has no relatives, but its influence both lexically and grammatically on other European languages is enormous. The Greek alphabet, derived from the Phoenician and Hebrew alphabets, is the ancestor of both the Roman and Cyrillic alphabets. The most ancient written Greek, a script known as "Linear B," is found in inscriptions from as early as 1300 B.C.E. The earliest extensive records of written Greek are the Homeric epics *The Iliad* and *The Odyssey*. Homer has his characters speak sometimes in various dialects. The two epics were written, however, in the "Homeric" dialect, an artificial literary dialect which is basically Ionic with elements from the other dialects. Including Homeric, there were five dialects of ancient Classic Greek: Ionic, spoken and written in the northern Aegean Islands; Aeolic, the dialect of Lesbos and the southern fringe of islands; Doric, spoken in Sparta and the other areas of the Peloponnese; and Attic, the dialect of Athens and the surrounding countryside. The dialect of Athens became perhaps the most important, and evolved into Byzantine Greek, widely used all over the ancient Mediterranean world in literature and administration, and eventually into Modern Greek. In the Hellenistic period, before the Byzantine Christian era, the New Testament was written in the *koine* (koy' ne), the standard spoken Greek of that period, a dialect differing from both Classic and Byzantine Greek.

Today there are two forms of Standard Modern Greek: "pure," a literary form; and Demotic, the *koine*, the spoken, popular form. The modern Greek alphabet is the same as the ancient one, but some of the letters are used differently. Greek is spoken by about 10 million people in Greece itself.

There are three methods of pronouncing Classic Greek. The first was devised by the Flemish Renaissance scholar Erasmus, and undoubtedly bore no resemblance to the true pronunciation. The second, no doubt almost equally egregious and inaccurate, is to pronounce it like Modern Greek. The third is an attempted reconstruction of the true classical pronunciation by linguists, and it may be as inaccurate as the other two. In other words, nobody knows how Ancient Greek was pronounced. Classic Greek proper names, as well as names from Greek mythology, were anglicized, sometimes almost out of all recognition, by Elizabethan scholars. *Aristotle* (a ri stA' tel), for example, is "A ri' sto te:' le:s" in Greek, *Aristophanes* (a ri stA' fe neez) is "A ri' sto fA' ne:s"; *Plato* (pLay' tO) is "plA' ton"; *Socrates* (sA' kRe teez) is "so krA' te:s", while *Aeschylus* (e, or, ee' ski lus) is "Aee' sKH<u>oo</u>' los" and *Sophocles* (sA' fe kLeez) is "so fo kle:s'." These anglicizations are not too far from the Greek, but *Euripides* (y<u>oo</u> Ri' pi deez) is not so close to "ay<u>oo</u>' ri pi:' de:s" and *Antisthenes* (an tis' the neez) is pretty far from "An ti:s the:' ne:s." Farther yet is *Thucydides* (thy<u>oo</u> si' di deez) from "thO k<u>oo</u> di:' de:s."

For good examples of Greek accents listen to Irene Pappas in *Zorba the Greek* (1964) and *The Trojan Women* (1971) and to Melina Mercouri in *Never on Sunday* (1960) and *Topkapi* (1964).

A Quick Reference

1) Pronounce "TH" and "th" correctly.
2) Substitute a soft "kh" for initial "h."
3) Use a lightly trilled "r" initially and drop "r" at the end of a word or before another consonant.
4) Use a retroflex "s," very characteristic of a Greek accent.
5) Substitute "A" for "u."
6) Substitute "e" for "a."

How to Do a Greek Accent

1) Position of the Vocal Apparatus
The mouth is fairly relaxed, but with the corners of the lips a bit tight. The mouth is slightly closed and the tongue generally held in a middle position, not too low, not too high. The main point of resonance, as well as the main focus of articulation, is middle to forward, not guttural.

2) The Most Important Sounds
Remember in particular that "TH" and "th" and initial "w" should be correctly pronounced. Greek is one of the few languages to contain "TH" and "th" sounds, so these are not a problem for Greeks learning English. The vowel "i:" is an important substitution for both "ee" and "i," as is the trilled "r" for the standard English "R."

Consonants
Most of the Greek consonants are very like their English counterparts.

h: This sound does not exist in Greek, and a soft "kh" similar to the Spanish *jota* is usually substituted for it.

L: This consonant is very close to the General American "L," but pronounced with a slight arching of the tongue which brings it close to a Slavic "L."

r: The "r" in Greek is lightly trilled; this is the sound heard in initial position in a Greek accent in English. At the end of a word and before another consonant it

310

tends to be dropped, as it is in British RP.

s: The Greek "s" is slightly retroflex, that is, the bottom of the tongue is turned up a bit towards the roof of the mouth as "s" is being said.

Vowels and Diphthongs
Every Greek vowel has a long and a short version. Vowels in a Greek accent in English tend to be lengthened slightly. The following system is the one used in Greek: A, e, i, o, u (oo). In addition there is a sound that need not particularly concern us in a Greek accent in English: the French "ü," used in words like *psyche*, (the soul).

a and e: The vowel "a" in *happy* usually shifts slightly, to become "e," so *happy* is pronounced "khe' pi:." The vowel "e" shifts on occasion to "a," so *every* is pronounced "a' vree."

i and ee: The vowel usually substituted for these two vowels, which do not have an exact equivalent in Greek, is the lengthened intermediate vowel "i:."

o: The usual substitution for this vowel in English *first* and *work* is "aw": fawrst, wawrk.

u: Since the vowel in *but* has no exact equivalent in Greek, it usually shifts to "A," so *but* is pronounced "bAt."

Stress

It is conjectured that in Classical Ancient Greek stress was indicated by an obligatory higher pitch, shown by a mark over the stressed syllable. This "pitch accent" and the complicated rules for determining where it falls have disappeared from Modern Greek, as have the very complicated rules for determining vowel length and the length of syllables by their position in a verse of poetry. In Modern Greek the stress is random.

Pitch

Greek has a musicality which consists of the usual Indo-European pitch patterns of an upper pitch on a stressed syllable and a lower pitch on unstressed syllables. Declarative sentences fall at the end and questions rise, but there is sometimes a falling pitch at the end of a question when it contains an interrogative word, and this pattern can carry over into the accent in English. Also, the most important stressed words in a Greek sentence, from the speakerís point of view, are often on a higher note than they would be in English, and this pattern too can be carried over into English.

Practice

Some Modern Greek words, transliterated from the Greek alphabet:
efkharisto (thank you); *parakolo* (please); *kalimera* (good morning); *kalispera* (good evening)
Phonetic pronunciations: ef khA' ri: sto'; pA rA ko Lo'; kA Li: me:' rA; kA li: spe:' rA
The opening of Book One of Homer's *The Iliad* (*Iliados* [i: li: A' dos] by (H)omeros [(h)o' me: ros]), transliterated from the Greek into the Roman alphabet:
Note that "(h)" represents the "rough" breathing sign, an obligatory diacritical mark, which looks like a backwards apostrophe (another Greek word) in Ancient Greek, over words beginning with a vowel; there is also an obligatory "smooth" breathing sign over the vowel and it does look like an apostrophe. The poems are written in dactylic hexameter, the usual Homeric metre: five feet of either long/short/short syllables (the dactyl) or long/long syllables (the spondee), always ending with a sixth of long/long syllables. A literal translation appears under each line. There is a wonderful translation of *The Iliad* by Robert Fagles, available in in paperback (Penguin Books, 1990).

　　Menin　　aeide,　　　　thea,　　Peleiadeo　　　　Akhileos
The wrath/rage sing,　　goddess, of the son of Peleus, Achilles,
oulomenen,
terrible/destructive/deadly {Note: rage, understood};

(h)e muri　　　　　　　　Akhaiois　　　　　alge　　　　etheken,
that numberless/countless upon the Achaeans woes/miseries/pains brought down,

　　pollas d iphthimous psukhas　Aidi　　　proiapsen
{and} many of valiant/mighty souls to Hades sent/precipitously hurled down
proon...
of heros/warriors...

(My) translation:
Of the wrath sing, goddess, the deadly wrath of Peleus' son Achilles,
that brought countless woes upon the Achaeans,
and hurled down many a valiant warrior's soul to Hades...

Phonetic pronunciation using Modern Greek phonetics (the long syllables are underlined):
me:̲ ' ni:n A e:̲ ' de̲, the:̲ A', pe:̲ le:i A' de: o A̲ KHi:̲ le:̲ ' os'
oo̲ lo̲ me:̲' nen, e:̲ moo̲ ri: AKH I̲ oys Al ge:̲' e:th' e:̲ ke:n,
po lAs' di:ph thi:̲' moos psü KHAs̲' Ai:̲' di: pro yAp' se:n pro̲' on'...

English Sentences
I don't know how to tell you this, but I'm very happy about everything.
Phonetic pronunciation: I do:nt no: khow too̲ te:l yoo̲ THi: s, bAt Im va ri: KHe'

312

pi: e bowt' a' vri: thi: ng'

He had to do it.
Phonetic pronunciation: khee khAd t<u>oo</u> d<u>oo</u> i: t

His father worked in the field.
Phonetic pronunciation: khi:s fa' THer wawrkt i:n THe feeld

How old did you say your daughter was?
Phonetic pronunciation: khow awld di:d y<u>oo</u> say yawr, or y<u>oo</u>r, daw ter waws

The only other thing that I thought was that he was too ambitious for his own good.
Phonetic pronunciation: THee awn' lee ATH' er thi:ng THet I thawt, or thOt, wAs THet khee wAs t<u>oo</u> em bi:' shes fawr khi: zawn g<u>oo</u>d

The ruins of the shrine of Apollo at Delphi on the slopes of Mount Parnassus, near the home of the Muses, is one of the most impressive and awe-inspiring in the whole world.
Phonetic pronunciation: THi r<u>oo</u>' i:ns awv THi shrIn awv a po:' lo at del' fI awn THi slawps awv mownt pAr na' soos neer THi khawm awv THi my<u>oo</u>' zes i:z wawn awv THi mawst aw i:n spI' ri:ng i:n THi khawl wawrld

So what do you want to eat?
Phonetic pronunciation: saw khwa d<u>oo</u> y<u>oo</u> wawnt t<u>oo</u> eet

Possible Pitch Pattern

```
      what
So       do you
              want to
                   eat?
```

I told her she shouldn't go there, but she insisted.
Phonetic pronunciation: I tawld kher shee shoo' dent gaw THe:r bAt shee i:n si:s' ted

Possible pitch pattern

```
   told                              sis-
      her she
               shouldn't         but she in-
I                    go there,            ted.
```

Chapter Twenty-Two

The Finno-Ugric (Ural-Altaic) and Baltic Languages: Hungarian, Turkish, Finnish, Estonian, Latvian (Lettish), Lithuanian; Basque; Albanian

This chapter represents a sort of grab bag of accents from various languages that have problematic relationships to other languages, or that have no relationship to other languages whatsoever. Basque, for example, is unique, in a group all by itself.

Although all the languages discussed in this chapter are European, only three—Albanian, Latvian and Lithuanian—belong to the Indo-European family of languages. Where did the other, non-Indo-European languages come from? Are they those of the original natives of the European continent, or are they, on the contrary, languages of peoples from farther to the east, from Asia, who conquered the European natives and then asserted their linguistic hegemony over them? Was Basque one of the languages of the original inhabitants of the Iberian Penninsula, or did the Basques arrive there from Gruzia, the name for the former Soviet republic of Georgia in the Caucasus Mountains? If these languages were native to Europe, did they survive in isolated pockets while those who spoke Indo-European languages took over the continent, ousting other speakers of now dead, irretrievably lost languages?

We shall possibly never know the solution to these historical mysteries. If there is a solution, it may lie in the realm of the study of linguistics, of the relationships of some of these languages to others, if they can be established. Lithuanian, for instance, is clearly closely related to Sanskrit and represents the survival of old, possibly even proto-Indo-European forms. Did the Indo-Europeans come west from the subcontinent of Asian India, or did they go east to Asia from Europe? The first surely appears more likely, but who can say with certainty in which direction the emigration occurred?

Hungarian

The relationship of Hungarian to other known languages is problematic. It is clearly a distant relative of Finnish, and is quite possibly related to Turkish and the Turkic languages of Central Asia, but that appears far more problematic, and some linguists deplore the suggestion as highly inaccurate. The Finnish, Estonian (clearly closely related to each other) and Hungarian languages, tenuous as their links to each other are, are among the languages known as the Finno-Ugaritic or Finno-Ugric, or alternatively as the Uralic or Ural-Altaic, languages. This complicated attempt at classification, with four names for what may possibly be one group of related languages, expresses the confusion of linguists. It is also possible that Mongolian is a member of this group. The only absolutely definite relationship of Hungarian to other languages is to the Vogul and Ostyak languages of Siberia, spoken more than two thousand miles away from Hungary, in a remote, isolated country, at least from the point of view of those unwary travelers trying to get there from outside.

Be that as it may, Hungarian is a fascinating language spoken by perhaps as many as 14 million people, not only in Hungary itself but also in the surrounding countries, notably in parts of Romania. Among its properties is agglutination, the building up of prefixes, suffixes and infixes into or onto a root word, so that an entire sentence may be expressed sometimes in one word.

Listen to the accents of Bela Lugosi in his many horror classics, such as *Dracula* (1931). Zsa Zsa Gabor can be heard in *Moulin Rouge* (1952) and *Death of a Scoundrel* (1956), among other films, and her sister Eva in such films as *Artists and Models* (1955). Paul Lukas, a fine actor who made more than 75 films, is wonderful in Alfred Hitchcock's *The Lady Vanishes* (1938) and Lilian Hellman's *Watch on the Rhine* (1943). All these actors provide fine examples of diverse Hungarian accents. Paul Lukas has the least exaggerated and most realistic accent of all of them, and is therefore probably the best one to listen to, along with another Hollywood movie actor of Hungarian background, Peter Lorre, in *Casablanca* (1942) and *The Maltese Falcon* (1941).

A Quick Reference

1) Stress the first syllable of most multi-syllable words.
2) Lengthen the vowel in monosyllabic words.
3) Substitute initial "v" for "w."
4) Substitute "aw" for "O."
5) Substitute "d" and "t" for "TH" and "th."
6) Use a lightly trilled "r" and do not pronounce final "r" or "r" before another consonant.

How to Do a Hungarian Accent

1) Position of the Vocal Apparatus
Say *work* with an initial "v" instead of a "w," drop the "R" and lengthen the vowel considerably: "vo:k vo:k vo:k." This will give you the feeling of Hungarian in the mouth and the correct position of the vocal apparatus. The mouth is in a relaxed position, slightly closed, with the lips slightly forward. Hungarian has a strong frontal articulation and the tongue returns to a position just on the gum ridge behind the upper front teeth.

2) Stress

It is very important to pay special attention to the stress patterns in a Hungarian accent. Fortunately for the actor who needs a Hungarian accent, the stress pattern in Hungarian is uniform. Hungarian words are always stressed on the first syllable. The following syllables are fairly evenly stressed. There is thus a tendency to stress the first syllable of words in English, no matter where the correct stress may fall. Zsa Zsa Gabor, in a travelogue on the Florida Everglades, described her trip through the swamps on a *bamboo raft*, and heavily stressed the first syllable of *bamboo*. Accent marks over Hungarian vowels always indicate vowel length, never stress.

3) Pitch

Also important are the pitch patterns of Hungarian. The pitch in Hungarian is quite even, a gentle rise on stressed syllables and a gentle fall on unstressed. The tone falls at the end of a declarative sentence and also, perhaps surprisingly, at the end of a question, which sounds like a very strong declaration. Sometimes it rises in a slightly unexpected place: In the question "Do you know what I mean?" there is an even stress on all syllables, a rise in pitch on the word *know*, and a falling tone on the word *mean*.

4) The Most Important Sounds

Vowels and Diphthongs

Vowels in Hungarian are long and short. The tendency is to lengthen vowels in stressed syllables, which usually means the first syllable; this is very important in a Hungarian accent. There are no diphthongs in Hungarian. As a consequence pure vowels are substituted for diphthongs very often, or else, alternatively, both halves are evenly stressed.

ay: This diphthong is usually pronounced as a lengthened "e:": *date* is pronounced "de:t." Alternatively, both halves of the diphthong are evenly stressed.

ee and i: Neither of these vowels exist in Hungarian. Usually the slightly lengthened intermediate vowel "i:" is heard in words with these vowels.

I: Since this diphthong does not exist in Hungarian, it is often pronounced with an even stress on both halves of the diphthong: "A'ee'." The first half of the diphthong is slightly more stressed.

O: This diphthong is pronounced either as a lengthened "aw" or with both halves of the diphthong evenly stressed: *home* is pronounced either "haw:m" or "haw'oom." The first half of the diphthong is slightly more stressed.

o: This vowel, which has long and short versions in Hungarian, is usually extra long in a Hungarian accent: *work* is pronounced "vo:k."

316

w and v: Since initial "w" does not exist in Hungarian, "v" is usually substituted for it. The number *one* is pronounced "vun" and *quite* is pronounced "kvIt." Sometimes (rarely) initial "w" is substituted for initial "v," so *very* is pronounced "we' ree."

y<u>oo</u>: This diphthong sometimes has its first half lengthened: *you* is pronounced "ee'<u>oo</u>'."

Consonants
qu: The English sound "kw" does not exist in Hungarian. The usual pronunciation in a Hungarian accent is "kv."

r: The "r" in Hungarian is spoken with one trill, and it is this sound heard in an accent in English. Before another consonant "r" is very lightly pronounced in both Hungarian, and in a Hungarian accent in English. The Hungarian accent is often non-rhotic.

TH and th: These sounds do not exist in Hungarian. Substitute "d" for the voiced "TH" in *this*, and "t" for the voiceless "th" in *think*.

Practice

Use both the Hungarian phrases and their English translations for practice. Notes: In Hungarian orthography "j" stands for the sound of the semi-vowel "y"; "sz" stands for the sound of the consonant "s." The letter "s" in Hungarian spelling is "sh" in English orthography, but this does not usually carry over into "s" being pronounced as "sh" in a Hungarian accent in English (as it does in a Portuguese accent). Remember to lengthen the vowels when practicing the English translations.

Jò napot kivànok. Köszönöm szépen. Nem értem.
Translation: Good day. Thank you very much. I don't understand.
Phonetic pronunciation: yaw' nA' pot ki:' vA nok ko' so nom se:' pen nem' e:r' tem
Phonetic pronunciation of translation: good' day. tank' ee'<u>oo</u>' ve' ree mAch. I' dawnt' An' der stand'

Certain sections of Budapest are extraordinarily beautiful, and the food in such renowned restaurants as Gundel's is superb.
Phonetic pronunciation: so:' ten sek' shens Av boo' dA pesht A ek' straw din er i: li: bee <u>oo</u>' ti: fool en di: food i:n sAch ri:' nAnd re' sto rawnts ez goon' delz i:z s<u>oo</u>' po:b, or pe:rb

Everything turned out the way it was supposed to.
Phonetic pronunciation: ev' e ree ti:nk to:nd' owd' de vay' i:t vAs s<u>oo</u>' pOs' t<u>oo</u>

317

Possible Pitch Pattern

```
                out                    posed
          turned                su-
Everything              the way it was          to.
```

My daughter was away on a wonderful trip to the Szeged area of Hungary.
Phonetic pronunciation: mI dO:' ter vAs *e* vay' on *e* vA:n' der fool tri:p t<u>oo</u> di se:'
get ay' ree *e* of hA:n' *ge* ree
Note: The vowels in stressed syllables should be lengthened slightly.

*Transylvania is the home of more than castles, you know, And the Carpathians are
most rugged there.*
Phonetic pronunciation: tran' si:l vay' nee A i:z de haw'<u>oo</u>'m awv mawr dan kA'
*se*Ls *ye* naw. an *de* kAr' pay' tee ents Ar most rA' get der

Turkish

For centuries the Ottoman Turks ruled their vast empire, which included among
other conquered territories, the capital city of Greek Orthodox Byzantium,
Constantinople, which the Turks renamed Istanbul, the capital of today's greatly
reduced Turkey. The Moslem Sultans ruled by a strict administrative system in
which everyone was classified according to their religion and social status. Everyone was technically a slave of the Sultan, from the Grand Vizier on down, but one
cannot say that the rule of the Sultans was more bloody or unhappy than that of
many of the monarchs of Western Europe. Indeed, discrimination against people
on religious grounds appears to have been less pronounced than it was in the West.

Turkish, an exception in this chapter of often isolated languages, has a great
many linguistic relatives, and is the most important of the Turkic languages, which
include Tatar and the Uzbek, Kirghiz, Azerbaijani and Turkmenian languages of
the former Soviet republics of Central Asia. Turkish may also be distantly related
to Hungarian, Finnish and Mongolian. Forty-five million people in Turkey are native speakers. Turkish used the Arabic alphabet until 1928, when a modified Roman alphabet was introduced.

A Quick Reference

1) Substitute "A" for the schwa in unstressed syllables.
2) Use a lightly trilled "r." Drop "r" at the end of a word and before another
consonant.
3) Substitute initial "v" for initial "w."
4) Substitute "d" and "t" for "TH" and "th."
5) Use a very slight schwa in between consonants in initial consonant clusters.
See below for an explanation.
6) Do a liquid palatal "l," a soft sound.

7) Stress words on the last syllable in a heavy accent, but use correct stress in a lighter accent.

How to Do a Turkish Accent

1) Position of the Vocal Apparatus
Say *aw aw aw naw naw naw*. This will give you the correct position of the vocal apparatus, in which the mouth is relaxed and slightly more open than in General American and the lips are slightly protruded.

2) The Most Important Sounds
Vowels and Diphthongs
Pay special attention to the vowels, to the characteristic rhythm produced by the shortness of the vowels, which in Turkish are all short. There is a compensatory, sometimes exaggerated lengthening of diphthongs. Also, vowels before "R" are lengthened.

A: This vowel is sometimes substituted for a schwa in unstressed syllables: *corners* is pronounced "kaw' nAz."

w: This semi-vowel does not exist. Substitute "v" for it in initial position especially.

Consonants
The Turkish of educated speakers is non-rhotic, that is, final "r" is not pronounced. In addition, the British model of English is the one most often learned by Turks, so the accent in English is usually non-rhotic. There are no initial consonant clusters in Turkish, so that it can be difficult for a Turkish speaker to learn them in English. A schwa ("e") is sometimes inserted between consonants in a cluster: *cluster* might be pronounced "ke lu' se ter," although it would not do to exaggerate this. The schwa should be only very slightly pronounced. In fact, a more accurate phonetic representation might be "ke lus' ter." Consonant clusters do occur in Turkish in final position, so it is generally no problem for Turkish speakers to learn to pronounce them. Voiced consonants "b," "d," "g," and "z" shift in final position to voiceless "p," "t," "k," and "s" in Turkish, and this carries over into an accent in English.

r: The Turkish "r" is trilled, and this is the sound in a Turkish accent as well. Before another consonant "t" is very lightly pronounced.

TH and th: These sounds do not exist in Turkish. The usual substitutions are "d" and "t": *this thing* is pronounced "dis ting."

Stress

The stress on Turkish words is most often on the last syllable, with the exception of certain word endings and almost all place names, which are never stressed on the last syllable, but either on the antepenultimate (next to the next-to-last) or the penultimate (next-to-last) syllable. The song says "It's I' stanbul', it's not Constantinople," but it's not "I' stanbul' " in Turkish—it's "I stan' bul."

Pitch

Stressed syllables are spoken on a higher pitch, unstressed on a lower pitch. Declarative sentences usually fall at the end, but sometimes they rise for emphasis. Questions rise at the end. All this is not very different from English pitch or intonation patterns.

Practice

Evet. Hayir. Allaha ismarladik.
Translation: Yes. No. Goodbye.
Phonetic pronunciation: e vet'; hA yi:r'; A la hA' i:s mAr lA di:k'

I'm going to Istanbul to visit that beautiful city on the Bosporus.
Phonetic pronunciation: Am gaw ing' te i:s tAn' bool te vi: si:t' dAt byoo' ti: fool si:' ti:

But, darling, it's wonderful to see you again.
Phonetic pronunciation: bu? dA:' li:ng i:ts wA:n' de fool ti see y<u>oo</u> A gen'

Possible Pitch Pattern

```
        dar-          won-
            ling,          derful to
But,          it's                  see you a-
                                        gain.
```

Of course my family was always on the right side of things.
Phonetic pronunciation: uv kos mI fa' mi: lee wos awl' ways awn THe rIt sId ef thi:ngz'

It was really so difficult at times.
Phonetic pronunciation: i:t wos ree' A lee sO di:' fi: kult at tIms'

Well, you know, we never had to worry about that sort of thing. We lived in the palace.
Phonetic pronunciation: wel y<u>oo</u> nO wee ne' vA had t<u>oo</u> wu' ree a bowt' THat sawt uf thi:ng   wee li:vd i:n THe pa' las

Finnish

Finnish is spoken by some five million people, mostly in the country of Finland, but also in Russia and the United States. It is a very complicated language,

320

which has 15 cases in noun declensions, for instance, and a complex system of verb conjugations, but, fortunately, it is a fairly simple accent to learn to do. It is written phonetically; once you know the sounds that the letters stand for you can read a page of Finnish and pronounce it correctly even without knowing what it means.

A Quick Reference
1) Stress words lightly on the first syllable.
2) Substitute "p" for "b" and "t" for "d" at the beginning of a word.
3) Substitute "v" for "f" at the beginning of a word.
4) Substitute "sh" and "s" for "zh" and "z" wherever they occur.
5) Substitute "s" and/or "t" for "TH/th" sounds.
6) Stress both halves of a diphthong evenly.
7) Pronounce initial "w" correctly.

How to Do a Finnish Accent
1) Position of the Vocal Apparatus
The position of the vocal apparatus is very much like that of General American, the mouth half open, half closed. However, the lips are slightly forward.

2) Stress
Finnish is uniformly stressed on the first syllable. There is a tendency for this phenomenon to be carried over into English, and this pattern makes the accent resemble Hungarian slightly.

3) The Most Important Sounds
Consonants
The consonants in Finnish are very similar to those of English, but there are a number of consonants in English that do not exist in Finnish, or are found only in words of foreign origin. Pay special attention to the **initial voiceless consonants**.

b: This sound does not exist in Finnish, and the voiceless "p" is sometimes substituted for it: *goodbye* is pronounced "goodpI."

d: This sound does not exist in initial position, and voiceless "t" is often substituted for it: *did* is pronounced "ti:t."

f: As this sound does not exist in initial position in Finnish, it is usually substituted for in English by "v": *five* is pronounced "vIv."

h: This letter in the Finnish alphabet stands for the sound "KH" and a soft version of it, similar to the Spanish *jota*, is used in initial position.

r: The "r" in Finnish is given one trill, and this is the sound heard in all positions.

TH and th: These sounds do not exist in Finnish. The usual substitutions are "s" or "t" for both voiced "TH" and voiceless "th" sounds: *this thing* is variously pronounced sis ting; tis sing; tis ting; sis sing. A "d" is sometimes substituted for the voiced "TH."

z and zh (as in the pronunciation of "s" in *pleasure*): These sounds do not exist in Finnish. Substitute "s" and "sh" for them in all positions.

Vowels and Diphthongs
Vowels are short and long, when in Finnish orthography they are doubled, and follow the system: A, e, i, o, <u>oo</u> (spelled "u"), plus "o." Finnish, like English, is rich in diphthongs, so Finnish speakers do not generally have much trouble learning English diphthongs correctly. In Finnish, however, both halves of the diphthong are evenly stressed, and this sometimes makes for an equally "careful" or evenly stressed pronunciation of diphthongs in English.

i and ee: The usual substitution for these vowels, which do not exist in Finnish, is the long intermediate vowel "i:."

u: This sound in such words as *but* and *love* does not exist in Finnish. The usual substitution is "A": "bAt"; "lAv."

w: This sound does exist in Finnish, and should be correctly pronounced in a Finnish accent in English.

Pitch

Once again there are no particular pitch patterns very different from English. The stressed syllables are on high pitches, the unstressed on lower pitches.

Practice

Note that double consonants in Finnish are pronounced doubled.
tammikuu, helmikuu, maaliskuu, sunnuntai, maanantai, kevät, kesä, syksy, talvi.
Translation: January, February, March, Sunday, Monday, spring, summer, fall, winter.
Phonetic pronunciation: ta' mmi: k<u>oo</u>, KHel' mi: k<u>oo</u>, mA' li: sk<u>oo</u>. soo' nnoon tI. mA' nAn tI. ke' vet, ke' se, sük' sü, tAl' vi:

The pleasure of doing such a thing as reading a good book demands leisure time and peace.
Phonetic pronunciation: di play' shoor ov t<u>oo</u>' ing sAch e ti:ng es ri:' di:ng e g<u>oo</u>d p<u>oo</u>k ti mAnds' lay' shoor tIm end pi:s

Helsinki is one of the cities you should make an effort to visit.
Phonetic pronunciation: khel' si:n ki: i:s wun uv ti: si:' ti:s y<u>oo</u> sh<u>oo</u>t mayk an e'

vut t<u>oo</u> vi:' si:t

Note: Although the usual substitution for "h" is a hard "KH," a soft "kh" is often heard as well, and, in fact, "h" can be and often is, learned by Finns.

But fertile lands are better to cultivate than barren lands.
Phonetic pronunciation: pAt ve' tIl lents A pe' tA t<u>oo</u> kAl' ti: vayt san pa' ren lents

Oh, there are old and new buildings of striking architecture in Finland.
Phonetic pronunciation: O se:r A Olt an ny<u>oo</u> pi:l' ti:nks uv strI' ki:ng A' ki: tek tye i:n vi:n' lAnt

Note: Remember to stress both halves of diphthongs evenly, giving a characteristic rhythm to the Finnish accent. Also, remember that "v" is the usual substitute for "f."

And of all the things you could do, listening to opera in Finland is one of the greatest pleasures. There are marvellous basses and singers in all categories, and they sing at the Savonlinna Festival in the summer, and we play the romantic, hauntingly evocative symphonies of Jean Sibelius as well.
Phonetic pronunciation: an uv awl ti ti:ngs y<u>oo</u> koot t<u>oo</u> li:' sen i:ng too aw' pe rA i:n vi:n lant i:s wun uv di gray' test play' shoors   ser A mA' vel us pay' ses ant si:ng' As i:n awl ka' te gaw rees an say si:ng at ti sA' von li:' nA ves' ti: val in ti sA' me an wee play si rO' man ti:k KHawn' ti:ng lee ee' vawk A ti:v si:m' vo nees uv shawn si:' be:' lee oos as wel

Estonian, Latvian (Lettish), Lithuanian

Latvian and Lithuanian, with its two principle dialects High and Low Lithuanian (alongside many others), are the two main surviving languages of the Baltic branch of Indo-European languages, while Estonian, spoken in the third Baltic republic, next door to the other two, is not related to them. Estonian has two main dialects: Reval, the standard literary language, spoken in the north, and Werre, spoken in the south. Those who speak the Reval dialect find it mutually intelligible with Finnish, to which it is related, and Estonian is, in fact, one of the Finno-Ugaritic languages. Standard Lithuanian is spoken in Kaunas and Vilnius, the capital. There are approximately two and a half million speakers of Lithuanian, two million of Latvian, and about one million of Estonian.

All three languages are very complicated. For example, Lithuanian has seven cases for nouns, and Estonian has 14. The phonetics of these languages, on the other hand, are fairly simple.

Lithuanian, which is close in some ways to Sanskrit, but has a vocabulary which may contain words which predate even that most ancient of Indo-European languages, is the oldest continually spoken Indo-European language. Linguists think that it may be the closest they will ever get to the theoretical ancestor language, Proto-Indo European.

A Quick Reference

1) **Lithuanian**: Palatalize consonants; pronounce "R" without the tongue being turned bottom up; pronounce "w" correctly at the beginning of a word; pronounce "z" correctly.

2) **Latvian**: Use a trilled "r" and pronounce all "r"s; pronounce "z" correctly; substitute "v" for "w" at the beginning of a word; stress the first syllable of words and the following syllables evenly. In a Latvian accent one sometimes hears a slightly Slavic "L," pronounced with the back of the tongue raised." Also, "s" instead of "z" at the end of a word is usual, as in the phrase lamp tables: Lamp tay' beLs. "R" can be correctly learned. Initial consonants can be quite soft; for example, the "p" in *perfectly*: peR' fekt Lee.

3) **Estonian**: Use a trilled "r" and pronounce all "r"s; substitute "v" for "w" at the beginning of a word; substitute "s" for "z" wherever it occurs; stress first syllables of words; see under "Stress" for the relationship between pitch and stress.

4) In all three languages substitute "d" and "t" for "TH" and "th."

How to Do Baltic Accents

Even though all three languages are not related to each other, they share some common phonetic characteristics, perhaps because of historical influence to geographic proximity. Pay special attention to the information on the phonetics of the three languages, which are compared below under "The Most Important Sounds."

1) Position of the Vocal Apparatus

For all three languages the mouth is fairly relaxed, and close to General American; the lips are slightly forward. For a **Latvian** accent, keep the mouth slightly closed, and the upper lip a bit down and forward.

2) The Most Important Sounds
Consonants

In **Lithuanian** all consonants can be palatalized, making the accent somewhat similar to a Russian accent. Palatalization consists of raising the blade of the tongue to the palate, or roof, of the mouth after pronouncing a consonant. Compare this with the limited number of consonants one can palatalize in a Russian accent (Chapter Seventeen). The consonants in Lithuanian are generally softer than in General American: "k," "p" and "t," for example, are pronounced without any extra breath, or aspiration, much as they are at the ends of English words, such as *tip*, *pit* and *kick*.

r and R: The attempt to pronounce a correct General American retroflex "R" leads on the part of **Lithuanian** speakers to the "R" being pronounced without the tip of the tongue being turned bottom up towards the palate. The resulting sound is unique to a Lithuanian accent. For **Latvian** and **Estonian** use a standard trilled "r" in all positions, although "R" is sometimes correctly learned.

z: This sound does not exist in **Estonian**. Substitute "s" for it. It does exist in **Lithuanian** and **Latvian**.

Vowels and Diphthongs

Estonian, like its relative Finnish and like English, is rich in diphthongs. So are **Lithuanian** and **Latvian**. This means that there is relatively little trouble in learning to pronounce English diphthongs correctly.

ee and i: Neither of these vowels exist in any of the languages, and the usual substitution for them is the intermediate lengthened vowel "i:."

w: This sound does not exist in **Estonian** or **Latvian**, and "v" is the usual substitution for it, both initially and in combination with other consonants, such as "qu": *queen* and *quick* are pronounced "kvi:n" and "kvi:k." In **Lithuanian**, on the other hand, "w" does exist, and is therefore pronounced correctly in English.

Stress

The stress in **Lithuanian** is random.

In **Latvian** stress is invariably on the first syllable, with following syllables evenly stressed, similar to Hungarian.

In **Estonian** there is a primary stress on the first syllable and secondary stresses on other syllables in longer words. Lengthened vowels tend to be spoken on different, slightly varied tones, of which there are four, as in the following examples, which you can use for practice:

1) *sada* (hundred; Phonetic pronunciation: sA' dA; short vowel; neutral tone)
2) *saada* (send, the imperative form; Phonetic pronunciation: sA: ' dA; medium length vowel, slightly higher tone)
3) *saata* (send, the infinitive form; Phonetic pronunciation: sA::' tA; very long vowel, slightly higher tone)
4) *tahan saada* (I will receive; Phonetic pronunciation: tA:' hAn sA::' dA; longest vowels, hghtest pitch)

Pitch

There are no particular pitch patterns to concern yourself with in either **Latvian** or **Estonian**. **Lithuanian** has obligatory rising and falling tones, indicated in Lithuanian orthography by accent marks. See "Stress," above, for the relation between lengthened syllables and pitch in **Estonian**. In all three languages, and this is true of the accents in English, the usual pattern of ending a declarative sentence on a falling tone and a question on a rising tone, obtains.

Practice

Estonian
Estonian Words
suur ramat (the large book; Phonetic pronunciation: soo:r rA:' mAt)
üks, kaks, kolm (one, two, three; Phonetic pronunciation: üks kAks kawlm; Note the French/German umlauted "u")

325

English Sentences
I will receive the letter some time this week.
Phonetic pronunciation: I vi:l ri: si:v' di: la' ter sAm tIm di:s vi:k

There is nothing so desparate you have to hurry about it.
Phonetic pronunciation: de:r i:s nA' ti:ng saw das' prit yoo khef too ha' ree a bA' ti:t

No, but why do you carry on so?
Phonetic pronunciation: naw bit vI dyoo kA' ree awn saw

In the zoo you can see zebras and quite a few other animals.
Phonetic pronunciation: i:n di soo yoo kAn si: si:' brAs an kvIt ay lawt awv A' de:r A' ni: mals

Whatever you want to do while you are here, wherever you want to go, do it.
Phonetic pronunciation: vAt' e ver yoo vawnt too doo vIl yoo Ar heer ve:' re: ver yoo vawnt too gaw doo i:t

Latvian (Lettish)
Latvian Words
viens, duas, tris (one, two, three; Phonetic pronunciation: vi:' ens doo' As tri:s)
pavasaris (spring, the season; Phonetic pronunciation: pA' vA sA ri:s)

English Sentences
Spring comes late to the beautiful Latvian countryside.
Phonetic pronunciation: spri:ng kAms lay:t te ze bi:' yoo ti: fool lAt' vi: en kAn' tri: sI:d
Note: Make all the syllables fairly even in length.

Castles, lakes and mountains make this a most romantic country to travel in.
Phonetic pronunciation: kA' sels layks an mAn' tins mayk zi:s ay mawst raw men' ti:k kAn' tri: te trA' vel i:n

This, that and the other, it's all the same to me.
Phonetic pronunciation: zi:s za:t an zi: aw' ze:r i:ts awl ze saym te mi:

Meat and potatoes and wonderful fruit and salads, that's what I like to eat.
Phonetic pronunciation: mi:t en paw tay' taws an vAn' de:r fool froot an sA' lAts zets vawt I lIk te i:t

Latvia suffered greatly during the World War Two.
Phonetic pronunciation: lAt' vi: yA sA' fert grayt' li: dyoo' ring ze vawlt vaw too

Lithuanian
Lithuanian Words and Phrases

Ar tu vedes? (Are you married?)
Phonetic pronunciation: Ar t<u>oo</u> ve' des
Note: Compare Old English "Art thou wedded?."
Alio, labas vakaras. Kaip sekasi? (Hello, good evening. How are things?)
Phonetic pronunciation: A' li: o lA' bAs vA' kA rAs kIp se' kA si:
Dekui, ne blogas. (Thanks, not bad)
Phonetic pronunciation: de k<u>oo</u>' i: ni blaw' gAs
Note: Compare Russian *nye plokha* (nyi pLaw' khA), meaning "not bad."

English Sentences
The head of the council wants to see you.
Phonetic pronunciation: zi: KHat Av zi: kAn' si:l wawnts te si: y<u>oo</u>

And just what did you want to see me about?
Phonetic pronunciation: an dgAs wAt di:d y<u>oo</u> wawn t<u>oo</u> si: mi: ay bowt
Note: Remember to keep the consonants in this and the other exercises quite
soft and unaspirated.

*It concerned a matter to be talked of in private. However, I have no secrets from my
wife.*
Phonetic pronunciation: i:t kon' sent ay mA' te t<u>oo</u> bee tawkt awv i:n pRI' vet
KHA e' veR I KHav naw si:' kRets fRawm mI wIf

Very well, we can proceed, if you wish.
Phonetic pronunciation: ve' ri: wel wi: ken pRaw' si:t i:f y<u>oo</u> wi:sh

I will get straight to the point.
Phonetic pronunciation: I wi:l get stRayt t<u>oo</u> di poynt

Basque

Basque is a language isolate, with no known relation to any other language. Its
origins are obscure, and it contains linguistic elements, such as the noun-verb or
verbal noun, which are to be found in some Asian languages, and verb conjugations
with suffixes of the sort found in Indo-European languages, without, however, being either an Asian or an Indo-European language. It is perhaps one of the surviving
ancient languages of the Iberian Peninsula, preserved because it is a mountain language, still spoken today on either side of the French/Spanish border in the Pyrenees
and on the coastal plains of France and Spain by approximately one million people.
In digs in the Iberian Peninsula archaeologists have found indecipherable inscriptions in ancient Iberian languages, and decipherable inscriptions written in Basque
in either the Greek or Roman alphabets. Georgian linguists in the former Soviet
republic have tried unsuccessfully to relate it to Georgian, an indigenous language
of the Caucasus, on the basis of a similarity of some place-names, such as Iberia,
which is also a name in the Caucasus, but this is probably purely coincidental.

Julius Caesar, conquering the Celtic-speaking Gauls and Belgians, disdained even to attempt the conquest of the Basques, whom he characterized as half-savage and intractable. If today and despite the existence of Basque separatist movements, the Basques are a peaceful people—farmers, shepherds and intellectuals—they were in ancient times fierce fighters by reputation and gave no quarter in battle.

As with every language, Basque has a number of dialects, and even Standard Basque, which its speakers call *Euskara,* is pronounced differently in Spain and France.

A Quick Reference

1) First decide whether it is a French or a Spanish Basque accent you wish to do.
2) Stress is fairly even on all syllables.
3) Substitute "f" for "p."
4) Drop initial "h."
5) Use a retroflex "s."
6) Use a dark liquid "l."
7) Vowels are mostly the same for both French and Spanish Basque accents, except for the use in French Basque itself of the French "ü," which can substitute for "yoo" as "yü."
8) Substitute "s" or "t" for both "TH" and "th."
9) Substitute "s" for "z."
10) Substitute "w" for "v."

How to Do a Basque Accent

1) Position of the Vocal Apparatus
The position of the vocal apparatus is with the mouth half open, half closed, as in General American, and the lips are slightly forward. The main point of resonance and articulation is forward.

2) Stress
Stress patterns are important here. In Standard Basque, and in the language of French Basque speakers, there is an even stress pattern; no syllable of any word is stressed more than any other syllable. This even-toned quality carries over into an accent in English, and every syllable tends to be evenly stressed. South of the Spanish border, some dialects of Basque stress some syllables more than others, and Spanish Basque speakers have a less even-toned quality in the accent in English.

3) Pitch
Pitch patterns go along with stress in creating a kind of even-toned accent. There is a soft, even quality to pitch patterns. Follow the usual pattern of a falling tone at the end of a declarative sentence and a rising tone at the end of a question.

4) The Most Important Sounds
Consonants

328

The consonants in Basque are soft and not harsh to the ear.

f: This consonant is very rare in Basque, and "p" is substituted for it when it is not correctly learned.

h: This consonant does not exist in Spanish Basque, and exists only in one dialect of French Basque. It is generally dropped in a Basque accent in English.

l: This sound is palatal, like the French "l."

r and R: One or other of these rhotic sounds is used, depending on whether Spanish or French Basques are speaking, and the same is true of either French or Spanish Basque accents in English. The "r" is softly trilled, or given one tap.

s and ts: Both these consonants are retroflex in Basque; the bottom of the tongue is turned up toward the palate when pronouncing them. The resulting sounds, somewhat like "sh" or "tsh," are the ones used in a Basque accent in English.

TH and th: The usual substitutes for these consonants are "s" or "t."

v: This voiced consonant, like its voiceless counterpart "f," does not exist in Basque, and "w" is substituted for it, so *very* is pronounced "we' ri:."

z: This voiced consonant does not exist in Basque, and "s" is the usual substitution, since this is what the letter "z" stands for in Basque orthography.

Vowels and Diphthongs
The vowel system of Basque is the following basic system: A, e, i, o, and u (oo). There are a number of diphthongs (with their phonetic pronunciations in parentheses) much like those of English: ei (ay), ai (I), au (ow), oi (oy), ui (wee), eu (yoo). Note that since initial "w," although rare in Basque, does exist, this sound should be correctly pronounced in a Basque accent in English.

i and ee: Since only the intermediate lengthened vowel "i:" exists in Basque, it is usually substituted for the short "i" or the long "ee."

ü: This sound, that of the French "u," is heard in the Basque spoken by French Basques, and occasionally in a French Basque accent in English, so *you* is sometimes pronounced "yü."

Practice

Basque Words and Phrases
oren bat (one hour; Phonetic pronunciation: o' ren bAt)
zer denbora da? (What's the weather like?; Phonetic pronunciation: se: den' bo rA dA)

Euskal gramatika bat baduzu? (Do you have a Basque grammar book?; Phonetic pronunciation: ay' oosh kAl grA' mA ti: kA bAt bA' doo soo)

English Sentences
It is very beautiful in the Basque country, with its high craggy mountains full of snow and cloudy skies.
Phonetic pronunciation: i:t i:s wa' ri: bi: oo' ti: fool i:n se bAsk kAn' tri: wi:s i:s I krA' gi: mAn' te:ns pool A snaw en klA' di: skIs

The Basques were some of the greatest explorers during the Age of Exploration, the greatest shipbuilders and the most wonderful fishermen, too.
Phonetic pronunciation: si bAsks we:r sAm Ap si grayt' es es plawr' ers di:' ring si aych Ap es plaw' ray shin si grayt' es shi:p bi:l de:rs an si maws wAn' de pool pi:sh' er man tsoo

The preservation of the Basque language and culture is of the utmost importance to the world as a whole.
Phonetic pronunciation: si pre' se way' shin Ap si bAsk lAn' gwesh an kAl tyoo i:s Ap si At' maws i:m pawr tents tsoo si wawrl as ay awl

Basque cooking is magnificent. If you have never had Basque chicken, flamed in cognac and braised with onions, garlic, peppers and ham from the Basque city of Bayonne in France, you have not lived. And don't forget the famous gâteau basque!
Phonetic pronunciation: bAsk kook' ing i:s mAg ni:' pi: sent   i:p yoo ap ne' per ad bAsk chi:' ken playm' ed i:n kaw' nyAc an brays' ed wit aw' nyawns gA' li:k pep' ers an am prum si bAsk si:' ti: A bI yun' yoo a nawt li:pt   an dawn paw ge' si pay' mOs gA taw: bAsk

Some cheese, some bread and some good red wine, and the bracing mountain air, and you have yourself a feast.
Phonetic pronunciation: sum chi:s sum bred an sum good red wIn an si bray' si:ng mAn' tsayn ayr an yoo a yoo sal ay peest

Albanian

Albanian is an Indo-European language in a class by itself, literally. Its exact origins and the amount of time it has been spoken are unknown, lost in the mists of time. It has no known relatives, despite the obvious heavy influence of Latin on its vocabulary. Linguists have conjectured that Albanian is an evolution of one of the ancient lost languages, either Illyrian or Thracian. There are two principal, very diverse dialects of Albanian: Tosk, in the south, and Gheg, in the north. The official dialect known as Standard Albanian is that of the capital, Tirana. There are isolated pockets of Albanian speakers in parts of Greece and Italy and the former Yugoslavia. Altogether perhaps four million people speak it. Its earliest written records date from the 15th century, and it was long supposed that it was a non-Indo-European language, until it was proved to be indeed Indo-European by linguists in the 1850s. In 1908 a standardized system of spelling was adopted using the Roman alphabet. Until then Greek, Cyrillic and Arabic had been used to write Albanian, and even when the Roman alphabet was used there was no standardized spelling in either Tosk or Gheg. Albanian has borrowed much vocabulary from Serbo-Croatian, Turkish and Greek.

A Quick Reference

1) Substitute "kh" for "h."
2) Use a trilled "r," sometimes very heavy in an Albanian accent.
3) Pronounce "TH/th" correctly.
4) Shift diphthongs to pure vowels. See below under "The Most Important Sounds."

How to Do an Albanian Accent

1) Position of the Vocal Apparatus
The position of the vocal apparatus is much as for General American, with the lips slightly protruded, however. The jaw is dropped, and the corners of the mouth are a bit taut.

2) The Most Important Sounds
It suffices to pay attention to the few phonetic changes or substitutions, as pitch and stress are of no particular importance here.

Consonants
The consonants are much as in English, with the following important exceptions:

h: The letter is used in Albanian to represent a soft "kh" sound, which is usually heard also in an Albanian accent in English.

j: In Albanian this letter represents the semi-vowel "y," and is sometimes heard initially where "j" is used in English spelling, so *just* is pronounced "yAst."

r: In Albanian the "r" is very strongly trilled or rolled, and this carries over into an accent in English.

TH and th: Albanian is one of the few languages where "TH" and "th" exist, and these sounds are therefore accurately reproduced in an accent in English. In Albanian the voiced "TH" is spelled "dh" and the voiceless "th" is spelled "th."

Vowels and Diphthongs
The vowels in Albanian follow the usual system: A, e, i, o, u (oo), plus "o," spelled with the letter "ë," and the French "u" (ü). The vowels are of medium length.

ay: This diphthong sometimes shifts to a lengthened "e," so *say* is pronounced "se:."

i and ee: Neither of these sounds exists in the exact versions they have in English, and the usual substitution for both is the long intermediate vowel "i:."

O: In an Albanian accent this diphthong usually shifts to the vowel "aw," so *home* is pronounced "khawm."

oo: This sound does not exist in Albanian, and "<u>oo</u>" is usually substituted for it, so *book* is pronounced "b<u>oo</u>k."

u: This sound does not exist in Albanian, and "A" is usually substituted for it, so *but* is pronounced "bAt."

w: This semi-vowel does not exist in Albanian, and "v" is usually substituted for it.

y<u>oo</u>: This diphthong exists in Albanian, and should be correctly pronounced in an Albanian accent in English, as should all combinations employing the semi-vowel "y."

Stress

The stress in Albanian is usually on the last syllable of a phrase and of a polysyllabic word, but there is generally no unusual problem encountered by Albanians in learning English stress patterns.

Practice

Albanian Words and Phrases:
nji, dy, tre (one, two, three; Phonetic pronunciation: nyi: dü tre:)
janar, shkurt (January, February; Phonetic pronunciation: yA nAr' shkoort)
zémërgjérë (generous; Phonetic pronunciation: ze: mer dge:r')

English Sentences
How are you doing? Fine? That's right, I'm just fine! Everything is great.
Phonetic pronunciation: khow Ar y<u>oo</u> d<u>oo</u>' ing fIn THets rIt Im yAst fIn a' vri: thi:ng i:s grayt

Just a minute. What are you talking about?
Phonetic pronunciation: yAst e mi:n' it vAt Ar y<u>oo</u> taw' ki:n a bAt'

For a long time Albania was isolated from the rest of the world.
Phonetic pronunciation: fawr ay lawnk tAm Al bay' nee A vaws A saw lay' tet frAm THe rest Av THe vawrlt
Note: Don't forget to trill the "r" heavily; give it at least two trills for a heavy accent.

Except for the coastal plains, where there is farming, the country is mostly mountains.
Phonetic pronunciation: ek sept' fawr THi kaws' tAl ple:ns we: THe:r i:s fAr' mi:ng THi kAn' tri: i:s mawst' li: mAn' te:ns

How did you come to be interested in the political system of our homeland?
Phonetic pronunciation: khA di:t y<u>oo</u> kAm t<u>oo</u> bee i:n' te res tet i:n THee paw li:' ti: kal si:s' tem awv Ar khawm' lAnt

Part Seven

Middle Eastern Accents

Introduction

The languages of the Middle East include two important Semitic languages, Arabic and Hebrew, and one Indo-European language, Persian or Farsee, a member of the Indo-Iranian branch, and thus a link with the languages of India and Europe, in between both. Arabic and Hebrew are called Afroasiatic languages because their area of distribution includes both continents. Arabic is the most widely spoken language in North Africa, and sometimes south of the Sahara as well, and the culture of Islam has certainly influenced those regions south of the great desert, inhabited by the Berbers and the Tuaregs and other nomadic peoples speaking a variety of African languages. In Ethiopia another prominent Semitic language, Amharic, is spoken. In the Middle East Persian has had an enormous influence, and in ancient days the Persian Empire spread from the Mediterranean to India. Once the spread of Islam began throughout the region the Persian hegemony gave way to the Ottoman Turks, and the Persians, whose present-day descendants are Iranians, were converted to the new religion. In the 20th century, after the dissolution of the Ottoman Empire following World War One, it was Arabic culture which came once again to dominate the region, although Turkish and Persian cultures and languages continued to remain prominent. The revival of the state of Israel and of the Hebrew language constituted another element in this mosaic of culture and language. All the accents associated with these languages are important in contemporary films and, to a lesser extent, in the theatre. English is widely spoken in the region as a second language.

Chapter Twenty-Three
Arabic Accents: Middle Eastern, Egyptian and Other North African Arabic Accents

Arabic is a Semitic language, related to Hebrew and Amharic, which last is spoken in Ethiopia. In its many varieties, Arabic, the standard version of which, Modern Classical Arabic, is one of the official languages of the U.N., is spoken by some 215 million people in North Africa and the countries of the Arabian Peninsula and the Middle East. It is the official language of 17 countries, including Tunisia, Morocco, Algeria, Saudi Arabia, Egypt, Jordan, Syria and Iraq. The liturgical, sacred language of Islam used in the Koran, Arabic is written in its own alphabet from right to left, like the Hebrew alphabet. The alphabet is also used to write Persian, and for a long time was the alphabet of the far-flung Ottoman Empire. Turkish was written with the Arabic alphabet, as were the Jewish languages of the Empire, Judeo-Persian and Judeo-Turkish, and Moslems in all countries are familiar with it through the Koran.

There has been a heavy influence of French culture in the Middle East and North Africa, ever since Napoleon invaded Egypt and France conquered Algeria in the 1830s, as well as of British culture. The contributions of Arabic culture to European culture from the Middle Ages to the present included the earliest modern methods of medicine and chemistry, as well as the preservation of ancient Greek philosophy. Such words as *algebra, alchemy, alcohol, alkali, amber, cotton, sherbet, syrup* and *sofa* come from Arabic. Contributions to mathematics include the Arabic numerals, and the concept of the *zero*, a word which comes to English from French, but is originally derived from Arabic *shifr*, meaning "cipher."

The Iberian Peninsula was home to a centuries long brilliant Islamic civilization, a Golden Age, which included Jewish and Christian Spain. In 1492 the Moslem Moors, like the Jews, were expelled from Spain by the Christianizing monarchs, Ferdinand and Isabella. The gorgeous contributions of Arabs there include a great literature and the magnificent architecture of the Moorish palaces of medieval Spain, such as the Alhambra.

With the conquest of territories by imperialist European powers and the later dissolution of the Ottoman Empire, the impoverishment of large sections of the populations of the Middle East and North Africa became widespread, particularly as modern technological developments aroused the need for oil from the oil-rich Middle East. An immensely rich, autocratic group of ruling families succeeded the Ottoman rulers, and in some countries, at least, did little to stop the imperialist takeover. A large, economically deprived underclass was thus created. For a picture of Egypt in the late 19th and early 20th centuries, read the classic novels and stories of Naguib Mahfouz, *The Palace Walk*, etc. Mahfouz, a brilliant writer, has been called the Egyptian Marcel Proust. In Paris there is today a good deal of prejudice against the many poor Arabs who live there, and this prejudice flourishes alongside an admiration for Arab culture and a delight in such superb dishes as *couscous*.

There are a number of important spoken varieties of Arabic. These include the Arabic spoken in Egypt and the variety used in Syria/Lebanon, as well as Iraqui and Palestinian Arabic, all of which are quite different from each other, and quite different from written Classical Arabic.

For a very light Egyptian Arabic accent, listen to Omar Sharif in any of his films. Anwar Sadat, who can be seen in documentary films, had a heavier Egyptian accent. If you need to use a heavier accent, watch the television news shows for the comments of Arab diplomats on the Middle East situation. Among people in the television news broadcasts, King Hussein of Jordan is a very good example of a medium accent, while Yassir Arafat has a heavier accent. A number of Arab diplomats have learned the British English model. See Chapter One for the system of vowels which you should follow.

A Quick Reference

1) Use a heavily trilled "r," sometimes aspirated to "hr." Drop "r" before another consonant and in final position.
2) Pronounce initial "h" and "TH/th" correctly.
3) Use a dark liquid "l."
4) Articulate final consonants very strongly and clearly.
5) Substitute "O" for both "aw." Substitute "aw" for "o."

How to Do Arabic Accents

1) Position of the Vocal Apparatus
The general position of the vocal apparatus is as follows: The mouth is half open, half closed, fairly relaxed, as in General American. The lips are slightly protruded, as in speaking standard modern Arabic. The language, despite the variety of guttural sounds, is frontally well articulated, and the tongue tends to stay in a forward, down position. Doing the practice exercises at the end of the chapter should give you a good idea of how the language feels in the mouth, and of the correct position of the vocal apparatus.

2) Stress
Stress can be very important in Arabic accents. Stress in Arabic is always on the syllable containing the long vowel, which means that for our purposes it is random, although there are rules. Almost never is it on the last syllable, for example, although often in anglicizations of Arabic words the stress is on the last

syllable, even where the stress should really be more even. In other words, learning correct stress patterns in English is usually not a problem for Arabic speakers. In fact the topic of stress in Arabic is a very complicated one, and it is possible for one Arabic speaker to tell where another Arabic speaker comes from by the way in which he stresses certain words, since the same word is stressed on a different syllable, depending on the dialect. Like French, and to some extent Hebrew, Arabic is spoken in "stress groups" or "breath groups," also called "rhythmic phrases." However, unlike French, the stressed syllable is most often not, I repeat, the last one in the group. There is nevertheless a tendency to group words together in a rhythmic phrase, words which go together to form a logical grouping, such as a noun with its adjectives, or a preposition with its object. A sentence like *Of course, I think so* consists of two groups, *of course* and *I think so*. The words *of* and *think* would be stressed, and the other non-stressed words glided over, giving the sentence the characteristic rhythm of an Arabic accent in English.

3) The Most Important Sounds
Consonants
The Arabic accent follows the British model in being non-rhotic. Final consonants are very well articulated, and it is usually the initial or middle version of "b," "d", "g," "k," "p," and "t" that is heard in final position. There are a number of back, guttural consonants in Arabic which need not concern us here, as they are hardly ever heard in an accent in English. Nevertheless I am including this information in case it should prove useful.

Arabic guttural consonants: "KH," as in Scottish *loch*; "gh" as in the French uvular "R." Both these consonants have variations, or, rather, several versions, farther back or more forward in the throat.

ch: This consonant is sometimes heard as "ty," so *church* could be pronounced "tye:rty," or "tyawrch."

h: Initial "h" exists in Arabic, and is usually pronounced in an accent in English.

l: There are two Arabic "l"s, one of which is palatalized; the blade of the tongue touches the palate when pronouncing the "l," which is dark and liquid. The other "l," with the blade of the tongue down and thickened and the tip of the tongue behind the upper front teeth, is similar to the Slavic "L." It is used mainly for the special way of pronouncing the name of God, Allah.

r: In Arabic the "r" receives from one to three trills. Often in English the attempt to pronounce the General American retroflex "R" results in a very aspirated trilled "r," sometimes pronounced with more than one trill: *right* is thus pronounced "hrIt" or "hrrIt." On the other hand, a simple trilled "r" is often the one heard in an Arabic accent in English. In a lighter accent, the General American retroflex "R" is well learned and correctly pronounced.

TH and th: These sounds exist in Arabic, however they are dentalized—pronounced with the tongue between the teeth, as opposed to standard English pronunciation, with the tongue just behind the upper front teeth.

Vowels and Diphthongs
schwa: An "i" often substitutes for a schwa, so *the* is pronounced "THi," whether before a vowel or a consonant.

aw: 1) Often "aw" in *law* or *talk* shifts to the diphthong "O," so that *law* and *talk* are pronounced "lO" and "tOk."
2) The vowel "aw" is also used instead of "o," so *work* and *first* shift to "wawrk" and "fawrst."

ay: In some speakers one hears "a" substituted for this diphthong: *enable* is pronounced "en a' bl."

e: This sound sometimes, but not always, shifts to "a," so *end* is pronounced "and."

o: See "aw" above.

Pitch

The stressed syllables are spoken on upper pitches, the unstressed on lower pitches. There are generally no unusual pitch patterns to concern yourself with. Questions rise in pitch at the end, and declarative sentences fall. There is an occasional pattern of rising at the end of a statement, for emphasis.

Practice

The following sentences are in spoken Egyptian Arabic, transliterated from the Arabic alphabet into the Roman alphabet.

Izzayyak? (said to a man); *Izzayik?* (said to a woman)
Translation: How are you?
Phonetic pronunciations: i:z zA:' yAk; i:z zA:' yi:k

kwayyis, il-Hamdu lillaah. (said by a man); *kwayyisa, il-Hamdu lillaah.* (said by a woman)
Translation: Fine, thank you.
Phonetic pronunciations: kwA' yi:s il hAm' d<u>oo</u> lil lAh'; kwA yi:s' A il hAm' d<u>oo</u> lil lAh'
Note that all the "h"s are pronounced, even in final position. The long vowels are really long. The initial "h" of *Hamdu* is very aspirated, very strong.

Misaa' il-xeer. Ahlan wa sahlan.
Translation: Good evening. Welcome.
Phonetic pronunciation: mi: sA?' il KHayr' Ah' lAn wA sAh' lAn
Note the glottal stop after the syllable "saa' " and the final "h," which is pronounced in Arabic.

English Sentences
The first glory of Ancient Egypt is seen today in the brilliance of her archaeological sites, and despite long occupations by the British and French, the independence of the country is assured.
Phonetic pronunciation: THi fawrst glO' ree Af e:n' tyen ee' dgi:pt i:s si:n ti day' i:n THi bri:l' yAnts Af hayr Ar kay O lO' dgi: kAl sIts end di spIt lOng Ok kyoo pay' shinz bI THi bri:' ti:sh end fransh THi in da pan' dants Af THi kAn' tree i:z a' shoord

(Heard on television) *We must go ahead and make the peace process more fruitful.*
Phonetic pronunciation: wi: mAst gaw A had' end me:k THa pi:s pRA' ses mawr froot' fool

It must be said that Arabia is very beautiful and that the Arabian cuisine is delicious.
Phonetic pronunciation: i:t mAst bi: sad THAt A ray' bi: a i:z va' ri: byoo' ti: fool
And THAt A ray' bi: An kwi: zi:n' i:z di li' shAs

This is really very serious and demands to be looked into.
Phonetic pronunciation: THi:s i:z ree' lee ve' ree see' ree es en dee mAndz' too bee lookt i:n' too

Possible Pitch Pattern

```
                                        mands to be looked
              really very seri-                          in-
This is                          ous and de-                   to.
```

The Mosque of Al Aksa, one of the holiest sites in all Islam, is on the Temple Mount in Jerusalem.
Phonetic pronunciation: THee mawsk awv Al Ak' sA wAn awv THee hawl' ee est sIts i:n awl i:s lAm' i:z awn THee tem' pel mownt i:n dge roos A lem

I don't care if he doesn't like it. That's just too bad. He has to accept what I say.
Phonetic pronunciation: I dawnt kaye:r i:f hee dAz' ent lIk i:t THet's dgAst too bed hee hez too ek' sept wawt I say

Chapter Twenty-Four
Hebrew

Hebrew, the language of the Bible and of Jewish religious education, was for long centuries confined to the area of religion, despite extensive borrowings from it in such Jewish languages as Yiddish and Ladino. Nevertheless, since it had been kept alive for so long, it was fairly easy to revive and modernize it as the official state language of Israel. The movement to revive Hebrew as both a spoken and a literary language began in the 19th century with the rise of Zionism, the political movement to found a state as a homeland for the world's Jews, whose ancestors had come mostly from the Middle East, that piece of land which forms a kind of bridge between Europe, Africa and Asia. Today in the state of Israel some three to four million people speak Hebrew and there is a flourishing Hebrew literature. Certainly there are many differences between modern spoken Hebrew and the Hebrew of the Bible. The language continues to evolve, but it is also possible for modern Israelis to understand the older version of the language, much more easily than, say, a modern Greek can understand Homer or Plato.

The Hebrew alphabet, written and read from right to left, consists of 22 consonants. A system of dots and dashes written below and sometimes above the consonants indicates vowel sounds. This alphabet, related to the Arabic alphabet, both of which were derived from the Phoenician alphabet designed for the lost Semitic tongue of those seafaring merchants, is the ancestor of the Greek alphabet, considerably simplified from the original Hebrew and easier to read, from left to right. It is therefore also the ancestor of the present Roman alphabet, perhaps the easiest to read of all the world's alphabets.

Because of the cosmopolitan and immigrant nature of the state of Israel, many people speak Hebrew with a foreign accent of one kind or another. We are concerned here with the accent of the Sabras, native-born Israeli Jews and Hebrew speakers, in English. Sabra refers to a kind of cactus, rough on the outside, sweet and tender on the inside. In Europe two different systems of pronunciation of Hebrew had developed, the Ashkenazic and the Sephardic. Ashekenazic comes from the Jews of Yiddish speaking background, mostly in Eastern Europe, and Sephardic from the Jews of Spain, who emigrated to North Africa, Turkey and Greece after their expulsion from Spain. There are some important differences: in the Ashkenazic system "A" is pronounced "aw," so *baruch atah* (the beginning of prayers, meaning "blessed [art, or be, *understood*] thou") is said as "baw rooKH' A taw", and in the Sephardic, where "A" is pronounced "A," it is said as "bA rooKH' A tA'." Final "th" is pronunced as "s" in Ashkenazic and as "t" in Sephardic, so the word *brith* (transliterated from the Hebrew alphabet; meaning "covenant," and usually referring to the circumcision ceremony) is pronounced "bri:s" in the Ashkenazic way and "bri:t" in the Sephardic. It is generally the Sephardic pronunciation that was adopted for modern Hebrew.

Hebrew is an ancient Semitic language of the Canaanite branch, and is some 3000 years old. Closely related to ancient Phoenician and to Arabic, it was one of the chief languages of the Jews of Biblical times, alongside Aramaic, which also contributed to the Judaic liturgy. The *Kaddish*, the prayer for the dead in which the word *death* is never mentioned, but the Creator is extolled, is in Aramaic. Jesus Christ probably spoke Aramaic, as opposed to Hebrew. Much of the New Testament is written, however, in Greek, the language of the Hellenized Jews, many of whom probably spoke more Greek than Hebrew by the time of the Roman occupation of Palestine, and certainly by the time the New Testament was written. Many of the upper-class Jews learned Latin as a matter of course, and many emigrated to Italy, where one of the oldest synagogues in Europe, at Ostia Antica near Rome, is to be found, on the outskirts of the city, away from the central temple area devoted to Jupiter and the other Roman gods. To speak Aramaic or even Hebrew, as opposed to using them only as liturgical, sacred languages, was then a mark of belonging to a lower class, and it is possibly in part the fact that Christ preached in Aramaic, as well as what he said, that led to his being viewed by the ruling Roman and Jewish classes as a heretical and dangerous rebel.

A Quick Reference

1) Last syllable stressing is a major part of the Hebrew language, and a prime aspect of an Israeli accent. Words should be evenly stressed as a compensation, especially when the last syllable contains a schwa, much as in the principle of stress in French.
2) A heavy retroflex "R" with a slight vibration of the uvula added is often heard in an Israeli accent.
3) Substitute "d" and "t" for "TH/th."
4) Substitute "e" for "a."
5) Substitute "i: " for "i" and "ee."

How to Do an Israeli Accent

1) Position of the Vocal Apparatus
The mouth is open to much the same position as in General American. The lips, however, are slightly protruded while speaking. English is spoken by many Israeli speakers with the lips in the position used for speaking Hebrew. You will get a feeling for this by doing the "Practice" exercises at the end of the chapter.

2) Stress
Stress is of paramount importance in doing a Hebrew or Israeli accent. The stress in Hebrew is on the last or on the penultimate (next to the last) syllable,

particularly in certain word endings indicating, for instance, possession (the genitive case), as in "el o hay' nu" (our Lord). As a result, and because of certain coincidental phonetic similarities, such as the use in Modern Hebrew of the uvular "R," there is a resemblance to French accents. There is a phenomenon in Hebrew, very similar to French, of speaking in somewhat rhythmical phrases. However every word in Hebrew retains its own stress, and this stress does not shift as it does in French. Still, in English the effect is often very similar to French rhythmic phrasing. If, for example, the last syllable of a word contains a schwa, it is usually not stressed.

3) The Most Important Sounds

Consonants

R: The "R" in Modern Hebrew is similar to the uvular "R" heard in French, but pronounced deeper in the throat, that is, the farther back part of the tongue is used to vibrate the uvula. The attempt to pronounce an English retroflex "R" correctly often results in the tip of the tongue being a little too far back, while the uvula is very slightly vibrated by the back of the tongue, which, as an automatic linguistic habit, is slightly raised. This pronunciation of "R" is specific to a Hebrew accent in English and serves to differentiate it from the otherwise somewhat similar French accent.

TH and th: These consonants do not exist in Hebrew. The usual substitutions in Israeli accents are "d" for the voiced "TH" and "t" for the voiceless "th": *this thing* is pronounced "di:s ti:ng."

Vowels and Diphthongs

Vowels in Hebrew are generally quite short, and this trait carries over into an accent in English.

a: As this vowel does not exist in the exact form it has in English, the usual substitution for it is "e."

ee: There is no vowel exactly like the "ee" in *meet* in Hebrew, so one often hears the intermediate vowel "i:" substituted for it.

i: This vowel also has no exact equivalent in Hebrew. Instead we usually hear, once again, a lengthened intermediate vowel "i:."

Pitch

There is a tendency for pitch to rise at the end of a declarative sentence, particularly if the speaker is making a point. Usually, however, there is a falling tone at the end. Questions rise at the end in Hebrew, just as they do in English. We are not talking here, of course, of the ritual chanting of the Jewish liturgy, which follows prescribed rules and is indicated in Biblical texts.

344

Practice

Hebrew Words Transliterated from the Hebrew Alphabet
Shalom aleichem
Translation: hello; Literal translation: peace to-you
Phonetic pronunciation: SHa lom' A lay KHem'

From the Passover *Haggadah: Ma nishtana halila hazeh mikol ha lilot?*
Literal translation: why different the-night the-this from the nights?; Translation: Why is this night different from all other nights?
Phonetic pronunciation: mA nish tA nA' hA lI' lA hA ze' mi: kol' hA lI' lot

The Book of Genesis, Chapter I, Verse 1: *Bereshit boroh elohim es hashemayim ve es haoretz*
Literal translation: In-the-beginning created lord both the-heavens and both the-earth. Translation: In the beginning God created the heavens and the earth.
Phonetic pronunciation: be re:' shi:t' bo ro:' el o hi:m' es ha she mA' yi:m ve es hA o:' rets'

From Psalm 23, Verse 4:
gam qi elech b'gay tsal moves, lo ira ra qi ata imodi
Literal translation: Though that I-walk in valley shadow of-angel-of-death not will-fear evil because you with-me
Translation (King James Version): Yea, though I walk through the valley of the shadow of death, I will fear no evil: for thou *art* with me
Phonetic pronunciation: gAm kee ay' leKH be gay tsAl mo' ves lo ee' rA rA kee A tA' i: mo dee'

English Sentences
I don't care. It's all right whatever you say.
Phonetic pronunciation: I dawn ke:R' i:ts awL rIt' wo te: ve:R yoo say'
Note: See the information under "R" in the section on consonants. Notice where the stress falls, at the end of a rhythmic phrase.

Tel Aviv is a city on the seashore and its name means the hill of spring.
Phonetic pronunciation: tel A vi:v' i:z e si:' tee awn THe see' shawR' end i:ts ne:m mi:nz di hi:l awv spRi:ngg'
Notes: The Hebrew "l" is close to the French liquid "l." For a heavier accent you can make the "R" sounds deeply guttural: "R." Remember that the retroflex "R" should be pronounced with the tongue curled farther back than it is in the General American version of this sound. Notice the extra "g" at the end of "spRi:ngg," which is meant to be pronounced after the nasal "ng."

One of the problems we have had in the last few years is the inability to find a peaceful solution to resolve the situation.
Phonetic pronunciation: wun uv THee pRAb' lems wee hev hed i:n THe lAst

345

fy<u>oo</u> yeeRs' i:s THee i:n A bi:' li: tee t<u>oo</u> fInd a pees' fool sO lyoo' shen too Ri zawlv' THee si: ch<u>oo</u> ay' shen

There is nothing to be done in such a situation except to grin and bear it.
Phonetic pronunciation: de: Ri:z nA' thi:ng t<u>oo</u> bee dAn' i:n sAch ay si: ch<u>oo</u>, or ty<u>oo</u>, ay' shen ak sap t<u>oo</u> gRi:n' en be:' Ri:t'
Note: Notice where the stresses fall, giving the sentence that characteristic sense of rhythmic phrasing. For a heavier accent use the deeply guttural uvular "R."

For thousands of years at every Passover seder Jews have said "hashanah haba'ah be yerooshelayim": "Next year in Jerusalem." This has been the dream of the exiled, persecuted Jews throughout the Diaspora.
Phonetic pronunciation: fawR thow zints Av yeeRz' et av Ree pas aw veR se:' deR dg<u>oo</u>z hev sed hA shA nA hA bA A' be ye R<u>oo</u> she lA' yi:m nakst yi:R' i:n dge R<u>oo</u>' sA lem di:s hez been di dReem Av eg zIld poR se ky<u>oo</u> ted dg<u>oo</u>s' tR<u>oo</u> owt THi dI, or dee, as' paw RA
Note: The inconsistency in the pronunciation of the "TH" and "th" sounds is deliberate, since people are often inconsistent even within their own accents, and find it easier to pronounce "TH" and "th" in certain phonetic contexts, not so easy in others.

One day there will be peace in the Middle East, and everyone will have their rights recognized.
Phonetic pronunciation: wAn day' THe:R wi:l bi: pi:s' i:n THe mi: del i:st' and av' ree wAn wi:l hev THe:R Rits' Re kawg nIst'

Possible Pitch Pattern

```
                                    East                          recog-
                    peace                      one          rights
         day                       in the Middle    every-   will have their
   One    there will be                         and                       nized
```

Chapter Twenty-Five

Persian

If you've ever worn a *shawl* or lounged in *pajamas* on a *divan* while sipping a mint *julep* and playing chess until you were able to say *checkmate* to your opponent, you were using words which came to English from Persian. *Checkmate* comes from the Persian words *shah mat*, meaning "the king dies."

Persian, spoken in Iran and in part of Afghanistan, is one of the Iranian languages of the Indo-European family. Fifty million people are native speakers of Persian. Since the conquest of Persia and the conversion of the Persians to Islam in the seventh century, Persian, written until then in its own alphabet, known as Pahlavi, has been written in a modified Arabic alphabet. Classical Persian developed in the capital city of Teheran in the early 13th century. Until the 19th century it represented the standard of written and spoken Persian, but has since been modified. Kurdish, spoken in northern Iraq and in parts of Iran, and Pashto (spoken in Afghanistan by the non-Persian speaking part of the population) are related languages of the West Iranian group of the Indo-Iranian branch. There are three main dialects of Persian: that of Iran; that of Afghanistan, called Dari; and a dialect used in Tadjikistan, the former Soviet Republic.

Persian is actually the simplest language of the branch. It has two genders (one for animate and one for inanimate objects), simple verb and adjectival forms, and no declensions for nouns. There is a great influence from Arabic on the Persian language, both in vocabulary and in certain forms such as the use of the Arabic plural endings for nouns. The sound system, close to that of English, but lacking certain sounds, is also relatively easy to master.

A Quick Reference

1) Use an "r" with one trill or tap and a dark liquid French-sounding "l."
2) Substitute "d" and "t" for "TH/th" and "v" for "w."
3) See below for the confusion of the vowels "A," "a" and "e" with each other.
4) Substitute "e" for both the "schwa (e)" and "o."

How to Do an Iranian Accent

1) Position of the Vocal Apparatus
It is much the same as in General American, but short vowels are "tight," that is, the mouth literally narrows and the muscles become taut when they are used. The main point of articulation is forward in the mouth; there are not many

back, guttural sounds in Persian.

2) The Most Important Sounds
Consonants
The consonants are very close to those of English. There is also a glottal stop in Persian, and this sound is heard, as in some accents native to English, replacing a "t" in such words as *but* and *bottle*.

l: The Persian "l" resembles the French "l" in being liquid. It is pronounced with the blade of the tongue down slightly and the tip of the tongue touching the upper gum ridge behind the upper front teeth.

r: The "r" is given one trill, and it is this sound heard in a Persian accent in English.

TH and th: Since these sounds do not exist in Persian, they are usually replaced by "d" and "t": *this thing* is pronounced "di:s ti:ng."

v: This is the usual substitute for "w," which does not exist in Persian.

Vowels and Diphthongs
The basic vowel system used in Persian consists of: A, e, i, o and u (oo). The vowel systems of the three dialects mentioned above are all slightly different from each other, but I think those complications need not concern us here. For instance, in both Iran and Afghanistan words with the vowels "a" and "e" and "o" are pronounced the same, and only in Tadjikistan do "e" and "o" shift to "i" and "u," respectively. In an accent in English "a" and "e" are sometimes confused with each other, however, and this creates the Persian accent. Diphthongs often change to pure vowels in a Persian accent, so "ay" shifts to a lengthened "e:" and "O" to a lengthened "o:" or "aw:."

A and a: These two vowels are sometimes confused with each other, so *father* is pronounced "fa' der" and *attack* is pronounced "e tAk' " (**Kurdish**) or "a tAk' " or "e tek' " (**Iranian**). This is not always the case, however, and the sound "A" is often the only one used in a Persian accent for words pronounced with both "A" and "a."
Practice words: Note: Practice these words using all the combinations just described. *attack, father, rather, can't bath, ask, asking, answer*

e and a: These two vowels are also sometimes confused with each other, and "e" always substitutes for "a" when this confusion occurs.
Practice words: *that, cat, hat, mat, bat, met, bet, debt, attack, rather, matter*

e and o: Neither of these vowels exist. The schwa can often be learned, however, and is heard not only in words with "o," ("vek," "fest" for *work, first*) but also in

348

words with "u" ("bet" for *but*). Instead of the schwa, however, an "e" is often substituted in those words: verk, ferst. *But* is pronounced "bet."

i and ee: The first of these vowels, as is so often the case, does not exist in Persian, and the usual sound for both "i" and "ee" is the long vowel "ee."

oo and oo: These vowels should be correctly pronounced.

w: This semi-vowel does not exist in Persian. The usual substitute in initial position is "v."

Stress

Although there are definite and clear rules of stress in Persian, for our purposes let us say that the stress is random. Stress in Persian can be on any syllable, depending on the rules, and is not uniformly on a particular syllable. In other words, learning to stress English words correctly presents no particular problem to the Persian speaker.

Pitch

There is no particular divergence from the usual rules that stressed syllables are spoken on an upper pitch and unstressed on a lower one, with declarative sentences falling at the end and questions rising in pitch. There is a tendency to rise at the end of a declarative sentence, for emphasis.

Practice

Persian Words and Phrases:
bahar (bA khAr'; spring, the season); *yakshanbeh* (yAk' shAn be:'; Sunday); *shab be-khair* (shAb' be KHA ir'; good night); *che khabar ast?* (What is the matter?; che KHA' bAr Ast)

English Sentences
(I heard the following sentence in a television interview given by a Kurdish military leader in Iraq, but the accent is very similar to the Persian, as Kurdish is a closely related language).
We are attacking the town.
Phonetic pronunciation: vee Ar e tA' keeng dee town
Notes: *The* is pronounced "dee" in all positions, even before a consonant. The "ee" in the syllable "-keeng" is perhaps a bit shorter than the other "ee"s, and more like the lengthened intermediate vowel "i:."

There would likely be some problem in the future regarding diplomatic relations.
Phonetic pronunciation: de:r vood lIk' lee bee sAm prawb' lem een dee fyoo' che ree gA' di:ng deep le mA' teek re le:' shens

No, but it's not that. Whatever you have to tell me will be of some help.
Phonetic pronunciation: nO bA di:ts, or di:s, nawt THat, or Thad wA dev' e yoo
hav too tel mee wi:l bee Av sAm help, or helb

It can be quite a wonderful work of art. You have to look at it in the right way.
Phonetic pronunciation: i:, or i:t, or i:d, kan bee kwI' *de* wun de' fool wok ev Art,
or Ard Yoo, or ye, haf too, or te, look a di: di:n de rId, or rIt, way

But of course you have to understand that this is the way things are.
Phonetic pronunciation: bA' dAv kawrs yoo hev too An' de stand THad THi:z i:z
THi way thi:ngz A
Note: In the exercises above, to lighten the accent pronounce final "R" in the
words *whatever, wonderful, work, art, course, understand* and *are* with the retrof-
lex, General American sound in its lightest version, avoiding the hard Middle
Western "R."

It's bad, very bad. The situation is really bad, that's all.
Phonetic pronunciation: i:ds ba:d ve' ree ba:d THi si:t yoo ay shin i:z ree' lee
ba:d THads aw:l

Possible Pitch Pattern

```
            ve-                        really
        ry                    tion is
                      situa-             that's
It's                  The                      all.
    bad,          bad.                  bad,
```

Part Eight

African Accents

Introduction

The languages of Africa account for almost a third of the world's languages, and there are 1300 or more African languages, according to David Crystal's *The Cambridge Encyclopedia of Language* (Cambridge University Press, 1987). (Other authors give different estimates.) On the Mediterranean coast of North Africa Arabic is ubiquitous and dominant, and in the Sahara the Berber languages predominate. The relationship among some of the various languages as one goes further south into the continent is extremely tenuous, although linguists have grouped some of them together into major families. To summarize a very complicated situation, the major language groupings are as follows:

1) Approximately 200 Afroasiatic languages, also known as Hamito-Semitic, because some of these languages, such as Arabic and Hebrew, are spoken in the part of Asia known as the Middle East, includes the Semitic language Amharic, spoken in Ethiopia, the Cushitic language Somali, spoken in Somaliland, and Coptic, spoken in Egypt; and the Chadic languages of East Africa, such as Hausa, spoken in Nigeria, and other Central and West African languages;

2) Niger-Kordofanian, including the Niger-Congo family of languages (1000 of them!), includes Ibo and Yoruba, spoken in Nigeria; the Bantu languages (500 or more of them), among which are the Zulu and Khosa of South Africa, and Swahili, spoken in Uganda and many parts of East and South Africa; and the Adamawa group of languages in the northern part of Central Africa. This language family, including 40 or even 50 more languages in various groups besides the ones mentioned, is the most important in Africa.

3) The Nilo-Saharan group of 100 languages spoken along the upper reaches of the Nile and in the Sudan, including Masai; these Sudanic languages, spoken in areas just north of the Niger-Congo languages, although all these language areas overlap, account for another 35 or 40 languages.

4) The Khoisan group of 50 languages, well known as the famous "click" languages, of the Kalahari desert and parts of South Africa, spoken by the Bushmen and Hottentots; the five or more Khoisan groups of South Africa are distinct from the Bantu languages Zulu and Khosa, which also have clicks, and are also spoken in South Africa, but which are Niger-Congo languages, as stated above; and

5) Various other groups of languages spoken in the interior of the continent.

All the above groupings of languages are further subdivided.

In countries formerly occupied by Great Britain English continues to be widely spoken, and is, in fact the official language of Uganda, Zambia (once called Northern Rhodesia), Zimbabwe (once called Southern Rhodesia), and Malawi (once called Nyasaland). In Kenya and Tanzania (formerly known as Tanganyika) and Zanzibar, English has all but official status; it is used in legal cases, on store signs and in advertisements, in newspapers and magazines and extensively in business dealings. English is also widely spoken as a second language in Ghana, Togoland and Nigeria. The accents of East and West Africa, which are developing into standardized forms of English, are extremely important. The other widely spoken European language in Africa is French, because of Belgian and French colonization, and French African accents in English are also quite common, and follow the general pattern of French accents, as outlined in Chapter Eight.

In North Africa there are alphabets milennia old, such as Egyptian hieroglyphics and Berber script, not to mention the use of the ancient Phoenecian and later Greek and Coptic alphabets. Many, if not most, of the languages of the continental interior had no alphabets. In the 18th and 19th centuries the imperialist powers, especially the missionaries, decided to write them down, and used a modified Roman alphabet to do so. The system used for spelling the 500 or so languages thus transcribed varied depending on the colonialist power. In 1836 the Royal Geographical Society in England decided to spell them using the so-called continental or Italian vowel system and the consonant system of English. In French areas the orthographic system of French was used. In Nigeria, however, for example, where there was a large Moslem population, Hausa had already been written using the Arabic alphabet, which had spread south below the Sahara. No attempt was made to account for the tonal nature of so many of these languages, and the transcriptions were in any case often inaccurate. Ewe (ay' way') is a case in point. It was differently transcribed by French and English missionaries in Ghana and Togoland, and its different dialects were misconstrued or incorrectly learned. The myth that Africa has no real history and Africans no past apart from their relationship to the European world dies hard, but it is as much an imperialistic, racist lie as the idea that Africa is nothing but jungle and desert and its people descended from primitive, savage nomads and hunters. Read Basil Davidson's *The Lost Cities of Africa* (Little, Brown and Company, 1987) and delve into the UNESCO 8-volume *General History of Africa*. For a look at the shameless, brutal exploitation of Africa by the imperialists see the 1998 **PBS** *Masterpiece Theatre* drama *Rhodes*, in which you can hear Ndebele (en de bee' lee), the Bantu language of the Matabele (mA te bee' lee) of Zimbabwe, formerly southwestern Rhodesia. Ndebele is spoken by about two million people. In the next chapter you will find information on East and West African accents, which have many phonetic features in common despite the widely differing sound systems of some of the languages on which they are based.

Chapter Twenty-Six

East and West African Accents: Notes on Sub-Saharan and Ethiopian; Nigerian; Ugandan (Swahili); Zaire and Congo: Lingala

There are, as I have said, 1300 or so African languages. The following information just touches the tip of the iceberg, but it may help to elucidate the problems involved in distinguishing African accents in English.

Let us take as an example of the linguistic complications of Africa the West African country of Nigeria, where the Chadic language Hausa, a member of the Afroasiatic (also called the Hamito-Semitic) language family, is spoken by about 25 million people. Hausas are largely Moslem, and Hausa used to be written in the Arabic alphabet. Ibo and Yoruba, the two other major Nigerian languages, are both Kwa languages, members of the Western Sudanic subgroup of the Niger-Congo branch of African languages. There is ethnic friction among all three language groups. Phonetically, however, there is not so much of a problem in doing Nigerian accents in English, because the vowel systems of these languages are quite similar. What need concern us here is that the vowel system consists of: A, e, i, o and oo, with closed and open versions of each. There are no schwas and no "u" as in *but*, no "o" as in *work*, and in Yoruba there are no diphthongs. Since there is no "oo," all words with this vowel are pronounced with "oo." Vowels at the end of a word ending in "n" are nasalized for Yoruba and Ibo. (See "Practice" at the end of this chapter.)

In Ghana and Togoland Ewe (ay' way') is spoken, and in Senegal, Wolof is perhaps the most important language spoken. These are both Niger-Congo languages; Wolof is one of the West Atlantic branch, and Ewe is one of the Kwa branch. Most of the Niger-Congo languages are tonal, and the number of tones varies from two to seven or even more.

In East Africa, the principal language of Ethiopia is Amharic, and it is a Semitic language, like the Ethiopic which it replaced in the 17th century, related to Hebrew and Arabic, and, more distantly, to the Hausa language of Nigeria. In Uganda the Bantu language Swahili is the official language, as it is of Rwanda and Zaire. Swahili, also used as a lingua franca in Tanzania and Kenya, is the most widely understood and spoken East African language, and is related to the South African languages Zulu and Xhosa and to many others. Approximately a third of the population of the continent speaks a Bantu language. The standard language is called Common Bantu, and serves with Swahili as a lingua franca in Africa. Lingala, one of the other official languages of Zaire and of the Congo, is a Bantu language in former French-speaking colonial possessions of France and Belgium. The accents in English tend to be French sounding on the non-rhotic Haitian Creole model, as the ancestors of Haitians came from Africa.

There are certain phonetic traits which East and West African accents in English have in common, due to the heavy influence of British English. All the present-day African countries in which English is one of the official languages were once colonies of Great Britain, except for Liberia, founded by the American Colonization Society in 1822 as a homeland for freed slaves from the United States. Although English is not the first spoken language of most Africans its use is widespread as a lingua franca, and it is very familiar to many Africans.

The vowel system of **Lingala**, to take one example of a Bantu language, consists of seven vowels: A, lengthened e:, e, i:, o, o: (close to aw), and oo. The same two semi-vowels, "w" and "y," exist, as in English, and there are no true diphthongs, but rather an even stress on two vowels which come together. There is no schwa. There is no "sh" or "zh," no "ch" or "dg." There is also no "r." This sound can, however, be learned, or replaced by a light "d" or sometimes in initial position by a French liquid "l." There are nasalized consonants with "m" or "n" in combination with all other consonants except "l." There is no "schwa (e)" or "h" and no diphthongs, and these are all determining factors in an accent in English. The consonant "h" is usually dropped, which is typical of **French** accents in general, and vowels are given a full value. In Lingala declarative sentences fall in tone at the end, and questions rise in tone, as in English. Lingala, unlike most African languages, is intonational, not tonal. The absence of the schwa is a typical phenomenon of **West African** accents, as you will see by consulting the information below. See "Practice" at the end of the chapter for some Lingala words and phrases.

Swahili has very similar phonetic characteristics. It is an intonational language. It has no true diphthongs; instead vowels next to each other are evenly stressed. The vowel system is virtually the same as in Lingala, and there is no schwa. There are nasal vowels preceded by "m" and "n." Also, there are some uvular consonants like Scottish "KH," unlike Lingala. All other consonants are much as they are in English, but there is no "zh." As in Lingala there is no "r," and this is often replaced with "l" in the interior. On the coast, where there has been more contact with the outside world, "r" is often learned and heard, but sometimes, as in a heavy Japanese accent, substitutes for "l." The consonants "z" and "s" often substitute for "TH" and "th," although these consonants exist, but are pronounced slightly differently, with the point of articulation slightly behind that of their English counterparts and closer to the place of articulation of "z" and "s."

From the foregoing information about the phonetic systems of Swahili and Lingala and the Nigerian accents you can see why African accents as described below are what they are, and the summary of phonetic information should be useful. There are so many languages in Africa that this book, being a survey, cannot possibly cover them all, but the information included here should give you what you need. See the next chapter for South African accents.

A Quick Reference

1) Most of the consonants of English are to be found in African languages, but they are very slightly harder in accents in English than in General American. Use hard "b," a very plosive "p," "d," a very plosive "t," etc.

2) Use a lightly trilled "r" for most African accents, and drop it before another consonant and at the end of a word, keeping the accents non-rhotic. For some **Bantu** accents (**Lingala, Swahili**) substitute a liquid "l" when "r" is not learned. Substitute "r" for "l" in coastal Swahili accents.

3) In some accents "TH" and "th" are correctly pronounced. For most accents substitute "d" and "t" for "TH" and "th."

4) Substitute "e: " for "o." (**Yoruba, Ibo, Hausa,** etc.)

5) Use the British RP "o" in such words as *hot*, instead of the vowel heard in General American.

6) Substitute "u" or "A" or "a" for the "schwa (e)." In the **Hausa** language "i" and the "schwa (e)" are often interchanged, and this carries over into a Hausa accent in English.

7) Substitute "A" for "a" in **West Africa** but not in **East Africa**.

8) Use the British model of pronouncing "A" in such words as *ask, bath,* and *can't,* but less open, for **East Africa**; use the American model for **West Africa**, but slightly more open. The word "heart" is pronounced "hAt" in East African accents, and "hat" in West African accents.

9) Nasalize vowels before "m" and "n." For accents of former **French** African colonies also do some of the rhythmic stressing described in Chapter Eight on French accents.

10) Substitute the intermediate lengthened "i:" for both "i" and "ee."

11) Shift the following diphthongs to pure vowels: "ay" to "e:"; "O" to "aw."

How to Do African Accents

1) Position of the Vocal Apparatus
The position of the mouth is much as it is in General American, half open, half closed, but with the lips slightly forward. English is a second language for millions of Africans, who are also familiar with it as a lingua franca in government and the media, but since many people speak it as a first language the West and East African accents can really be considered native to the English language by this time.

2) The Most Important Sounds
Consonants
The accents are usually non-rhotic, following the British RP model. There is a tendency to pronounce all syllables in a word, as it is written, "-ed" verb endings, for example. The final consonant in a consonant cluster is sometimes

dropped. In a **Hausa** accent there is a tendency to insert a shwa between consonants of an initial consonant cluster. In many accents final voiced "b" and "v" shift to voiceless "p" and "f."

r: The "r" is trilled in initial position, although a retroflex "R" is also often correctly learned. See "A Quick Reference" for more information about this consonant.

t: This consonant is dentalized sometimes, and sounds like "ts."

TH and th: 1) **East African** accents: In **Swahili** these consonants exist, and should therefore be correctly pronounced in a **Ugandan** accent, and in other East African accents. In **Amharic**, which is also East African, an initial consonant cluster consisting of "t" followed by "th" exists, and in an **Ethiopian** accent this is sometimes substituted for both "TH" and "th," although the correct sounds are easily learned by Amharic speakers and often correctly pronounced. 2) In **West African** accents, such as those of **Nigeria**, the consonant "d" substitutes for voiced "TH" and "t" for voiceless "th." This information applies to **Ibo** and **Yoruba** speakers; speakers of **Hausa** tend to pronounce "TH" and "th" as "z" and "s."

zh: In **Swahili** this consonant does not exist. Substitute its voiceless counterpart "sh." The same thing is true for the **Ibo** and **Yoruba** speakers of **Nigeria**, but not for **Hausa** speakers, who use the voiced sound preceded by "d": dzh.

Vowels and Diphthongs
The vowel systems of African languages can be quite complicated. Those of the Bantu languages are simpler, and all quite similar, which helps the mutual intelligibility of many of the group. They generally follow the system: A, e, i, o, <u>oo</u> (u). There is also an "a" and an intermediate "i:," but not "ee." For purposes of learning English the British RP vowel system is the preferred one.

a: In **East African** accents this vowel often shifts to "A," so *that, am,* and *cat* are pronounced "THAt," "Am," and "kAt." In **West African** accents it remains as "a."

A: This vowel is less broad and open-throated than its British RP counterpart, but in the following partial list it is pronounced:
1) in **East African** accents like the "A" in *father;*
2) in **West African** accents like the "a" in *that.*
advantage, after, words beginning and ending with *after: afternoon, afterwards, hereafter,* etc., *answer, ask, aunt, banana, basket, bastard, bath, blast, branch, brass, broadcast, calf, can't, cask, casket, cast, caste, castle, chance, chancellor, chant, clasp, class,* words beginning with *class: classmate, classroom, classy,* etc., *command, countermand, daft, dance, demand, disaster, downcast, draft, enchant, entrance* (verb), *example, fast, fasten, gala, ghastly, glass, graft, grant,* words ending

in *graph*: *telegraph*, etc., *grasp*, *grass*, *half*, *lance*, *last*, *lather*, *laugh*, *lithograph*, *mask*, *mast*, *master*, *nasty*, *outcast*, *paragraph* ("a" in first syllable, "A" in last syllable: pa' Re gRAf), *pass*, *past*, *pastor*, *pastoral*, *path*, *perchance*, *phonograph*, *photograph*, *plant*, *plaster*, *prance*, *raft*, *rascal*, *rasp*, *raspberry*, *rather*, *reprimand*, *salve*, *sample*, *shaft*, *shan't*, *slander*, *slant*, *staff*, *stanch*, *surpass*, *task*, *tomato* (Note: the "a" in *potato* is as it is in American), *trance*, *transport* and other words beginning with the prefix "trans," *vast*, *waft*, *wrath*

e: Instead of a schwa, especially in unstressed syllables before "R," a "u" as in *but* or, alternatively, an "A" as in *father* is heard, or one hears an "a" as in *cat*. In stressed syllables with the vowel "o," such as in the word *services*, the same thing applies, so *services* is pronounced "su' vee sees" or "sA' vee sees" or "sa' vee sees." The "-es" and "-ed" word endings are pronounced with the "ee" in *meet* or, alternatively, like the "e" in *met*.

i: The short "i" in *bit* is usually either like the intermediate lengthened vowel "i:," or sometimes as long as the "ee" in *meet*. You can use a lengthened "i:" for both "i" and "ee."

o: Following the model of British RP, in which this vowel is pronounced like a short "aw," the "o" in *not*, etc., is pronounced like "aw," but considerably lengthened.

o: Instead of the usual sound in General American or British RP, the lengthened vowel "e:" is heard, especially before "r," so *learned* and *first* are pronounced "le:nd" and "fe:s." See "*e*" just above; these sounds are very close.

oo and <u>oo</u>: The long vowel "<u>oo</u>" often shifts in African accents to the shorter "oo," so *fool*, *pool*, and *mule* are pronounced "fool," "pool," and "myool."

u: This vowel sometimes shifts to "aw," so *but* is pronounced "bawt," and rhymes with *bought*.

Stress

There are two general rules to remember for these accents: 1) For **West African** accents, in words of three syllables, stress the antepenultimate syllable, and in longer words stress the syllable farthest from the end: In the word *relation*, for example, stress the first syllable; in the word *community* stress the first syllable. 2) For **East African** accents, in words of three syllables, stress the penultimate syllable: In the word *continual*, for example, stress the syllable "-u-." These are not hard and fast rules, however, and, generally you should stress most words correctly. See the "Practice" section, below.

Pitch

Many of the African languages are tonal languages. This results in a kind of disorientation when trying to learn the pitch patterns of English. The confusion is compensated for by high and low pitches, but no rising pitch at the end of questions, for instance. By and large there is not much to concern yourself with here, but bear in mind that tones can go higher or lower than in standard spoken varieties of English.

Practice

Lingala Words and Phrases

nalingi yo (I love you; nA li ngee yo'); *talatala ya ngai* (the mirror is mine; tA lA tA' lA yA ngA' ee); *natondi yo* (thank you; nA to' ndee yo'); *pilipili* (pepper; pi: li: pi: li:); *facture, soki olingi* (the check, please; fAk ti: re so' ki:' o li: ngee)
Note that *facture* is directly from French, meaning "bill." Note also the nasalized consonants and the absence of diphthongs.

English Sentences

This thing clearly resulted in a breakdown in services.
Phonetic pronunciations:
General East African, Ethiopian: dees teeng klee' u lee ree zAl' teed <u>or</u> re zAl' ted een u brayk' down een su' vee sees
Swahili Coastal (Zaire): di:s ti:ng kree' a ree li: zAr' ti:d i:n a ble:k' dAn i:n se:' vi: si:z
Ugandan Interior: di:s tsi:ng klee' a lee lee zAl' tseed i:n a ble:k' dAn i:n se:' vi: si:z

English Sentences

I am encouraged. It is special from God.
Phonetic pronunciation, **Former French Colonies, Nigeria**: I Am en kaw' rA jed'. i:ts iz spe' shal fron gaw:d'
Note the dentalized "t" and the nasalized vowel in *from*.

The first thing I learned at work was how to use the computer.
Phonetic pronunciations:
East African: THi: fe:s thi:ng I le:' ned, or le:nd, at we:k wawz how t<u>oo</u> y<u>oo</u>z THi: kawm py<u>oo</u>' te:
West African: de fe:s ti:ng I le:' ned At we:k wawz how t<u>oo</u> y<u>oo</u>z de kawm py<u>oo</u>' te:
Note the absence of the schwa and the substitution of "e:" for "o." Final "n" could also be nasalized for **Nigerian** and **French African** accents.

My aunt came to see us this afternoon. She had a swim in the pool and afterwards she went home again. She likes to listen to the birds singing, too.
Phonetic pronunciations:
East Africa: mI Ant ke:m too see As di:s Af te:' noon   shee hAd ay swi:m i:n dee pool and Af te:' we:dz shee went hawm i: gen'   shee lIKs t<u>oo</u> lis' en t<u>oo</u> dee be:dz sing' gin t<u>oo</u>
West Africa: mI ant ke:m too see us di:s af' te: noon   shee had ay swi:m i:n di pool and af' te: we:dz shee went hawm e: gen'   shee Liks te Lis' en te de be:dz sing' in t<u>oo</u>

Every person can cross the border into a community.
Phonetic pronunciations:
East Africa: ev' ree pe:' sen kan krAs dee bA' du i:n' too ay kawm yoo' ni: tee
West Africa: ev' ree pe:' sun kan kraws dee baw' du i:n too ay kum' yoo ni: tee

Thank you for being a part of this.
Phonetic pronunciation (**East Africa**): tank yoo fA bee' i:ng e pA duv di:s
Note: For **West Africa** say "faw" *for* the word for and "pat" for *part.*

We cannot do that.
Phonetic pronunciation (**East Africa**): wee ka' nod doo dat

The fact that you are discounting this theory is interesting. I would like to know what you think. How does it apply? Or rather not apply.
Phonetic pronunciation (**East Africa**): de fakt dat yoo A di:s kAn' ting di:s tee' O ree i:z i:n ter est' ing   I wood lIk too nO wAt yoo tink   how dooz i:t a plI' A rA' de nAt a' plI'

These are orders from the government.
Phonetic pronunciations:
West Africa/Nigeria: deez A aw' dez frAm dee gav' ment
East Africa: dees A aw' des frAm di goov' A ment

This is how they create, but we waste some of those things, and then the community doesn't benefit.
Phonetic pronunciation (**West Africa**): di:s i:z how day kree ayt' bAt wee we:st sum uv daw:z ti:ngs an den dee kum' yoo ni: tee dawz' ent ben' ee fi:t

That school of thinking lets you protect yourself.
Phonetic pronunciation (**West Africa**): dat skool uv ti:nk' ing lets yoo prO tekt' yaw self'
Note: For **East Africa** say "yA self' " for the word *yourself.*

So I go through the tunnel to find the train.
Phonetic pronunciation (**West Africa**): saw I gaw troo dee tu' nel too fIn dee trayn

The describe it as a landmark.
Phonetic pronunciation (**West Africa**): day dee skrIb' i:t az ay land' mAk

In the third floor reading room people want quiet, so don't talk too much.
Phonetic pronunciation (**West Africa/Nigeria**): in dee te:d flaw reed' i:ng room pee' pel wawnt kwI' et saw dawn tawk too mAch
Note: Remember that one of the keys to this accent is the shift of the vowel "o" to "e:" as in the word *third.*

360

Chapter Twenty-Seven

South African Accents:
British, Dutch (Boer), and Zulu

In 1488 the Portuguese explorer Bartolomeu Diaz was the first European to see South Africa, but it was not until 1652 that the Dutch East India Company established the settlement later known as Cape Town. Its natural harbor made it an international, cosmopolitan center for European traders, who stopped to resupply their ships on voyages round the Cape of Good Hope. Captain Cook stayed there on his exploratory voyages, and enjoyed the hospitality of the Dutch administrators and the British Consul. When gold was discovered in the Transvaal, the Orange Free State was established by Boers in the 1830s. In 1841 the British decided it was time for them to take over the Dutch colony, and they fought bloody wars to quell the Zulus and the Dutch. The Boer War of 1899 to 1902 resulted in British victory, and the establishment of the Union of South Africa. The system of apartheid ("separateness" in Afrikaans) grew gradually, resulting in increasingly restrictive, Nazi-like racial laws directed against the black population, and this horrible system of oppression, dire poverty and misery was only abolished in 1990, after decades of UN sanctions and embargos.

There are three major distinct groups of accents in South African English:
1) the Boer accent, from Afrikaans, a language intimately related to Dutch. *Boer* means "farmer" in Dutch, and they were the first Europeans to invade and settle what later became South Africa;
2) the native English speaker's accent, which slightly resembles that of Australia and New Zealand in its vowels and diphthongs, but has certain striking differences in the consonants and is generally lighter and softer than either; and
3) the Black accents derived, among others, from the languages of the Zulu and Xhosa nations, and from the Sotho and other languages of nations native to the area, the original sole occupants of South Africa before the European takeover. Many of these languages, whether Bantu or Sotho, are mutually comprehensible, and therefore similar phonetically.
All three accents have much in common, as they are all based on the native English speaker's accent.

For good examples of South African accents see videos of Athol Fugard's plays, for example *Master Harold and the Boys*, with the South African actor Zakes Mokae, who has an authentic Black accent. There are also many newsreels of Nelson Mandela and Bishop Tutu, as well as of de Klerk, with his Boer accent, and English members of the South African legislature.

Zulu is a fascinating language, known among other things for its "clicks," which do not, of course, concern us much here, since they don't exist in English and do not affect the accent in English. (For more information on clicks see Arnett Wilkes and Nicholias Nkosi's *Teach Yourself Zulu*, Teach Yourself Books, London, Chicago, 1995.) Among the interesting features of Zulu is the existence, in the absence of masculine and feminine genders, of 18 classes of nouns, singular or plural, and two neutral (neither singular nor plural) classes. Adjectives agree with the class and number of the nouns they modify. Personal pronouns form constituent parts of words. There is a great variety of greetings and forms of address. Zulu, a Bantu language of the Nguni branch, has about eight million speakers. It is closely related to Xhosa, which is also spoken by about eight million people. There are in South Africa approximately 20 million speakers altogether of the various Nguni languages, and several million speakers of the Sotho languages. The Bantu languages fall into 31 groups, but they are all pretty closely related and sometimes mutually intelligible—closer, according to linguists, than Spanish and French are, for example.

A Quick Reference

1) The specific differences among the three major accents are compared for each sound under "The Most Important Sounds."
2) For English and Zulu accents do not pronounce "R" before another consonant or at the end of a word. For Boer accents do a lightly trilled "r" in all positions.
3) Vowels and diphthongs are generally short. Consonants are generally "soft."
4) Substitute a short "I" for "ay."
5) In a Boer accent substitute "u" or a "schwa (*e*)" for "i."
6) In English and Zulu accents substitute "a" for "ow." In a Boer accent substitute "A" for "ow."
7) Substitute "aw" for "A," especially in a Boer accent, but see below under "A" for complications.
8) *Been* rhymes with *bean*.

How to Do South African Accents

1) Three Positions of the Vocal Apparatus
A) **Boer**
The mouth is slightly closed, the lips tightly held and slightly protruded. The corners of the mouth are slightly contracted.
B) **English**
The mouth is slightly closed and drawn back a bit, as in a smile.
C) **Black (Zulu)**
The mouth is more relaxed and slightly more open than in either Boer or English accents.

362

2) The Most Important Sounds
Consonants
As with other African accents the sound system of British RP is the preferred model for English. The **English** and **Zulu** accents are strongly **non-rhotic**, but the **Boer** accent is usually **rhotic**. Certain voiceless initial consonants often shift to voiced in a Boer accent, or, more accurately, to a very soft, slightly voiced version of the consonant, so "p" becomes "b"; "t" becomes "d"; and "k" becomes "g." Consonants are, in fact, generally softer in all three accents than in either General American or British RP.

Practice

The king put a cup of tea on the table.
Phonetic pronunciations:
Boer: THe ging boo da gA pe dee awn THe dI' bL
Zulu, English: THe king poo de kA pe tee awn THe tI' bL

r and R: In **Boer** and **Zulu** accents the "r" is usually trilled, in the case of Zulu in initial position only. In the Boer accent the "r" is often strongly aspirated and shifts to "hr." In the South African **English** accent the standard retroflex "R" (with the bottom of the tongue turned upwards toward the roof of the mouth) is retained in all initial positions, but not, of course, in final position or before another consonant, since, as stated above, the accent is non-rhotic. Occasionally a trilled "r" with one flap may be heard between two vowels: *very* is said as either "ve' ree" or "ve' Ree." There is little tendency to an intrusive "R," as there is, for example, in British RP, so one is more likely to hear *drawing* rather than "drawRing." A linking "R" is sometimes heard: *there is* is pronounced either "THe Riz" or "THe: iz."

Vowels and Diphthongs
Vowels and diphthongs tend generally to be short and closed. Short vowels are usually given a full value in unstressed syllables. The schwa is largely absent, except where it naturally occurs in words like *the* before a consonant.

Practice

I am very concerned about that situation.
Phonetic pronunciations:
Boer: oy am ve' ree gAn so: nd A bowt THat si ty<u>oo</u> ay, or I, shun
English: oy am ve'ree kAn sond A bowt THet si ty<u>oo</u> ay, or I, shun
Zulu: I am ve' ree kAn send e bowd THet si ch<u>oo</u> ay shun

A: This vowel usually shifts to "aw" in a **Boer** accent, and sometimes in an **English** accent, where it can also be heard as a long "a" as in American *cat*. "A" is less broad and open-throated than its British RP counterpart, but in the following partial list of **Practice Words** it is pronounced like the "a" in American *father*:

advantage, *after*, words beginning and ending with *after*: *afternoon*, *afterwards*, *hereafter*, etc., *answer*, *ask*, *aunt*, *banana*, *basket*, *bastard*, *bath*, *blast*, *branch*, *brass*, *broadcast*, *calf*, *can't*, *cask*, *casket*, *cast*, *caste*, *castle*, *chance*, *chancellor*, *chant*, *clasp*, *class*, words beginning with *class*: *classmate*, *classroom*, *classy*, etc., *command*, *countermand*, *daft*, *dance*, *demand*, *disaster*, *downcast*, *draft*, *enchant*, *entrance* (verb), *example*, *fast*, *fasten*, *gala*, *ghastly*, *glass*, *graft*, *grant*, words ending in *graph*: *telegraph*, etc. (But note that *graphic* and words ending in "graphic" are pronounced with the "a" in *cat*), *grasp*, *grass*, *half*, *lance*, *last*, *lather*, *laugh*, *lithograph*, *mask*, *mast*, *master*, *nasty*, *outcast*, *paragraph* ("a" in first syllable, "A" in last syllable: pa' Re gRAf), *pass*, *past*, *pastor*, *pastoral*, *path*, *perchance*, *phonograph*, *photograph*, *plant*, *plaster*, *prance*, *raft*, *rascal*, *rasp*, *raspberry*, *rather*, *reprimand*, *salve*, *sample*, *shaft*, *shan't*, *slander*, *slant*, *staff*, *stanch*, *surpass*, *task*, *tomato* (Note: the "a" in *potato* is as it is in American), *trance*, *transport* and other words beginning with the prefix "trans," *vast*, *waft*, *wrath*

a: This vowel often shifts either to a longer version of itself (**English**) or to "e" (**Boer**; some **English**; **Zulu**).
Practice Words: *cat, mat, that, hat, sat, bat, rat*

ay: This diphthong, similarly to Australian and Cockney accents, shifts to "I," in **Boer** and **English** accents, but is much shorter than it is in Cockney. It usually remains "ay" in a **Zulu** accent.
Practice Words: *paper, maybe, say, day, lay, play, berate, engage*

e: This vowel often shifts to "i" or a lengthened "i:" or sometimes to "ee" in **English** and **Boer** accents, but remains as "e" in **Zulu** accents.
Practice Words: *met, let, debt, get, fret, set, pet, tremble, assembly, merit*

i: This vowel often shifts in a **Boer** accent to either a schwa ("e") or a "u" (as in the word *but*) giving it a distinct resemblance to a New Zealand accent. Even when it remains "i" it is a very short vowel. In **English** and **Zulu** accents it remains "i."
Practice Words: *dinner, six, pick, stick, it, is, miss, kiss, bliss*

o: The British pronunciation of this vowel, a short "aw," in such words as *hot*, *not*, and *got* is also the South African preferred pronunciation for all accents.

O: A short version of the British pronunciation of this vowel is the usual one for all accents: *home* is pronounced "he_oo_m."
Practice Words: *home, alone, bone, roam, known, drone, throne, dome*

oo: This vowel shifts sometimes to "i," so *whom* is pronounced "him" (**Boer**; **English**); and sometimes to "O" (see above; **English**). In a **Zulu** accent it remains as "_oo_."
Practice Words: *whom, boom, loom, broom, doom, moon, June, spoon*

364

ow: This diphthong is often shifted to a pure vowel, "a" in the **English** and **Zulu** accents and "A" in the **Boer** accent, and sometimes broadened and turned into a triphthong, "aow," similar to the Cockney sound, but tighter and more closed. **Practice**: "South African" is pronounced: (**English**) saowth or sath a' fRi: ken; (**Zulu**) sath e' free kAn; (**Boer**) sATH e' fri: kun.

y: All the South African accents customarily insert this semi-vowel after a consonant and before "<u>oo</u>" in such words as *newspaper* and *duke*.

Stress

There are no particular stress patterns which need concern the actor doing Boer or English accents. The short vowels and diphthongs give these accents a characteristic "clipped" feeling. In Zulu, itself, the penultimate (next to last) syllable of a word is lengthened, that is, the vowel is slightly drawn out. This can carry over into English, where a corresponding syllable will be lengthened slightly, giving a long/short rhythm to the accent.

Practice

Let's practice the material.
Phonetic pronunciation (**Zulu**): lets pre:k', or prA:k', tees THe mA tee:' ryAl

Ever since Captain Cook landed in Table Bay there have been a great many tales of English merchantmen circulating in Capetown.
Phonetic pronunciations:
Boer: i' ver si:ns kep' tn k<u>oo</u>k len' dud un dI' bL bI THay ruv been e grIt mi' nee dIlz v ing' leesh mo' chnt mn so' ky<u>oo</u> LI' deng en kIp' down

English: ee' vA si:ns kep' tn kook len' ded en tI' bl bI THee Rev been e gRIt mi' nee tILz ev ing' leesh mo' chent men so' ky<u>oo</u> LI ting in kIp taown

Zulu: e' vA seens kep' tn kook len' ded i:n tay' bL bay THe rev been A grayt mi' nee taylz Av ing' leesh mo chent men so' ky<u>oo</u> lay teng in kayp town

Note that the Zulu pronunciation could possibly also be used for a Boer accent, and that the English pronunciation could be used for a Zulu accent, depending on the social class of the speaker (de pind' eng awn THe se<u>oo</u>' shL kLAs ev THe sbee' kA (or) spee' ke). Remember that the "b" really stands for a very soft "p."

There were silver and diamonds to be found there in great abundance amidst the great silence of the minefields, bathed in sunlight. It is more beautiful than there is power in me to tell of it.
Phonetic pronunciation (**Boer**): THe: wer sel ver en doy' menz t<u>oo</u> bee fownd THe: i:n grIt e bAn' dints a mi:dst' THe grIt soy' lints ev THe moyn fee' eldz bIeeTHd i:n sAn loyt i:t i:s mawr bee<u>oo</u>' ti: fool THan THe ri:s' par i:n mee t<u>oo</u>

tel *ev* i:t

I ate far too much for my own good.
Phonetic pronunciation (**Boer**): oy hIt faw ty<u>oo</u> mAch f*e* moy hown good
Notice the intrusive "h" in the words *ate* and *own,* an occasional phenomenon
in the **Boer** accent.

Eventually everything turned out great and I had a wonderful time.
Phonetic pronunciation (**English**): i vin' ch<u>oo</u> *e* Lee i' vRee thing to:nd owt
gRayt and oy hed *e* wAn' d*e* fooL toym

I have to travel extensively for my work, you see.
Phonetic pronunciation (**English**): I hev t*e* tRe' veL ik stin' siv Lee f*e* mI wok
y<u>oo</u> see

In the homelands and the villages people are happy to be free at last of the hated
system of apartheid.
Phonetic pronunciation (**Zulu**): i:n THe hawm Landz And THe vi:' LA dgez pi:'
peL A he' pee t<u>oo</u> bee free at Last uv THe he:' ted sis' tem uv A pA' tayt

It was a long time coming, and there is a long road still to travel, but we are in
sight.
Phonetic pronunciation (**Zulu**): i:t wuz a lawng tIm kum' i:ng An THe:R i:z *e*
Long Rawd sti:L t<u>oo</u> tRA' vel bAt wee A i:n sIt

Part Nine

Asian Accents

Introduction

Of the great number of Asian languages, three important, widely spoken languages are "isolates," with no known related languages: Japanese, Vietnamese and Korean. Japanese and Korean are both "intonational" languages, but Vietnamese, like the vast majority of Asian languages, is "tonal." The Chinese languages of the Sino-Tibetan group (also known as Tibeto-Burman), which includes Tibetan, Burmese, Laotian and Thai, are "tonal." Indonesian, on the other hand, is "intonational."

Many members of the Tibeto-Burman family remain to be studied. Some of these languages are being studied for the first time. In 1996, for example, the first *Hani-English/English-Hani Dictionary* (by Paul W. Lewis and Bai Bibo (Piu Bo), Kegan Paul International) was published. Hani is spoken by approximately 1.3 million people in Yunnan province on the Burma-Laos-Vietnam border with China.

Hindi, Bengali, and Gujurati are among the languages of India, discussed in Chapter Five, which are Indo-European intonational languages, descended from Sanskrit and distantly related to English. There are also, in Pakistan and India, the Dravidian languages, of which the most widely spoken in the South are Telugu and Tamil, while in the North we have Gondi and Oraon, spoken in southern Pakistan.

Another, smaller language group is the Munda, of which Santali, spoken by some six million people in the interior of the subcontinent, is the most important. The Dravidian and Munda languages apparently evolved in India itself, centuries before the Indo-European conquest, although the Munda languages may be related to the Khmer languages of Cambodia and other Southeast Asian countries. Where the Indo-Europeans originated is not known, but probably they came from the west and in their wars of conquest forced the speakers of Dravidian southwards, where, in fact, most speakers of Dravidian languages live to this day. The speakers of Munda languages, who live mostly in mountainous regions, were probably driven up into the hills, where they survived and preserved their cultures. The Indo-Europeans may have come from Mesopotamia and spread out both to the east and to the west, or gone from the valley of the Tigris and Euphrates first to the East, and then back from India to the west again—vast migrating, conquering armies of them, taking over all of Europe.

Chapter Twenty-Eight
Chinese Accents: Mandarin, Cantonese

China, the third largest country in the world, can be justly proud of a rich culture thousands of years old. This vast land was once ruled from the gorgeous palaces of Beijing's Forbidden City by Manchu emperors, who lived in isolated splendor and superb luxury, rigidly bound by court etiquette. The last of them, Henry Pu Yi, eventually became a gardener in Beijing, and died there in 1967. His fascinating story is told in Bernardo Bertolucci's film, *The Last Emperor* (1987), which you should see for excellent examples of Chinese accents.

More than a billion people speak a Sino-Tibetan language. There are so many spoken languages in China that not all of them have even been studied, and nobody seems to know how many there are. Some remote villages in the interior of the country, only 20 miles distant from each other over rugged mountain terrain, apparently have their own mutually unintelligible languages, and on the south coast of China dialects are separated sometimes by only a few miles.

A characteristic common to all the Chinese languages is that they are "tonal," that is, the lexical or dictionary meaning of a word changes depending on the "tone," or musical note, on which it is pronounced. This is quite different from European languages, in which this phenomenon seldom occurs. For an example of tonal qualities in an Indo-European language, see the chapter on Swedish. All languages have tone, or pitch, which occurs in certain patterns; in other words, all languages, whether tonal or intonational, have "intonation," through which the emotional as well as actual meaning of what is being said is conveyed. For information on the tones in Chinese, see the section in this chapter on "Pitch."

The **Mandarin** of Beijing, a Han Chinese language, is the Standard Chinese of today, the language of administration and education. It is also one of the official languages of the United Nations. **Cantonese**, or Yue, is, however, also spoken by millions of people.

The Chinese alphabet is ideographic: The characters represent images, objects or ideas, as opposed to the letters which represent sounds in western alphabets, such as the Roman, Greek, or Hebrew. The Chinese alphabet, which is a unifying factor in creating Chinese literary and philosophical culture, evolved over many centuries. Although based on Mandarin, it can be read in any of the Chinese languages by anyone who knows the characters, except where these have been modified locally with words from different dialects added. The words may be different, but the pictures remain the same. The closest example in the west is, perhaps, the symbols which stand for numbers: "1" is read by an English speaker as *one*, by a French speaker as *un*, by an Italian or Spanish speaker as *uno*, and by a German as *eins*, etc.

It is difficult, certainly, to talk of a single Chinese accent, because the many people of different dialect backgrounds will have different accents in English. The information which follows, however, should be useful in helping the actor to create a recognizable Chinese accent.

A Quick Reference

1) Keep the rhythm and stress fairly even. Pitch, on the other hand can vary considerably, and there is occasionally a kind of singing quality to the accent. Normally unstressed words (prepositions, some verbs, etc.) are sometimes stressed.

2) Drop final "R" and "R" before another consonant, especially in a **Cantonese** accent. Final "R" may be pronounced lightly in a **Mandarin** accent. The consonants "R," "sh" and "ch" are all retroflex, with the bottom of the tongue curved up towards the roof of the mouth.

3) Drop most final consonants both singly and in clusters, except for "n," "ng," and "s" in a **Mandarin** accent. Add to these final consonants "k," "m," "p," and "t" for a **Cantonese** accent.

4) In a heavy **Cantonese** accent substitute "L" for "R." Retain "R" in a **Mandarin** accent.

5) Substitute "d" and "t" for "TH" and "th."

6) In a **Mandarin** accent keep voiced consonants voiceless or only very lightly voiced in initial position, so "b," "d," "g," "v," "z" and "zh" shift to "p," "t," "k," "f," "s," and "sh." For a **Cantonese** accent retain the voiced consonants, except that "zh" and "sh" do not exist. Substitute a sibilant "s" for them.

7) You can often replace final consonants with a glottal stop, and use a glottal stop to replace "t" in the middle of a word like *bottle*, as in New York, Cockney or Glasgow accents.

8) You can often substitute "A" for the "schwa (*e*)" in unstressed syllables, and use only the briefest of schwas between consonants in an initial consonant cluster.

9) Shift diphthongs to pure vowels in a **Mandarin** accent, or pronounce them with an even stress on both halves. In a **Cantonese** accent pronounce diphthongs correctly, except for "O." See below for details.

10) Keep vowel sounds short.

Different Chinese Accents

1) For a **light** accent, pronounce "R" and "TH" and "th" correctly, but keep the even-toned stressing. Keep consonants either voiceless or aspirated or only lightly voiced.

2) For a **medium** accent, add more tones, as under "Pitch."

3) For a **heavy** accent, do everything suggested for either Mandarin or Cantonese. Very important is the information under Consonants and Pitch.

How to Do a Chinese Accent

1) Position of the Vocal Apparatus
The position of the tip of the tongue, to which it so often returns, is on the upper gum ridge just before the opening into the upper palate. English feels to the speaker of Chinese as if it is generally spoken with the tongue in that position, which is not actually true of accents native to English. This is due to the nature of articulation of Chinese consonants. The mouth is fairly open when speaking Chinese, but the lips are not protruded, except for the sound of "oo."

2) Stress
The stress pattern of Chinese accents is quite even in rhythm, and stress is heard more as a lengthened vowel, rather than a particular accentuation. The Chinese stress pattern is different from that of English. In Chinese, where stress depends as much on tone as on emphatic loudness, the way of stressing words in English must be learned as another concept, and often is, by Chinese speakers. There is nevertheless a kind of even stressing of all syllables, with only a slightly greater emphasis on stressed syllables.

3) The Most Important Sounds
Note that the sound system is quite similar in both Mandarin and Cantonese. The Mandarin word for *tea*, pronounced "tay" (approximately) accounts for the pronunciation in Ireland, which is the old English pronunciation, whereas in Cantonese the word is *chai*, pronounced "chI," and it is this pronunciation which gives the Russians their word for tea, *chai*, and the name of the country *China* to much of the world.

Consonants
There is an initial "R" and a final "R" in Mandarin Chinese, but no "R" in Cantonese. Chinese accents in English are most often non-rhotic.

Consonant clusters are lacking in all Chinese languages. There is a tendency to put schwas between consonants in a cluster in a Chinese accent in English. *Princeton University* is pronounced "pA Lin sA ten yoo ni ve si tee" (**Cantonese**) or "pA rin', or Rin', sA ton yoo ni: vA' si: tee" (**Mandarin**).

Final consonants are often dropped in a Chinese accent, or only very lightly pronounced, if at all, or replaced by a glottal stop. The only final consonants which occur in **Mandarin** are "n" and "ng." In **Cantonese**, which has nine tones, "k," "m," "p" and "t" are also found in final position, along with "n" and "ng." These are the only endings clearly pronounced in a **heavy** accent in English. Also, in final consonant clusters the tendency is to drop the final consonant, so

371

that, for example, the final "t" in *don't* is dropped, leaving the final "n," which is a comfortable ending for a Chinese speaker. The final "t" is also dropped, to take another example, in *last*, and the "s," which the speaker has learned how to pronounce fairly comfortably, is retained. **Initial consonants** often shift from voiced to voiceless; see "A Quick Reference."

R and L: The sound of the retroflex "R" exists in both an initial and a final position in **Mandarin,** as in the word, spoken on a slight rising tone, "shR," which means *yes* in Mandarin. In a **Cantonese** accent "L" is often substituted for "R" in a middle or initial position in an accent in English. "L" is often dropped in a final position, as in the word *milk*, where it is replaced by "<u>oo</u>." "R" does not exist in the Cantonese consonant system. I have heard people on the New York City subway platform say "Lush owA subway cLowded" (Rush hour subway crowded). Another example: Chinese people who have not learned to pronounce "R" correctly in English say "lada" (lay' dA'), which sounds like *later* with the final "R" dropped and a soft "d" instead of a "t," for *radar*. Final "L" is sometimes barely pronounced or else heard as "<u>oo</u>": milk (mi<u>oo</u>k); feel (fee<u>oo</u>).

TH and th: These consonants do not exist in Chinese, and the usual substitutions for them are "d" for the voiced "TH" and "t" for the voiceless "th."

Vowels and Diphthongs
Vowels in Chinese are fairly short, generally speaking, including such open vowels as "A." **Mandarin** has no true diphthongs, and all vowels are pronounced distinctly, even when next to each other. In a Mandarin accent the tendency is to substitute pure vowels for diphthongs, or to pronounce diphthongs with an even stress on both halves. Remember that both the vowels, or the vowel and the semivowel, in the diphthongs should be short in length. Vowels end almost every syllable, with the exceptions noted above under "Consonants." Diphthongs with the semi-vowels "w" and "y" should be pronounced with both halves stressed, so *yet* would be pronounced "ee'e?' " and *you* "ee'<u>oo</u>," and *what* would be pronounced "<u>oo</u>'a'?" (Note the glottal stop "?" in this last pronunciation.) **Cantonese,** on the other hand, does have diphthongs, and combines vowels with the semi-vowels "y" and "w." Diphthongs should be correctly pronounced and lengthened slightly. In a **Mandarin** accent "<u>oo</u>" is sometimes pronounced "ü," so *you* becomes "iü'."

A and *e*: The attempt to pronounce clearly and to eliminate schwas results in an open-throated shift from the schwa to "A": *exhibition* (ex' A bi' shAn). Note the even stressing. On the other hand, a vowel similar to the English schwa does exist in Chinese, and is often used in unstressed syllables, so the choice is the actor's.

ay: The diphthong "ay" shifts to a lengthened "e:" in a **Mandarin** accent, but may be correctly pronounced in a **Cantonese** accent.

O: This diphthong usually shifts to a pure vowel, either "aw" or a long "o."

oy and ow: These diphthongs exist in **Cantonese** and should be correctly pronounced in English.

Pitch

Standard Chinese (Mandarin) has four tones:
1) long high level pitch: —
2) high rising, from low to high: /
3) low falling-rising: V
4) starting high and falling abruptly: \
Cantonese has nine tones:
1) high level pitch: —
2) high rising, from low to high: /
3) long middle level, or neutral: —-
4) high falling-rising, from high to low to high: V
5) middle level falling, from middle level to low: -\
6) long low level: __
7) abrupt high: \
8) abrupt middle level: -
9) abrupt low level: _
You see how complicated this is for non-Chinese speakers to learn, particularly as tone makes a difference in the meaning of words. It can be done, however. In a Chinese accent in English there is sometimes a musicality, a rise and fall in pitches, to compensate for the lack of certain pitches in English.

Practice

There is sometimes, you know, a lot to do, and sometimes less. I think that's right.
Phonetic pronunciations:
Cantonese: de: i su tIm y<u>oo</u> naw a LA t<u>oo</u> d<u>oo</u> an sum tIm Les. I tink das LIt, or LI?
Notes: Keep the stress fairly even on all syllables. Note the glottal stop. This is a very heavy Cantonese accent.

Mandarin: deR i su tA'ee' ee'<u>oo</u>' naw a LA t<u>oo</u> d<u>oo</u> a su tA'ee' Les. A'ee' tin das RA'ee'
Note that for a Mandarin accent you should stress both halves of the diphthongs evenly, keeping the diphthongs and the vowels short.

Possible Pitch Pattern:

```
          some-                           do                 less.
     is                              to          some-
There            times    know   lot         and        times
                     you       a
```

It's very nice, very delicious dish.
Phonetic pronunciation (**Mandarin**): is ve' Ree nIs ve' Ree dee' Li' shus dish

Possible Pitch Pattern

<pre>
                    de-   dish.
          nice,   licious

It's very   very
</pre>

Note: Notice the double stress in the word *delicious*.

I went away to town.
Phonetic pronunciation *(Mandarin)*: I wen', or wen', a way t<u>oo</u>' town
Note: Look at the stress pattern, as indicated by the apostrophes.

Possible Pitch Pattern

<pre>
          way∨
     a-   to-\
   went   to
I   wn.
</pre>

Of all the many Chinese festivals, one of the most well known is the Chinese New Year, a wonderful occasion celebrated over many days in New York and all over the world wherever there is a Chinese community. We have special foods and also parades with dragons.
Phonetic pronunciation (**Mandarin**): uf aw de me nee chI nees fes' ti v<u>oo</u>s wun uf dee mOs we:<u>oo</u>, or weL, nOn i:s de chI nees ny<u>oo</u> yi:e ay wun' de foo O kay' shen se' Li bRay' di O' fe me' nee days in ny<u>oo</u> yawk an aw O' fe de weL we e ve de is ay chI' nees kum y<u>oo</u>' ni: tee wee haf, or ha, spe' sh<u>oo</u> foods an aw' sO pa Rayts wi dRa' gens

Through the centuries the brilliant schools of philosophy, such as Confucianism and Taoism, have provided inspiration to millions of people around the world.
Phonetic pronunciation (**Mandarin**): sR<u>oo</u> de sen ch<u>oo</u> Rees de bRi' yan sk<u>oo</u>s uv fi law *se* fee sush as kon fy<u>oo</u> shan i:s em an dow i:s em ha pRO vI' de di:n spi: Ray shun t<u>oo</u> mi yans uv pee p<u>oo</u> a Rown di weL

Any time you want to come over to my house we can have a good time and good food.
Phonetic pronunciation (**Cantonese**): e' nee tI y<u>oo</u> wAn ne kum O' fA te mI hows wee kan ha e goo tIm an goo f<u>oo</u>

Possible Pitch Pattern

```
                                          good ti-\
                          we can have a              good fo-\
                   house\                    me and
Anytime you want to come over to my                      od.
```

What do you want to watch television for anyway. The programs are terrible.
Phonetic pronunciation (**Cantonese**): wA yoo wA' ne wAch te' Le vi' shu faw e'
nee way   di: pLO gLans A teL' i: beL
Note: The "L" for "R" substitution is certainly heard often enough, but keep the
"L" fairly light; the attempt is to pronounce "R" correctly.

Chapter Twenty-Nine
Japanese Accents

Japanese is the native language of more than 125 million people in the home islands of Japan. Its use as a literary language goes back to before the eighth century C.E. From the 12th to the 16th centuries the language evolved into its present form. As the center of government power shifted between the cities of Kyoto and Kamakura, so did the standard language, spoken in Tokyo,which is essentially the modernized dialect of Kyoto.

Japanese is a language isolate, without a known relationship to any other languages. It is written in a modified, simplified Chinese alphabet. There are actually two versions of a standard language: masculine and feminine. The principal difference is in vocabulary and intonational patterns, which reflect the hierarchy prevalent throughout centuries of Japanese culture, when the sexes were often segregated. The modes of address in the Japanese language also reflect the system of class culture which still prevails to some extent, and is very similar to European class structure and older modes of address.

Japanese is written in its own alphabet, or, rather, alphabets, adapted from the Chinese alphabet. There are more than 40 thousand *Kanji* (Phonetic pronunciation: kAn' dgee'), or characters, which come directly from the Chinese alphabet. In addition there are the phonetic syllabary alphabets, *Hiragana* and *Katagana* (Phonetic pronunciations: hi: rA gA nA; kA tA gA nA), the 48 symbols of each of which represent Japanese syllables, consisting of a vowel, or of a vowel and a consonant. Hiragana is a more rounded script, while Katagana is square. There is also a system of Roman letters, called *Roomaji* (Phonetic pronunciation: ro o ma dgee), which is also phonetic, that is, the symbols represent sounds. It is necessary to know all four of these alphabets in order to be able to read Japanese.

The excellent Japanese actor Sessue Hayakawa in *Bridge on the River Kwai* (1957) and in other films is a fine source for an authentic Japanese accent. To hear the language itself watch the many great Japanese films, such as those of Kurosawa, who made *Seven Samurai* and *The Throne of Blood* in 1957 and *Ran*, based on Shakespeare's *King Lear* in 1987.

A Quick Reference

1) Keep the stress even on all syllables.
2) Substitute "r" for "L."

3) Insert a very brief schwa between consonants in a consonant cluster, and after a consonant at the end of a word when the next word begins with a consonant.
4) Keep the consonants light and aspirated.
5) Substitute pure vowels for diphthongs, or stress both halves of a diphthong evenly. See below.

How to Do a Japanese Accent

For a really **light** accent pronounce a correct English "L" and pronounce the other consonants lightly. Also very important is the information under "Stress."

1) Position of the Vocal Apparatus

For the general position keep the mouth open slightly wider than in General American. The lips are slightly rounded. The main point of resonance is just back of center, but the softly articulated frontal, sometimes almost palatalized, consonants make the tongue stay generally slightly up and forward. This upper position is constantly compensated for by the fact that Japanese vowels are pronounced with the tongue a bit lower in position than it is for English vowels.

2) Stress

In Standard Japanese stress is even on all syllables. Lengthened and shortened vowels appear to give one or another syllable greater stress because of the pitch on which the syllable is spoken. This phenomenon gives the characteristic even-toned quality of a Japanese accent in English. Incidentally, in some Japanese dialects there are stress patterns closer to those of English, in that certain syllables are emphatically stressed more than others, and this is also related to Pitch patterns (see below).

3) The Most Important Sounds

Consonants

The Standard Japanese dialect is non-rhotic, or the final "r" is very lightly pronounced; usually it is assimilated with or dropped altogether before a following consonant. The Japanese accent in English tends to be strongly non-rhotic, with all "r" sounds dropped at the end of a word or before another consonant.

For the most part consonants do not end a syllable, except for two consonants, "ng," sometimes heard in Japanese as "m" also, and a kind of doubling or prolongation of voiceless "k," "p," "s," "sh" and "t." These are often heard in a syllable in the middle, as opposed to the end, of a word, but the phenomenon does two things: 1) it gives the impression that the syllable in which it occurs is stressed (but see below under Stress); and 2) it means that these consonants can be correctly pronounced in word endings in English.

There are few real **consonant clusters** in Japanese, except those including a nasal consonant, "m" or "n"; the first consonant of what would be a cluster tends to disappear, as it is assimilated into the consonant which follows it. In a **heavy** Japanese accent, as a result, a schwa is sometimes inserted between consonants in an initial consonant cluster, so, for example, *break* is pronounced "be

377

re:k." In a final consonant cluster the last consonant is often dropped, so *last* is pronounced "las"; this is even easier to do if the consonant cluster is followed by another consonant, so that *last thing*, for example, might be pronounced "las ting" or "la' *se* ting," or, in a heavier accent "ra' *se* ti:ng." A schwa is also inserted for phonetic comfort between a consonant which ends a word and a consonant which begins the next word, forming a kind of consonant cluster once again.

Japanese consonants are pronounced more softly than their English counterparts, and they are sometimes almost palatalized; the blade of the tongue approaches the upper palate.

b: Since this consonant does not end syllables in Japanese, it can either be correctly learned, or else substituted for by an aspirated "p."

d: This consonant does not end a word in Japanese, but in an accent in English it can be correctly learned, or substituted for by an aspirated "d" or by the voiceless "t."

g: This consonant, except in the nasalized combination "ng," does not end a syllable in Japanese. The usual substitution for it is "k."

L: There is no "L" in Japanese, which does not mean Japanese people cannot learn it, and in fact many do. A lightly trilled "r" substitutes for "L."
Practice: *Please light the light.*
Phonetic pronunciation: pe reez' rl' te ze rlt

r: The Japanese "r" is lightly trilled, and this is the sound we hear in a Japanese acent in English.

TH and th: These sounds do not exist in Japanese. Either "d" or "z" for the voiced "TH," and either "s" or "t" for the voiceless "th" are the usual substitutes for them.

zh: This consonant, heard in *measure* does not exist in most Japanese dialects, although it does exist in some; not, however, in the Standard Japanese of Tokyo. Its voiceless counterpart is substituted for it, so *measure* is pronounced "me' shA" or "me' she." The combination "dg," on the other hand, does exist, but is not usually heard as a substitution for "zh." This does mean, however, that words like *just* and *edge* should be correctly pronounced in a Japanese accent.

Vowels and Diphthongs
The Japanese vowel system consists of the five classical vowels: a (A), e, i, o and u (oo), plus "o" and "ü." Japanese vowels are pronounced with the tongue slightly lower in the mouth than their English counterparts, and this phenomenon can carry over into a Japanese accent in English. The vowels each have two versions, long and short. Vowels can be replaced by a schwa in syllables with shorter vow-

els, giving the impression that syllables with long vowels are stressed, but see below, under "Stress."

Vowels in the Tokyo dialect are voiced, but in some other dialects, such as those of Okinawa, their pronunciation has an aspirated, almost whispered quality, making them devoiced. This can be a very useful character choice for a **heavy** Japanese accent.

Lengthened vowels are sometimes spoken with a glottal stop, and this makes a difference in the meaning of the word. This phenomenon, while interesting, is not terribly important for a Japanese accent in English, except that a glottal stop can be used when necessary, since it does exist in Japanese.

More important is that there are no real diphthongs in Japanese. Diphthongs in a Japanese accent in English will, therefore, sometimes be evenly stressed on both halves, or shifted to pure vowels.

ay: This diphthong tends to shift to a lengthened "e:."

I: This diphthong has both halves evenly stressed, with a slightly stronger stress on the first half, so "I" is pronounced "A'ee."

O: This diphthong tends to shift to a lengthened "aw" or else to be pronounced like "o" in British RP *not*.

w: The sound in Japanese which is closest to this semi-vowel does not exist in English. One might describe it as a sound intermediate between "w" and the consonant "v." To pronounce it the upper teeth must very lightly touch the upper inside of the lower lip, higher than in making an English "v." This is the sound to use in a Japanese accent in English. Incidentally, in Japanese "w" can be a final consonant, which is not the case in English.

y<u>oo</u>: The semi-vowel "y" exists in Japanese, but the diphthong, as noted above, would tend to be stressed evenly on both halves, so *you* might be pronounced "ee'<u>oo</u>' ." The stress on "<u>oo</u>" is slightly stronger.

Pitch

Japanese is sometimes referred to as a "pitch accent" language, rather than a strictly intonational language. Certain pitches are obligatory on specific syllables, and these, rather than simple emphatic stress, create stress patterns, much as stress and pitch were related, at least so it is conjectured, in ancient Greek. In the many dialects of Japanese there are numerous variations, and some dialects almost appear to be tonal languages, because of the number of words in them which change their meaning according to the pitch on which they are spoken. For our purposes the important dialect is the Standard Japanese of Tokyo, which is not a tonal language. To some extent the meaning of a word is changed if it is spoken on a high or low tone, but it is not in any case a true tonal language. The pitch of a syllable is predictable if one knows the complicated rules of Japanese phonetics, and pitch also varies along expressive, emotional lines.

Syllables with long vowels are spoken sometimes on an upper pitch, those with short vowels on lower pitches. This is not a hard and fast rule. Sometimes multisyllable words can be spoken on all high or all low pitches. At the end of a declarative sentence the tone often falls, but it can also fall in questions. In general there are only a few pitches used in ordinary Japanese statements, but, as one can see in Japanese kabuki movies, there is a wide range of pitches available to express emotion, such as the famous loud high *Hah!* before a fight. In Japanese television costume dramas the men often have a rougher, more emphatic way of speaking than the women characters, apparent even to someone who does not understand Japanese. This phenomenon is related more, perhaps to character and is the actor's choice.

Practice

Japanese Sentences
Omeni kakarete ureshii desu.
Translation: I am very pleased to meet you
Phonetic pronunciation: o: me: ni: kA kA re: te: oo re shee: de *se*
Note the extra long vowel in the syllable "shee:." The other vowels are rather short. To pronounce this phrase correctly remember to assume the correct position of the vocal apparatus. The syllables "me:," "re:" "shee:" and "de" are all spoken on an upper pitch, and this appears to make them stressed syllables, but in reality all the syllables are evenly stressed.

Arigato gozaimasu.
Translation: Thank you very much
Phonetic pronunciation: A ri:ng A to go zA i: mA *se*
Note the nasalized vowel in the second syllable of *arigato*, often pronounced simply as "A ree gA to" by American speakers. The syllables "A," "zA," and "mA" are spoken on upper pitches, appearing, once again, to make them stressed syllables, but they are not. The combination "ai" in *gozaimasu* does not result in the diphthong "I"; each vowel is pronounced separately.

English Sentences
You know that what I tell you is true.
Phonetic pronunciation: ee'oo' no zat wAt A'ee' ter ee'oo' i' se troo
Note: In a light accent the schwa may be dropped in the syllable "se" and the diphthongs correctly pronounced. Also, the "z" substitution for "TH" can be changed to an "s," and the "r" for "L" substitution eliminated, in favor of a very lightly pronounced, liquid "l," with the tongue quickly drawing away from the "l."

Of course you can tell me this is true, but I don't know.
Phonetic pronunciation: uf kaws eeoo' ka ne ter mee di:s i: se troo bAt I dawn naw

Possible Pitch Pattern

```
                                        I don't
  course                      true
        you can                     but
Of                tell me this is                   know.
```

Under the circumstances it will be possible to do everything you ask, so do not worry.
Phonetic pronunciation: un dA dee so kum stan ses i:t wi:r bee po si: ber t<u>oo</u> d<u>oo</u> e ve ree si:ng y<u>oo</u> ask saw d<u>oo</u> naw' te wA ree

It is very beautiful workmanship, very artistic and well fashioned, a lovely piece of work.
Phonetic pronunciation: i:t i: *se* ve ree bee <u>oo</u> ti: f<u>oo</u>r wo:k ma' ne shi:p   ve ree A ti:s ti:k a ne we' re fash en   ay ru' ve ree pees u' ve wo:k

The tea ceremony is meant to be calming and to soothe the nerves in a harried, fast-paced modern world.
Phonetic pronunciation: dee tee se re maw nee i: *se* men t<u>oo</u> bee kA mi:ng en ty<u>oo</u> s<u>oo</u> dee nofs i:n ay ha ree de fas te, or fas, pays maw de ren wawr, or wawrd

In Japan and in America the television show "The Iron Chef" is very popular.
Phonetic pronunciation: i: ne dga pan an i:n a me ri: ka di te re vi shun shaw di I An shef i: *se* ve ree po p<u>oo</u> rA

Possible Pitch Pattern

```
                me-                                          pop-
                              vision              Chef"  very
        pan and in A-              tele-        "The Iron    is         ular.
In Ja-                   rica the          show
```

There is old-fashioned competition and delicious tasting of food by the judges, who have a wonderful time, like the audience.
Phonetic pronunciation: de i:s O fash u ne kawm pe ti: shun an di ri shus tays ti:ng awf food bI di dgu dges h<u>oo</u> haf ay wun de foo re tIm rI ke di aw dee ens

381

Chapter Thirty
Korean Accents

Korean, a language isolate whose relationship to other languages has been explored but never established, is spoken by some 65 million people in Korea, and by more than three million more people worldwide, including approximately six hundred thousand in the United States. It has the only phonetic alphabet in Asia, based on the correlation of symbol to sound, as in the European and Middle Eastern alphabets. There is also a system of romanization of Korean, called the McCune-Reischauer system. These are the same linguists who devised a system for the romanization of Chinese. The system is used in pronouncing dictionaries of Korean and is very useful for any researcher who does not read the Korean alphabet.

The standard accent in Korean is that of the province of Kyôngsang, from which the ruling classes emanate. It is the accent used by the professional classes and by intellectuals. The peasant, working-class accent of the Chôlla provinces is considered vulgar and déclassé. Quite a number of immigrants to this country who speak Korean with this accent came here in part to avoid the discrimination and lack of opportunity which they faced in Korea because of the way they speak. People from the Chôlla provinces were not permitted to work in government jobs, for example. To be exiled to those provinces and their capital city, Kwangju, an industrial metropolis, was to be exiled to the hinterlands of social neglect and massive poverty. The prejudice against these people is centuries old, stemming from their rebellions against the ruling dynasties and the unification of Korea under the mistrustful Silla emperors, who ruled with the help of the Chinese T'ang dynasty. It is the language of the Silla and the *yangban* (aristocrats) who looked down on manual labor and mercantile activity, much as their European counterparts did in the 18th and 19th centuries, which became Standard Korean. In Korean television dramas people in positions of authority speak with Kyôngsang accents, and workers, low-class criminals and the uneducated use the Chôlla provincial accents. Of course there were many other reasons for emigrating as well. The massive tragedy of the Korean War, which ruined countless lives and separated families, is certainly a major contributing factor, as is the repressive nature of the dictatorships in both North and South Korea.

There are other forms of discrimination in Korean society. Age discrimination and the emphasis on age-appropriate activities, is apparently quite common. Honorific forms of address, as in Japan, are the linguistic codification of this attitude. Younger children are expected to address older children as *hyông*, meaning "older brother," for example. The *hyông* may call the younger person by his name, but not vice versa. There are also feminine modes of address not employed by males and vice versa.

Korean is a fascinating language, with some features which make it easy to learn. There are no genders for nouns, and no indication of singular or plural number. Korean follows one of the standard word orders for sentences: subject, object, verb. (English word order for a simple sentence follows another such model: subject, verb, object.)

A Quick Reference

1) Stress is fairly even and pitch is even-toned.
2) The "r" is pronounced with a light tap. Final "r" and "r" before another consonant are not pronounced. A correct retroflex American "R" can be learned and should be used in a light Korean accent.
3) Do the Korean liquid "l." At the beginning of a word replace it, occasionally, with "r."
4) Substitute "sh" for "zh" wherever it occurs.
5) Substitute "z" and "s" or "d" and "t" for "TH" and "th."
6) Pronounce initial "h," "w" and "y" correctly.

How to Do a Korean Accent

1) Position of the Vocal Apparatus
The mouth is slightly closed, more than in General American. The tongue tends to seek a forward, upward position. The main point of resonance is in the center to slightly forward of center part of the upper palate.

2) Stress
Pay special attention to stress, even in a lighter Korean accent. The stress pattern in Korean is very even on all syllables, but the last syllable receives a slightly greater stress. This even stressing, and an occasional confusion about the correct stress on English words is very important in a Korean accent in English.

3) Pitch
Pitch is also very important in this accent. There are no great variations in pitch, which is fairly even-toned, but the standard pattern of rising at the end of a question and falling at the end of a declarative sentence is the one found in Korean, so it should also be used in a Korean accent in English.

4) The Most Important Sounds
Consonants
Some Korean consonants are heavily aspirated. The initial English versions of "ch," "k," "p" and "t" are the versions to use in all positions in a Korean accent. There are glottalized versions of these consonants and of "s" as well; the glottis is tensed, as for a glottal stop, and the air released as the consonant is pronounced. This is not generally a problem, however, in an accent in English, since English

does not have glottalized consonants. Since "r" does not occur in final position in Korean, the accent in English is generally non-rhotic. A Korean name like *Park* is pronounced "pA:k" in Korean, with the vowel slightly, but only slightly, lengthened. There are a number of final consonant clusters in Korean (including some that do not exist in English), so they can generally be learned in English.

h: There is an initial "h" in Korean, and it should be retained in a Korean accent in English.

l: The Korean "l" is a liquid sound, with the unthickened blade of the tongue approaching the upper palate and the tip of the tongue forward. In Korean it occurs in final position only, including final consonant clusters. However, because the sound exists it can be learned and used, instead of the General American "L," in initial position. There is an occasional tendency to substitute "r" for "l" in initial position, in a heavy Korean accent. The final consonant cluster "lp" exists, so *help* should be correctly pronounced.

r: The initial "r" is a slight trill. There is no final "r" in Korean, which has "l" in final positions and in consonant clusters, but this has no particular bearing on an accent in English.

s: Because "s" is often glottalized, as described above, there is a possibility of doing a slightly more sibilant, or hissing, "s" in a Korean accent. This is the actor's choice.

zh: This sound does not exist in Korean. Substitute "sh," which does occur in Korean, so *measure* is pronounced "me' she'."

Vowels and Diphthongs
The vowel system of Korean is the usual a (A), e, i, o, u (oo), plus the schwa (e) and o. There are also nasal vowels in Korean, indicated in the romanized Korean alphabet by the letters "ng." Vowels are long and short, but even the longer Korean vowels are a bit shorter than English long vowels, and this phenomenon carries over into an accent in English, where all vowels tend to be a bit shortened. The majority of Korean syllables end in a vowel, but there are some final consonant clusters, as described above.

ee and i: There is no vowel quite as long as "ee" in Korean, which has a short "i" and the intermediate vowel "i:," and it is this vowel which should be used instead of "ee" in a Korean accent. Since "i" exists in Korean, it should usually be correctly pronounced, but if there is some confusion in the mind of the Korean speaker as to when to use it, substitute "i:" for it, so *it* can be pronounced either "it" or "i:t."

w: This semi-vowel exists in initial position in Korean, and forms diphthongs, so it should be correctly pronounced in English in such words as *well, where* and *when*.

y: This semi-vowel also exists in initial position in Korean, so words like *yes* and *yet* should be correctly pronounced in English.

Practice

Korean Phrases
Annyong haseyo. Yojum ottoshimnikka?
Translation: Greeting meaning "good morning," "afternoon," or "evening"; How are you?
Phonetic pronunciation: An nyawn(g)' hA say yo' yo dgem' o:t to shim ni:k' kA
Note the double "n" in the word *annyong* and the nasal vowel in the final syllable "nyawn(g)." The vowels "aw" and "o" are quite short. The "(g)" is barely pronounced. All syllables are evenly stressed, but there is a slightly stronger stress on the syllables "nyawn(g)," "yo, "dgem" and "ni:." You will notice also that the "i" in the syllable "shim" is very short and the "i" in the syllable "ni:k" is lengthened. Also, the "tt" and "kk" in *ottoshimnikka* are doubled, and both are pronounced, but in such a way as to make them sound as if the vowels preceding them are long.

English Sentences
So how are you today? Do you need some help?
Phonetic pronunciation: so how A yoo too day' doo yoo ni:d sum help'
Note that all syllables should be evenly stressed, the stress on *day* and *help* being slightly stronger. Note also the absence of the schwa, even though it exists in Korean.

I don't agree with your point.
Phonetic pronunciation: I dO' nA gRee' vis yooR poyn'
Note: A retroflex "R" can be accurately learned by Koreans, and is sometimes heard in this accent instead of a lightly trilled "r."

What you are telling me is not true.
Phonetic pronunciation: vat yoo AR te' li:ng mee i:s nO tRoo

It is a pleasure to read by the light of such a beautiful lamp.
Phonetic pronunciation: i: di:s a ple' shoor too ri:d bi de rIt awf sush ay byoo' di: fool lamp, or ramp

Possible Pitch Pattern

```
                  read                    beau-
                               such a          ti-
It is a          to       by the light of          ful
     plea-
        sure                                            lamp.
```

How was your trip to New York?
Phonetic pronunciation: how wAs yaw tri:p t<u>oo</u> ny<u>oo</u> yawk

It is very clear that the tragedy of the separation of North and South Korea must be brought to a peaceful solution to the satisfaction of all concerned.
Phonetic pronunciation: it is ve' ree klee' e dat se tra' dge di: Av di se pa Ray' shun Av nawrs an sowt kaw Ree' A mAs bi: bRaw t<u>oo</u> ay pi:s' fool saw ly<u>oo</u>' shun t<u>oo</u> de sa tis fak' shun Av awl kAn seRnd'

Chapter Thirty-One

Vietnamese, Burmese, Indonesian and Singaporean, Philippines (Tagalog), and Thai Accents

This chapter is devoted to a miscellany of Southeast Asian and Pacific Asian island accents, of which there are a great many indeed. There are hundreds of Malayo-Polynesian languages, spoken on islands and archipelagos all over the Pacific. Some of them are: Indonesian, spoken in Indonesia and Java; Malaysian; Malagasi, one of the two official languages of Madagascar, along with French; and Tagalog, spoken in the Philippines. Vietnamese, like Korean and Japanese, is a language isolate. Burmese and Thai are related to each other, but belong to two separate branches of the Sino-Tibetan language family, and are also related to Chinese. In that vast area of the continent and the islands off its coasts some 86 major and minor languages are spoken.

A General Note About Pitch

It is perhaps paradoxical that the intonational patterns of English, the inflections which indicate a question or a statement, are largely absent in three of the Southeast Asian accents covered here: Vietnamese, Burmese and Thai, (as well as in those of Laos and Cambodia, not covered in this book). The paradox is that these languages are all tonal, and full of their own music, but there is perhaps a confusion as to the meanings of English intonations, and it is probably difficult to distinguish the pitches. Instead there is a higher pitch on stressed syllables and a low pitch on unstressed syllables, but no other pitch pattern. Instead of a rise in pitch on either *you* or on the last syllable of *today* in "How are you today?," indicating different emphasis in the questioner's mind, typically the Southeast Asian intonation is monotonal, flat, on one pitch, with no rise at the end of the question. This information does not apply to the accents of the Philippines or Indonesia.

Vietnam

Though more than half its vocabulary is derived from Chinese, Vietnamese has absolutely no proven language relative. It is not related to Chinese, and its origin is unknown, but it is spoken by more than 65 million people.

Vietnam, with its long Pacific seacoast, is rich in natural resources, among them tin and rubber. These interests were considered vital to the United States, as they had been to France and Japan, both of whom had in succession occupied Vietnam, and were eventually expelled. Vietnam had been an occupied country for several hundred years at the point when it was finally divided in two by the northern Communist and the Southern capitalist dictatorships. Vietnam was founded between 1940 and 1945 in the area called Indochina. It was in 1954, after the defeat of the French at Dienbienphu and as a result of a Geneva Conference, that the division of the country took place.

In the 1960s the tragic and horrible Vietnam War broke out, with all its terrible consequences for both Vietnam and the United States. The carnage and the devastation, the loss of life on both sides, and the general horror and deep, wounding divisions which resulted are with us to this day, though, slowly, they are healing. There has been a Vietnamese immigration to America, and an article in *The New York Times Magazine* for Sunday, January 12, 1997, talks about Saigon, the capital of the former South Vietnam, with its flavor of France, as being a new haven for young American expatriates. Vietnamese food is also increasingly popular in such metropolitan centers as New York City. The Vietnamese accent is important in Broadway shows like *Miss Saigon* and in innumerable movies about the Vietnam War, such as *Platoon* (1986).

A Quick Reference

1) Do a non-rhotic (final "R" dropped) British-sounding accent with a relaxed jaw. Do a lightly trilled "r."
2) Shift final voiced consonants to voiceless.
3) Substitute "v" for initial "w."
4) Keep the consonants "soft."
5) Substitute "d" and "t" for "TH" and "th."
6) There is no "schwa (e)" in Vietnamese, so all vowels, even when unstressed, receive a full value.

How to Do a Vietnamese Accent

1) Position of the Vocal Apparatus
The mouth is relaxed and open, very similar to the position of General American. The main point of resonance is the middle of the mouth, although there is very clear articulation of frontal consonants. The tongue tends to remain in an upward position.

2) Stress
Stress in the English sense does not exist in Vietnamese, which is a tonal language. Stress is either correctly learned or not, depending on the character. The tendency is to stress every syllable pretty evenly and to give all vowels a full value.

3) The Most Important Sounds

Many of the sounds of English exist in Vietnamese, as well as sounds particular to Vietnamese, which do not exist in English, such as the use of "ng" in initial position, so the actor may want to do only a very light accent. The model of British RP is often the one followed, so do British vowels.

Consonants

Final consonants in Vietnamese are either nasal ("m," "n," "ng") or voiceless ("ch," "k," "p," "t"). In English the voiced consonant endings ("b," "d," "g") shift, in a Vietnamese accent, to voiceless endings ("p," "t," "k"). Otherwise the consonants are much the same as in English. The accent is largely non-rhotic, since a final "r" does not exist in Vietnamese.

l: The Vietnamese "l" is liquid, with the blade of the tongue unthickened and approaching the palate.

r: The Vietnamese "r" is lightly trilled. It is this sound that should be used in a Vietnamese accent in English, although a uvular "R," as in French, is also heard.

t: Final "t" in a consonant cluster is often dropped, son *don't* is pronounced "dOn" or "dOn," and *moment* is pronounced "mo' mun."

TH and th: These consonants do not exist in Vietnamese. They can be learned, but usual substitutions are "d" for the voiced consonant and "t" or "s" for the voiceless.

Vowels and Diphthongs

Most of the vowels and diphthongs of English also exist in Vietnamese. The exceptions are:

e: The schwa does exist in Vietnamese, but in an accent in English the full value of vowels is often given to them in unstressed syllables: "a" is always "a," "u" is always "u," etc.

I: This diphthong is usually learned accurately, but both halves should be evenly stressed: A'ee'.

O: This diphthong, when not correctly pronounced, which it can be, tends to shift either to the pure, lengthened vowel "aw:" or to the shorter "o."

w: This semi-vowel is usually heard as an initial "v," although it can be, and is, correctly learned and pronounced.

Pitch

Vietnamese has six tones:

389

1) high: —
2) low:__
3) middle or neutral: -
4) rising from middle to high: -/
5) rising from low to high: __/
6) heavy falling: \

See "A General Note About Pitch" at the opening of this chapter. Because of the tones, questions sometimes rise at the end, and sometimes end on a falling tone. The same phenomenon is true of declarative sentences.

Practice

We are all aware of the right thing to do in the circumstances, but we don't always do it.
Phonetic pronunciation: vee a awl a ve: uv de rA'ee't ti:ng t<u>oo</u> d<u>oo</u> in de so kum stan ses but vee dawn awl ve:s d<u>oo</u> i:t
Note the even stressing of almost all syllables. A possible choice for pitch is to say syllables that are slightly stressed, as well as the word *it* on a rising tone.

Saigon was a French city, and still retains a French flavor.
Phonetic pronunciation: sA'ee gawn vus a french si:' tee *an* sti:l ri: tayns a french flay va

Vietnam has a history of being occupied, but we are now free.
Phonetic pronunciation: vee et nAm' has a hi:s taw ri: af bee' i:ng a' ky<u>oo</u> pA'eet bat vee A now free

Wounds take a long time to heal and there is much that needs to be forgiven.
Phonetic pronunciation: v<u>oo</u>ns tayk a lawng tIm t<u>oo</u> heel *an* der i:s mach dat ni:ds t<u>oo</u> bi: faw gi:' fen

Vietnamese, like most of the world's languages, is tonal.
Phonetic pronunciations: vee et nA' ni:s lA'eek maws awf di vawlts lan' gwe ches i:s taw' nal

Southeast Asia has wonderful, varied cuisines, becoming better known in the West.
Phonetic pronunciation: sow tees ay' shA has vun' de fool va' reet kwi: si:ns' bi kam' ing be' ta nawn i:n di wes

Burma

Burma is a country of Southeast Asia centered around the fertile, densely populated valley of the Irrawaddy River. Its capital is Rangoon (*Yangoon* in Burmese), and Burma is famously celebrated in the west by Rudyard Kipling's popular "The Road to Mandalay," with its picture of the "old Moulmein pagoda" and the Burmese girl waiting for the British soldier she loves to return while the temple bells ring out and the wind blows through the palm trees. The paddle steamers ply their way slowly up and down the river in the steamy heat and the flying fishes leap out of the water in this romantic fantasy.

Imperialist sentiment notwithstanding, it evokes the great beauty of the Burmese landscape. A more disturbing picture is painted in the film *Beyond Rangoon* (1995), with its story of political unrest and oppressive tyranny. This film, based on a true story, is excellent for hearing authentic Burmese accents in English. Indeed the principal Burmese character, Aung Ko, is a highly cultivated intellectual, and the actor playing him, U Aung Ko (Phonetic pronunciation: <u>oo</u> An(g) ko:), speaks superb, non-rhotic British-accented English, with a correct "R," as well as a trilled "r" and an American diphthong for "O."

A Quick Reference

1) Drop final consonants in consonant clusters.
2) Do a Burmese "l."
3) Substitute "y" for "R" in a heavy accent, a light tapped "*d*" otherwise. Alternatively, a "w" is a possible substitute for "r."
4) Substitute "hp" and "ht" for initial "b" and "d."
5) Substitute "hd" and "ht" for "TH" and "th."
6) Substitute "p" for "f" and "b" for "v."

How to Do a Burmese Accent

1) Position of the Vocal Apparatus
The mouth is drawn very slightly to the side, as in a smile, and is otherwise relaxed downward. The tongue is held slightly forward and is relaxed and down.

2) Pitch
Pitch is very important in this accent, and the attempt is to give English the same music as Burmese. There are three tones in Burmese, indicated in the language itself by accent marks: a neutral tone, midlevel; a higher tone, abrupt and short; and a lower tone, called a "heavy" tone, during which the vowel is also lengthened. The tones change the lexical meaning of a word, as does the length of vowels in both stressed and unstressed syllables, so that there are a great number of meanings possible for any combination of, say, the same three syllables in the same order. There are no intonational patterns as in English, and a question, for instance, does not rise at the end, but is indicated by a stressed, prolonged tone on a particular interrogative affix at the end of a sentence, which is not higher in pitch than the other tones of the sentence. Questions can also begin with an interrogative word, in which case the obligatory word *leh*, pronounced "le:," is used at the end of the sentence; still, the tone does not change.

3) The Most Important Sounds

Consonants

Final consonant clusters are largely absent in Burmese, and the last consonant of a cluster tends to be dropped in a Burmese accent in English, so *don't* is pronounced "dO*n*," with a slightly nasalized "O." Certain consonants of English do not exist in Burmese, but they can be accurately learned, and often are. Initial voiced consonants are sometimes aspirated and voiceless, sounding as if they have "h" before them, so the "b" in a word like *bed* sounds like "hp" (hpet), and initial "d" like "ht," or "hd" so *this* is pronounced "hti:s" or "hdi:s." The following information applies to a very heavy Burmese accent in English.

f and v: Neither of these consonants exists in Burmese, and "p" and "b" are the usual substitutions for them, respectively, so *very* is pronounced "bay" (see "r," below) and *fright* is pronounced as either "pdIt" or "pyIt."

l: This sound exists in Burmese, but in pronouncing it the tip of the tongue is pushed forward against the back of the upper front teeth. This sound is the one heard in a Burmese accent in English. The effect is that of a simultaneously dentalized and palatalized "l," with the blade of the tongue up toward the palate.

r, R, R: There are no rhotic sounds in most Burmese dialects, except for Arracanese. The semi-vowel "y" is substitued for "R" in a Burmese accent in English, so, for example, *Brahmin* is pronounced "byA' mi: n" and *democratic* is pronounced "de' mo kyA' ti:k." *True* is pronounced "ty<u>oo</u>." A tapped "d" can also be substituted, so *true* would be pronounced "td<u>oo</u>." Someone whose linguistic background is Arracanese, on the other hand, will pronounce the English "R" correctly, or as "r" with one trill. Perhaps in general, for the sake of clarity, the actor should pronounce the "r" correctly in any case. This phenomenon in Burmese reminds one of certain aristocrats in England, who have some difficulty in pronouncing "R," and pronounce words like *very* as "vay," and the phrase *very true* as "vay tw<u>oo</u>," although the Elmer Fudd "w" (Elmer Fudd also pronounces his "L's as "w") is not a true "w," but is, rather, a retroflex semi-vowel, with the bottom of the tongue curled up toward the palate in an attempt to say the "R" correctly.

Vowels and Diphthongs

Vowels in Burmese are long and short, and follow the usual system: A (a), e, i, o, <u>oo</u> (u).

w: This semi-vowel exists in initial position in Burmese, and is therefore to be correctly pronounced in English. You may hear "w" substituted for "R."

Stress

Stress is intimately bound up with pitch, as is often the case with tonal languages. The length of vowels also helps to creates stress patterns. The three tones described below act as creators of rhythm as well as pitch, since the tones are either abrupt or more drawn out, and the meaning of a word depends on them as well.

That's very true. I'm very frightened. Let us have light. You don't have good light in here.
Phonetic pronunciation: hdas bay ty<u>oo</u>, or be' *di* td<u>oo</u>. Im bay pyI' tin, or be' *di* pdI' tin. let As hep lIt. y<u>oo</u> dO*n* hep goo lIt in hee
Note: See "l" under "Consonants." Notice also that the final "d" in *good* is dropped, because "d" and the following "l" in *light* would form an unacceptable, or very difficult, consonant cluster, not permitted in Burmese, or in English either, for that matter, in initial position.

This thing that I am telling you is the right course of action, so hold on.
Phonetic pronunciation: hdi:s hti:ng hda I am tel' i:ng y<u>oo</u> i:s hti rI, or yI, kaws Ab ak' shen saw hawl awn

To be hard and fast as a rule is to be too inflexible and very rigid.
Phonetic pronunciation: t<u>oo</u> hpee hA an fas as a r<u>oo</u>l, or y<u>oo</u>l, or w<u>oo</u>l, i:s t<u>oo</u> bee t<u>oo</u> i:n plek' si: hp*e*l an be' yee, or bay, yi:', or wi:', dgit
Note: Remember that in the Arracanese dialect rhotic sounds do exist, so you can pronounce "R" sounds to lighten the accent. The accent in these exercise is very **heavy**; to make it **light** restore some of the accurate sounds of English, especially "R" and "th." You might want to substitute "w" for "R" instead of "y" in the words *rule* and *rigid*, as shown.

The Irrawaddy River is wide and the water traffic in the steamy heat is enormous.
Phonetic pronunciation: hdi i: yA wA' dee ri', or yi', or wi', ba i:s wId an hdi waw ta tyA', or twA', fi:k i:n hdi sti:' mee hi:t i:s i: naw' mus

Like other countries Burma has suffered over the centuries from imperialism.
Phonetic pronunciation: lIk a' hde kAn' tri:s hpoo' mA has sAf' et aw bA hdi sen' ty<u>oo</u> ri:s, or yi:s, or sen' tyi:s, pyAm, or pwAm, i:m pi:' yi: li:s em

The lot of mankind is to live and love and to die in the end, making way for others.
Phonetic pronunciation: hdi lawt awb ma*n* kI*n* i:s t<u>oo</u> li:b a*n* lAb an t<u>oo</u> dI in hdi e*n* me:' kin way paw A' hdes

Indonesia and Singapore

Indonesia, with its capital Djakarta, located on the island of Java, is a country of more than three thousand islands in the Malay Archipelago. Its official language is Indonesian. The Portuguese, the British and the Dutch in turn all occupied Indonesia, which was called, after the Dutch East India Company was dissolved and the country was directly ruled from Holland beginning in 1798, the Netherlands East Indies. In 1949, after years of terrible and bloody war, the imperialist yoke was finally thrown off, and Indonesia achieved its independance.

Its political troubles hardly ceased at that point, however, and they continue to this day. For authentic examples of Indonesian accents, see the Australian film *The Year of Living Dangerously* (1983), which concerns the politics of the island nation. Linda Hunt is magnificent as an Indonesian male journalist.

Indonesian and Malaysian, the official languages of the Federation of Malaysia and the Republic of Indonesia are closely related Malay languages, and the accents are virtually the same in English. Singapore, with its immensely large English-speaking population (the English spoken there has its own dialectical features), also counts Malaysian as an official language, as it is in the Sultanate of Brunei. Altogether Indonesian and Malaysian are spoken by a total of about 180 million people. The history of Malaysian and Indonesian as written languages dates back to seventh-century inscriptions.

A Quick Reference

1) Substitute "p" for "f."
2) Pronounce "r" (Indonesian) or "R" (Malaysian) in all positions. For Singapore follow the British non-rhotic model of English.
3) Generally, shift voiced consonants to voiceless.
4) Substitute "d" and "t" for "TH" and "th."
5) Substitute initial "w" for initial "v" in a Singaporean accent.
6) Vowels and semi-vowels should be correctly pronounced, but diphthongs should shift to pure vowels for Indonesian and Singaporean accents. In a Singapore accent do not use a schwa, but pronounce pure vowels as written. See below for details.
7) See "Stress" and "Pitch," very important in these accents.

How to Do an Indonesian Accent

Pay special attention to the differences between an Indonesian and a Singaporean accent.
1) Position of the Vocal Apparatus
The mouth is slightly closed, the lips slightly protruded, the tongue a bit upward in general position.

2) The Most Important Sounds
Consonants
The **Indonesian** accent is largely rhotic, because final "r" is pronounced in Indonesian. However, in **Singapore** the accent, following the British model, is non-rhotic. In an **Indonesian** accent voiced consonants often shift to voiceless, although both the voiced and voiceless pairs exist in Indonesian. So "d" shifts to "t," and *padded* is pronounced "pa' tet"; g" shifts to "k," and *magnet* is pronounced "mak' net"; "z" shifts to "s," so *is* is pronounced "i:s," instead of "iz." This is true at the ends of words as well as initially.

f and p: As in Tagalog in the Philippines, "p" is often the usual substitution for "f."

r and R: In **Indonesian** the "r" is trilled, but in **Malaysian** it is much like the French uvular "R," pronounced with the tongue down, its tip behind the lower front teeth, its back raised to vibrate lightly against the uvula. This is the principal difference between an Indonesian and a Malaysian accent in English, the particular rhotic sound of either language being the one maintained in English.

t: The **Indonesian** "t" is dentalized, sounding almost like "ts." In **Singapore** a glottal stop (?) is often substituted for final "t" and for "p" as well: *stop* (stA?); *what* (wA?).

TH and th: These sounds do not exist in Indonesian. The usual substitutions are "d" for voiced and "t" for voiceless, in Singapore.

v: In **Singapore** English "v" often shifts to "w." However, "v" exists in **Indonesian**, and should be correctly pronounced in English.

Vowels and Diphthongs
Indonesian vowels are classified as "high class" and "low class." This really means that they are long or short, and their use is governed by the particular consonants surrounding them. While this is a fascinating linguistic phenomenon, it need not concern us overly in doing an Indonesian accent in English. Diphthongs in a Malaysian, Indonesian and Singapore accent all tend to shift to pure lengthened vowels: "ay" shifts to "e:" and "O" to "aw:." The schwa is largely absent in the **Singapore** accent. Vowels in Singapore before "r" are often lengthened, so *more* is pronounced "maw:" and *pair* is pronounced "pe:."

e and e: The schwa (e) and "e" are two vowels which exist in Indonesian, but which are easily confused, perhaps because of English orthography, and the schwa is usually substituted for by "e," so *forever* is pronounced "faw re: ver."

w: This semi-vowel exists in **Indonesian**, and should be correctly pronounced in English. However, in **Singapore** "v" and "w" are often shifted, so *very* is pronounced "we' ree."

y: This semi-vowel exists in Indonesian and should be correctly pronounced in English.

Stress
Stress differs occasionally from the standard accents of English. Stress in Indonesian is generally on the penultimate (next to the last) syllable, but in Java it is on the last syllable, leading to an accent similar in pattern to French or Hebrew. In the English of **Singapore** the stress is even on all syllables, tending to last-syllable stressing, so that the distinction between the noun "in'sult" and the verb "insult' " is lost; the usual pronunciation of both words is the latter. There is also a kind of rapid-fire staccato rhythm, similar to that of a native Hawaiian accent.

395

See the section on Hawaiian in Chapter Six. Because of the rhythm of Singaporean speech, there are some non-standard stresses, as in "disadvan' tageous," "econ' omic," "charac' ter," and "facul' ty" and "latchkey'." This phenomenon reminds one of the stress in some Indian accents.

Pitch

Pitch is also important here. In Indonesian accents and in Singapore English the pitch range is much more limited than it is in Standard British or American English. It is louder, as well, on a high pitch, and the syllable on a high pitch has its vowel lengthened slightly.

Practice

Indonesian Words and Phrases
Doubling, or repetition, of a syllable or words is a phenomenon in Indonesian, and can either change the meaning, or simply make the word plural.
mata (eye; mA' tA); *mata-mata* (spy; mA' tA mA' tA'); *bangun* (awake; bA' ngoon); *bangun-bangun* (as soon as they were awake; bA' ngoon bA' ngoon); *ibunda bangun* (respected-mother awoke; i: b<u>oo</u>n' dA bA' ngoon)

English Sentences
Yes, that is what I told you. It is very true indeed. Very fine.
Phonetic pronunciations
Indonesian: yes dats is wAts I tawlts y<u>oo</u>. i:ts is ve: ree tsr<u>oo</u> i:n tsi:ts. ve ree pIn
Note that this is a heavy accent. For a lighter accent, pronounce the "t" without dentalizing it.
Singapore: yes' dat is wAt I tawld' y<u>oo</u>. it i:s we ree tr<u>oo</u>' i:n deed'. we ree pIn
Note that this should be said in a staccato rhythm, with the stressed syllables on an upper pitch.

Just step up here and do what I tell you.
Phonetic pronunciations
Indonesia: dgus stsep up hee' A an dz<u>oo</u> wAts I tsel y<u>oo</u>
Singapore: dgus ste? U pee*e* an d<u>oo</u> wA? I teL y<u>oo</u>

So he went downtown yesterday morning.
Phonetic pronunciations:
Indonesia: so hee wen dzAn tsAn yes' tsA dzay mA' ning
Singapore: so hee wen? dAn tAn yes' di day maw' ning

There was a big to do about all that.
Phonetic pronunciations:
Indonesia: de wAs a bi:k ts<u>oo</u> d<u>oo</u> a' bow' dawl dat
Singapore: de wAs a bi:g t<u>oo</u> d<u>oo</u> a bowt' awl dat

Right away he wanted to come back with me to my house.
Phonetic pronunciations:
Indonesia: RI *da* way hi: waw' net t<u>oo</u> kAm bek wi:t mee t<u>oo</u> mI hows
Singapore: rI' ta vay hee vAn' tet t<u>oo</u> kAm bak vi:t mee t<u>oo</u> my hows

There aren't too many things to complain about, and the city is very interesting and fine.
Phonetic pronunciations:
Indonesia: de:r AR' ent t<u>oo</u> me' nee ti:nks t<u>oo</u> kAm ple:n' a bowt an di si:' dee i:s ve' ree i:n te Res' ti:nk an pIn
Singapore: de Ant t<u>oo</u> me' nee tsi:nks ts<u>oo</u> kAm ple:n' a bowt an di si:' tsee i:s we' ree i:n te res tink an pIn

Thailand

The Kingdom of Thailand was founded in the seventh century, and was for centuries a satellite of China, paying tribute to the emperors. With the arrival of the Portuguese in the 16th century the country came under the sway of Europeans, and, especially in the 19th century, the British and French competed for its rich natural resources. Thailand has been ruled by the Chakkri monarchs since the 18th century. They still reign today on the throne of the capital city of Bangkok, a city of golden pagodas and temples and slender, graceful spires.

If you are going to play the King of Siam, which is the old name for Thailand, in Rodgers and Hammerstein's *The King and I*, a Thai accent is a very useful, not to say absolutely necessary, thing to know how to do. It is often ignored in productions and in film versions, unfortunately. The accents in the Hollywood film *Anna and the King of Siam* (1946) are totally inauthentic, not to say nonexistent. Rex Harrison as the king didn't even try, but he was delightful. However, Lee J. Cobb as his adviser is a positive disgrace. There was also no attempt to do authentic accents in the film of the musical *The King and I* (1956). Yul Brynner, wonderful as the king, simply used his own Russian accent.

A Quick Reference

1) Drop final consonants in consonant clusters.
2) Shift final voiced consonants to voiceless.
3) Do an "r" with one light trill, and drop final "r" and "r" before another consonant. The consonants "l" and "r" are often confused with each other, and in the Thai language they are often used for each other.
4) Use voiceless "th" for both "TH" and "th."
5) Substitute "a" for "A."
6) Shift diphthongs to pure vowels.

How to Do a Thai Accent

1) Position of the Vocal Apparatus

The mouth is half open, half closed, much as in General American. The tongue tends to be held in an upward position.

2) The Most Important Sounds
Consonants
Most of the consonants of English have Thai counterparts. There are consonant clusters in Thai, but only in initial position, never at the end of a word, so some part of a final consonant cluster is often dropped. *Don't* is pronounced "dO*n*," with a slightly nasalized diphthong, and *last* is pronounced "la:t," since "s" does not occur in final position in Thai. Final voiced consonants do not exist in Thai either, only voiceless, except for "m," "n," and "ng." The Thai accent is non-rhotic. See below under "r."

b: This consonant exists in initial position, but at the end of a word it shifts to voiceless "p," so *cab* is pronounced "kap."

d: It shifts in final position to "t," so *bad* is pronounced "bat."

g: This consonant is found at the beginning of Thai words, but at the end of a word it is the voiceless "k," so *dig* is pronounced "di: k."

l: The Thai "l" is a liquid consonant, with the blade of the tongue up toward the palate and the tip of the tongue on the upper gum ridge a little way behind the teeth. Use this "l" for all words, instead of the American "L."

r: This consonant is pronounced with one trill, and it is the sound to use in a Thai accent. It never occurs in final position in Thai.

TH and th: The voiceless "th" exists in Thai, but without its voiced counterpart. Use the voiceless "th" for both voiced and voiceless, unless the character is supposed to have learned the "TH" well.

v: This consonant does not exist in Thai. The usual substitution is the semi-vowel "w," which exists in Thai, so *very* is pronounced "we' ree."

Vowels and Diphthongs
Vowels are long and short. The usual basic system is followed, except for "A": a, e, i, o, <u>oo</u> (u). There are only six diphthongs in Thai, the second half of which is "a," among them the English diphthongs "ya" (yam) and "wa" (water), which consequently should be correctly pronounced in English. The other four are particular to Thai, and make no difference to an accent in English.

A: This vowel does not exist in Thai. The usual substitution is "a."

ay: Since this diphthong does not exist in Thai it is usually substituted for with a lengthened "e:."

ee and i: Neither of these vowels exist. The long intermediate vowel "i:" is the usual substitution.

O: This diphthong does not exist in Thai. A lengthened "aw:" is the usual substitution for it.

u: The exact vowel heard in English in *but* does not exist in Thai. The usual substitutions are either the schwa or the "a," both of which exist in Thai: bet; bat.

Stress

Primary stress in Thai is on the final syllable. There are secondary stresses as well, but the tones play an important part in establishing the rhythmic quality of the language, especially because of the length of the vowels on which they occur.

Pitch

Thai is a tonal language. There are five tones:
1) a middle tone, even or level or neutral in quality;
2) a low tone, even or level or neutral in quality;
3) a high tone, even or level or neutral in quality;
4) a rising tone, which rises from the low tone to the high tone;
5) a falling tone, which falls from the high tone to the low tone.
There is also a phenomenon called *tone splitting*, which means that a tone can change from low to high, rising or falling, thus further complicating the tonal system. As a result, in English there is often a lack of intonation differentiating questions and declarative sentences. See "A General Note About Pitch" at the beginning of the chapter.

Practice

But I don't think that you can tell me what to do about these problems.
Phonetic pronunciation: bet a dawn thi:nk that yoo ken tel mi: wA too doo a bowt thi:s prawp lems', or plaw' prems, or plaw' plems, or praw prems'

To dig ditches and to labor for one's bread is very honorable work.
Phonetic pronunciation: too di:k di:' ches ant too le: be faw wawns bret i:s we' ree hawn' a bel wawk
Note: Notice the "h" at the beginning of *honorable*. An "h" is sometimes heard in this accent where it is normally silent in native accents of English.

Thailand, which used to be Siam, and its capital Bangkok, are known for golden spires.
Phonetic pronunciation: ta lant, or ran, wich yoos too be sa am' an i:s ka' pi: tal bang' kok' a nawn faw gaw:l' den spa' yas

Note: Since "A" does not exist in Thai, the usual substitute for it being "a," the diphthong "I" is sometimes difficult to learn, and "a" is sometimes substituted for "I."

The answer to this thing that I want to ask you is very important in its implications.
Phonetic pronunciation: thee an' se t<u>oo</u> thi:s thi:ng that a wawn t<u>oo</u> ask y<u>oo</u> i:s we' lee i:m paw tan i:n i:s i:m pri:, or pli:, ke:' shens

In the old days we led charmed lives and we ate wonderfully well.
Phonetic pronunciation: i:n thi: awr, or awl, de:s we red, or led, chawmt rafs, or lafs, an wi: e:t wen de foo' ree, or lee, wel, or wer

We can say this is true, but de we really know?
Phonetic pronunciation: wi: kan se: thi:s i:s tr<u>oo</u>, or tl<u>oo</u>, be d<u>oo</u> wi: ri:' li:, or li:' ri:, or li:' li:, or ri:' ri:, naw

The Philippines (Tagalog)

The linguistic situation in the Philippines is complicated by the fact that these islands were occupied for more than three centuries by Spain, so that Spanish became predominant as the official language and the language of administration. Then, after the Spanish-American War, the United States occupied the Philippines, and continued to do so for more than half a century, until after World War Two. Tagalog, a Malayo-Polynesian language, but much influenced lexically by Spanish and English, is the official language of the country, spoken by more than 15 million people. There are approximately 80 other Philippines Islands languages!

A Quick Reference

1) Substitute "p" for "f."
2) Do short vowels even where long ones would normally be used in General American.
3) Eliminate the schwa, which does not exist in Tagalog. Instead do pure vowels in unstressed syllables. The word *the* before a consonant, for example, is pronounced "dee."

How to Do a Tagalog Accent

1) Position of the Vocal Apparatus
The position of the mouth is relaxed, half open and half closed, much as in General American. The lips are protruded fairly far forward.

2) Stress
Stress is extremely important, and the short vowels and rhythms create this accent. The rules of stress in Tagalog are somewhat complicated, but in general the

stress is on either the penultimate (next to last) or last syllable, so for purposes of developing an accent in English it is random. The length of the long vowels influences the stress patterns in an accent in English, where the long vowels tend to be really long. When words in Tagalog end in short vowels they end quite abruptly. Stress is an important element in determining meaning in Tagalog, along with vowel length, and a three-syllable word has three meanings depending on which syllable is stressed, and perhaps more meanings depending on which stressed and unstressed vowels are short or long.

3) The Most Important Sounds
Pay special attention to the consonants, especially to the notable absence of "f" in Tagalog and the "p" which substitutes for it; and to the absence of the schwa under vowels.

Consonants
Final voiced consonants tend to shift to voiceless, and even voiceless final consonants tend to be very lightly pronounced. Final consonant clusters are largely absent in Tagalog, and are hard to pronounce in English, so the second consonant is usually dropped. *Don't* is pronounced "dOn," for example, and *last* is pronounced "las."

f: There is no "f" in Tagalog, and "p" is the usual substitution for "f" in an accent in English, so *Philippines* is pronounced "pi: li: pi: ns." Final "p" is barely pronounced, so *lip* is said as "li:(p)." *Philosophy* is said as "pi: law' so pi:."

R and r: Either of these rhotic sounds can be used for a Tagalog accent.

TH and th: Pronounce these sounds correctly, or substitute "d" and "t" for them.

w: There is no "w" in Tagalog. The usual substitute, when the sound is not learned correctly, is "v."

z: Final "z" shifts to "s," so *is* is pronounced "is." Likewise, voiced "zh" shifts to "sh," so the word *pleasure* is pronounced "ple' shoor" or even "play' shoor."

Vowels and Diphthongs
Vowels in Tagalog are long and short, the long vowels being very long, and the short very abrupt, shifting to a schwa. In an accent in English the vowels tend to be fairly short.

e and i: There is no vowel "e" in Tagalog, and these two vowels are often confused in a Tagalog accent in English, so that, for example *get* is pronounced "git" and *pen* and *pin* are both pronounced "pin."

ee and i: The intermediate lengthened vowel "i:" is usually heard in words with either "ee" or "i."

Pitch

The pitch is fairly high, but the usual rule of dropping a declarative sentence at the end and rising on a question are followed. Were it not for centuries of Spanish and English occupation, the "General Note About Pitch" might apply here as well.

Practice

Tagalog Words
magutang (to lend; mA g<u>oo</u>' tAng); *magpautang* (to lend with good will; mAg pA <u>oo</u>' tAng); *dumalita* (to last or endure; d<u>oo</u> mA li: tA'); *sumilang* (to rise; s<u>oo</u> mi:'lAng); *sumilang* (to go between; s<u>oo</u> mi: lAng')
Note that the change in stress in the last two words changes their meanings.

English Sentences
(Heard on a TV news broadcast) *We don't have any flights that is leaving on schedule.*
Phonetic pronunciation: vee dOn hav e' nee pLIts dat is lee' vi:ng on ske' dg<u>oo</u>L

Did you know that the English word "boondocks" comes from the Tagalog word "bundok" meaning mountain?
Phonetic pronunciation: did yoo nO dat dee ing' lish vord boon doks kums prum dee tA gA' log vord boon dok mi:n' ing man' ten

Remember that in Tagalog the vowels are short.
Phonetic pronunciation: Ri mem' bur dat i:n tA gA' log dee vals Ar short

It has been a great pleasure to meet you, such a fine person.
Phonetic pronunciation: i:t has been ay grayt ple' shoor t<u>oo</u> mi:t y<u>oo</u> sAch ay pIn por' sun

The three of them went together to the art exhibition.
Phonetic pronunciation: di tree uf dem ven t<u>oo</u> ge' door t<u>oo</u> dee Art ek' si bi' shun

Did you know that there are hundreds of languages spoken in the Philippine Islands?
Phonetic pronunciation: di:t y<u>oo</u> naw dat der Ar hAn' dreds awp lan' gwA shes spaw' ken in di pil' i pin I' lans

Chapter Thirty-Two
More Asian Accents: Armenian, Georgian, Mongolian, Uzbek

The languages in this chapter vary tremendously and are not related to each other, though they are all spoken on the continent of Asia. Armenian is an Indo-European language and thus related distantly to English. Mongolian, the language of Mongolia in the east of Asia, and spoken as far west as Central Asia, is an Altaic language, related to Manchu (now almost a dead language), and possibly to Turkish, and therefore perhaps to Uzbek, which is a Turkic language. Georgian is one of the many languages of the Caucasian group, spoken in the Caucasus Mountains between the Caspian and Black Seas.

Armenian

Armenian is an Indo-European language, with its own alphabet, invented by the Christian missionary Mesrop Mashtots in the fifth century. It is spoken in what was the Soviet republic of Armenia by most of its population of three and one half million, and by another half million elsewhere. The tragic history of the Armenians, who have a civilization that is more than two millenia old, has been all too sadly documented, and there is no question that they suffered horribly in the First World War when the Turks attempted genocide. Armenia has been invaded and occupied from ancient days, first by the Medes and Persians, then by the Byzantines, and later by the Ottomans and the Russians. Its literary tradition dates back to the early part of the fifth century, but as a nation Armenia is mentioned in ancient inscriptions even earlier. Armenians are perhaps of ancient Greek origin, having emigrated eastward in the days of the Hittites.

The Armenian language contains a large Persian vocabulary, so much so that until 1875, when a great deal of work was done on studying Armenian, many linguists thought it a dialect of Persian. Armenian also contains unique words found in no other Indo-European languages. These words are thought to be from extinct and long-forgotten tongues. Latin shares some 26 percent of its basic vocabulary items with Old Armenian, and Greek and Armenian have certain morphological and lexical affinities.

Armenian, which has two dialects, Eastern and Western, both mutually intelligible, contains a remarkable repertoire of sounds, more than in any other language, in fact. Included are all the consonants of English as well as the various rhotic sounds.

A Quick Reference

1) Pronounce final "r" and "r" before other consonants. You can also use the retroflex "R" of General American, lightly pronounced.
2) Pronounce "TH" and "th" correctly.
3) Substitute "e" for "a."
4) Substitute a long "aw" for the diphthong "O."
5) Substitute "v" for initial "w."

How to Do an Armenian Accent

1) Position of the Vocal Apparatus
This is much as in General American, with the mouth half open, half closed. The tongue is relaxed downward.

2) The Most Important Sounds
Consonants
The accent tends to be rhotic. The reason for this is that the stress is on the last syllable, when it ends in a consonant.

h: This consonant exists in Armenian, and should be correctly pronounced in English.

R, r, R: All three of these rhotic consonants exist in Armenian. In English it is the second, trilled "r" that is usually used, except when the rhotic is the second part of a consonant cluster, so *crown* is pronounced "kRown." It is also certainly possible to pronounce a retroflex "R" lightly, particularly at the end of a word.

TH and th: Both these sounds exist in Armenian, and should be correctly pronounced in English.

Vowels and Diphthongs
The usual system of vowels is the one found in Armenian: A, e, i,o, oo (u). There are many diphthongs as well.

a and e: These two sounds tend to be confused, and it is usually "e" that is heard, so *cat* is pronounced "ket."

i and ee: These sounds do not exist in Armenian, and the usual substitution for them is the long intermediate vowel "i:."

O: This diphthong does not exist in Armenian. Substitute a long "aw" for it, so that *home* is pronounced "hawm."

w: This semi-vowel exists in Old Armenian in initial position, but in Modern Armenian it has merged with "v," and it should be so pronounced in English.

Stress

The stress in Armenian is uniform, always on the last syllable of words ending in consonants, and on the penultimate (next to last) syllable of words ending in vowels. For the purposes of doing an accent in English, this means that the stress is random enough so as not to cause a problem in learning correct English stress patterns. Incidentally, the stress pattern of Armenian means it is easy for Armenians to learn French rhythmic phrasing correctly.

Pitch

The usual pitch pattern of falling at the end of a declarative sentence and rising at the end of a question is followed in Armenian, and is typical in general of the basic pitch pattern of Indo-European languages. In Armenian, however, the high and low pitches are very close to each other, so that the end of a question does not rise as high as it normally would in English.

Practice

Armenian Words and Phrases
hackagortzutsyun (counteraction; hA ka gawR ts<u>oo</u> tsi: <u>oo</u>n'); *hatshuykov* (with pleasure; hAt sh<u>oo</u> i: kawv'); *patahackanutsyun* (chance; pA tA hAk A n<u>oo</u> tsi: <u>oo</u>n'); *razmaget* (strategist; rAz mA get'); *jrel* (water; zhrel); *verjk gcin* (traces of the lines; veRdgk ge tsi:n'); *mer hayr or erknk'umn es* (our father who art in heaven; meR hayR awr eRk ne koo men es)

English Sentences
The elections will be free and democratic. There is no need to fear for the home-land.
Phonetic pronunciation: THi: el ek' shens vi:l bi: fri: end dam aw kRA' ti:k. THe:r i:z naw ni:d te fi:r fawr THe hawm' lend

Shish kebab and rice are just some of the delicious dishes of Armenia.
Phonetic pronunciation: shi:sh ke bap' end rIs Ar dgust sum awv THi di li' shis dish' is awv Ar mi:n' i: yA

The cat jumped out of the bed and landed on her feet.
Phonetic pronunciation: THe ket dgumpt owt awv THe bed end lend' ed awn her fi:t

Such red and gold sunsets you never saw before in your life.
Phonetic pronunciation: sAch red end gawld sun' sets y<u>oo</u> ne' ver saw bi fawr i:n y<u>oo</u>r lIf

Armenia has had a history of some tragic proportions, and the 1915 attempted genocide by the Turks is never to be forgotten, and the victims are always to be mourned.

Phonetic pronunciation: Ar mi:n' i: yA hez hed *e* hi:s' taw ri: awv sum tre' dgi:k praw pawr' shens end THi nIn' ti:n fi:f' ti:n e temp' ted dgen' aw sId' bI THi toorks i:z ne' ver t<u>oo</u> bee fawr gaw' ten end THi vik' ti:ms Ar awl' vays t<u>oo</u> bee mawrnd

The peaceful life we have found in America, to live with our gardens and in our vineyards, is a source of great harmony in our lives.

Phonetic pronunciation: THe pi:s' fool lIf vee hev fownd i:n A me' ri: kA t<u>oo</u> li:v vi:th owr gAr' dens end i:n owr vi:n yARdz i:z *e* sawrs awv grayt hAr' maw nee i:n owR lIvs

Georgian

"V *padlyednyi zhar, v dalinye Dagyestana,*
S svintsom v grudyi lyezhal nyedvizhim Ya"
—by Mikhail Lyermontov, "Son" ("Dream"); written in 1841; transliterated from the Cyrillic alphabet into the Roman alphabet.
Literal translation: "In the midday heat, in a gorge of Dagestan, With a bullet in my breast lay unmoving I"
Phonetic pronunciation: fpAd lyed' nyee zhAr, vdA lee' nyi dA gyi stAn' A, s(*e*)svi:n' tsom vgr<u>oo</u>' dyee lyi zhAl' nyed vi:' zhi:m yA

In 1841 Lyermontov, the Russian Romantic poet and novelist, was killed in a duel in the Caucasus. He had composed the poem which begins above only a few months before his death, when he was a soldier in the Czar's army. Dagestan, whose language is Avar, is a neighboring Caucasian country, formerly a Soviet republic, like Georgia, which the Russians call Gruzia. Throughout the 1830s Russia was subduing pockets of rebellion in the Caucasus, especially the marauding rebels hiding in the mountains, and completing its conquest of the region, begun in the 18th century. Georgia had been occupied many times before, by the ancient Persians, the Armenians and the Turks, all of whom had a linguistic influence. The ruins of a great hilltop fortress overlook Tbilisi, a beautiful city of broad, tree-lined avenues and lovely parks. That fortress is still called by its Turkish name, the Naragala. There are even borrowings from Indo-European languages for modern scientific and technological words as well as other kinds of words, such as the Georgian words for *lampshade, abazhur* (A bA' zh<u>oo</u>r), or *aggressive, agresiuli* (A gre see <u>oo</u>' lee) from French. There was a Georgian ambassador at the court of Louis XIV in 17th-century France.

Georgian, written in its very own alphabet, is a South Caucasian language spoken by about four million people, many of whom belong to the Georgian Orthodox Church. There is also a large population of Moslems and Jews. Georgian has only a tenuous relationship to the other Caucasian languages, which may or may not be indigenous to the Caucasus Mountain region, and most of which are not related to each other. They include Abkhasian, Chechen, Ossetian and several languages loosely classified as Circassian. In fact, it is only because of geography that all these languages are classified as Caucasian languages, not for reasons having to do with linguistics.

Georgian is probably one of the last surviving members of a language family whose ancestor is conjectured to be Ancient Sumerian, and the Georgians may have come from Colchis, the mythological home of Medea, on the Black Sea. The earliest known literature in Georgian, rich to this day in poetry of all kinds, dates from the fifth century. Possibly the most famous Georgian is Joseph Dzhugashvili (dgoo' gA shvi: lee; there is a secondary stress on the syllable "shvi:"), the former seminarian turned revolutionary and dictator who christened himself *Stalin*, which in Russian means "Man of Steel."

A Quick Reference

1) Study the information about Pitch below. Use a falling tone on the first syllable of some words.
2) Do a strongly trilled "r."
3) Pronounce "TH" and "th" correctly.
4) Substitute "aw" for "O."
5) Substitute "A" for "ow."
6) Pronounce initial "w" correctly.

How to Do a Georgian Accent

1) Position of the Vocal Apparatus
Say *true true true blue blue blue* to get the correct position of the vocal apparatus, in which the mouth is slightly closed, and the lips slightly protruded. The tongue, which has a tendency to be high in the mouth when used for speaking, seeks the upper gum ridge behind the front teeth as a natural position, because of all the agglutinative consonant clusters.

2) Pitch
Pitch is very important in a Georgian accent. In initial consonants, or rather on the vowel following, there is usually a falling tone. To put it another way, stressed syllables are usually spoken on a falling tone. There is also a marked falling tone at the end of a Georgian sentence, and it goes lower than the fall at the end of an English declarative sentence. Questions rise at the end.

3) The Most Important Sounds
Consonants
r: The Georgian "r" is strongly trilled, and this is the sound carried over into a Georgian accent in English.

TH and th: The voiceless "th," strongly aspirated, exists in Georgian, but its voiced counterpart, "TH," does not. Occasionally the voiceless "th" is pronounced like a "t" or else like the voiced "TH," but mostly both sounds, "TH" and "th," are pronounced correctly in an accent in English.

Vowels and Diphthongs
Almost every word in Georgian ends in a vowel, and the vowel system is the simple standard: A (a), e, i, o, <u>oo</u> (u). There are no diphthongs in Georgian, which leads to an even stressing of both halves of a diphthong in English. Also, very importantly, diphthongs often shift to pure vowels.

ay: This diphthong shifts to a lengthened "e:."

i and ee: These vowels exist in Georgian, but in a Georgian accent in English the long intermediate vowel "i:" is often substituted for both of them.

I: In this diphthong stress both halves evenly: "A'ee'."

O: This diphthong shifts to a lengthened "aw:." *I know* is pronounced "A'ee' naw:."

ow: This diphthong shifts to "A," so *now* is pronounced "nA."

w: This semi-vowel exists in Georgian, so it should be correctly pronounced in English.

Further Phonetic Information

Consonants
There are some incredible initial consonant clusters in Georgian (at least from the point of view of native English speakers), but almost every word in Georgian ends in a vowel. There are, among many others, the combinations: "mtsKH," as in the name of the ancient capital of Georgia, *Mtskheta* (mtsKHe' tA); "tb," as in the name of its present capital, *Tbilisi* (tbi:' li: si: ; there is a secondary stress on the second syllable); "mKH," as in the name of the Georgian alphabet, *Mkhedruli* (mKHe dr<u>oo</u>' li:); "mg" as in *mgazuri* (traveler; mgA z<u>oo</u>' ree); "mszh" as in *mszhelobu* (discussion; mszhe lo' b<u>oo</u>); "mtr" as in *mtredi* (pigeon; mtre' dee); and."rchkvn" as in *gapfurchkvna* (blossoming; gA pf<u>oo</u>' rchkvnA). Consonants ending a word in a Georgian accent in English are linked to the following word when it begins with a vowel, so *that is a boy* is pronounced "THa ti zA boy." If a word ends in a consonant, even if it ends a sentence, a schwa is often added after the consonant, so *house* is pronounced, at least in a heavy Georgian accent, "KHAse." Of course in English, too, we have a number of difficult consonant clusters, such as "dzf," as in the phrase *God's forgiveness*, and "xtst," as in *next stop*, which is sometimes pronounced with all its consonants in Great Britain, but which in the United States is usually pronounced "nek stAp." The pronunciation of these consonant clusters is made easier by the fact that they are not in initial position, but between vowels.

408

k and KH: The sound of "k" is very strongly aspirated, with almost a "KH" sound, but not quite. The sound in Scottish *loch* (KH) also exists in Georgian.

Stress

The stress in Georgian is almost always on the penultimate (next to last) syllable. Correct stressing in English is easily learned.

Practice

Georgian Words

Note: See the words under Further Phonetic Information for further practice.
msahiobi (actor); *msubukad* (slightly); *mtkiuneuli* (painful); *sashemodgomo* (autumnal); *ra tkma unda* (of course); *sakhvareli* (dear, darling)
Phonetic pronunciations: msA hee o' bee; ms<u>oo</u> b<u>oo</u>' kAd; mtkee <u>oo</u> ne: <u>oo</u>' lee; sA she mo dgo' mo; rA tkmA oo' ndA; sA KHvA re:' lee
Note: In the word *sakhvareli* note the derivation from *sakhar* (sA' KHAr), *sugar* in Russian, and *shakhari* (shA KHA' ri:), *sugar* in Georgian.

English Sentences

That's right. I want to go home. It's what I told you an hour ago.
Phonetic pronunciation: THa tsrA'\eet'. A'ee' waw'\ nt<u>oo</u> gaw KHaw'\ me. ee ts wA\ tA'ee' taw'\ ldy<u>oo</u>\ a nA'\ ra gaw\
Note the falling pitches on certain syllables followed by the sign "\."

How do you know what you are talking about or that anything you say is true—a philosophical question.
Phonetic pronunciation: KHA d<u>oo</u> y<u>oo</u> naw THat wAt y<u>oo</u> Ar taw' king e bAt or THat a' nee thing y<u>oo</u> say i:z tr<u>oo</u> e fi:l aw saw' fi: kal kwes' chun

On the other hand, who really cares?
Phonetic pronunciation: awn THee u' THer KHand KH<u>oo</u> ree' a lee kayrs

Georgian poetry, Georgian literature and history are all fascinating.
Phonetic pronunciation: dgawr' dgan paw' e tree dgawr' dgan lit' e rA ty<u>oo</u>r and KHi:s taw ree AR awl fas' i: nay ti:ng

The splendor of the Caucasus is legendary.
Phonetic pronunciation: THe splen' dawr awv THi kaw' ka zus i:z le dgen' da ree

No wonder the Russians wanted to conquer us, and succeeded, under the Czars, in spite of everything. In the end, of course, it was not possible.
Phonetic pronunciation: naw vun' der THi Ru' shenz vawn' ted t<u>oo</u> kawn' ker us and suk' si:d ed un' der THe zArz i:n splt awv ev' e ree thing   i:n THee end awv kawrs i:t vAs nawt paw' si: bel

409

Mongolian

Mongolian, a member of the Altaic family, which is possibly related to Turk- ish is spoken in Mongolia, parts of China and parts of Russia by about four to five million people. A closely related language, Manchu, has by now almost dis- appeared. There are three major dialects of Mongolian, of which Khalkha (Pho- netic pronunciation: KHAl' KHA) has become Standard Mongolian, the lan- guage of the capital, Ulan Bator. Mongolian has its own alphabet, Uyghur, de- scended apparently, from the Ancient Syriac alphabet of the Middle East. This alphabet is related to the Phoenician and Hebrew alphabets, but how and by whom it was invented in Mongolia, *if* it was invented there, and whether Phoenicians went to what is now Mongolia, or whether Asians went to the Middle East, remain impenetrable mysteries.

A Quick Reference

1) Substitute "p" for "f."
2) Do a lightly trilled "r."
3) Substitute "d" and "t" for "TH" and "th."
4) Substitute "w" for initial "v" and pronounce initial "w" correctly.
5) Shift diphthongs "ay" to "e:"and "O" to "aw."

How to Do a Mongolian Accent

1) Position of the Vocal Apparatus
The mouth is fairly relaxed, with the tongue down, and the lips slightly forward.

2) The Most Important Sounds
Pay attention to the consonant substitutions especially, and to the long and short vowel alternation, which gives the accent its characteristic rhythm.

Consonants
Certain consonants of English simply do not exist in Mongolian.

f: This consonant does not exist in Mongolian, and "p" is the usual substitution for "f," so *fight* is pronounced "pIt."

l: There is a liquid "l" in Mongolian, and it should be used instead of the Gen- eral American "L" in a Mongolian accent.

r: There is a lightly trilled "r" in Mongolian, and this is the sound heard in English.

TH and th: These sounds do not exist in Mongolian. Substitute "d" and "t" for them.

v: This consonant does not exist in Mongolian. Instead substitute the semi-

410

vowel "w," so *very* is pronounced "we' ree."

Vowels and Diphthongs
The basic vowel system, with long and short vowels, is the following: A, e, i, o, <u>oo</u> (u). There are quite a number of diphthongs, among them: I, ay, oy and y<u>oo</u>. Vowels in unstressed syllables tend in Mongolian itself to become a schwa (*e*). As is usual with Altaic languages, there is a phenomenon known as "vowel harmony," too complicated to go into here in detail, according to the principles of which front and back, long and short vowels alternate.

ay: This diphthong, which exists in Mongolian, is sometimes pronounced as a lengthened pure vowel "e:" in an accent in English.

O: This diphthong does not exist in Mongolian, and should be shifted to a pure, lengthened vowel "aw."

w: This semi-vowel exists in Mongolian, and it is easily learned when English is spoken, and should be correctly pronounced.

Stress

The stress in Mongolian is random, but there is a marked rhythm to the language, a kind of music which carries over into English, based on the extra length of long vowels and the brevity of the short vowels.

Pitch

The pitch patterns are similar to those of Indo-European, with a falling tone at the end of a declarative sentence, and a rising tone at the end of a question.

Practice

Mongolian Words
tiim (yes); *ugui* (no); *bayarlaa* (thanks); *khairtai* (love); *bi chamd khairtai* (I love you)
Phonetic pronunciations: teem; <u>oo</u> gooi: '; bA yAr lA'; khIr' tI; bi chAmd khIr' tI

English Sentences
The tents are pitched near Ulan Bator. There is no fighting. The horses stand idly by munching their hay.
Phonetic pronunciation: di: tents Ar pi:cht ni:r <u>oo</u>' lAn bA' tawr   de:r i:s naw pI' ting   di: khawr si:s stend I' dli: bI mAnch' ing de:r khe:

Ulan Bator is the capital of Mongolia.
Phonetic pronunciation: <u>oo</u>' lAn bA' tawr i:s di kA pi:' tAl awp mawn gaw' lee yA

Five times I went there and five times I came home.

411

Phonetic pronunciation: pIp tIms I wen der an pIp tIms I ke:m khɔwm

It is a very controversial matter.
Phonetic pronunciation: i:t i:s *e* we' ree kawn traw wer' shil mA' ter

Would you rather be very hot or very cold?
Phonetic pronunciation: wood y<u>oo</u> rA' der bee we' ree khawt awr we' ree kawld

No home is more precious to me than my own home.
Phonetic pronunciation: naw khawm i:s mawr pre' shus t<u>oo</u> mee dan mI awn khawm

Uzbek

Uzbekistan, formerly one of the Soviet republics, is a country of Central Asia. Its capital, Tashkent, was destroyed by an earthquake in the 1950s, but has since been rebuilt. Other cities include Bukhara, famous for its rugs and ancient marts, and the fabled and gorgeous Samarkand, located along the silk and spice route from East Asia, and known for its caravansary and its ancient mosques of blue, turquoise and gold, with their superb domes, spires and minarets. To stand in the *Registan*, "area" or "square of sand" in Uzbek, ("-stan" is an ending meaning "area") on a bright, sunny day is to have an overwhelmingly beautiful sense of the ancient days, the times of Marco Polo, the intrepid Venetian who journeyed to Asia and stopped in Samarkand in the 14th century. Indeed the dry desert air has preserved buildings a thousand years old in a perfect state.

The Uzbeks are largely a Moslem people, and several very important Moslem holy sites are to be found in Samarkand. Their language, Uzbek, written in the Cyrillic alphabet, is an Altaic language of the Turkic family, and is therefore distantly related to Turkish. Some other Turkic languages of Central Asia are Azerbaijani, Kazakh, Tartar, Turkmenian, and Kirghiz. Uzbek is also possibly related to Mongolian. (Tadzhik, geographically in the same region of Central Asia is, however, an Indo-European language, related to Persian.) The Turkic languages, including Turkish, are very closely related to each other, so much so as to be often mutually intelligible. This intelligibility is much helped by the fact that the phonetic systems and other characteristics of the different languages are very similar in all of them.

Because of Islam, Uzbek, which is spoken by about 18 million people, has been heavily influenced by Arabic, the alphabet in which Uzbek was once written. The Russian language has also had an influence on Uzbek, first under the Czars, to whom the Emir of Uzbekistan paid tribute, and then under the Soviets. Uzbek has been written in the Cyrillic alphabet since 1940.

A Quick Reference

1) Use a trilled "r" and pronounce it in all positions.

412

2) Substitute a light "kh" for "h."
3) Substitute "d" and "t" for "TH" and "th."
4) Substitute "v" for initial "w."
5) Shift diphthongs to pure vowels. See below for specifics.

How to Do an Uzbek Accent

1) Position of the Vocal Apparatus
The mouth is relaxed, similar to the position in General American, with the lips slightly forward.

2) The Most Important Sounds
Consonants
Most of the consonants of English exist in Uzbek, but there are some which do not. The accent is usually rhotic, as final "r" is pronounced in Uzbek.

h: This consonant is not heard in Uzbek. Substitute a soft "kh" sound for it, much like the Spanish *jota*.
r: The "r" in Uzbek is trilled, and this is the sound that should be used in English.

TH and th: These sounds do not exist in Uzbek. The usual substitutions are "d" and "t."

Vowels and Diphthongs
Vowels are long and short, and follow the usual system: A, e, i, o, oo (u). There are few diphthongs, except those beginning with the semi-vowel "y." All vowels are pronounced, so a word like *used* might be pronounced "yoo' zed." Do not use a schwa in this accent; instead, give vowels a full value.

ay: This diphthong does not exist in Uzbek. Substitute a lengthened "e:."

ee and i: These vowels do not exist in Uzbek. Substitute the lengthened intermediate vowel "i:" for both of them.

I: This diphthong also does not exist. Substitute "A" for it.

O: This diphthong does not exist in Uzbek. Substitute the pure vowel "aw."

ow: Both halves of this diphthong should be evenly stressed: A'oo'.

u: The sound of "u" in *but* has no exact equivalent in Uzbek. Substitute "A" in stressed syllables, or "e," when the vowel occurs in an unstressed syllable.

w: This semi-vowel does not exist in initial position. Substitute the consonant "v" for it.

Stress

The stress is mostly on the last or penultimate (next to last) syllable, so for our purposes it is random, and English stress correctly learned.

Pitch

The pitch tends to be low in tone, but otherwise follows the oft-repeated pattern of a falling tone to conclude a declarative sentence and a rising tone to terminate a question.

Practice

Uzbek Words Transliterated from the Cyrillic alphabet
syevmoq (verb meaning "to love"); *yakhshi körmoq* (a phrase meaning "to love"; literal meaning: kindly to see, or, to look on someone with kindness or tenderness); *mukhabbat* (noun meaning "love"); *childirma* (tambourine); *osmon* (heaven); *lazzat* (noun meaning "taste; delight")
Phonetic pronunciations: syef mok'; yAKH shee' kor' mok; m<u>oo</u> KHAb bAt'; chi: l di: r' mA; os' mon'; lAz' zAt

Note that the "q," a special Uzbek letter transliterated from the Cyrilic alphabet, represents a "glottalized" consonant which does not exist in English. To pronounce it correctly, say "k" while moving the glottis, that is, making a slight swallowing sound on the consonant. Note also the last syllable stressing on most of these words, typical of Turkish and the Turkic languages generally.

English Sentences
The Emir of Uzbekistan lived in Bokhara in a beautiful palace, which is now a tourist attraction.
Phonetic pronunciation: de e: mi:r' ov <u>oo</u>z bek i: stAn' li:' ved i:n baw KHA rA' i:n a bi: y<u>oo</u>' ti: f<u>ool</u> pA lAs' vi:ch i:z nA'<u>oo</u>' a t<u>oo</u> ri:st' A trA' kshen

Note, by the way, that the city of Bokhara is Bukhara in Russian, and is pronounced "boo KHA' rA."

The oldest observatory in the world, or one of the oldest, is in Samarkand, with its gorgeous blue, gold and turquoise mosqes and minarets, on the fabled spice and silk route.
Phonetic pronunciation: dee awl' dest ob ser' vA taw ree i:n di veld awr vAn Av dee awl' dest i:s i:n sA' mAr kAnd' vi:t i:ts gawr' dges bl<u>oo</u> gawld en tA kwoys' mi:n A rets' awn dee fe:' beld spAs end si:lk root

The architecture of the cities in the central Asian countries is exquisite.
Phonetic pronunciation: de A ki: tek' choo Av dee si:' dees i:n dee sen' trAl e:' shen kAn' trees i:s eks' kfi: si:t

414

Why they ever built an opera house in the middle of Samarkand I will never know. Nobody goes to it. And they sang all the operas in Russian, even La Traviata. *When the curtain rose, I said "Oh! Interesting! There is Oscar Wilde. They try to recreate the period in Paris." But he turned out to be the tenor! Later on when the soprano started to sing "Ya stradayu," which means "I suffer" in Russian, I turned to my friend and I said "So do we!" Of course you can say we could have walked out, but we didn't somehow. We stayed to the bitter end.*

Phonetic pronunciation: vA day e' ve bi:lt an o' pe: rA hows i:n di: mi:' del awv sA' mAr kAnd' A vi:l ne:' ver naw naw baw dee gaws t<u>oo</u> i:t an day sang awl dee o' pe: rAs i:n rA' shin ee ven lA trA' vee A tA ven di kawr' tayn raws A sad aw i:n te ras' ti:ng de:r i:s aws' kAr vAld day trA t<u>oo</u> re' kree ayt di: pi:' ryawd i:n pA' ri:s bAt khi: tawrn' ed At t<u>oo</u> bi: di: ta' nawr lay' tA awn ven di: saw prA' naw stA' tet ti: sing yA strA dA' y<u>oo</u> wi:ch mi:nz A sA' fer i:n RA' shin A tawrn' ed ti mA frend end A sad saw d<u>oo</u> vee awv kawrs vee kood hev vawk' ed At bAt vee di:d' ent sAm' khA vee stayt ti di bi:' ter ent

Most people here don't speak Russian, no more than a few words. They speak Uzbek.
Phonetic pronunciation: mawst pi:' pel kheer dawnt spi:k rA' shin naw mawr dan ay fy<u>oo</u> vets day spi:k ooz' bek

There are no more exercises. That's it. Now you can go to the Bibliography.
Phonetic pronunciation: de:r Ar naw mawr ek' ser sIz is dats i:t na yi kAn gaw ti di bib' lee a' gru fee

Selected Bibliography

1) Video and Audio Recordings;
Books on Speech and Accents for Actors

BBC records:
1) *English With an Accent*, BBC 22166 (23 accents).
2) *English With a Dialect*, BBC 22173 (British Isles accents).
(All the accents on these records are with native speakers.)

Record:

Great Actors of the Past, compiled by Richard Bebb, Argo Records, SW 510. London, England: The Decca Record Company Limited, 1970. Voices of Ellen Terry, Henry Irving, Sarah Bernhardt, Sir Herbert Beerbohm Tree, Edwin Booth, Lewis Waller, Alexander Moissi, Julia Neilson and Fred Terry, Constant Coquelin, Joseph Jefferson, Tomasso Salvini, Cyril Maude.

Cassettes:

Accents for Actors: Ireland, Wales, Scotland and England, compiled and directed by Christopher Casson, with a commentary by Joseph D. Pheiffer. Cassette SAC 1027. New Rochelle, NY: Spoken Arts, Inc., 1983. These are recordings by native speakers.

Skinner, Edith. *Speak With Distinction*, ed. by Lilene Mansell (accompanying cassette). New York: Applause Theatre Book Publishers, 1990.

Stern, David Allen. Series of tapes, published by Dialect Accent Specialists. Los Angeles, 1970s.

Videotape:

PBS television series. *The Story of English*, videotape, host: Robert MacNeil. 1986.

Compact Discs:

About a Hundred Years: The History of Sound Recording, Symposium CD 1222. East Barnet, Hertfordshire, England: Symposium Records, 1997. Voices of Arthur Conan Doyle, Sarah Bernhardt, Thomas Alva Edison, Johannes Brahms, Mahatma Gandhi, Field Marshall von Hindenburg, Neville Chamberlain, Winston Churchill, Leo Tolstoy, etc.

The Art of the Savoyard, Pearl, Gemm CD 9991. Wadhurst, East Sussex, England: Pavilion Records, 1993. Authentic Victorian English: Voices of singers who worked with Gilbert and Sullivan themselves in their comic operas; in-

417

cludes the voices of Richard Temple, who was the first Mikado and Pirate
King, and of Sir Arthur Sullivan.

Great Shakespeareans, Pearl, Gemm CD 9465. Wadhurst, East Sussex, England:
Pavilion Records, 1990. Voices of Edwin Booth, Sir Herbert Beerbohm Tree,
Arthur Bourchier, Lewis Waller, Ben Greet, John Barrymore, Sir Johnston
Forbes-Robertson, Sir John Gielgud, Henry Ainley, Maurice Evans.

In Their Own Voices: The U.S. Presidential Elections of 1908 and 1912, Marston
CD 52028-2. U.S.A.: Marston Records, 2000. Voices of William Jennings Bryan,
William H. Taft, Theodore Roosevelt, and Woodrow Wilson.

Othello, with excerpts from *Sanders of the River*, Pearl, Gemm CD 0037.
Wadhurst, East Sussex, England: Pavilion Records,1998. Voices of Paul
Robeson, Uta Hagen, Jose Ferrer, Alexander Scourby, etc. Recorded in 1944.

Le Théâtre parisien de Sarah Bernhardt à Sacha Guitry, EMI Classics, 6 CDs,
CZS 7 675392. EMI France, 1992. For francophones; the voices of Sarah
Bernhardt, Coquelin Ainé (the first Cyrano), Jean Cocteau, and many others.

Books

Blunt, Jerry. *Stage Dialects*. New York: Harper and Row, 1967.

Blunt, Jerry. *More Stage Dialects*. New York: Harper and Row, 1979.

Herman, Lewis Helmer, and Marguerite Shalett Herman. *Manual of American
Dialects for Radio, Stage and Screen*. Chicago and New York: Ziff Davis Publishing Co., 1947.

Herman, Lewis Helmer, and Marguerite Shalett Herman. *Manual of Foreign
Dialects for Radio, Stage and Screen*. Chicago and New York: Ziff Davis Publishing Co., 1943.

Molin, Donald H. *Actor's Encyclopedia of Dialects*. New York: Sterling Publishing Co., 1984.

The voices and accents of various people, such as the ones listed below, mentioned in this book can be found on cassettes, CDs or videocassettes:

Alda, Frances
Booth, Edwin
Eames, Emma
Gilbert, Sir William Schwenck
Irving, Sir Henry
Nightingale, Florence
Roosevelt, Franklin D.
Sullivan, Sir Arthur Seymour
Tennyson, Alfred, Lord

2) Language Books and Tapes

The following series were all published over many years, and are currently
available in bookstores.

The *Colloquial* series of books, available with or without accompanying cassettes, Routledge.

The *ES* (*Educational Services*) series of cassettes with accompanying booklets, 22 languages.

The *Listen and Learn* series of cassettes with accompanying booklets, Dover Publishing.

The *Teach Yourself* series of over 50 paperback textbooks, many with accompanying cassettes or CDs.

3) Technical Books on Languages, Phonetics and Linguistics

Allen, W. Sidney. *Vox Graeca, A Guide to the Pronunciation of Classical Greek*, 3rd edition. Cambridge and New York: Cambridge University Press, 1987.

Baldi, Philip. *An Introduction to the Indo-European Languages*. Carbondale and Edwardsville: Southern Illinois University Press, 1983.

Barber, Charles. *Early Modern English*. Edinburgh: Edinburgh University Press, 1997.

Barber, Charles. *The English Language A Historical Introduction*. Cambridge and New York: Cambridge University Press, 1993.

Battye, Adrian, and Marie-Anne Hintze. *The French Language Today*. London and New York: Routledge, 1992.

Baugh, John. *Black Street Speech*. Austin: University of Texas Press, 1983.

Brook, G.L. *A History of the English Language*. New York: W.W. Norton and Company, Inc., 1958.

Brook, G.L. *Dialects of English*. New York: Oxford University Press, 1963.

Brook, G.L. *Varieties of English*. London and Basingstoke: Macmillan St. Martin's Press, 1973.

Bryson, Bill. *Made in America: An Informal History of the English Language in the United States*. New York: Avon Books, 1994.

Bryson, Bill. *The Mother Tongue: English and How It Got That Way*. New York: Avon Books, 1990.

Canfield, D. Lincoln. *Spanish Pronunciation in the Americas*. Chicago and London: The University of Chicago Press, 1981.

Cavalli-Sforza, Luigi Luca. *Genes, People and Languages*. New York: North Point Press, A division of Farrar, Straus and Giroux, 2000.

Comrie, Bernard, ed. *The World's Major Languages*. Oxford and New York: Oxford University Press, 1990.

Comrie, Bernard, Stephen Matthews and Maria Polinsky, consultant eds. *The Atlas of Languages*. New York: Facts on File, Inc., 1996.

Castiglione, Pierina Borrani. *Italian Phonetics, Diction and Intonation*. New York: S. F. Vanni, 1957.

Cruttenden, Alan. *Intonation*. Cambridge and New York: Cambridge University Press, 1986.

Crystal, David. *The Cambridge Encyclopedia of Language*. Cambridge and New York: Cambridge University Press, 1987.

Crystal, David. *The Cambridge Encyclopedia of the English Language*. Cambridge and New York: Cambridge University Press, 1995.

Dalby, Andrew. *Dictionary of Languages*. New York: Columbia University Press, 1998.

De Mauro, Tullio. *Storia linguistica dell'Italia unita*. Roma, Bari: Editori Laterza, 1998.

De Mauro, Tullio, and Mario Lodi. *Lingua e dialetti*. Rome: Editori Riuniti, 1993.

Dillard, J. L. *Black English*. New York: Vintage Books, 1973.

Dixon, R.M.W. and Alexandra Y. Aikhenvald, eds. *The Amazonian Languages*. Cambridge and New York: Cambridge University Press, 1999.

Ellis, Alexander J. *On Early English Pronunciation with Special Reference to Shakspeare and Chaucer*, in three volumes "*on the Pronunciation of the XIVth, XVIth, XVIIth and XVIIIth Centuries.*" London and Berlin: Asher and Company, 1869 (reprinted 1929).

Fisher, John H. *The Emergence of Standard English*. Lexington: The University Press of Kentucky, 1996.

Giegerich, Heinz J. *English Phonology*. Cambridge and New York: Cambridge University Press, 1992.

Gimson's Pronunciation of English, 5th edition, revised by Alan Cruttenden. London: Edward Arnold, 1994.

Gramley, Stephan, and Kurt-Michael Pätzold. *A Survey of Modern English*. London and New York: Routledge, 1992.

Harris, Martin and Nigel Vincent, eds. *The Romance Languages*. Oxford and New York: Oxford University Press, 1988.

Heine, Bernd and Derek Nurse, eds. *African Languages: An Introduction*. Cambridge and New York: Cambridge University Press, 2000.

Hewitt, George. *Georgian, A Learner's Grammar*. London and New York: Routledge, 1996.

Hirst, Daniel and Albert Di Cristo, eds. *Intonation Systems: A Survey of Twenty Languages*. Cambridge and New York: Cambridge University Press, 1998.

Holloway, Joseph E., and Winifred K. Vass. *The African Heritage of American English*. Bloomington and Indianapolis: Indiana University Press, 1997.

Holm, John. *Pidgins and Creoles*, in two volumes. Cambridge and New York: Cambridge University Press, 1988.

Hughes, Arthur, and Peter Trudgill. *English Accents and Dialects*, third edition. London: Edward Arnold, 1996.

Jones, Daniel. *The Pronunciation of English*, definitive edition. Cambridge and New York: Cambridge University Press, 1992.

Katzner, Kenneth. *The Languages of the World*, new edition. London and New York: Routledge, 1995.

Kökeritz, Helge. *A Guide to Chaucer's Pronunciation*. New York: Holt, Rinehart and Winston, 1962.

Kökeritz, Helge. *Shakespeare's Pronunciation*. New Haven: Yale University Press, 1953.

Kreidler, Charles W. *Describing Spoken English: An Introduction*. London and New York: Routledge, 1997.

Ladd, D. Robert. *Intonational Phonology*. Cambridge and New York: Cambridge University Press, 1996.

Ladefoged, Peter. *A Course in Phonetics*, 3rd edition. Fort Worth, Philadelphia, etc.: Harcourt Brace College Publishers, 1993.

Ladefoged, Peter. *Preliminaries to Linguistic Phonetics*, Midway Reprint. Chicago and London: The University of Chicago Press, 1971.

Ladefoged, Peter, and Ian Maddieson. *The Sounds of the World's Languages*. Oxford, England and Cambridge, Mass.: Blackwell Publishers, 1996.

Lambert, Pierre-Yves. *La Langue Gauloise*. Paris: Editions Errance, 1995.

Lass, Roger. *Phonology*. Cambridge and New York: Cambridge University Press, 1984.

Laver, John. *Principles of Phonetics*. Cambridge and New York: Cambridge University Press, 1994.

Lynch, John. *Pacific Languages: An Introduction*. Honolulu: University of Hawai'i Press, 1998.

McArthur, Tom, ed. *The Oxford Companion to the English Language*. Oxford and New York: Oxford University Press, 1992.

McCrum, Robert, William Cran and Robert MacNeil. *The Story of English*, a companion to the PBS television series. New York: Elizabeth Sifton Books, Viking, 1986.

Masica, Colin P. *The Indo-Aryan Languages*. Cambridge and New York: Cambridge University Press, 1991.

Mencken, H.L. *The American Language: An Inquiry into the Development of the English Language in the United States* (together with its two supplements). New York: Alfred A. Knopf, 1936.

Nielsen, Hans Frede. *The Germanic Languages, Origins and Early Dialectical Interrelations*. Tuscaloosa and London: University of Alabama Press, 1989.

Norman, Jerry. *Chinese*. Cambridge and New York: Cambridge University Press, 1988.

Palmer, L.R. *The Latin Language*. Norman and London: University of Oklahoma Press, 1988.

Pei, Mario A. *The World's Chief Languages*. New York: S. F. Vanni, 1946.

Pinker, Steven. *The Language Instinct*. New York: William Morrow and Company, 1994.

Pleasants, Jeanne Varney. *Pronunciation of French, Articulation and Intonation*. New York: privately printed, 1964.

Posner, Rebecca. *The Romance Languages*. Cambridge and New York: Cambridge University Press, 1996.

Price, Glanville, ed. *Encyclopedia of the Languages of Europe*. Oxford and Malden, Massachusetts: Blackwell Publishers, 1998.

Ramsey, S. Robert. *The Languages of China*. Princeton: Princeton University Press, 1987.

Rickard, Peter. *A History of the French Language*, 2nd edition. London and New York: Routledge, 1993.

Ruhlen, Merrit. *A Guide to the World's Languages*, Volume 1: Classification. Stanford, California: Stanford University Press, 1991.

Ruhlen, Merritt. *On the Origin of Languages: Studies in Linguistic Taxonomy*. Stanford, California: Stanford University Press, 1994.

Ruhlen, Merritt. *The Origin of Language: Tracing the Evolution of the Mother Tongue*. New York, Chichester, Brisbane, Toronto, Singapore: John Wiley and Sons, Inc. 1994.

Russ, Charles V. J. *The German Language Today*. London and New York: Routledge, 1994.

Sáenz-Badillos, Angel. *A History of the Hebrew Language*, trans. John Elwolde. Cambridge and New York: Cambridge University Press, 1993.

Shibatani, Masayoshi. *The Languages of Japan*. Cambridge and New York: Cambridge University Press, 1990.

Sneddon, James Neil. *Indonesian, A Comprehensive Grammar*. London and New York: Routledge, 1996.

Thomas, Cyrus, assisted by John R. Swanton. *Indian Languages of Mexico and Central America and Their Geographical Distribution*. Seattle, Washington: The Shorey Bookstore, facsimile reprint, 1975.

Trudgill, Peter. *The Dialects of England*. Oxford, England and Cambridge, Mass.: Blackwell, 1990.

Upton, Clive, and J. D. A. Widdowson. *An Atlas of English Dialects*. Oxford and New York: Oxford University Press, 1996.

Wells, J.C. *Accents of English*, in three volumes: *1, Introduction; 2, The British Isles; 3, Beyond the British Isles*. Cambridge and New York: Cambridge University Press, 1982.

Wolfram, Walt and Natalie Schilling-Estes. *High Tide on the Outer Banks: The Story of the Ocracoke Brogue*. Chapel Hill and London: The University of North Carolina Press, 1997.

Zilyns'kyj, Ivan. *A Phonetic Description of the Ukrainian Language*, translated and revised according to the author's emendations by Wolodymyr T. Zyla and Wendell M. Aycock. Cambridge, Mass.: Harvard University Press, 1979.

4) Some Dictionaries

There are many pronouncing dictionaries for English and for other languages, all useful: Larousse for French and Duden for German, for example. Cassel's and Harper Collins' foreign language dictionaries are excellent. Every dictionary has its own phonetic system of pronunciation; some use the IPA system. The American Heritage, Webster and Random House dictionaries of the English language have many biographical and geographical pronunciations, and Webster's old *New International Dictionary* (first and second editions, but not the third edition), is especially useful for everything, including the correct anglicized Latin pronunciations of the names of biological species, of mythological personages, and of scientific and literary terms. The unabridged *Oxford English Dictionary* (Oxford University Press) is in a class by itself. For an account of how it was put together read the fascinating, superbly written *The Professor and the Madman: A Tale of Murder, Insanity, and the Making of the Oxford English Dictionary* (HarperCollins Publishers, 1998) by Simon Winchester. After reading that, you may be inspired to read the dictionary itself!

Akowuah, Thomas A. *Lingala-English/English-Lingala* New York: Hippocrene Books, 1996. One of a series of Hippocrene dictionaries, which includes such languages as Armenian, Georgian, Polish, Sicilian, Tatar, Uzbek, etc.

Barnhart, Clarence L., ed. *New Century Cyclopedia of Names*, in three volumes. Englewood Cliffs, NJ: Prentice-Hall, Inc., 1954.

Colloiani, Louis. *Shakespeare's Names: A New Prounouncing Dictionary*. New York: Drama Publishers, 1999.

Edelstein, Debra. *Pronouncing Dictionary of Artists' Names*, The Art Institute of Chicago 3rd revised edition. Boston, New York, Toronto, London: Little, Brown and Company, 1993

Ehrlich, Eugene and Raymond Hand, Jr., revised and updated by. Introduction by Edwin Newman. *NBC Handbook of Pronunciation*, 4th edition. New York, Harper and Row, 1984.

Graham, William. *The Scots Word Book*, 3rd revised edition. Edinburgh: The Ramsay Head Press, 1980.

Greet, W. Cabell. *World Words: Recommended Pronunciations*, second edition, revised and enlarged. New York: Columbia University Press, by arrangement with the Columbia Broadcasting System, 1948

Irvine, Theodora Ursula. *How to Pronounce the Names in Shakespeare*. New York, Philadelphia, Chicago: Hines, Hayden and Eldredge, Inc., 1919.

Jacobus, Melancthon W., Elbert C. Lane, Andrew Zemos, with the assistance of Elmer J. Cook. *Funk and Wagnall's New "Standard" Bible Dictionary*, 3rd revised edition. New York: Funk and Wagnalls, Inc., 1936

Jones, Daniel. *An English Pronouncing Dictionary*, 15th edition, eds. Peter Roach and James Hartman. Cambridge and New York: Cambridge University Press, 1997.

Kökeritz, Helge. *Shakespeare's Names: A Pronouncing Dictionary*. New Haven and London: Yale University Press, 1977.

Merriam-Webster's Biographical Dictionary. Springfield, Massachusetts: Merriam-Webster. Incorporated, 1995

Merriam-Webster's Geographical Dictionary, 3rd edition. Springfield, Massachusetts: Merriam-Webster, Incorporated, 1997.

Merriam-Webster's Medical Desk Dictionary. Springfield, Massachusetts: Merriam-Webster, Incorporated, 1996.

Moss, Norman. *British/American Language Dictionary*. Lincolnwood, Illinois: Passport Books, 1984.

Pei, Mario and Salvatore Ramondino, in collaboration with Laura Torbet. *Dictionary of Foreign Terms*. New York: A Laurel Original, Dell Publishing Co., 1974

Pointon, G.E., editor and transcriber. *BBC Pronouncing Dictionary of British Names*. Oxford and New York: Oxford University Press, 1990. This dictionary includes English, Scottish, Irish and Welsh names of people and places.

Pullum, Geoffrey K., and William A. Ladusaw. *Phonetic Symbol Guide*. Chicago and London: Chicago University Press, 1986.

Seltzer, Leon E., ed. *The Columbia Lippincott Gazetteer of the World*, with 1961 supplement. New York: Columbia University Press, by arrangement with J.B. Lippincott Company, 1962.

Thomas, J. *Universal Pronouncing Dictionary of Biography and Mythology*, in two volumes. Philadelphia: J.B. Lippincott and Company, 1870; republished by Gale Research Company, Book Tower, Detroit, 1976.

Zimmerman, J. E. *Dictionary of Classical Mythology*, 18th printing. Toronto, New York, London, Sydney, and Auckland: Bantam Books, 1985.

About the Author

Robert Blumenfeld lives in New York City, where he has worked as a professional actor and a private and production dialect coach for more than twenty-five years. He has been on the faculty of both the Stella Adler and National Shakespeare Conservatories. He created the roles of the Marquis of Queensberry and two prosecuting attorneys in the Off-Broadway hit play *Gross Indecency: The Three Trials of Oscar Wilde*, for which he was also the Dialect Coach. On Broadway he was Dialect Coach for the musicals *Saturday Night Fever* and *The Scarlet Pimpernel* (the third version and the national tour). Mr. Blumenfeld has used accents extensively as an actor on stage, and in film, television voice-overs and radio commercials. He has also recorded more than two hundred books for Talking Books at the American Foundation for the Blind. He is the winner of the 1997 Canadian National Institute for the Blind's Torgi Talking Book of the Year Award, for his recording of Pat Conroy's *Beach Music*. Mr. Blumenfeld holds a B.A. from Rutgers University and an M.A. from Columbia University in French Language and Literature. He also speaks German and Italian fluently, and has a good smattering of Yiddish, Spanish and Russian. Having toured for almost four years with the National Theatre of the Deaf, he is also fluent in American Sign Language.